W9-DDD-343

ROADSIDE HISTORY OF
Illinois

STAN BANASH

2013
MOUNTAIN PRESS PUBLISHING COMPANY
MISSOULA, MONTANA

ROADSIDE HISTORY OF ILLINOIS

Cover painting: *Transforming the Prairie* by Ken Holder. Panel from mural at Illinois State Capitol, Springfield, one of four panels commissioned for the capitol's centennial celebration in 1988. Photo by Heather Hayes, courtesy of the Office of the Secretary of State.

Maps by James Lainsbury.

Library of Congress Cataloging-in-Publication Data

Banash, Stan, 1940-
Roadside history of Illinois / Stan Banash.
    pages cm. — (Roadside history series)
Includes bibliographical references and index.
ISBN 978-0-87842-599-0 (paperback : alkaline paper)
1. Illinois—History—Anecdotes. 2. Illinois—History, Local—Anecdotes. 3. Cities and towns—Illinois—History—Anecdotes. 4. Historic sites—Illinois—Anecdotes. I. Title.
F541.6.B36 2013
977.3—dc23
                                                            2013002316

PRINTED IN THE UNITED STATES

Mountain Press
PUBLISHING COMPANY
P.O. Box 2399 • Missoula, MT 59806 • 406-728-1900
800-234-5308 • info@mtnpress.com
www.mountain-press.com

For my children, Maria, Stan Jr., Dina, Patrice, and Katherine, all of whom weathered motor trips through Illinois to visit most of the memorials and monuments on the Illinois state map. Hopefully, these experiences left within them a better appreciation for and an under-standing of the people, places, and events that played a significant role in the development of the Prairie State.

Contents

Preface

Illinois comprises more than 1,200 incorporated cities, towns, and villages, each with a history of its own. Writing about each municipality would be a Herculean task, and I had to omit many more stories than I would have liked. The communities selected for this book were associated, for the most part, with people and events that helped to mold and define our state. I established criteria for each choice—maybe it was the site of a major event, or perhaps a prominent person was born there, lived there, or contributed in a significant way to its regional history.

When I began researching this book, I found myself asking: Is it possible that one person—Abraham Lincoln—actually made such a profound impact in all corners of Illinois? The answer is a resounding "yes." Lincoln's role in this state's history was monumental, and his influence extended the length and breadth of Illinois. Among Lincoln's many contributions were his service as a soldier, a traveling attorney, a state representative, a U.S. Congressman, and an American president.

I felt it was important to include troubling events along with positive ones. Slavery and its prejudicial laws; the Trail of Tears; Indian depredations at Fort Dearborn, Hutsonville, Wood River, and other early settlements; the Haymarket Square Riot; the St. Valentine's Day Massacre; and many more distasteful happenings are still subjects of heated debate and intense emotion. Yet the innovations that came out of Illinois were momentous: the G.I. Bill of Rights; the *Plan of Chicago;* Hull-House; modern dentistry; and myriad agricultural inventions as well as cultural creations from the Ferris Wheel to the fly swatter and from Raggedy Ann to Dairy Queen. All, for good or bad, were part of our state's history, and all have the potential to help us better understand the past, appreciate the present, and plan the future.

As with the other titles in the Roadside History series, this book is organized along roadways. Some trips stick to major interstates, others follow official scenic byways, and a few wind along county roads. Many of these routes trace old Indian trails, wagon roads, military roads, or railroad lines. The view from some of these motorways has not changed much in more than a century, rolling through the same countryside where early settlers drove their wagons and livestock. Along the way, the contributions of hardworking pioneer families are reflected in small communities and modern cities alike. In addition, these drives will reveal to travelers Illinois's incomparable scenic beauty—verdant farms and wildflower prairies, idyllic lakes and rushing rivers, dense conifer forests and sleepy cypress swamps.

This book's tours are designed to help both visitors and residents discover and savor the historical, cultural, and natural opulence of this great state. It is my hope that readers will find *Roadside History of Illinois* entertaining, informative, and even enlightening. If it inspires just one person to further explore the Prairie State and its remarkable history, it will have served its purpose.

Illinois Chronology

Before 300,000 BC	Pre-Illinoian glacial and interglacial activity in North America
300,000– 125,000 BC	Illinoian Glacial Period; glaciers cover more than 70 percent of the future state of Illinois
125,000– 75,000 BC	Sangamonian Interglacial Period
75,000– 12,000 BC	Wisconsinan Glacial Period; glaciers cover about 35 percent of Illinois, including most of the northern and northeastern part of the future state
12,000– 8000 BC	Paleo-Indians (hunter-gatherer cultures) migrate into Illinois
8000– 1000 BC	Archaic Indians appear in Illinois, living in semipermanent seasonal villages; they develop specialized tools and begin to cultivate plants
1000 BC– AD 1000	Woodland Indian Cultures evolve and develop agriculture, weapons, social structures, and intertribal trade
AD 900–1450	Mississippian Indians build cities along rivers with flat-topped ceremonial and burial mounds; in southeastern Illinois, Mississippians extract salt from Saline River
Circa 1600	Illiniwek tribes begin migrating into Illinois; by the mid-1600s, the Illiniwek Confederation dominates the future state
1655	Iroquois Indians invade Illinois country and conduct raids against the Illiniwek and other local tribes
1673	Frenchmen Père Jacques Marquette and Louis Jolliet explore the Mississippi River and other rivers in Illinois, gathering information and interacting with the natives
1680	René-Robert Cavalier, Sieur de La Salle, builds Fort de Crevecoeur on the Illinois River near present-day Peoria; it is destroyed a few months later
1682	René-Robert Cavalier, Sieur de La Salle, builds Fort St. Louis at Starved Rock on the Illinois River, near present-day Ottawa
1691–92	Henri de Tonti relocates Fort St. Louis to a site near Lake Pimiteoui (Peoria Lake), across the Illinois River from the demolished Fort de Crevecoeur
1696	Père Pierre François Pinet establishes the Guardian Angel Mission in future Chicago; it is abandoned six years later
1699	Priests of the French Seminary of Foreign Missions establish Holy Family Mission at Cahokia, founding the first European village in Illinois

1703	French Jesuits establish mission at Kaskaskia
1717	September 27: Illinois becomes part of the French colony of Louisiana
1719	The French build Fort de Chartres near present Prairie du Rocher and establish it as the seat of their military and civil government in Illinois
1754	May 28: The French and Indian War, a struggle between France and England for colonial supremacy in North America, begins in the Ohio River Valley
1763	February 10: (First) Treaty of Paris signed, ending the French and Indian War; France cedes its North American colonial possessions east of the Mississippi River to Great Britain
1775	April 18: American Revolution begins
1778	George Rogers Clark leads a seven-month campaign against the British in Illinois; after his victory in Kaskaskia on July 4, the state of Virginia assumes control of Illinois Country
1779	Jean Baptiste Point de Sable builds first permanent settlement at future site of Chicago
1783	September 3: The (Second) Treaty of Paris ends the American Revolution; western boundary of the United States extends to the Mississippi River
1784	March 1: Virginia relinquishes its claim to Illinois Country
1787	July 13: Congress passes the Northwest Ordinance, establishing a government for the Northwest Territory, which includes Illinois
1795	August 3: A confederation of Midwestern Indian tribes signs the Treaty of Greenville, establishing the borders of Indian territory and allowing the U.S. government to build forts at designated sites in the Northwest Territory, among which are the future locations of Chicago and Peoria
1800	May 7: Congress creates Indiana Territory, which includes Illinois
1803	July 4: Louisiana Purchase extends U.S. territory west of the Mississippi River
	August 13: Kaskaskia Indians sign treaty at Vincennes, relinquishing their claim to all land in the Illinois Country except a small area around Kaskaskia
1803–4	Winter: American troops build and occupy Fort Dearborn on the future site of Chicago
	Meriwether Lewis and William Clark establish winter quarters at Camp Dubois, near present-day Hartford, before embarking on their expedition with the Corps of Discovery
1804	March 26: Congress approves the establishment of a U.S. land office in Kaskaskia, the first of ten U.S. land offices in Illinois, for the purpose of selling land to settlers
	November 3: Members of the Sauk and Mesquakie (Fox) tribes sign Treaty of St. Louis, ceding most of their land between the Mississippi and Illinois Rivers to the U.S. government

1809	March 1: Congress creates the Illinois Territory, which includes the present states of Illinois and Wisconsin and portions of Michigan and Minnesota; Kaskaskia is designated first territorial capital and Ninian Edwards of Kentucky is appointed territorial governor
1812	June 18: The United States declares war on Great Britain, launching the War of 1812, in which Americans battle the British and their Indian allies for trade rights and territorial control
	August 15: Indians attack U.S. troops and civilians as they flee from Fort Dearborn, killing 52; the episode becomes known as the Fort Dearborn Massacre
1814	December 24: Great Britain signs the Treaty of Ghent, ending the War of 1812
1816	United States rebuilds Fort Dearborn in Chicago and builds Fort Armstrong on Rock Island
1817	U.S. government begins issuing land grants in Illinois Military Tract to veterans of the War of 1812 as payment for their service
1818	April 18: Congress passes Illinois Enabling Act, allowing for the establishment of the state of Illinois
	August 26: At the Illinois Constitutional Convention in Kaskaskia, the state constitution is adopted and Kaskaskia is named the first state capital
	October 6: Shadrach Bond is inaugurated as the first governor of Illinois
	December 3: Illinois becomes the twenty-first state
1819	July 30: Kickapoo Indians sign a treaty ceding most of their land in Illinois
1820	December 1: Vandalia becomes the new state capital
1825	August 19: Representatives of several regional tribes sign the (First) Treaty of Prairie du Chien, establishing tribal boundaries to reduce intertribal conflicts
1827	September 3: After a six-month uprising, Winnebago Indians in Illinois Territory surrender to the U.S. army; tribe cedes land to the government
1829	July 29: Potawatomi, Ottawa, and Chippewa Indians sign the (Second) Treaty of Prairie du Chien, ceding more than 3,000 square miles in northern Illinois to the state; the Winnebago (Ho Chunk) sign a separate treaty on August 1
1830	March: Abraham Lincoln and his family move to Macon County, Illinois, from southern Indiana
1832	May 14: The Black Hawk War, an Indian rebellion led by Sauk leader Black Hawk, begins with Battle of Stillman's Run
	August 27: The Black Hawk War ends with Black Hawk's surrender
	September 15: In a treaty signed at Fort Armstrong, the Sauk resisters and their allies cede their land in Illinois, Wisconsin, and Iowa and are forced to move to reservations in the West

1833	September 26: The Treaty of Chicago, the last Indian treaty in the state; all remaining Potawatomi, Ottawa, and Chippewa Indians agree to leave Illinois
1836	July 4: Construction of the Illinois & Michigan Canal begins
1837	February 25: State capital is moved from Vandalia to Springfield; the cornerstone of first capitol in Springfield is laid on July 4
	March 4: Chicago is incorporated as a city
	November 7: A mob in Alton slays Elijah P. Lovejoy, editor of the abolitionist newspaper the *Alton Observer*
1838	April: Mormons begin arriving in Commerce (later dubbed Nauvoo) after being driven from Missouri
	September 4–November 4: Potawatomi Trail of Death; nearly 1,000 Indians are forcibly marched across central Illinois to Indian Territory; at least 40 die en route
1838–39	Winter: Cherokee Trail of Tears; more than 10,000 Cherokees pass through southern Illinois on their forced march to Indian Territory; thousands die en route
1844	June 27: An anti-Mormon mob kills church founder Joseph Smith and his brother, Hyrum, at the Carthage jail
1846	February: Mormons depart Nauvoo for Winter Quarters (near present-day Omaha, Nebraska), under the leadership of Brigham Young
1848	March 5: Illinois adopts its second constitution, which among other things abolishes slavery in the state
	April 10: Completion of the Illinois & Michigan Canal, linking Lake Michigan with the Illinois River
1851	February 10: The Illinois Central Railroad receives its charter; construction begins on December 23
1856	September 27: Illinois Central Railroad is completed with the final spike driven near Mason
1858	August 21: U.S. Senate candidates Abraham Lincoln (Republican) and Stephen A. Douglas (Democrat) square off in Ottawa for the first of seven debates held throughout the state; the final debate is held in Alton on October 15
1860	May 18: Abraham Lincoln of Illinois is nominated as Republican candidate for U.S. president; he wins the election in November, becoming the 16th president
	September 8: The steamship *Lady Elgin* collides with the schooner *Augusta* on Lake Michigan near Highwood and sinks; about 300 people die
1861	March 4: Abraham Lincoln is inaugurated
	April 12: The Civil War begins when Confederate forces fire on Fort

	Sumter, South Carolina; Illinois sends more than 250,000 troops to join the Union forces during the four-year conflict
1864	November 8: Abraham Lincoln is elected to a second term as president
1865	February 1: Illinois is the first state to ratify the Thirteenth Amendment to U.S. Constitution, outlawing slavery
	April 9: Civil War ends with Robert E. Lee's surrender
	April 14: John Wilkes Booth assassinates Abraham Lincoln
	May 4: Lincoln's body is placed in a vault at Oak Ridge Cemetery in Springfield
	December 25: Union Stock Yard opens in Chicago
1868	October 5: Cornerstone of the current capitol in Springfield is laid
	November 3: Ulysses S. Grant, a former resident of Galena, is elected 18th president of the United States
1871	October 8–9: The Great Chicago Fire destroys 3.5 square miles of the city, with a loss of more than 300 lives and $200 million in property
1874	July: Joseph F. Glidden and Isaac L. Ellwood, both of DeKalb, form the Barb Fence Company and begin manufacturing Glidden's barbed wire design; the product will soon alter the landscape of the West
1886	May 4: During a labor gathering in Haymarket Square in Chicago, a bomb explodes, killing seven police officers and several others
1889	January: Jane Addams and Ellen Gates Starr, both Illinois natives, found Hull-House in Chicago
1892	July: Construction of Illinois & Mississippi (Hennepin) Canal begins
1893	May 1: World's Columbian Exposition, commemorating the 400th anniversary of Christopher Columbus's discovery of America, opens in Chicago
1894	May 10: Pullman Car Company employees strike, disrupting mail delivery; federal troops called out in July; violence erupts, killing at least 12 strikers
1898	April 25: Spanish-American War begins after Spain destroys the U.S. battleship *Maine* in Havana Harbor in February; Illinois sends 12,000 men to the conflict
	October 12: Violence erupts during a coal strike in Virden; 7 strikers and 6 guards are killed
	December 10: Spanish American War ends with signing of the 1898 Treaty of Paris
1900	May 2: Main channel of the Chicago Sanitary and Ship Canal to Lockport opens, reversing the flow of the Chicago River
1903	December 30: A fire engulfs the Iroquois Theater in Chicago, causing the death of 571 people; the tragedy leads to improved building-safety laws throughout the country

1905	June 27: Industial Workers of the World is founded in Chicago
1907	November 8: Illinois & Mississippi (Hennepin) Canal completed
1909	July 4: Daniel H. Burnham and Edward H. Bennett publish the *Plan of Chicago*, the first comprehensive urban-development plan ever created for an American city
	November 13: Explosion at the Cherry Mine in Cherry kills 259 miners
1914	November 12: The first "seedling mile" of concrete is poured in Malta for a transcontinental roadway that ultimately becomes the Lincoln Highway
1915	July 24: The excursion steamer *SS Eastland* capsizes at its wharf in the Chicago River, killing 812 passengers
1917	April 6: The United States enters World War I; Illinois sends more than 350,000 men to war
1918	November 11: Armistice with Germany signed, ending World War I
1920	January 17: The Volsted Act (Prohibition) goes into effect
1922	June 21–22: Violence erupts during a general coal strike in Herrin; 22 are killed
1925	March 18: The Tri-State Tornado hits Missouri, Illinois, and Indiana; 695 people die, making it the deadliest tornado in U.S. history
1929	October 24–29: U.S. stock market collapses, launching the Great Depression
1933	April 7: Repeal of the Volsted Act goes into effect, ending alcohol prohibition in the U.S.
	May 27: A Century of Progress International Exposition, celebrating Chicago's 100th anniversary, opens at Burnham Park
1937	May 30: Chicago police fire into a crowd of striking steel workers on the South Side, killing ten; the episode becomes known as the "Memorial Day Massacre"
1941	December 8: The United States declares war on Japan and, on December 11, on Germany and Italy; Illinois will send about 670,000 men and women for the war effort
1942	December 2: At the University of Chicago, Enrico Fermi directs the world's first controlled nuclear reaction, paving the way for development of the atomic bomb
1945	April 29: Germany surrenders; Japan surrenders on September 2, officially ending World War II
1946	July 7: Mother Frances Xavier Cabrini, who died in Chicago in 1917, is declared a saint, becoming the first U.S. citizen to be canonized by the Roman Catholic Church
1947	March 25: A coal mine explodes in Centralia, killing 111 miners
1950	June 25: U.S becomes involved in the Korean War

1951	December 20: Argonne National Laboratory near Darien produces the world's first nuclear-generated electricity
1953	May 2: The first Baha'i Temple in the Western Hemisphere is dedicated in Wilmette
	July 27: Armistice signed, ending the Korean War
1955	April 20: Richard J. Daley assumes office, beginning the first of six consecutive terms as mayor of Chicago; he serves until his death on December 20, 1976
	October 29: O'Hare International Airport in Chicago begins commercial passenger operations
1964	August 7: U.S becomes involved in the Vietnam War
1968	August 28: Violence erupts between protesters and city police during Democratic National Convention in Chicago, making headlines around the world
1970	December 15: Illinois voters ratify a new state constitution
1973	January 27: Peace agreement signed, ending U.S involvement in the Vietnam War
	May 3: The Sears Tower, the world's tallest building until 1998, is completed in Chicago
1979	April 3: Jane M. Byrne elected as first woman mayor in Chicago history
1980	November 4: Native Illinoisan Ronald Reagan elected president
1983	April 5: Harold Washington elected as first black mayor in Chicago history
1992	November 3: Carol Moseley Braun of Illinois becomes the first black woman to be elected to the U.S. Senate
1995	July 12: A newly renovated Navy Pier reopens as a public attraction
2005	April 19: Abraham Lincoln Presidential Library and Museum opens in Springfield
2008	February 14: A lone gunman commits a mass shooting at Northern Illinois University, killing 5 students and wounding 21
	November 4: U.S. Sen. Barack Obama of Illinois elected president, becoming the first African American U.S. president
2009	January 29: Gov. Rod Blagojevich becomes the first Illinois governor to be impeached and removed from office
2011	February 22: Rahm Emanuel elected first Jewish mayor in Chicago history
	March 9: Gov. Pat Quinn abolishes the death penalty in Illinois

Illinois Facts

Area:	57,926 square miles (including Illinois share of Lake Michigan)
Population:	12,830,632 (2010 census)
Territory established:	February 3, 1809
Statehood granted:	December 3, 1818
Capital:	Springfield (named capital 1837; originally Kaskaskia, 1818–20; Vandalia, 1820–37)
Nickname:	Prairie State
Slogan:	Land of Lincoln (adopted 1955)
Motto:	State Sovereignty, National Union
Flag:	Original adopted 1915; amended design adopted 1970

State Symbol	Year Adopted
Amphibian: Eastern tiger salamander	2006
Bird: Cardinal	1929
Dance: Square Dance	1990
Fish: Bluegill	1987
Flower: Violet	1908
Fossil: Tully monster	1990
Gem: Calcium fluorite	1965
Grass: Big bluestem	1989
Insect: Monarch butterfly	1975
Mammal: White-tailed deer	1982
Reptile: Painted turtle	2006
Snack: Popcorn	2003
Soil: Drummer silty clay loam	2001
Tree: White oak	1973

State song: "Illinois"

Official state song by Charles H. Chamberlin, 1925
Music by Archibald Johnston
New verses by Win Stracke, 1968, in celebration of the Illinois Sesquicentennial

(VERSE 1)
By thy rivers gently flowing, Illinois, Illinois,
O'er thy prairies verdant growing, Illinois, Illinois,
Comes an echo on the breeze,
Rustling through the leafy trees,
And its mellow tones are these, Illinois, Illinois,
And its mellow tones are these, Illinois.

(VERSE 2)
From a wilderness of prairies, Illinois, Illinois,
Straight thy way and never varies, Illinois, Illinois,
Till upon the inland sea,
Stands thy great commercial tree,
Turning all the world to thee, Illinois, Illinois,
Turning all the world to thee, Illinois.

(ORIGINAL VERSE 3)
When you heard your country calling, Illinois, Illinois,
Where the shot and shell were falling, Illinois, Illinois,
When the Southern host withdrew,
Pitting Gray against the Blue,
There were none more brave than you, Illinois, Illinois,
There were none more brave than you, Illinois.

(ORIGINAL VERSE 4)
Not without thy wondrous story, Illinois, Illinois,
Can be writ the nation's glory, Illinois, Illinois,
On the record of thy years,
Abraham Lincoln's name appears,
Grant and Logan and our tears, Illinois, Illinois,
Grant and Logan and our tears, Illinois.

(NEW VERSE 3)

Eighteen eighteen saw your founding, Illinois, Illinois,
And your progress is unbounding, Illinois, Illinois,
Pioneers once cleared the land
Where great industries now stand,
World renown you do command, Illinois, Illinois,
World renown you do command, Illinois.

(NEW VERSE 4)

Let us pledge in final chorus, Illinois, Illinois,
That in struggles still before us, Illinois, Illinois,
To our heroes we'll be true
As their vision we pursue
In a biding love for you, Illinois, Illinois,
In a biding love for you, Illinois.

Illinois Originals

The first African American settlement in the nation (Brooklyn, 1825); in 1873 Brooklyn became the first incorporated African American town in American history

The inventor of the steel bladed plow (John Lane of Lockport, 1833)

The first town in the United States platted and registered by an African American (New Philadelphia, founded by Free Frank McWorter, 1836)

The first racially integrated private school in the nation (Otterville, Hamilton Primary School, opened 1836)

The first and only U.S. president to receive a patent for an invention (Abraham Lincoln of Springfield, May 22, 1849)

The first completed land-grant railroad (Illinois Central Railroad, September 27, 1856)

The inventor of the two-horse cultivator (William Weir of Monmouth, 1862)

The first council meeting of the Union League of America (Pekin, June 25, 1862)

The first post of the Grand Army of the Republic (Decatur, April 6, 1866)

The first woman in the nation to receive a law degree (Ada Miser Kepley of Effingham, graduated from Union College of Law in Chicago, June 30, 1870)

The first retail mail-order catalog company in the world (Chicago, Montgomery Ward & Company, founded 1872)

The inventor of the upright grain silo (Fred Hatch of Spring Grove, 1873)

The first skyscraper in the world (Chicago, Home Insurance Building, designed by William Le Baron Jenny, 1885)

The first African American Catholic priest in the United States (Fr. Augustine Tolton of Quincy, ordained April 24, 1886)

The inventor of the automatic dishwasher (Josephine Garis-Cochran of Shelbyville, 1886)

The inventor of the game of softball (George Hancock of Chicago, 1887)

The first African American–owned and –operated hospital in the United States (Chicago, Provident Hospital, founded by Daniel Hale Williams, 1890)

The inventor of the mechanical Braille writer (Frank H. Hall of Jacksonville, 1892)

The first successful open-heart surgery in the world (Chicago, Provident Hospital, performed by Daniel Hale Williams, 1893)

The inventor of the Ferris Wheel (George Washington Gale Ferris of Galesburg, 1893)

The first eighteen-hole golf course in the United States (Wheaton, Chicago Golf Club, 1894)

The first automobile race in the United States (Chicago to Evanston and back, November 28, 1895)

The first juvenile court system in the nation (created by state legislature in Springfield, 1899)

The inventor of the fly swatter (Robert R. Montgomery of Decatur, 1900)

The first Walgreens drugstore (Chicago, founded by Illinois native Charles Walgreen, 1901)

The first 24-hour solar-powered generator (Olney, Willsie Power Company, founded by Henry E. Willsie and John Boyle Jr., 1902)

The first African American–owned film production company (Chicago, Foster Photoplay Company, founded by William Foster, 1909)

The creator of the Tarzan stories (Edgar Rice Burroughs of Oak Park, 1912)

The inventors of nonperishable processed cheese (Kraft brothers of Stockton, 1914)

The first mile of the Lincoln Highway, the nation's first trancontinental concrete roadway (Malta, November 14, 1914)

The creator of the Raggedy Ann stories and doll (John Barton Gruelle of Arcola, 1915)

The inventors of the pickup-style mechanical hay baler (Horace M. Tallman and Raymore McDonald of Shelbyville, 1929)

The creator of the cartoon sailor Popeye (Elzie C. Segar of Chester, 1929)

The inventor of the [Hostess] Twinkie (James Dewar of Oak Park, 1930)

The discoverer of Pluto, then considered the ninth planet (Clyde Tombaugh of Streator, 1930)

The first American woman to be awarded the Nobel Prize for Peace (Jane Addams of Chicago, December 10, 1931)

The first Dairy Queen soft-serve ice cream shop (Joliet, 1940)

The first controlled nuclear chain reaction (Chicago, University of Chicago, December 2, 1942)

The first American Roman Catholic saint (Mother Frances Xavier Cabrini of Chicago, canonized July 7, 1946)

The first African American Pulitzer Prize winner (Gwendolyn Brooks of Chicago, May 1950)

The first Baha'i Temple in the Western Hemisphere (Wilmette, dedicated May 2, 1953)

The first McDonald's franchise restaurant (Des Plaines, opened April 15, 1955)

The first ultrasound images of the human body (Lemont, Argonne National Laboratory, 1957)

The first African American U.S. president (Barack Obama of Chicago, elected November 4, 2008)

Special Introduction

By *Dee Brown*

> **Author's Note:** *American writer and historian Dee Brown wrote these remarks after reading this book's original draft, shortly before he died in 2002, poignantly noting, "This is the last piece of formal writing from my pen." I am deeply grateful for his guidance and encouragement during the project's embryonic stage and sincerely regret that he is unable to see its completion. It is my hope that I have lived up to his expectations.*

Good fortune afforded me an opportunity to live in Illinois for a quarter of a century. When I first arrived there I was under the false impression that the state's past was a series of rather dull incidents spread over monotonous prairies, occasionally illuminated by the celebrated Rail Splitter, Abraham Lincoln. Perhaps our greatest president.

After a few explorations of the differing areas of Illinois (and how different they are!) I discovered that had Lincoln never existed, or had he lived in another state, the myriad of historical events, the sites and scenes, still formed a fascinating pattern—challenging to historians, storytellers, and poets.

Nevertheless, any exploration of the Illinois past should probably begin with the Lincoln story, and for that we need a trustworthy guide. No better pilot is likely to be found than the author of this book because Stan Banash believes in accuracy combined with an interesting and informative narrative. Banash not only includes the basics but brings Lincoln into related actions and places where his presence adds interest.

The Lincoln basics of course take place in New Salem and Springfield, where the participating characters in the events are presented with the flair that is made possible for the re-creation of the town where Lincoln spent his youth and the city where are preserved various places where the great man came to maturity.

So many important matters originated in Illinois, so many great human beings began their lives here—outstanding personalities who often made their marks elsewhere in the world with original ideas and actions and inventions galore, [such as the] great agricultural revolution that made it possible for the American Middle West to feed the world occurred within and around this energetic state.

Among the most important events that originated here, but proceeded across the American West was the Lewis and Clark expedition. Below present-day Alton on Wood River near Bellefontaine, the expedition was planned, recruited, outfitted, and organized. With all the care that modern astronauts used for the first journey to the moon, Lewis and Clark built a keel boat, trained their young soldiers, and began their incomparable journey.

A half century later, another event that culminated outside the state originated at Mattoon. Here occurred a portentous incident that forecast the conquest of Mississippi, Tennessee, and finally Virginia and the Union victory in the Civil War. In June 1861, with the war going badly for the Union, Ulysses S. Grant came to Mattoon to muster an infantry regiment into state service. At the time Grant was considered a failure in civilian life, with no outstanding record as a military officer. A [decade] and a half later, Grant was honored in Mattoon for service to the nation.

Illinois provided more than its share of Civil War generals, some outstanding, [others] occasionally mediocre. Perhaps the state's most dramatic commander is celebrated at Jacksonville, in Morgan County. They celebrate Benjamin Grierson, a musician who hated horses but became one of the Civil War's greatest cavalrymen. Grierson led a daring raid through Mississippi, an operation designed to take Confederate pressure off Grant at Vicksburg. Because of the daring drama of the raid, Grierson has been memorialized in history, fiction, and film.

In his arrangement of this book, Mr. Banash has cast the Illinois past into regions: southern, western, central, eastern, northern, and greater Chicagoland; Chicago, being Chicago, has a section all its own. Here are the pioneer French and their relations with the nation's tribes. Stephen Douglas achieved fame, there was a great fire and a martyred cow, politics, politics, politics, the Union Stock Yard, and an early movie industry.

Illinois has not been blessed with such a book as this for more than half a century. But here we come to the old saying, the proof is in the pudding and let us proceed to the main course.

—Dee Brown
Little Rock, Arkansas

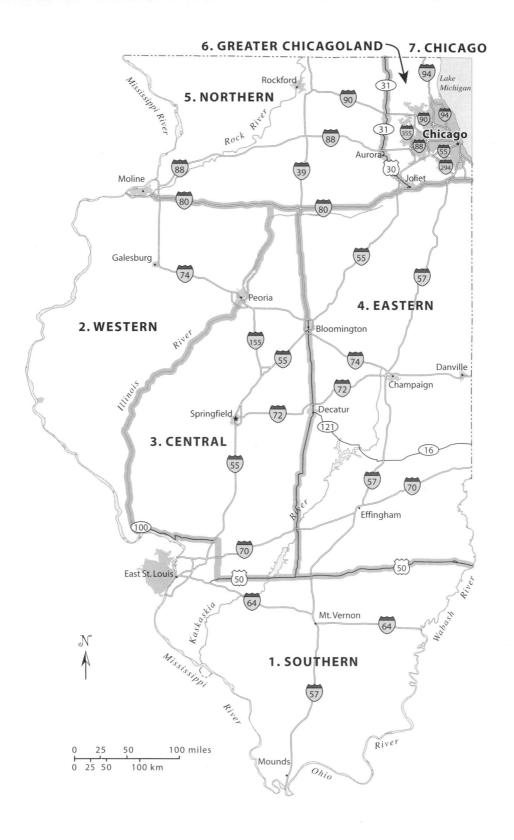

Overview:
A Brief History of Illinois

The land that became the state of Illinois began under layers of ice. Over a period of about 250,000 years, climatic changes melted and moved the glacial ice that once covered about 75 percent of the existing state's landscape. By around 12,000 BC, the glaciers that formed during the Illinoian and Wisconsinan periods had exposed flat lands, meandering rivers, lakes, swamps, rolling hills, and other geographical formations, in addition to rich soil, an abundance of bituminous coal, and scattered deposits of oil in the future Prairie State.

Early Native American Cultures

Paleo-Indians arrived in future Illinois around 12,000 BC and remained about 4,000 years, moving throughout the Mississippi River Valley and other riverside locations. They often stayed in small, temporary camps as they followed migrating large game, but they sometimes set up larger villages. These prehistoric Native Americans fashioned primitive stone tools, woven baskets, and clothes of animal skins. Succeeding them was the Archaic Culture, which evolved through Early, Middle, and Late periods. Less nomadic than the Paleo-Indians, the Archaic peoples cultivated native plants in addition to hunting and gathering.

Around 1000 BC, the Early Woodland Culture began to take over, followed by the Middle and Late Woodland Cultures. The Woodland peoples, who inhabited the Illinois and Mississippi River Valleys for about 2,000 years, are believed to be the first to build burial mounds in Illinois. They also eventually developed pottery, long-distance trade, rock art, and the bow and arrow. During the Woodland period, around 200 BC, the Hopewell Culture, another mound-building society, also emerged in Illinois' river valleys. The last prehistoric native group were the Mississippians, who lived throughout Illinois and whose mounds can still be seen at Cahokia Mounds, Dickson Mounds, and other sites.

When Europeans arrived in the late 1600s, the Illiniwek Confederation—a loose alliance of Algonquian tribes who shared the same language and culture—dominated

1

the northern Illinois River Valley region. Made up of the Cahokia, Kaskaskia, Michigamea, Moingwena, Peoria, Tamaroa, and related tribes, the Illiniwek numbered about 25,000 members in total.

European Explorations and Territorial Disputes

In May 1673 French explorer Louis Jolliet and Jesuit missionary Père Jacques Marquette, along with a crew of seven, paddled their two large canoes along the Fox, Mississippi, and Arkansas Rivers in an unsuccessful attempt to find a river route to the Pacific Ocean. They returned via the Mississippi, Illinois, and Des Plaines Rivers, portaging to the Chicago River and Lake Michigan, where they paddled north to Green Bay. In the spring of 1675, Marquette returned to the Illinois country and established the Church of the Immaculate Conception on Kaskaskia Island.

Seven years after the Jolliet and Marquette expedition, René-Robert Cavalier, Sieur de La Salle, accompanied by his friend, Henri de Tonti, and others, came to Illinois to lay claim to the Mississippi River Valley for France. In 1680, near today's Peoria, they built Fort Crevecoeur. Only a few months later, however, when both La Salle and de Tonti were away, the post's small garrison mutinied and destroyed the fort. La Salle and de Tonti returned to the region in 1682 and built Fort St. Louis atop what is now called Starved Rock. De Tonti later built a second Fort St. Louis (also called Fort Pimiteoui) near Lake Peoria. But France was unable to hold onto the region for long. In 1763, after the French and Indian War, France surrendered its claims east of the Mississippi River to the British.

Great Britain, too, soon lost its control of Illinois country and all its American colonies after its defeat in the Revolutionary War. In 1778 Virginian George Rogers Clark captured Fort Kaskaskia for the colonies, and a year later, as commander of the Kentucky and Illinois militias, he seized control in Vincennes. With Illinois in American hands, Virginia took over the region. Other states laid claim to parts of the territory as well, but by 1786 they had all relinquished their claims in the Northwest Territory to the federal government.

From Territory to State

Illinois country remained part of the Northwest Territory until 1800, when it became part of Indiana Territory. Nine years later, Illinois Territory, which encompassed present Illinois as well as Wisconsin and parts of Minnesota and Michigan, was established, with Kaskaskia as its capital. Ninian Edwards was appointed the first governor of the Illinois Territory, and Nathaniel Pope was named the first territorial secretary. The latter was influential in establishing the northern boundary of the future state of Illinois. Illinois won its statehood in 1818, with Shadrach Bond elected governor. The territorial capital of Kaskaskia became the state's first capital.

In 1820 the state capital was moved to Vandalia, reflecting a population shift inward. Illinois was growing, and state leaders began to focus on improving infrastructure such as roads and bridges, railroads, and the Illinois & Michigan Canal. Federal funds were needed. After several failed attempts, Daniel Pope Cook, U.S. Congressman from Illinois (and namesake of today's Cook County), succeeded in passing legislation in 1827 that granted the state nearly 150,000 acres on each side of the canal route.

Nathaniel Pope, first territorial secretary —Courtesy Schaumburg Township District Library, Illinois Collection

Daniel Pope Cook, first Attorney General of Illinois —Courtesy Schaumburg Township District Library, Illinois Collection

By dividing the land and selling parcels, Illinois was able to finance the canal construction, which began in 1836 and was completed twelve years later. Much of Chicago's early growth has been attributed to the Illinois & Michigan Canal. In the meantime, a young state legislator named Abraham Lincoln helped lead the push to relocate the state capital from Vandalia to Springfield. This time the move, which took place in 1839, was permanent.

Indian Relocation

In 1815 the Sauk and Mesquakie (Fox) tribes agreed to end hostilities against settlers and move west of the Mississippi River, but a splinter group of about 400 or 500 warriors along with some 2,000 women and children under the leadership of Ma-ka-tai-me-she-kia-kiak (Black Hawk) stayed firm. After a short-lived rebellion failed, Black Hawk's followers tried again in the spring of 1832. The Black Hawk War, a three-month conflict that ended in early August, resulted in Black Hawk's defeat and the relocation of his people. The following year, the Potawatomi, Ottawa, and Chippewa tribes signed the Treaty of Chicago, which ceded northeastern Illinois to the United States, pushing out most of the few remaining Indians in the state.

In the late 1830s, under the authority of the Indian Removal Act of 1830, the federal government completed its systematic relocation of all Indians east of the Mississippi to reservations in the West. In the summer of 1838 about nine hundred Potawatomi were forcibly marched from north-central Indiana across central Illinois to a reservation in present Kansas. The treacherous journey, which cost the lives of more than forty Potawatomi (mostly children), became known as the Trail of Death. Several months later, the tragedy was repeated when about 13,000 Cherokee were forced from their homelands in Georgia and North Carolina to march across southern Illinois to Indian Territory in present Oklahoma; about 3,000 died en route. This march came to be called the Trail of Tears.

Increasing Settlement and Development

Although some intrepid settlers and fortune seekers had braved moving into Illinois as early as the 1820s, the removal of the Indians in the late 1830s marked the beginning of widespread settlement in the state. In 1837 the town of Chicago incorporated as a city, attracting easterners and European immigrants. In southern and central Illinois, settlers established homes and industries along the rivers and ventured inland to establish ethnic and religious colonies, such as the Swedes at Bishop Hill, the Mormons at Nauvoo, and the Amish at Arthur.

Meanwhile, transportation was expanding, contributing greatly to Illinois' growth. The completion of the nearly one-hundred-mile Illinois & Michigan Canal in 1848 enabled goods to be shipped from Chicago to New Orleans and elsewhere through the canal to the Illinois and Mississippi Rivers. Around the same time, overland transportation took a giant stride when the Northern Cross Railroad, the first railroad in the state, began its eight-mile first run in 1838. Eighteen years later, the final spike of the Illinois Central Railroad was driven in at Mason, linking Chicago with Cairo.

It was also a time for innovation. John Lane of Will County invented the steel-bladed plow, which was further developed and marketed throughout the Midwest by John Deere of Moline. In Chicago, Cyrus Hall McCormick manufactured his mechanical reaper. Later, other Illinoisans developed such agricultural innovations as the mechanical hay baler, hybrid corn, the vertical silo, and barbed wire.

Slavery and the Underground Railroad

At the time Illinois became a state, slavery was a murky issue. Much of Illinois was abolitionist, but many citizens, especially in the southern part of the state, supported slavery. In 1824 the proslavery faction proposed a constitutional amendment to legalize the dubious institution, but Illinois' second governor, Edward Coles, and others ultimately defeated the referendum.

Despite pockets of slavery sympathizers, Illinois was a major part of the Underground Railroad. Runaways from slave states entered Illinois at riverfront towns such as Alton, Cairo, Chester, and Quincy and headed north through Chicago to Canada and freedom. Along the way, abolitionists hid the fugitives in their homes, businesses, churches, and barns. Slave catchers continued to be a threat even after the adoption of the 1848 state constitution, which prohibited involuntary servitude in Illinois. Slavery was still a contentious issue in 1858, when Abraham Lincoln and Stephen A. Douglas held their legendary senatorial debates in seven cities across the state.

The War of the Rebellion

Aside from a few proslavery areas, Illinois overwhelmingly supported the Union cause as the nation prepared for war, and the state exceeded its quota of volunteers to serve in the Union Army. Illinois' central location put it north of the major battlefields, so its citizens feared little from Confederate forces. Moreover, Chicago's secure location enabled it to become a major hub for producing and transporting food and supplies for Union troops.

In addition to soldiers, Illinois produced some extraordinary battlefield nurses, notably Mary Ann Bickerdyke of Galesburg and Mary Newcomb of Effingham. The Prairie State was also the home of two major figures of the Civil War era, President Abraham Lincoln and General (later President) Ulysses S. Grant.

During the war, four prisoner-of-war camps were established in Illinois. The largest was Camp Douglas, on the outskirts of Chicago; this prison became notorious for its unhealthy conditions and high death toll, but improvements were later made to mitigate the problems. Camp Douglas, along with the prisons in Alton, Rock Island, and near Springfield, were all closed by the summer of 1865.

The Industrial Era

After the Civil War, Illinois saw years of industrial expansion and prosperity. Chicago in particular became a railroad, manufacturing, and commercial behemoth and a magnet for immigrant workers. Although the Great Chicago Fire of 1871 devastated the city, it soon rebuilt with bigger and better-constructed buildings while expanding its manufacturing and meatpacking industries. By 1893 Chicago was ready to showcase itself at the World's Columbian Exposition, a huge international event that elevated Chicago in the eyes of the world.

The late nineteenth century also saw the emergence of modern retailing, with Chicago's Marshall Field's, Carson Pirie Scott, Walgreens, and others in the vanguard. Elsewhere in the state, agriculture remained the paramount industry, augmented by the mining of coal and other minerals in central and southern Illinois.

While mining benefitted the state's economy, it was a dangerous occupation. After numerous mining accidents, labor activists began clamoring for protections and benefits, fostering the rise of unions and other labor organizations. Workers in Illinois' railroad, steel, meatpacking, and other industries joined in the union movement as well. Violent conflicts occurred during strikes in Chicago, Virden, and elsewhere in the late 1800s and early 1900s. As a result, laws to improve working conditions in Illinois were passed, and Chicago became a strong union town. Meanwhile, deplorable living conditions and injustices in Chicago's struggling neighborhoods were brought to light by Jane Addams, Julia Lathrop, Ida B. Wells, Mary Augusta Safford, and others who helped improve the lives of the poor and working classes. These women also worked for universal suffrage in America, a goal that would finally be achieved in 1920.

The dawn of the twentieth century brought new vision to art, culture, and urban development in Chicago. In 1909 architects Daniel H. Burnham and Edward H. Bennett created their *Plan of Chicago*, one of the first urban-development plans in the United States. The plan recommended the creation of public parks and beaches, public transportation systems, cultural facilities, and public art. While not everything in the proposal was implemented, its ideas influenced not only the development of modern Chicago but the field of city planning itself.

As the automobile came into greater use, a need for improved roadways emerged in Illinois and the rest of the nation. In 1914, just west of Malta, the first seedling mile of a transcontinental roadway later known as the Lincoln Highway was laid down using a new construction material called concrete.

War, Peace, and Progress

Some 300,000 Illinoisans joined the service during World War I, and thousands of Midwestern recruits were trained at Fort Sheridan and the Great Lakes Naval Training Center. In addition, the Rock Island Arsenal produced weapons, artillery, and ammunition for American troops, and the facility continued to develop military technology during World War II and subsequent wars.

Prohibition and the 1920s was an unsettling time in parts of Illinois as Al Capone and other gangsters terrorized the Chicago area, and the Charlie Birger and the Shelton Brothers' gangs ran amok in the south-central part of the state. Then the Great Depression hit, creating hardships for many Illinois families. President Franklin Roosevelt's federal New Deal programs helped mitigate the crisis by providing jobs through the Civilian Conservation Corps, and federal art, writing, and theater programs promoted culture in both urban and outlying areas. Another bright spot during the Depression was Chicago's Century of Progress Exposition in 1933 and 1934, in which the Windy City celebrated its first one hundred years and even turned a profit from the event.

World War II was a technological turning point for Illinois and the nation as the work of Enrico Fermi and other scientists in Chicago gave birth to the atomic age. With the discovery of how to split the atom, scientists created the two atomic bombs that ended the war in the Pacific in 1945. Returning World War II veterans eager to build new lives received support through the newly created G.I. Bill of Rights, which was drafted in downstate Salem in 1943 and signed into law the following year.

Modern Times

After World War II, Illinois and the rest of the nation saw the expansion of interstate highways, suburban development, commercial aviation, and myriad new technologies. In Chicago, the opening of O'Hare International Airport made the city a national aviation hub. Over the next fifty years, the city continued to develop while wrestling with racial tensions, social unrest, and a changing economy.

As more and more highways crisscrossed the state, both large cities and small towns gained access to outside resources and populations became more diverse. Housing construction sprawled into what had been farmland and traditional manufacturing slowly gave way to high-tech and service-oriented industries. Increased energy needs led to the construction of seven nuclear power stations in the state, beginning in the 1960s. More recently, in the early twenty-first century, wind farms began appearing along the roads and highways, especially in central Illinois.

In 1970 Illinois ratified its fourth constitution, which addressed issues far different from those of earlier decades. Among other things, the document updated rules for voting, taxes, the legislature, the courts, and government responsibilities. The year 1980 saw the election of Ronald Reagan, the only U.S. president born in Illinois. Twenty-eight years later, former Chicago community organizer and U.S. Senator from Illinois Barack Obama became the nation's first black president.

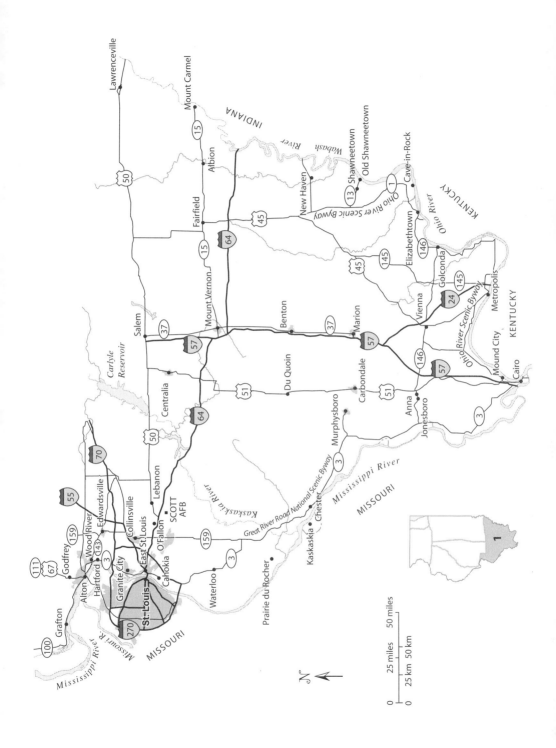

Southern Illinois

BETWEEN THE GREAT RIVERS

Southern Illinois covers nearly 11,000 square miles between the Mississippi, Ohio, and Wabash Rivers. This region was one of the first parts of the state to be developed, and its history is distinct from that of the rest of Illinois. The earliest settlers made their homes in the Ohio River Valley; later, some ventured farther west to the Mississippi River Valley. Their independence and optimism, triumphs and sorrows are woven into the fabric of regional lore.

Some people refer to southern Illinois as "Little Egypt." The source of this moniker may be in the region's geography, as the mighty Mississippi seemed as imposing as the Nile, and the Mississippi and Ohio River Valleys were thought to be as lush as the valley of the Nile. Furthermore, the area's ancient Indian mounds, such as Cahokia Mounds, were somewhat reminiscent of the Pyramids. Egyptian town names in the region, including Cairo, Karnak, Thebes, and others, may have either inspired or reinforced the nickname. Some historians and local residents maintain that Little Egypt was so christened in the 1830s, when droughts in the north drove people to turn to southern Illinois for corn—just as people traveled to Egypt to buy corn in Biblical times.

The region discussed in this chapter extends across the southern part of the state from the St. Louis metropolitan area to the state's eastern border. Major features include rolling agricultural farmland, coal mines, recreation on three large man-made lakes, and higher education at two campuses of Southern Illinois University.

Beginnings

Around 300,000 years ago, about 75 percent of the land that later became Illinois was covered with ice. The southern one-quarter, however, was unglaciated and retained its natural topography. Rolling prairies—now mostly farmland—extend from the Mississippi River on the west to the Wabash River on the east, plus a small pocket at the southern tip of the state. South of today's IL 13 are the Shawnee Hills, which stretch across the state from the Mississippi to the Ohio River. Some know this area as the "Illinois Ozarks," with its heavily timbered wilderness and rocky cliffs that tower above the valley floor. Still farther south, the land extends into steep valleys, foothills, swamps, lakes, and the floodplains of the Mississippi and Ohio Rivers.

The first occupants of these hills, valleys, and prairielands were various Indian cultures who roamed freely, moving according to the season and the availability of game. Traces of prehistoric civilizations are evident at the Cahokia Mounds, near Collinsville. The disappearance of these prehistoric peoples remains a mystery, though theories abound.

By 1673, when the first French explorers arrived in Illinois, only a few thousand Indians, mostly associated with the Illiniwek Confederation, lived in this region. Concentrated in the Illinois River Valley, the local tribes included the Cahokia, Kaskaskia, Michigamea, Moingwena, Peoria, and Tamaroa. But later, as tribes from the north, south, and east felt the pressure of European encroachment, they pushed into the southern part of the Illinois country. Tribal warfare ensued among the Cherokee, Delaware, Iroquois, Kickapoo, Miami, and Shawnee, and raids on white settlers increased with the population.

European Settlement

In the 1670s, French explorers Père Jacques Marquette, Louis Jolliet, and René-Robert Cavelier, Sieur de La Salle, explored the lands along the Illinois and Mississippi Rivers, seeking to establish trade routes and claim land for France. Their explorations laid the groundwork for white settlements at Cahokia and Kaskaskia in the early 1700s. To strengthen their hold on the region, the French ringed the southwestern perimeter of the Illinois country with military outposts—Fort de Chartres, Fort Kaskaskia, and Fort Massac. These forts became centers of military and political life on the frontier. In 1763 the French ceded some of their holdings in North America, including future Illinois, to the British, who held the region only until the American Revolution, less than twenty years later.

After the war, Easterners began to hear about the vast country west of the Wabash and Ohio Rivers, and some were lured by the opportunities for enrichment there. In 1782 a number of English-speaking settlers established Bellefontaine (near present Waterloo), adding to the settlements of Kaskaskia, Cahokia, and Prairie du Rocher.

Another early settlement, just east of St. Louis, Missouri, was established by Col. Samuel Judy in 1801. Known as Goshen Settlement, about a mile south of present Glen Carbon, it became a major community in the early days. In 1808 the Goshen Road, a wagon road, was built between the settlement and the saltworks near (Old) Shawneetown, on the Ohio River. The road, which crossed southern Illinois diagonally, mostly along Indian trails, was the region's main east-west road in the early 1800s. Traces of parts of the road still exist, but the exact route of much of the road is uncertain.

It was in the southern region that the roots of Illinois grew. In 1804 Congress chose Kaskaskia as the site of the first federal land office (established to sell land to settlers) in Illinois. Five years later, the federal government created the Illinois Territory and designated Kaskaskia as its first territorial capital. In 1814 the territory's first newspaper, the *Illinois Herald*, was published in Kaskaskia.

The land office in Kaskaskia and, later, those in other southern Illinois towns attracted settlers, who claimed land, built cabins, established farms, raised livestock, and eked out a living while maintaining a watchful eye for roaming Indians. Many gathered together to form villages and towns. When Illinois became a state in 1818, the territorial capital of Kaskaskia was selected to be the first state capital.

At first, as settlement developed, the region's Indians were, for the most part, peaceful. But as westward expansion continued, some young tribal members responded to the white man's encroachments by occasionally raiding isolated cabins, sometimes murdering settlers and travelers. Most of these actions were not sanctioned by tribal leaders, but the whites still held them accountable. Finally, as part of national policy, during the winter of 1838–39, thousands of Cherokee men, women, and children were forcibly marched across the sparsely settled southern part of the state to Indian Territory in the West. More than 3,000 died en route, earning the relocation program notoriety as the Trail of Tears. By the early nineteenth century, nearly all Native American tribes in Illinois had been relocated to reservations west of the Mississippi River.

Slavery and War

Throughout the first half of the nineteenth century, slavery was a contentious issue in Illinois, though relatively few slaves ever lived in the state. Slavery had been prohibited in Illinois from its inception as a territory, and the first state constitution, adopted in 1818, also banned the slave trade, though people who already owned slaves were allowed to keep them. Nevertheless, political battles over slavery raged in the state until the Civil War. Many slaveholders and slavery sympathizers lived in southern Illinois, and some landowners there held slaves illegally. The proslavery factions tried several times to reverse the prohibition against involuntary servitude, but they were unsuccessful.

In the meantime, abolitionists in southern Illinois were also actively fighting for their beliefs. Southern Illinois' geographical location made it a gateway for the Underground Railroad. The river crossings at Cairo, on the Ohio River, and Alton and Chester, on the Mississippi River, were major entry points on the freedom trail of secret havens inside the houses, barns, caves, churches, and cabins of many towns in Illinois.

When the Civil War broke out, Illinois declared itself a Union state, even though pockets of Confederate sympathy remained, especially in the southern region. The war drew military attention to this area due to its proximity to several slave states and, equally crucial, the strategic importance of the Ohio and Mississippi Rivers. In 1861 Cairo, the southernmost city in Illinois, became the site of several Union army camps as well as a naval base. The city's Fort Defiance served as headquarters for Gen. Ulysses S. Grant, a resident of Galena, Illinois. Although no battles were fought in Illinois, river towns such as Cairo were important supply bases and tactical posts for the Union.

Industrial Era and Beyond

During the Civil War, railroads proved their inestimable value. Afterward, Illinois' rail lines were expanded, opening up the state's interior to broader markets, fostering economic growth, and establishing new towns. The steam-powered locomotives and riverboats drew on southern Illinois' vast timber and coal reserves until both fuels were replaced by diesel power. The timber industry continues to feed the region's economy, though to a lesser degree after nearly two centuries of tree harvesting and clear cutting. Coal, too, is still mined in some counties.

With the accessibility of fuel and river transportation, manufacturing also flourished in the southwestern part of the state. The industrialization of the late nineteenth century attracted immigrants, especially Europeans, to southern Illinois. While Germans mostly took to farming, establishing towns that reflected their culture, Welsh, British, and Eastern Europeans sought work in the coal mines and factories. During World War I, black workers from the South often filled manufacturing jobs left by whites called to active service, especially in the East St. Louis area.

By the late twentieth century, coal and lumber production in southern Illinois had dropped to nearly nothing, and manufacturing had seriously declined as well. While industrial and mining activities continue today in varying degrees, agriculture has remained the mainstay of the economy throughout southern Illinois. Recently, however, community leaders have been putting more emphasis on tourism and recreation, fostering the development of large parks and recreation facilities, museums, visitor accommodations, and even "wine trail" tours of local vintners.

Ohio River Scenic Byway (IL 37, IL 169, US 45, IL 145, and IL 146)
CAIRO–GOLCONDA
76 miles

Connected to the Great River Road Scenic Byway at Cairo, the Ohio River Scenic Byway extends nearly 1,000 miles across Illinois into eastern Ohio. Following the byway for its entire route is a long and winding journey along various US highways, state routes, and county roads. For this tour, we shave off a bit between Metropolis and Golconda by taking IL Routes 145 and 146. This trip ends at Golconda; the other half of the byway in Illinois, from Golconda to Shawneetown, will be described on a later trip.

CAIRO

Cairo (pronounced KAY-ro), at the confluence of the Mississippi and Ohio Rivers, has a rich history as a transportation center. Throughout the nineteenth century, it thrived as a river port and railroad hub. Yet in 1990, the principal of Cairo High School advised the graduating class to leave town, saying the city had nothing to offer them. What happened to Cairo's potential?

The town's original landholders envisioned it as a mecca for trade and immigration. In 1817 founder John G. Comegys, a St. Louis merchant, purchased 1,800 acres on the future site of Cairo. He incorporated his land as a city the following year, naming it Cairo for the area's resemblance to the Nile delta. Comegys planned to sell lots and use the monies to build a levee. He also wanted to connect Cairo by rail with the proposed Illinois & Michigan Canal. Unfortunately, he died shortly thereafter, and so did his plans for Cairo. The federal government took back most of his land.

In 1834 Cairo got a second chance when a group of investors acquired Comegys's land and some additional adjacent acreage, determined to fulfill the promise of this well-located river port. Soon Cairo had levees, a dry dock, a shipyard, warehouses, and other operations. Due to financial setbacks and political shenanigans, however, construction of the railroad was delayed until the 1850s. Finally, on September 27, 1856, Cairo and Chicago were linked by rail, providing an inland alternative to steamboat transportation. Now a hub for both rail and water routes, Cairo flourished.

An artillery battery at Fort Defiance (Camp Prentiss) near Cairo
—Courtesy Schaumburg Township District Library, Illinois Collection

Its excellent transportation made Cairo a key transfer station for fugitive slaves from the South heading to Chicago and beyond along the Underground Railroad. The runaways were secreted in safe locations in area homes and businesses. Once safe passage could be arranged on the Illinois Central Railroad or on steamboats, the fleeing slaves continued their trek north.

The Civil War changed the complexion of Cairo. When the war broke out, the Union Army established a number of military encampments here, including the well-armed Fort Defiance, originally called Camp Prentiss. Due to its location, Cairo was a crucial strategic position for maintaining control of the Mississippi and Ohio Rivers. Brig. Gen. Ulysses S. Grant of Galena used the city as his headquarters while commanding the District of Southeast Missouri, Western Department. Fort Defiance served as a major supply base and as a staging area for military actions in the South. The post also handled wounded Union soldiers and Confederate prisoners arriving from southern battlefields. The original site of Fort Defiance was about one mile north of present Fort Defiance State Park.

A yellow fever epidemic in 1878 didn't slow Cairo's dynamic growth, but progress eventually did. The river trade died down, and the traffic that remained was mostly composed of barges, which had no need to stop at Cairo for refueling or letting off passengers. After its peak in the mid-1880s, the city entered a steady decline.

Cairo's death knell may have come in the 1960s. Due to its proximity to southern states, Cairo was strongly influenced by the culture of the South, and many white residents supported racial segregation. Three days of race riots in July of 1967 were followed by years of racial unrest and civil rights protests. A ten-year organized boycott of white-owned businesses drove many merchants out, and Cairo's downtown became a cluster of abandoned storefronts.

Today Cairo struggles to regain its economic and social stability. Helping this effort is the preservation of its downtown and its historical structures. The Cairo Historic District was listed on the National Register of Historic Places (NRHP) in 1979, and the city contains several buildings of historic significance.

Historic Cairo: Magnolia Manor and Other Unique Buildings

Magnolia Manor, a fourteen-room brick mansion of Italianate design, testifies to the charm and beauty of Cairo in its heyday. Built between 1869 and 1872, the four-story home featured winding staircases and opulent furnishings, including gold-washed chandeliers. Its original owners were Charles and Adelia Galigher, who lived there until 1905. Galigher was a prominent citizen of Cairo who made a fortune selling flour to the government during the Civil War. He befriended Gen. Ulysses S. Grant while the latter was stationed in Cairo, and their friendship lasted after the war. But it was not until 1880 that Grant returned to Cairo to visit the Galigher family and stay at Magnolia Manor.

Magnolia Manor, the crown jewel of Victorian-era historic houses in Cairo—Author's collection

Only three other families occupied the home after the Galighers, and it sat empty until 1952, when the newly formed Cairo Historical Association began restoration of the home. Seventeen years later, it was added to the NRHP.

Two other architecturally significant buildings in Cairo are the U.S. Custom House and the A. B. Safford Memorial Library. The former, a limestone structure of Romanesque design, was completed in 1872 and speaks to Cairo's former importance as a river port. One distinct artifact on display is the flagpole from the *Tigress*, the river packet that carried Maj. Gen. Ulysses S. Grant up the Tennessee River to the Battle of Shiloh. The ship was sunk in 1863 near Vicksburg, Mississippi, but the crew survived. Later, they recovered the flagpole and presented it to the city of Cairo.

The A. B. Safford Memorial Library is an imposing red brick structure designed in Queen Anne style. It was built in 1883 by Mrs. Anna E. Safford as a memorial to her husband, Alfred. Statues of Greek goddesses flank the entrance and stained-glass windows all around depict classical authors. The library's Special Collections Room counts among its treasures more than six hundred books on the Civil War.

MOUND CITY

Indian burial mounds, the only remnant of the native villages that once stood at the confluence of the Cache and Ohio Rivers, gave Mound City its name. Among the first white settlers in the area were the Clark and Phillips families, who arrived from Tennessee in 1811. The two families lived peacefully in neighboring cabins until their tranquility was shattered less than two years later.

On February 9, 1813, a band of about ten Creek Indians stopped at the Clark homestead asking for food. After sharing a meal, some of the Creeks stayed at the Clark place while others walked over to the Phillips cabin. Mr. Phillips was away, but Mrs. Phillips was there with her two teenage children and a boarder. Suddenly the Indians attacked, murdering all six settlers. A visiting neighbor who had stopped by for some whiskey was wounded but escaped the slaughter and alerted a nearby settlement. Local militia tracked the Indians to Kentucky but lost their trail in a snowfall. The victims were buried by soldiers from nearby Fort Massac (see next stop). Today, there are no traces of the event that became known as the Mound City Massacre or the Cache River Massacre.

The area remained sparsely settled until the early 1850s, when Virginia native Gen. Moses M. Rawlings, a wealthy businessman, purchased about twenty acres of land in what would soon become Mound City. He platted a town on the cleared land and erected a cabin that served as his home, a boardinghouse, and a hotel. In 1854 he chartered a short-line railroad connecting Mound City with the Illinois Central line; it was completed two years later. At the time, the settlement had seven residents; by 1860, two years after Mound City was incorporated, it had nearly nine hundred.

In the meantime, a group of Cincinnati investors formed Emporium Real Estate & Manufacturing Company and purchased a forty-square-mile tract of land near Mound City. The partners' plan was to build a metropolis "grander than all the cities built since the downfall of ancient Rome," according to the *History of Pulaski County*. Naming their community Emporium City, the partners constructed houses, several warehouses, a foundry, and a shipyard. But in 1857 the company went bankrupt, and Emporium City eventually merged with its neighbor.

In 1861, as a war between the North and South became imminent, the federal government looked to Mound City as a possible base of operations. Its location on the Mississippi River, along with the shipyard and large sturdy warehouse that the Emporium Company had already established here, made it ideal. Later, Gen. Ulysses S. Grant established his headquarters in nearby Cairo.

The government leased the Mound City Shipyard from Hambleton, Collier & Company, who had purchased it after Emporium Real Estate went under, and outfitted it for naval support. The facility housed the Mississippi River Squadron, which included more than 150 gunboats, transports, mortar boats, and tugboats. During the war, some 1,500 contracted employees repaired vessels, converted steamers into armored boats, and built new ships. The shipbuilders produced three ironclad warships, including the *U.S.S. Mound City*.

In 1862 the *Mound City* captured a Confederate steamer, the *Red Rover,* and the Union refitted it as a hospital vessel. The *U.S.S. Red Rover,* which transported wounded troops to the Mound City Naval Hospital, was the U.S. Navy's first hospital ship. It is believed that the ship carried the first female military nurses, some of them black women who were actually contraband slaves retroactively listed as naval nurses.

The Union also took over Emporium's empty factory-warehouse and converted it into the Mound City Naval Hospital, whose staff provided medical care to thousands of Union soldiers and sailors. Those who died at the hospital were buried in Mound

This barracks (left foreground) was part of the Mound City Navy Yard.
—Courtesy Public Library of Cincinnati and Hamilton County

City National Cemetery, established in 1864, about a mile south of town. It was the first national cemetery in Illinois. The 10.5-acre grounds include the graves of 1,644 troops, including Union soldiers killed on nearby battlefields, a number of Confederate soldiers, and a Confederate spy (J. Purveyor). Union Brig. Gen. John Basil Turchin (born Ivan Vailovitch Turchinoff in rural Russia) is interred here alongside his wife, Nadine. Nearly fifty nurses and civilian employees who served at the hospital are also buried here. The seventy-two-foot high Illinois Soldiers and Sailors Monument, erected in the mid-1870s, lists many of those interred, but almost 3,000 graves are those of unknowns.

The hospital building was placed on the NRHP in 1974, but it burned down two years later. The Mound City Shipyard, a.k.a. Mound City Marine Ways, passed through several private owners until it was abandoned in the 1970s. Visitors to the site today will find only remnants of its concrete foundations, rails, and sliding launch ramps.

METROPOLIS

Metropolis makes a point of telling the world that in 1972, the city was declared the "Hometown of Superman." A fifteen-foot-tall statue of the DC Comics hero stands before the county courthouse, and residents hold an annual Superman Celebration. In 2010 a statue of Lois Lane was unveiled nearby. A museum dedicated to the "Man of Steel," the Super Museum, features movie props and collectibles.

While the fictional Superman draws in tourists, two real-life heroes of Metropolis are less well known. Oscar Micheaux (1884–1951), an author and independent film-maker, was the first African American to produce a feature-length film (1919) and a feature-length talkie (1931). His works aimed to counter racism and raise consciousness in a segregated society. (See also under North Center and Roscoe Village in Region 7.)

Another black pioneer from Metropolis was Annie Turnbo Malone (1869–1957), a chemist and entrepreneur who developed and manufactured a line of hair products for black women. She started by selling her products door-to-door and later set up shop in St. Louis, eventually becoming a millionaire. In 1918 she founded a cosmetology school, Poro College, in St. Louis. A dedicated philanthropist, Malone gave much of her fortune to charitable causes, including the St. Louis Orphans Home, later renamed the Annie Malone Children and Family Service Center.

The town of Metropolis was established in 1839 near the site of Fort Massac (see below), which had been abandoned twenty-five years before, and it was named the seat of Massac County in 1843. The site of Fort Massac was established as a state park in 1908, making it the first state park in Illinois.

Fort Massac State Park

In 1757, during the French and Indian War, French Army commander Charles-Phillippe Aubrey was leading an expedition on the Ohio River to intercept English troops when he discovered a strategic location near the confluence of the Ohio and Tennessee Rivers. Here he built a temporary outpost, which he called Fort Ascension because construction began on that religious holiday. The post soon became a permanent stronghold, renamed Fort Massiac.

After Illinois and the rest of the French territory in North America were ceded to Britain in 1763, Fort Massiac was abandoned and later burned down by the Chickasaw. In 1794 President George Washington ordered the fort, now spelled Massac, rebuilt and garrisoned to repel any attempt by the Spanish to expand their territory. Two years later, post commander Capt. Zebulon Pike strengthened the fort's defenses in anticipation of Spanish imperialist encroachment. In 1803 Meriwether Lewis and William Clark, seeking men for their trek westward, visited Fort Massac. Here local resident George Drouillard joined the expedition as a hunter, trapper, and interpreter.

Indian unrest in the early 1800s led to increased military activity at the fort until its structures were damaged in the New Madrid earthquake of 1811. The fort was soon repaired and regarrisoned to meet British threats in the War of 1812. Two years later, however, the post was abandoned; its military equipment was shipped to St. Louis, and materials from the buildings were scavenged by area residents and passing riverboats. At the outbreak of the Civil War, a Union army camp was briefly established at the Fort Massac site, but a measles epidemic forced its evacuation. These were the last troops ever stationed on the grounds of Fort Massac.

In 1908, through the efforts of Joseph Cullen Blair and the Daughters of the American Revolution, Fort Massac became the first state park in Illinois. The achievement earned Blair the sobriquet "Father of Illinois State Parks."

BROOKPORT

Located on the Ohio River and surrounded by abundant forests, Brookport came of age with the steamboat. When wood-burning steamers plied the river, Brookport, originally called Pellonia but chartered in 1855 as the village of Davis Landing, was a fuel stop.

When boats and barges converted from wood fuel to coal in the mid-1800s, the rapidly expanding railroad kept Brookport going, at least for a while, as the town supplied timber for railroad ties. Eventually, though, the forests became depleted and Brookport began its decline. After the ferry between Brookport and Paducah, Kentucky, was destroyed in an ice storm in 1918, it was replaced by a bridge connecting Paducah to Metropolis, leaving Brookport struggling. A new highway and bridge in 1929 helped the town for a few decades, but when I-24 was built in the 1970s, it bypassed Brookport, limiting future prospects. Most residents don't seem to mind, however. Today's Brookport maintains an old-fashioned small-town atmosphere where its 1,000-plus residents walk most everywhere and catch up on gossip at the beauty shop or hardware store.

GOLCONDA

Revolutionary War veteran Maj. James Lusk and his wife, Sarah, along with thirty-two other settlers left Waxhall, South Carolina, in 1796, intending to settle in Livingston County, Kentucky. Lusk planned to build a ferry across the Ohio River to Illinois, then part of Indiana Territory. Upon learning that the newly established state of Kentucky would allow slavery, however, Lusk, a rabid abolitionist, decided to reverse direction and settle on the Indiana side of the river.

Lusk applied for a ferry license in Indiana, but his request was denied. Undeterred, he built and operated his ferry business illegally in present Golconda. At the time, the Lusks were the only settlers between Kentucky and Kaskaskia, a distance of about eighty miles. Their ferry house doubled as an inn, providing lodging and meals for travelers. When James died in 1803, Sarah continued the business. She reapplied for a ferry license and the application was approved, making her the first woman to be granted a ferry license in Illinois. Two years later, Sarah married Thomas Ferguson and sold the ferry, though the couple stayed in the area. Ferguson platted the land around his cabin and named it Sarahsville, later renamed Golconda. Steamboats continued to stop at the ferry house for fuel, and the settlement thrived.

In the winter of 1838–39, about 13,000 Cherokee people, forced to march from their homes in the South to the western Indian Territory, reached the Ohio River at Golconda. They crossed into Illinois on the still-operating ferry before continuing their trek west. So many Indians died on this march that it became known as the Trail of Tears (see next trip).

Despite a devastating flood in 1937, Golconda survives, protected by a floodwall. The entire city is designated a state historic district.

IL 146
GOLCONDA–IL 3
53 miles

IL 146 runs east and west between IL 3 at Ware, just west of Jonesboro, and Golconda. The highway follows the approximate route of the forced Cherokee exodus known as the Trail of Tears.

Trail of Tears

In 1830 President Andrew Jackson signed the congressionally approved Indian Removal Act. After four other Indian nations had been forcibly marched from their lands, in early 1838 it was the Cherokee's turn. Brevet Maj. Gen. Winfield Scott was placed in charge of the operation, a forced relocation of approximately 13,000 Cherokee people from their ancestral homelands in North Carolina, Georgia, Tennessee, and Alabama to Indian Territory in present Oklahoma.

During the roundup, the Indians were divided into groups of about a thousand and held at thirteen crude forts in southeastern Tennessee before moving westward on one of four routes. The northern route passed through Illinois, extending from Golconda on the Ohio River to Ware and Reynoldsville along the Mississippi River. The first group taking the northern route left Tennessee in August 1838 to begin the eight-hundred–mile journey, mostly on foot. Other parties followed later in the fall. The trail was primitive even when dry, but heavy autumn rains made it nearly impassable. Along the way, at least 3,000 Indians died—largely from starvation, exposure, and disease. Their bodies were buried in shallow, unmarked graves along the trail.

After entering Illinois, the Cherokee marchers' hardships were compounded when ice floes and melting snow prevented ferries from transporting the more than 10,000 tribal members across the Mississippi River at Elijah Willard's ferry landing. The Cherokee families languished along the eastern shoreline, near Jonesboro, for the entire winter, sleeping on hard ground or in flimsy shelters, huddling together around campfires with only thin blankets to ward off the cold; a few were able to find lodging with homesteaders. When the weather improved, the survivors were ferried across and continued the trek through southern Missouri, arriving at their reservation by mid-March 1839.

The Cherokee called their tragic journey *Nunahi-Duna-Dio-Hilu-I*, which means "Trail Where They Cried."

In 1987 Congress established the Trail of Tears National Historic Trail. Through the efforts of private citizens, nonprofit groups, and government agencies, much of the original route is identified and marked with official National Historic Trail markers. Today, travelers can visit the crossing site at Willard's Landing (near Ware), across the Mississippi River from the Trail of Tears State Park in Missouri, and imagine what the Cherokee people endured during that brutal winter. Nearby, about five miles northwest of Jonesboro, is Illinois' 5,000-plus-acre Trail of Tears State Forest.

GOLCONDA
See previous trip

VIENNA

As a reminder that thousands of Cherokee people trekked through Vienna (pronounced VY-enna) on the Trail of Tears in the 1830s, a commemorative totem pole depicting the seven clans of the Cherokee Nation, carved by local artist Terry Bittle from a one-hundred-year-old cedar tree, was erected in Vienna City Park in 1998.

Another place of interest to history buffs is the Paul Powell Museum and Research Center, the former home of eccentric Illinois politician Paul Powell. Born in Vienna in 1902, Powell was a leading force in downstate politics in the 1950s and 1960s. He served six years as mayor of Vienna, four terms as Illinois House minority leader, three terms as Speaker of the Illinois House, and two terms as Illinois Secretary of State. During his tenure as Secretary of State, his office was investigated for corruption, but he was cleared. He died in Minnesota in 1970, while a patient at the Mayo Clinic.

After Powell's death, his suite at Springfield's St. Nicholas Hotel was found to hold more than $800,000 in cash, stuffed in shoeboxes, as well as forty-nine cases of whiskey, two cases of creamed corn, and other strange items. His estate turned out to be worth millions, including about a million dollars in racetrack stock. His Vienna home displays memorabilia from his life and serves as the headquarters for the Johnson County Genealogical and Historical Society.

JONESBORO

Jonesboro lies amid the rolling hills that surround the Shawnee National Forest. When Union County was formed in 1818, the same year Illinois became a state, Jonesboro was created as the county seat. Illinois politician John Grammer donated land for the new town and its first county courthouse, a modest log cabin.

But the Jonesboro's real booster was the Willard family. The recently widowed Nancy Willard had three children, a daughter, Anna, and two sons, Elijah and Willis. The family established a general store, Willard & Company, and built the first good county road and the first steam-powered flour mill and sawmill. Elijah Willard built a ferry landing on the Mississippi River. In 1839 this ferry was used by the Cherokee during their forced march on the Trail of Tears (see above).

In 1857 a new courthouse replaced the original log cabin. The building was only a year old when Abraham Lincoln and Stephen A. Douglas debated in their U.S. Senate campaign. The site of the debate is commemorated in a twenty-two-acre park on the edge of town.

Third Lincoln-Douglas Debate (Jonesboro, September 15, 1858)

Jonesboro was in Democratic, proslavery country, giving Douglas comfortable support at his third debate with Lincoln. The town's population was about eight hundred, but the crowd at the event was nearly double that number. Even so, the turnout was the smallest of all the debates.

The debate took place in a grove a short distance from town. Because of the small crowd, nearly everyone in the audience was able to hear the candidates' remarks, though they were periodically interrupted by a brass cannon that Douglas's backers had brought to the event.

Douglas opened by blasting Lincoln for inflaming the nation's divisions over slavery. Lincoln denied this and pointed out that some Democrats also favored the abolition of slavery. Douglas also claimed that his opponent presented himself as more conservative the farther south he traveled. In spite of Douglas's accusations to the contrary, Lincoln's speeches were remarkably consistent, and many historians believe that this consistency enhanced his image in Illinois and throughout the nation.

Ohio River Scenic Byway (IL 146, IL 1, and IL 13)
GOLCONDA—SHAWNEETOWN
64 miles

From Golconda, the Ohio River Scenic Byway continues north along various state and county roads to the Indiana state line near New Haven, but we will end our tour in Shawneetown. Along the way we'll visit Cave-in-Rock, once an ambush spot for pirates and bandits.

GOLCONDA
See earlier trip

CAVE-IN-ROCK

Cave-in-Rock State Park, established in 1929, offers beauty and solitude near the eastern edge of the Shawnee National Forest, along the banks of the Ohio River. The cave is just east of the tiny village of Cave-in-Rock. In 1962 the cave and its unspoiled surrounding area were on-location settings for the movie *How the West Was Won*.

The park's serene setting belies the activities that take place there every summer. The first "Hogrock River Rally" was held in the area in June 1997, and it has become an annual tradition for a decidedly untraditional crowd. Geared to bikers and restricted to persons eighteen and older, the four-day, three-night gathering features live "hardcore" music, vendors, and nightly contests. Other events at Cave-in-Rock include various outdoor rock concerts and the river rally's autumn counterpart, "Hogrocktoberfest."

Wild times have always been part of Cave-in-Rock's history. Beginning in the late eighteenth century, the huge cave was a notorious hideout and ambush site for outlaws and river pirates.

Pirates on the Ohio River

In the late 1780s, bands of outlaws operated from the caves along the Ohio River, just beyond the edge of civilization. They preyed on unsuspecting travelers passing by on flatboats and the crews of cargo-laden keelboats, robbing them of goods, money, livestock, and often their lives.

Probably the most vicious of these pirates were the Harpe brothers—Micajah "Big" Harpe and Wiley "Little" Harpe. For a while, they were part of the Samuel Mason gang, who operated out of Cave-in-Rock in the early 1800s. In the late 1790s Mason, a former officer in the American Revolution, converted the fifty-five-foot-wide, two hundred–foot-deep cave into a tavern called Cave-in-Rock. The "hospitality" offered there was but a ruse to lure in passersby, whom the bandits would rob and usually murder.

While at Cave-in-Rock, the Harpe brothers once went too far. They stripped a captured traveler, placed him naked atop a blindfolded horse, and sent both horse and rider over a cliff to crash against the rocks below, in full view of Mason's gang members. Subsequently banned from the Mason gang, the Harpe brothers moved on to Kentucky, where they went on a killing spree. In the meantime, a volunteer militia unit captured or killed most of the Mason Gang except their leader, who escaped to operate along the Natchez Trace in Mississippi.

In time, travelers on the Ohio River were warned to look out for the pirates, often recognizable by "an absence of ears." In those days, criminals were sometimes punished with the amputation of one or both of their ears, depending on the severity of the offense. In the case of Samuel Mason and the Harpes, however, it was not their ears they lost, but their heads.

After the Harpes' rampage in Kentucky, local settlers captured Big Harpe, cut off his head, and mounted it at a crossroads to send a message to other marauders. Little Harpe escaped and rejoined Mason at Cave-in-Rock, but a few years later, hearing of a $500 reward for Mason, Harpe and a cohort, James May, killed him. The pair severed Mason's head and brought it to Natchez to collect the reward money. As the outlaws were leaving with their cash, someone recognized them. Both men were arrested, convicted, and executed at the gallows. Some historians contend that after the hanging, the two bodies were treated just as Big Harpe's had been—the heads were cut off and placed on poles.

By the late 1820s, lawmen and citizen posses had all but purged the area of organized piracy and other criminal activity, including that of the Sturdivant gang of counterfeiters. Among the last to ply his trade at Cave-in-Rock may have been gang leader James Ford, who led a double life. He maintained an upstanding public image as a legitimate ferry operator while secretly directing a gang of pirates. Ford met his fate in 1833, when he was murdered by some of his own cronies.

SHAWNEETOWN AND OLD SHAWNEETOWN

As the closest port on the Ohio River to the salt springs on the Saline River, the site of Old Shawneetown was a prime spot for settlement. The Shawnee Indians had a sacred burial site and winter village at that location, but they never lived there permanently. The first American settler was Michael Sprinkle, a hunter and meat supplier, who arrived around 1800. Sprinkle made friends with the Shawnee and, because of his gun-repair and blacksmith skills, was allowed to build a cabin and settle among them.

After the Shawnee were forced out, Sprinkle remained to conduct business with traders, trappers, and arriving settlers.

The settlement grew quickly as a harbor for flatboats and steamboats and as an early industrial center for salt refining and logging. In 1810 the village of Shawneetown was platted by the federal government; it and Washington, D.C., are the only two municipalities in the country to hold that distinction. When Gallatin County was formed two years later, Shawneetown was designated the seat. A courthouse was built in 1815; it would be replaced by a sturdier structure in 1857.

In 1812 a federal land office opened in Shawneetown, attracting lawyers, bankers, and other professional people. Two years later, the Illinois legislature chartered the first state bank, the Bank of Illinois, in this village. The original bank was in a room at the 1808 brick residence of early settler John Marshall, who served as the first bank president. This structure is now the John Marshall House Museum.

By the early 1830s, the thriving metropolis of Shawneetown was "thumping its chest" while the settlement known as Chicago, 350 miles north, was only a cluster of buildings. In 1838 a small group of Chicago businessmen came to Shawneetown hoping to obtain a loan to make improvements to their fledgling city on Lake Michigan. The bank officials refused their request, however, stating that, due to an overly high demand for funds, they were not making any new loans. (Contrary to popular legend, the reason

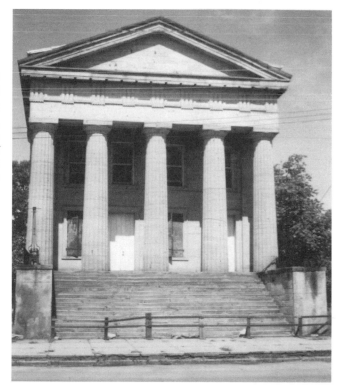

The Bank of Illinois in Shawneetown, completed in 1841; this photo was taken in the 1930s.
—Courtesy Farm Security Administration, Office of War Information Photograph Collection

for the refusal had nothing to do with the bankers' belief that Chicago would never amount to anything.) The Greek Revival–style Bank of Illinois building replaced the one in John Marshall's home in 1840. This imposing structure, now a state historic site, reflects the city's onetime financial influence.

After surviving major floods in 1882, 1883, 1898, and 1913, Shawneetown received a fatal blow in 1937, when the rising waters of the Ohio River engulfed the village. The floodwaters crested at sixty-six feet, reaching the second floor of the Bank of Illinois building. With the flood having destroyed more than 75 percent of Shawneetown's buildings, the entire town was rebuilt on higher ground, about three miles northwest of the old one. Old Shawneetown continues to exist, but its population is less than 500.

Though its location had changed, Shawneetown remained the county seat. The bell from the 1857 courthouse in Old Shawneetown was moved to the new courthouse, built in 1939. This building, the current Gallatin County Courthouse, features three murals by New Deal artist Earl Ledyard. The showpiece mural, titled "History of Gallatin County," depicts the salt industry.

IL 13
OLD SHAWNEETOWN—MURPHYSBORO
71 miles

This is a fairly long trip on IL 13 that heads west from Old Shawneetown to Murphysboro, passing through Equality, the site of an old slave house and home of the Ohio River Visitor Center, and the largish cities of Harrisburg, Marion, and Carbondale.

SHAWNEETOWN/OLD SHAWNEETOWN
See previous trip

EQUALITY

Equality's history begins with salt. A large, horseshoe-shaped salt lick here attracted deer, antelope, buffalo, and other animals, making them easy to hunt. Indian tribes and early colonizers took advantage of this, and they also valued the salt for their own use. It was essential for curing and preserving meat and hides, and it was prized as a trade item. Later settlers recognized its potential for profit.

In the early 1700s, French fur traders established a fortified saltworks and tannery atop the bluff near Half Moon Lick, at the future site of Equality. Eventually, however, local Indians drove them away and destroyed their work site. But the French post would not be the last saltworks at Half Moon Lick.

In an 1803 treaty, the native tribes of the Indiana Territory ceded two million acres of land to the United States, including the salt deposits around Equality. The government leased the land to private interests wanting to establish commercial saltworks, and the site of the old French saltworks was selected for a new settlement. The post office at the base of the cliff opened under the name "U.S. Salines," but in 1827 the town was dubbed Equality. Some believe the name was culled from the motto of the French Revolution, "Liberty, Equality, Fraternity." The name was ironic considering that slavery was permitted in salt mines, an exception to the territorial laws against it.

Slavery was completely abolished in the 1848 state constitution, but slaveholding continued illegally for some years afterward. A case in point was that of John Crenshaw, owner of Hickory Hill, better known as the Old Slave House.

Crenshaw House

With its numerous Underground Railroad routes, Illinois offered many safe havens to runaway slaves. Lesser known, however, is Illinois' role in what has been dubbed the "Reverse Underground Railroad," in which free black citizens were abducted and sold as slaves in the South. In addition, runaway slaves attempting to cross into this free state were sometimes intercepted by residents and either turned in for a reward or simply resold in the South. In Equality, one building, in particular, remains a physical reminder of the sordid treatment of slaves by some Illinoisans.

The Crenshaw House, a.k.a. Hickory Hill, a.k.a. the Old Slave House, was built in the 1830s; additions were completed in 1842. Its owner, John Hart Crenshaw, allegedly snatched escaping slaves as they entered Illinois or even kidnapped black freemen and held them in cells on the third floor of the house, then put them to work in his saltworks or sold them in the South.

The three-story building is reminiscent of a stately plantation manor house of the Old South, with its tall wooden columns in the front, a wide two-door entrance with flanking windows and transom, and a second-story balcony. A steep, narrow stairway leads to the windowless third floor, which is divided into small cubicles on either side of a long hallway. Some rooms, equipped with two-foot-wide bunks, housed entire families of slaves. Ventilation was poor and the air inside was oppressive. On display are iron rings to which rebellious slaves were secured for punishment.

Crenshaw was brought to trial in the 1840s but, since blacks could not testify against a white man and no other witnesses came forward, he was freed. His salt business, however, was already in decline. He lost his lease to the saltworks in 1846 for unpaid taxes and eventually sold the house and its surrounding acreage. Crenshaw died in 1871 and was buried in Hickory Hill Cemetery, northeast of the house.

The Sisk family bought the house from the Crenshaw family in 1906. By the 1930s it had become a tourist attraction, and rumors spread that the house was haunted. In 2000 the state of Illinois acquired the building from George M. Sisk, Jr., and is planning to restore it as a state historic site. As of this writing, an archaeological survey has been completed but restorative work remains to be done, and the house is closed to the public.

HARRISBURG

Founded as a village in 1853, Harrisburg became the seat of Saline County, moved from Raleigh, in 1859. By then coal had been discovered in the area, and Harrisburg grew quickly as a mining and industrial town, incorporating as a city in 1889. The Saline County Area Historical Museum is located on part of the city's former poor farm; the museum complex includes the 1877 Old Pauper Home as well as other historic structures.

Harrisburg, known as the "Gateway to Shawnee National Forest," profits from its proximity to the 270,000-acre preserve. This national forest includes seven wilderness areas and recreational facilities throughout. The most popular spot is Garden of the Gods, with its spectacular limestone bluffs, accessible via IL 34 south of Harrisburg.

Harrisburg's most notorious era was the 1920s, when gangsters battled for territorial control in Saline, Franklin, and Williamson Counties.

Birger-Shelton Gang War

Prohibition in southern Illinois sometimes made for unusual alliances. In one such case, law officers, Prohibitionist citizens, and members of the Ku Klux Klan banded together to fight Charlie Birger, Carl Shelton, and their gangs of bootleggers, who were running rampant throughout south-central Illinois in the 1920s.

Charlie Birger, a native Russian and former U.S. cavalryman, was a saloon owner in Harrisburg when national Prohibition took effect. Seeing opportunity in the illegal liquor trade, he allied with moonshiners, bribed public officials, and set up a speakeasy near Harrisburg. He shared some of his wealth with the community's less fortunate, earning him a Robin Hood image.

Many of Harrisburg's citizens, however, were not so fond of Birger and his activities. These "do-gooders" and the ineffective local lawmen sought help from the Ku Klux Klan. Due to their largely Southern Baptist tradition, the Klan supported Prohibition and associated drinking with Catholic immigrants. Led by Seth Glenn Young, a gun-toting enforcer with a cowboy persona, the Klan became the champions of decency and law and order. Klan raiders targeted illegal drinking establishments and the people associated with them, including Birger. The bootleggers fought back, and the tri-county region became a war zone. In January 1925 Young and two bodyguards were gunned down in nearby Herrin. Young's tombstone in Herrin Cemetery is easily identifiable by its bullet holes; Birger's henchmen often used it for target practice.

Birger, seeking to drive out the rest of his Klan opposition and to expand his territory, allied with a rival gang, the Shelton Brothers—Carl, Bernie, and Earl (see also Fairfield on later trip). The partnership soon soured, however, and Birger and the Sheltons became enemies again. All-out war ensued. The brothers once dropped sticks of dynamite from an airplane to bomb Birger's speakeasy, Shady Rest. Though the dynamite missed its target, this attack is often considered the first aerial bombardment in the United States. The Birger-Shelton turf war lasted six months, leaving more than twenty dead.

In 1927 Birger was arrested for engineering the murder of West City mayor Joe Adams, a Shelton ally. Birger was tried in Franklin County and, with the testimony of his accomplices, convicted and sentenced to hang. Thousands of people flocked to Benton to watch the April 19, 1928, execution. It was the last hanging in Illinois before the gallows was replaced by the electric chair. Birger's final words were "It's a beautiful world."

The Sheltons continued operating in southern Illinois until Carl and Bernie were killed in the 1940s; Earl moved to Florida and lived to age ninety-six. Birger's Harrisburg home was demolished about seventy-five years after his death, and the Shady Rest speakeasy no longer exists, either. A stone marker that once identified the site of Shady Rest was moved, due to vandalism, to the old jailhouse in Marion (see below).

WILLIAMSON COUNTY AND MARION

Marion, the seat of Williamson County, is playfully promoted as "the hub of the universe." It is the second-largest city in southern Illinois outside the St. Louis metro area and is the retail center of the region. The city also prides itself on its award-winning cultural and civic center, which was built in 2004 on the site of the 1922 Orpheum Theatre.

Marion was created in 1839 specifically to be the county seat and was named for Revolutionary War hero Gen. Francis "Swamp Fox" Marion. A pioneer of modern guerilla warfare, the general got his nickname from his method of eluding the enemy by traveling through swamps. Marion still celebrates its namesake with an annual Swamp Fox Festival. Beginning in the late 1800s, Marion, like many towns in this region, grew steadily after the opening of area coal mines.

While coal is still produced in the area, mining is no longer the dominant industry in Marion. A veterans' hospital and a maximum-security federal penitentiary, along with numerous retail businesses, provide economic stability. Tourism and recreation have also become primary industries. Several large nearby lakes, the Crab Orchard National Wildlife Refuge, and the adjacent Shawnee National Forest, all have hiking trails and facilities for boating, camping, and swimming.

While city and county residents have seen some good times, they have also had their share of bad ones, from decades of violence in the late nineteenth and early twentieth centuries to the tornado of 1982, which killed ten Marion residents and destroyed some $100 million in property.

From the 1870s to the mid-1920s, a series of violent episodes across the county gave it the moniker "Bloody Williamson," signifying an era that most locals would prefer to forget. Six separate events reflected the lawlessness that once reigned in the region. The first one, known as the "Bloody Vendetta," was an eight-year family feud that began over a card game in 1868 and culminated in 1876 after taking seven lives. The next three incidents were labor strikes that occurred during Williamson County's peak coal-mining years. Five people were killed in the 1899 Carterville Massacre, and a few years later, the Coal Strike of 1906 left many injured over a period of months. The worst of them was the 1922 Herrin Massacre, in which three striking union miners and nineteen scab workers lost their lives over a two-day period.

The fifth violent episode was the Ku Klux Klan war of 1924–26, and the last, in 1926, was a feud between rival gangs of bootleggers (see Harrisburg above and Benton on next trip). The former county jail, where many offenders were held over the years, now houses the Williamson County Historical Society.

CARBONDALE

The mainstay of this city of 26,000, often described as the "Capital of Southern Illinois," is Southern Illinois University, whose presence helps Carbondale maintain its status as the commercial and cultural center of the region.

In 1852 three investors—Daniel Harmon Brush, John Asgill Conner, and Dr. William Richart—bought 360 acres along the Illinois Central Railroad right-of-way between the established communities of Marion and Murphysboro, with the express purpose of founding a town. With large coal deposits in the area, after which the settlement was named, as well as rich farmland, Carbondale was brimming with economic potential, and after the railroad arrived two years later, Carbondale became a central shipping point for both fossil fuels and produce.

With Carbondale's economic success, town leaders, at the urging of the Presbyterian Church, resolved to establish a college in their community. The school, straightforwardly named Carbondale College, held its first classes above the local general store while a brick school building was being erected. The building, begun in 1858, was completed in 1861, but the college had financial problems and closed after a few years.

The building was used for public school classes until investors revived the college, which was chartered as Southern Illinois College in 1867. This school, too, ran into financial difficulties and closed only three years later. By this time, however, Carbondale had been chosen as the site of a new state teachers' college, Southern Illinois Normal University, which opened in 1869. It was the teachers' college that would become Southern Illinois University (SIU) in 1948, when schools of law, medicine, and dentistry were added. Today, SIU Carbondale is recognized as one of the premier universities in the state.

Carbondale continued to thrive into the twentieth century, and its population grew by leaps and bounds as the university expanded. Today the city's university-based economy is supplemented by tourism, as the town's boosters promote fishing and boating on nearby lakes, hiking and camping in the Shawnee National Forest, and tours of local wineries on the Shawnee Hills Wine Trail.

Carbondale's historic sites, too, bring in visitors. One residential neighborhood, the West Walnut Street Historic District, has more than fifty historic homes, some dating to the early 1850s. It was designated a National Historic District in 1975. The campus of SIU Carbondale has several of its own historic buildings, the oldest one being the castlelike Altgeld Hall, built in 1896.

One of the city's historical attractions is a bit unusual—Woodlawn Cemetery. In 1866 the first Memorial Day service in Illinois—many maintain it was the first such event in the nation—was held in Carbondale's Woodlawn Cemetery to honor fallen Union soldiers. The cemetery includes the remains of sixty Union veterans and about thirty freed slaves.

MURPHYSBORO

In 1810 William Boon established the first commercial coal mine in Illinois Territory, along the Big Muddy River near what is now Murphysboro. This mine, plus another near Belleville, led to the construction in 1833 of the first two railroads in Illinois. These primitive rail lines, which consisted of mules pulling cars on crudely built iron tracks, carried coal to New Orleans–bound flatboats on the Mississippi River. Later, several more mining companies set up shop nearby, promoting further growth in the area.

Murphysboro was founded in 1843 as the new Jackson County seat after a fire destroyed the county courthouse in the original seat, the now-defunct community of Brownsville. Area resident Dr. John A. Logan (father of future general John A. Logan) donated twenty acres of his farm to establish the new town and courthouse. The town's name was decided by putting the names of the three county commissioners into a hat— William C. Murphy's name was chosen.

Murphysboro grew and prospered, and it was incorporated as a city in 1867. In 1888 the Mobile & Ohio Railroad built a depot here as well as railyards, car-repair shops, and a roundhouse, and many small industries followed. Before long, Murphysboro became known as "the Chicago of Southern Illinois."

All was well in Murphysboro until tragedy struck on March 18, 1925, when the deadliest tornado in U.S. history hit the area. The Tri-State Tornado killed a total 695 people in southeastern Missouri, southern Illinois, and southwestern Indiana. Illinois was the hardest hit, with 541 fatalities. In Murphysboro alone, the twister killed 234 residents, injured more than 800, and destroyed over 1,200 homes. Some of the other southern Illinois towns affected included Gorham, De Soto, West Frankfort, Maunie, and Parrish.

Although the tornado devastated Murphysboro's downtown and drained the population, the city rebuilt and regenerated. In fact, for decades afterward, into the 1960s, Murphysboro was a retail hub for the region. In 1957 another tornado hit, killing 2, injuring 61, and destroying 110 homes, but even this did not diminish the city's spirit. Nevertheless, progress, namely the completion of I-57 in 1971, eventually broke Murphysboro's back. Built about twenty-two miles east of town, the interstate left the town out in the cold as businesses and residents moved elsewhere. By the late 1970s, shuttered storefronts, depleted coal mines, a bypassed railroad station, and relocated factories signaled the end of the city's prosperous era.

Despite these reversals, Murphysboro looked to the future. The brick train depot was transformed into a restaurant, part of the roundhouse was adapted to manufacturing, and the Illinois Main Street program restored business facades to their century-old look. Today, Murphysboro remains economically viable as a bedroom community of neighboring Carbondale and as a city in its own right. Light manufacturing still hums in the Technology and Industrial Park, and visitors to nearby Shawnee National Forest provide the city with a modest tourist trade.

One of the city's attractions is the John A. Logan Museum, dedicated to Murphysboro's most prominent native son. The complex includes several renovated historic buildings, the site of Logan's birthplace, and a walking trail.

Maj. Gen. John A. Logan

Of all his achievements—Civil War major general, U.S. senator, vice presidential candidate, and commander of the Grand Army of the Republic (GAR)—John A. Logan is probably best known for General Order 11, which officially established Memorial Day as a national holiday. Logan, who wanted a genuine tribute to the thousands of men killed in the recently ended Civil War, called for "decorating the graves of comrades who died in defense of their country during the late rebellion." The first Memorial Day, originally called Decoration Day, was May 30, 1868.

Born in future Murphysboro in 1826 to city founder Dr. John Logan and his wife, Elizabeth, the younger Logan joined the Union cause as a civilian and member of Congress in 1861. Later that year, after fighting in the First Battle of Bull Run, he entered the U.S. Army as colonel of the 31st Illinois Infantry Regiment. Badly wounded at the Battle of Fort Donelson, he was promoted to brigadier general for his actions on the battlefield.

*Union general John A. Logan,
resident of Murphysboro*
—Author's collection

Later, he fought at the Battle of Corinth and in the Vicksburg and Atlanta campaigns. After the war, Logan returned to Congress, serving as a congressman (1867–71) and as a U.S. senator (1871–77 and 1879–86). He was a candidate for vice president on the Republican ticket with James G. Blaine in 1884. He died on December 26, 1886.

IL 37
MARION—SALEM
67 miles

IL 37, which parallels I-57 north of Goreville and passes through numerous small towns, is a more scenic, leisurely route than the interstate. Alternatively, travelers can take I-57 to the same stops. Beginning at Marion, we head north to historic Salem.

MARION
See previous trip

BENTON

Benton was not organized as a village until it became the Franklin County seat in 1839. The site was simply referred to as "a hill at the south end of Rowling's Prairie" until a village was platted in 1841 and named Benton, after renowned Missouri senator Thomas Hart Benton.

The tranquil fledgling community sought to find its niche among the many small towns in southern Illinois. Soil conditions did not encourage farming, but high-sulfur coal existed in large quantities near the surface. The arrival of the Illinois Central Railroad in 1879, followed by other rail lines later, helped to sustain Benton and its natural resources for decades afterwards.

The execution of notorious bootlegger Charlie Birger put Benton on the map in the 1920s (see under Harrisburg on previous trip). Birger's exploits are highlighted in the former Franklin County jail, now a museum in Benton, where visitors can see the noose used in Birger's hanging, some of his weapons, and other related items.

Later in the twentieth century, Benton was the home of Louise Harrison Caldwell, sister of Beatle George Harrison, who was yet little known in the United States when he and his brother, Peter, visited Louise in September 1963. While in Benton, George bought a guitar at a neighborhood shop and played with a local band, the Four Vests, at the VFW Hall in nearby Eldorado. It was only a few months later that Beatlemania hit the States. Louise's bungalow is now A Hard Days Nite Bed & Breakfast, featuring 1960s-era furniture and Beatles memorabilia.

The early 1970s saw the completion of the 19,000-acre Rend Lake, built by the Illinois Department of Natural Resources, the Rend Lake Conservancy District, and the U.S. Army Corps of Engineers. The reservoir not only controls flooding on the Big Muddy and Mississippi Rivers, it also offers sport fishing, boating, and wildlife watching, boosting the area economy.

MOUNT VERNON

Zadok Casey, former lieutenant governor, U.S. Congressman, and state senator for whom the city of Casey was named, donated land for the founding of Mount Vernon in 1817, and it was designated the seat of Jefferson County in 1819. Like Benton (above), Mount Vernon became a county seat before it officially became a village, which happened eighteen years later.

In 1848 Mount Vernon was chosen as one of three sites for the Illinois Supreme Court. Having the state court in Mount Vernon brought many prominent judges and lawyers, including Abraham Lincoln, into town. After a day in the courtroom, it wasn't unusual for Lincoln and his colleagues to gather at the Mount Vernon Inn for some libations. After the Illinois high court was consolidated in Springfield in 1897, the regal gray brick state courthouse became an appellate courthouse.

In the 1870s, Mount Vernon banned the sale of alcohol. In response, antitemperance backers established East Mount Vernon and allowed saloons. After a lengthy court fight, East Mount Vernon was ruled an illegal village. The pro-whiskey forces then mounted a campaign to reinstate the sale of liquor in Mount Vernon, and they won. East Mount Vernon was subsequently annexed to the city.

A devastating tornado struck the city in 1888, killing more than 30 people, destroying about 500 buildings, and leaving more than 1,200 residents homeless. Some of the relief supplies came from the newly formed American Red Cross, under the personal direction of Clara Barton. It was one of the organization's first disaster responses.

One of the operations built after the tornado was the Mount Vernon Car Manufacturing Company, which made railroad cars. It became the area's major employer and remained so for more than six decades, finally closing in 1954. Mount Vernon's economy did not falter for long, however, as the 1950s and 1960s brought two interstate highways through town, and with them came a plethora of light manufacturing, an industry that continues to grow in the Mount Vernon area.

SALEM

Sometime in the early 1800s, settlers established a tavern in Salem, where the well-traveled Vincennes Trail met the road to Vandalia. In 1823 Salem was founded as the seat of newly formed Marion County, and it was incorporated as a village in 1855.

With its abundant game, rich soil, and sandstone deposits, the town thrived. The arrival of the railroad ensured stability, though there was only modest development until the 1930s, when oil was discovered. After this, oil companies rushed in to lease land and mineral rights, making some Salem farmers instantly wealthy. Workers came in from all parts of the United States and from foreign countries.

Today the city's economy is quite diverse, from transportation to telecommunications and from manufacturing to retail. The oil industry continues to play a role, though on a more limited scale. Another significant part of modern Salem's economy is tourism, especially historical tourism. The Marion County Historical Society offers a map of a historical driving tour of Salem that includes twenty-nine sites of interest, including several historic homes, such as the 1854 Badollet House. Also on the tour is the former Max Crossett's Cafe, supposedly the birthplace of Miracle Whip salad dressing, though the historical society says this legend has no basis in fact.

The highlights of this or any other Salem history tour are the childhood home of famed lawyer and politician William Jennings Bryan and American Legion Post 128, birthplace of the 1940s G.I. Bill of Rights. Both are described below.

William Jennings Bryan Birthplace

William Jennings Bryan was born in Salem on March 19, 1860. Reared in a Christian environment and home-schooled by his mother during his childhood, at age fourteen he was sent to Whipple Academy in Jacksonville. He graduated from Illinois College in 1881 and attended Union Law College (which later became Northwestern University School of Law). After passing the bar, he practiced law in Jacksonville for a time before moving to Lincoln, Nebraska.

Bryan was elected to the U.S. House of Representatives in 1890 and again in 1892. He ran for president in 1896, 1900, and 1908. Although he never won, it was at the 1896 Democratic National Convention in Chicago that he gained national fame. In his fiery "cross of gold" speech, he rallied supporters of "bimetallism," a movement to jettison the gold standard and reinstate silver as legal tender in addition to gold. Advocates saw "free silver" as the solution to the serious economic problems of the day. At the convention, Bryan brought the crowd to its feet when he said, "You shall not press down upon the brow of labor this crown of thorns. You shall not crucify mankind upon a cross of gold." Although the silver faction lost the battle and Bryan lost the election to William McKinley, William Jennings Bryan became a household name.

Bryan also published a newspaper, the *Commoner*, from 1901 to 1913. He served as U.S. Secretary of State from 1913 to 1915, under President Woodrow Wilson. After resigning from that post, he returned to private practice but remained involved in politics as a campaigner for Prohibition, women's suffrage, and other issues.

As an attorney in 1925, Bryan faced renowned trial lawyer Clarence Darrow in one of the most infamous courtroom dramas of the twentieth century. Bryan was the prosecutor in the case against science teacher John T. Scopes, who taught Darwin's theory of evolution to his high school classes, violating Tennessee state law. Derisively known as the "monkey trial," the case was widely publicized, and observers from both sides closely watched the proceedings. In spite of Darrow's razor-sharp questioning of Bryan, which made Bryan look foolish, the latter won the case. Later, however, the state supreme court overturned the verdict.

Coincidentally and ironically, Salem was the hometown of both Bryan and Scopes. In fact, Bryan had been the commencement speaker at Scopes's graduation from Salem High School in 1919.

Bryan, who suffered from diabetes, died on July 26, 1925, only five days after the Scopes trial ended, at age sixty-five. He was buried at Arlington National Cemetery. His childhood home, built in 1852, is now the William Jennings Bryan Birthplace Museum.

The Salem Eight and the G.I. Bill of Rights

During World War II, President Franklin Roosevelt spoke of the need for government assistance for the nation's veterans. "We are laying plans for the return to civilian life of our gallant men and women in the armed services," he said. "They must not be demobilized into an environment of inflation and unemployment, to a place on the bread line or on a corner selling apples." On November 4, 1943, eight men gathered in Luther B. Easley American Legion Post 128 in Salem to flesh out Roosevelt's idea. Dubbed the Servicemen's Readjustment Act, the proposed law would provide all U.S. veterans with education and training, loan guarantees for home purchases, and unemployment pay, among other benefits.

With the support of newspaper baron William Randolph Hearst, the proposal gained momentum and national attention. It was introduced to Congress in January 1944. In spite of some opposition, the bill, popularly known as the G.I. Bill of Rights, passed on June 13, 1944, and was signed into law nine days later.

IL 15
MOUNT CARMEL–MOUNT VERNON
65 miles

From Mount Carmel, hometown of a surprising number of scientists, IL 15 passes through mostly small towns to Mount Vernon.

MOUNT CARMEL

Beginning in 1905 and for several years, Mount Carmel was known as the "Pearl of the Wabash," producing more than $1 million in freshwater pearls. At one time, as many as 4,000 men dragged the Wabash River for mussels, hoping to find a pearl to rival the marble-sized one found by "Jumbo" Adams, which was set in a necklace for England's Queen Mary. More realistic mussel hunters collected the shells to sell to button makers in the region and around the world. Within a few years, the mussels were fished out and the boom was over.

Mount Carmel was founded in 1818 by three Methodist ministers from Chillicothe, Ohio, fulfilling their vision of a community "based upon Christian faith and the principles as taught by John Wesley." The founders named their settlement for the biblical Mount Carmel because a nearby bluff reminded them of "the Holy Land mount that juts out into the Great Sea." The community was incorporated as a village in 1825 and as a city forty years later.

Throughout its history, Mount Carmel suffered disasters. The city burned twice, endured several major floods—including two consecutively in 1875 and 1876—and was hit by tornadoes in 1877, 1887, and 1990. Nevertheless, the city has held on.

Mount Carmel was the hometown of four leading American scientists—Robert and John Ridgway, Lucien M. Turner, and Dr. Jacob Schneck. Robert Ridgway (born 1850) was a world-renowned ornithologist. He accompanied a major expedition to Alaska with John Muir; served as curator of birds at the United States National Museum; participated in numerous scientific organizations; and published extensively on birds, other wildlife, and plants. Today near Olney is the Robert Ridgway Memorial Arboretum and Bird Sanctuary (see Olney on next trip). His brother, John Ridgway (born 1859), was an important scientific illustrator, author of the classic text *Scientific Illustration* and chief of illustrations at the U.S. Geological Survey.

The third local scientist was Lucien Turner, a close friend of the Ridgway brothers, who explored Alaska as a member of the U.S. Army Signal Corps and later as a naturalist. He prepared numerous reports on his findings related to native people, wildlife, and plants. Finally, Dr. Jacob Schneck was a longtime resident of Mount Carmel. Born in New Harmony in 1843, Schneck moved to Mount Carmel in 1871 to practice medicine. In addition, he pursued a passion for botany and entomology, identifying and recording rare plants and researching bees and other insects. All four men are honored at the Famous Americans Memorial, installed in 2004 outside the Mount Carmel Public Library.

ALBION

Albion was founded in 1818 by immigrants from Great Britain and named poetically after ancient England. These settlers established Illinois' first chamber of commerce (called the Albion Market Club) at the time of the town's founding, and they built the state's first public library the following year. The Albion Public Library still serves the community in the same location today, making it the oldest continuously operated public library in Illinois. Both the library and the chamber of commerce were significant achievements for an early-nineteenth-century rural community of one square mile.

Albion cofounder George Flower came to America following the Napoleonic wars, a time of civil strife and a poor economy in England. He sailed to the New World in 1816 to scout for settlement opportunities. Another like-minded Englishman and friend of Flower, Morris Birkbeck, emigrated the following spring. Birkbeck opposed the class disparity of England and saw America as a place where all people could be equal. He and Flower jointly explored the Midwest for a site to establish a colony of their countrymen.

In Illinois, they came upon Boltinghouse Prairie, which reminded them of the English countryside. They purchased as much land as their funds allowed and notified potential settlers back home. In an 1817 letter to a friend in England, Birkbeck wrote, "I have secured a considerable tract of land, more than I have any intention of holding, that I may be able to accommodate some of our English friends. Our soil appears to be rich . . . [and] so easy of tillage as to reduce the expense of cultivation below that of the land I have been accustomed to in England, notwithstanding the high rates of human labour. . . . Our main object will be live stock, cattle, and hogs, for which there is a sure market at a good profit."

While Birkbeck established his settlement at Boltinghouse Prairie, calling it Wanborough, Flower returned to England for a while. The following summer, two more groups of British immigrants, one led by Flower and the other by Charles Trimmer and James Lawrence, arrived at Boltinghouse Prairie and created their own settlements. Trimmer and Lawrence dubbed their community Village Prairie, and Flower called his Albion. The general area became known as English Settlement.

After a long-simmering dispute of uncertain causes, Birkbeck and Flower ended their association and never spoke to each other again. In the fall of 1818, Flower met with James Lawrence and one or two other settlers to discuss the future of their villages. They decided that, rather than having separate settlements, combining Village Prairie and Albion into one town would better serve the interests of all the families. They agreed to designate a central location in a wooded area as the merged community's public square and to use the name Albion. The town was platted a few months later, in 1819. After two years, the colony had 1,100 residents—about 400 English and 700 Americans. In 1824 it was chosen to be the seat of Edwards County.

Meanwhile, Birkbeck concentrated on developing Wanborough. During his second year, he and future governor Edward Coles started an agriculture society that advised Illinois settlers on better farming methods. In 1825, while returning from a visit to New Harmony, Indiana, Birkbeck drowned crossing a river. Without Birkbeck, the residents of Wanborough lost interest in their settlement, which within a few years ceased to exist. George Flower died circa 1862, leaving Albion as his monument to Illinois development.

The city of Albion is still an agricultural community, with a population under 2,000; hogs are the dominant commodity.

FAIRFIELD

The peacefulness of today's Fairfield reflects the serenity that arriving settlers felt in the 1810s when they halted their wagons atop a small plateau, gazed upon an expansive flowing prairie, and proclaimed that "no fairer field" could be found. The city of Fair-field was founded as the seat of Wayne County in 1819.

Beginning in the 1920s, the serenity of this farming community was interrupted by three hometown boys—brothers Carl, "Big" Earl, and Bernie (a.k.a. "Red") Shelton. With their gang of Fairfield bootleggers, the Sheltons ran roughshod over Franklin, Wayne, and Williamson Counties during Prohibition. The gang concentrated its liquor, gambling, and prostitution operations in East St. Louis, and later Peoria, though the brothers' reach extended throughout southern Illinois. While they were convicted of several crimes over the years, none of the Sheltons served much time behind bars.

The Sheltons had a local rival, Williamson County's Charlie Birger, with whom they fought for territory until Birger was hanged in 1928 (see under Harrisburg and Benton on previous trips). Even after Prohibition was repealed, the Shelton gang con-tinued illegal activities, and turf wars periodically erupted for the next two decades. Finally, rival gangsters from Chicago took care of the brothers. Carl was ambushed on a rural road in Wayne County and shot dead in 1947, and Bernie was gunned down outside his Peoria headquarters in 1948. Big Earl was the target of repeated assassina-tion attempts and was wounded several times, but he survived. He eventually moved to Jacksonville, Florida, and lived to age ninety-six.

Even as Fairfield endured its crime problem, a boom hit the city after the Pure Oil Company produced the first successful oil well in the area in March 1937. For the next thirty years, oil production, light manufacturing, and agriculture all contributed to Fairfield's prosperity and brought positive changes to the area.

Fairfield's development from the 1800s to the early 1900s is the focus at the Early History Museum, and relics from the 1920s to the present are showcased in the Hanna House Museum.

MOUNT VERNON
See previous trip

US 50
LAWRENCEVILLE—SALEM
81 miles

Between St. Louis and Vincennes, near the Missouri and Indiana state lines, respectively, US 50 roughly follows the old Vincennes-to-St. Louis Trail. Originally an Indian trail, it sometimes served as a military road and became a mail and stage route around 1805. Displaced by the rail line in the 1850s, the road still served the region in the early twen-tieth century as part of the Midland Trail, a primitive interstate highway. US 50 was built along this part of the Midland Trail corridor in 1926.

We begin this trip in Lawrenceville and pass through a number of small rural com-munities, stopping at a couple of historic sites along the way. Much of the drive is quite scenic as well.

LAWRENCEVILLE

Lawrenceville was a nine-year-old frontier village when a twenty-one-year-old Abraham Lincoln, accompanied by his father and stepmother, crossed the Wabash River from Indiana and entered Illinois in March of 1830. From there, they moved up the Vincennes-to-St. Louis Road to Lawrenceville and proceeded west to settle a homestead on the Sangamon River, a few miles southwest of Decatur (see under Decatur in Region 3). A monument, dedicated in 1938, marks the site where the future president first entered Illinois, at the west end of the Lincoln Memorial Bridge on US 50 in Lawrenceville. It consists of a life-size bronze statue of Abe in front of a limestone wall carved with a family leading an ox-drawn wagon and an angel above leading the way.

When the Lincolns arrived, the Wabash River was high and icy, difficult to cross with the wagons. Thirty years later, at the 1860 Republican convention in Decatur, a local supporter asked Lincoln about his memory of Lawrenceville. The candidate's reply was recounted in a letter from a local resident to his cousin:

> *I crossed the Wabash at Vincennes, and the river being high, the road . . . was covered with water a half mile at a stretch and the water covered with ice. . . . When I came to the water I put a favorite dog I had along into the wagon and got in myself and whipped up my oxen and started into the water to pick my way across as well as I could. After breaking the ice and wading about a quarter mile, my little dog jumped out of the wagon, and the ice being thin, he broke through and was struggling for life. I could not bear to lose my dog and I jumped out of the wagon and waded waist deep in the ice and water got hold of him and helped him out and saved him.*

Among the earliest settlers in this area was French Canadian Toussaint Dubois, an officer in the Revolutionary War and the War of 1812, who by the time of his death in 1816 had become the largest landowner in the region. When Lawrence County was formed in 1821, Dubois's heirs donated fifty acres to start Lawrenceville, the designated county seat. The family's home served as the county courthouse until 1824, when the first courthouse was erected; this was replaced by a larger, brick structure in 1846. Toussaint Dubois's son, Jesse K. Dubois, served with Abraham Lincoln in the Illinois legislature from 1835 to 1841 and from 1843 to 1845 and was a pallbearer at Lincoln's funeral.

Lawrenceville was incorporated as a town in 1835 and as a city in 1895. The discovery of oil in the region in the early 1900s set off a boom that lasted until the mid-1980s. During World War II, the military acquired 3,000 acres of farmland for an advanced twin-engine pilot training school. The base, named George Field, existed for about three years before it was transferred to the city of Lawrenceville in 1948. It is now the Lawrenceville-Vincennes International Airport.

Perhaps the most notorious episode in Lawrenceville's history was the 1845 trial and subsequent hanging of local settler Elizabeth "Betsy" Reed.

The Hanging of Elizabeth Reed

In April 1845, Elizabeth "Betsy" Reed, who lived in a log cabin near Heathsville, was convicted of murdering her husband, Leonard. The crime occurred over a five-day period in August 1844, as Mrs. Reed mixed small amounts of arsenic into her husband's sassafras tea, nursing him tenderly during his "illness" until he died. At his funeral, she was seen crying bitterly but, as it was soon discovered, this was a charade.

Following an inquest on August 20, 1844, Reed was arrested and incarcerated in the Crawford County jail in nearby Palestine. While confined to the log jailhouse, she tried to escape by setting it on fire. With the jail burned down, Reed was transferred to the home of the county sheriff, where she was shackled to a bedpost in the attic. She was later moved to the Lawrence County jail in Lawrenceville.

The trial, which took place in Lawrenceville, began on April 25, 1845, before a packed courtroom. Of the state's six witnesses, the Reeds' neighbor, Eveline Deal, presented the most damaging testimony. Deal said that she saw Betsy Reed take some white powder wrapped in paper and empty it into a cup of tea, which she served to Mr. Reed. It "seemed to make him very sick and caused him to vomit immediately and it continued for about a day and a half," Deal testified.

After Betsy emptied the powder, she tried to throw the paper away, but it fell on the doorsteps, where Deal found it and grew suspicious. She looked around the house and found more powder wrapped in similar paper. She turned the items over to authorities, who identified the powder as arsenic. On April 28, the jury found Elizabeth Reed guilty of premeditated murder. Judge William Wilson sentenced her to hang.

The sun was shining on May 23, the day of the hanging. Thousands of men, women, and children had come to Lawrenceville from miles around to witness the event, riding in wagons or on horseback, or coming on foot. Some camped out for days. As the time neared, a white-robed Betsy Reed rode in on a wagon, sitting beside her own casket. She mounted the scaffold singing hymns and praising God, and while the local minister delivered an hour-long sermon, the prisoner listened, enraptured and calling out in concordance. Near midday, the black execution hood was placed over Reed's head and she calmly stepped up to the noose. The sheriff cut the rope, and within a minute, Elizabeth Reed was dead. She was the first and only woman ever hanged in Illinois.

OLNEY

The early history of the small city of Olney, Illinois, is unremarkable. Like a number of other towns in the state, it was created as a county seat—in this case, of Richland County, in 1841. Settlers followed, and Olney was incorporated as a village in 1848 and as a city in 1867. It survived the usual ups and downs and grew into a stable community. But the twentieth century brought a few surprises to the city, including Olney's unusual claim to fame: squirrels.

In the early 1900s, at least two white squirrels were discovered somewhere in the area. No one knows exactly where the critters came from, but in 1902 a pair of young albino squirrels were somehow captured and either given or sold to saloon owner Jasper Banks, who put them in the window of his tavern as an attention-grabbing display. Not surprisingly they multiplied, and the squirrels were released into the wild a few years later to become a self-sustaining population and the pride of Olney, "Home of the White Squirrels."

Because of their standout coloring, albino animals are particularly vulnerable to predators, so city officials passed a variety of ordinances to protect the treasured creatures. In Olney, both dogs and cats must be leashed; white squirrels may not be killed, captured, or moved out of town; and the critters always have the right-of-way on city streets. The squirrel's image can be seen everywhere, including on the shoulder patches of the local police. Each October, the city conducts a squirrel count to keep an eye on the population. The best spot to see the snowy rodents is said to be Olney City Park, on the west side of town.

Squirrels aren't the only safeguarded species in the Olney area. The Robert Ridgway Memorial Arboretum and Bird Sanctuary, a small reserve near East Fork Lake, just northwest of Olney, is a bird lover's paradise. Ridgway, born on July 2, 1850, in Mount Carmel (see Mount Carmel on previous trip), learned about wildlife from his nature-loving father. He began sketching birds at age three. He grew up to become, among other things, the curator of birds at the U.S. National Museum (now the National Museum of Natural History), a branch of the Smithsonian Institution; president of the American Ornithologists' Union; a respected wildlife artist; and the author of more than four hundred books and articles.

In 1906 Ridgway bought eight acres of land near Olney for an arboretum, which his wife named "Bird Haven." Two years later, a local nature lover donated ten additional acres. The property served as a bird sanctuary and an experimental farm to test the viability of various nonnative trees and plants in Illinois. Ridgway died on March 25, 1929, and was buried on the land that remains a monument to his scientific research. In 1976 the Ridgway chapter of the Audubon Society officially renamed Bird Haven the Robert Ridgway Memorial Arboretum and Bird Sanctuary, but it is still referred to as Bird Haven.

Another remarkable, if less well known, fact about Olney's history is that the city was the site of the world's first solar power plant, which was built—amazingly—in 1902. Two St. Louis engineers, Henry F. Willsie and John Boyle, Jr., chose Olney as the location for their experimental plant, based on an 1885 French plan. After several years of research and experimentation, Willsie and Boyle patented their design in 1903. The Olney facility was a limited success—it heated water during the day and kept it warm throughout the night by using a huge insulated basin. Due to high costs, however, the project had to be abandoned after six years. A historical marker stands at the site, at the northwestern edge of Olney City Park.

Today, visitors can learn about the rich heritage of Olney and Richland County at the Richland Heritage Museum, housed in a restored 1870s brick home. Also part of the museum complex is another restored historic building, the 1904 Carnegie Library. Because many of Olney's first settlers were from New England and painted their houses the way they had done back East, Olney was once known as the "Painted Town." Olney's South Elliott Street Historic District, on the NRHP, contains some of these colorful old homes as well as other historic structures.

SALEM
See earlier trip

US 51
CARBONDALE—CENTRALIA
61 miles

US 51 runs the entire length of Illinois, dividing east and west. This trip begins in Carbondale and heads north to Centralia, once the major rail hub of the region.

CARBONDALE
See earlier trip

DU QUOIN

The original Du Quoin was established around 1831. The first white settler here, Jarrold Jackson, established a toll bridge over the Little Muddy River in the early 1800s, and the town gradually grew up around it. Originally the site of the Kaskaskia tribe's winter camp, the settlement was named after eighteenth-century Indian chief Jean Baptiste Ducoigne, leader of the Illiniwek Confederation, made up of the Kaskaskia, Cahokia, Peoria, Michigamea, Moingwena, and Tamaroa tribes.

Around 1850, when word arrived that the new Illinois Central Railroad would be running several miles west of Du Quoin, most of the residents began moving their homes and businesses to be closer to the train route. The site of the first settlement, now called Old Du Quoin, is today a dot on the map.

Not long after the new Du Quoin was founded, it was discovered that the town lay atop a major coalfield, which provided a steady stream of mining jobs for the next several decades. By the 1920s, after less-costly strip mining had displaced shaft mining, Du Quoin's landscape had been strip-mined into ugliness. In 1923 forward-thinking local businessman William R. Hayes reclaimed a piece of strip-mined land and developed it into the Du Quoin State Fairgrounds. Among other events held there were harness races, a sport that became increasingly popular in the twentieth century.

In 1957 Hayes's sons, Gene and Don, brought the Hambletonian, harness racing's premier thoroughbred contest, to Du Quoin from New York. For the next twenty-three years, the Hambletonian was a major event in downstate Illinois and drew national attention. After being outbid by the Meadowlands in New Jersey, however, Du Quoin lost the Hambletonian, and the last Hambletonian race in Du Quoin was held in 1981. In the meantime, however, Du Quoin began hosting three other races—the World Trotting Derby, the Filly World Trotting Derby, and the Hayes Memorial Races. But in 2010, after twenty-nine years, all three events were cancelled due to the state of Illinois' precarious financial situation.

In spite of these disappointments, the city is still "proud to be the home of the Du Quoin State Fair" and of the fairgrounds themselves, where the town continues its longstanding tradition of holding community events. The fairgrounds' 1,200 beautifully landscaped acres remain a year-round recreational and entertainment center for the region.

IRVINGTON

Irvington, a small village on US 51, was once the site of Illinois Agricultural College, the first school in the state to focus on scientific methods to improve agricultural production. The college, chartered in 1861, opened in 1866 and endured financial difficulties from the beginning, finally closing in 1878. For the next three decades, the campus remained mostly vacant. From 1904 to 1936, an orphanage, the Hudelson Baptist Children's Home, occupied the property, but a fire in 1934 ravaged the administration building, and a year later, a boiler explosion killed two employees, leading the orphanage to close the Irvington facility. The remaining buildings, materials, and land were eventually sold off. All that remains of the lofty educational experiment known as Illinois Agricultural College is a historical marker in Irvington's Fortmeyer Memorial Park.

CENTRALIA

Centralia, on US 51 about five miles south of US 50, once claimed the title of "railroad crossroads of southern Illinois," as three lines—the Illinois Central Railroad, the Chicago, Burlington & Quincy Railroad, and the Southern Railroad—all passed through the city. The first, the Illinois Central, saw the area as a pivotal location for railroad operations; consequently, the name Centralia was deemed apt. In late 1853, the railroad platted lots and constructed a roundhouse, shops, a hotel, and other relevant structures for work crews and staff. The Centralia House, built in 1850, housed workers and then railroad travelers.

While the city owes its early growth to the railroad, in 1874 Centralia became a coal-mining town. That year, a seven-foot-wide seam of coal was discovered, ushering in more than seventy-five years of coal mining in Centralia. During Centralia's railroad era, its population was predominantly made up of German and Dutch immigrants, but the mines attracted new immigrant workers from Ireland, Germany, Italy, Poland, and Russia.

In 1947 a terrible underground explosion killed 111 miners. Following an investigation, more stringent safety standards were adopted statewide. But by that time, the coal was nearly exhausted, and most of the mines in Centralia were closed within a few years. In the meantime, however, in the late 1930s, other natural resources were discovered in the area. Large oil and natural-gas fields boosted employment and aided Centralia's economy. Oil production soon waned, but natural gas is still produced in abundance in the Centralia area.

Great River Road National Scenic Byway (IL 3)
MURPHYSBORO–WATERLOO
74 miles

This trip takes us along part of the Great River Road National Scenic Byway, the southern portion of the Great River Road, between the Murphysboro area (via IL 149) and Waterloo. In its entirety, the byway follows IL 3 for approximately 175 miles between Cairo and the Alton area. For most of the way, this scenic route hugs the Mississippi River and is dotted with historical sites that preserve reminders of early French settlement, economic change, political disputes, and war.

MURPHYSBORO
See earlier trip

CHESTER

Chester's position on the Mississippi River made it a convenient location for shipping goods. It was also a convenient location for fugitive slaves to enter Illinois. Along with Alton and Quincy, the Chester area was a major entry point for slaves escaping from bondage in Missouri. It is believed that runaways who made their way to the Underground Railroad station at the Allan Plantation in Missouri crossed the Mississippi River to a cave near the Harvey Clendening farm just south of Chester, from which point they continued to Eden (near Sparta) and gradually on to Chicago.

John McFerron was the first settler to purchase land in Chester, but it was Samuel Smith who founded the town in 1829 when he established Smith's Landing, a ferry and flour mill. Smith's wife, a native of Chester, England, gave the settlement its name. Chester prospered as a minor river port and a manufacturer of wheat flour and castor oil.

Chester is the burial place of Illinois's first governor, Shadrach Bond. The grave is marked with a granite monument, the Governor Bond State Memorial, erected in 1883. Born in Maryland in 1773, Bond came to Illinois Country in 1794, joining his uncle, also named Shadrach Bond, and eventually settled on a farm near Kaskaskia (see next stop). He served as an Illinois territorial representative from 1812 to 1814, and as Illinois

Shadrach Bond, the first governor of Illinois, 1818–22
—Courtesy Schaumburg Township District Library, Illinois Collection

governor from 1818 to 1822. After his term as governor, he returned to his farm, where he died in 1832, at age fifty-eight.

Today the city's main claim to fame is its status as the hometown of Popeye, or rather of his creator, Elzie Segar, who invented the spinach-eating cartoon sailor in 1929. In 1977 a six-foot-tall bronze statue of Popeye was erected in Elzie Segar Memorial Park, near the Chester Bridge. The Popeye & Friends Character Trail now includes Olive Oyl, Bluto, and others. Two historic homes in the Chester area are the 1802 Pierre Menard Home and the 1855 William Cohen Home. The Southern French Colonial mansion of Pierre Menard, the first lieutenant governor of Illinois, has often been called the "Mount Vernon of the West."

KASKASKIA

It is ironic that Kaskaskia, Illinois' original territorial capital and its first state capital, is now geographically removed from the rest of the state and all but abandoned. Repeated flooding through the nineteenth century destroyed most of the town and cut off the peninsula on which it was built, creating an island. This island—or what is left of it after subsequent deluges—is now on the west side of the Mississippi River and is no longer accessible from Illinois.

After the first of these severe floods, in 1844, Kaskaskia was rebuilt a short distance to the south, but the new settlement, also prone to flooding, failed to thrive and continued to lose population over the succeeding decades. A century and a half later, the great flood of 1993 submerged Kaskaskia under nine feet of water and pushed out most of the remaining residents. Nevertheless, according to the 2010 census, fourteen people still live here, and the area has several points of interest.

The most prominent icon in Kaskaskia is a 650-pound bronze church bell, often referred to as the "Liberty Bell of the West." Cast in France in 1741, the bell was a gift from King Louis XV to the settlement's Immaculate Conception Catholic Church, built when Kaskaskia was a French colonial village. French Jesuits had founded the settlement in 1703 when they moved their Indian mission from Des Peres (present-day St. Louis) to this site near the mouth of the Kaskaskia River. The congregation built its first church, a stone structure, in 1714.

The French began to build a military post, Fort Kaskaskia, here in 1759, but it was destroyed during the French and Indian War, which ended in a victory for Great Britain in 1763. England erected a new post, Fort Gage, nearby, but the Brits would not remain there for long. On the night of July 3, 1778, during the American Revolution, Lt. Col. George Rogers Clark and a company of Virginia colonial militia raided and captured Fort Gage and the village of Kaskaskia. The next day, July 4, local residents rang the bell to signal their independence from fifteen years of British rule. It was sounded every Fourth of July until 1993, when the great flood of that year enlarged a hairline crack that a previous flood had produced, permanently silencing the bell. The remains of Fort Kaskaskia and its old cemetery can be seen north of town at nearby Kaskaskia State Historic Site, which also offers expansive picnicking and camping grounds.

Kaskaskia was the territorial capital from 1809 to 1818, but the town served as the state capital for only two years, from December 1818, when statehood was achieved, to December 1820, when the honor was given to Vandalia. A two-story brick building

This building in Kaskaskia served as the first capitol of Illinois.
—Courtesy of Schaumburg Township District Library, Illinois Collection

served as the statehouse. It was here that the first constitution was drafted. The building was gutted by a fire in 1824, and the remaining structure was washed out in a flood in 1881. By that time, the town of Kaskaskia had been virtually abandoned. The surrounding area, however, remained vibrant with farms, including that of Shadrach Bond, Illinois's first governor (see Chester above).

PRAIRIE DU ROCHER

Prairie du Rocher was founded in 1722 by French colonists near Fort de Chartres, a newly built French fort on the Mississippi River. The fort was completed in 1720 to strengthen French presence in the "American Bottom." The first Fort de Chartres was made of vertical logs and surrounded by a dry moat along the perimeter. Prone to flooding, the fort had to be rebuilt in 1727 and again in 1732. By 1752 the fort housed about a hundred soldiers and served primarily as a supply center for other French forts on the Ohio and Mississippi Rivers.

The community of Prairie du Rocher that grew up around the fort, like many other early French towns in the rich Mississippi River Bottom, produced corn and wheat for New Orleans and other French communities in Louisiana Territory. Exhaustion of the soil caused some residents to leave in the 1750s.

In 1763, with the Treaty of Paris that ended the French and Indian War, the British gained control of most of Louisiana Territory east of the Mississippi. Great Britain took formal possession of Fort de Chartres two years later. The post, renamed Fort Cavendish, continued to contend with frequent flooding. In 1771, with its structures deteriorating and the troops suffering from sickness and squalor, the fort was abandoned and the garrison moved to nearby Fort Gage in Kaskaskia (see Kaskaskia above).

In the meantime, the British and, later, American control of the area inspired further exoduses of the French inhabitants. Nevertheless, some people remained, and Prairie du Rocher now represents one of the oldest French colonial communities still surviving. One historic building in town, the Creole House, dates to 1800 and reflects French Creole design that was common in this region at that time.

Fort de Chartres deteriorated until only one structure, the powder magazine, was left. The magazine was restored in 1917, and many years later, further restorations were done and buildings were added at the site, creating a partial replica for visitors.

WATERLOO

During their march through Illinois country, troops led by George Rogers Clark saw a region previously unknown to them. After the war, many of them returned there to settle. Among the first was Capt. James Moore, who led a contingent of pioneers from Virginia and Maryland to southwestern Illinois in 1782. This group included Shadrach Bond and his namesake nephew; the younger Bond would later become the first governor of Illinois. The settlers chose a place the French called "La Belle Fontaine," or "beautiful spring," in what is now Waterloo. Bellefontaine is thought to have been the first American settlement in what would come to be called the Northwest Territory.

Because the remote settlement was vulnerable to Indian attacks, Moore built a fort, attracting additional settlers. By 1800 Bellefontaine had a population of nearly 300. A few years later, Emory Peters Rogers built a settlement called Peterstown across the spring creek from Bellefontaine, erecting a combination store, tavern, and inn called Peterstown House. In 1818 politician George Forquer founded another town, dubbed Waterloo, nearby. Eventually Bellefontaine and Peterstown were absorbed into Waterloo, which was designated the seat of Monroe County in 1825. In the 1840s, an influx of German settlers multiplied Waterloo's population. The town still takes pride in its German heritage.

Emery Peters Rogers's Peterstown House, built in the early 1800s, still stands. Listed on the NRHP in 1977, it is now a museum in Waterloo's historic district. The historic Bellefontaine spring still flows on the southern edge of town, near two other buildings of interest—the Bellefontaine House, a nineteenth-century red brick structure, and the more recently built History Museum of Monroe County. The trail that once led through briars and bushes to the spring has been transformed into a groomed walkway lined with greenery and park benches.

I-64 and US 50
EAST ST. LOUIS–LEBANON
20 miles

This trip, short in length but long in history, follows I-64 and US 50. This part of Illinois is in the St. Louis, Missouri, metropolitan area, and some of the cities and towns in this region are essentially suburbs of the larger city across the Mississippi River. Many, however, have an economy—and a history—of their own. On this trip, we will visit three of them. We begin at the commercial riverfront city of East St. Louis and continue to Scott Air Force Base, ending in Lebanon, home of McKendree University, one of the oldest colleges in the state.

EAST ST. LOUIS

Nearly two hundred years ago, a small settlement called Illinoistown (or Illinois City) stood on the Cahokia Commons near Piggot's Ferry. After a flood in 1849, the fourth since 1785, inundated the village, Illinoistown was forced to give up on agriculture and transform itself into a commercial and industrial center. Rail lines, which had connected Illinoistown to area coal mines since 1838, helped the transition, as did the steamboats that plied the Mississippi River. During the Civil War, East St. Louis became a transfer point for Union troops and supplies. As civic improvements were made and a municipal government established, Illinoistown was chartered as a city, renamed East St. Louis, in 1865.

The expansion of the railroad after the Civil War furthered industrial growth in East St. Louis. Among the first major industries here was the National Stock Yards, established in 1871. Meatpacking quickly followed, along with ironworks, grain mills, breweries, and factories manufacturing everything from syrup to roof shingles. In 1874 the completion of the James B. Eads Bridge, which spanned the Mississippi to connect St. Louis and East St. Louis, opened the area to further road and railway traffic, fostering more industrial growth.

The year America entered World War I, 1917, was a turning point for East St. Louis. To replace men called to serve in the military, employers hired black workers from the South. This led to a fear among whites that their jobs would not be available at war's end. The racism of the time fueled the fears, and soon rumors of interracial sexual unions began to fly. Random attacks on black men, women, and even children escalated into full-fledged race riots that destroyed millions of dollars in property and left dozens (by some accounts, hundreds) dead. The National Guard was called in twice during the summer of 1917 to quell the unrest, which was finally put down in July. It was an ominous sign for the future of East St. Louis.

In spite of the racial tensions, the city continued to grow, especially after World War II. The new arrivals were mostly white, and black residents were pushed to the fringes of town. East St. Louis reached a population high of more than 82,000 in 1958, and the next year it was named an "All-American City." But within a decade, the picture had become dramatically different. Due to the economic, industrial, and transportation changes of the 1960s, factories closed, businesses moved, and neighborhoods were split up by the new interstate highways, leading to soaring unemployment, crime, and urban blight. Whites, especially, fled to other places, mostly the suburbs of St. Louis, in search of work, better public schools, and more agreeable environments. By the mid-1960s, the city's population was less than half of its mid-twentieth-century peak. Conditions only grew worse during the 1970s as company after company left East St. Louis, leaving thousands jobless.

Since the 1990s, however, positive changes have been taking place in East St. Louis. In 1994 the *Casino Queen* riverboat casino opened, bringing a new revenue source to the city. The following year, the Gateway Geyser, a 630-foot-high fountain on the East St. Louis waterfront, designed to complement the Gateway Arch in St. Louis, was completed. Billed as the tallest fountain in the world, its waters reaching the same height as the Arch, the geyser is now part of the thirty-four-acre Malcolm W. Martin Memorial Park, which opened in 2009. In addition, the community has begun several "urban farming" projects, modeled after Detroit's green development of vacant land. With these ventures, combined with other urban-renewal endeavors, East St. Louis hopes to prosper once again.

Success Stories
Beginning in the 1920s and into the 1960s, even in bad times, East St. Louis was a hot bed of musical innovation. Many jazz, blues, and rock musicians got their start in the Metro East area in the mid-twentieth century, including Tina Turner and Chuck Berry. Perhaps the city's most celebrated son is jazz trumpeter Miles Davis, who was born in Alton but grew up in East St. Louis. Several athletes, too, hail from East St. Louis, notably Olympic gold-medal-winning runner Jackie Joyner-Kersee and tennis great Jimmy Connors.

SCOTT AIR FORCE BASE
Scott Air Force Base, which today serves as headquarters for a number of U.S. military units, was established in 1917 as Scott Field, a training school for pilots. The government built the 640-acre field on leased land. It was named for Corp. Frank S. Scott, the first enlisted man to die in an airplane crash. The accident, caused by engine failure, occurred in College Park, Maryland, during a test flight on September 28, 1912; Scott was a passenger.

In 1920 the War Department purchased the property, and eighteen years later, Scott Field became the general headquarters for the U.S. Army Air Corps, focusing on technical training. After World War II, the Air Force was established as its own military branch, and Scott Field was renamed Scott Air Force Base in 1948. Since then, the base has served the nation in both wartime and peacetime and through a staggering number of technological innovations.

LEBANON
The first inhabitants of the Lebanon area were the Mississippian Indians. About a mile and a half northeast of the city is the nearly two-acre site of Emerald Mound, the second-largest Indian mound in Illinois. Archaeological digs support the belief that it was used for ceremonial rather than burial purposes during the Mississippian period (AD 900–1450). The mound, though inaccessible to the public, can be seen from IL 4; it stands about one mile away from the road.

The founder of Lebanon was William H. Bradsby, who arrived in the area from Kentucky with a handful of friends and family members in 1804. The settlers built a shelter and planted crops, and when harvest time came, the rest of the Bradsby family joined them. The multiskilled William Bradsby farmed, taught school, practiced medicine, and held various public offices in Illinois. By 1814 the settlement of Lebanon was well populated; it was incorporated as a town in 1857 and as a city seventeen years later.

Early in its history, Lebanon became the home of McKendree University. Founded as Lebanon Seminary in 1828, the school, whose charter was acquired with the assistance of Abraham Lincoln, was renamed in 1831 for Bishop William McKendree, the first American-born Methodist bishop. Many of the buildings on campus are listed on the National Register of Historic Places.

In 1830 former sea captain Lyman Adams built the Mermaid House Hotel in Lebanon. The two-story frame hotel still stands, and it was listed on the NRHP in 1975. The hotel received its most famous guest in April of 1842—English author Charles Dickens. During a four-month visit to America, Dickens took a sixty-mile round-trip stagecoach ride through southwestern Illinois to see the open prairie. He described nearby Looking Glass Prairie as "lonely and wild, but oppressive in its barren monotony." On April 12, he stayed overnight at the Mermaid. In his subsequent travel book, *American Notes*, he described the inn: "In point of cleanliness and comfort it would have suffered by no comparison with any English alehouse."

In the late nineteenth century, an interurban trolley connected Lebanon to St. Louis. By that time, Lebanon had become a resort town for wealthy St. Louis families, who built many of the town's still-standing English Country, Georgian, Gothic, Greek Revival, Italianate, Queen Anne, and Southern Colonial homes. The Lebanon Historic District was added to the NRHP in 1978.

I-55/I-70 and IL 159
EAST ST. LOUIS–EDWARDSVILLE
20 miles

Like the previous trip, this one is a short drive going east from East St. Louis. The route passes through places with prehistoric beginnings, dating to the first century. The famous Cahokia Mounds State Historic Site preserves the remains of the largest known ancient Native American city in the nation.

Between Collinsville and Edwardsville is the site of Goshen Settlement, the earliest white settlement in this area. Established in 1801, Goshen Settlement, near present-day Glen Carbon, was the main community outside St. Louis in the early 1800s. Within a few years, Collinsville and Edwardsville—both of which are now cities of around 25,000 residents—had grown up nearby.

EAST ST. LOUIS
See previous trip

CAHOKIA MOUNDS

Indians of the Woodland and Mississippian Cultures flourished on the Mississippi River floodplain for centuries, the former until about AD 1000 and the latter until about AD 1450. Remnants of their cultures are reflected in the seventy remaining ceremonial and burial mounds preserved in Cahokia Mounds State Historic Site.

The people of the Late Woodland culture, who existed from about AD 200 to about AD 1000, lived in compact villages. It was the Late Woodland Indians who first began using bow and arrow. They combined hunting, fishing, and gathering wild plant foods with farming, cultivating corn and other crops. The Mississippian Culture, which emerged about AD 900, also combined hunter-gatherer practices with agriculture. This later culture developed a sophisticated community of social, political, and religious activities. Their 3,500-acre city had an estimated 120 mounds and as many as 20,000 inhabitants. Around AD 1100, the people here erected a circle of vertical wooden posts that, when viewed in relation to the sun, indicated the changing seasons and time of day. The collection of posts is often called "Woodhenge," as a play on England's Stonehenge.

Open plazas and clusters of dwellings graced the inner perimeter of the city, and a twelve- to fifteen-foot-high log wall, added around AD 1200, enclosed the two-hundred-plus-acre "central ceremonial precinct." The construction of the wall, which was rebuilt three times, depleted the nearby woods, contributing, some archaeologists believe, to the culture's ultimate disappearance from the region. Whether the residents died off or simply moved away is a matter of continuing debate.

Cahokia Mounds as it might have looked in the 1100s is depicted in this 1991 painting by William R. Iseminger. —Courtesy Cahokia Mounds State Historic Site

Monks Mound, Cahokia Mounds State Historic Site
—Courtesy Cahokia Mounds State Historic Site

The largest surviving remnant of this prehistoric civilization is Monks Mound, a one-hundred-foot high, four-tiered platform containing about 22 million cubic feet of earth. Its base covers fourteen acres, and the project was built in stages over three hundred years. Atop this plateau lived the principal ruler who governed the city and conducted ceremonies.

Monks Mound was named to commemorate a group of French Trappist monks who established a monastery on the mound around 1809. The cloister included several cabins, a chapel, and a refectory, with stables, granaries, cribs, and other structures around the base. In early 1812 and again in 1813, however, a "very pernicious fever" spread through the monastery and took its toll on the inhabitants. Physically and materially devastated by the epidemic, the surviving monks abandoned the property, returning to Pennsylvania, then New York, and finally France. The land was sold, but the name remained.

Cahokia Mounds was designated a United Nations World Heritage Site in 1982. As a cultural landmark of international significance and importance, it shares this honor with the city of Rome, Italy; the Great Wall of China; the Great Pyramids of Egypt; and the Taj Mahal in Agra, India.

COLLINSVILLE

Virginian John Cook built the first permanent log cabin on the land that eventually became Collinsville in 1810, but the credit for founding the community that evolved here belongs to three brothers—Anson, Augustus, and Michael Collins. The Collins brothers arrived from the East in 1817 and purchased Cook's property the following year. Within a short time, the brothers, along with other members of their family, had established a distillery, a gristmill, and a sawmill, along with several shops. The family initially called their settlement Downing's Station, but the name was changed to Collinsville by popular vote in 1825. Dr. Octavius Lumaghi opened the area's first coal mine in 1870, and Collinsville was incorporated as a city two years later.

Today the city's attractions include Fairmount Park Race Track, two amusement parks, and America's largest catsup bottle. The 170-foot-tall water tank shaped like a bottle of Brooks Catsup, restored in 1993 to its original 1949 appearance, is considered a prime example of twentieth-century roadside Americana.

GLEN CARBON

Founded in 1892 as a railroad and coal-mining town, Glen Carbon originally had three rail lines passing through it—the Chicago & North Western, the Norfolk Southern, and the Illinois Central. The name Glen Carbon, another way of saying "Valley of Coal," came from the area's mineral activity. Because of the mines, Glen Carbon attracted immigrants from all over, and it remains an ethnically diverse community to this day. Although all the major mines in the area had closed by the 1930s, Glen Carbon survived, eventually becoming a bedroom community for Edwardsville, Collinsville, and St. Louis. The Glen Carbon Heritage Museum displays artifacts and photos from the village's mining days and beyond.

The village of Glen Carbon grew up near the site of Goshen Settlement, one of the earliest non-Indian settlements in the region.

Goshen Settlement

Goshen Settlement, named for the biblical Land of Goshen, was established in 1801 by Swiss immigrant Col. Samuel Judy, the first permanent resident of Madison County. About twenty years later, as the area became more populated, Goshen Township was divided into five smaller townships, where additional settlements, including Edwardsville and Collinsville, had sprung up.

Helping to spur this growth was the Goshen Road, a wagon road built in 1808 between Goshen Settlement and the salt mines near Old Shawneetown, some 150 miles away on the eastern border of Illinois. Salt was a rare and valuable commodity on the frontier, so the road, which mostly followed Indian trails and animal migration paths, created wealth and facilitated development throughout southern Illinois. Today's Goshen Road south of Edwardsville, between IL 159 and IL 143, is believed to have been part of the original wagon road, and a historical plaque marks the road's end point, just northeast of the site of Goshen Settlement. Short segments of the road also still exist outside of Carlyle and near McLeansboro, as well as several places in Jefferson County, where sections of the original road are marked with signs.

EDWARDSVILLE

James Gillham, a South Carolinian by birth, entered the Illinois country in 1797 in search of his family, who had been kidnapped from their Kentucky farm by Kickapoo Indians several years earlier. With the help of two French traders, Gillham located his wife and three sons and recovered them after paying a ransom. Deciding he liked Illinois, then still part of Indiana Territory, Gillham settled about ten miles west of present Edwardsville. Several years later, his wife received 160 acres in the area from the federal government as remuneration for enduring captivity, expanding their property. Soon Gillham's four brothers joined him at the homestead.

Although the Gillhams were the area's first settlers, the founder of Edwardsville was Thomas Kirkpatrick, who arrived here from North Carolina in 1805. In 1812, when Madison County was established, territorial governor Ninian Edwards chose Kirkpatrick's crude but centrally located cabin as the county seat. Kirkpatrick then platted his land into a town, naming it Edwardsville in honor of his benefactor. Edwardsville was incorporated as a city in 1818.

One early settler in Edwardsville, Edward Coles, was a leader in the antislavery movement and later became the second governor of Illinois. Born in Virginia in 1786, Coles came to Illinois Territory in 1815, purchasing 6,000 acres near Edwardsville. From his family's Virginia estate, he took his twenty inherited slaves to free soil, where he gave each a certificate of freedom.

Working at the federal land office in Edwardsville, Coles built a reputation of fairness and honesty. In 1822 he ran as the only abolitionist of four candidates for governor. When the ballots were counted, slavery supporters found that they had split their votes, enabling Coles to win with 33 percent. In his inaugural address, Coles outlined his plan to abolish the indenture system and eliminate the "Black Codes" in Illinois. After losing his bid for a second term and with his political influence waning, Coles moved to Philadelphia, Pennsylvania, where he lived until his death in 1868.

Edwardsville prospered after the Civil War, when several railroads linked the city with distant places and supported its nearby coal mines. The railroads also stimulated

Edward Coles, second governor of Illinois, 1822–26
—Courtesy Schaumburg Township District Library, Illinois Collection

manufacturing in Edwardsville, which produced cigars, garments, carriages, bricks, and more. In the early twentieth century, an intercity train offered service to St. Louis, Decatur, Peoria, Springfield, and other towns until it ceased operations in 1955.

In 1957 Edwardsville became the home of the sprawling, 2,500-acre campus of Southern Illinois University, an extension of SIU Carbondale. Students from nearby cities, including St. Louis, easily reach the campus via several interstate highways.

Fort Russell and Gen. Samuel Whiteside

About two miles northwest of Edwardsville is the site of Fort Russell, a wooden stockade built during the War of 1812. The post was named after its commander, Col. William Russell of Kentucky, whose ten companies of mounted rangers were established in 1812 to defend the Illinois Territory against local Indians who had aligned with the British. The fort served as a base of operations for the Illinois militia and for a time as the seat of government for the territory.

Among the rangers stationed at Fort Russell was Edwardsville resident Capt. Samuel Whiteside, who commanded one of the companies. Whiteside had a personal hatred for Indians that began in his childhood. When he was about ten years old, a small band of Indians attacked his home near Edwardsville and killed two of his family members while he himself escaped. He grew up to become a dedicated Indian fighter.

Toward the end of the War of 1812, in July 1814, Whiteside's company pursued a band of renegade Indians who had murdered a woman and six children at the fork of the Wood River (see under Wood River on next trip). Catching up to them along the Sangamon River, the rangers killed one of the raiders, but the others escaped.

A month after the massacre, Whiteside commanded one of three boats on a water expedition when it was attacked by British artillery. Another boat, commanded by Capt. Stephen Rector, ran ashore and fell under attack by Indians. Disregarding his own safety, Whiteside and his men fought the warriors hand-to-hand while lashing the boats together and pushing them back into open water. This courageous act saved Rector's men and showed Whiteside's ability to keep his head in a crisis.

After the War of 1812, Whiteside moved to Galena and later fought Indians in the Winnebago War of 1827 and, as a brigadier general, in the Black Hawk War of 1832. After the latter war, he settled in Mount Auburn, Illinois, with his wife and nine children. He died on January 13, 1866, and was buried in Hunter Cemetery, northeast of Mount Auburn. Whiteside County in northwest Illinois is named in his honor.

Great River Road National Scenic Byway (IL 3, IL 143, and IL 100)
CAHOKIA—GRAFTON
45 miles

The Great River Road National Scenic Byway passes through the Illinois side of the St. Louis metroplitan area, mostly along IL 3 (called Lewis and Clark Boulevard between Granite City and East Alton) and IL 143, before continuing west and north on IL 100. The section of IL 100 between Hartford and Grafton is officially called the Meeting of the Great Rivers National Scenic Byway. This route is more than scenic—it's abundant with history too. Whether you are interested in Native American lore, eighteenth-century architecture, the Lewis and Clark Expedition, or Civil War prisons, this trip has something for every history buff.

CAHOKIA

The site of Cahokia was discovered in 1698 by explorer Henri de Tonti while he was guiding an expedition of Jesuits down the Mississippi River. The following year, priests of the French Seminary of Foreign Missions in Quebec established a mission at Cahokia, named after a subtribe of the Illiniwek Confederation. The priests established the Holy Family Parish and built a log church. The church that replaced it one hundred years later still stands and holds services to this day. The Holy Family Parish is the oldest continuously active Catholic parish in the United States, and its 1799 church was named a National Historic Landmark in 1970.

By the mid-eighteenth century, the settlement of Cahokia had become a center for trading between the French and the Indians, and its population had grown to more than 3,000. In 1787 Cahokia was named seat of the newly created St. Clair County. The old Cahokia Courthouse, built as a private residence in the late 1730s, served as the county courthouse until 1814, when the county boundaries changed and the seat was moved to Belleville. By that time, Cahokia's role was diminishing as neighboring towns—St. Louis and Belleville—grew in influence. For the next 150 years, Cahokia's population never exceeded 1,000.

Restoration of the 1799 Church of the Holy Family in Cahokia
—Courtesy Schaumburg Township District Library, Illinois Collection

Sketch depicting the original courthouse in Cahokia. Built as a private home around 1737, the structure served as the St. Clair County courthouse from 1787 to 1814.
—Courtesy Schaumburg Township District Library, Illinois Collection

After World War II, Cahokia revived as a suburb of St. Louis. Today its population is about 16,000. Among the village's historic treasures, in addition to the Church of the Holy Family and the Old Cahokia Courthouse, is the 1810 Jarrot Mansion, built by wealthy French immigrant Nicholas Jarrot.

Jarrot arrived in the United States around 1790 and settled in Cahokia about four years later. It was Jarrot who owned the property on which Lewis and Clark, with permission, established Camp River Dubois in 1803 (see Hartford later on this trip). Jarrot designed his mansion, begun around 1807 and completed about 1810, in American Federal style, in contrast to the French architecture of its neighbors, to reflect his wealth and prominence. Jarrot's frequent guests were treated to lavish entertaining in the second-floor ballroom, which Jarrot lent out during the day to serve as Cahokia's first schoolhouse.

The mansion remained occupied by members of the Jarrot family until 1886, when it was donated to the nearby Holy Family Church for use once again as a school. The building had begun to deteriote when a private buyer purchased it in the 1970s and partially restored it as a home. In 1976 the village of Cahokia bought it, and four years later, the Illinois Historic Preservation Agency took it over to develop as part of the Cahokia State Historic Site complex. In 1999 the agency launched a meticulous restoration project that remains ongoing today. Named a National Historic Landmark in 2001, the mansion is open periodically for special events while restoration work continues.

Even older than the Jarrot Mansion and the Holy Family Church is the old Cahokia Courthouse. Built as a private home by an unknown settler in the late 1730s, the large vertical-log house reflected the French architecture of the period—slab flooring, cantilevered roof, and vertical log walls chinked with crushed limestone and clay. In 1792 the home's second owner sold it to the government for use as a county court-house. After the county seat was moved to Belleville in 1814, the structure was used variously as a home, a saloon, a storehouse, and the town hall. Over the years it deterio-rated and was eventually abandoned. The historic courthouse stood empty until 1901, when East St. Louis businessman Alexander Cella bought it at auction. The building's second century would prove to be even more eventful than its first had been.

Cella had the structure dismantled and reconstructed it at half-size at the 1904 World's Fair in St. Louis. The exhibit bore little resemblance to the original building. After the fair, the reduced building was again sold and dismantled, this time recon-structed in Chicago's Jackson Park, where it remained for the next thirty years. In 1939 the courthouse was returned to Cahokia and reconstructed on its original site using as many of the original logs as possible. The Old Cahokia Courthouse was added to the NRHP in 1972 and was named an Illinois State Historic Site in 1985.

GRANITE CITY

Granite City, a town built "by and for industry," was named for the graniteware pro-duced by the enameling factory that spawned the city. Figuratively, however, "granite" could easily refer to the spirit of the central European immigrants who settled here. These intrepid souls overcame depressions, wars, and natural disasters to build their industrial community.

The first settlement here was a farming community called Six Mile Prairie, later named Kinder, or Kinderhook. In 1874 German immigrants Frederick and William Niedringhaus, who had established a metal-stamping company in St. Louis that pro-duced kitchen utensils, patented a process of using ground granite in enamelware and started a new business. Wanting to expand, the brothers purchased 3,500 acres near Kinder in 1892. After platting and selling a number of lots for homes, they incorporated the property and named it Granite City in honor of their own business. Three years later, they also opened a new stamping plant and a metals factory, Granite City Steel Works.

The brothers chose the site wisely, as Granite City's abundant water supply, good roads, access to river and railroad transportation, moderate taxes, and large pool of immi-grant labor made it an attractive location for heavy industry. During the early 1900s, many companies built factories here, and Granite City grew accordingly. But swings in the economy eventually caused some plants to close, including the Niedringhaus enamel factory in 1956. Their steel company, however, survived and, now a division of U.S. Steel, is still a major employer in the area.

In 1953 the nearly eight-and-a-half-mile-long Chain of Rocks Canal was com-pleted to skirt the Mississippi River's shallow rock ledges and shelves near St. Louis, allowing continuous navigation of the river. Later, two bridges were built to provide automobile access over the river and the canal. These structures helped sustain the region's economy even as manufacturing continued its free fall through the later twentieth century.

Despite setbacks, Granite City managed to survive. Recent commercial expansion and redevelopment efforts have seen some success, and the city's future is relatively promising. Meanwhile, the immigrants who helped to develop Granite City over nearly two centuries are not forgotten—the flags of seventeen European nations in downtown Memorial Park call attention to their contribution.

HARTFORD

Here, near the confluence of the Missouri and Mississippi Rivers, groves of ash and elm once meshed with the farmlands in the valley to the east. The Hartford area remained virtually unchanged until the turn of the twentieth century, when a handful of homes sprang up to house railroad employees and a few farm families. On March 6, 1920, these fifty-odd residents voted to incorporate as the village of Hartford. With its railroad, river, and highway access, Hartford soon became an industrial and commercial community. The adjacent farmland is now consumed by sprawling oil refineries, power plants, and chemical-production facilities.

Hartford's main historical attraction is the Lewis and Clark State Historic Site, established at what may have been the approximate site of Camp River Dubois, the launching point of one of the greatest exploratory ventures in U.S. history.

Lewis and Clark State Historic Site

In December 1803, Capts. Meriwether Lewis and William Clark and their men set up a winter camp on the east side of the Mississippi River near the mouth of the Missouri, in the vicinity of present-day Hartford. During their stay at Camp River Dubois, Lewis often visited nearby St. Louis to purchase supplies and recruit men for the expedition. Back at the camp, Clark put his men to work building shelters and boats, performing drills, and doing chores, punishing those who fell out of line.

The final thirty-two-man crew was officially assembled and enlisted on March 31, 1804. On the afternoon of May 14, 1804, Clark and his men boarded the boats and set sail on the Missouri River. Lewis joined the group on May 20 in St. Charles, Missouri. Two days later, the Corps of Discovery left behind the civilization they knew and began their nearly two-and-a-half-year exploration of the uncharted land and rivers of the western frontier.

Today, due to natural changes in the course of the Mississippi River, the actual site of Camp River Dubois probably lies beneath the river's muddy waters. Nevertheless, to commemorate this remarkable piece of Illinois history, Lewis and Clark State Park was established in the 1950s as near to the campsite as possible. The park, expanded and renamed Lewis and Clark State Historic Site in 2002, now includes a large interpretive center with a reproduction of the Corps' fifty-five-foot-long keelboat as well as a replica of the winter camp. Nearby, the recently built, 150-foot-tall Lewis and Clark Memorial Tower, with its open-air viewing decks, provides a panoramic view of the Mississippi and Missouri Rivers.

Historical reenactors at Lewis and Clark State Historic Site in 2004 recreate the tableau from the painting "Shooting for the Red Leggings" by Michael Haynes, which depicts an 1804 shooting match. —Courtesy Lewis and Clark State Historic Site

WOOD RIVER

Throughout the nineteenth century, the Wood River Valley retained much of its virgin habitat, interrupted only by the homesteads of a few adventuresome settlers. That era ended in 1907, when Standard Oil established a refinery here along the Mississippi River, producing asphalt, coke, fuel oil, kerosene, paraffin, and later, gasoline. The company established the community of Wood River as a family-oriented place for its employees to live.

Meanwhile, local entrepreneur Amos E. Benbow built another housing development near the plant. His town, called Benbow City, offered worker housing along with saloons, brothels, and gambling houses. In 1911 Wood River and an adjacent community called East Wood River merged as the city of Wood River, which annexed Benbow City six years later. By the 1920s, Standard Oil employed about 90 percent of Wood River's population.

To meet its housing needs, Standard Oil turned to Sears, Roebuck & Co. "catalog" homes, prefabricated house kits available by mail order, produced between 1908 and 1940. Many of these catalog homes still remain in central Wood River, giving the city one of the largest concentrations of these architectural treasures in the nation.

One of the isolated homesteads that dotted the Wood River area before the city was founded was, in 1814, the target of the most brutal Indian attack in Madison County history.

Wood River Massacre

About eight pioneer families, most of them related, arrived on the Illinois frontier around 1810 and settled near the east fork of the Wood River, about four miles north of the present city of Wood River. Among them were the families of William Moore, his brother Capt. Abel Moore, and their brother-in-law, Reason Reagan.

On the morning of July 10, 1814, Reagan left for church, several miles away, leaving his wife, Rachel, and their two children at the home of Abel Moore, about one mile from his own residence. William Moore's wife and two children were also visiting at Abel's house, where the families all planned to have supper that evening. Later that afternoon, Rachel left the Moore home to get some food from her own place. She took her two children and the four children of the two Moore families, promising to return shortly.

As evening fell, William Moore returned to his cabin to find no one there, so he went to his brother's house to look for his family. There he found his wife, Polly; Abel's wife, Mary; and Mary's sister, Hannah Bates. When William heard that Rachel and the children had left hours earlier but had not returned, he and Polly set out on different paths for the Reagan home. In the darkness, William discovered a body on the ground. Fearful that the attackers might still be nearby, he did not stop to identify it but hurried back to Abel's house with word of his grisly discovery. He urged everyone to seek shelter in the nearby blockhouse owned by another brother, George Moore. The families groped their way through the dense woods to the blockhouse, where other neighbors who had heard the news joined them.

At three o'clock in the morning, a messenger was sent to Fort Russell, about ten miles east, with the alarming news. A party of troopers was sent out at daybreak. The soldiers soon found the scalped and stripped bodies of Rachel and five of the children. Near Rachel's body was her three-year-old son, alive but badly wounded. The child was rushed to the post doctor, but he died the next day.

Meanwhile the soldiers, led by Capt. Samuel Whiteside (see under Edwardsville on previous trip) pursued the raiders. Although the War of 1812 was still on and some local tribes fought for the British, the Wood River raiders are thought to have been renegades bent on driving white settlers from their hunting grounds. Years later, Elias K. Preuitt, the son of one of the men in the pursuing party, described the chase, and his account appeared in the *History of Madison County, Illinois*:

> *The weather was extremely hot, and some of [the soldiers'] horses gave out and fell beneath their riders. . . . It was on the second day in the evening that they came in sight of the Indians, on the dividing ridge of the Sangamon River. . . . [The Indians] separated and went in different directions, all making for the timber.*

Two soldiers, James and Abraham Preuitt, overtook one of the fleeing raiders and shot him. In the Indian's pouch they found the scalp of Rachel Reagan. Whiteside's men continued their pursuit, but the rest of the Indians escaped. It is believed that after the chase, however, most of the Indians in the raiding party died of heat exposure and exhaustion.

In 1910 descendants of the victims erected a memorial at the massacre site, near the entrance to today's Gordon F. Moore Community Park. Nearby is the small cemetery where the settlers' bodies were buried, on Abel Moore's original property.

ALTON

A mythical bird, a shocking murder, a state prison turned prisoner-of-war camp, a very tall man, and nearly a dozen floods are only a few of the elements in the eventful history of Alton.

In 1814 St. Louis land developer Rufus Easton saw the solid-rock shoreline of future Alton, on a bend in the Mississippi River between the Illinois and Missouri Rivers, as a perfect spot for steamboat landings. Easton platted a town, naming it after his son, Alton, and sold lots, though he never lived there. He established a ferry across the river to Missouri in 1818, and other ferry businesses followed. Soon Alton became a major port for shipping goods between St. Louis and New Orleans, and by 1835 the city had a population exceeding 2,000.

Just across the Mississippi River from the slave state of Missouri, Alton was a major hub for the Underground Railroad in the decades before the Civil War. Not everyone in Alton was an abolitionist, however, and tensions between pro- and antislavery factions ran high in the town. The 1837 murder of abolitionist newspaper editor Elijah P. Lovejoy was a severe blow to Alton residents. Lovejoy was shot to death while trying to protect his printing press, which had been attacked several times before, from an armed and angry mob of slavery supporters. The incident made a martyr of Lovejoy and heated up the slavery debate as well as debates regarding freedom of the press. The second Illinois constitution, drafted in 1848, finally outlawed slavery altogether.

Alton was the site chosen for Illinois' first state penitentiary in 1833 (see below). The prison was closed in 1860 but was revived as a prison camp during the Civil War. In the meantime, in October 1858, Alton hosted the seventh statewide debate between U.S. senatorial candidates Abraham Lincoln and Stephen A. Douglas (see below). The twentieth century brought Alton its quirkiest claim to fame when the city became known as the home of the tallest man in the world.

Robert P. Wadlow, whose father would become the city's mayor from 1945 to 1949, was born on February 22, 1918. He was a normal baby in weight and height but within a few years that changed. By age eight, he was over six feet tall and weighed nearly two hundred pounds. At thirteen, he was the tallest Boy Scout in history, measuring seven feet, four inches.

As a young man, Wadlow toured the country with his father, visiting schools and giving lectures. For a short time, he also worked for the Ringling Brothers Circus. While on a tour in Michigan, his foot became infected and he developed a high fever. He died in his sleep on July 15, 1940, at the age of twenty-two. At the time of his death he was eight feet, eleven inches tall and weighed 490 pounds.

Robert Wadlow's remains were returned to Alton. All the businesses in town closed the day of his funeral, which drew a crowd of 40,000. Visitors to Alton can see his statue on the campus of Southern Illinois University School of Dental Medicine.

Throughout Alton's history, the seasonal unpredictability of the Mississippi River created havoc at the town's low-lying riverfront. The first major flood took place in 1844, and others occurred in nearly every decade of the twentieth century, despite efforts to control them with levees. The most devastating was the Great Flood of 1993, which caused severe damage and shut down the city's water supply for more than three weeks.

In spite of flood problems, the Mississippi has served Alton well, from its early days as a river port to today. In 1990 Illinois passed a law allowing offshore casino gambling for the first time since the days of the great riverboats. The first floating casino in the state, the *Alton Belle*, opened here in 1991. The *Alton Belle* has since been replaced by the Argosy Casino Alton, a permanently docked facility. In addition, Alton remains a stop for the *Delta Queen* and the *Julia Belle Swain*, two old-fashioned paddle-wheelers that tour up and down the Mississippi River.

Long before the city of Alton existed, when this area was home to the Illini Indians, a large and mysterious mural graced a nearby bluff overlooking the Mississippi River. At least one of the images depicted a mythical bird known as the Piasa.

Legend of the Piasa Bird

According to Illini lore, the Piasa (pronounced PIE-a-saw) was a flesh-eating bird that could carry a full-grown human in its talons. In 1673 Père Jacques Marquette, in his diary account of his exploratory journey down the Mississippi River with Louis Jolliet, noted two huge rock paintings on a bluff near today's Alton. He describes the images as "monsters . . . on which the boldest Indian dare not gaze long."

> *They are as large as a calf, with horns on the head like a deer, a fearful look, red eyes, bearded like a tiger, the face somewhat like a man's, the body covered with scales, and the tail so long that it twice makes the turn of the body, passing over the head and down between the legs, and ending at last in a fish's tail.*

Marquette's description does not mention wings or any birdlike features, but the images were later identified as "Piasas." In 1836 John Russell, a professor at Shurtleff College, put the Piasa legend into writing, recounting the tale in detail in an article for *Family Magazine*:

> *Having obtained a taste of human flesh, [the Piasa] would prey upon nothing else. He was artful as he was powerful; would dart suddenly and unexpectedly upon an Indian, bear him off into one of the caves in the bluff, and devour him. . . . Whole villages were nearly depopulated, and consternation spread through all the tribes of the Illini.*

Russell went on to describe the dream of the great warrior chief Ouatoga, in which the Great Spirit visited him and outlined a plan for destroying the dreaded creature. Ouatoga was to select twenty warriors, armed with poison arrows, to lay in wait while Ouatoga offered himself as bait. As soon as the Piasa swooped down to take his

Restored painting of the mythical Piasa Bird on a limestone cliff near Alton
—Photo by Burfalcy, Wikimedia Commons

prey, the hidden warriors rushed out and killed it. In memory of this event, the image of the Piasa was engraved on the face of the bluff.

The Piasa painting was eventually destroyed, but in 1998 the American Legends Society and volunteers created a forty-eight-by-twenty-two-foot replica on a limestone bluff along IL 3 (the Great River Road), just north of downtown Alton.

First State Prison

Illinois built the first state penitentiary in Alton in 1833. The prison's original capacity of twenty-four cells had been expanded to nearly three hundred cells by 1857. In the meantime, however, the facility's poor management, inadequate care of prisoners, and unsanitary conditions drew the attention of Dorothea Dix, a leading advocate of prison reform. Her persistent national efforts along with sympathetic local voices led to the prison's closing in 1860. The Alton prisoners were relocated to the new state penitentiary in Joliet.

With the Civil War imminent, the Union Army recognized the abandoned prison's potential as a detention camp for Confederate prisoners. In 1862 the army garrisoned the building, and in early February the first contingent of 650 Confederate prisoners arrived from an overcrowded facility in St. Louis. By 1865 the prison held nearly 2,000 (some accounts say 3,000) detainees, of which about 80 percent were Confederates and the remainder civilians, including three women.

Diseases were common in the crowded conditions of war prisons, and in December 1862 smallpox struck the Alton camp hard. The afflicted prisoners were quarantined on a nearby island in the Mississippi River (then called Sunflower Island), where they were housed in a makeshift hospital in an abandoned building. Thousands died before the epidemic subsided in March 1864. The island is now under water and, along with it, an unknown number of graves. Some smallpox victims and other Confederates who died at the prison were buried at the Confederate Cemetery in Alton, where a granite obelisk, about forty feet high, was erected in 1909 by the War Department.

The prison itself was closed on July 7, 1865, and sold to private interests, who demolished the buildings and sold the stone blocks for reuse. In 1973 a remnant of a cellblock was preserved as a monument to the inmates and guards. The prison property was converted into a city park, but it is now a paved parking lot.

Seventh Lincoln-Douglas Debate (Alton, October 15, 1858)

A large crowd was expected to turn out for the final senatorial debate between Democratic U.S. Sen. Stephen A. Douglas and Republican challenger Abraham Lincoln, held in the small river town of Alton. Yet in spite of warm, sunny weather, the anticipated throng never materialized. For whatever reason, the event drew only about 5,000 spectators, the second-smallest gathering of the seven debates.

Lincoln and Douglas arrived early on the morning of the debate. Douglas was given a rousing welcome, while Lincoln's was more subdued. The audience gathered in a semicircle at the debate site, adjacent to the city hall. Vendors hawked souvenirs while the band played rousing tunes and spectators cheered their respective candidates.

The exchange began with Douglas pouncing on repeated themes—Lincoln's opposition to the Mexican War, his support of Whig candidates, and his supposed hypocrisy concerning black equality. Lincoln, for his part, attacked Douglas for refusing to take a moral position on slavery.

GRAFTON

Near the confluence of the Illinois and Mississippi Rivers lies Grafton, billed as "A Real American River Town." Founded in 1832 by developer James Mason and named for Mason's hometown of Grafton, Massachusetts, the city's population peaked in 1850 at 10,000; today, the count is less than 10 percent of that number.

In its first century, Grafton boomed with stone quarries, boat-building shops, and commercial fishing operations. All of these industries have since disappeared, and in the late twentieth century, the town began to concentrate on developing tourism. Plans suffered a setback in 1993, when the Great Flood caused serious damage to Grafton's buildings and infrastructure. Nevertheless, the city continued to build upon its past to create economic security for the present and future. The Old Boatworks, which built paddle-wheelers in the nineteenth century and PT boats during the Korean and Vietnam Wars, was converted into a restaurant, boat harbor, and events center. The town also holds seasonal events and offers tours, ferry rides, and recreational facilities.

For nature lovers, Grafton, known as the "winter home of the bald eagle," is a prime spot for eagle-watching from late December to early March. In warmer weather, the 8,000-plus-acre Pere Marquette State Park, the largest state park in Illinois, attracts visitors from all over. The park, named for Jesuit priest and explorer Jacques Marquette, lies five miles west of Grafton.

OTHER COMMUNITIES AND SITES
OF INTEREST IN SOUTHERN ILLINOIS

Brooklyn (IL 3): In 1825 "Mother" Priscilla Baltimore, a Missouri slave who had bought her freedom and that of her mother and husband, led a group of eleven free black and fugitive slave families across the Mississippi River into Illinois and established the first African American settlement in the nation. Originally known as Freedom Village, its name was changed to Lovejoy in the late 1830s to honor martyred abolitionist newspaper publisher Elijah P. Lovejoy (see under Alton on earlier trip and under Princeton in Region 2). The settlement was incorporated as the village of Brooklyn in 1873, becoming the first incorporated African American town in U.S. history. Throughout the pre–Civil War era, Brooklyn's churches and homes were stations on the Underground Railroad.

In 1836 Mother Baltimore and Rev. William Paul Quinn established Quinn Chapel, the first African Methodist Episcopal (AME) church in the region. Although the original church building no longer stands, the congregation still meets in a brick church built in 1839. Baltimore died in 1882 and was buried in an unmarked grave in Bellefontaine Cemetery in St. Louis. In 2011 the Historical Society of Brooklyn, Illinois, founded four years earlier, placed a marker at her gravesite.

Brooklyn's current population of less than 1,000 remains primarily African American. In recent years, the Illinois State Archaeological Survey along with the University of Illinois began archaeological excavations to find out more about the original village.

Elizabethtown (IL 146): The first settler in the Elizabethtown area, Capt. James McFarlan, established a ferry here sometime before the War of 1812. The village that grew up around the ferry was probably named for McFarlan's wife, Elizabeth. The captain soon expanded his ferry's brick tollhouse into an inn and trading post called McFarlan's Tavern. The inn was further enlarged over the years, and in 1884 it was renamed for its new owner, Sarah F. Rose. Among other improvements, Mrs. Rose added a gazebo atop a rocky promontory overlooking the Ohio River. In 1989 the Illinois Historic Preservation Agency refurbished the building, grounds, and gazebo as the Grand Rose Hotel bed-and-breakfast.

Elsah (IL 100): The entire village of Elsah was listed on the NRHP in 1973, so most of its nineteenth-century buildings are preserved. In fact, more than two dozen structures in Elsah were built before the Civil War. The Village of Elsa Museum is located in the 1887 Village Hall. In 1935 Elsah became the home of Principia College, the only Christian Science college in the nation. Although this liberal-arts school is not officially affiliated with the church, "the practice of Christian Science is the cornerstone of campus life." The area around the campus was designated a National Historic Landmark in 1993. The school's most famous alumnus is actor Robert Duvall (class of 1953).

Iuka and Halfway Tavern State Historic Site (off US 50 at County Road 27): Near Iuka, a village of about 600 residents incorporated in 1882, is the Halfway Tavern

State Historic Site. This stagecoach inn was midway between Vincennes and St. Louis on the old Vincennes-to-St. Louis Trail, hence the name Halfway Tavern. The simple log structure was built in 1818 or 1819 by early settler John Middleton. A replica inn now stands on the site, though visitors are not allowed inside.

New Haven (IL 141): In the early 1800s, Jonathan Boone (brother of Daniel Boone) ventured to Illinois from Kentucky and settled along the Little Wabash River. He built a few cabins enclosed in a stockade, calling the place Boone's Fort; he also erected a three-story gristmill. Today a historical marker identifies the Boone's Mill site.

Tamaroa (US 51): The village of Tamaroa, named for a local Indian tribe, began around 1839, when pioneer educator, lawyer, farmer, and abolitionist Benajah Guernsey Roots purchased a large homestead here. In the 1850s Roots established a school called Locust Hill Academy. He also built a stately, sixteen-room mansion that became a stop on the Underground Railroad. It featured secret passageways and a fake cistern that held no water—instead it was equipped with seating for hidden slaves. A ladder in the attic led to a trapdoor to the roof, where residents could keep a lookout for slave catchers. Some of the fugitive slaves who passed through Locust Hill later returned to live and work on Roots's farm.

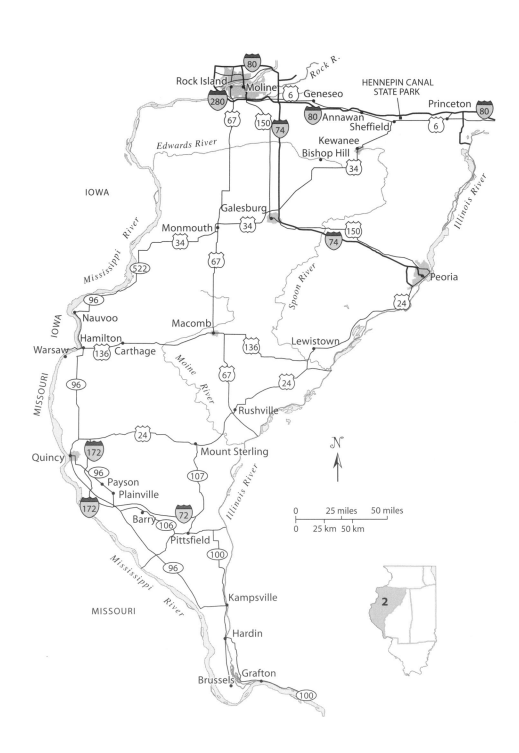

Western Illinois
UTOPIA ON THE PRAIRIE

The phrase "Utopia on the Prairie" was coined by Swedish colonists for their religious utopian community of Bishop Hill, near Kewanee, but the idyllic peacefulness of western Illinois makes the name an apt one for the whole region. As we define it here, western Illinois is roughly the area between the Mississippi and Illinois Rivers up to the northern boundary of Interstate 80. It includes all or part of nineteen counties and covers about 9,600 square miles. Two major scenic river routes grace this part of the state: the western side of the Illinois River National Scenic Byway (IL 29 and US 24) and the central part of the Great River Road National Scenic Byway (IL 96 and other roadways).

The flat and fertile landscape reflects the movement of the Illinoian glaciers, which covered the entire region with ice between 300,000 and 125,000 BC. As the glacier retreated over thousands of years, it left a level, mineral-rich surface with undulating hills and wooded areas along the rivers and streams. For centuries, the prehistoric Hopewell and Mississippian Cultures gathered wild plants, cultivated maize, fished, and hunted the bountiful game of western Illinois. Remnants of early Indian cultures have been found near Lewistown and Kampsville.

French explorers claimed much of the land around the Illinois and Mississippi Rivers through the mid-eighteenth century. The presence of French, Canadian, and Franco-Indian trappers and the building of Forts Crevecoeur and Pimiteoui along the Illinois River solidified France's hold on the region, but the French did not have the resources to protect such a vast territory. Following the French and Indian War, France relinquished control of Illinois to the British as part of the 1763 Treaty of Paris, and the United States seized control of the region during the American Revolution. In the 1810s western Illinois was singled out to become one of three military tracts established by Congress after the War of 1812.

Illinois Military Tract

To stimulate development of the western frontier and to pay soldiers for their service in the War of 1812, Congress established three military tracts in present Illinois, Missouri, and Arkansas. The Illinois Tract contained 3.5 million acres within boundaries close to those used to designate western Illinois in this book—the area between the Illinois and Mississippi Rivers south of today's I-80. After the land was surveyed in 1815 and 1816, it was opened for settlement.

Each veteran was awarded 160 acres as partial payment for his military service. Some settled on their land despite the threat of Indian unrest, while others sold their parcels to land speculators. But settlement of the region was stalled in 1832, when the warrior-leader Black Hawk led a band of Sauk and Mesquakie (Fox) to retake a region comprising parts of present Illinois and southwestern Wisconsin (then part of Michigan Territory). Fort Armstrong, built in 1816 on the southern tip of Rock Island, served as the launching point for army regulars and Illinois militia during the fifteen-week conflict. After the Black Hawk War, the treaty at Fort Armstrong ended the Indian threat to settlers on the Illinois prairies.

Settlement and Civil War

Much of the northern part of the military tract in western Illinois was settled by New Yorkers and New Englanders seeking to overcome economic depression in the Northeast and take advantage of the area's rich farmland, while arrivals from southern states often remained in the southern part of the tract. Other settlers included members of the newly created Mormon Church, who in 1839 arrived at Commerce (later named Nauvoo) on the Mississippi River. In 1846, the same year the Mormons were driven out of Nauvoo, a coterie of Swedish immigrants led by Erik Jansson established the colony of Bishop Hill, just west of present-day Kewanee. In the mid-1850s, the building of several railroads opened up further economic opportunities in western Illinois.

As settlement expanded, the slavery issue was coming to a head in the region and throughout the country. When the Civil War erupted, most Illinoisans remained loyal to the Union, and many young men from the Prairie State volunteered to fight. No major battles were fought in Illinois, but many towns became important supply bases, and there were several prison camps established throughout the state, including the Rock Island Prison Barracks at Arsenal Island. After the war, development resumed in most of Illinois, including the western tracts.

Postwar Growth

With the war over, manufacturing centers emerged in Galesburg, Macomb, Moline, Peoria, Quincy, and Rock Island. By the turn of the twentieth century, Peoria and Rock Island had become industrial giants, as had Moline, home of John Deere's manufacturing operations. In 1907 the Illinois & Mississippi Canal (a.k.a. the Hennepin Canal) was completed. Extending from Hennepin to the Mississippi River, the canal reduced the shipping distance between Lake Michigan and the Mississippi River by several hundred miles. The canal's usefulness, however, turned out to be limited as other shipping options—especially railroads—superseded water transportation in the early twentieth century.

A steamer passes through Lock 22 of the newly completed Illinois & Mississippi (Hennepin) Canal, early 1900s. —Courtesy Hennepin Canal Parkway State Park

Quiet Progress

In the 1930s and early 1940s, western Illinois was the site of several New Deal public-works projects, but by the 1970s, the infrastructure there had become so inadequate that the region was dubbed "Forgottonia." A campaign to secure government funding for public improvements was modestly successful in getting highways and bridges built, expanded, or repaired and in improving train service. The completion of I-74 in the 1970s provided access to the northern part of this region; the new highway ran north and south between the Quad Cities area and Galesburg, then on to Peoria. But it wasn't until 1991 that west-central Illinois was opened up with the completion of I-72, which connected Quincy with Springfield. This interstate opened this much-neglected region to expanded tourism, economic development, and commerce.

Much of western Illinois is still rural, and agriculture remains the economic mainstay. The more populated areas—Rock Island, Moline, Peoria, and Quincy—rely on manufacturing and urban industries such as retail trade, services, government, and health care.

Illinois River Road (County Rte 1 and IL 100) and IL 106
BRUSSELS—PITTSFIELD
57 miles

This scenic trip begins in tiny Brussels, home of the visitor center for the Two Rivers National Wildlife Refuge (part of the Mark Twain National Wildlife Refuge), and heads north. From Brussels we will follow the Illinois River Road (County Hwy 1), which becomes IL 100 at Hardin, and continue on IL 100 to IL 106, where we turn westward to the Pike County seat in Pittsfield.

To begin this trip from the Alton-Grafton area (see Region 1), take IL 100 to the Brussels Ferry and cross the Mississippi River; from there, follow the Illinois River Road/County Hwy 1 to Brussels.

BRUSSELS

A visit to Brussels is akin to returning to the nineteenth century. Surprisingly little has changed in this historic village since it was first settled in 1822. Even today, the population is less than two hundred. Chartered in 1847, Brussels was named after the Belgian city that was the hometown of its first parish priest, Fr. John Moliter.

The eighty-building Brussels Historic District includes several buildings dating back to the village's founding in 1847. Among these are the Wittmond Trading Post (eventually expanded into today's Wittmond Hotel) and the Brussels Village Jail, which was used as a detention cell until 1952. Local homes—fine examples of Greek Revival, Italianate, and Queen Anne architectural styles—also grace the historic district.

Headquartered in Brussels is the 8,501-acre Two Rivers National Wildlife Refuge, which attracts bald eagles to its five separate bottomland parcels of riverine wetlands. The refuge, managed by the U.S. Fish and Wildlife Service, extends from here in Calhoun County into neighboring Greene and Jersey Counties.

PITTSFIELD

Pike County (named for explorer Zebulon Pike) was carved from Madison County in 1821. As one local chronicler described the region, "the prairies were a vast wilderness covered with a rank growth of prairie grass, and much of the land . . . was covered with heavy forests." The county's original seat was a now-defunct town called Cole's Grove; the seat was moved a few years later to another extinct town, Atlas, which conducted county business in an unfinished courthouse. Pittsfield, so named by local settler Col. William Ross for his hometown in Massachusetts, was established as the permanent county seat in 1833.

Colonel Ross and his brothers had arrived in 1820 to claim their land payment for service during the War of 1812. The colonel had served in the Black Hawk War as first aide to Brig. Gen. Samuel Whiteside and as commander of a company of Mounted Rangers, and he later served in the Illinois House and Senate. One of his brothers, Henry, was a prominent physician in Pike County, and another brother, Leonard, served as Pittsfield's first sheriff. The colonel himself built Pittsfield's first bank, Ross & Company, in 1854. By the Civil War, the bank had closed along with many others, but it reopened twenty-five years later as Pittsfield Bank, later changed to Farmers State Bank. Descendants of Col. William Ross continue to operate the bank in the same building.

Visitors to Pittsfield will find many unique historic buildings. The current Pike County Courthouse—the third in Pittsfield—was designed by master mason Robert Franklin. This often-photographed, 136-foot-high, octagonal structure was completed in 1894. Noted architect John M. Van Osdel designed the Pittsfield East School, listed on the NRHP in 1971. Built between 1863 and 1866, the school building now houses the Pike County Historical Society and the Pike County Historical Society Museum. Pittsfield also boasts nine pre-Civil War buildings tied to Abraham Lincoln. One of these is the former home of John Hay, Lincoln's personal secretary and later Secretary of State under presidents William McKinley and Theodore Roosevelt.

I-72/US 36, I-172, and IL 96
PITTSFIELD–HAMILTON
89 miles

This route from Pittsfield to Hamilton takes motorists through the "micropolitan" area of Quincy, historically and currently the hub of this region. From Pittsfield, we can take any one of a number of roads a short distance north to I-72, where we'll head northwest past the site of the extinct town of New Philadelphia, a little-known but important place in African American history. From I-72, we'll hop onto I-172, one of many roads leading to the lively city of Quincy. Here we can pick up scenic IL 96, which leads us all the way to the riverside town of Hamilton.

PITTSFIELD
See previous trip

NEW PHILADELPHIA HISTORIC TOWN SITE

Most maps of Illinois show a small town called New Philadelphia, population 100, east of Macomb in McDonough County. But the original New Philadelphia, Illinois, which stood three miles east of Barry, no longer exists as a community and does not appear on current maps—not yet, anyway. Several local preservation groups, including the Free Frank New Philadelphia Historic Preservation Foundation and the New Philadelphia Association, have been working in recent decades to share with the world the story of New Philadelphia and its founder, Free Frank McWorter.

Results of their efforts include the listing of McWorter's burial place, just off US 36, on the NRHP in 1988; the naming of a section of I-72 as Free Frank McWorter Historic Memorial Highway in 1990; and the designation of the town site as a National Historic Landmark in 2009. In the meantime, the preservation foundation has spearheaded a project to build a replica of this racially integrated frontier town as an interactive living history museum called the Free Frank New Philadelphia Historic Frontier Town.

The story of Free Frank McWorter and his settlement begins in 1836, when New Philadelphia became the first town in the nation to be platted and registered by a black man. McWorter was born a slave in South Carolina in 1777. He later moved with his master to Kentucky, where he met his wife, Lucy, and had a family. Hired out as a farm hand on the side, Frank saved up his meager earnings and opened his own small business, a modest saltpeter production facility, around 1812. From this venture, he accumulated enough money to purchase freedom for Lucy in 1817 and for himself in 1819.

In 1830 McWorter bought land in the rolling hills of Pike County, between the Illinois and Mississippi Rivers. In 1836 he had the land surveyed, platted, and registered as New Philadelphia, then, using monies from the lot sales, purchased the freedom of more family members in Kentucky. Free Frank died in 1854, but his town continued to grow. The population of New Philadelphia, according to some records, may have been as high as 170 by the end of the Civil War. Residents were both black and white, and the town's school was integrated.

After the Hannibal & Naples Railroad built a station at Barry, bypassing New Philadelphia, in 1869, many of the latter town's businesses relocated to Barry, and New Philadelphia's population began a steady decline. The town was legally dissolved in 1885, although a few residents remained until the 1920s.

In 1996 local organizers formed the New Philadelphia Association and brought in archaeologists to survey the site for possible preservation. The efforts of the association, along with many supporting organizations, have already borne significant fruit. As their work continues, Illinois may see a full-fledged historical museum develop on what is still an open field. As of 2012, there is even legislation pending that could lead to the site's being designated a National Park.

BARRY

A bright red water tower, the Apple Basket farm, and an annual apple festival all serve as reminders of the apple orchards that once fed Barry's economy. Most of the orchards are gone now, but the city still honors its agricultural heritage, which began in 1836, when the first settlers arrived in the newly platted village of Worchester. The town was renamed Barry, after one prominent resident's hometown of Barre, Vermont (mistakenly recorded as Barry), three years later.

The arrival of the Hannibal & Naples Railroad in 1869 spurred more than two decades of growth and development in Barry, but in 1894 a fire destroyed about half of the town's businesses as well as some homes. Residents rebuilt their downtown within a few months, but a second fire in 1913, though less devastating, caused similar damage. Undaunted, the locals rebuilt, determined to preserve their community. Barry's business district is now listed on the NRHP, and the Barry Museum, located on the second floor of the Barry Public Library, shares the history of this tenacious town.

PLAINVILLE AND PAYSON

Plainville, founded as Stone's Prairie in 1856 and incorporated under its current name in 1896, and its larger neighbor Payson, founded in 1835, are both small farming communities southeast of Quincy in Adams County. The two villages share a mostly quiet history of agriculture and rural seclusion. But during the 1860 presidential election, the county was a hotbed of political activity, and both towns participated in a rally that eventually erupted into injurious violence.

The Stone's Prairie Riot

On August 25, 1860, in the village of Stone's Prairie, a political rally was held in support of presidential candidate Abraham Lincoln. Initially, backers of Democrat Stephen A. Douglas had been invited to the gathering, advertised as a forum for debate. Four days before the event, however, the Republican organizers decided to withdraw the invitation and focus instead on firing up their own base, leaving the Democrats little time to notify their people.

In those days, it was customary for supporters of a candidate, in preparation for a political demonstration, to erect in their town square tall poles bearing flags, banners displaying their candidate's name, and effigies of the opposing contender. On the day of the rally, a group of Republicans, part of a paramilitary group known as the "Wide Awakes," marched through Payson, where local Democrats had put up banners backing Douglas and an effigy of Lincoln. The Republican procession carried its own banner, which portrayed Douglas as a drunk. Both sides may have grumbled at each other, but the Republicans passed through the town without incident.

The rally attracted droves of area residents, reportedly reaching a peak of 7,000 to 10,000 people. Music played, speakers delivered speeches, and picnic lunches were distributed from wagons. As the event continued into the afternoon, a number of Democrats, realizing that their faction wouldn't be allowed to talk, began disrupting the Republican presenters. Fistfights broke out, and a general melee involving several hundred men ensued. After things settled down, the Wide Awakes left on their return march. As the procession passed through Payson, the Democrats fired gunshots at the Republicans, piercing their flag and wounding a man in the arm. The twin incidents became known as the Stone's Prairie Riot of 1860. While no one was killed, the episode added to the animosity between the supporters of the two parties.

QUINCY

Quincy's founder and first settler was New Yorker John Wood, who in 1822 purchased 160 acres from a veteran of the War of 1812 for sixty dollars. Three years after Wood settled there, Quincy became the seat of the newly formed Adams County and was incorporated as a city in 1840. Wood, a private in the Black Hawk War, later served as mayor of Quincy (1844–48, 1852–53, and 1856), Illinois state senator (1851–55), lieutenant governor (1857–60), and governor (1860–61) upon the death of Gov. William H. Bissell in 1860. In addition to Wood, the city fostered two other future Illinois governors—Thomas Carlin (1838–42) and Thomas Ford (1843–49).

Sitting atop a 125-foot-high bluff with a natural harbor below, Quincy was ideal for docking freight boats. This harbor, Quincy Bay, also inspired a group of local businessmen to launch a new industry—the harvesting and shipping of ice. During the winter months, pristine ice formed in the bay's spring-fed waters. The Quincy entrepreneurs, who began their enterprise in 1857, were among the earliest Midwesterners to recognize the potential of ice harvesting as an industry. Before long, nearly twenty ice companies sprang up in Quincy, shipping ice throughout the region and down the Mississippi River to New Orleans and other southern cities. Naturally, other towns soon followed suit and began cutting and selling the ice that formed on their own inland lakes.

As ice prices increased to as much as eight dollars per ton, companies competed to meet the demand, enlarging their ice storehouses and stepping up production. The ice industry in the region flourished into the twentieth century, until advancements in refrigeration technology provided alternatives.

With its rich farmland, abundant timber, easy access to water (and ice), and ideal shipping location on the Mississippi River, Quincy grew rapidly before, during, and after the Civil War. Before the war, Quincy was known as an abolitionist city. Located just across the river from the slave state of Missouri, it became the first stop on the Underground Railroad that led northeast toward Chicago and Canada. The slavery issue was naturally a paramount subject for debate when Abraham Lincoln and Stephen A. Douglas squared off in Quincy in October 1858 (see below).

During the Civil War, Quincy was represented in the Union Army with four general officers—Brevet Maj. Gen. James D. Morgan, Maj. Gen. Benjamin M. Prentiss, Brevet Brig. Gen. William A. Schmitt, and Brig. Gen. John Tillson. In 1861, just after the war began, a family of escaped slaves arrived in Quincy. One of the children, seven-year-old Augustine (Gus) Tolton, grew up to become the nation's first African American Catholic priest (see below).

By the 1870s Quincy had become so prosperous it was known as the "Gem City." In 1879 the town had more than seventy-five businesses, and at one time, as many as eight railroads connected Quincy with Chicago and the East Coast. In 1886 the state's first veterans' home was established here, one of five now located in Illinois to provide health care and housing to former service members and their spouses. The facility also has a museum.

Four historic districts in Quincy—the Downtown Historic District, the South Side German Historic District, the East End Historic District, and the Northwest Historic District—offer various architectural styles and tree-lined streets. Among the highlights in town are the Quincy Museum; the John Wood Mansion; Dr. Richard Eels House, a major Underground Railroad site; the Gardner Museum of Architecture and Design; and the Villa Katherine Castle, a rare example of Mediterranean architecture in the Midwest.

Sixth Lincoln–Douglas Debate (Quincy, October 13, 1858)

Both Abraham Lincoln and Stephen A. Douglas were seasoned debaters by the time they appeared in Quincy. The event, which took place in present-day Washington Park (then called John's Square), was memorialized in 1936 with a bronze bas-relief panel created by famous sculptor Lorado Taft.

The candidates traveled on separate trains from Macomb, both arriving the evening before the debate. Douglas was greeted by an enthusiastic crowd who provided a torch-light parade from the station to the Quincy House hotel. Lincoln's followers ushered him through town, serenaded by an all-ladies chorus. Throughout the town, an array of colorful banners and signs extolled each side's allegiances.

Spectators from as far away as Keokuk, Iowa, and Hannibal, Missouri, traveled in wagons, on horseback, and on foot over roads turned into quagmire by uninterrupted rains. In all, 10,000 to 15,000 people assembled in John's Square. Before it began at

2:30 p.m., in separate incidents, the railing around the platform broke and a bench with seated ladies collapsed. Calm was soon restored and the debate began.

Lincoln hammered home his theme that Negroes are entitled to human and civil rights and that he personally opposed slavery and its expansion. Nevertheless, he stated that "I have no purpose directly or indirectly (to) interfere with the institution of slavery in the States where it exists." Furthermore, he said, "I have no purpose to introduce political and social equality between the white and the black races. There is a physical difference between the two, which, in my judgment, will probably forever forbid their living together upon a footing of perfect equality, and inasmuch as it becomes a necessity that there must be a difference, I, as well as Judge Douglas, am in favor of the race to which I belong having the superior position."

Fr. Augustine Tolton

Quincy was the home of Augustine (Gus) Tolton, who overcame great adversities to become the first African American Catholic priest. Born a slave on April 1, 1854, in Brush Creek, Missouri, Tolton was the property of his mother's master. When the Civil War began, his father, Peter, fled to join the Union Army, and his mother, Martha, escaped with their three children to Quincy, rowing across the Mississippi River at Hannibal.

Arriving in Quincy after a forty-one-mile trip evading Confederates and slave catchers, the Tolton family sought refuge among a colony of blacks on the city's east side. For several years, Martha eked out a living making cigars in the Harris Tobacco Factory while sharing shelter with another family. When Gus was nine, he and his brother, ten-year-old Charles, joined their mother at work. Charles died later that year, leaving only Gus and his sister, Anne, age four. Their father, they learned when the war ended, had died of dysentery.

As members of St. Boniface Catholic Church in Quincy, Martha enrolled Gus in the all-white St. Boniface School, but his attendance sparked such insults and threats that he was withdrawn. When Gus was fourteen, Fr. Peter McGirr, pastor of St. Lawrence Church (later St. Peter Church), insisted that the boy attend St. Lawrence School, assuring the family that no abuses would be tolerated.

As a student at St. Lawrence, Gus showed a keen interest in religious matters. The priests in Quincy, seeing a promising future for him in the priesthood, tutored him privately to prepare him for the seminary. Despite his talent and the support of the priests, he was denied entry into several seminaries because of his race. In the meantime, however, he was able to continue his studies at St. Francis College (later Quincy University). While a student, Gus attended daily Mass, served Mass, taught the catechism to children, and counseled black parishioners about alcohol abuse.

In 1880, with the help of the Bishop of Alton and one of his Quincy tutors, Fr. Michael Rickard, Gus was admitted to the College of Sacred Propaganda in Rome, Italy. After six years of study, he was ordained a priest, celebrating his first Mass on Easter Sunday in St. Peter's Basilica in Rome. He believed he would be sent to a mission in Africa, but instead church officials sent him back to the United States. Cardinal Giovanni Simeoni stated, "America has been called the most enlightened nation in the world. We shall see if it deserves that honor. If the United States has never before seen a Black priest, it must see one now."

On July 18, 1886, Father Gus returned to Quincy to celebrate Mass at St. Boniface, and the following Sunday he was installed as pastor of the Negro Church of St. Joseph in Quincy. His stirring sermons drew many white parishioners, and attendance at St. Joseph grew considerably. But his very success incited renewed resentment and racial prejudice in Quincy. In 1889 he was transferred to Chicago.

Reporting to Archbishop Patrick Augustine Feehan, Father Gus was given "full pastoral jurisdiction over all Negro Catholics in Chicago." In a poor, racially mixed neighborhood, he opened a storefront church called St. Monica's Chapel. Later, with financial assistance from Katherine Drexel, founder of the Sisters of the Blessed Sacrament for Indians and Colored People, he began construction on a permanent church. Services were held there, though the building was never finished.

On a very hot Chicago day in 1897, Father Gus, returning from a retreat, collapsed on the sidewalk while walking home from the train. A few hours later at the hospital, he was pronounced dead of heat stroke and uremia. He was only forty-three. His body was returned to Quincy and buried at St. Peter Cemetery.

In March 2010, the Archdiocese of Chicago announced that the Cause for Sainthood has been opened for Fr. Augustine Tolton, representing the first step in a lengthy, multistage process toward canonization. It is likely to take decades before

Father Augustine Tolton of Quincy in 1887, less than a year after his ordination
—Courtesy Quincy University

the Catholic Church can make a final decision. Although dozens of black Catholics have been canonized by the church, as of this writing, none were American, though the Cause for Sainthood is open and currently under inquiry for another African American, Mother Henriette Delille of New Orleans.

WARSAW

Warsaw has an indirect connection to several U.S. presidents. John Hay, who moved to Warsaw with his parents in the late 1830s, was Abraham Lincoln's private secretary and later served as Secretary of State under both William McKinley and Theodore Roosevelt. Roosevelt's grandfather, William H. Roosevelt, also lived in Warsaw. In September 1814, more than twenty years before Warsaw was platted, Maj. (later President) Zachary Taylor led more than 400 troops up the Mississippi River to fight the British and their Indian allies. On a sloped, sixty-foot-high bluff just below the Lower Rapids, opposite the mouth of the Des Moines River, the men built Fort Johnson, a rough stockade with four blockhouses. Less than two months later, the fort was burned and abandoned.

In October 1815 the U.S. Army sent an expedition to build a string of forts along the Mississippi. Cantonment Davies (or Davis), a collection of lean-tos and crude cabins near the site of Fort Johnson, was hurriedly built to provide shelter for the upcoming winter. In the spring, some soldiers stayed at the camp to build a more permanent post, Fort Edwards, named in honor of Illinois territorial governor Ninian Edwards. Despite its marginal value as a military outpost, the fort was garrisoned until 1824. During the Black Hawk War, the abandoned fort was used as a refuge for settlers and a rendezvous spot for state militia. Eventually, local settlers dismantled the stockade and buildings.

With Indian troubles over, several investors platted the town of Warsaw in 1834. Its location on the riverfront was ideal for ferry and freight-boat landings, and soon Warsaw was the busiest port between St. Louis and St. Paul. The arrival of the Toledo, Peoria & Warsaw Railroad in the 1860s further strengthened the local economy. Eventually, however, modern highways ended Warsaw's importance as a port and railroad center. The Warsaw Historic District, which includes buildings of Federal, Italianate, and Greek Revival design, was placed on the National Register of Historic Places in 1977.

HAMILTON

The 160-acre tract of land acquired by settler John Gordon in 1833 and platted in 1852 was named after Artois Hamilton of Carthage, in honor of his support of the town. The settlement was incorporated as a town in 1854 and it was reincorporated as a city five years later.

A ferry transported people and livestock across the Mississippi River until the Keokuk-Hamilton iron bridge opened in 1871. Over subsequent decades, various industrial and commercial enterprises thrived in downtown Hamilton and along the riverfront, but the city continued to rely on its economic mainstay—agriculture.

Probably Hamilton's most influential citizen was Mary Augusta Safford, who became known as "Queen Mary" for her leadership in the Iowa Sisterhood, a group of female Unitarian ministers dedicated to women's rights. The Safford family, natives of Massachusetts, arrived in Hamilton in 1855, when Mary was about three years old. She spent her adult life setting up congregations throughout the Midwest and working for universal suffrage and social justice. Shortly before her death in 1927, Mary funded the construction of the Hamilton High School auditorium, which is currently being restored.

A major employer in Hamilton is Dadant & Sons Beekeeping Supplies, a family-owned business that began in 1863, when French-born Charles Dadant settled on the tallgrass prairie here and started keeping bees. He developed the Dadant beehive, with a roomy movable-block design that proved very popular. Today, the Dadant company's ten U.S. branches serve the beekeeping industry worldwide.

Since 1968 Hamilton has been home to the Western Illinois Threshers, an organization devoted to preserving the region's agricultural heritage. Each August, crowds gather at the Threshers' forty-acre headquarters near Hamilton to examine their collection of antique farm equipment, visit their minivillage of early buildings, and ride the group's own Western Illinois Shortline Railroad. The Threshers also sponsor events throughout the year.

US 136 and US 24
HAMILTON—PEORIA
112 miles

Crossing the heart of western Illinois on US 136, we pass through Carthage, which like Nauvoo is an important site in Mormon history. Just south of Lewistown we pick up US 24 to Peoria. This section of the highway is part of Illinois River National Scenic Byway, also known as the "Route of the Voyagers." For the most part, it parallels the Illinois River, providing views of the bluffs, forests, prairies, and wetlands formed thousands of years ago by melting glaciers. For those who wish to continue on this scenic route, it leads, via IL 29, to Princeton.

HAMILTON
See previous trip

CARTHAGE

First settled in 1831, Carthage was designated the Hancock County seat in 1833 and incorporated as a town four years later. The first courthouse was a log cabin that served the county until 1839, when it was replaced with a sturdier building. The second courthouse lasted sixty-seven years before it was razed in 1906 and replaced by the building that remains in use today. The current courthouse features a large rotunda, marble staircase, and stained-glass windows, reflecting the grandeur of early twentieth-century government architecture.

Early in its history, Carthage gained notoriety as the site of the murder of Mormon Church founder Joseph Smith (see also Nauvoo on later trip). As Smith's power in Nauvoo grew, he directed his followers to squelch opposition both inside and outside the church. In June 1844, after Smith's supporters destroyed the press of a newly formed opposition newspaper, his opponents filed a complaint against him and his brother, Hyrum, in Carthage. Rather than resist arrest, the brothers rode to Carthage and surrendered to authorities there on June 25, hoping to defend themselves at their

The jail in Carthage, where in 1844 Joseph and Hyrum Smith were being held when a mob broke into their cell and killed the two brothers —Author's collection

hearing. Shortly afterward, Gov. Thomas Ford visited Carthage to talk to the Smiths in jail. Upon leaving, he ordered the local state militia, the Carthage Greys, to protect the Smith brothers from harm.

On the afternoon of June 27, a mob stormed the jail (some believe with the complicity of the Carthage Greys) and shot first Hyrum, then Joseph Smith, who fell out the window and landed next to a well. The Carthage jail and its environs are now historic landmarks maintained by the Mormon Church.

In 1870 Illinois State University moved from Springfield to Carthage and was renamed Carthage College. An early landmark of the school was the Old Main Bell, which hung in a tower atop Old Main, the first building on the Carthage campus. Students regularly rang the bell to celebrate athletic victories. Another campus icon was "kissing rock," a 2.5-ton granite boulder located at the entrance to Evergreen Walk. The rock became a rendezvous point for young lovers as well as a graffiti magnet.

Carthage College moved to Kenosha, Wisconsin, in 1962, retaining its name. Shortly thereafter, fraternities retrieved both the bell and the rock and moved them to the new campus along Lake Michigan. The old campus buildings in Carthage were utilized for various other purposes over the years. They now sit vacant, but city officials are considering plans for their renovation and future use.

MACOMB

At the time of its founding, Macomb, then called Washington, had only one resident, Rev. John Baker, whose home also served as a tavern and general store. Four years after McDonough County was created in 1826, Baker's cabin in Washington, the most centrally located site in the county, was designated the seat. Later that year a town, renamed Macomb, was platted and lots were sold. Both the county and the town were named for War of 1812 leaders—McDonough County for Commodore Thomas McDonough (also spelled Macdonough) and Macomb for Maj. Gen. Alexander Macomb.

In 1855 the Northern Cross Railroad's line through Macomb brought further population and economic growth. Various attempts to establish a school of higher learning in Macomb were unsuccessful until 1899, when Western State Normal School (now Western Illinois University) was built as a teachers' college. Later it broadened its curriculum and became part of the state university system. The administration building, Sherman Hall, was listed on the NRHP in 1998.

Macomb is also the home of the Western Illinois Museum, whose exhibits pertain to the history and culture of the region. The museum, the 1872 McDonough County Courthouse, and the Old Bailey House, built by banker William S. Bailey around 1887, are good places to stop on a historical tour through west-central Illinois.

LEWISTOWN

Hundreds of square miles of the Military Tract remained unclaimed by veterans of the War of 1812 until 1821, when Maj. Ossian M. Ross became the first to claim his 160 acres. Originally from Seneca, New York, Ross brought his wife, three children, and a party of settlers that included a blacksmith, a carpenter, a shoemaker, some laborers, and their families. The following year, Ross platted a town site, which he named for his first son, Lewis.

When Fulton County was established in 1823, Lewistown became the county seat. It was incorporated as a town in 1857 and as a city around 1882. The original Fulton County courthouse, where Stephen A. Douglas served as a circuit court judge and where Abraham Lincoln delivered a speech in 1858, was set afire by an arsonist in 1894. The building's two front columns were salvaged and placed in front of the Civil War monument at Lewistown's Oak Hill Cemetery.

The Peoria & Hannibal Railroad reached Lewistown in 1862, but in 1880 local residents warmly welcomed the Fulton County Narrow Gauge Railway, affectionately known as the "Peavine," which ran along a curvy route between Lewistown and Fairview, later extending northwest to Galesburg and southeast to West Havana. In 1905 the Chicago, Burlington & Quincy Railroad acquired the sixty-one-mile-long rail line, converting the track to standard gauge. The CB&Q operated the Peavine until 1934 and ran passenger trains until 1961.

In 1880 Hardin W. Masters, father of poet Edgar Lee Masters, moved with his family from Petersburg to Lewistown, when Edgar was twelve (see also Petersburg in Region 3). The elder Masters was a prominent attorney and four-term mayor who also established the town's public library. As a young man, Edgar worked in his father's law office before moving to Chicago in the early 1890s. He later became a partner in the Chicago law firm of Clarence Darrow.

In time, Edgar Lee Masters became better known as a writer than as a lawyer. In 1915 he published his most famous book, *Spoon River Anthology.* The book was a series of short freeform poems set in the cemetery of the fictional town of Spoon River, based on Petersburg and Lewistown. The poems, presented as monologues delivered by the dead, revealed small-town pettiness, prejudice, and hypocrisy. The book won nationwide critical acclaim, but many locals were offended at the way it presumably portrayed them, their neighbors, and dearly departed citizens. Masters wrote over fifty books in his lifetime. He spent his final years in Pennsylvania, where he died in 1950 at age eighty-one. His body was returned to Petersburg for burial.

Lewistown's Oak Hill Cemetery, the setting of Masters's *Spoon River Anthology,* is a popular attraction for visitors. Other historic sites in the city include the Rasmussen Blacksmith Shop Museum, still at its original 1893 location; the Carnegie Public Library, built in 1906; and Dickson Mounds, an ancient Indian burial site about five miles south of Lewistown.

Dickson Mounds

Thousands of years ago, nomadic Indians of the Paleo-Indian (12,000 to 8000 BC) and Archaic (8000 to 1000 BC) periods roamed the Illinois River Valley near present Lewistown. These peoples were followed by the more sedentary Woodland Cultures (about 1000 BC to AD 1000). By the beginning of the twelfth century, the Mississippian Culture dominated southwestern Illinois.

The Mississippian peoples often buried their dead in earthen mounds. One of these burial sites was discovered on the farm of William Dickson, who in the 1860s uncovered bones and other artifacts while clearing brush and trees from his land, near the juncture of the Illinois and Spoon Rivers. Little was done about the discovery until 1927, when Dickson's son Don, a chiropractor and student of pathology, excavated the mounds.

Working in a scientific manner, Don Dickson carefully cleared dirt away from the bones while leaving the skeletal remains intact. Charging admission fees to view the excavation, he collected enough money to erect a building over the site and establish the private Dickson Mounds Museum. In 1945 he sold the mounds to the State of Illinois, and twenty years later the property was transferred to the Illinois State Museum, which added a new museum and research facility.

By the 1980s, however, the exposure and display of Indian skeletal remains became controversial as modern tribes sought to protect ancestral burial sites. In response to complaints and protests, the state enacted the Human Skeletal Remains Protection Act in 1989 to protect old, unregistered graves on private or public land, and the federal government passed the Native American Graves Protection and Repatriation Act in 1990.

In the meantime, the Dickson Mounds Museum became a lightning rod for activism, and in September 1993 the museum closed its doors to revamp its displays and educational programs. Reopening one year later, the museum is now a respected center for archaeological research and education.

PEORIA

"Will it play in Peoria?" This question originated during the vaudeville era, when stage shows considering a national tour had a good chance of success if Peorians, with their Midwestern values and mainstream culture, liked it. Peoria soon became the definitive test market for political pundits, advertising agencies, TV and movie producers, and others to judge the viability of their programs and products.

The seeds for this all-American city were sown in 1680, while the Illinois country was under French control. To establish France's presence in the territory, French explorers René-Robert Cavalier, Sieur de La Salle, and Henri de Tonti built the first white settlement in the vicinity of future Peoria, Fort Crevecoeur (see Creve Coeur in Region 3). The fort was destroyed only a few months later, but in 1683 the Frenchmen built a new post, Fort St. Louis, on the Illinois River at what is now known as Starved Rock (see Starved Rock State Park in Region 4). Nine years later, in 1691, Indian attacks compelled the French to relocate the post to Peoria Lake, then called Lake Pimiteoui, not far from the site of Fort Crevecoeur.

France used the new Fort St. Louis off and on until the British took control of Illinois in 1763, but French settlers remained in the Lake Pimiteoui area for another fifteen years. Around 1778 Jean Baptiste Maillet established a new French village called La Ville de Maillet near present downtown Peoria. This settlement lasted until American forces burned it down in 1812, and the following year, the U.S. government built Fort Clark at the site. This post grew into a settlement, which was dubbed Peoria in 1825. Twenty years later, with a population of nearly 2,000, Peoria was incorporated as a city.

From its founding until the enactment of the Volstead Act (Prohibition) in 1920, Peoria was known as the "Whiskey Capital of the World." Twenty-four breweries and seventy-three distilleries once operated in the city, with its convenient rail and river transportation and its ample supply of corn, barley, and cool spring water. During the golden years of Peoria's liquor industry, some of the city's whiskey and beer barons used their fortunes to help fund local projects such as the construction of the G.A.R. Hall, the Orpheum and Palace Theaters, and the Jefferson Hotel; the organization of the Peoria Public Library; the expansion of Peoria Park District lands; the creation of public artworks; and other endeavors. Prohibition, however, forced Peoria's breweries and distilleries to close, and even after the Eighteenth Amendment was repealed in 1933, the city never regained its prominence in the alcohol industry.

In the 1940s Peoria played an important role in world medicine. With the advent of World War II, a greater supply of penicillin, discovered in Great Britain in 1928, was needed. The Northern Regional Research Laboratory in Peoria, where researchers had been studying molds and bacteria, was selected to develop a method for mass-producing the drug. Because of the abundance of corn in the region, scientists at the laboratory experimented with corn steep liquor to make naturally fermented penicillin. The process they developed allowed mass production of the life-saving medication.

In 2000 Peorians suffered a tragic blow when three workers performing maintanence on the McClugage Bridge, which spans the Illinois River between Peoria and its eastern suburbs, were killed after falling from a scaffold that suddenly collapsed. Several others were injured in the accident. The following year, a memorial marker honoring the three men who died was dedicated at the western end of the bridge.

Notable Peorians

Peoria has produced a lengthy roster of celebrities and notable figures in sports, entertainment, politics, and other fields. This robust city is or was the hometown of a dozen

Major League Baseball players as well as a good number of professional football and basketball players and a couple of Olympic medalists. Legendary comedians Richard Pryor and Sam Kinison hailed from Peoria, and musicians Dan Fogelberg, Bruce Johnston of the Beach Boys, and Elaine "Spanky" McFarlane as well as actors David Ogden Stiers and Camryn Manheim were all either born in Peoria or grew up there.

A major celebrity from Peoria was Archbishop Fulton J. Sheen, who in his time was not only a leader in the Catholic Church but also a household name. His radio programs in the 1930s and '40s and his television programs of the 1950s and '60s made him a "star" among Catholics and Protestants alike in America and throughout the western world. Peter John Sheen (known as Fulton) was born in El Paso, Illinois, in 1895, and his family moved to Peoria when he was an infant. He was ordained as a priest in 1919 and was consecrated as a bishop in 1951. After a life dedicated to education, civil rights, and peace, Archbishop Sheen died in 1979 at age eighty-four. In 2002 his Cause for Canonization was opened under the authority of the Diocese of Peoria, and in 2012 he was declared "venerable," the second step toward sainthood, by Pope Benedict XVI.

Though they represent opposite poles on the political spectrum, activists Betty Friedan and Nancy Brinker, both born and raised in Peoria, were dedicated to the well-being of women. Renowned feminist leader Betty Friedan is probably best known for her seminal book, *The Feminine Mystique*, published to wide acclaim as well as controversy in 1963. She went on to found the National Organization for Women in 1966, and she remained active in the women's rights movement for the rest of her life. Friedan died in 2006.

Nancy Brinker, a conservative Republican, is the founder of Susan G. Komen for the Cure. Named for Brinker's sister, who died of breast cancer in 1980, this nonprofit organization provides funding for research, education, and health services in support of the fight against breast cancer worldwide. The recipient of dozens of awards and honors, Brinker currently serves as the World Health Organization's Goodwill Ambassador for Cancer Control.

Great River Road (IL 96 and IL 522) and US 34
HAMILTON–GALESBURG
89 miles

The first half of this enjoyable trip follows the Great River Road National Scenic Byway, which continues north all the way to Galena (see Region 5). Our route, however, follows the byway through Nauvoo, a major site in Mormon history, to US 34, where we will head east to Monmouth and Galesburg, two sites on the Ronald Reagan Trail (other Reagan sites include Eureka in Region 3 and Tampico and Dixon in Region 5).

The scenic byway is IL 96 from Hamilton to the tiny village of Lomax, and from there to US 34, it is IL 522. Those interested may pick up IL 164 from US 34 near Gladstone and continue north to Oquawka, another charming river town chock-full of local historic sites and structures, then follow the same highway east to Monmouth and Galesburg.

HAMILTON
See earlier trip

NAUVOO

The place that later became Nauvoo was once the village of the Sauk chief Quashquema, or Jumping Fish. The first white settler here was Capt. James White, who arrived in 1823 or 1824 and purchased the Indians' land on the banks of the Mississippi River for 200 sacks of corn. He established a post near the river to trade with the local natives, and a small settlement called Venus grew up around White's store. In 1834 Venus was absorbed into the newly platted town of Commerce. Commerce, however, was not the success its planners had envisioned, and most of the would-be settlers left the area within a year or two.

In 1839 the followers of Joseph Smith, known as Mormons, purchased several hundred acres of bargain-priced land in the floundering Commerce, changing the name to Nauvoo (which in old Hebrew means "beautiful place"). By 1845 Nauvoo had become the "promised land" for many members of the Church of Jesus Christ of Latter-day Saints (LDS) and was one of the largest cities in the state.

Mormon Settlement

The Church of Jesus Christ of Latter-day Saints (Mormons) was founded near Fayette, New York, in April 1830, by Joseph Smith Jr., a self-proclaimed prophet who claimed to have found golden tablets that contained previously unknown Christian doctrine. At Smith's urging, believers regrouped in Kirtland, Ohio, and in western Missouri. The church in Kirtland fell apart, mostly because of internal conflicts, and Smith left to join the colony in Missouri. This community did not last long, however. The colonists' non-Mormon neighbors were infuriated by the church's unconventional beliefs and secretive practices, as well as their growing political power. Violent conflicts erupted, and in the fall of 1838 the Mormons were expelled from Missouri altogether. The outcasts crossed the Mississippi River into Illinois, spending the winter in Quincy.

By spring the church had purchased the land in Commerce and the "Saints" were ready to start their new colony. They drained the swampy land to rid the area of malaria-infected mosquitoes and proceeded to build the city they had rechristened Nauvoo. In 1841 they began work on a large temple, designed by architect William Weeks and built of native limestone. Their troubles, however, would soon erupt anew.

As the new religion developed, its controversy grew. Smith's opponents established their own newspaper, *The Nauvoo Expositor*, publishing one issue before Smith destroyed their presses on June 10, 1844. The incident sparked a public outcry for Smith's arrest. Joseph and his brother, Hyrum, turned themselves in to authorities in nearby Carthage and were taken to the jail there to await a hearing. On June 27, an angry mob attacked the jail and murdered both brothers. (See also Carthage on previous trip.)

The death of Joseph Smith left the church with a leadership vacuum. Several contenders emerged, but ultimately the majority of colonists rallied around Brigham Young, a charismatic member of the church's missionary council. Splinter groups formed around some of the other candidates, including Joseph Smith's eleven-year-old son, Joseph Smith III. Several of these groups moved on to form their own versions of

Joseph Smith addresses local Indians in Nauvoo, June 1843
—Courtesy Schaumburg Township District Library, Illinois Collection

the church in Illinois (see Amboy and Plano in Region 5), Iowa, Missouri, Wisconsin, Pennsylvania, and elsewhere. Young would eventually lead his Saints to Utah, where they again began rebuilding their dream—this time successfully.

In the meantime in Nauvoo, while the church struggled to restore order within its ranks, the hostility from outside had not abated. Mormon families continued to be harassed, and in January 1845 the state of Illinois revoked the city's charter. By the spring of 1846 nearly all of the LDS colonists had left, most of them following Brigham Young. A small number stayed, however, including Joseph Smith's widow, Emma. These few continued construction on the Nauvoo Temple, which had been only partially finished when Joseph Smith was murdered. The temple was officially dedicated on May 1, 1846. In October 1848 arsonists set fire to the temple, causing extensive damage, and two years later, all but one wall was destroyed by a tornado. The remaining portion was razed.

In 1858 Joseph Smith III returned to Nauvoo, moving into his father's two-story log cabin, now known as the Joseph Smith Homestead, which he expanded. His mother, Emma Smith, still occupied the large frame house her husband had built in 1842, known as the Smith Mansion House. Emma later moved into the brick-and-stone Nauvoo House, an unfinished boardinghouse that she and her second husband converted into a home in 1871.

In 1937 the LDS Church bought the lot on which the original Nauvoo Temple had stood, intending to build a new temple at the site. Construction of the new temple, modeled after the original, did not begin until 1999, however. The completed new temple, known as the Nauvoo Illinois Temple, was dedicated in June 2002. The temple is the centerpiece of Nauvoo's Joseph Smith Historic Site complex, which includes the homestead, the mansion, Nauvoo House, the Smith family cemetery, and a reconstructed store, as well as an information center for visitors. Most of the city was designated a National Historic Landmark District in 1961.

The Mormons weren't the only group to attempt to establish an idealogical colony in Nauvoo. Only three years after the Mormon exodus, a society known as the Icarians arrived here hoping to settle.

The Icarians

In 1849 a French utopian socialist named Etienne Cabet and his followers moved into the Nauvoo area to start a communal colony based on Cabet's manifesto, *Voyage en Icarie*. In this book, Cabet advocated a society founded on political equality and communist principles. Among other properties, the Icarians purchased Temple Square, where they used limestone blocks from the destroyed Mormon Temple to construct a school.

As Cabet, a megalomaniac, vied for increasing power, dissension erupted among his followers. Within ten years, the Icarians had split up, many moving to Iowa, others returning to Europe, and some staying in Nauvoo as conventional settlers. Cabet himself died of a stroke in St. Louis in 1856. By 1895 the Icarian movement had ceased to exist in the United States.

Wine and Cheese

German immigrants began settling in Nauvoo at the same time as the Mormons. A few of them were LDS, while others were Catholic or Protestant. Many of these German settlers remained in the area after most of the Mormon and Icarian colonists had left Nauvoo. Together with Swiss, Belgian, French, and other European immigrants, they helped Nauvoo develop into a stable community.

Early in Nauvoo's history, these European settlers recognized that the climate and soil, similar to that in their native countries, was favorable for grape growing. In 1851 two immigrants, John Sillar of Germany and Alois Rheinberger of Liechtenstein, planted grape cuttings and established Nauvoo's first commercial vineyard. This vineyard, now located in and operated by Nauvoo State Park, is the oldest in Illinois and still produces grapes.

Along with the vineyards came wineries, and by 1900, forty-plus limestone wine cellars dotted the hills surrounding Nauvoo. Icarian Emile J. Baxter built a winery here in 1857, and the fifth generation of his family continues to operate the business, the oldest winery in the state.

Enactment of the Volstead Act (Prohibition) in January 1920 devastated Nauvoo's thriving wine industry. Most of the local vintners moved on to other livelihoods, though some hobbled through the Prohibition era selling fresh grapes. After the act was repealed in December 1933, only Baxter's winery resumed operations.

In the meantime, Nauvoo was left dotted with abandoned wine cellars. They did not remain empty for long, however. Iowa cheesemaker Oscar Rohde discovered that the cool, damp wine cellars provided the perfect conditions for making blue cheese. He opened the Nauvoo Blue Cheese Company in 1937, and the factory continued to operate into the twenty-first century under various ownership. In 2003 the food giant ConAgra, who had owned the Nauvoo company since 1999, sold the brand to Saputo Cheese, which promptly shuttered the factory and tore it down. Some efforts are under way to resurrect the production of blue cheese in Nauvoo, though on a much smaller scale, in the near future.

As a reminder of the city's delicious heritage, the Nauvoo Grape Festival, an annual celebration that began in 1938 and features a pageant called "the Wedding of the Wine and Cheese," continues today.

MONMOUTH

According to local lore, the first settler in what is now Monmouth won his property claim in a New Orleans poker game. In 1827 an unnamed War of 1812 veteran wagered and lost his land warrant to John Talbot, a plantation owner from Kentucky. Talbot and his cousin, Allen Andrews, set out to identify their claim in western Illinois and determine its condition. Pleased, they built a one-room cabin about eight miles northeast of present day Monmouth and invited friends from Kentucky to join them in settling the area.

When Talbot's settlement was selected in 1831 as the new Warren County seat, the name Monmouth was supposedly drawn from a hat. The first railroad arrived in the 1850s, and the community grew quickly into a center of agriculture, coal mining, limestone quarrying, and manufacturing. The town was also known for its maple trees, earning it the nickname the "Maple City."

Monmouth College (originally Monmouth Academy), founded in 1853, was one of the earliest coeducational American colleges. The school was the birthplace of Pi Beta Phi, founded in 1867 as I. C. Sorosis, the first sorority modeled after men's Greek fraternities in the United States. Kappa Kappa Gamma was established here three years later.

One notable early Monmouth resident was farmer, inventor, and industrialist William Weir, who invented the two-horse cultivator, patented in 1862. Soon afterward, Weir opened the Weir Plow Company. He later helped found the Weir Pottery Company in 1899. Weir's wares, marked with the "Old Sleepy Eye" Indian head trademark, are now valuable collectors' items.

In 1906 both Weir Pottery and Monmouth Pottery Company, established in 1893, merged with five other companies to form Western Stoneware Company, which eventually consolidated its various factories into one plant in Monmouth. For more than a century and through numerous changes in ownership, the Western Stoneware facility continued to produce pottery until it was shut down in 2006. A short time after the factory closed, three former employees purchased some of the production equipment and opened a shop in the vacant building, operating as WS Inc. under a contractual agreement with the city of Monmouth, which currently owns the rights to the Western Stoneware name and logo.

William Weir was only one of many achievers from the Maple City. Others include a Wild West legend, a billiards champion, and even a president. Some two dozen historical markers in town identify significant places and commemorate events including visits from Abraham Lincoln and Stephen A. Douglas, the hotel where French dancer Loie Fuller lived, and the Main Street Café, where future billiards legend Ralph Greenleaf (1899–1950) honed his skills in a second-floor poolroom. The Monmouth native went on to become the National Pocket Billiard Champion twenty-one times between 1919 and 1937, and he was one of the first three inductees into the Billiard Congress of America Hall of Fame. Monmouth also has the oldest continuously operated airport in the state. Six homes, two stores, and the city's commercial district are listed on the NRHP.

As impressive as all of this may be, Monmouth's historical credentials don't stop there. The Maple City was also one of Ronald Reagan's boyhood homes in Illinois. The Reagan family lived here from 1918 to 1919, when the future president was seven years old. The Ronald Reagan exhibit at the Monmouth Chamber of Commerce is one of several stops on the Ronald Reagan Trail, as is Reagan's childhood home, which is not open to the public but is marked with a historical plaque. Another plaque graces Lincoln Elementary School, then called Central School, where little Ronnie Reagan attended second grade.

Among all of Monmouth's historical treasures, however, the best known may be the birthplace of famous frontier lawman Wyatt Earp. The 1841 frame house is now operated as the Wyatt Earp Birthplace museum, open by appointment.

Wyatt Earp

Three generations of the Earp family emigrated from Ohio County, Kentucky, to Monmouth in 1845. The settlers included Wyatt's grandparents, Walter and Martha Earp, their son Nicholas Earp and his wife, Virginia, and Nicolas's three sons. Walter served as a justice of the peace in Monmouth, while Nicholas farmed and worked as a cooper.

In 1846, with the Mexican War looming, Nicholas Earp joined a volunteer unit commanded by local merchant Wyatt Berry Stapp. Earp had such high esteem for his commander that he named his next child Wyatt Berry Stapp Earp, born March 19, 1848. The following year, Nicholas moved his family to a horse farm near Pella, Iowa. They moved back to Monmouth in 1856, but Nicholas had trouble earning a living there. He also had trouble with the law—he had been convicted of bootlegging and still faced several lawsuits for debt. The court auctioned his house to pay his fines. In 1859 Nicholas, angry and broke, left Monmouth and returned to Pella. Wyatt was eleven.

In 1864 Nicholas guided a wagon train of settlers from Iowa to California. Wyatt, now a young man, accompanied his father. In California Wyatt worked as a stage driver and a teamster. He also made money as a gambler, an occupation he continued throughout his life.

In 1872 Wyatt was arrested in Peoria for running a floating brothel on the Illinois River. He subsequently returned to the West and served as a lawman in several frontier towns, notably Wichita, Dodge City, and Tombstone. He is most known for participating, along with two of his brothers and Doc Holliday, in the gunfight at the OK Corral in Tombstone, Arizona Territory, on October 26, 1881.

In the mid-1880s Wyatt and his common-law wife, Josie Marcus, moved to San Diego, where he ran several saloons. Over the years, he also had considerable investments in mining, real estate, and horse racing. During the Alaska gold rush, he and Josie moved to Nome for a few years, then they returned to California, where they fraternized with early Hollywood stars. Wyatt Earp died in Los Angeles on January 13, 1929, at age eighty.

GALESBURG

Presbyterian minister George Washington Gale and his friend Sylvanus (also spelled Silvanus) Ferris, both of New York state, arrived in western Illinois in the 1830s to scout for a place to establish an abolitionist community. In 1836 they purchased seventeen acres on a government-owned tract known as Log City and established their settlement, naming it after Gale. Later that year, the men organized the first Antislavery Society in Illinois in Galesburg. Ferris so admired Gale that he named his son George Washington Gale Ferris. George's son, G.W.G. Ferris Jr., would grow up to invent the Ferris Wheel.

The founders of Galesburg set aside part of their settlement to build the "Prairie College," a school founded on principles of manual labor in the service of God and of antislavery activism. They chartered Knox Manual Labor College, which admitted both white and black students, in 1837; the first classes were held in 1841, and the Female Collegiate Department opened six years later. In 1857 the school's name was changed to Knox College, and the following year, the college was chosen to be the site of the fifth Lincoln-Douglas debate (see below).

Two Knox College students would become pioneers in African American achievement. Hiram Rhodes Revels, who attended the college in the 1850s and studied at several other seminaries, became the first black U.S. senator in 1870. Barnabas Root graduated from Knox College in 1870, making him the first African American to receive a bachelor's degree in Illinois.

The Chicago, Burlington & Quincy Railroad arrived in Galesburg in 1854 and built rail yards here. Other rail lines soon followed, expanding the city's economy and prestige. In 1873, after much political maneuvering, the seat of Knox County was moved from Knoxville to Galesburg. Galesburg prospered throughout the twentieth century, and it remains the principal city in the vicinity, with a population of more than 32,000.

Galesburg has had more than its share of notable residents, among them Civil War nurse Mary Ann Bickerdyke (see below), Ferris Wheel inventor George Washington Ferris Jr., poet Carl Sandburg (see below), and President Ronald Reagan. The short and tumultuous life of George Washington Ferris Jr., grandson of Galesburg cofounder Sylvanus Ferris, began in Galesburg in 1859, though his family moved to Nevada when he was five. After graduating from Rensselaer Polytechnic Institute in Troy, New York, he established an engineering company in Pittsburgh.

Although for a brief time, during the 1893 World's Columbian Exposition in Chicago, he was considered a great American genius as the inventor of the fair's spectacular, twenty-six-story-high Ferris Wheel (see also under Hyde Park in Region 7), he died young, broke, and alone. He received virtually nothing for his invention and failed to achieve further success. Shortly after his wife left him, he died in Pittsburgh in 1896, probably of typhoid fever, at the age of thirty-seven.

In the late 1910s, Ronald Reagan attended first grade and part of second grade at Silas Willard School in Galesburg. Interestingly, Reagan's future wife, Nancy Davis, also spent time in this city. Her stepfather, Dr. Loyal Davis, grew up in Galesburg, and Nancy spent many summers and holidays at the home of Dr. Davis's parents. Although Ron and Nancy never crossed paths in Galesburg, they are the only president and first lady to have spent part of their childhood in the same community. Both Reagan's boyhood home and the Davis home are still standing; both are now privately owned but are identified with historical markers. The Galesburg Welcome Center has a permanent Reagan exhibit.

Fifth Lincoln-Douglas Debate (Galesburg, October 7, 1858)

Those who arrived in Galesburg on October 7, 1858, for the fifth debate between senatorial candidates Stephen A. Douglas and Abraham Lincoln were greeted by high winds, cool temperatures, and wet ground from the previous day's rain. Locals were surprised when 15,000 to 20,000 spectators turned out, more than three times the city's population. Many families had arrived early and pitched tents throughout the town.

Both candidates arrived to much fanfare. A three-team hitch pulled Douglas in a carriage, while Lincoln was escorted by a string of wagons nearly long enough to encircle the town. The debate began at 1:30 p.m. at Knox College's Old Main building.

Douglas and Lincoln argued their positions on slavery in the new states of Kansas and Nebraska, the Mexican War, and Negro rights under the Constitution. The hardy spectators followed the presentations intensely, offering enthusiastic cheers when their favored candidate made points against his rival.

"Mother" Mary Ann Bickerdyke

Early in the Civil War, Dr. Benjamin Woodward, a Union army surgeon stationed in Cairo along with about five hundred other Galesburg volunteers, wrote to his pastor, Rev. Edward Beecher, that due to unsanitary conditions, many soldiers were dying from diseases before ever seeing a battlefield. Beecher read the letter from the pulpit to members of Galesburg's First Congregational Church. Taking note of this plight, widowed mother Mary Ann Bickerdyke and other Galesburg residents collected medical supplies and other items to transport by rail to Cairo. Bickerdyke herself accompanied the shipment, leaving her two sons, ages eleven and thirteen, with friends. Unbeknownst to her, it was the beginning of a long and storied career as a nurse, social reformer, and humanitarian.

Born Mary Ann Ball in Knox County, Ohio, in 1817, the future "Mother" Bickerdyke was orphaned at a young age and raised by relatives. In 1847 she married widower Robert Bickerdyke in Cincinnati. They had two sons before moving to Galesburg in 1856, then a daughter. Robert Bickerdyke died suddenly in 1859, and the little girl died the following year, at age two. The widow Bickerdyke supported herself and her sons in part by selling herbal medicines.

Galesburg's indefatigable "Mother" Mary Ann Bickerdyke —From steel engraving by A. H. Ritchie

When Bickerdyke arrived at the army tent hospital in Cairo, she immediately set to work organizing chores, cooking, washing clothes, and tending to the sick. Although she had intended to return to Galesburg right away, she decided to stay in Cairo to help at the hospital. While she had no official authority, her bold determination and unwavering tenacity commanded the respect of doctors and officers, who often stepped aside when she bypassed military procedures in order to get the job done. Her assertiveness did not please everyone, however, and she sometimes had confrontations with line officers. But she soon acquired friends in high places, including army generals William T. Sherman and Ulysses S. Grant, both of whom recognized her contributions.

In 1862 Mother Bickerdyke was allowed to travel with Grant's army into Tennessee to set up hospitals. On the general's order, she took charge of the Gayoso Block Hospital in Memphis, later renamed the Mother Bickerdyke Hospital. As Grant moved south, Bickerdyke followed. She later accompanied Sherman's army, tending to the wounded after the capture of Atlanta. Throughout the war, she helped raise funds and acquire food and supplies for the soldiers. Her wartime service included caring for the wounded of nearly twenty battles and establishing over three hundred hospitals.

After the war, Bickerdyke moved to Kansas, where she had claimed a homestead for her two sons. There she opened a boardinghouse and raised donations for poor farming families. She later traveled to the slums of New York to aid the impoverished there, and then to California, where she helped Civil War veterans get their pensions from the army. Around 1899, Bickerdyke returned to Kansas, where she died on November 6, 1901. Her remains were transported to Galesburg and interred next to her husband at Linwood Cemetery. A bronze statue depicting Bickerdyke tending to a wounded soldier was erected in the Knox County courthouse square in 1906.

Carl Sandburg

Carl Sandburg was born in Galesburg on January 6, 1878, the second of seven children. His parents, August and Clara Anderson Sandburg, were Swedish immigrants. August's salary as a blacksmith's helper on the Chicago, Burlington & Quincy Railroad barely provided for the family. After graduating from the eighth grade, Carl quit school to work. He delivered milk, harvested ice, and shined shoes in Galesburg's Union Hotel, among other things, before setting off to travel as a hobo at age nineteen. He continued working odd jobs throughout the Midwest until 1898, when he enlisted in the army to serve in the Spanish-American War. Stationed in Puerto Rico, he never saw action.

Upon his return from the army, Sandburg enrolled in Galesburg's Lombard College, where he studied for three years. While there, he honed his writing skills under the tutelage of Prof. Phillip Green Wright, who influenced Sandburg's political views as well as his writing. Wright compiled many of Sandburg's poems and short prose pieces into a small book, *In Reckless Ecstasy*, printed in 1904 on a basement press. Wright later published two more books of Sandburg's poetry.

From 1907 to 1912, Sandburg worked in Milwaukee. Here he met his future wife, Lillian Steichen, sister of famed photographer Edward Steichen, about whom Sandburg later wrote a biography. The couple had three daughters. Around 1910 Sandburg embarked on his first trip across America, playing guitar and singing folk songs, reciting poetry, and giving talks. He continued these tours throughout his life. In 1912 he moved

*Carl Sandburg, poet laureate
of Illinois, 1962–67*
—Courtesy Library of Congress
(digital ID cph.3c15064)

his young family to suburban Chicago, where he worked as a journalist and continued to write poems and other works.

By 1920 Sandburg had become well known for his free-verse poetry as well as for nonfiction. The writer's lifelong interest in Abraham Lincoln led to his two-volume biography, *Abraham Lincoln: The Prairie Years*, published in 1926. In 1939 he published the second four volumes of the six-volume set, *Abraham Lincoln: The War Years*, for which he received a Pulitzer Prize in 1940. In 1950, he produced *Complete Poems*, for which he received a second Pulitzer.

In 1945 Sandburg moved to a farm in Flat Rock, North Carolina, where he continued to write while his wife, Lillian, managed her herd of prize-winning goats. Although he no longer lived in the state, he was named poet laureate of Illinois in 1962, a nonsalaried position that he held until his death on July 22, 1967. His ashes are buried beneath Remembrance Rock behind his boyhood home in Galesburg. The house is now a state historic site with a museum next door.

I-74
GALESBURG—ROCK ISLAND
52 miles

This trip follows the interstate, but as a more scenic alternative, travelers can take US 150 from Galesburg to Moline and Rock Island, a route that passes through the bucolic countryside and a number of quaint farm towns.

GALESBURG

See previous trip

MOLINE

Moline, one of the Quad Cities (the others being Rock Island, Illinois, and Bettendorf and Davenport, Iowa), was founded on industry, thrived on it, and still reflects its potent force around the world. The Quad Cities employ more than 30,000 people in the manufacturing industry; Moline alone contains more than a hundred manufacturing facilities, including the world headquarters of the John Deere equipment company. Moline is also the region's primary retail center.

Moline began when New York-born David B. Sears visited the Rock Island waterway in 1836 and recognized its potential for industry. The following year, Sears partnered with fellow entrepreneurs John W. Spencer and Spencer H. White to build a brush dam across Sylvan Slough from Rock Island (later known as Arsenal Island) to the Illinois mainland. The dam generated power for a two-story mill (sawmill on the lower level and a flour mill on the second floor). Several years later, the brush dam was replaced with a wooden dam. The water power attracted the attention of industrialists, who began to build factories in the area even before the town of Moline was platted.

Massachusetts-born Charles Atkinson arrived in the area in 1843 and joined Sears, Spencer, and White to purchase land from a local farmer to plat a new town. Atkinson chose the name Moline, meaning "city of mills," from the French *moulin* (windmill). He also helped bring a stagecoach line and later a railroad to Moline, attracting more industry as well as immigrant workers, particularly from Sweden.

In 1848, five years after the village was established, Deere & Company relocated their plow factory from Grand Detour to Moline. As the factory grew, so did Moline. Dimock & Gould Lumber Company, established in 1851, produced timber products well into the late twentieth century and survives as Dimock, Gould & Co., manufacturing bricks and other construction products. The founder of the company, New Hampshire native John Maxfield Gould, became one of Moline's most active and beloved citizens.

Gould moved to Moline in 1848 to work for John Deere, and the following year he persuaded a telegraph company to set up a line in Moline by offering to personally back up any financial losses. Over the years, Gould served as a Rock Island County judge, organized the city's first volunteer fire department, helped plan and build the county jail, and established the First National Bank of Moline and the Moline City Hospital. Gould also held numerous executive positions in public and private enterprises throughout the city and county. Known affectionately as "Judge Gould," he died on October 10, 1912, leaving a record of civic accomplishment unequaled in the history of Moline.

After Moline was incorporated in 1872, more industries moved in. By the turn of the twentieth century, Moline was the world's largest producer of agricultural machinery, becoming known as the "Farm Implement Capital of the World." The city was also the site of some of the earliest automobile plants.

Today Moline's recently redeveloped riverfront includes a large civic center and the John Deere Commons complex, which contains hotels, restaurants, offices, retail stores, entertainment venues, and even a history museum. Plans for further development are currently in the works.

ROCK ISLAND

Just west of Moline on the Mississippi River, the city of Rock Island lies atop a plain that offers picturesque views of Davenport, Iowa, to the northwest. This plateau was originally the site of a large Sauk and Mesquakie (Fox) Indian village called Saukenuk, which prospered until the War of 1812. During the conflict, the area was opened to white settlement to help defend it from the British. Tribal members were divided about whether to stay in the village or to leave. Most moved west across the river, but one band, under the Sauk leader Black Hawk, chose to stay and fight for the British. Black Hawk and his people would eventually be driven out of Illinois after the Black Hawk War of 1832.

In 1816, to counter the problems with local Indians and encourage further settlement, the government built a heavily fortified post, Fort Armstrong, on the southwestern tip of the river island now known as Arsenal Island, on the north side of the current city of Rock Island (see Fort Armstrong below). The post sutler, George Davenport, who was friendly with local tribes, built a trading post near the fort the following year. Later he met fellow trader Russell Farnham, and around 1826 the two men partnered to build a tavern and stage station on the mainland. Davenport and Farnham founded the settlement of Farnhamsburg, which along with neighboring Stephenson would eventually grow into the city of Rock Island, so named in 1841. (See also "The Murder of Col. George Davenport" below.)

In January 1854, the first railroad, the Chicago & Rock Island line, reached the Mississippi River, bringing growth and prosperity to Rock Island. By 1860 it was the fifth-largest city in Illinois. In subsequent years, Rock Island's economy continued to flourish, particularly in the lumber industry.

Only a year after the railroad's arrival, construction began on a single-track railroad bridge that linked Rock Island to Davenport, Iowa, via Arsenal Island. Steamboat companies, which saw the bridge as a dangerous impediment to river traffic, petitioned the government to stop the project, but construction proceeded, and the bridge was completed in April 1856. Only a month later, the steamboat *Effie Afton* crashed into a bridge pier, damaged a span, and caught fire, burning most of the bridge's wooden support structure.

James Hurd, owner of the *Effie Afton*, sued the railroad company in federal court, charging that the bridge was hazardous to navigation. The Rock Island Railroad Company hired Abraham Lincoln to represent them because of his acute knowledge of railroad litigation. His strong presentation caused the jury to deadlock. Similar lawsuits also failed, and the bridge remained until 1866. It was later replaced several times by stronger bridges at different locations. Today two bridges, the Arsenal Bridge, or Government Bridge, and the Rock Island Centennial Bridge, join Rock Island and Davenport.

Present-day Rock Island has numerous landmarks of historical and general interest. Among these are the Broadway Historic District, the Rock Island Public Library, the Quad City Botanical Center, and the Quad City Hindu Temple. At the south end of town is the Black Hawk Forest Nature Preserve, where the Black Hawk State Historic Site honors the Sauk leader and the area's original inhabitants. The historical complex includes the John Hauberg Museum of Native American Life, the Civilian Conservation Corps Museum, and the Singing Bird Nature Center, which offers educational programs on the region's natural history.

Much of Rock Island's history occurred on Arsenal Island, still owned by the U.S. government. The island has an abundance of historic sites, including a replica of one of Fort Armstrong's blockhouses, the Colonel Davenport House museum, the Rock Island Prison site, and the Rock Island Arsenal itself.

Fort Armstrong

In the middle of the Mississippi River, Arsenal Island, originally called Rock Island, was a natural site for a military post. Its high limestone bluffs at the southwestern tip provided a clear, panoramic view of both sides of the river.

Built in 1816, Fort Armstrong, named for Secretary of War John Armstrong, was truly a fortress. It was laid out in an approximate square with two-story blockhouses at three corners. Two sides were built along the bluffs, while two four-hundred-foot-long walls, with openings for cannons and musketry, created the other two sides. Within the fort were enlisted men's barracks, officers' quarters, a powder magazine, and a storehouse, all protected by eight-foot-high stone walls along the perimeter. The fort remained peaceful until 1832, when Black Hawk's followers attempted to retake their land east of the Mississippi. During the Black Hawk War, the fort served as a base for U.S. regulars and Illinois militia. It was also the place where the so-called Black Hawk Purchase—the agreement that ceded Sauk, Mesquakie (Fox), and Winnebago lands in Illinois, Wisconsin, and Iowa to the federal government—was signed in September 1832.

Fort Armstrong was abandoned as a military outpost in 1836 but served as an ordnance depot from 1840 to 1845, when its supplies were transferred to St. Louis to support American troops in the Mexican War. In 1855 a fire destroyed the empty fort. Modern visitors to Arsenal Island can see a replica of one of the post's blockhouses, constructed at its original site in 1916.

The Murder of Col. George Davenport

In 1835 area resident Col. George Davenport, a major developer of the Quad Cities region, bought a tract of land across the river from Rock Island, in the future state of Iowa. The following year, the settlement of Davenport was founded. Davenport did not live to see his namesake city evolve, however. In July 1845 he was murdered in his home on Arsenal Island by members of the outlaw gang known as the Banditti of the Prairie (see also Ogle County in Region 5).

On July 4, Colonel Davenport stayed home while his family went into town for an Independence Day celebration. Several Banditti members, who had mistakenly heard that Davenport had $20,000 in his safe, thought the house was empty and broke in. The sixty-two-year-old colonel caught them in the act of robbing his safe, which in fact contained only a few hundred dollars. The burglars shot him in the leg, then tied him up, beat him severely, and left him for dead. Although neighbors found him and called in a doctor, Davenport died a few hours later.

Five men were arrested and charged with the murder. One of them escaped, but the others were convicted and sentenced to hang. One of the accused, John Baxter, appealed his case, and his sentence was commuted to life in prison. The other three, John and Arron Long and Granville Young, were hanged on October 19, 1845. The historic role of Col. George Davenport in developing the Quad Cities area was not forgotten. The home in which he was killed is preserved as the Colonel Davenport House museum.

Rock Island Prison Barracks

Early in the Civil War, both sides agreed to exchange prisoners of war shortly after each battle. But by the third year of the war, these agreements had broken down and captured soldiers were held in semipermanent prison camps. The Union, looking for suitable sites, chose Rock Island (now Arsenal Island), which, as the former site of Fort Armstrong, was already owned by the U.S. government. The island was relatively isolated from the battlefields yet near a rail station, simplifying the transporting of prisoners. In July 1863, the Union army constructed barracks at the northern end of the island, facing the widest part of the Mississippi River. The compound was designed to house 10,000 prisoners.

The crude barracks buildings were arranged in fourteen rows of six buildings, each one equipped to house 120 prisoners. Each one-hundred-by-twenty-two-foot building had twelve windows, two heating stoves, and a kitchen with a cooking stove. Surrounding the camp was a twelve-foot-high stockade with sentries positioned outside the stockade and along an eight-foot-high walkway overlooking the compound. Among those assigned as guards were members of the 108th Regiment, U.S. Colored Infantry, a fact that the Southern prisoners resented.

On December 3, 1863, following the Battles of Lookout Mountain and Missionary Ridge, both in Tennessee, the first prisoners arrived at the still unfinished camp. The winter was bitterly cold, and blankets were scarce. Furthermore, some of the prisoners were sick when they arrived. Twenty percent of the 5,600 new inmates were diagnosed with smallpox, but healthy prisoners were housed together with the sick. Within three

Confederate prisoners at Rock Island Prison
—Courtesy Dee Brown Collection

months, 679 prisoners and 17 guards had died from smallpox, pneumonia, or diarrheal diseases.

An inspection by Assistant Surgeon General Ambrose M. Clark in February 1864 led to some reforms. Clark ordered that six "pesthouses" be built to contain inmates with malignant diseases, and that eleven adjacent barracks be converted into a temporary prison hospital until a new permanent, 560-bed hospital was completed.

A follow-up report by Surgeon William Watson in March 1864 noted some improvement. According to Watson, the "great want of cleanliness among the patients and attendants" was "disappearing under stringent regulations requiring the regular use of bath tubs and the labors of a permanent detail as laundrymen." After another inspection a few months later, Surgeon Inspector Charles T. Alexander reported that "the camp is well managed."

During the Rock Island compound's twenty-month existence, a total of about 12,400 Confederate prisoners were confined there. Of that total, 73 were transferred, 3,876 were exchanged, 1,964 died, 41 escaped, and 5,581 were released. Some 3,000 Rebel prisoners chose to join the Union cause in exchange for release; these defectors, known as "Galvanized Yankees," were sent to the western frontier to replace regulars who had been transferred east during the war. The prison released its last detainees in July 1865.

The only reminder of the Rock Island Prison Barracks today are two cemeteries: the Confederate Cemetery, which contains the identified remains of 1,964 prisoners, and the Rock Island National Cemetery, with the graves of 125 guards, sixteen galvanized Yankees who died before their release, and other Union dead. On Memorial Day, an American flag is placed on each grave at Rock Island National Cemetery, and Confederate battle flags are set on the graves in the Confederate Cemetery.

Rock Island Arsenal

Rock Island Arsenal was established by an act of Congress in 1862, during the Civil War, but the first building was not finished until 1865, after the war was over; the rest of the complex was not completed until 1886. At first, the arsenal overhauled Civil War surplus arms and gear and also manufactured new equipment, though production was limited. Initially, the reconditioned gear was shipped to forts on the frontier. The first international conflict to utilize weaponry and equipment from Rock Island was the ten-week Spanish-American War in 1898.

Over the years, Rock Island Arsenal's production was expanded or reduced as military needs dictated. The armory's stock included the Model 1903 .30-06-caliber bolt-action rifle, a stable shoulder weapon that served as the backbone for American troops during World War I. Also during WWI, the facility manufactured more than 167,000 howitzer shells; this was the only time the arsenal made ammunition.

Between the World Wars, the arsenal developed and tested tanks and artillery pieces, becoming a major producer of artillery carriages and machine guns. The facility also developed parachuted containers for air-dropping supplies. It continued to advance military technology during the Korean, Vietnam, and Gulf Wars. During peacetime, the average number of employees was about 2,400; employment reached a high of over 18,000 workers during World War II. Today the Rock Island Arsenal remains the nation's largest government-owned and -operated military production resource.

Visitors to the facility may tour some of the grounds, which include the Fort Armstrong blockhouse replica, the Davenport House, the Civil War prison site, the Union and Confederate cemeteries, and the Rock Island Arsenal Museum. The museum, established in 1905, is the second-oldest U.S. Army museum after the West Point Museum. Exhibits focus on the history of the island as well as displays of various arms, artillery, and military vehicles.

US 34
GALESBURG—PRINCETON
74 miles

Few people know that in 2003, US Route 34 in Illinois was designated the Walter Payton Memorial Highway, after the beloved longtime Chicago Bears running back (number 34). This trip follows the highway from Galesburg to Princeton. From there it continues northeasterly to Berwyn, just outside Chicago, where it merges with Ogden Avenue.

One of the interesting stops on this stretch of US 34 is Sheffield, home of the Hennepin Canal visitor center. The main east-west route of the obsolete canal, now a state park and recreational trail, very roughly parallels I-80 between the Mississippi and Illinois Rivers.

GALESBURG
See earlier trip

BISHOP HILL

The rolling prairie of west-central Illinois offered abundant land for Erik Jansson, an outspoken preacher from Sweden, to start a colony. He and several hundred followers, who clashed with the Lutheran Church of Sweden over doctrine and beliefs, "resolved to immigrate to the United States of America, and into this land of liberty," as explained in the preamble to the Bishop Hill Colony charter.

Jansson designated Olof Olson and a few other men to sail to America and find an appropriate spot in 1845. Upon arriving in New York, Olson met and befriended fellow Swede Rev. Olof Hedstrom, who suggested he visit his brother, Rev. Jonas Hedstrom, founder of the Swedish Methodist Church in western Illinois. Impressed with the area, Olson relayed his findings back to Jansson, encouraging him and his followers to come there. Followers had contributed cash to a common fund, from which they purchased 544 acres of land in southern Henry County.

In 1846 Jansson gathered the first group of colonists and sailed to New York. The pilgrims continued on the Hudson River through the Erie Canal to Buffalo, then across the Great Lakes to Chicago. From there they walked southwest for more than a hundred miles to the site of their new colony. Many in this group of immigrants and in subsequent groups perished on the journey from diseases or shipwrecks. Upon their arrival, the colonists immediately set to work building shelters, storehouses, and a large but crude church. Jansson named the colony Bishop Hill, derived from Biskopskulla, his birthplace in Sweden.

The first winter was difficult, and dozens of colonists died of disease. But the following year brought successful crops of corn, wheat, flax, and vegetables. Eventually the colonists produced enough crops, cloth, and other goods to sustain themselves as well as surpluses to sell to outsiders. Over the next few years, as additional Janssonists arrived from Sweden, the community stabilized. More-refined structures and neatly laid wooden sidewalks were built, reflecting the colonists' commitment to making a permanent home here. In 1849 the "tent church" was replaced by a sturdy two-story structure that still stands.

Three years into the social experiment, the colony experienced a devastating epidemic of Asiatic cholera. The death rate exceeded the colonists' ability to build coffins. Nearly 150 people died during the three-month epidemic, including Jansson's wife and their two youngest children. Jansson soon remarried, wedding the thrice-widowed Sophia Gabrielsson.

In spite of the hardships, the community continued to grow. By 1850 Bishop Hill had a population of over five hundred. But even as the colony prospered, dissension began to appear among its ranks. Many found Jansson despotic, corrupt, and indifferent to the needs of his flock.

In early 1850, John Root, disgusted with Jansson's leadership, wanted to leave the colony with his wife, Charlotte Louise, who was Jansson's cousin. Jansson forbade her to go, and, unwilling to disobey him, she refused her husband. Root left, but he soon returned, attempting to kidnap Charlotte and their infant son. Unsuccessful, he tried twice more to abduct his wife and child, but he was thwarted each time. The second time, Root led a mob of men who already distrusted the Janssonists to attack Bishop Hill, but the colonists fought them off. Finally, Jansson sought legal protection against Root, but this step would also prove to be futile.

On May 13, 1850, Root found Jansson at the Henry County Courthouse in Cambridge. He fired two shots. One bullet struck Jansson just above the heart, killing him instantly. Root was found guilty of manslaughter and served one year in the Alton Penitentiary before being pardoned by Gov. Joel A. Matteson.

The Colony Church in Bishop Hill
—Photo by Kepper66, Wikimedia Commons

With Jansson's death, his widow, Sophia, assumed responsibility for the colony and anointed Andrew (Andreas) Bergland as colony custodian until Jansson's son, age twelve, came of age. Some colonists were fine with this, believing the right of succession was hereditary; others wanted one of Jansson's adult male followers to be in charge. The latter group prevailed, choosing Jonas Olson, brother of Olof and close friend of Jansson, to be the leader of the colony. Olson set up a board of seven trustees to help administer the affairs of Bishop Hill.

Under Olson, the colony thrived for several more years, but its prosperity did not last. Bad investments and a national financial panic in 1857 drove Bishop Hill to the brink of ruin, causing infighting among the trustees and discord among the colonists. In 1861 the Bishop Hill experiment collapsed. The colony was dissolved, and the 14,000 acres the Janssonists had acquired were divided among the members, some of whom chose to stay while others moved elsewhere.

In 1946 the state of Illinois acquired the Old Colony Church and the two-acre village park and began to restore the site. The Bishop Hill Heritage Association was formed in 1962 to preserve and restore the remaining buildings. Among the first to be restored was Steeple Building, formerly a school for new immigrants. Restoration of the Bjorklund Hotel began in 1973. Both of these buildings as well as the church now house museums. The Bishop Hill Historic District was added to the NRHP in 1970, and the town was named a National Historic Landmark in 1984. Some residents are descendants of the original Swedish colony, and the community still takes pride in its Swedish heritage.

KEWANEE

Taking its name from the Winnebago word for prairie chicken (the birds gathered there during mating season), Kewanee was incorporated in 1854. The town grew out of Wethersfield, a colony of New England Protestants who also founded nearby Andover and Geneseo in the 1830s. In 1853, when the Central Military Tract Railroad (later called the Chicago, Burlington & Quincy Railroad) was extending its route from Chicago to Galesburg, the people of Wethersfield learned that the line would bypass their town about two miles to the north, so they bought land and platted a new community, dubbed Kewanee, near the train route. Within a few years, the population of Kewanee had swelled to 1,500, while Wethersfield shrunk to a smattering of homes, farms, and orchards. Wethersfield was finally annexed to Kewanee in 1921.

In the late 1860s, coal was discovered near Kewanee, and the city expanded its economy with extensive coal mining. Over the next few decades, three manufacturing companies also became significant to the town's economic development—the Kewanee Boiler Company, the Walworth Company, and Good's Furniture Company. The first two closed in the later twentieth century, but Good's Furniture Company, founded in 1895, is bigger than ever. Comprising twelve historic buildings, totaling 250,000 square feet, the current complex includes furniture showrooms, a gift shop, a bistro and bakery, and even a bed-and-breakfast.

Another big part of Kewanee's economic base was, and still is, agriculture. The city was declared the "Hog Capital of the World" in 1948, and residents continue to celebrate "Hog Days" every year. To learn more of this town's story, visitors may check out the Kewanee Historical Society, which contains three floors of exhibits, artifacts, photos, and records related to local history.

SHEFFIELD

The village of Sheffield, founded in 1852, was named after Joseph Sheffield, an engineer on the Chicago & Rock Island Railroad. One of the village's landmarks is St. Peter's Danish Evangelical Lutheran Church, established in 1869 and recognized as one of the oldest Danish Lutheran Churches in the United States. It was listed on the NRHP in 1973.

Nearby is Hennepin Canal Parkway State Park, whose visitor's center provides interpretive displays to help the public understand the canal's place in Illinois history and its pioneering role in canal engineering. Outside, a half-acre plot of wildflower prairie provides a sampling of big bluestem bunchgrass, the official state prairie grass, and other plants that welcomed early settlers to the Illinois landscape.

Hennepin (Illinois & Mississippi) Canal

The idea for a canal between Hennepin and Rock Island was conceived in 1834. Jacob Galer, a resident of Geneseo, Illinois, stood up at a courthouse meeting in Hennepin and reported, according to an article he later wrote for the *Geneseo Republic*, that he had "viewed the country through from Hennepin to the Mississippi River near Rock Island and thought it a natural pass for a canal as there was a depression all the way across with high land on either side." Indeed, the natural depression was an ancient channel of the

Dueling dredges scoop dirt during the construction of the Illinois & Mississippi Canal (Hennepin Canal), early 1900s. —Courtesy Hennepin Canal Parkway State Park

Mississippi River. "I reported my discovery but was much ridiculed for holding such ideas," he recalled.

By the 1860s, the idea for a canal through this region was taken seriously, but the state's financial problems hampered development of the project. Congress finally authorized preliminary surveys in 1870, but financial, logistic, and political issues delayed the canal's construction for years. Building finally got under way in 1890.

Nearly 4,000 Americans and immigrants from Germany, Ireland, Denmark, Sweden, and elsewhere worked on the canal. During the construction, local people along the route got an economic boost from working on the project or catering to the workers. The engineering team, which included a woman engineer, a rarity in the late 1800s, was the first to try using concrete as a cheaper substitute for cut stone in building locks and other structures. The experiment was a success, and this cost-saving technology was used in later projects, including the Panama Canal.

The Illinois & Mississippi Canal was completed in 1907. The main canal was seventy-five miles long; the feeder line, from the Rock River at Rock Falls south to the main canal line, was almost thirty miles long and provided a continuous flow of water. The canal system included thirty-three locks and nine aqueducts, most of which can still be seen.

The engineering team for the Illinois & Mississippi Canal included a woman. —Courtesy Hennepin Canal Parkway State Park

Ironically, by the time the project was completed, railroads were traversing the region and water transportation had become less desirable. The canal's marginal usefulness lasted until the mid-1930s, but it remained open for boat traffic until 1951. The state of Illinois took possession of the obsolete waterway in 1970 and reopened it as a state park.

Hennepin Canal Parkway State Park is nearly one hundred miles long, spans five counties, and covers more than 5,000 acres, including the 1,450-acre Lake Sinnissippi near Rock Falls. A walking trail runs nearly the entire length of the main canal as well as that of the feeder. Much of the trail, portions of which are newly paved, is also open to biking and horseback riding. A 4.2-mile segment of the canal between Lock 15 and Bridge 11 is a historic zone.

PRINCETON

Among the first settlers in the Princeton area were members of the Hampshire Colony, a group of Congregationalists from New England and the mid-Atlantic states. To select a name for their parcel of land in 1832, the trustees' suggestions were dropped into a hat. The name Princeton, for the hometown of a trustee from New Jersey, was drawn. Princeton was incorporated as a city in 1884.

Before the Civil War, several homes in Princeton served as stations on the Underground Railroad, including those of poet John Bryant and Rev. Owen Lovejoy, a fervent abolitionist and perhaps Princeton's most prominent citizen. Reverend Lovejoy's white frame house, built in 1837 just east of Princeton, is a National Historic Landmark. The Lovejoy Homestead opened as a museum in 1972. In 2002 it was designated part of the National Underground Railroad Network to Freedom program.

Rev. Owen Lovejoy

On November 7, 1837, Rev. Elijah Lovejoy, publisher of the abolitionist *Alton Observer*, was attacked and killed by a proslavery mob (see under Alton in Region 1). His murder inflamed the convictions of his like-minded younger brother, Owen. The following year, at age twenty-seven, Owen Lovejoy moved to Princeton and became the second pastor of the seven-year-old Hampshire Colony Congregational Church, where he remained for the next seventeen years. Shortly after he arrived, Lovejoy spearheaded the Underground Railroad in Princeton, and the village became a refuge for runaway slaves.

A bachelor at the time, Lovejoy boarded with Mr. and Mrs. Butler Denham. Butler Denham died in 1841, and two years later, Lovejoy married his widow, Eunice. The couple remained in the Denham home, which ultimately became the Lovejoy Homestead historical site and museum. Lovejoy farmed the 1,280-acre property during his ministry, but he never owned it.

Throughout his career, Lovejoy made antislavery speeches and held meetings, often in defiance of the law. During a sermon in Princeton, Lovejoy vowed: "Come life or death, I will devote the residue of my life to the anti-slavery cause. The slaveholders and their sympathizers have murdered my brother, and if another victim is needed, I am ready."

Lovejoy's election to the Illinois legislature in 1854 and to the U.S. Congress two years later broadened his audience. As a Congressman, Lovejoy authored a bill to abolish slavery in all U.S. territories, and Lincoln called upon him to introduce the Emancipation Proclamation to Congress.

When Lovejoy became seriously ill in 1864, Lincoln was a frequent visitor to his home. Upon learning of Lovejoy's death on March 25 of that year, Lincoln remarked to artist Francis B. Carpenter, "Lovejoy was the best friend I had in Congress." Owen Lovejoy was buried in Princeton's Oakland Cemetery.

OTHER COMMUNITIES AND SITES OF INTEREST IN WESTERN ILLINOIS

Kampsville (Illinois River Road): In 1869 Capt. Michael L. Kamp established Farrow Town, later renamed Kampsville, where he operated a general store. In 1902 he built a new store, which the Kamp family ran until 1952, and other owners continued it until the building was acquired by the Center for American Archeology (CAA) in 1991. The CAA Visitor's Center offers information about the region's archaeology and includes a museum with artifacts that reflect human occupation in the Lower Illinois River Valley dating back to about 10,000 BC. The center conducts ongoing excavations nearby as well as educational programs.

Knoxville (I-74 and US 150): Originally called Henderson (or Henderson Town), founded in 1828 and named the Knox County seat in 1830, this city became Knoxville in 1833. Though the seat was moved to Galesburg in 1873, Knoxville's original 1839 Knox County Courthouse still stands as a museum, as does the 1832 John G. Sanburn Log Cabin, the town's first store. The city's most famous native is Charles Walgreen, founder of the Walgreens drugstore chain, born in Knoxville in 1873 (see also Dixon in Region 5 and Bronzeville in Region 7).

Mount Sterling (US 24): Incorporated in 1837, Mount Sterling became the seat of Brown County two years later. In its peak years, the city served as a rail hub for the area's farmers and ranchers. In 1976, as a bicentennial project, Mount Sterling's historic Quincy & Toledo railroad station, built around 1868, was moved to the Brown County Fairgrounds and is now known as the Whistle Stop Depot Museum.

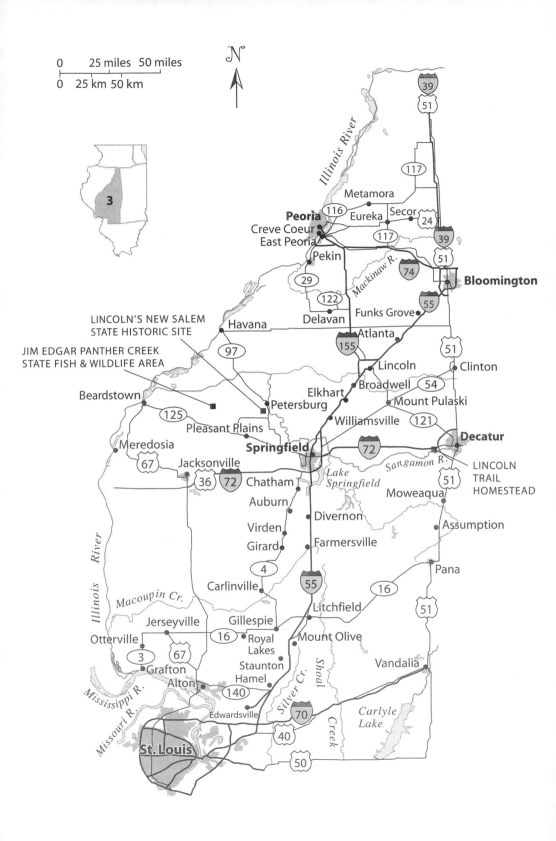

Central Illinois
LINCOLN'S LEGACY

Abraham Lincoln dominates the history of central Illinois. It was here that Lincoln left his parents' home along the Sangamon River southwest of Decatur, enlisted in the Black Hawk War, was elected to the state legislature, practiced law, married, served as a U.S. Congressman, patented an invention, campaigned for the U.S. Senate, was elected president, and was laid to rest.

The Lincoln Heritage Trail, which crisscrosses Kentucky and Indiana as well as Illinois, is not one road but a network. Originally, some 3,000 markers dotted the route, but today most of the signs have been removed or replaced or have become obscured from weathering or overgrowth. Nevertheless, historic-minded travelers may map out a route that encompasses many of the sites along the trail, not only those related to Lincoln but also other sites of historic interest, many of which will be discussed in this section of the book. The sites on the eastern part of the trail, representing Lincoln's early years in Illinois, will be discussed in Region 4.

Another legendary road passing through central Illinois is the historic US Route 66, the "Mother Road," which starts in Chicago and goes to Los Angeles. Several historic associations have pamphlets, maps, and Web sites with specific directions for the route. The Illinois section, which mostly parallels I-55, is well marked with signs. Several trips in this chapter follow sections of the southern part of the route. The northern section will be covered in Region 4. Also running through this region is the eastern side of the Illinois River National Scenic Byway; the western side was discussed in Region 2.

From Glacial Grounds to Land of Lincoln

Several hundred thousand years before trails, roads, and highways snaked through the region, central Illinois was covered with the ice sheets of the Illinoian and Wisconsinan glacial periods. The melting ice nearly leveled the land and exposed mineral deposits. Around 12,000 BC, prehistoric peoples migrated from the distant northwest. These nomadic hunters spread across the country, including the future state of Illinois.

The arrival of Europeans in the seventeenth century introduced new elements to the Indian way of life. Some hunters and planters became fur traders, involving themselves in European alliances and disputes over territories. Others remained true to their native culture. The westward migration of European Americans throughout the eighteenth and nineteenth centuries infiltrated Midwestern Indian territories, pushing tribes ever farther west.

Early French exploration skirted much of central Illinois. This left most of the area unsettled until the early 1800s, when adventuresome pioneers arrived to eke out a living on farms, taking their chances with roaming bands of Indians. Many were never bothered, but some, like the Hutson family near the Wabash River, were not so lucky.

After the Black Hawk War of 1832, the "Indian question" was settled with the 1833 Treaty of Chicago, making central Illinois more attractive for white settlers. The 1830s and 1840s were a period of filing land claims, establishing settlements, building roads, advancing education and religion, and promoting statewide development.

During this period, Abraham Lincoln's growing political stature mirrored the state's development. During his four terms in the Illinois General Assembly (1834–41), he was instrumental in passing legislation to improve the state's infrastructure. In 1836 he and eight other state representatives, known as the "Long Nine," successfully worked to relocate the state capital from Vandalia to Springfield.

Although the question of slavery in Illinois was permanently settled during the 1848 state constitutional convention, it remained a thorny issue through the 1850s and beyond. Slavery was one of the major questions addressed by Lincoln and Stephen A. Douglas during their 1858 U.S. senatorial debates. As president, Lincoln had the backing of numerous Springfield friends throughout the Civil War, especially Illinois governor Richard Yates and future governor Richard Oglesby.

After the war ended, central Illinois resumed its role as part of the nation's breadbasket. The region weathered the numerous financial panics of the late 1800s and early 1900s, the Great Depression, and other downturns. Even today, agriculture is the driving economic engine of central Illinois.

The Railroad Revolution

As central Illinois entered the second half of the nineteenth century, a new prosperity was on its way, arriving, as it were, by train. The Illinois Central Railroad (ICRR), built between 1850 and 1856, connected southern and northern Illinois, from Cairo to Galena, and linked farmers and businesses in the heartland to the network of rail lines that would soon crisscross the continent, making it easy to reach any number of outlying markets. For the rest of the nineteenth century and into the twentieth, the ICRR continued to expand into other states, going as far west as Sioux Falls, South Dakota, and extending south to New Orleans. Parts of the route follow various modern highways, and many ICRR trains (as of a 1999 merger, the Canadian National Railway) still run along the same tracks today.

The Role of Coal

In addition to agriculture and the railroad, coal has played a significant role in central Illinois' development. Coal was first mined commercially in Illinois in 1810, but most surface and underground mining in this part of the state occurred between 1864 and

1928. In the early days, steamboats, railroads, and households all relied on this abundant fuel source. Railroads represented a double benefit for the coal industry: as rail lines expanded, the railroad companies bought more coal to fuel their trains while providing low-cost shipping for the coal itself, allowing coal companies to reach more distant markets. By the late 1800s, coal was also being used to generate electricity for both industry and residences. Business was booming.

Into the early twentieth century, the bituminous ("soft") coal of Illinois remained the primary fuel source for everything from giant factories to home furnaces. More than a thousand coal mines once operated in central Illinois, providing employment for locals and newly arrived immigrants into the 1920s. But eventually coal found itself competing against oil, natural gas, petroleum, and other newly developed fuels. Labor disputes and safety issues took a toll on the industry as well. Later, evolving transportation technologies, federal and state pollution standards, and the development of modern fuel and power alternatives such as nuclear power and wind energy all helped push coal further into the margins. Coal is still mined in parts of central Illinois, but its uses are much more limited than they were in its heyday.

Modern Landscapes

Today central Illinois has a diverse economic base. Agriculture is still at the top, but manufacturing, retail, research, education, health services, and government all play significant roles. Tourism, both recreational and historical, also thrives in many places, especially in Springfield and in communities along historic and scenic routes.

IL 3, Otterville Road (County Rte 9), and IL 16
GRAFTON–HILLSBORO VIA JERSEYVILLE
64 miles

This trip takes us from Grafton to IL 16 via Otterville, home of the first free, racially integrated private school in the nation. On IL 16, a major east–west artery in this part of the state, lie several communities and sites of historical interest. One of them, Litchfield, has a number of old Route 66 landmarks. For more Route 66 fun, the next two trips also follow sections of the old highway.

GRAFTON
See Region 1

OTTERVILLE

About six miles north of Grafton on County Hwy 9 (Otterville Road) is Otterville, home of the Hamilton Primary School, the first racially integrated tuition-free private school in the United States. Although the school closed in 1971, the building still stands and was placed on the NRHP in 1998. The partially restored, two-story stone building is available for tours by appointment.

Hamilton Primary School was founded by and named for Dr. Silas Hamilton, a humanitarian former slave owner who had moved north from Mississippi in the 1820s and freed all his slaves. Three of his former slaves continued to live with him, however,

Otterville's original Hamilton Primary School, built in 1835, was replaced by this more modern building in 1873. The historic school closed in 1971. —Courtesy Jersey County Historical Society

and the four of them settled in Otterville in 1830. Upon his death in 1834, Hamilton left a trust fund to build and operate a primary school in Otterville. His former slave, George Washington, oversaw the construction of the school in 1835, and it opened the following year, enrolling both black and white students. In 1872 the original building was razed, and a new, larger school was erected on the previous structure's stone foundation.

Washington himself attended the school and became a successful farmer. When he died in 1864, he left a sizable estate, from which was established a perpetual educational fund for "colored persons or Americans of African descent." He also left money to build a memorial to his erstwhile master, Silas Hamilton, next to the school; it is the only monument in the country dedicated to a master by his slave. In another unique gesture, Washington's body was placed in a crypt alongside Hamilton's remains, making it the only grave in the United States where master and slave are buried side by side.

JERSEYVILLE

The first building in the Jerseyville area was a small, two-story frame cabin, known locally as the "Little Red House," built by settler James Faulkner in 1827. The structure served not only as a home for Faulkner and his family but also as a stagecoach station, tavern, school, and bank for the settlement that grew up around it, known as Hickory Grove.

Not long after the settlement formed, New Jersey natives John Lott and Edward Daley took an interest in Hickory Grove. They surveyed and platted some of the surrounding land and successfully promoted the area to merchants and settlers from their home state. When Hickory Grove was ready for a post office in 1834, the settlers decided to change the name to Jerseyville, in honor of the Garden State.

When Jersey County was created in 1839, Jerseyville became the county seat. The first courthouse, built in 1840, was destroyed by fire in 1884 and replaced by a small frame building that served the county until 1894, when a fine new courthouse was completed. This magnificent Romanesque Revival structure with its imposing tower still serves as Jersey County's courthouse today. It was placed on the NRHP in 1986.

Jerseyville was an abolitionist community, and the Little Red House that originally served as the town center was also an Underground Railroad station until the end of the Civil War. After the war, the house was incorporated into a larger home built by Prentiss Dana Cheney, and it became known as the Cheney Mansion. The twelve-room Victorian structure, completed in 1878, is now part of the Jersey County Historical Museum complex, which also includes a one-room schoolhouse, a small log cabin, a restored 1920 church, and a newer structure that houses additional exhibits and a research center.

The first rail line to reach Jerseyville was the Chicago & Alton Railroad in 1866, and the succeeding years brought the young city unprecedented growth. Most of Jerseyville's commercial buildings were erected during the railroad period, from the 1870s to the 1910s. The Jerseyville Downtown Historic District, an approximately nine-square-block area of mostly Romanesque commercial and retail buildings, was added to the NRHP in 1986. Jerseyville continues to grow and expand its local economy, which is still based partly on agriculture and supporting businesses.

Just one mile north of Jerseyville on US 67 is the Fulkerson Mansion & Farm Museum. The museum's fifty-eight acres include the Hazel Dell Farm, a portion of which still produces crops, and the fourteen-room, Italianate-style Fulkerson Mansion, originally the home of Confederate Lt. Col. William H. Fulkerson and his wife, Cornelia. Built in 1866 and expanded in 1872, the house is decorated with period furnishings as well as displays of Civil War artifacts, many of them from Fulkerson's own collection. Among the prominent visitors to the Hazel Dell estate were Gen. Robert E. Lee, cowboy artist Charles M. Russell (Cornelia's nephew), and even outlaws Frank and Jesse James. The property was added to the NRHP in 1998.

About sixteen miles east of Jerseyville on IL 16 is the Southwestern Farm and Home Museum in Shipman. Dedicated to the history and ongoing contribution of agriculture in America, this small museum features antique farming equipment and displays of rural life.

ROYAL LAKES

In 1956 Chicago developer Seymore Goodman purchased 320 acres of formerly agricultural land, excavated three recreational lakes, and divided the remaining acreage into more than 2,000 lots to be sold as affordable resort properties. Goodman promoted Royal Lakes primarily to African Americans in the St. Louis metro area. Buyers, who arrived to find a community without roads, sewers, or basic services, learned that the developer had simply abandoned the project. Some families stayed and tried to make the best of it, while others simply gave up and left. The community soon deteriorated.

In 1958 St. Louis resident Rosetta Gee and some friends purchased most of the remaining lakefront lots in the community and formed the Royal Lakes Club. The following year, Mrs. Gee's husband died, and she decided to move to Royal Lakes permanently. Later, with the help of volunteers from Southern Illinois University at Edwardsville, she organized and built a community center. In the meantime, residents formed the First Baptist Church of Royal Lakes in 1961, holding services in an old chicken house until 1968, when a church was built and renamed the First Community Baptist Church.

Royal Lakes was incorporated as a village in 1972. At that time, the community had about 300 residents and its homes, streets, and roads were in shambles. Improvements came slowly as appeals for government funds were often denied and residents had to depend on private donations and local fundraising efforts to pay for basic improvements and maintenance. Eventually, however, the fortitude of Royal Lakes citizens paid off. The village now boasts a modern sewer system, good roads, and a 50,000-gallon water tower. Many old homes have been restored and new ones built. A renovated village hall, a new children's park, low-income senior housing, and a rebuilt bridge all testify to this community's determination to thrive.

LITCHFIELD

Often called the hub of central Illinois, Litchfield lies midway between St. Louis, Missouri, and Springfield, Illinois. This city of approximately 6,600 residents, at the junction of IL 16 and US 66, boasts several landmark sites on or near the original US Route 66, the "Mother Road," as well as a train station from the early twentieth century.

Before Litchfield was established in 1854, a settlement called Hardinsburg, about two miles to the southwest, was founded in anticipation of the St. Louis, Alton & Terre Haute Railroad. When it became clear that the rail line would be built two miles away, Hardinsburg residents moved their homes and businesses to the site, where eighty acres had recently been platted in a cornfield. The new community, named after railroad executive Electus Baccus Litchfield, incorporated as a village in 1856.

After the Civil War, additional rail lines were built in Litchfield, ensuring the town's future prosperity. The Wabash Railway Company constructed a roundhouse and repair shops here in addition to a passenger depot. Meanwhile, coal, oil, and natural gas were discovered in the region, creating an industrial boom for several decades. Two coal mines opened in the area, the first one in the late 1860s and the second one a few years later. Among Litchfield's major enterprises during this period of growth were the Car Works, manufacturer of railroad freight cars; the American Radiator & Standard Sanitary Corporation, which built cast-iron radiators; the Zuber cigar factory, maker of "Zuber's Favorite" and "Blue Bonnet" cigars; and several wheat mills. Litchfield also saw a spate of civic improvements including a water reservoir, gas lines, and electric lights.

Litchfield's progress hardly slowed down through the twentieth century, and it remains a thriving city today. Its two industrial parks contain more than twenty manufacturers, sales offices, and distribution centers.

Route 66 Icons

IL 16 intersects with old US Route 66 in Litchfield, and several landmarks from the old highway's heyday are major attractions. Two of them have been inducted into the Route

66 Hall of Fame: the Ariston Café, one of the oldest operating restaurants (some sources claim *the* oldest) on Route 66, and the Skyview Theater, the last functioning drive-in movie theater on the Mother Road. The Ariston Café was originally established in Carlinville in 1924; it was relocated to its current building in Litchfield in 1935. The Skyview, which has had several owners since its opening in 1951, remains a time capsule for nostalgic moviegoers.

Another Route 66 landmark is the Belvidere Café, Motel, and Gas Station, constructed in 1929 as a service station and expanded several years later to include a motel and a café. Owned and operated by the Cerolla family, the Belvidere was not only a stop for travelers but also a popular local hangout with a jukebox, a small dance floor, and sometimes even live music. Completion of I-55 in the 1970s sounded the death knell for this classic roadhouse. Even though the business closed, the buildings remain. Most of the space is now used for storage, although a few of the motel rooms can still be rented. The Belvidere was listed on the NRHP in 2007.

HILLSBORO

Founded as the seat of Montgomery County in 1823, Hillsboro, today a small city of fewer than 4,500 residents, is home to a sizable number of sites, museums, and events related to the history of both the city and the county. Downtown Hillsboro contains more than twenty historic buildings, most built in the late 1800s and early 1900s. The jewel among these is the Montgomery County Courthouse, a handsome brick structure built between 1868 and 1872. During its construction, fragments of the county's original 1823 log courthouse were incorporated into the new building. Until 1909 the courthouse held the county jail and, right below the jail, the county sheriff's living quarters. The building is still partly in use, though most county offices are in the nearby annex building, erected in 1993.

While a few of Hillsboro's historic buildings are vacant and in disrepair, many are occupied and well maintained. One recently refurbished structure is the 1920 Orpheum Theatre, which now features state of the art projection and sound equipment. The 1902 Red Rooster Inn, near the courthouse, is nicely preserved and still operates as a hotel.

At least a dozen historic homes may also be viewed along the streets of Hillsboro, several of them built before the Civil War. Most are privately owned, but the oldest home in Hillsboro—the Solomon Harkey House, built in 1834—is open to the public. This two-story Federal-style residence was built by early settler Solomon Harkey, a tanner from North Carolina. It was donated to the Historical Society of Montgomery County in 1968, at which time it was moved to a new site a block away. The society undertook a massive restoration, finally opening the house as a museum in 1979.

Hillsboro's early history included frequent visits from Abraham Lincoln. Joe and Jane Eccles, personal friends of the Lincoln family from Kentucky, resided in Hillsboro and often hosted the young lawyer when he was in the area. Lincoln tried a number of cases at the county courthouse, and during his senatorial campaign in 1858, both he and his rival, Stephen A. Douglas, gave speeches at the Hillsboro Fairgrounds, now the site of Beckemeyer Elementary School. To commemorate Hillsboro's connection to the Rail-splitter, a bronze statue of him stands in Hillsboro Plaza, across the street from the courthouse. The almost seven-foot-tall figure, created by Illinois artist John McClarey, was dedicated in 2009.

Old Route 66 (IL 157), I-55, and IL 4
EDWARDSVILLE–SPRINGFIELD
80 miles

Like many early roads in the state, IL 4 started as an Indian trace, later known as the Pontiac Trail. The Chicago & Alton Railroad tracks followed an approximately parallel route from St. Louis to Chicago, and the road was almost fully paved by 1924.

This trip leads north from Edwardsville (see Region 1) to Springfield, the heart of Lincoln country. In 1926 these sections of IL 4 and IL 157 became part of the original US Route 66. The section of IL 4 between Auburn and Springfield was listed on the NRHP in 1998, and the stretch between Girard and Nilwood was listed in 2002. Travelers following old Route 66 may extend their trip southwest on IL 157 through Edwardsville to Chain of Rocks Road, which goes through Mitchell and beyond into Missouri. Later this stretch of US 66 was rerouted; the alternate Route 66 roughly follows what is now I-55 (see next trip).

EDWARDSVILLE
See Region 1

HAMEL

The earliest settlers in the Hamel area may have been former members of George Rogers Clark's military expedition to capture Kaskaskia in 1778. After completing their enlistments in 1781, some of them returned to claim their 300 acres as a reward for their military service, but it is uncertain if any of them stayed. It is known that a group of pioneers came from Massachusetts in 1817, later joined by settlers from Kentucky, Tennessee, Virginia, and the Carolinas. These early residents grew wheat and ran sawmills and gristmills. The area's first apple orchard was planted in 1819. A wave of German immigrants arrived in the 1830s, fleeing unrest in southern Germany; the addition of these settlers more than doubled the population of Madison County.

After the Mexican War ended in 1848, Andrew Jackson "Jack" Hammel, an Indiana farmer and enterprising businessman, moved to Madison County and bought up various tracts to sell in the settlement that came to be called Hamel's Corner, usually spelled with only one *m*. In 1868 Hammel opened a general store, which he sold three years later and moved away. Jack Hammel was never heard from again, but his misspelled name remained, and the unincorporated community became known as Hamel.

In spite of a nearby railroad, Hamel's growth was slow. In fact, the population mostly decreased until the mid-twentieth century. Hamel was not officially incorporated as a village until 1955; within a few years it had a post office, a bank, water and sewer lines, and a fire department. By that time, residents had easy highway access to larger cities for employment, shopping, and entertainment, so the economy of the village itself has remained modest. Its current population is just over 800, and many residents commute to work in one of several nearby cities. Yet symbols of the village's agricultural ties endure. One grain elevator built in 1911 is still operating. Another local historic site is the Hamel School Log Cabin, once the community's only school, now a museum.

Since the late twentieth century Hamel has embraced tourism, especially promoting its attractions related to old Route 66. Every June the Illinois Route 66 Motor Club winds its way through Hamel on the historic Mother Road. The main stop is Weezy's Route 66 Bar & Grill, formerly known as Tourist Haven Restaurant, built by George Cassens in 1937; between then and now, the café operated under various names including Village Inn, Ernie's Roadhouse, and Scotty's Route 66 Bar & Grill.

Two other remnants of the Mother Road are on I-55, part of the rerouted US 66 north of Hamel. In the daytime, travelers can see one of the few remaining advertisements for Missouri's Meramec Caverns painted on the side of a barn. A little farther up the road, nighttime motorists may notice a blue-neon-lighted concrete cross atop the entrance to St. Paul Lutheran Church, placed there as a memorial in 1946 by the parents of Oscar Brunnworth, a soldier who died in World War II. The surprisingly lovely cross is meant to serve as a "beacon of hope to cross-country travelers."

STAUNTON

This city of about 5,000 residents was named for James and Thomas Stanton, early settlers who donated land for a public square in 1836. When the settlement applied to Washington for a post office, a clerk misspelled the name as Staunton, and it was never corrected. Farming was Staunton's economic mainstay for decades, but after the Civil War, coal mining became the major industry, attracting hundreds of European immigrants in search of jobs. Staunton prospered, and in 1891 it was incorporated as a city.

Coal mining in this area continued for the next fifty years, reaching its peak around 1910, but over subsequent decades the coal industry steadily declined, and the last mine closed in 1951. Today, Staunton's economy is based mostly on manufacturing and trade. Tourism, too, plays a modest role. Many of the city's downtown buildings date to the early 1900s and comprise its historic district, which some describe as "what small towns used to be."

Just south of Staunton is the site of DeCamp, an old coal-mining town. The only remaining building from DeCamp's mining days is the old Riddel Store, now used as a private residence. Several history-minded Staunton-area residents are currently working on creating a replica mining town called DeCamp Settlement at the site.

Near DeCamp is an original Route 66 icon, the still-operating DeCamp Junction bar and restaurant. Formerly known as Duda's Restaurant, this roadhouse opened in 1931 and was a popular stop on the Mother Road. In addition to rental cabins, the place once had a dance hall, gambling, and, some say, a brothel.

The biggest draw for visitors to the Staunton area is probably Henry's Rabbit Ranch (sometimes written as Ra66it Ranch), developed along old Route 66 as a tourist attraction in 1995. In addition to the rabbit farm, owners Rich and Linda Henry also built a visitor center—a replica of a classic mid-twentieth-century gas station—for travelers on the Mother Road. Inside is a souvenir shop and displays of road memorabilia.

CARLINVILLE

Unlike many towns on old Route 66, most of Carlinville's attractions are related to the history of Macoupin County, of which Carlinville is the seat, rather than to the Mother Road. Among the city's many historical highlights are the Macoupin County

Courthouse, believed to be the most expensive courthouse of its time; the "Standard Addition" neighborhood, one of the largest concentrations of Sears catalog homes in the country; and the Anderson Mansion Museum, home of the Macoupin County Historical Society. Founded in 1828, Carlinville was named for Thomas Carlin, a state legislator who was instrumental in creating Macoupin County; he was later elected governor of Illinois.

Among Carlinville's notable former residents are Union general and Illinois governor John Palmer, author and naturalist Mary Hunter Austin, and prominent entomologist Charles Robertson. Robertson, who specialized in the habits of bees, identified more than one hundred new species of bees and wasps in Illinois. He is best known for his 1928 study, *Flowers and Insects*.

Historic Carlinville

Carlinville's most identifiable landmark is probably the Macoupin County Courthouse, dubbed the "Million Dollar Courthouse" because of the cost overruns in its construction, which placed the county in debt for more than forty years after the building's completion in 1870. The county had originally approved $50,000 to build the 191-foot-tall, Classic Revival structure, but due to its lavish design and luxurious materials, in the end it cost nearly $1.4 million. City officials borrowed money, issued bonds, and levied taxes

The historic Macoupin County "Million Dollar" Courthouse
—Courtesy Macoupin County Enquirer-Democrat

to pay the balance. The burning of the last bond in 1910 was marked with a two-day celebration in Carlinville, with Gov. Charles Deneen in attendance.

Because of its size, the courthouse—the county's third—was built several blocks east of the public square on eight lots. Among its many extravagant features are marble floors, iron interior doors, ornamental iron stair railings, a seven-foot-high judge's chair of hand-carved walnut, and a six-hundred-seat courtroom; the exterior features forty-foot-high Corinthian columns and a large silver-colored dome on top. With its impressive look and quirky history, the Macoupin County Courthouse is one of the region's major attractions.

Near the courthouse is a related but less ornate structure, the Old County Jail, completed in 1869. Small but heavily fortified, the jail was built with one-inch iron plates embedded between twenty inch thick walls of solid stone. In the early years, the jailer and his family lived in an apartment above the cells. In its 119-year history, only one inmate ever escaped. Listed on the NRHP in 1976, while it was still actively housing prisoners, the jail was used until 1988, when the new county jail was built. Along with the Macoupin County Courthouse, the old jail is open for tours by appointment.

Not far from the courthouse and jail, in the center of town, is Carlinville Square, the city's old downtown district, which includes a number of historic buildings. One of these is Loomis House, originally a fifty-room hotel built in 1870 by Judge Thaddeus L. Loomis, who was a major player in the construction of the county courthouse. Loomis later sold the hotel, which then operated as the St. George Hotel until 1964. The building now houses several local businesses. In the center of the square, a green space that is actually circular and surrounded by old brick-paved streets, is a lovely large gazebo, donated to Carlinville by a local family in 1993. The entire district around the square was placed on the NRHP in 1976.

On the northwest side of Carlinville is the Anderson Mansion Museum, home of the Macoupin County Historical Society. The historical society, which was formed in 1970, bought the two-story Victorian dwelling in 1973 to house its collection of antiques, artifacts, and documents related to the county's past. The house was originally built in 1883, with the second story added in 1892. The museum complex's outbuildings include an old one-room schoolhouse, a blacksmith shop, and a small church. A newer building accommodates an assortment of antique vehicles and farm machinery collected by the Macoupin Agricultural Antique Association.

On the northeast edge of town is Blackburn College, founded as Blackburn Theological Seminary in 1837 by Presbyterian minister Gideon Blackburn. While the land for the campus was deeded in 1837, due to funding problems the seminary did not open until 1859. Reverend Blackburn died in 1838, so he never got to see his school built. Eventually the theological classes were discontinued, and Blackburn officially became a liberal-arts college in 1950.

Blackburn College had only a handful of students when it established its student work program in 1913, allowing undergraduates to work on campus to help pay for their tuition. One of the student workers' first projects was constructing campus buildings. Ten of the college's existing buildings were erected by students, making Blackburn unique in this respect. The college is also unique in that its work program is the only one in the nation to be entirely managed by students. Thanks to this program, Blackburn, which currently has an enrollment of about 600 students, is the least expensive private four-year college in Illinois.

The Standard Addition

Just west of the Blackburn campus is a nine-block neighborhood of Sears catalog kit homes known as the "Standard Addition." Today, 152 of the original 156 catalog homes still exist, giving Carlinville the largest contiguous concentration of occupied Sears kit houses in the nation. The neighborhood was built by Standard Oil of Indiana in 1918 to house the workers at its two recently acquired coal mines south of the city.

At the time, Carlinville was a modest town of about 4,000; Standard Oil knew it would need to bring in hundreds of workers for the mines, but Carlinville did not have adequate housing to shelter the newcomers. To solve the problem quickly, the company bought a 500-acre farm northeast of town and placed an order for nearly 200 mail-order homes from the Sears Roebuck Company, 156 of which would be shipped to Carlinville, while the others were sent to nearby Schoper and to Wood River. Within a year, the company had built and outfitted all the homes, selling them to the miners for $3,000 to $4,000 each, including the lot. Only a few years later, however, Standard Oil closed the mines, and many of the houses were then abandoned. The company sold off its surplus of houses during the Great Depression for an astonishing $350 to $500 each.

Many of the Sears homes fell into serious disrepair over the years, but in the late twentieth century, a renewed interest in old kit houses stimulated a spate of restorations, and in 1987 Carlinville began to conduct tours of the Standard Addition neighborhood. The tours were a hit, prompting further renovations. These restoration efforts continue today, and the neighborhood is now one of the area's most popular attractions.

VIRDEN

First settled in 1829 as a farming community, the city of Virden was founded in 1852. It was named for early resident John Virden, proprietor of the settlement's first inn. After the first coal shaft opened in 1868, Virden saw steady growth through most of the late 1800s. In 1898 Virden was the site of a bloody labor dispute known as the Battle of Virden.

Coal Mine Wars and the Battle of Virden

Nineteenth-century coal companies were notorious for exploiting and mistreating their workers with long hours, unfair wage scales, and neglect of health and safety issues. The 1897 coal miner strike in Pana, supported by the United Mine Workers of America (UMWA), was the union's first successful strike (see Pana on later trip). But after the agreement with the union was reached, the Chicago-Virden Coal Company and a few other Illinois coal companies refused to abide by its terms, provoking another strike in 1898. Work stoppages occurred throughout the nation, with central Illinois at the center.

After three months, coal company officials threatened to reopen the mines with nonunion labor. As strikers surrounded the mines with mass picket lines, the mine owners recruited black workers in Birmingham, Alabama, and transported them by train to central Illinois. To shield the strikebreakers, the coal companies had erected stockades around several of their mines and posted armed guards.

The first trainload of southern black workers to arrive in Virden, in September 1898, was turned back by protesters. A month later, after successfully installing strikebreakers in Carterville and Pana, the mine owners decided to try again in Virden, this time protecting their train with armed guards. But the miners were ready for them. Supporters from Mount Olive, Springfield, and other mining towns across the state poured in to help stop the scabs from entering Virden, lining up all along the tracks.

On October 12, as the train of black workers came to a stop in front of the mine, gunfire broke out between the strikers and the guards. The train engineer, wounded in the melee, drove the train on to Springfield. The rioters spread out and continued their battle. By the end of the fight, six guards and seven miners lay dead and some thirty-five people were wounded. Upon hearing of the riot, Gov. John Riley Tanner sent the National Guard into Virden to restore order.

After the incident, the coal companies stopped bringing in strikebreakers, though it took another year to reach a final agreement. In November 1899 mine owners agreed to pay laborers according to the original contract that had been laid before them fifteen months earlier, and the UMWA's local union was officially recognized.

A six-foot-tall granite monument in Virden's town square, dedicated in 2006, commemorates the conflict with a detailed bronze bas-relief.

SPRINGFIELD

The first known settlers in the Springfield area were the Elisha Kelly family, who arrived from North Carolina around 1820 with several other families. The homesteaders built cabins amid the rolling prairie and timber groves along the Sangamo (today called Sangamon) River. A year later, the county of Sangamon was organized and the cluster of cabins by the river, dubbed Springfield, was chosen to serve as the county seat. In 1823 additional land was purchased, and the expanded settlement was platted as Calhoun, in honor of John C. Calhoun, President James Monroe's Secretary of War. The new name never caught on, however, and many locals continued to call the place Springfield. When the community incorporated as a town in 1832, it took Springfield as its official name.

In 1837 a steamrolled vote led by State Representative Abraham Lincoln led to the relocation of the state capital from Vandalia to Springfield, ensuring its future prosperity. Three years later, Springfield was incorporated as a city.

Famously rich in Lincoln lore, Springfield was the Railsplitter's home from 1837 to 1861. Sites related to the sixteenth president include Lincoln-Herndon Law Office State Historic Site, the Lincoln Home National Historic Site, the Lincoln Depot, and Lincoln's Tomb State Historic Site, all described below. In 2005 the city dedicated its newest Lincoln attraction, the Abraham Lincoln Presidential Library and Museum.

Springfield also offers a number of historic buildings unrelated to Lincoln. One of these is the former home of socialite Susan Lawrence Dana. The Dana-Thomas House, designed by Frank Lloyd Wright and a prime example of his early Prairie style architecture, contains the world's largest collection of original Wright art glass and furniture. Another point of interest is a plaque identifying the departure point of the ill-fated Donner-Reed Party, who left for California from Springfield on April 14, 1846. The plaque is on a brick wall that runs along Old State Capitol Plaza. The plaque was installed in 1957 by the Children of the American Revolution.

Springfield's status as the state capital gives visitors three other sites of interest—the Old State Capitol State Historic Site (see below); the current capitol, completed in 1888; and the governor's mansion (Illinois Executive Mansion). The latter, a sixteen-room Georgian-style home, was completed in 1855 and first occupied by the tenth Illinois governor, Joel Matteson. The main part of the mansion is maintained as a historic site and is regularly open for tours, while the governor and his family live in a large private apartment on the second floor. The building was listed on the NRHP in 1976.

The current four-story domed capitol is adorned with artwork, including twelve murals on the first floor, eight of which were commissioned during the building's construction. In 1988, as part of the capitol's centennial celebration, Secretary of State Jim Edgar commissioned four additional mural panels. The new murals were meant to "reflect historical and social changes in Illinois from the mid-1800s to the twentieth Century," according to the official description.

Artist Ken Holder of Bloomington, now professor emeritus at Illinois State University, was chosen to paint one of the murals, depicting the theme "Transforming the Prairie" (shown on the cover of this book). "My aim was to present . . . an imaginary slice of the Illinois landscape as it might have looked in the 1870s," Holder explained. "The field hands are employed using the newly invented machinery of the times, on farmscapes that were based on typical layouts of the day," symbolizing, he said, "the transformation: the loss of the prairie as a sacrifice in exchange for the agricultural boon."

Lincoln-Herndon Law Office State Historic Site

In 1843 Abraham Lincoln, then a young attorney, and his partner Stephen T. Logan established a law office in a three-story brick building in Springfield. A year later, the firm of Logan & Lincoln broke up, but Lincoln stayed in the same office, taking on a new junior partner, William Herndon. Lincoln & Herndon used this office from 1844 to 1852. Although part of the original building, constructed in 1841, was torn down in 1872, Lincoln's third-floor office was preserved. The refurbished building became the Lincoln-Herndon Law Office State Historic Site in 1985.

It is a little-known fact about Abraham Lincoln that he was an inventor. It was in his law office and its neighboring shop that Lincoln developed the design for his first and only patented invention, an "Improved method of lifting Vessels over Shoals."

The inspiration for the invention came on September 29, 1848. Lincoln was aboard a steamboat on the Detroit River when he observed another ship stuck on a sandbar. To solve the problem, the captain ordered empty barrels, boxes, and casks to be forced under the hull to lift the boat and clear the sandbar. This process took three days. Pondering the problem, Lincoln conceived the idea of a device to solve it. Back in Springfield, he whittled a wooden model of his invention.

Lincoln sometimes worked on his invention model in his law office and sometimes in the nearby cabinet shop of a friend, Walter Davis. A U.S. representative at the time, Lincoln returned to Washington, D.C., in December 1848 with a working model of his invention in hand and applied for a patent. He received Patent No. 6469 on May 22, 1849. Lincoln's invention was never used or even tested on a navigable waterway, but its principles may have been incorporated into the design of the submarine decades later.

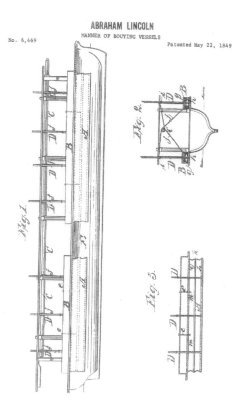

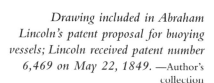

Drawing included in Abraham Lincoln's patent proposal for buoying vessels; Lincoln received patent number 6,469 on May 22, 1849. —Author's collection

Old State Capitol State Historic Site

During its 1832–33 session, the Illinois state legislature debated the question of a new location for the state capital. Among the contenders were Alton, Jacksonville, Peoria, and Springfield. Another option was to leave the capital in Vandalia.

The question remained unresolved until the 1836–37 legislative session. Supporters of each candidate city argued their cases. Representing Springfield were Senators Job Fletcher and Archer G. Herndon and Representatives John Dawson, Ninian W. Edwards, William F. Elkin, Abraham Lincoln, Andrew McCormick, Dan Stone, and Robert L. Wilson. Because these men all happened to be tall (their combined height totaled exactly fifty-four feet), they became known as the "Long Nine." The group secured votes in exchange for various public-works projects.

In spite of the concerted efforts for Springfield, the competition hung tough. It took four ballots before Springfield emerged as the winner of the capital race. After the victory, the city conveyed two acres of land on which to build a new capitol, and citizens pledged $50,000 for its construction, which began in 1837.

By 1840 construction expenditures for the capitol exceeded $180,000, and the building was still far from finished. Construction continued, as did cost overruns. Over the next fourteen years, the state legislature had to appropriate additional monies five times in order to complete the project. In the interim, the nearby Second Presbyterian

Church was used for meetings of the House of Representatives, and the Methodist and Episcopal churches were used for Senate and Supreme Court sessions, respectively. The capitol was finally finished in 1853, at an estimated cost of $260,000—twice the original projection.

Lincoln served his last legislative term and tried cases before the Illinois Supreme Court in this building, and he delivered his famous "House Divided" speech here on June 16, 1858. On May 3 and 4, 1865, his body was laid in state at the capitol prior to the funeral procession to Oak Ridge Cemetery.

In 1867, due to the rapid growth of Illinois' population, legislators authorized the construction of a new statehouse. In 1876 the state government moved into the new capitol while it was still under construction; the building was finally completed in 1888. Meanwhile, the Old State Capitol was sold to Sangamon County, serving as the county courthouse for nearly a hundred years. In 1961 it was resold to the state of Illinois and restored to its original appearance as a State Historic Site. Today, visitors can take a tour of the places where Abe Lincoln walked, spoke, and worked.

Lincoln Home National Historic Site

When Abraham Lincoln married Mary Todd on November 4, 1842, he was working in Springfield as a lawyer and a legislator. For the first two years of their marriage, the Lincolns rented quarters in the Globe Tavern. In 1844 they purchased the one-and-a-half-story, Greek Revival cottage on South Eighth Street. At the time of their move, the couple had a son, Robert Todd Lincoln, born August 1, 1843. During the time the Lincolns lived in this home, three more children were born: Edward, born in 1846; William (Willie), born in 1850; and Thomas (Tad), born in 1853. Also during this period, in February 1850, the family suffered their first tragedy, the death of little Edward, not yet four years old.

In 1856, having outgrown the small house, the Lincolns added a full second floor at a cost of $1,300, the same price they had paid for the original house twelve years earlier. When the newly elected president departed for Washington in 1861, he bid farewell to his beloved Springfield at the train depot, now a historic site (see below). At the time, Robert, age eighteen, was a freshman at Harvard University, while Willie, eleven, and Tad, eight, moved with their parents into the White House.

With the death of Willie in the White House on February 20, 1862, the president's death on April 15, 1865, and Tad's passing on July 15, 1871, the grieving Mary Lincoln, having no further need for the house in Springfield, moved out. After a few years of traveling in the United States and abroad, Mary grew increasingly unstable. In 1875 Robert had his mother committed to a mental institution in Batavia (see also under Batavia in Region 6). After her release a few months later, Mary moved in with her sister in Springfield, where she died on July 16, 1882. After her death, Robert, as the sole surviving son, inherited the Lincoln Home, which he donated to the state of Illinois in 1887.

Over the subsequent decades, visits of famous personages to Springfield almost always included a tour of the Lincoln Home, which was elevated to the level of a shrine. But this shrine soon showed signs of wear. Souvenir stands and gift shops encroached upon the home's appearance, as did unsightly above-ground power lines and other anachronistic features. In 1971 the house was designated a National Historic Site and the National Park Service took over its management. In 1987 the building was closed for extensive restoration work. Even the lightning rods that Lincoln installed to calm Mary's fear of electrical storms were replicated. On June 16, 1988, the home was reopened to the public.

Lincoln Depot

The morning was dismal and rainy as the crowd gathered at Springfield's Great Western Railway depot to bid farewell to Abraham Lincoln, who was about to board the last car of a special inaugural train bound for Washington. It was a few minutes before 8 a.m. on Monday, February 11, 1861, when he made his way through the hundreds of friends and neighbors who eagerly grasped his hand and called out words of encouragement. Reaching the platform of the last car, the president-elect "turned towards the people, removed his hat . . . and then slowly, impressively, and with profound emotions," delivered his remarks to the group. Despite the rain, hats were removed and heads leaned forward to hear:

> *Friends, no one who has ever been placed in a like position can understand my feelings at this hour, nor the oppressive sadness I feel at this parting. For more than a quarter of a century I have lived among you, and during all that time I have received nothing but kindness at your hands. Here the most sacred ties of earth were assumed; here all my children were born; and here one of them lies buried. To you, dear friends, I owe all that I have, all that I am. . . . Let us all pray that the God of our fathers may not forsake us now. To him I commend you all. Permit me to ask that with equal sincerity and faith you will all invoke His wisdom and guidance for me. With these few words I must leave you—for how long I know not. Friends, one and all, I must now bid you an affectionate farewell.*

At the conclusion of his remarks, precisely at 8 a.m., the train pulled away from the station while Lincoln stood on the rear platform, his hand raised in goodbye. The old train station in Springfield, built in 1852, has been restored and opened to the public as the Lincoln Depot historic site.

Lincoln's Tomb State Historic Site, Oak Ridge Cemetery

The death of Abraham Lincoln on April 15, 1865, evoked a national outpouring of sorrow. Across the nation, federal, state, and city offices, as well as many private homes and businesses, were draped in commemorative black and white bunting, American flags, and other symbols of patriotism and memorial as church bells tolled and choirs sang somber hymns. Nowhere was the mourning more apparent than in the late president's adopted home of Springfield.

The date for Lincoln's funeral was set for May 4. The nine-car funeral train, draped in black bunting, left Washington on April 21, carrying the president's body along with that of his son, William, who had died in the White House. The boy's body had been buried in Washington but was exhumed to be interred next to his father in Springfield. The train traveled 1,662 miles across the country, making stops in Baltimore, Harrisburg, Philadelphia, New York, Albany, Buffalo, Cleveland, Columbus, Indianapolis, and Chicago, arriving in Springfield on May 3.

This sketch by William Waud (from Harper's Weekly, *May 27, 1865) depicts President Abraham Lincoln being laid to rest in a tomb at Oak Ridge Cemetery in Springfield.* —Author's collection

That morning in Springfield, population 15,000, a crowd of more than 150,000 assembled to meet the train. The roads into the city were congested with mourners and curiosity seekers. The funeral train was scheduled to arrive at 8 a.m., and crowds had been gathering for hours along the tracks of the Chicago & Alton Railroad as well as at the depot to catch a glimpse of it. Cannons manned by Battery K, Second Missouri Light Artillery, fired salutes at precise intervals. The pilot engine that preceded the funeral train reached the depot an hour behind schedule.

The reception committee, led by Brig. Gen. John Cook, and a delegation of dignitaries took their positions. As the funeral train slowed to a stop, the president's remains were transferred from the funeral car to a black hearse drawn by six horses. Both hearse and horses were adorned with black plumes.

At the Hall of Representatives in the State Capitol, the casket was placed on a catafalque (platform) at the head of the semicircular chamber for public viewing. Shortly after 10 a.m., the doors were opened and the mourners flooded in. It is estimated that 25,000 people paid their respects during the first ten hours. At sundown, twelve gas-burning globe lamps were lit, emitting a soft light for the steady stream of mourners that poured in through the night.

When the coffin was closed at 10 a.m. the following day, a 250-member choir sang hymns on the steps of the Capitol while the casket was carried from the hall to the hearse. Behind the hearse, Lincoln's horse, Old Bob, walked riderless. The procession traveled past Lincoln's former residence and the Governor's Mansion to the east entrance of Oak Ridge Cemetery, a distance of one and a half miles.

At the tomb, the choir sang, passages from scripture and from Lincoln's own speeches were read, remarks were made, and prayers were offered. While the tomb was prepared for closure, military participants and the fire department marched in formation back to the city. The president was laid to rest with William in a temporary vault, where his son Edward's body had already been placed.

In 1871 the remains of the three Lincolns were moved to a permanent tomb, as were those of the recently deceased Thomas. Later, due to vandalism and deterioration, a new tomb was built, and the bodies of the Lincoln family—which now included that of Mary Lincoln—were moved there in 1901. Robert Lincoln, who died in 1926, was interred in Arlington National Cemetery in Virginia.

Camp Butler National Cemetery

Camp Butler was an interim military facility established in August 1861 to muster and train urgently needed infantry, artillery, and cavalry regiments for the Union army. About one-third of all Illinois troops underwent training here.

After the Union victory at Tennessee's Fort Donelson on February 16, 1862, part of the post became a prison camp for about 2,000 of the 14,000 Confederate prisoners taken at the battle. Another 1,500 prisoners were added after the capture of Island Number Ten in the Mississippi River. Camp Butler processed more than 200,000 men during the war and remained in use until June 19, 1866.

The camp's adjacent cemetery contains 1,642 Civil War graves, more than half of which are those of Confederate prisoners, the remainder being Union soldiers. Later interments include veterans of subsequent wars. Today's Camp Butler National Cemetery, placed on the NRHP in 1997, contains a portion of the original site of the camp.

I-72/US 36 and US 67
SPRINGFIELD–BEARDSTOWN
34 miles

This route takes motorists through a very historically significant part of the state, beginning in Springfield and passing through Jacksonville, home of Illinois College (founded in 1829), and other communities to Beardstown, site of Abe Lincoln's famous "Almanac Trial."

SPRINGFIELD

See previous trip

JACKSONVILLE

To some, Jacksonville is the "Athens of the West," a slogan created in the 1800s to boost interest in settlement here. But to poet William Cullen Bryant, the village was "a horrid little town" with "a dingy square" and "the ugliest possible Court House." Even Julian Sturtevant, the second president of Illinois College, chimed in by referring to Jacksonville as a "realm of confusion and religious anarchy."

Indeed, Jacksonville is a city of seeming contradictions—historic and political, religious and educational, industrial and agricultural—meshing into a mosaic of what is special about Illinois. The town is unusual in its number of educational institutions per capita; many of these schools were established shortly after the town was established. Illinois College, founded in 1829, was soon followed by Jacksonville Female Academy (1830), now part of Illinois College; the Illinois School for the Deaf (1839); Illinois Conference Female Academy (1846), now MacMurray College; and the Illinois Institute for the Education of the Blind (1849), now the Illinois School for the Visually Impaired.

In addition to its educational institutions, Jacksonville has produced an impressive number of prominent citizens from the past two centuries. Among them are educator Jonathan B. Turner, creator of the land-grant college concept; Brig. Gen. Benjamin H. Grierson, leader of the "most brilliant expedition of the [Civil War]"; Dr. Greene Vardiman Black, "the father of modern dentistry"; Frank H. Hall, inventor of the Hall Braille Writer; Democratic presidential candidates Stephen A. Douglas and William Jennings Bryan; William E. Sullivan, manufacturer of Ferris Wheels and other amusement rides; world-champion heavyweight boxer Ken Norton; and three Illinois governors—Joseph Duncan, Richard Yates, and Richard Yates, Jr.

In 1825, two years after Morgan County was formed, local settlers deeded forty centrally located acres to establish a seat. The land held a single cabin, the home of a hatmaker, where early circuit-court sessions were held. The town was dubbed Jacksonville in honor of the War of 1812 hero and future president Andrew Jackson.

While still in its infancy, Jacksonville endured seven feet of snow during the winter of 1830–31, a cholera outbreak in 1833, and a period of frigid temperatures and high winds in December 1836. In 1838, during the event later known as the "Trail of Death," Jacksonville families offered food and comfort to the Potawatomi Indians who were being forced to cross the state on foot to a reservation in Osawatomie, Kansas (see under Danville in Region 4). Jacksonville citizens also offered aid to runaway slaves. Many townspeople provided "safe houses" for escaped slaves headed north on the Underground Railroad; other runaways were harbored among free blacks in a part of Jacksonville called "Africa."

Some of the city's early-twentieth-century industries included a brickworks, a textile mill, a manufacturer of amusement rides, and thirteen cigar factories. The city and surrounding farmland continued to draw newcomers throughout the first half of the twentieth century. It remains a lively town with education, health services, manufacturing, and government providing its economic backbone.

Illinois College

The first school in the state to grant a four-year degree was Illinois College, founded in 1829 by a group of Yale men who wanted to establish a liberal-arts college on the western frontier. Classes began in 1830, with Edward Beecher serving as the school's first president. The Illinois legislature granted the college a charter in 1835, the same year the school graduated its first class, which consisted of only two students—Richard Yates and Jonathan Edward Spilman. The former would eventually be elected governor of Illinois (see below). Other famous alumni include explorer John Wesley Powell (attended 1855) and politician William Jennings Bryan (graduated 1881), along with two U.S. senators, twenty congressmen, and six governors (including Yates).

Illinois College's Beecher Hall, the oldest college building in the state
—Courtesy Schaumburg Township District Library, Illinois Collection

College president Edward Beecher, brother of Harriet Beecher Stowe, was ardently opposed to slavery and expressed his views forthrightly. Most students and faculty supported his position, and some may have helped hide runaway slaves before and during the war. Although Beecher resigned in 1844, the college never abandoned its opposition to slavery. In 1903 the nearby Jacksonville Female Academy merged with Illinois College, making the school coeducational.

Beecher Hall, the oldest college building still standing in the state, has served as a chapel, science laboratory, dormitory, library, and center of the state's first medical school. Listed on the NRHP, the 1829 brick structure is now home to the Phi Alpha and Sigma Pi Literary Societies.

Today Illinois College offers more than forty academic programs and enrolls over a thousand students per year. It remains a private liberal-arts school affiliated with the Presbyterian Church and the United Church of Christ.

Richard Yates: War Governor

Richard Yates was born on January 18, 1815, in Warsaw, Kentucky. His family moved to Sangamon County when he was a teenager. After graduating from Illinois College in 1835, he studied law at Transylvania University in Lexington, Kentucky, was admitted to the bar in 1837, and returned to Jacksonville to open his practice.

Yates was a grammarian and a gifted orator, two skills that aided him in politics. He campaigned for Whig candidate William Henry Harrison in 1840 and began his own political career shortly afterward.

Yates served three terms in the state legislature (1843–47 and 1849–51) and two in the U.S. Congress (1851–55). He was defeated for reelection after opposing repeal of the Missouri Compromise and espousing strong antislavery views. Though originally a Whig, he was appointed as a delegate to the Republican National Convention in 1860 and was elected governor as a Republican later that year, taking office January 14, 1861.

A staunch Unionist, Yates opposed any compromise with the South and vowed to use all resources to defend the U.S. Constitution. When President Lincoln requested volunteers for the army, Yates used his charismatic appeal to raise twice the expected number. He was credited for plucking Ulysses S. Grant from oblivion, overseeing his early promotions.

Yates left the governor's office on January 16, 1865, and took a seat in the U.S. Senate seven weeks later. He and his wife were invited to join President and Mrs. Lincoln to see *Our American Cousin* at Ford's Theater on April 14. They declined due to a previous engagement and so were spared witnessing Lincoln's assassination.

After completing one term as U.S. senator, Yates was appointed a federal commissioner to oversee land-subsidy railroads. On his way home from a trip to Little Rock, Arkansas, he suddenly took ill in St. Louis and died there on November 27, 1873. He was buried in Diamond Grove Cemetery in Jacksonville. His son, Richard Yates, Jr., served as governor of Illinois from 1901 to 1905.

Dr. Greene Vardiman Black: Father of Modern Dentistry

During the 1800s, dentistry gradually went from a tooth-pulling trade performed by blacksmiths and barbers to a technical and scientific profession, thanks in part to Dr. Greene Vardiman Black. Black was born August 3, 1836, on a farm near Winchester, Illinois. In his late teens, he became interested in medicine and studied with his elder brother, physician Thomas G. Black. He later studied with a practicing dentist in Mount Sterling. After serving with the Union Army, he moved to Jacksonville in 1864 and started a dental practice while continuing his research in dentistry. He was a kindly man, devoted to his family and his patients as well as to his field.

As a member of the Missouri and Illinois state dental societies, he presented his first important paper in 1869 and the following year was elected president of the Illinois State Dental Society. With his brother Thomas, he co-authored Illinois' Medical Practice Act, requiring physicians to be licensed, in 1877. Four years later, he helped write and pass the state's first Dental Practice Act. Black became the first dentist in Illinois to receive both a medical and a dental license.

Black authored several books that became seminal contributions to medicine and dentistry. *The Formation of Poisons by Micro-organisms* (1884) is considered one of the most important works on bacteriology ever published, and his two-volume *Operative Dentistry* (1908) was the standard text of dental school students for seventy-five years.

In addition to holding many other positions and offices, Black was one of the founders of the Northwestern University Dental School in Evanston in 1891. He became dean of the school in 1897 and served in that position until his death in 1915. He was also the inventor of several dental instruments and devices. During his lifetime, Black made over 1,000 scientific contributions to the field of dental medicine. A year after Black's death, H. E. Friesell, writing in the *National Dental Journal*, described the

Dr. Greene Vardiman Black in his Jacksonville office
—Courtesy Northwestern University Archives

doctor's life's work as "marking an age in dentistry as does that of Euclid in Mathematics, Archimedes in Mechanics, or Homer in Poetry."

Dr. Greene Vardiman Black died on August 21, 1915, at age seventy-nine, and was buried at Diamond Grove Cemetery in Jacksonville. He is memorialized with a life-size statue, sculpted by Frederick Cleveland Hibbard, in Chicago's Lincoln Park. The monument was unveiled in 1918, during the sixtieth anniversary of organized dentistry. Black was also among the nineteen innovators honored with a special plaque at the 1933 Century of Progress Exhibit for Dentistry.

The Northwestern University Dental School that Black helped found in 1891 closed in 2001. Ironically, the great-granddaughter of Greene Vardiman Black, Elizabeth Malott, graduated with the school's last class in subdued ceremonies on the Evanston campus.

MEREDOSIA

With steamboats chugging up and down the Illinois River, Morgan County was already well settled when Meredosia was founded on the riverbanks in 1832. The little river village received a boost five years later, when the construction of the eleven-mile Northern Cross Railroad, the first rail line in Illinois, was completed between Meredosia and Morgan City, a now-defunct town near Chapin. The railroad was later extended across the state.

Meredosia developed steadily with the addition of several sawmills, a whiskey distillery, and other businesses, including a seventy-five-room hotel built in the 1840s. For a time, pecans were a major industry for the town, as wild pecan trees once grew in abundance until a devastating flood in 1926 killed most of them off.

Other early industries in Meredosia were based on the Illinois River and nearby Lake Meredosia. In the 1890s, beds of freshwater mussels were discovered in the river. These were harvested for their shells, from which buttons were made. Meredosia once had four button factories, the last one closing in 1948. Commercial fishing was another significant part of the local economy until the 1950s, and ice was harvested from the river until the 1930s. These three river-based industries faded over time as conditions changed; the fish and mussels were overharvested, and ice cutting became an obsolete industry with the advent of refrigeration.

Meredosia Island—technically not an island but a tract of wooded wetland that becomes surrounded by water when the river and lake waters are high—was another natural resource exploited by early residents. The area was a cornucopia of waterfowl and wetland mammals such as beaver, muskrat, and mink. Commercial duck hunting on the island was a profitable business in the late 1800s, and fur trapping was a going concern until the 1920s. The Kappal Brothers Furriers, established in Meredosia in 1905, was once the second-largest fur company in the Midwest. The old Kappal building downtown now serves as headquarters for the Meredosia Historical Society and River Museum.

In the 1970s, much of Meredosia Island was donated to the National Wildlife of Game and Fisheries, which created the Meredosia National Wildlife Refuge, a managed habitat for waterfowl, migratory birds, and native plants. Recreational tourism at the lake and the wildlife refuge helps sustain Meredosia's economy, though agriculture remains its mainstay.

BEARDSTOWN

One of the first settlers in this part of Illinois was Thomas Beard, who built a cabin on the Illinois River in 1819. He originally made a living trading with the local Kickapoo Indians, then in 1826 he opened a ferry, around which a small settlement grew. Three years later, Beard's Ferry was platted as a town and renamed Beardstown. Beard built a two-story brick building that functioned as a store and inn for eighty-five years before it was torn down. The ferry ran till 1888, when it was supplanted by a wooden toll bridge.

As with many towns in downstate Illinois, Beardstown's economy was based on agriculture. Beardstown watermelons are still known far and wide, and the city is also noted for its sweet corn. But its best-known agricultural product may be pork. In the early days, hogs and hog slaughtering were the town's chief industry; in fact, for a time Beardstown was nicknamed "Porkopolis." Even today, pork is important in Beardstown, as it is the home base of Cargill Meat Solutions, the largest pork-processing plant in Illinois and a major employer.

As a river port, Beardstown grew rapidly through the nineteenth century. Besides its transportation benefits, the Illinois River also provided the city with several harvest industries. Fishing was a significant part of the economy for a time, as was gathering mussels, whose shells were used for making buttons. The collecting of ice from the river also brought income into Beardstown until the early twentieth century.

Due to its success, Beardstown served on and off as the seat of Cass County from 1837 until 1875, when the seat was permanently established in Virgina, Illinois. The former county courthouse, built in 1844, now houses several local museums, while the courtroom is still used for hearings and trials. On the first floor is the Chamber of Commerce Visitors Center, home of the Beardstown River Museum. Upstairs is the Rudy Black Museum, which has an extensive collection of guns, Indian artifacts, and local memorabilia. Also on the second floor is the historic courtroom, referred to as the Old Lincoln Courtroom Museum, where Abraham Lincoln often argued cases, including the famous 1858 "Almanac Trial."

Beardstown had its first contact with Abraham Lincoln in 1832, during the Black Hawk War, when a company of soldiers was mustered near what is now Schmoldt Park and nominated young Abe Lincoln as its captain. A marker in the park commemorates the event. Beardstown would encounter Lincoln again as a lawyer trying cases at the county courthouse. The most significant of these took place in May 1858, when Lincoln, by then a seasoned attorney, argued for the defense in what became known as the Almanac Trial.

The defendant was a young man named Duff Armstrong, accused of beating to death local farmer James Metzger during a drunken brawl in Petersburg on August 29, 1857. A witness named Charles Allen claimed to have seen Armstrong delivering the death blow. The crime occurred late at night, but Allen testified that he could see clearly from 150 feet away by the light of the full moon. As part of his argument, Lincoln produced an almanac indicating that the moon was not full that night, nor was it high enough in the sky at that hour to provide adequate light to see clearly from such a distance. Armstrong was acquitted.

This ambrotype of Abraham Lincoln was taken in Beardstown after he won a famous court case known as the "Almanac Trial" on May 7, 1858. —Author's collection

In addition to the courthouse and its three museums is the Grand Opera House, built in 1872. As the building neared completion, a tornado struck and destroyed most of it. Undaunted, local volunteers helped rebuild it, and it opened later that year. The opera house passed through various owners over the years, and it was placed on the NRHP in 2000. In 2004 it was purchased by the Beardstown Grand Opera House Heritage Preservation Foundation and is currently undergoing restoration. Most recently, the opera house was the subject of a paranormal investigation for the cable TV show "Ghost Hunters," and private ghost tours are sometimes given there.

Visitors to Beardstown may also enjoy recreational opportunities at Sanganois State Wildlife Area and its numerous large lakes, just north of town. At the junction of the Sangamon and Illinois Rivers (the name *Sanganois* came from combining the names of the two rivers), this area has a history of its own. Once privately owned, it was a popular getaway for gangster boss Al Capone in the 1920s and early '30s when things got too hot in Chicago. The state purchased the main property in 1948, adding parcels through 1970.

In the 1990s, little Beardstown made a splash when the "Beardstown Ladies Club" became an American sensation. This independent investment club of sixteen local Beardstown women formed in 1983. Nine years later, the group claimed they had amassed annual stock gains of more than 20 percent, gaining them national media attention. They appeared on television shows and published several books until a *Chicago* magazine article in 1998 concluded that their actual gain was only about 9 percent, discrediting their previous reports. The numbers weren't presented fraudulently—the gains were merely a miscalculation. Since its meteoric rise and fall, the Beardstown Business and Professional Women's Investment Club continues to meet, stressing its original intent "to learn how to better manage their personal assets."

IL 125, IL 123, and IL 97
SPRINGFIELD–HAVANA VIA PLEASANT PLAINS
58 miles

On this trip we follow IL 125, an old stagecoach route, and IL 97, going slightly out of our way to stop at Pleasant Plains and the Clayville Historical Site.

SPRINGFIELD
See earlier trip

PLEASANT PLAINS

The village of Pleasant Plains is primarily known for two historic sites, the nearby Clayville Historical Site (a.k.a. the Broadwell Tavern), one of the oldest brick buildings in Illinois, and the Peter Cartwright United Methodist Church, built in 1857 (see below). Pleasant Plains was the home of the renowned Reverend Cartwright from 1826 to 1872.

The village, platted in 1854 and incorporated ten years later, grew slowly on the Springfield-to-Beardstown stage route. The Baltimore & Ohio Southwestern Railroad arrived in Pleasant Plains in 1890, but a later rerouting bypassed the village. Pleasant Plains has remained a quiet farming community with a current population of fewer than eight hundred.

Clayville Tavern Historical Landmark

Early travelers on the stagecoach route that is now IL 125 enjoyed the comforts of Broadwell Tavern, a warm and inviting inn built in 1834. The original tavern was a two-story brick structure in the settlement of Clayville, about a mile southeast of Pleasant Plains.

John Broadwell, son of wealthy New Jersey native Moses Broadwell, founded Clayville, named for Whig politician Henry Clay, and built the tavern on his farm there. The unusually large and comfortable inn served stagecoach passengers, cattle drovers, teamsters, migrating families, and others, including a circuit-riding lawyer named Abraham Lincoln. The cost of a room and a meal ranged from fifty cents to a dollar. Broadwell later built two more brick buildings and added a brick kiln, a brickyard, a blacksmith shop, and a tannery in Clayville.

The success of the village was short-lived. After the 1860s, as railroads bypassed the stagecoach road, business declined. Eventually, the little community and its cozy tavern were abandoned. Some buildings were razed, while others were destroyed by fire. Only the tavern and a few outbuildings remained intact.

The former Clayville Tavern (a.k.a. Broadwell Tavern) stagecoach stop is now known as the Clayville Historical Site. The building has been partially restored by volunteers.
—Courtesy Schaumburg Township District Library, Illinois Collection

At various times during the twentieth century, the old tavern was used for craft festivals and as a rural-history center before it was closed and sold to a private interest in the 1990s. By the early twenty-first century, the tavern was considered one of the most endangered historic sites in Illinois.

In 2009 the Pleasant Plains Historical Society formed, aiming to buy and restore the Broadwell Tavern and the village site, now called the Clayville Historical Site. Within a year, volunteers had cleared the property of trash and overgrown brush, stabilized the tavern's structure, and upgraded its electrical system. By fall they had opened Clayville to the public, though work remains to be done. The society hosts several events here throughout the year, including a Halloween hayride and haunted house.

Rev. Peter Cartwright

"For as long as I can remember, the name of Peter Cartwright has been a household word in our western country. Bold, honest, earnest and untiring, he has stood on the frontier of advancing civilization to proclaim the truth of God and history." So wrote Gov. Richard B. Oglesby in an 1869 letter to commemorate Cartwright's election as presiding elder of the Methodist Church. Although Cartwright's roots were in the East, he made his mark in central Illinois and his home in Pleasant Plains.

Rev. Peter Cartwright
—Author's collection

Born in Amherst County, Virginia, on September 1, 1785, Cartwright converted to Methodism at age sixteen, began circuit riding in 1803, and was ordained in 1806. Twenty years later, he moved to Pleasant Plains, where he held church services in his home until 1838, when he built a log chapel. Cartwright attracted a large following with his fiery oratory and down-home wit.

In 1828, believing he could serve God and country simultaneously, Cartwright ran for and was elected to the state legislature as a Democrat. During his term, he successfully repealed some of the so-called black codes that restricted the activities of free blacks. He was reelected in 1832, defeating Abraham Lincoln. In his second term he passed laws prohibiting the sale of liquor within one mile of colleges and camp meetings. When the Mormons arrived in Illinois in 1839, Cartwright vigorously preached against their practice of polygamy. In 1846 he ran for U.S. Congress against Lincoln but lost.

Back in Pleasant Plains, Cartwright built a new church, now called the Peter Cartwright United Methodist Church, in 1857. He remained in Pleasant Plains until his death on September 25, 1872. A large marble tombstone marks his grave at Pleasant Plains Cemetery.

The Cartwright Church still stands, and the pulpit from which the reverend delivered his fiery sermons remains intact. The church also contains a small museum with Cartwright family artifacts.

LINCOLN'S NEW SALEM STATE HISTORIC SITE

New Salem (not to be confused with the hamlet just north of Pittsfield) existed for only eleven years—from 1829 to 1840—but its memory lives on as the home of Abraham Lincoln during his formative years, from 1831 to 1837, a time when he grew physically, intellectually, and politically.

James Rutledge and John M. Camron, both skilled craftsmen from the South, founded New Salem in 1828. Settling along the Sangamo (Sangamon) River, they built a dam, sawmill, and gristmill. Soon a store and saloon opened, serving mill workers and attracting further settlers. Within two years, the village had a post office, a ferry, a school, several general stores, and other services. At its peak, New Salem had about twenty-five families and an equal number of buildings.

New Salem had been around only a few years when the young Abraham Lincoln moved there in 1831, taking a job guiding flatboats down the river to New Orleans. He later worked (and slept) in the general store of a friend, Denton Offutt. When the store went out of business, Lincoln turned to politics. He announced his candidacy for the state legislature in a March 15, 1832, letter to the *Sangamo Journal*.

The Black Hawk War that began only two months later interrupted Lincoln's election campaign. He enlisted immediately and served for about eighty days. When his tour of duty ended on July 10, he returned to New Salem to renew his campaign. Though he ran strong in his own precinct, he was largely unknown elsewhere and lost the election. A few months later, he partnered with William F. Berry to open a store. He also served as New Salem's postmaster and performed various odd jobs, including surveying, splitting rails, and harvesting crops. He also began to study law. In 1834 Lincoln again ran for the state house, and this time he won.

It was around this time that Lincoln allegedly fell in love with Ann Rutledge, daughter of New Salem cofounder James Rutledge. Lincoln's supposed romance with the young woman ended when she contracted an illness, probably typhoid fever, and died in 1835 at age twenty-two. It is known that Lincoln and Rutledge knew each other, but historians continue to debate the veracity of the love story.

Although his first term in the General Assembly had been lackluster, Lincoln was reelected in 1836. It was during his second term that he first expressed his public opposition to slavery, voting against resolutions that hindered abolition groups. In the meantime, he had earned his license to practice law. In March 1837 he decided to move permanently to Springfield. Atop his horse and with a few possessions in his saddlebags, he rode out of New Salem, never to return.

Not long after Lincoln left New Salem, so did everyone else in town. As nearby Springfield and Petersburg began to show promise, residents began to move to these larger towns. When Petersburg was named the seat of the newly created Menard County in 1839, the few remaining settlers departed, and within a year New Salem had ceased to exist.

The re-creation of New Salem as a historic site began when the Old Salem Lincoln League was formed in 1917 to restore the old buildings here. New Salem was named a state historic site in 1919; a museum opened in 1921, and thirteen log structures were added in 1933. After a period of inactivity, the New Salem Lincoln League formed in 1981 and resurrected development efforts at the site. Today, New Salem contains a replica of the village and seven hundred acres of recreational grounds.

PETERSBURG

In 1836, three years after real estate speculators Peter Lukins and George Warburton chose this site for a new town, young surveyor Abraham Lincoln surveyed and platted the city of Petersburg. Its name, according to legend, was determined by a drunken card game between the two developers—Lukins won and dubbed the town Petersburg. When it was designated the seat of Menard County in 1839, Petersburg's success was all but assured. Residents of nearby New Salem moved lock, stock, and barrel to the new county seat, abandoning their settlement to the elements (see previous stop).

One particularly fun fact about Petersburg is that it was once the winter home of a traveling circus. In 1880 juggler and equestrian Henry Lamkin, who toured with different circuses in the summer but spent winters in his hometown of Petersburg, constructed a large barn here, where he and fellow performers practiced their acts. A few years later Lamkin's brother-in-law, Edwin Schipp, organized Schipp's Indoor Circus, which presented shows in the barn in the cooler months and toured the Midwest during the summer. Schipp's Circus operated under various names until about 1905. A few years later, brothers Patrick and Dan Kelly, who ran their own circus until the early 1920s, took over the barn. At one time, circus performers made up about 10 percent of Petersburg's population, and many of their descendants live in the area to this day. The barn, however, is gone.

Today Petersburg's economy is tied mainly to government and agriculture, but it also has a lively tourism industry. The city's lovely downtown historic district is dotted with Victorian homes and even a few cobblestone streets. One popular site is the Edgar Lee Masters Memorial Museum, former home of writer Edgar Lee Masters, best known for his *Spoon River Anthology*. Masters lived in Petersburg as a child before moving to Lewistown at age twelve, in 1880 (see under Lewistown in Region 2). After his death in 1950, his body was returned to Petersburg and buried in Oakland Cemetery. Besides Masters, a number of other Illinois notables are buried in this historic cemetery, including Ann Rutledge, Abe Lincoln's purported sweetheart, and other New Salem friends of the future president.

This area's history can be explored further at the Menard County Historical Society Museum, housed in the former Frackelton Bank. This 1889 Victorian-style brick structure faces another historic building, the 1896 Menard County Courthouse. A recently added feature for visitors to Petersburg is a replica trolley car that tours the city and nearby sites of interest.

HAVANA

Visitors to Havana will find what early settlers discovered: an island (Belle Rose Island) at the mouth of the nearby Spoon River that is shaped like Cuba. Local residents called it "Cuba Island," which led settlers to refer to their adjacent village as Havana.

In 1821 Maj. Ossian M. Ross of Seneca, New York, was the first War of 1812 veteran to lay claim to his 160 acres in the Military Tract. The following year, Ross founded Lewistown, naming it for his son (see Lewistown in Region 2). In 1827 he moved to a site near the mouth of Spoon River, where he established a canoe ferry and had the land surveyed for the village that would become Havana. The post office was established as "Ross' Ferry" in 1829, about the same time the first steamboats arrived. Upon Ross's death in 1837, another son, Harvey, tended to his father's business ventures in Havana. Within two years, Harvey had opened the Ross Hotel, which also housed the town's first store and at times served as a courthouse. Havana was incorporated as a town in 1848 and as a city in 1873.

True to its name, Havana was known for its fine cigars. Early in the town's history, some clever businessmen decided to take advantage of the Havana name. For nearly a century, dozens of cigar factories operated in the city, using tobacco from Connecticut. While production had greatly diminished by the mid-1950s, an annual festival still celebrates the city's smoky past.

By the turn of the twentieth century, Havana was a bustling city with hotels, stores, restaurants, and theaters as well as saloons and gambling houses. In fact, gambling and wild entertainment were so rampant in Havana that the city was often called "Little Reno." One of Havana's more prominent guests was Al Capone, who frequented the city in the late 1920s as a retreat from the heat of the law and pressure from rival gangs in Chicago. In 1953 state police raided fourteen Havana gambling establishments and closed them down, virtually ending the city's wild days.

I-55 and US 66
HAMEL–LAKE SPRINGFIELD
68 miles

In the 1930s and 1940s, parts of US Route 66 were realigned on or near what is now I-55. As on IL 4, segments of the original highway are listed on the NRHP. The stretch between Mount Olive and Litchfield was listed in 2001, and the few remaining fragments of the road around Lake Springfield were listed in 2009.

HAMEL
See earlier trip

MOUNT OLIVE

The forty acres that German immigrant John C. Neimann purchased in 1846 would eventually become the nucleus for the city of Mount Olive. Neimann was soon joined by his brothers Fred and Henry, who bought adjoining acreage, and afterward by other German settlers. Around 1852, John Niemann opened a store and post office to serve the fledgling community, then known as Niemann's Settlement.

In 1868 Corbus J. Keiser purchased a half-interest in Neimann's store and, along with his partner Mient Arkebauer, platted Neimann's original forty acres into a town site, which he named Oelburg (roughly translated as Mount of Olives). When the Wabash Railroad arrived in 1870, Oelburg became Drummond Station, which was incorporated as a village in 1874. The name was finally changed to Mount Olive in the 1880s, and it was incorporated as a city in 1901.

It was Keiser who developed the area's first coal mine in 1875. The coal industry brought a new influx of immigrants to the region along with increasing prosperity. But it wasn't long before the miners, rallying against low pay and harsh working conditions, organized into a union. In 1898 the Mount Olive miners joined in the strike in Virden (see Virden on earlier trip), about forty miles north. In the resulting conflict, four miners from Mount Olive were killed.

These miners were originally buried in Mount Olive's town cemetery, but the owner of the land insisted the bodies be exhumed and reburied elsewhere. After the Lutheran cemetery refused to take the remains, the local union purchased a one-acre site at the edge of town in 1899 and established the Union Miners Cemetery, where the four fallen miners were finally laid to rest for good. Later, in 1930, famed labor advocate Mary Harris "Mother" Jones was buried here per her own request. A monument to Mother Jones and to the slain miners of the Battle of Virden was erected here in 1936. The Union Miners Cemetery was listed on the NRHP in 1972.

Also on the NRHP is the Soulsby Service Station, a Route 66 icon listed in 2004. This mom-and-pop gas station was also among the first sites to be inducted into the Route 66 Association of Illinois Hall of Fame in 1990. Henry Soulsby opened the station in 1926, investing most of his life savings in the promise of the new highway. The gamble paid off, and Soulsby's business thrived, operating for the next sixty-seven years. A modest white frame building with a canopied front and cheerful red and yellow trim, the station had two gas pumps and a drive-up ramp for oil changes and minor repairs.

The business continued to operate, if at a slower pace, after I-55 was built in the late 1950s. After Henry Soulsby retired, his children, Russell and Ola, kept it running until 1993. The station remained intact as a Route 66 landmark and was later sold to a neighbor, Michael Dragovich. Beginning in 2003, the Soulsby Station Society worked with Dragovich to restore the station to its pre–World War II appearance. It now serves as a modest museum with limited tours; plans for further improvements are under way.

LITCHFIELD

See earlier trip

DIVERNON

Through numerous economic and transportation developments, Divernon has remained a quaint rural community, its village square comprising buildings old and new. Located seventeen miles south of Springfield, the village functions in part as a suburb of the state capital but retains an identity of its own. Many of Divernon's businesses are still family owned and operated.

The town's name came from an unusual source. Its founder, Henry C. Barnes, was a fan of Sir Walter Scott's historical novel *Rob Roy*, whose heroine was named Diana (Di) Vernon. The village was incorporated in 1897. Two years later, the Illinois Central Railroad arrived and Madison Coal Mine #6 opened, giving Divernon an instant economy. In 1925 the coal mine closed, and by the early 1960s ICRR passenger and freight service had ended, but Divernon continued to survive as a stop on US Route 66, which expanded Divernon's access to Springfield and other cities, keeping the community stable. Although trains no longer stop at Divernon, the tracks are still there and the original Illinois Central Railroad depot, restored in 1999, still exists as a museum.

LAKE SPRINGFIELD

In 1931, as the Great Depression tightened its grip on America, the city of Springfield was outgrowing its water supply, which came largely from the Sangamon River. With funding from the federal government's Civilian Conservation Corps (CCC), construction began on a 4,260-acre reservoir to be called Lake Springfield. Workers stationed at nearby CCC camps cleared the land and set to work building the Spaulding Dam across Sugar Creek. The dam was named after the project's main booster, Willis J. Spaulding, commissioner of Springfield's utility company, City Water, Light & Power. In addition to the dam, workers built roads and bridges; water, sewer, and power lines; a public beach and recreational facilities; a new electrical power station; and a water-filtration plant. The jobs created by the Lake Springfield project helped the community survive the Great Depression.

In December of 1933, the reservoir was ready to be filled. It was estimated that this process would take about seven months, but due to a drought it took eighteen months for water from Sugar and Lick Creeks to slowly seep into the lake. In the meantime, residents began to doubt the wisdom of undertaking the $2.5 million project, and critics dubbed it "Spaulding's Folly." The lake did fill up, however, topping the spillway in May 1935. Lake Springfield was now ready to provide not only city water but also recreation for the community. Many historians credit Willis Spaulding with saving Springfield.

Civilian Conservation Corps workers bolster the shoreline during the construction of Lake Springfield in the 1930s. —Courtesy City Water, Light & Power

Today, the shores of Lake Springfield are dotted with public parks and recreational facilities. One of the most interesting spots is the one-hundred-acre Lincoln Memorial Garden, designed in 1936 by noted landscape architect Jens Jensen as a living memorial to the sixteenth president. The woodland and prairie nature preserve features native plants of Kentucky, Indiana, and Illinois—the states where Lincoln lived—and numerous wooden benches inscribed with quotes from Honest Abe. The garden was added to the NRHP in 1992. Nearby is the Henson Robinson Zoo, which opened in 1970. The zoo features more than ninety species from all over the globe, housed in a naturalistic setting.

IL 54
SPRINGFIELD–CLINTON
49 miles

IL 54 traces the route of the Gilman, Clinton & Springfield Railroad line, later acquired by the Illinois Central Railroad. This trip takes travelers over part of that route, stopping in Mount Pulaski, where visitors will find one of only two surviving courthouses on the Eighth Judicial Circuit, the old legal beat of Abraham Lincoln.

SPRINGFIELD
See earlier trip

MOUNT PULASKI

In 1836 Springfield businessman Jabez Capps, having heard about a beautiful high hill amid rolling countryside twenty-three miles northeast of Springfield, visited the place and decided it was an ideal site for a town. Capps joined with several other businessmen to purchase 480 acres at the site, including the mound, and laid out a new settlement, which they named in honor of Revolutionary War hero Casimir Pulaski. Later that year, the word *Mount* was added to the name.

The village blossomed around a public square, part of which was occupied by Capps's general store and cabin. Within a decade, Mount Pulaski's population had surpassed that of Camden (Postville), then the Logan County seat. In 1848 the seat was moved to Mount Pulaski and a two-story brick, Greek Revival courthouse was built (see below). Only seven years later, however, the seat was moved to Lincoln (see Lincoln on next trip) and the railroad opted to run its tracks through the new seat rather than Mount Pulaski, hindering the latter town's further development. The Peoria, Lincoln & Decatur Railroad finally built through Mount Pulaski in 1871, helping it to grow again. It was reorganized as a city in 1893.

Prohibition brought Mount Pulaski an unexpected revival as thirteen speakeasies sprang up in the city. Thirsty customers arrived daily by rail, and as the train neared Mount Pulaski, conductors called out, "Next stop, Vinegar Hill." The nickname, code for a "wet" town, came from the Prohibition practice of secretly refilling empty pickle and vinegar barrels with liquor or beer.

Three downtown buildings are listed on the NRHP—the 1847 Mount Pulaski Courthouse; the 1860 Theodore H. O. Mattfeldt House (a.k.a. St. Pierre House), a private home; and the 1917 Robert Buckles Barn, one of eighteen round barns in Illinois listed on the NRHP. Of these, the most historically significant is the courthouse, a State Historic Site.

Mount Pulaski Courthouse State Historic Site

For the seven years that Mount Pulaski was the seat of Logan County, the Mount Pulaski Courthouse served county residents as part of the Eighth Judicial Circuit, the district in which attorney Abraham Lincoln served. The courtroom was on the second floor, while the offices of the circuit clerk, county clerk, school commissioner, sheriff, surveyor, and treasurer comprised the first floor. The historic courtroom as Lincoln knew it is preserved and furnished as a museum.

Two years after the county seat was relocated to the city of Lincoln in 1855, the Mount Pulaski Courthouse was turned over to a group of three trustees, who transferred it to the Board of Education for use as a school in 1859. During this period, the stairway in the main entrance was changed, ground-level windows were installed, and a cupola was added on the top.

When Mount Pulaski's students moved to a new, larger school building in 1878, the courthouse was recycled again. The basement was converted into a jail, city offices were established on the first floor, and the second floor became a public meeting room.

Eleven years later, the first floor was revamped to accommodate a post office, while the second floor served as a civic center and library.

In 1936 the town of Mount Pulaski deeded the old courthouse to the state of Illinois, which restored the building to reflect the period in which Lincoln practiced law. It is one of only two surviving courthouses of the original fifteen on the Eighth Judicial Circuit. The other is in Metamora (see under Metamora on later trip).

CLINTON

In the mid-1830s, land speculators James Allen and Jessie Fell, encouraged by talk of a north-south railroad connecting Cairo with the western terminus of the proposed Illinois & Michigan Canal, purchased land in central Illinois along the projected route, laid out a town, and sold lots, hoping to make a quick profit. Only a handful of families resided in Clinton when it was named the DeWitt County seat in 1839, with no guarantees that the railroad would come. In the county court's first year, Stephen A. Douglas and Abraham Lincoln jointly defended the accused in the county's first murder trial, which they won.

The Illinois Central Railroad (ICRR) finally arrived in Clinton in 1854. Soon afterward, two competing east-west railroads built repair shops here, and the ICRR moved its division headquarters to Clinton. By 1920 six passenger trains a day passed through the city, and more than 100,000 cars per month moved through the freight yards. Nearly 25 percent of Clinton's population worked for the railroad. But the 1929 Great Depression began a downward spiral from which the city never recovered. By 1955 all of Clinton's railroad facilities had closed, and the town turned to agriculture to sustain itself.

Clinton remains a proud city. Among its noteworthy buildings is the Prairie School–style Vespasian Warner Library. In 1906 five-term Congressman Warner donated the 8,000-volume private library of his father-in-law, attorney Clifton H. Moore, to his hometown of Clinton and funded the construction of a two-story brick building to house the collection. Moore's homestead, another Clinton landmark, became the DeWitt County Historical Museum in 1967. The home, built in 1867 and expanded in 1887, was added to the NRHP in 1979.

Just east of the city is the 9,300-acre Clinton Lake State Recreation Area. This reservoir, created by damming Salt Creek in the 1970s, was built not only for recreation but also for cooling the Clinton Nuclear Generating Station, which began operations in 1987.

Between the city of Clinton and the lake, a little to the south, is Weldon Springs State Park, which has an interesting history of its own. In 1901 Judge Lawrence Weldon of Clinton leased his forty-acre estate to establish a Chautauqua, a program designed to provide educational, cultural, and entertainment opportunities for rural residents. The Chautauqua group created Weldon Springs Lake, with boathouses and docks, and numerous other facilities on the property, including a 5,000-seat amphitheater. Among the notables who appeared at the Weldon Springs Chautauqua were William Jennings Bryan, Carrie Nation, Pres. William Howard Taft, Helen Keller, and Rev. Billy Sunday. After the Chautauqua program ended in the early 1920s, the Weldon family donated the property to the city of Clinton. The state of Illinois took ownership in 1948 and developed what is now the 550-acre Weldon Springs State Park.

I-55
SPRINGFIELD–BLOOMINGTON-NORMAL
72 miles

For the most part, I-55 runs parallel to old US Route 66 from Springfield to Bloomington, and motorists on the interstate can still get a feel for the surroundings that earlier
travelers passed through on the Mother Road. Remaining landmarks include The Mill
restaurant in Lincoln and the Palms Grill and Atlanta Museum in Atlanta. This trip is not
all about Route 66, however. The towns along this stretch of the interstate boast many
historic sites, including the Postville Courthouse State Historic Site (Lincoln) and the
Funks Grove Pure Maple Sirup store (Funk's Grove).

SPRINGFIELD

See earlier trip

WILLIAMSVILLE

Williamsville was originally platted in 1853 as Benton, named for U.S. Senator Thomas
Hart Benton of Missouri, but a year later the town changed the name of its post office
to honor Col. John Williams of Springfield. Benton was incorporated as the village of
Williamsville in 1865.

Benton's first railroad depot was built in 1854, and by 1855 the village had about
twenty houses, several stores, a post office, and a school. Over subsequent decades the rail
station served various rail lines until it burned down in 1900. Rebuilt a few years later,
the new depot continued to serve passengers and freight into the 1970s.

Although trains don't stop in Williamsville anymore, remnants of the village's railroad days continue to play a role in the local economy. After rail service ended in 1977,
the village purchased the depot and rented it out for social events. Later the building
was used as a senior center, and in 2006 it became the Williamsville Public Library. Next
door, two converted boxcars from the Gulf, Mobile & Ohio Railway house the Williamsville Historical Museum.

The original US Route 66 passed through Williamsville from 1926 to 1940. Keeping the Mother Road's legacy alive is the Old Station museum, a converted 1930s gas
station that displays Route 66 memorabilia. Until recently, Williamsville also boasted the
Route 66 Dream Car Museum, but it closed in 2010.

ELKHART

Around 1819 James and Richard Latham built a double cabin along the old trail that
connected Cahokia to Fort Clark (Peoria), later known as the Edwards Trace. A major
landmark on the trace was Elkhart Hill, a glacial ridge that juts up prominently from
the surrounding prairie. The hill served as a lookout for Indians and as a guidepost for
westbound pioneers. Around 1830 the Lathams added a four-horse mill and built Kentucky House, a stagecoach stop about one mile south of their cabin on the Edwards
Trace. Today the Under the Prairie Museum stands at the site of the Kentucky House
tavern. The museum holds one of the largest collections of archaeological and frontier
artifacts in the Midwest.

In 1850 John Shockey, a Pennsylvania cattleman, purchased 5,000 acres near the Latham property and moved there with his family. He bought the Latham brothers' farm in 1853, the same year the Chicago & Alton Railroad arrived. Two years later, he and his wife, Catherine, platted part of their land as the village of Elkhart City.

Elkhart City's development was stagnant until livestock mogul John Dean Gillett arrived. Gillett, known in the Chicago stockyards as the "Cattle King," purchased part of the Shockey property to start a ranch, where he selectively bred Durham cattle from Scotland. With his move to Elkhart, Gillett made the town the largest shipping point on the Chicago & Alton Railroad, transporting over 1,500 head of cattle and about the same number of hogs to Chicago and beyond. Today the Gillett Memorial Bridge honors the man who put Elkhart on the map.

Elkhart was officially called Elkhart City until 1979, when the word "city" was dropped. Famous residents, besides Gillett, include three-term Illinois governor Richard J. Oglesby and world wing-shot champion Adam H. Bogardus. In 1891 Governor Oglesby and his second wife, Emma, daughter of city founder John Dean Gillett, built a forty-six-room mansion known as Oglehurst on the original Latham cabin site in Elkhart. They used the cabin's still-standing chimney and fireplace as the nucleus of their home. Oglehurst burned down in 1891, but the Oglesbys built a new home nearby, where the governor and his wife lived until their deaths in 1899 and 1928, respectively. Both are interred at Elkhart Cemetery. The second Oglehurst eventually fell into disrepair, and in November 1984 it was burned to the ground by the Elkhart Fire Department as a practice exercise.

Not well known outside of the trap-shooting world, Bogardus made indelible marks on the sport. An excellent marksman, Bogardus won a trap-shooting contest in 1868 against Hough Stanton, considered the best shot in the world. By 1871 he had become the wing-shot champion and was performing exhibitions all over the country. When the clay pigeon was introduced in 1880, Bogardus was instrumental in popularizing it, saving an untold number of live birds. For a short time in the early 1880s, he performed with Buffalo Bill Cody's Wild West Show. He retired from show business in 1891 and returned to Elkhart to spend his final years. He died in 1913 and is buried in Elkhart Cemetery.

LINCOLN

Few if any public officials have had a town named for them before they were elected to office, but Abraham Lincoln was the exception. The city was conceived by three Springfield developers—Robert B. Latham, Virgil Hickox, and John Dean Gillett, the cattle baron who helped develop Elkhart (see previous stop). The partners chose the site of a proposed Chicago & Alton Railroad depot in Logan County, near the former county seat of Postville, and met at the Lincoln-Herndon law office to discuss possible names for the community. Latham suggested it be named after Lincoln because of the lawyer's longstanding association with the county. Lincoln responded: "You'd better not do that, for I never knew anything named Lincoln that amounted to much." Nevertheless, the name was adopted.

The lanky lawyer was in attendance when lots for his namesake city were placed on sale in August 1853. Near the town square, he purchased two watermelons from a street vendor, broke them open for the juices to run free, and invited the three founders to join him in "christening" the new community.

In 1855 Lincoln was incorporated as the Logan County seat, moved from Mount Pulaski (see Mount Pulaski on previous trip). By then the old Postville courthouse, which served Logan County from 1840 to 1848, had been sold and converted into a store, so a new courthouse was built. Ten years later, Postville was absorbed into the city of Lincoln.

Lincoln preserves the heritage of the old county seat with the Postville Courthouse State Historic Site, a replica of the original 1840 courthouse. As a circuit-riding lawyer, Abraham Lincoln made frequent appearances at the courthouse in Postville. When the county seat was moved to Mount Pulaski in 1848, the courthouse was sold, and it was used for various purposes over the years. In 1929 the building was purchased by automobile mogul Henry Ford, who dismantled it and rebuilt it in Dearborn, Michigan, as a museum.

In the early 1950s, Lincoln residents received funding from the state of Illinois to build a replica of the Postville Courthouse. The building was reconstructed from the original plans as a State Historic Site in 1953. The first floor is a reception area and gallery, and the second floor is furnished to resemble a mid–1800s courtroom.

The present Logan County Courthouse, built in 1905 to replace an earlier structure, is part of a National Register historic district, so designated in 1985. The courthouse contains a statue of Abraham Lincoln, and his portrait can be seen beneath the rotunda's dome, reflecting the city's pride in its connection to the sixteenth president. Numerous artifacts from Abraham Lincoln's life and times are housed in the Lincoln College Museum. Nearby is a bronze statue of Lincoln as a young man.

In addition to Lincoln's association with its namesake, the city also has remnants of old US Route 66, which went right through the city's downtown from the 1920s to the 1960s. Among the old landmarks from the Mother Road are the pillar supports over Salt Creek and The Mill restaurant, currently undergoing restoration.

ATLANTA

The first settlement in the future Atlanta area was called New Castle, platted in 1836. Here early settlers built several stores, a church, a blacksmith shop, and a smattering of homes. In May 1853, anticipating the arrival of the railroad, three developers bought land about a mile northwest of New Castle and platted their own town, dubbed Xenia. Also wanting to be by the railroad, most of the residents of New Castle moved their homes and businesses to Xenia.

The Chicago & Alton Railroad arrived in 1855, and the town was incorporated the same year with a new name—Atlanta. In 1856 the *Logan County Forum* reported that Atlanta had a population of about 1,500, with fifty-six businesses, twelve professionals, and four ministers. A year later, the *Springfield Register* commented that "the growth of Atlanta is without a parallel in the county."

In spite of its early promise, Atlanta did not fare well in the long run. New building ceased during the economic panic of 1857, and many families moved away. A series of fires over the next ten years contributed further to Atlanta's decline. In 1872 the Illinois Midland Railroad, an east-west line, crossed the north-south Chicago & Alton Railroad at Atlanta, enabling shipping in four directions, but it wasn't enough to revitalize the town. Even coal mining was unable to stimulate significant growth. Atlanta's population today remains nearly the same as it was in 1856.

In the mid-twentieth century, Atlanta was one of the cities along the legendary US Route 66. A few decades after the highway was rerouted, the nation began to show a nostalgic interest in the old Mother Road, and towns both thriving and dying saw tourism potential in resurrecting some of its landmarks. In Atlanta, the 1867 Downey Building, originally a bank, housed a popular Route 66 cafe called the Palms Grill from the 1930s through the 1960s. The building was added to the NRHP in 2004, and the Palms Grill reopened in 2009 as the Palms Grill and Atlanta Museum.

Atlanta's newly created Route 66 Park and Tourism Center features a piece of classic roadside Americana: a nineteen-foot-tall statue of Paul Bunyan holding a hot dog. The statue, affectionately called "Tall Paul," was one of the many Paul Bunyan figures produced by a California fiberglass company in the 1960s. Most were designed as a giant "Muffler Man" for a service-station chain, with the lumberjack holding a muffler instead of an ax. This one, however, was altered to hold a hot dog rather than a muffler for Bunyon's hot dog stand in Cicero, Illinois, in 1965. After the restaurant closed in 2003, the owners donated their Hot Dog Man—which had stood in front of Bunyon's for nearly forty years—to the town of Atlanta.

Downtown Atlanta also offers a number of historic buildings that predate Route 66, including the octagonal 1908 Atlanta Public Library and Clock Tower and the sixty-foot-tall, 1904 J. H. Hawes Grain Elevator; both buildings are listed on the NRHP and are now museums. In addition, many of the old murals that graced Atlanta's downtown buildings have recently been restored by the Letterheads, a national group of historic-minded sign painters.

FUNKS GROVE

Before Funks Grove became famous for its maple syrup, it was the center of an agriculture empire. When Kentucky native Isaac Funk arrived in central Illinois in 1824, he had little education and was $2,000 in debt. Eventually, however, Funk's reputation for fair dealing helped make him one of the leading cattlemen in central Illinois.

Upon his arrival here, Isaac Funk, along with his brother Absalom and a friend named William Brock, built a twelve-by-fourteen-foot log cabin, which sheltered eighteen people during the settlers' first winter. Over the next few years, Isaac and his family experimented with crops and raised pedigreed Polled Angus cattle, Shropshire sheep, and Chester-White hogs. Before the arrival of the railroad in the 1850s, Funk drove his livestock along dirt trails to Chicago, 140 miles away. By the time of his death at age sixty-seven, Isaac Funk had amassed an estate of $2 million and more than 25,000 acres of land.

Although he lacked formal schooling, Funk helped found Illinois Wesleyan University in nearby Bloomington in 1850. He also served alongside Abraham Lincoln as a state representative from 1840 to 1842, and he later became a state senator, serving from 1862 until his death in 1865. Several of Isaac's nine sons were elected to public office as well. Benjamin Franklin Funk served as mayor of Bloomington (1871–76 and 1884–86) and as a representative in U.S. Congress (1893–95), among other things. Lafayette Funk, one of the founders of Chicago's Union Stock Yard, was also a state legislator, as were his brothers George, Frank, and Elijah. Many of Isaac's other children and descendants also became prominent citizens.

Modern visitors to Funks Grove are often unaware of the extent of the Funk family's impact on world agriculture. The Funk Brothers Seed Co., founded by Lafayette Funk's son Eugene in 1901, became internationally recognized for developing the first commercially viable hybrid corn seed. In conjunction with the U.S. Department of Agriculture, the company cultivated high-yield corn that resisted disease, insects, and cold weather. Funk Brothers was bought out by the Ciba-Geigy Corporation in 1974.

In addition to livestock and corn, Funks Grove became known for another agricultural product—maple syrup. When Isaac Funk bought his homestead, it contained an extensive grove of sugar maple trees, which the family tapped to make maple syrup for their own use. In 1891 Isaac's grandson, Arthur, began producing maple syrup commercially. In the 1940s the grove of maple trees was placed in trust to preserve the business for future generations, and the Funk family has continued to produce Funks Grove Pure Maple Sirup to this day. The trust documents contained the stipulation that the word *sirup* in Funks Grove Pure Maple Sirup would always be spelled with the letter *i* to distinguish it from sugar syrup.

When US Route 66 passed through the Funk property in 1926, the motoring public discovered Funks Grove Pure Maple Sirup. Today's travelers can still buy maple syrup at Funks Grove, but there's also much more. Among its attractions are the Sugar Grove Nature Center, which opened in 2004; the Funk Prairie Home and Gem Museum; and the still-standing Funks Grove Church, built by the Funk family in 1865. Adjacent to the old church is the "Chapel of the Templed Trees," a wooded sanctuary that has become a popular spot for outdoor weddings. The grove itself was designated a National Natural Landmark in 1974.

BLOOMINGTON-NORMAL

Amid the rich farmland of central Illinois lay the twin cities of Bloomington and Normal. The first to develop was Bloomington, originally called Keg Grove after a group of Indians (probably Kickapoo) discovered a trapper's stockpile of liquor here. The first settlement, established in the 1820s, was named Blooming Grove as a reflection of the area's fertility and natural beauty. When McLean County was created in 1830, a Blooming Grove landowner donated 22.5 acres at the north end of the settlement for a county seat, and the name was changed to the more substantial-sounding Bloomington. Proceeds from lot sales funded the construction of its first courthouse.

The original McLean County courthouse was built in 1832, but it was replaced just four years later with a sturdier structure that housed the county courts and offices until 1868, when a third courthouse was erected. Yet another new building was constructed in 1900, but it burned down the same year. Immediately rebuilt at the same site, the still-standing fifth courthouse was dedicated in 1904 and served McLean County until 1976. Today the county's business is handled at the McLean County Law and Justice Center, while the "Old Courthouse" is now the McLean County Museum of History. The latter building was listed on the NRHP in 1973, and the neighborhood surrounding it is one of several National Historic Districts in Bloomington-Normal.

As the county seat, Bloomington progressed steadily in its first two decades. It got an extra boost in 1853 with the arrival of two railroads—the Illinois Central and the Alton & Sangamon Railroad (later the Chicago & Alton Railroad). Additional railroads followed and the city grew, becoming known as a railroad town.

In 1854 an adjacent community was established as North Bloomington, often called "the Junction" because of its intersecting railroads. Jesse Fell, North Bloomington's main developer, placed restrictions on the lots he sold, such as requiring that the new owners maintain the trees he had planted and prohibiting the sale of alcohol on the properties.

Even in the early stages of the twin cities' development, local leaders sought to bring higher education to the area. Illinois Wesleyan University, the first liberal-arts college in the state, was founded in Bloomington in 1850. Much of the school's early financial support came from the United Methodist Church, so "Wesleyan," for Methodism founder John Wesley, was added to its name. Old North Hall, the school's first building, was completed in 1856.

In 1857, when the state of Illinois sought to establish its first normal school, or teachers' college, Jesse Fell successfully lobbied for the institution to be located in North Bloomington. Illinois State Normal University held its first classes in Bloomington until Old Main, the first building on the North Bloomington campus, was completed in 1861. In 1865 North Bloomington officially changed its name to Normal in honor of the college, today's Illinois State University.

Besides the colleges, Bloomington-Normal boasted a variety of industries including nurseries, canneries, and manufacturers. A fire in 1890 destroyed several of downtown Normal's businesses, and ten years later, another fire destroyed much of that city's downtown—including the just-completed new courthouse. In both cases, however, the cities quickly rebuilt. The twentieth century brought new industries to the area, including State Farm Insurance, founded in Bloomington in 1922. With two universities, numerous factories, flourishing farms, and good transportation, the twin cities thrived even through the Great Depression.

In the 1930s the twin cities saw the creation of two culinary phenomena. The first came in 1934, when Gus and Edith Belt added a dining room to their Shell's Chicken business in Normal. Looking for a way to distinguish themselves from competitors, the Belts created the "steakburger," a burger made from ground steak cuts, along with a hand-dipped, real dairy milkshake, and the Steak 'n Shake restaurant was born. The enterprise expanded into franchises, and today, more than four hundred Steak 'n Shake restaurants operate in eighteen states.

Not long after that, in 1937, Bloomington entrepreneurs Edward and Arlo Shirk created a glazed peanut they called "Redskins," later marketed as Shirk's Glazed Peanuts. The snack became popular in taverns and bars, so in the 1950s the product's name was changed to Beer Nuts. The Beer Nuts plant still operates in Bloomington.

With all they had to offer, Bloomington and Normal flourished even through the Great Depression, and growth in the area has continued almost nonstop up to the present time. Evidence of the twin cities' colorful past can be seen in the abundant historic structures and museums of the metro area. Bloomington in particular has an interesting record as a spawning ground for American political development.

Political Hotbed

After the 1854 passage of the Kansas-Nebraska Act, allowing slavery in some of the western territories, a number of the law's opponents in Illinois united under the newly created Republican Party. The first meeting of Illinois Republicans, on September 13, 1854, was sparsely attended, but two years later, the party held a fully representative state convention.

The 1856 Republican State Convention, called the Anti-Nebraska State Convention, was held in Majors Hall in Bloomington. The gathering officially established the Republican Party in Illinois. At this meeting, Abraham Lincoln gained greater prominence thanks to the eloquence of his speech, which his law partner, William H. Herndon, later called "the grand effort of his life." Although the main content of this speech was repeated a few months later in Peoria, during an early debate with Stephen A. Douglas, there is no written record of his exact words from the Bloomington convention, thus it is remembered as Lincoln's "lost speech."

Bloomington was not only the birthplace of the Republican Party in Illinois, but it was also the hometown of a vice president (Adlai Stevenson I), a U.S. Supreme Court justice (David Davis), a governor (Adlai Stevenson II), and several U.S. legislators. While the Stevenson family produced one of the most prominent political dynasties in the nation's history, less well known is Judge David Davis, whose impact on the development of Bloomington, the Republican Party, and Abraham Lincoln's political career was monumental.

Davis arrived in Bloomington in 1835, at the age of twenty-one, to practice law. Five years later, he ran unsuccessfully for state senator, but he was elected a state representative in 1844. From 1848 to 1862, he presided over the courts of the Eighth Judicial Circuit, the stomping grounds of Abe Lincoln, with whom he became good friends. Davis was Lincoln's campaign manager during the 1860 presidential election, and in 1862 President Lincoln appointed him an Associate Justice of the U.S. Supreme Court. He remained on the court until 1877, when he was elected as an Independent to the U.S. Senate. After serving one term, Davis retired and returned to Bloomington. He died in 1886, at age seventy-one, and was buried in Bloomington's Evergreen Cemetery.

Judge Davis's 1870s home, Clover Lawn, became a state museum in 1960. The three-story, thirty-six-room mansion was named a National Historic Landmark in 1975. The grounds include a formal garden and the original wooden carriage house, barn, and stable.

Born in Kentucky, the first Adlai Ewing Stevenson moved to Bloomington with his parents in 1852. He enrolled at Illinois Wesleyan University in 1854 and later attended Centre College in Danville, Kentucky. After being admitted to the Illinois bar in 1858, he opened a law office in Metamora. In 1868 he was elected district attorney for the region and returned to Bloomington.

A Democrat, Stevenson made several runs for congressional office, winning elections in 1874 and 1878. In 1892 he headed the Illinois delegation at the Democratic National Convention in Chicago, where he was named Grover Cleveland's running mate. Cleveland won, and Stevenson served as U.S. Vice President from 1893 to 1897. In 1900 he became the running mate of William Jennings Bryan, who lost to William McKinley. Eight years later, Stevenson made an unsuccessful bid for Illinois governor.

Bloomington resident Adlai E. Stevenson I served as vice president under Grover Cleveland from 1893 to 1897. This portrait appeared in Harper's Weekly, *July 2, 1892.* — Author's collection

Stevenson died in Bloomington in 1914, but his political legacy was carried on by his grandson, Adlai E. Stevenson II, born in 1900. The younger Stevenson served one term as governor of Illinois (1949–53), and he ran for president twice, in 1952 and 1956, both times losing to Republican Dwight D. Eisenhower. He was later appointed U.S. Ambassador to the United Nations by John F. Kennedy. Stevenson died of heart failure in 1965. His eldest son, Adlai III, born in 1930, served one term each as state representative and state treasurer, and ten years as a U.S. senator.

I-155, IL 122, and IL 29
LINCOLN–CREVE COEUR VIA DELAVAN
52 miles

The junction of I-55 and I-155 lies just northwest of the city of Lincoln. From there we will make our way north and west to the small city of Delavan, then continue west to pick up IL 29, which leads north to Pekin and Creve Coeur, both in the Peoria metropolitan area. Alternatively, travelers may stay on the interstate all the way to Creve Coeur.

LINCOLN
See previous trip

DELAVAN

Recognizing the Peoria area's potential as a trading center, James A. Gale of Providence, Rhode Island, and fellow New Englander Edward Cornelius Delavan, a retired merchant and land promoter, established a settlement in 1836. The plat for the town, named Delavan for its cofounder, was recorded in 1841.

Delavan residents welcomed the Petersburg & Tonica Railroad in 1857 and the Pekin, Lincoln & Decatur Railroad in 1870. With this boost, Delavan grew, incorporating as a city in 1888.

Over the years, Delavan has preserved much of the historical architecture downtown and throughout its neighborhoods. Several homes were known to have served as havens on the Underground Railroad from Alton to Chicago.

Throughout its history, Delavan has supported and been supported by agriculture. The community's fertile environs have attracted farmers since its founding. In the late 1800s, one of these local farmers, James L. Reid, developed a high-production seed corn that revolutionized the crop.

James L. Reid's Corn

James Reid was only nine years old when he learned how to work a farm, taking over the family's corn crops after his father, Robert, fell ill in 1853. The Reid family had moved to the Delavan area from Ohio in 1846. Their first two crops, grown from the Gordon Hopkins variety of seeds they had brought from Ohio, were disappointing. Robert Reid began to plant the local Little Yellow corn alongside the Gordon Hopkins, and the cross-pollination resulted in a new, high-yield variety that he dubbed Yellow Dent corn.

James Reid continued to grow his father's Yellow Dent and committed himself to further developing the seed. In 1893, after years of experimentation and careful selection, he entered a sample of his Yellow Dent corn at the World's Columbian Exposition in Chicago, where it received the gold medal. Afterward, the demand for the seed was nearly overwhelming.

James Reid's Yellow Dent remains one of the most popular corn varieties in the country, and it has been the source of many modern hybrids. Even though his contribution to corn growing may be compared to Henry Ford's impact on the automobile industry, Reid likely earned no more than a few thousand dollars from his seed during his lifetime. A plaque affixed to a boulder outside Delavan, dedicated in 1955, commemorates his achievement. The marker is located about two miles northeast of Delavan on Dillon Road.

PEKIN

When Jonathan Tharp built the first cabin here in 1824, a large Potawatomi village still stood along a ridge near today's Pekin Lake. About five years later, the county surveyor platted parcels for a yet-unnamed town. Most of the lots were sold in 1830 to Maj. Nathan Cromwell and three other men. Mrs. Cromwell, joking that the settlement was on the opposite side of the world from Peking (today called Beijing), China, suggested the name Pekin.

The seat of Tazewell County was moved to Pekin from Mackinaw, about seventeen miles east, in 1831, but it was moved again, this time to nearby Tremont, only a few years later. The honor would eventually be reinstated, and in the meantime, Pekin grew into a stable community with a number of businesses. Its future, however, was far from assured. The Black Hawk War of 1832 posed a threat to the fledgling village, and residents converted the one-room schoolhouse, built in 1831, into Fort Doolittle. The fort never came under siege and the war did little damage in the town, but a cholera epidemic in 1833 infected many residents and nearly ended Pekin's existence. Ten years later, an epidemic of strep throat and scarlet fever swept through the village, during which 60 percent of the population became ill and fifty-two people died over a four-month period. Nevertheless, Pekin held on.

By the time it was reinstated as the Tazewell County seat in 1849, Pekin's population had swelled to 1,500, and it was incorporated as a city the same year. The first rail line to arrive in Pekin was the Peoria, Pekin & Jacksonville Railroad in 1865. Within a few years, several other railroads converged here, and additional lines were built into the early twentieth century, bringing further growth to the city.

The first courthouse in Pekin, built in 1849, was torn down in 1914 and replaced with the current structure, which was listed on the NRHP in 1985. Other local buildings on the NRHP include the 1906 Pekin Federal Building, a.k.a. the Old Post Office; the 1912 Carl Herget Mansion, now a bed-and-breakfast; and the 1894 Chicago & Alton Railroad depot, currently undergoing renovation.

A bronze plaque in downtown Pekin commemorates one of the most significant episodes in the city's history—the founding of the Union League of America in 1862. During the Civil War, the South found support through the Knights of the Golden Circle and other Klan groups; the North countered with the Union League of America (ULA). The first ULA council was established in Pekin on June 25, 1862. The oath of membership outlined five directives, among which were to "support, maintain, protect, and defend" the Union and to help elect Union loyalists to local, state, and national offices. The group also worked to provide aid to Union soldiers and to promote equality for black citizens. Oaths were taken on the Bible, the Declaration of Independence, and the U.S. Constitution.

The league soon branched to other counties, and its first statewide council was held in Bloomington three months later. Membership at the time was between 3,000 and 5,000; within a few months, that figure had mushroomed to 50,000. A National Grand Council was established in Cleveland, Ohio, on May 20, 1863, and soon ULA membership peaked at more than two million. The league continued its support of the Union for the duration of the war, recruiting and training nurses and raising funds for sick and wounded soldiers. After the war, the ULA ceased its political activities but continued its charitable and patriotic ones, spearheading such projects as the Metropolitan Museum and Grant's Tomb in New York, the Art Institute of Chicago, and numerous other large and small civic ventures. The ULA still exists as a charitable foundation.

CREVE COEUR

It was not until 1921 that this farming community along IL 29, a few miles north of Pekin, became an incorporated village. Within a decade or so, the little family farms in the area began to be subdivided and developed into residential neighborhoods, and by the mid-twentieth century, the village had become a suburb of Peoria, across the Illinois River to the west.

Creve Coeur is primarily known for its namesake, a precolonial French fort built in the late seventeenth century. Today the fort site is part of Fort Crevecoeur State Park, an eighty-six-acre state park along the river on the west side of town. Its main feature is a replica of the post and a visitor center, surrounded by campgrounds and recreational areas. While actual location of the fort is still debated among historians, the approximate site is marked with a stone monument.

Fort Crevecoeur, the first white settlement in this area, was built in January 1680 by French explorers René-Robert Cavalier, Sieur de La Salle, and Henri de Tonti. They established the post to bolster France's presence in the fur trade and strengthen its claim on the newly explored territory. Fort Crevecoeur had a twenty-five-foot-high stockade and deep ravines on three sides imbedded with iron-spiked timbers; the fourth side opened to the river. Inside were two barracks, a cabin, a forge, and a couple of tents.

Less than four months after the post was built, while La Salle and de Tonti were away, five members of the garrison mutinied, destroying the fort and pillaging its contents. The Frenchmen moved their base to Fort St. Louis at Starved Rock (see Starved Rock State Park in Region 4).

French explorer René-Robert Cavalier, Sieur de La Salle
—Courtesy Schaumburg Township District Library, Illinois Collection

IL 116, IL 117, and US 24
CREVE COEUR—I-39/US 51 VIA METAMORA
41 miles

This trip heads north and east from the Peoria metro area to I-39/US 51 at El Paso. Historical stops on this route include sites related to two familiar Republican presidents—Abraham Lincoln (Metamora Courthouse) and Ronald Reagan (Eureka College).

CREVE COEUR
See previous trip

EAST PEORIA

While East Peoria's name makes it sound like little more than a suburban extension of the city across the Illinois River, this community of more than 23,000 residents has a significant history of its own.

East Peoria began as Bluetown, a riverside village founded in the 1860s. Bluetown grew out of a farming settlement established in the early 1830s by a group of War of 1812 veterans from Vermont. A few years later, a family of immigrants from Alsace-Lorraine in France, the David Schertz clan, settled here to farm. In 1840 Schertz built a three-and-a-half-story structure that served as a combination inn and corn mill. Over the next twenty-four years, the settlement grew and became more structured, organizing as the village of Bluetown in 1864. While the reasons for choosing that name are uncertain, the most widely accepted explanation is that the appellation refers to the blue smocks worn by the settlers from Alsace-Lorraine.

In the meantime, the city of Peoria was growing. In the 1860s, Peoria businessman Capt. Almiron S. Cole acquired some land across the river and built a toll bridge that connected the two sides. On the east side, between Bluetown and a village called Fondulac, the captain founded a settlement he named Coleville. In 1884 the three communities merged and incorporated as the village of Hilton. Five years later, the name was changed to East Peoria, which was finally incorporated as a city in 1919.

While East Peoria started as an agricultural community, it soon became an industrial town after coal was discovered nearby and railroads began building through the region. From the late 1890s to the late 1930s, more than ten coal mines operated at different times, and local industry grew in tandem. In 1899 Frederick R. Carter established the Peoria Brick & Tile Company, which continued through five generations of the same family. The company manufactured bricks until 1982, after which it remained in business as a distributor, and it remains as the largest brick distributor in central Illinois.

Heavy manufacturing arrived in East Peoria when two companies, the Colean Manufacturing Company and the R. Herschel Manufacturing Company, built factories here, the first in 1902 and the other the following year. Both plants were built on a former dairy farm that had been converted into an industrial site. The Colean Company's factory went bankrupt after only a few years, but in 1909 a Stockton, California, firm, the Holt Manufacturing Company, purchased the Colean plant and began producing its newest product: an innovative tractor trademarked under the name Caterpillar.

The Caterpillar tractor was a great success. Later adapted to pull artillery, this tractor was used during World War I. In 1925 Holt Manufacturing merged with its main competitor, C. L. Best Gas Tractor Company, to form the Caterpillar Tractor Company. During World War II, the company's diesel-powered heavy equipment was used extensively for building airfields and other facilities in the Pacific. But it was its peacetime farming equipment that made the Caterpillar Company the leader in its industry. After more than a century, the company's manufacturing facilities remain in East Peoria, occupying more than four hundred acres on what was once riverside swampland.

METAMORA

Records of Metamora's earliest settlers show that William and Solomon Sowards settled in future Metamora in 1823, though little is known about them. Another family, the Bantas, homesteaded near the settlement, originally called Hanover, in 1831. Two years after Woodford County was formed in 1841, the seat at Versailles was relocated to Hanover, which was incorporated as the village of Metamora in 1845. Metamora served as the county seat until 1894.

Like many towns in this part of Illinois, Metamora was mainly an agricultural community in its early days, but the coal boom that began in the 1860s came to Metamora a decade later, boosting the village's economy and stimulating its growth. Even so, Metamora remained a small town surrounded by farms. Today, most of its businesses, many housed in buildings from the early 1900s, are still located around the village square. The focal point of downtown Metamora is the former Woodford County courthouse, now known as the Metamora Courthouse State Historic Site.

After Metamora (then called Hanover) became the Woodford County seat in 1843, the town got to work building a stately Greek Revival courthouse, which was completed two years later. This building was one of fifteen county courthouses within the Eighth Judicial Circuit in which Abraham Lincoln represented clients between 1845 and 1856. Lincoln also visited Metamora in conjunction with his 1858 U.S. Senate campaign. Today the Metamora Courthouse is one of only two remaining Eighth Judicial Circuit courthouses.

When voters elected to move the Woodford County seat to Eureka in 1894, the Metamora Courthouse was closed and ownership of the building reverted to the village. For a while, the first floor was used for storage and civic meetings and the second floor for concerts, movies, community theater, and social events. But soon the historic structure began to deteriorate.

In 1921, hoping to save the building, former Illinois governor Joseph Fifer and some concerned local residents convinced the state to purchase the site and help fund restorations. The renovated building became a museum dedicated to local history and frontier courts of law. The second floor is furnished as a replica of the 1850s courtroom.

EUREKA

The small city of Eureka, home of Ronald Reagan's alma mater, Eureka College, is one of thirteen Illinois towns on the Ronald Reagan Trail. Others include Monmouth and Galesburg (two of Reagan's boyhood homes), discussed in Region 2 of this book, and Tampico (Reagan's birthplace) and Dixon (another boyhood home), both of which will be examined in Region 5.

Eureka was once known as Walnut Grove. In 1835 Thomas Bullock led about sixty families from Kentucky to start a settlement along Walnut Creek, but it was never chartered as a town. Ohioan John Darst came here and purchased land in 1851, and four years later, upon learning that the Peoria & Oquawka Railroad would be building tracks through the area, he platted the property and began to sell lots. The community, renamed Eureka, was incorporated as a village in 1859 and as a city in 1880. It was chosen to be the Woodford County seat in 1894. Eureka's elegant courthouse, completed in 1898, still stands.

Eureka is best known for Eureka College, from which future president Ronald Reagan graduated in 1932.

Eureka College

Eureka College was founded before the town of Eureka was even platted. Originally opened as a multigrade one-room schoolhouse in 1848, the school was incorporated as Eureka College in 1855. The school's founders were Kentucky abolitionists who believed in equality for all, and it was the first college in the state to educate women and men on an equal footing.

Of its many students over the years, one particularly stood out: Ronald "Dutch" Reagan, class of 1932. As a participant in athletics, drama, and student life at Eureka College, he developed the leadership qualities that later helped propel him to state and national office. By the 1950s, Reagan was a popular actor in Hollywood; in the 1960s he turned his attention to politics. He was elected in 1966 to the first of two terms as governor of California, and in 1980 he was elected to the first of two consecutive terms as U.S. president.

During his first presidential term, Reagan chose Eureka College as the setting for one of his most important speeches—the 1982 announcement of his new arms-control program, known as START (Strategic Arms Reduction Treaty). This address became known as the "Eureka Speech." He also delivered the commencement addresses for the classes of 1982 and 1992.

In 1994 the college opened the Reagan Museum. This exhibition space and repository contains more than 2,000 items from Reagan's life, from his student days to his presidency, the largest collection of Reagan memorabilia outside the Reagan Presidential Library in Simi Valley, California. The college also honors the fortieth president, who died in 2004, with the Ronald W. Reagan Leadership Program, the Reagan Physical Education Center, the Ronald Reagan Society, and the Ronald Reagan Peace Garden, which includes a large piece of concrete from the Berlin Wall.

SECOR

A year after the Peoria & Oquawka Railroad ran its eastern extension through this area in 1856, this sparsely settled community was officially incorporated as a village, named for engineering executive Charles A. Secor, whose company had designed the extension. The village thrived for a time, but today it has a population of less than four hundred and only one business, the Secor Saloon.

Despite Secor's modest size, one resident reached international acclaim in the 1930s for her lifesaving role in the Nanjing Massacre, also known historically as the "Rape of Nanjing." Wilhelmina (Minnie) Vautrin was born in Secor in 1887 and grew up here, attending Illinois State Normal University in Normal and graduating from the University of Illinois in Champaign in 1912. Joining the United Christian Missionary Society, she began a six-year mission in Nanjing (or Nanking), China, where she helped found Ginling Girls College in 1916.

Vautrin later became the dean of education at the Nanjing girls' school, and she was still there when, in December 1937, the Japanese invaded the city, which was then the Chinese capital. During the siege, the Japanese soldiers indiscriminately murdered and raped hundreds of thousands of Chinese men, women, and children. No one was spared from the atrocities.

As foreigners and Chinese civilians fled the city, Vautrin and about twenty other foreigners courageously stayed and established a three-square-mile safety zone in the western part of the city, encompassing Ginling Girls College among other buildings. Originally meant to provide food and shelter for a limited number of Chinese for a few weeks, the safety zone was forced to accommodate hundreds of thousands of people as panicked Nanjing citizens poured in. While the Japanese army agreed to respect the safety zone, soldiers nevertheless invaded sporadically, hauling off men and women, including a few students from the Ginling school, who were then tortured, raped, and killed. In addition to making repeated appeals at the U.S. Embassy, Vautrin personally confronted soldiers to repel the incursions, earning her the title "Goddess of Mercy."

After six weeks of occupation, the fall of Nanjing was declared completed, and the civilians were ordered out of the safety zone. Vautrin stayed two more years, helping survivors put their shattered lives back together. She aided the women in finding food, shelter, and lost family members and continued to teach classes as best she could. In May 1940, an exhausted and depressed Vautrin returned to the United States, where she received psychiatric care. Nevertheless, she became increasingly distraught, and on May 14, 1941, Minnie Vautrin committed suicide. Later, the Chinese government posthumously awarded her its highest civilian honor, the Emblem of the Blue Jade, for her heroic actions during the Nanjing Massacre.

After World War II ended, a number of the Japanese officers involved in the massacre were tried for war crimes by an international military tribunal, but only two were convicted and hanged.

US 51
VANDALIA–DECATUR
66 miles

This stretch of US Route 51 is the focus of a major improvement project spearheaded by an organization called the US 51 Coalition, a group of local citizens, business owners, government officials, and others that formed in 1994. The goal is to widen the entire highway into four lanes through Illinois, and while progress has been made, work remains to be done.

VANDALIA

Beginning in 1820 and for the next twenty years, this city on the west bank of the Kaskaskia River was the state capital. Formerly known as Reeve's Bluff, Vandalia was selected as the Illinois capital during the First General Assembly meeting in Kaskaskia in 1818–19. It was the state's second capital, moved from Kaskaskia to a more central location. At the time, the town site was unoccupied frontier land. The entire city was built solely to be the Illinois state capital.

Today the Old State Capitol—the last of three statehouses built in Vandalia—is a historical museum (see below). Another Vandalia site worth a visit is the Fayette County Museum. The museum building started as a church, the House of Divine Worship, built in the 1820s. Moved to its current site in 1867, the structure is a rare example of Early Gothic Revival architecture. The church was converted into a history museum in the late 1970s.

Old State Capitol

The first building constructed as the state capitol was a plain two-story frame structure, approximately thirty by forty feet. The House of Representatives met on the first floor, and the Senate and Council of Revision assembled on the second floor. Executive offices were located in other buildings, many in the state bank building.

A fire on January 23, 1823, destroyed the bank building along with most of the state's financial records. On December 9 of the same year, another fire consumed the statehouse. Some suspected arson, committed for political reasons.

Fearing they might lose Vandalia's capital status to another town, local residents hastily built a new capitol nearby. Legislators kept meeting at the slipshod new building even as it deteriorated. Recognizing the structure's shortcomings and hearing of plans to relocate the capital elsewhere, Vandalians built a third, substantial statehouse.

Using some materials from the previous capitol, workers began construction on the new Federal-style building in the summer of 1836. It was still unfinished when the legislature convened on December 3, 1836, for the Tenth General Assembly. But a serious movement was already under way to move the capital to Alton or Springfield. On February 28, 1837, legislators voted to relocate the capital to Springfield. In the meantime, the General Assembly met at the extravagant new building in Vandalia for the 1838–39 session.

No longer used by the legislature, the new capitol was adapted to serve as a school for a number of years. From 1856 to 1933, the building was used as the Fayette County Courthouse. Now a historic museum, the old capitol remains as a landmark of an earlier time in Illinois history.

Madonna of the Trail Monument and the National Old Trails Road

On the grounds of the old state capitol in Vandalia is Illinois' "Madonna of the Trail" statue, one of twelve pink granite monuments erected by the Daughters of the American Revolution in 1928 and 1929 along the National Old Trails Road from Maryland to California. The National Old Trails Road Association (NOTRA) formed in 1912 around the idea of uniting various historic westward trails as the National Old Trails Road, also called the Ocean-to-Ocean Highway. Much of the western part of the route traced the old Santa Fe Trail, while the eastern part mostly followed the Old Cumberland Road, a.k.a. the National Road (the approximate route of today's US 40), whose construction began in Cumberland, Maryland, in 1811. The National Road was supposed to reach the Mississippi River and beyond, but lack of funding stopped the construction at Vandalia in 1839.

The Madonna of the Trail Monument, a tribute to the settlers of early Illinois, adorns the grounds of the Old State Capitol in Vandalia, which can be seen in the background. —Photo by Lyle Kruger

The original goal of NOTRA was to place markers at regular intervals from coast to coast, but the plan was jettisoned. In 1927 the Daughters of the American Revolution, a partner in the association, made a new suggestion—to place a monument honoring pioneer women in each of the twelve states traversed by the road. Harry S Truman of Missouri, then president of NOTRA, secured congressional funding for twelve identical statues, at a cost of $1,000 each.

The monuments were ten feet tall and mounted on a six-foot-high base. The sculpture depicts a pioneer mother wearing a sunbonnet and long dress, holding a baby in one arm and a rifle in the other. At her side, a small boy grasps her skirt. In Vandalia, the monument marks the western terminus of the Cumberland Road. The other statues were placed in Maryland, Pennsylvania, West Virginia, Ohio, Indiana, Missouri, Kansas, Colorado, New Mexico, Arizona, and California.

PANA

Pana was founded as Stone Coal Precinct in 1845. A few years later the name was changed to Pana, probably derived from the name Pawnee, one of the tribes in the area. Construction of the Illinois Central Railroad through Pana in 1853 established it as a settlement. Pana was incorporated as a village in 1857. Twenty years later, it was chartered as a city.

Beginning in 1884 and continuing well into the twentieth century, coal played a major role in Pana's economy. In July of 1897, the local union called a strike to demand a better wage scale, which they won in September. The work stoppage, supported by the United Mine Workers of America, was the union's first successful strike.

After the wage increase became effective, however, several Illinois mining companies—the primary ones being the Chicago-Virden Coal Company and the Pana Coal Company—refused to abide by the agreement, inciting another strike. This one, supported by miners nationwide, eventually escalated into a riot in Virden (see under Virden on earlier trip).

Events in Pana paralleled those in Virden, with the coal companies bringing in black strikebreakers from Alabama. The first trainload arrived on the grounds of Pana's Springside Mine on August 24, 1898. The strikebreakers, protected by a stockade around the mine, proceeded to work, but both striking miners and local residents deeply resented their presence. Several armed and unarmed skirmishes occurred, though there were no fatalities. In September Gov. John Riley Tanner sent the state militia to restore order. A few weeks later, the riot in Virden broke out, leaving thirteen dead and dozens wounded. By the fall of 1899, after a year of violence and public pressure throughout the state, the coal companies finally capitulated, signing a new agreement in October.

A fascinating historical site in Pana is Kitchell Park, one of the very few parks listed in the National Register of Historic Places. The original park, which opened in 1908, featured a large swimming pool and a track for horse racing. Some believe that Frank James, brother of famous Missouri outlaw Jesse James, was hired to appear at the horse race in an effort to hype attendance at the 1906 Tri-County Fair, but James's attendance remains undocumented. The first Chautauqua Institution meeting in the county was held at Kitchell Park in 1907, and the round Chautauqua Pavilion was built in 1911. Some of the speakers at the pavilion included William Jennings Bryan, Billy Sunday, and WWI hero Sgt. Alvin York.

Pana's nickname, the "City of Roses," was coined in the early 1900s, when the town's booming floral industry began. Pana experiences very little hail, making it ideal for greenhouse growing. Pana once accommodated dozens of greenhouses, which by the 1950s were shipping about 19 million roses annually. By the mid-1990s, however, primarily due to rising utility costs and competition from foreign markets, growers had stopped cultivating roses in Pana. Still, for tradition's sake, the town retains its flowery title.

MOWEAQUA

The first settler in this area may have been North Carolinian Jacob Traughber, who homesteaded near Moweaqua in 1831. German immigrant Michael Schneider bought land in this area in 1836 and 1849, and it was he who founded the village in 1852. Settler Chester Wells built the first sawmill here, and his son, Mattie Wells, helped bring the Illinois Central Railroad through town in 1855 and named the town Moweaqua, an Indian word whose meaning is uncertain. In 1890 the name was erroneously recorded as Moweaqua, and the variation stuck.

British-born cattleman Tom Candy Ponting settled near Moweaqua around 1850. Between 1853 and 1854, he and his partner, Washington Malone, conducted one of the longest cattle drives in history. Driving 350 longhorns from Texas, the partners wintered the herd on Ponting's Moweaqua homestead, then drove about 150 of them on foot and by rail to New York City, arriving in July 1854. These were the first Texas cattle ever brought to New York. The total journey covered 1,500 miles on foot and horseback, plus another 600 miles by railroad. Ponting continued his cattle business in Moweaqua, introducing Herefords to central Illinois in 1879. He died in 1916 and was buried in West Side Cemetery, just down the road from his original homestead.

Coal was discovered in Moweaqua in 1889, and the coal mine opened in 1892. The mine operated successfully for forty years until a tragic explosion killed more than fifty miners and devastated the community, ending coal mining in the town.

The tragedy occurred on Christmas Eve morning 1932. Miners at the Moweaqua Coal Mine, Shelby County's largest mining operation, were just settling into their daily routine when a loud explosion reverberated underground. As the shrill warning sirens shattered the stillness of the unseasonably warm day, the mine supervisors hastened to the site of the blast, but below ground the damage was done. In a matter of seconds, poisonous gases had entered the mine and, ignited by the miners' open-flame carbide lights, exploded.

After several days, scores of volunteers felt their hopes of rescuing the trapped men drain away. They did succeed, however, in recovering all the bodies. Fifty-four miners lost their lives in the disaster. A lengthy investigation determined that an unprecedented drop in barometric pressure had forced the methane into the main entries of the mine. The accident ended the use of open-flame carbide lights in underground mines.

Today, the mine is closed and a simple stone monument marks the accident site. The Moweaqua Coal Mine Museum, opened in 1986, contains artifacts from the town's mining days.

A crowd of locals await news from rescue operations after the Moweaqua coal mine disaster in 1932. —Courtesy Moweaqua Coal Mine Museum

DECATUR

Visitors to Decatur may be astonished by the city's twenty-seven monuments, eight honoring Abraham Lincoln and seven paying tribute to the Civil War and its veterans. The city also contains examples of ten pure architectural styles, mostly in the downtown historic district.

Economically, Decatur is a driving force in agriculture and crop processing. Known as the "Soybean Capital of the World," the city processes about one-third of the state's soybean crops. Two of Decatur's principal employers are Archer Daniels Midland (corn and soybean processing) and Tate & Lyle (corn processing). Two other major companies in town are industrial manufacturers—Caterpillar (industrial and agricultural equipment) and Mueller Company (industrial fittings and equipment).

Located near the center of the state, Decatur was founded in 1823. It was named for Commodore Stephen Decatur, whose leadership in the Barbary Coast War and the War of 1812 is less familiar than the words he exclaimed at a banquet upon his return: "Our country, right or wrong!"

When Macon County was created in 1829, Decatur became the county seat. Abraham Lincoln tried cases at the original courthouse (1829–38), at which site a marker now stands. Decatur built its second courthouse in 1837, completed the following year. In 1854 the Chicago Great Western Railroad built a large depot, and the Illinois Central Railroad arrived later the same year, establishing Decatur as the railroad crossroads of central Illinois.

Abe Lincoln's name pops up over and over again in Decatur's history. Lincoln Trail Homestead State Park, a few miles southwest of town, is believed to have been the site of the small log cabin built by Abraham's father, Thomas Lincoln, in 1830 (see below). Although the family lived here only a year, the park is part of the Lincoln Heritage Trail in Illinois.

In 1860 Decatur hosted the convention of the Illinois Republican Party, at which Lincoln was named the party's presidential candidate. The event took place in a hastily constructed, seven-hundred-square-foot, single-floor building called a Wigwam. Decatur residents Richard J. Oglesby, future Illinois governor, and John Hanks, a close friend and distant cousin of Lincoln, brought in two rails that Lincoln had split and stretched across them a banner that read "Abraham Lincoln, the Railsplitter Candidate, for President in 1860." The city honors Oglesby with the Richard J. Oglesby Mansion museum (see below), and Hanks is remembered with a statue and a marker.

The historical significance of Decatur does not end with Lincoln. In addition to being the longtime home of Governor Oglesby, the city was the birthplace of the Grand Army of the Republic (GAR) in 1866. It was also the birthplace of the fly swatter, invented in 1900 by Decatur businessman Robert R. Montgomery. Millikin University was founded in Decatur in 1903, and in the 1920s the city produced the Decatur Staleys—forerunners of the Chicago Bears. All of these people and occurrences are discussed in further detail below.

Lincoln Trail Homestead

Just off I-72, a few miles southwest of Decatur along the Sangamon River, is Lincoln Trail Homestead State Park. Within the 162-acre park is the probable site of the eighteen-by-eighteen-foot log cabin built by Thomas Lincoln for the twelve members of his extended family, including his twenty-one-year-old son, Abraham. The family moved here from southern Indiana in March 1830. Twelve months later, after a poor crop of corn and a harsh winter, the Lincoln family pulled up roots again and moved southeast to Coles County (see Lincoln Log Cabin Historic Site in Region 4). Abraham embarked on his own, becoming a flatboatman on the Sangamon River and settling in New Salem.

The Lincoln cabin, later used as a schoolhouse and a farm building and largely forgotten until after the president's death, was reclaimed, dismantled, moved, and rebuilt for display in various locations during the late 1800s and early 1900s before it was somehow lost. The farmstead property was occupied by another family for several generations until the state of Illinois bought the land in the 1930s and transformed it into a state park. The exact site of the Lincoln family's cabin has never been certainly determined; some believe it may have stood just outside the park's boundaries.

Richard Oglesby: Three-time Governor

The political, military, and personal life of Richard J. "Uncle Dick" Oglesby spanned much of the nineteenth century. This self-taught lawyer was comfortable in a courtroom, but he ended up in politics, later stating "I was never much of a lawyer."

Born in Kentucky in 1824, young Richard was orphaned at age eight, and four years later he was sent to live with his uncle in Decatur. In 1844 he went to Springfield to study law. When the Mexican War began in 1846, the twenty-one-year-old Oglesby enlisted as a first lieutenant in the Fourth Illinois Infantry Regiment, participating in the battles of Vera Cruz and Cerro Gordo.

Back in Decatur, Oglesby married Anna White in 1859. He was elected to the Illinois Senate the following year. When the Civil War broke out, he resigned his seat and joined the Union Army, forming the Eighth Illinois Infantry Regiment, of which he was named colonel. During his tour, he participated in the battles of Forts Henry and Donelson, was wounded at Corinth, and received promotions of brigadier general and major general.

In 1864 Oglesby left the army to run for governor, a race he won. One of his first acts was to lead the legislature in ratifying the Thirteenth Amendment to the Constitution, abolishing slavery. During his term, the legislature also ratified the Fourteenth Amendment, granting citizenship to black people.

Coincidentally, Oglesby was Lincoln's last official business appointment on April 14, 1865. He was invited to join Lincoln at Ford's Theater but declined due to fatigue. Later that evening, he was summoned to Lincoln's deathbed at the Peterson house, where he witnessed the president's death.

In 1869, near the end of Oglesby's first gubernatorial term, his wife, Anna, died. He was elected governor again in 1872 but resigned a short time later, after being elected to the U.S. Senate. The following year, he married Elkhart widow Emma Gillett Keays. One of their sons, John G. Oglesby, would serve two terms as Illinois lieutenant governor in the early twentieth century. In 1874 the newlyweds expanded Richard's seven-room frame house in Decatur into an elaborate Italianate-style mansion. The family occupied this home until 1882, when they moved to Lincoln and later to an estate called Oglehurst in Elkhart (see Elkhart on earlier trip). The Decatur house, restored in the 1970s, is now the Richard J. Oglesby Mansion historical museum.

In 1884 Oglesby was again elected governor. After his final term ended in 1889, he retired to Oglehurst in Elkhart. He died on April 24, 1899, and was buried in Elkhart Cemetery. Among the many dignitaries attending the funeral were Abraham Lincoln's son, Robert T. Lincoln, and former vice president Adlai E. Stevenson.

Founding of the Grand Army of the Republic

During the Civil War, two members of the Fourteenth Illinois Infantry Regiment—Dr. Benjamin F. Stephenson, surgeon, and Rev. William J. Rutledge, chaplain—discussed the future of Union veterans. An organization was needed, they felt, that would "preserve the friendships and the memories of [soldiers'] common trials and dangers." After the war the pair formed the Grand Army of the Republic (GAR), on April 6, 1866, in Decatur.

At first, the GAR was mostly a fraternal organization for veterans, but within a few years, the members began to organize to petition the government to provide benefits for Union Army veterans and their families. By the end of the nineteenth century, the GAR had over 400,000 members and was a potent political force.

During its ninety-year history, the GAR counted five future presidents among its members: Ulysses S. Grant, Rutherford B. Hayes, James A. Garfield, Benjamin Harrison, and William F. McKinley. One of the organization's most noted accomplishments was the designation of May 30 as a day of remembrance for soldiers who died during the Civil War. Established in 1868, Memorial Day (originally called Decoration Day) became a legal federal holiday a hundred years later, by which time the day commemorated fallen American service members of all wars.

The last surviving Union veteran of the Civil War, Albert Woolson, died in 1956, after which time the GAR was formally dissolved. Subsequent organizations using the GAR model included Sons of Union Veterans of the Civil War, the American Legion, and Veterans of Foreign Wars. GAR memorials can still be found throughout the country. Illinois has markers in Chicago, Hoopeston, Minier, Murphysboro, Watseka, and Springfield; Decatur has five.

New Century Movers

The dawn of the twentieth century brought further innovations to Decatur. The first was the fly swatter, invented by local businessman Robert R. Montgomery in 1900. Montgomery noticed that using a solid object, such as a newspaper, to kill a fly was ineffective. The sudden swoosh of air provided advance warning for the fly to escape. Instead, he attached a piece of wire mesh to a wooden handle. The air passed through the mesh, so the fly remained unaware of the threat and the swat landed fatally on its victim. On January 9, 1900, Montgomery received Patent No. 640,790 for the "Fly-Killer."

Montgomery set up shop in the basement of his home in Decatur, where his sons helped assemble the gadgets. By 1902 his company was producing 500,000 swatters annually and shipping worldwide. A few years later, Montgomery sold his operation to the United States Wire Mat Company. The company, later renamed U.S. Manufacturing Corporation, produced about 75 percent of the world's fly swatters. When the patent

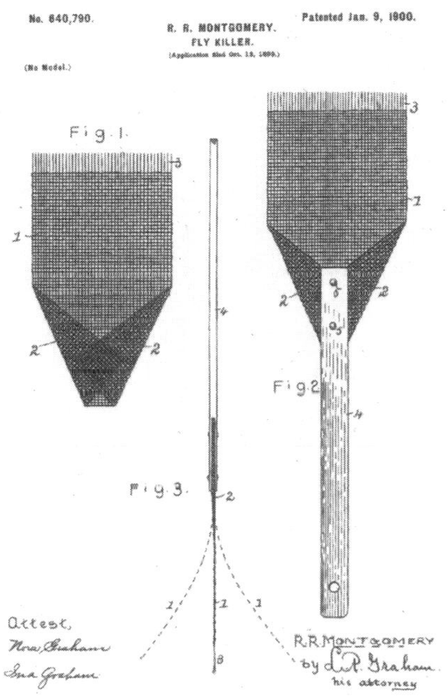

No. 640,790.
(No Model.)

R. R. MONTGOMERY.
FLY KILLER.
(Application filed Oct. 13, 1899.)

Patented Jan. 9, 1900.

Fig. 1.

Fig. 2.

Fig. 3.

Attest,
Nora Graham
Ina Graham

R. R. Montgomery
by R. Graham
his attorney

Sketch of the "Fly Killer," designed by Decatur resident Robert Montgomery; Montgomery received patent number 640,790 on January 9, 1900. —Courtesy U.S. Patent and Trademark Office

expired, other companies entered the field, increasing competition, and plastic swatters eventually superseded the wire-mesh kind. In 1959 U.S. Manufacturing Corporation filed for bankruptcy.

As Montgomery was getting his business under way, another creation was coming to fruition in Decatur. In the late spring of 1903, James Millikin, seventy-six-year-old owner of the Millikin National Bank of Decatur and a leading citizen of the city, realized a vision he had conceived more than fifty years earlier—Millikin University.

At age twenty, Millikin vowed that if he ever became wealthy, he would open an institution of higher learning that all students could afford. After successful ventures in banking, real estate, and industry, he donated Oakland Park, a substantial plot of land, and $200,000 to the city of Decatur to build the university. On June 4, 1903, President Theodore Roosevelt delivered the dedicatory address. Three months later, the university opened its doors to 562 students, and the school began its first century. Today the school encompasses a seventy-five-acre campus and has an enrollment of 2,400 students.

Another innovator came to Decatur in 1920. Contrary to popular legend, George S. Halas did not invent the game of football, nor did he coach or play in the first game. In fact, the first recorded football game was played in 1895, the year Halas was born. He did, however, change the game forever. His impact on professional football as a player, coach, owner, and visionary was legendary. Also a key organizer at the first meeting of the American Professional Football Association (later named the National Football League), Halas is sometimes called the "Father of the NFL."

In 1920 the Chicago-born Halas was recruited by A. E. Staley, a Decatur starch manufacturer and booster of sports teams, to recruit players for and coach a football team in Decatur. Halas had been a star in college sports (football, basketball, and baseball) and a top organizer of U.S. military football and basketball teams during World War I. He had also played briefly for the New York Yankees. For these accomplishments, he had earned the nickname "Mr. Everything."

Halas came to Decatur and helped develop the football team, known as the Decatur Staleys, for their 1920 season. Although the Staleys had an excellent record that year, the economy took a downturn and Staley had to drop his company's football program the following year. Rather than disband the team, Staley offered the franchise to Halas, who moved the team to Chicago. In their first season, 1921, the Chicago Staleys won the championship. The next year, Halas—who was not only the team's owner, manager, and coach but also a star player—renamed the team the Chicago Bears as a tribute to the Cubs, who allowed the Staleys to play their early games in Wrigley Field. For this reason, Halas was known as "Papa Bear."

Halas served ten years as a player, forty years as a coach (during which time he had only six losing seasons), and sixty-three years as an owner. Throughout his career, he pioneered new concepts, standards and practices, strategies, techniques, and plays. He was a charter member of the Pro Football Hall of Fame, formed in 1963. He retired in 1967, at age seventy-two (the oldest coach in football history), and died in 1983, at age eighty-eight. To this day, the Chicago Bears wear a patch on the sleeve of their uniform that bears the initials of their founder, GSH.

OTHER COMMUNITIES AND SITES OF INTEREST IN CENTRAL ILLINOIS

Auburn (IL 4 and IL 104): The first coal mine was established in the Auburn area around 1880, and by 1915, four mines were operating in the vicinity. The city's coal economy diminished in the 1920s, however, and the last mine closed in 1944. Luckily, by then Auburn had a self-sustaining local economy of its own, supported in part by its proximity to Springfield and by US Route 66. Today, just north of Auburn, Route 66 travelers can see the 1.53-mile-long Auburn Brick Road, listed on the NRHP in 1998. Nearby, on Snell Road, is Becky's Barn, a vintage-style Route 66 visitor center, gift shop, and snack bar.

Broadwell (I-55): The village of Broadwell was platted in 1856, the same year the railroad came, and it was incorporated in 1869. By the time railroad service was discontinued, Broadwell had become a stop on US Route 66. In 1937 Ernie and Frances Edwards opened a small café that would become a Route 66 icon, the Pig Hip restaurant. This family-run eatery started as the Harbor Inn, but the owners changed the name to the Pig Hip the following year, after a hungry farmer pointed to a steaming pork roast and asked for a sandwich "off that pig hip." Sadly, like so many original stops on the Mother Road, the Pig Hip no longer exists—the building burned down in 2007. Today, a stone memorial with a bronze plaque marks the site where thousands of barbecue sandwiches were served for more than fifty years.

Chatham (IL 4): The village of Chatham was founded in 1836, and the railroad arrived in 1852. The town's 1902 train depot, which closed in 1972, was restored by the Friends of the Depot in 1991. Eight years later, the local chapter of the National Railway Historical Society took over and, after further renovations, opened the Chatham Railroad Museum.

Farmersville (I-55): The now boarded-up Art's Motel and Restaurant, inducted into the Route 66 Association of Illinois Hall of Fame in 1995, dates back to 1920, when Hendricks Brothers' Café and Service Station opened here. In 1937 Art McAnarney took over the business, which included several cabins for overnight guests. After several attempts to renovate and reopen both the motel and the restaurant in the 2000s, the establishment closed for good in 2012. The old neon sign for Art's Motel and Restaurant, which had stood idle and rusting for more than fifty years, was refurbished in 2007 by the Route 66 Association of Illinois.

Glenarm (I-55) was once the home of the first settler in Sangamon County, Robert Pulliam, who arrived in 1817. A metal plaque commemorating this fact stands at the entrance to Pioneer Park, which also boasts the Sugar Creek Covered Bridge, believed to be the oldest remaining covered bridge in Illinois. Built in 1827, the bridge remained in use until 1984.

McLean (I-55 and US 136): With the building of US Route 66 in the 1920s, McLean seized the opportunity to cater to automobile travelers. The Dixie Truckers Home started as a mechanic's garage that also sold sandwiches, but it soon grew into a full-service restaurant and remained in continuous operation from 1928 to 2003. Until it was sold in 2003, Dixie stood as the oldest (and some say the best) truck stop in the state. It once housed the Route 66 Hall of Fame, founded in 1990, but in 2004 the museum was moved to Pontiac. After passing through several owners, an extensively remodeled Dixie Travel Plaza reopened in 2009, retaining the Route 66 theme and displaying artifacts from its history.

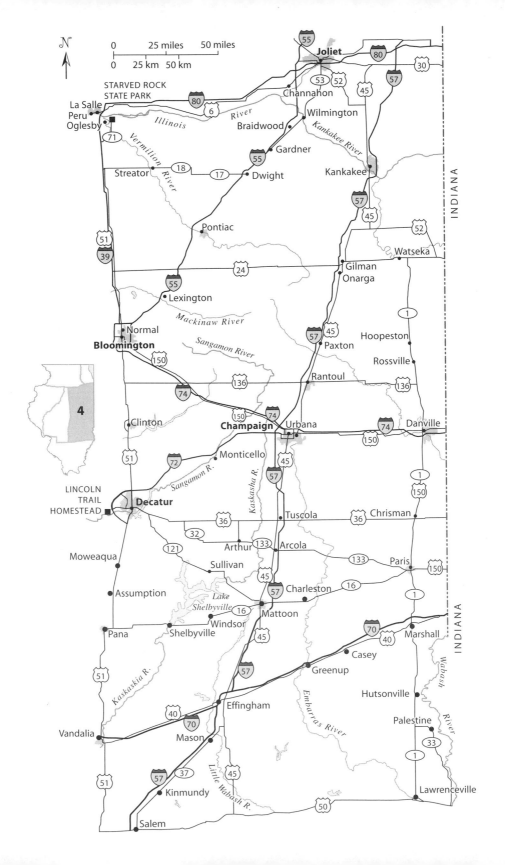

Eastern Illinois
MORE THAN YOU EXPECT

Eastern Illinois may be flat geographically but not historically. Visitors to this region will be pleasantly surprised to find many significant but often overlooked places that played important roles in the state's development. This part of Illinois has been home to individuals from inventors to war nurses to cattle kings, and it has been the site of events from the Potawatomi expulsion to public hangings to prison riots. Travelers will find landmarks along old Route 66, the "Mother Road," as well as locales associated with the life of Abraham Lincoln, especially his early years. In addition to history, the region offers recreational areas, college campuses, farmlands, museums, wildlife reserves, shopping centers, scenic drives, local festivals, and friendly people. There is certainly more to eastern Illinois than one might expect.

The original inhabitants of this region were mostly the tribes identified with the Illini Confederation (Kaskaskia, Cahokia, Peoria, and others). The earliest Europeans in eastern Illinois were French explorers and fur traders, who began arriving in the seventeenth century. The Fox, Kickapoo, Potawatomi, and other tribes migrated into eastern and central Illinois in the 1700s and early 1800s, until westward expansion forced them out. Many of the towns and cities here were founded shortly after the Indians were expelled in the 1830s. Once the railroads arrived in the 1850s and '60s, more communities sprang up and thrived. Coal mining in the area, which began near Braidwood in the 1860s and expanded through the region in subsequent decades, spurred additional growth.

As in many other downstate regions, agriculture was the dominant industry in eastern Illinois and remains so. The largest city is Champaign, home of the University of Illinois, a land-grant college and one of two major educational institutions in the region. The other is Eastern Illinois University in Charleston. About halfway between these two urban areas are Arthur and Arcola, centers for a large Amish community. Unexpected diversity, natural beauty, and an abundance of convenient but unhurried small communities are among the many reasons that eastern Illinois is a favorite among vacationers and the beloved home of old-timers and newcomers alike.

IL 37 and US 45
SALEM—EFFINGHAM
45 miles

This section of IL 37, which parallels I-57, follows the route of the Illinois Central Railroad, the nation's first land-grant railroad, which arrived in the 1850s. The northern and southern work crews of the railroad met near Mason, driving the final spike on September 27, 1856. Also on the trip is Kinmundy, with its re-created pioneer village, and Effingham, a major downstate transportation center with Civil War ties.

SALEM
See Region 1

KINMUNDY

By the time it was incorporated as a city in 1867, only ten years after its founding, Kinmundy had dozens of stores, two sawmills, several machine shops, a two-story school, three churches, and three doctors. Although a devastating fire destroyed most of its downtown businesses in 1903, the city rebuilt, and within five years it was again thriving, with a population of more than 1,500. Over subsequent decades, however, economic conditions changed, and while nearby Centralia, Mount Vernon, and Effingham developed into large cities, Kinmundy leveled off. Today its population is less than a thousand.

Although many of the old buildings in Kinmundy were torn down over the years, the city still has a number of beautiful old homes, including a pre–Civil War brick mansion called Fleetwood (later known as the Leach Mansion), built in 1857 by Kentuckian Michael Wolff. This stately, eight-room house with twelve-foot-high ceilings once served as an Underground Railroad station for fugitive slaves. The house, which has had more than a dozen private owners over the last century and a half, is still a private family residence.

Just east of Kinmundy is Ingram's Log Cabin Village, a re-created pioneer settlement. Erma Ingram, a retired Kinmundy schoolteacher, established the living museum in 1977 with the help of family members and students. The village, on seventy-four acres of wooded ground, contains seventeen original log cabins built between 1818 and 1860, most of which are authentically furnished and open to the public. The buildings include a cobbler's shop, a doctor's office and apothecary, a general store, and a stagecoach inn that allegedly hosted Jesse James, Abraham Lincoln, and others.

MASON

In the early 1850s, the residents of a town named Bristol, about a mile southeast of present-day Mason, moved their homes and business to the new train station called Mason. The station and surrounding town were named for the chief engineer of the Illinois Central, "Colonel" Roswell B. Mason. Both the military title and his middle initial were fictitious, added to dignify his image. Mason later moved to Chicago and was elected that city's mayor, serving from 1869 to 1871.

The colonel's namesake town was not just another railroad stop. On September 27, 1856, the northern and southern work crews of the Illinois Central Railroad met at Mason, driving the final spike just northeast of town. The spike linked the rails of the nation's first land-grant railroad, completing 705 miles of track that traversed the state's entire length. The route extended from Cairo to LaSalle-Peru, with branches to Galena and Chicago. By the early 1870s the Illinois Central Railroad had branched out beyond the state.

EFFINGHAM

Present-day Effingham is a few miles northeast of the site of Ewington, the first county seat of Effingham County, established in 1831. On the western bluffs of the Little Wabash River, Ewington flourished for twenty-seven years, reaching a population of about two hundred. But when the railroad arrived in the area in the 1850s, the line skirted Ewington, sealing the town's fate.

Meanwhile, nearby Effingham (then called Broughton) was only a small village until the Illinois Central Railroad began laying track in the area. Residents expanded their town along the railroad right-of-way to ensure its growth. Incorporating as a village in 1854, Broughton began to build its case to become the county seat. When voters approved the change in 1859, Broughton changed its name to match that of the county. The loser, Ewington, soon ceased to exist.

In time, four other rail lines were built through Effingham, making the town a major railroad hub in the region. The restaurants, hotels, and shops built to accommodate travelers created a hospitality industry that defined the city's identity for decades. In the twentieth century, though the railroads declined, highways came in to take their place. Several major highways converge in Effingham, enabling the town to keep its place as a transportation center.

Among Effingham's notable residents was Ada Miser Kepley, who held the distinction of being the first woman in the nation to receive a law degree. She graduated on June 30, 1870, from Union College of Law, predecessor of Northwestern University Law School. Illinois law banned her from obtaining a license to practice, however, until 1881.

Another Effingham woman to carve a place in history was Mary Newcomb, a Civil War nurse whose dedication put her in the company of Clara Barton, Dorothea Dix, and fellow Illinoisan Mary Ann Bickerdyke (see under Galesburg in Region 2). After her husband enlisted, Newcomb headed to southern Illinois to offer her assistance as a nurse. Her tender and meticulous care of the wounded and dying on both sides at the battles of Fort Henry, Fort Donelson, Shiloh, and Vicksburg made her a legend.

Newcomb's commitment to duty brought her to the attention of Maj. Gen. Ulysses S. Grant, Maj. Gen. Ambrose E. Burnside, and even President Abraham Lincoln. In her memoirs, *Four Years of Personal Reminiscences of the War*, "Mother" Newcomb described the daily challenges and triumphs of caring for those wounded in the bloody conflict. After the war, in which her husband, Hiram, was mortally wounded, she moved to Effingham, where her son, Sidney, operated a business. Mother Newcomb died on December 23, 1892, and is buried with other family members in Oak Ridge Cemetery in Effingham.

US 40
EFFINGHAM–MARSHALL
51 miles

For most of its length through Illinois, US 40 parallels I-70. More interestingly, between Marshall and Vandalia, it follows the historic National Road, also known as the Cumberland Road, the Great Western Road, Ohio's Road, or Uncle Sam's Road; part of the route is now a National Scenic Byway.

Established in the early 1800s, the National Road was a major thoroughfare from Cumberland, Maryland, to Vandalia, Illinois. The road was supposed to extend to California, but funds ran out in 1840, so construction was stopped at Vandalia. The old roadway now forms the main streets of Marshall (East National Road, Archer Avenue), Martinsville (Cumberland Road), Casey (Main Street), and Greenup (IL 121/Cumberland Street), all of which the interstate skirts.

President Thomas Jefferson authorized the creation of the National Road in 1806, and construction began in 1811. The first highway built with federal funds, the National Road was a major route for settlers, freighters, stagecoaches, and other travelers. Most of the original road was unpaved, but some sections were later paved with brick and others with concrete; small sections of both brick and concrete pavement are still visible in Illinois.

In 1912 the National Old Trails Road Association was formed to develop the National Old Trails Road, a coast-to-coast historic route combining the National Road with the old Santa Fe Trail and various other pioneer trails. Over the years, the group erected a number of stone markers and, later, metal signs along the route. Replica signs and even a few originals can still be seen in places. In the 1920s, Vandalia received one of twelve "Madonna of the Trail" monuments that were placed across the country to commemorate the National Road and other pioneer routes (see under Vandalia in Region 3).

EFFINGHAM
See previous trip

GREENUP

William C. Greenup, the man for whom this village was named, was known in Illinois even before it became a state. He served as a court clerk in the first two territorial legislatures, and in 1809 he joined the Illinois militia as a lieutenant; by the end of the War of 1812, he had been promoted to colonel. After the war Greenup served as secretary of the First Constitutional Convention in Kaskaskia, at which the original state constitution was adopted.

In the 1830s William Greenup was the construction superintendent for the one-hundred-mile section of the National Road from the Indiana state line to Vandalia. He used various inns along the route as offices, keeping money in a chest under his bed. In 1834, during the road construction, Greenup teamed up with Joseph Barbour, who owned an inn in what is now the town of Greenup. The partners bought the surrounding land and platted the settlement of Greenup. The National Road served as the town's main street.

The village of Greenup saw modest growth in its early years, serving as the Cumberland County seat from 1843 to 1857. In the late 1860s, the St. Louis, Vandalia & Terre Haute Railroad built through the area, sparking a boom for the community, which incorporated as the village of Greenup in 1869. A depot built in 1870 served the several railroads that soon ran through town, including the Illinois Central, which arrived in 1880.

Today, the only reminders of Greenup's once-dominant railroads are the CSX Railway that passes south of town and the Greenup Depot, housed in the original 1870 rail station building. The depot is part of a museum complex operated by the Cumberland County Historical and Genealogical Society. The complex also includes Greenup's former Carnegie-funded library, built in 1904, and the 1895 Johnson Building, where the society has its main museum, headquarters, and library. Greenup's central business district was named to the NRHP for its many surviving 1860s-era buildings. Many of these structures feature New Orleans–style overhanging porches and iron railings, earning Greenup the nickname "Village of Porches." On the west end of town, travelers may cross over the Embarras River via the Jackson Truss covered bridge, a replica of a bridge built in 1832.

MARSHALL

Marshall was the easternmost of the many Illinois towns established along the National Road during and after its construction through the state in the 1830s. Politician and former army colonel William B. Archer and Illinois governor Joseph Duncan founded the city shortly after Duncan took office in 1834, naming it for U.S. Chief Justice John Marshall.

As construction on the National Road progressed, traffic through the area increased, and Marshall grew apace. The Clark County seat was moved to the three-year-old Marshall in 1838. The first courthouse was a small wooden structure; it was replaced by the current courthouse, a large and elegant brick building, in 1903.

The National Road provided steady east-west traffic through town, and the north-south Vincennes-to-Chicago stagecoach road intersected the National Road here, making Marshall a transportation center for decades. In 1870 the St. Louis, Vandalia & Terre Haute Railroad laid tracks parallel to the old National Road, extending Marshall's life as a hub. The discovery of oil nearby in the early 1900s provided the city an additional, if short-lived, boom as well.

Marshall may be best known as the home of the Handy Writers' Colony from 1949 to 1964. Its most famous participant was James Jones, author of *From Here to Eternity*, who was born in Robinson, Illinois. Much of Jones's work was done at the colony in Marshall, where in 1953 he built a large house he called his "bachelor palace." The grounds of the colony compound—which started as a group of tents in a cow pasture—and Jones's nearby house are memorialized with a Literary Landmark marker placed by the Friends of Libraries USA.

Most of the buildings in Marshall's historic downtown date from the late 1800s and early 1900s, including the stately 1903 courthouse. One of Marshall's eight landmarks on the NRHP is the Archer House. Originally a stagecoach stop and now a bed-and-breakfast, it is one of the oldest hotels in Illinois. Other sites on the NRHP include the Old Stone Arch Bridge, constructed in 1831 and still in use, as well as the segment of the National Road that passes over the bridge. Harlan Hall, an 1872 opera house with adjoining livery stable, was listed on the NRHP in 2001. This building now houses a community center on the ground floor, and plans are under way to turn the second floor into a National Road Welcome Center.

IL 16
PANA–PARIS
80 miles

On this trip, travelers can visit several sites related to Abraham Lincoln, including the Lincoln Log Cabin State Park, where Lincoln's parents had a farm, and Charleston, the site of the fourth Lincoln-Douglas debate. In addition, we will stop at Shelbyville, the hometown of two major inventors; Mattoon, with its colorful history; and the verdant and romantically named city of Paris.

PANA
See Region 3

SHELBYVILLE

Shelbyville sits atop a bluff overlooking the Kaskaskia River Valley, a vista of rich farmland, verdant woodlands, and the seventeen-mile-long Lake Shelbyville. The first settlers, mostly from the Southern states, arrived here in the mid-1820s and, with help from the Kickapoo Indians, established an unnamed settlement. When Shelby County was organized in 1827, this site was chosen to be the location of the county seat, which was to be called Shelbyville. The county and its new seat were named for Revolutionary War general Isaac Shelby, who later became the governor of Kentucky. A group of area settlers donated twenty acres of land for a public square.

The cabin of settler Barnett Bone, who had arrived in 1825, served as a temporary election site and courthouse until a log courthouse could be erected in 1828. The county's second courthouse was a two-story brick building that stood in the center of the town square from 1832 to 1883. The third and current courthouse, a Victorian structure north of the square, features two Grecian statues representing the goddesses of liberty and justice. Inside hangs a painting by renowned Illinois artist Robert Root; it depicts a famous debate between Abraham Lincoln and Judge Anthony Thornton that took place in Shelbyville in 1855.

Located on the Vandalia-to-Springfield postal route, Shelbyville was originally served by stagecoach. The Indianapolis & St. Louis Railroad arrived in 1858, and the Chicago & Eastern Illinois Railroad was built through the city in 1891. Through the years, agriculture sustained much of Shelbyville's economy, boosted for a time by coal mines, which operated in the area from the mid-1890s to the 1940s. Another boost came with the construction of nearby Lake Shelbyville, the third-largest manmade lake in the state, in the 1960s. The Shelbyville Dam on the Kaskaskia River created this 11,000-acre reservoir, one of the premier lakes in the region for boating, fishing, and other recreational activities.

The Shelbyville Historic District, a multiblock area downtown, includes Italianate, Greek Revival, and Late Victorian structures dating from 1825 to 1924. The Old County Jail, built around 1892, now houses the Shelby County Historical and Genealogical Society. Another historic site in Shelbyville, near the edge of a large city park, is the Chautauqua Auditorium, a 5,000-seat cultural center built in 1903. Listed on the NRHP in 1978, it is the largest building of its kind in the world.

Shelbyville Innovators

Illinois was the home of many agricultural innovations. One of these, the first commercial pickup-style mechanical hay baler, was invented by prominent Shelbyville businessman Horace M. Tallman in 1929, shortly before his death. Fellow Shelbyville resident Raymore McDonald is credited with the baler's design and development; Tallman conceived of the original idea and financed the project. Tallman had bought the Ann Arbor Agricultural Machine Company in 1921, relocating the factory to Shelbyville. After Tallman's death in 1929, his sons took over the company's operations until they sold it in the 1940s. The company began manufacturing and marketing the baler, known as the Ann Arbor baler, in 1932. The machine, attached to a tractor, picked up cut hay from the field and pressed it into bales. The Ann Arbor baler revolutionized the industry and became one of the most popular balers in America.

Tallman and McDonald's invention did not go unappreciated. In 1980 Shelbyville was designated one of forty-seven National Historic Agricultural Landmarks by the American Society of Agricultural and Biological Engineers. Horace M. Tallman's home, built in 1905, was listed on the NRHP in 1988 and restored the following year. The sprawling, two-story Victorian structure now serves as the main office for the Shelby Historic House and Inn.

Another inventor from Shelbyville was a clever housewife. In 1886 Josephine Garis Cochran (also spelled Cochrane) invented the first successful automatic dishwasher. With the help of a local mechanic, Mrs. Cochran developed her creation in a woodshed behind her home. After patenting the design, she sold a few early models to friends and neighbors, then a few more to area restaurants and hotels. Finally, after founding the Garis-Cochran Dish-Washing Machine Company, Cochran took her machine to the 1893 World's Columbian Exposition in Chicago, where it won an award for best design and construction.

Although housewives did not immediately embrace the dishwashing machine, as it had limited home adaptability, Cochran found a huge market among large hotels and restaurants. After Cochran's death in 1913, the Garis-Cochran Dish-Washing Machine Company was sold to a major manufacturer, and in 1949 it became KitchenAid, now owned by Whirlpool.

WINDSOR

The first settlers arrived in Windsor Township in 1826, homesteading on what became known as Carr's Creek, a branch of Sand Creek, just north of present Windsor. When the railroad arrived in 1856, Windsor was one of four towns founded in this area; the others were Pana, Tower Hill, and Gays. Today, Pana is the largest of these communities, with nearly 6,000 residents. Windsor's current population is around 1,000 and Tower Hill's is about six hundred, while Gays is now a dot on the map with fewer than three hundred residents. In the late nineteenth century, however, all four were thriving municipalities. By 1880 Windsor had a full range of retail and grocery stores and a broad assortment of butchers, bakers, tailors, shoemakers, blacksmiths, doctors, dentists, and other service providers.

From Windsor's earliest days as a community, religion was important. The first church in the settlement was Ash Grove Christian Church, founded in June 1832. The first meeting place was a log cabin with seats of rough hewn logs. The log church was used until 1856, when a new frame building was dedicated. In 1887 the frame church was replaced with a larger structure, which lasted eighty years until it burned down in 1967. It was rebuilt the following year, and it is in this structure that parishioners attend services today.

Another Windsor church, the Sand Creek Church of Christ, had an interesting history of its own. Founded in 1834, this congregation built its first log church in 1838, near Sand Creek, about five miles north of Windsor. The original congregation had eleven members, but it soon outgrew its log cabin, and a frame building replaced it in 1851. In 1874 a sturdy brick structure was erected; by then the membership was eighty-five and counting. Around 1904, the congregation split into two factions, one conservative and the other progressive. A dispute arose over which group should have possession of the 1874 church building. The progressives sued, and the case was eventually taken to the state supreme court. The court decided in favor of the defendants, the conservative congregation, and the progressives began meeting in a nearby schoolhouse. The church, which held services until about 1950, still stands, partially restored by a local resident in 2002.

Not all Windsor residents were pious, however. In the 1860s and '70s, according to *Yesteryears of Windsor*, published in 1956, "The righteous went to temperance meetings and to Church on Sunday. The rest of the town got drunk and went to the horse races." The races were held northwest of town near what is now IL 32, and, according to an item from an unidentified newspaper dated May 30, 1870, the events produced more than their fair share of rowdiness: "There is much fighting and drunkenness. Ladies are obliged to walk in the middle of the street to avoid fights going on outside saloons. Men may be often seen lying full length on the sidewalk, dead drunk. There is horse racing every Saturday afternoon and at that time much drinking and fighting occurs."

In the end, the Christians prevailed. Many of Windsor's early congregations endure to this day, while the horse races eventually faded away.

MATTOON

The convergence of the St. Louis, Alton & Terre Haute Railroad (east and west) and the Illinois Central (north and south) in Mattoon, then called Pegtown, placed the settlement in a strategic commercial position. The residents were so happy about the railroads' arrival in 1855 that they named their community after William Mattoon, the chief of railroad construction. Within a year, Mattoon had at least one hundred buildings.

At the beginning of the Civil War, Ulysses S. Grant took his first post in Mattoon, training recruits on the spacious lawn in the town square. Given the rank of captain,

Grant commanded the unit that became the 21st Illinois Infantry. After the war, the arrival in 1870 of the Decatur, Mattoon & Sullivan Railroad further strengthened the local economy, and a number of smaller rail lines were built through Mattoon as well. In 1881 the discovery of coal nearby provided another boost to the city's prosperity, and Mattoon became a bastion of manufacturing.

The twentieth century brought interesting changes both good and bad. The summer of 1901 saw a series of sixteen fires around town. Arson was suspected but never proved. In 1914 the Illinois Central Railroad routed tracks underground to preserve Mattoon's downtown, a project derogatorily described as the "million dollar ditch." A few years later, in May of 1917, a tornado hit Mattoon, killing more than a hundred people and leaving some 2,000 residents homeless. It was the third-deadliest tornado in Illinois history. The downtown area, however, was virtually untouched.

In 1944 a strange criminal terrorized Mattoon residents. Called the "Mad Gasser," he sneaked up on homes and sprayed toxic nerve gas through the windows, inducing illness and temporary paralysis in the victims, but no deaths. Both the identity of the perpetrator and the reasons for his behavior remain mysteries to this day.

Later in the mid-twentieth century, the discovery of petroleum gave yet another economic boost to Mattoon and led to even more manufacturing in the area. Recently a clean coal power plant was built here, making the town a major energy center.

In 1986 Lender's Bagels built their factory in Mattoon, whereupon the town declared itself the "Bagel Capital of the World." Each year, the community serves about 60,000 bagels at the Lender's Bagelfest, with the world's biggest bagel on display.

CHARLESTON

Named for Charles Morton, the first postmaster, Charleston was established as the seat of Coles County in 1831, the same year that Abraham Lincoln settled in Illinois. Charleston has several connections to Lincoln. In 1840, after occupying three other homes in Coles County, Thomas and Sarah Lincoln, Abraham's father and stepmother, started a farm a few miles south of Charleston (see below). Abe, who was an adult by the time his family moved to Illinois, had established his own home in New Salem, but he occasionally returned to Charleston to visit Thomas and Sarah, to try cases at the county courthouse, and, in 1858, to debate with Stephen A. Douglas (see below).

During the Civil War, Charleston was the scene of a deadly riot. In March 1864, a band of Confederate sympathizers known as the Copperheads attacked Union soldiers near the courthouse. The fight, which lasted only a few minutes, left nine dead and twelve wounded before the Copperheads fled the city. Some fourteen Copperheads were indicted for murder, but only two were ever captured, and both of them were later exonerated. A historical marker now stands near the site.

In the late 1880s, Illinois' population had grown to the point that it faced a teacher shortage, and the state legislature began plans to establish more normal schools (teacher-training programs) in Illinois. In 1895 funds were set aside to create Eastern Illinois State Normal School, but the site for the school was left undecided. Of the twelve cities that competed for the privilege, Charleston offered the infrastructure, natural resources, transportation, and general support needed to outdistance its rivals. The first building on the Eastern Illinois State Normal School campus, informally known as Old Main, was erected in 1899.

The original normal school offered a two-year degree for teachers. As the school expanded its curriculum and degree programs, its name was changed. It became Eastern Illinois State Teachers College in 1921, Eastern Illinois State College in 1947, and Eastern Illinois University—its current moniker—in 1957. The university today offers a full range of undergraduate and master's degree programs. Famous former students include folk singer Burl Ives, actor John Malkovich, and Illinois governor Jim Edgar, who grew up in Charleston.

In addition to a number of historic structures—including the Coles County Courthouse, the Dudley House Museum, the Greenwood School Museum, and the Five Mile House—the Charleston area has several attractions related to Abraham Lincoln. In addition to the Lincoln Log Cabin State Historic Site and the Lincoln-Douglas debate site, both described below, is a goofy, seventy-foot-tall fiberglass statue of Honest Abe, the tallest (and, many say, the ugliest) Lincoln statue in the world. (Unfortunately, the campground on which the statue stands, three miles east of Charleston in Ashmore, is closed as of this writing, and motorists can catch no more than a glimpse of Abe's head from the road.)

Those looking for a more serious Lincoln experience will want to visit the Lincoln Log Cabin State Historic Site in Lerna, nine miles south of town, and the Lincoln-Douglas debate site, which includes a museum devoted to the historic 1858 senatorial debates, at the Coles County Fairgrounds in Charleston.

Lincoln Log Cabin State Historic Site

The mid-1800s homestead of Abraham Lincoln's father and stepmother, Thomas and Sarah Bush Lincoln, stands in a still-rural area south of Charleston. To reach it, take Lincoln Highway Road south from Charleston. About a mile north of the Lincoln cabin is the Reuben Moore Home State Historic Site, the home of Abraham's stepsister and her husband.

This homestead was the last of five places in Illinois where the Thomas Lincoln family lived. Their "saddlebag" cabin—two connected one-room cabins—originally housed Thomas, Sarah, and Sarah's three children. As more relatives moved in, the home contained as many as eighteen people at one time.

On the 120-acre farm, Thomas Lincoln grew corn, oats, and potatoes and maintained a menagerie of geese, horses, hogs, dairy cows, and sheep. His farm was not profitable, however, and Abraham often helped his father financially. In October 1841 the younger Lincoln bought about 40 of his father's 120 acres to keep the overstretched family afloat.

After Thomas died in 1851, Sarah continued to live on the farm until her own death in 1869. Abe was on good terms with his stepmother, and he visited her at the Moore home before leaving for the White House in early 1861. It would be the last time he ever saw Illinois.

Thomas and Sarah Lincoln were buried side-by-side in what is now the Thomas Lincoln Cemetery (formerly Gordon's or Shiloh Cemetery), a short distance west of the homestead. Today the Lincolns' farm, combined with the adjacent Stephen Sargent home and the nearby Reuben Moore home, is a living history museum and state historic site.

Fourth Lincoln-Douglas Debate (Charleston, September 18, 1858)

The day before their Charleston debate, Abraham Lincoln and Stephen A. Douglas, each surrounded by a bevy of supporters, traveled in separate carriages along the dusty road from the train station in Mattoon to Charleston. Among those in Lincoln's parade was a cadre of thirty-two women dressed in white, representing the states of the Union. The next day, a crowd of about 12,000 formed a semicircle around the makeshift platform at the county fairgrounds, just west of town. The event began at 2:45 p.m.

Lincoln opened by responding to his opponent's incessant charge that he favored equal rights for black people, a central issue among the electorate. Lincoln maintained, "I am not nor ever have been in favor of bringing about in any way, the social and political equality of the white and black races . . . of making voters of the negroes, or jurors, or qualifying them to hold office, or having them to marry with white people." While his statements may have assuaged some voters' worries that Lincoln was a radical proponent of Negro equality, it led others to question his commitment to ending slavery.

Visitors may learn more about this historic event at the Lincoln Douglas Debate Museum, near the debate site at the Coles County Fairgrounds in Charleston. Opened in 2001, it is the only museum devoted to the famous senatorial debates of 1858.

PARIS

When Edgar County was founded in 1823, one of the area's first settlers, Samuel Vance, donated twenty-six acres in future Paris to found the seat. Paris was incorporated as a village in 1849 and as a city twenty years later. The current Edgar County courthouse—the city's third—is a striking Gothic structure completed in 1983. Ornate both inside and out, the building features a statue of Lady Justice atop a four-faced clock tower.

Sources conflict about how the town got its name; one oft-told story holds that the word "Paris" had been carved, by an unknown person for unknown reasons, into a large jack-oak tree that stood in the center of the proposed new town, and the name was adopted. But according to a 1923 article in the *Paris Daily News*, the honor of christening the town was given to county commissioner Col. John Houston, who was quoted as saying, "I came from Paris, Kentucky, the best town in the whole country, and I therefore name this new town 'Paris' in honor of my hometown."

One of Paris's most prominent citizens was Milton K. Alexander, a Georgia native and War of 1812 veteran who constructed the first buildings in Paris, a cabin and a general store. He later built the town's first brick home, erected in 1842 and still standing today. Following the Black Hawk War of 1832, in which he served as a brigadier general, Alexander returned to Paris and committed himself to local development. He served as president of the Board of Commissioners of Public Works from 1837 to 1842, during which tenure he oversaw the $10 million development of river improvements and the construction of railroads. Following a stroke in 1846, Alexander spent the last ten years of his life as an invalid. He died on July 7, 1856. Originally buried in the Presbyterian Yard, his remains were exhumed and reburied in Edgar Cemetery in 1870. Alexander's former home now houses the Bicentennial Art Center.

By the turn of the twentieth century, Paris had more than 150 storefront businesses and factories and a population of more than 6,000. Today it is a small but lively city of 9,000. A number of historic buildings, including the arts center and the county courthouse, as well as several city parks make Paris worth a stop.

IL 32 and IL 133
WINDSOR–ARCOLA VIA ARTHUR
40 miles

IL 32 and IL 133 roughly trace an old stagecoach road between Paris and Springfield and traverse the Amish country of Illinois. Much of the prairie on both sides of the Kaskaskia River was settled by Old Order Amish from Pennsylvania, who arrived around 1864. These settlers followed the simple traditions and practices established in the 1690s by Swiss Mennonite bishop Jacob Amman. Today, the Amish colonies founded here still adhere to those traditions and practices.

WINDSOR
See previous trip

SULLIVAN

In the 1830s, early settler Asa Spencer Rice came across a tract of tall trees standing among the timber grass. "Of all the country I've seen," he wrote, "this is my choice." The settlement he began was known as Asa's Point until it was designated the seat of Moultrie County in 1845, whereupon it was renamed Sullivan, after Sullivan Island, the site of Col. William Moultrie's victory over the British fleet during the Revolutionary War.

Primarily an agricultural community, Sullivan was served at various times by the Illinois Central, the Wabash, and the Chicago & Eastern Illinois Railroads. Today it is a small city of under 4,500 people. While agriculture continues to play a prominent role in the local economy, manufacturing, service industries, and tourism also contribute. History lovers will find many sites of interest in Sullivan.

The historic courthouse—the county's third—was built between 1904 and 1906 and contains a mural depicting a young Abraham Lincoln, a frequent visitor to Moultrie County. During Lincoln's 1858 senatorial campaign against Stephen A. Douglas, a near riot broke out between the two factions on the town square in Sullivan. No one was seriously hurt, but the incident highlights the passion of that election. Today a large bronze plaque, erected in 1921, stands in the courthouse lawn to commemorate the event.

Sullivan is also the home of several museums, including the Moultrie County Heritage Center museum and research library and the Ward Museum, where 10,000 seashells, antique glassware, frontier furniture and household items, and other diverse articles are displayed. The city's public library, the Elizabeth Titus Memorial Library, houses an unusual display of automobile hood ornaments.

Another point of interest in Sullivan is the Little Theatre on the Square, where, during its fifty-plus-year history, a surprising number of stars have performed, including Mickey Rooney, Betty Grable, Ann Miller, Vincent Price, Alan Alda, Leonard Nimoy, and Ben Affleck. Sold to a local nonprofit corporation in 1981, the theater has expanded both its space and its programs, including an educational outreach program and a regional touring program.

ARTHUR

Although the Old Order Amish community lives on the flat, fertile farmland surrounding the village of Arthur, the town itself is mostly occupied by the "English" (non-Amish). The first Amish families arrived from Pennsylvania in 1865 and purchased farmland near two branches of the Kaskaskia River, avoiding the mosquito-ridden "big slough" in between. The village of Arthur came later, after the arrival of the Paris & Decatur Railroad in 1872. The railroad needed to place a passing switch and water tank west of Arcola, so they built one on the border of Moultrie and Douglas Counties, with the tracks built to circumvent the wetland. This rail stop, originally called Glasgow, became Arthur when it was incorporated as a village in 1877. Later, the swampy lands were drained, exposing rich and tillable soil and leading to further settlement.

For the next seventy-five years, Arthur maintained a light industrial economic base in addition to the agricultural production of its environs. Various companies manufactured tile, machinery, wire fencing, and other products. Fires in 1879 and 1901 destroyed many downtown businesses, but most were rebuilt. In the meantime, the Amish colony quietly continued farming, as it always had, outside of town.

Today, in addition to its own manufacturing and retail operations, Arthur functions as a trading center for the Amish, who produce handmade foods, crafts, and furniture, among other things. The Amish emphasize family bonds and live, work, and worship communally. The household language for many of them is Pennsylvania Dutch, a variation of German. Many Amish families shun such modern trappings as electronics, commercially produced food and clothing, and automobiles. Indeed, horse-drawn buggies are as prevalent as cars in this area.

Horse-drawn buggies—shown here tethered to a hitching rail in the Arthur area—are the primary means of transportation for the Amish. —Author's collection

ARCOLA

Arcola began as Bagdad, a start-up village that included a brickyard, blacksmith shop, gristmill, and country store in the early 1850s. When the Illinois Central Railroad laid its track between Centralia and Chicago, the route bypassed Bagdad, so the residents hoisted their buildings, minus the brickyard, onto large makeshift sleds and slid them along the snowy ground and across the frozen Okaw River (the local pronunciation of Kaskaskia River) to rebuild their village beside the rail line. In 1855 the county surveyor platted the town of Okaw, encompassing a quarter-mile tract on either side of the railroad. When the U.S. Post Office rejected the name Okaw, someone proposed Arcola. The first city council convened under the new name in 1858, and Arcola was incorporated as a city in 1873.

Arcolans are proud of their nickname, the "Broomcorn Capital of the World." For nearly a hundred years, the city was the undisputed king of broomcorn production, growing nearly half of the nation's supply. Dating from the end of the Civil War, Arcola's broomcorn growing and shipping operations were the oldest in the country. As its name implies, broomcorn was used for making brooms, but contrary to its name, the plant is actually a variety of sorghum, not corn. The dried stalks were (and still are, though less commonly) utilized to make brooms, while the seeds are harvested for livestock feed. By the 1950s, broomcorn production in Illinois fell off as cheaper brooms were imported from China, Mexico, and elsewhere. Nevertheless, Arcola continues to hold its annual Broom Corn Festival as a reminder of its agricultural heritage.

Like neighboring Arthur, Arcola helps serve the area's large community of Amish, and it is known as the gateway to the region's Amish country (see below). The city has also produced several interesting personalities. Among them are the "Lawn Rangers," a precision lawn-mower drill team who perform during the Broom Corn Festival and other special events. Arcola was also the birthplace of Raggedy Ann originator John Gruelle and the longtime home of Bob Moomaw, creator of the world's only "hippie memorial." Both are described below.

Amish Country

Arcola is the home of the Amish Interpretive Center, where visitors can learn more about the history and culture of the Amish branch of Mennonites. Many members of the sect emigrated from Switzerland and Germany to Pennsylvania in the early 1700s, and later the church established colonies in the Midwest and parts of Canada. The Old Order Amish believe in maintaining a simple agricultural way of life, rejecting modern technologies and mainstream American culture.

While some Amish have accepted certain modern-day conveniences, the majority continue to travel by horse and buggy, dress in their traditional, unadorned garb, and eat only their own farm-raised food. The Amish and "English" (non-Amish) in this region are mutually supportive. The Amish operate hundreds of cottage industries at their colonies, while downtown Arcola offers its own eclectic mix of businesses.

The Amish Interpretive Center is located at Rockome Gardens, a two-hundred-acre farm and living museum just west of Arcola. The gardens were originally a private homestead in the early twentieth century. The owners, Arthur and Elizabeth Martin, donated their property to the Mennonite Board of Missions in 1952. A few years later, it was sold to a private family, who developed the farm as a tourist destination, offering tours of the farm, buggy rides, a museum, gift shops, and other attractions. Under new ownership today, Rockome Gardens continues to bring in visitors. Its Cheese Factory and Bulk Food Store facility serves travelers and locals alike with its homemade baked goods, deli sandwiches, fresh cheeses, site-harvested honey, and bulk groceries.

Famous Dolls

Another of Arcola's claims to fame is its status as the birthplace of Raggedy Ann creator John Barton "Johnny" Gruelle. Born in Arcola in 1880, Gruelle originally worked as an illustrator and cartoonist for newspapers in Indianapolis, Cleveland, and New York. He is best known, however, for his children's books and his doll creations, Raggedy Ann and her brother, Raggedy Andy.

According to the story most often told, sometime in the early 1900s, Gruelle's young daughter, Marcella, found a dusty old rag doll in her grandmother's attic and showed it to Gruelle. The doll, which Gruelle's mother had made for his sister, was faceless, so Gruelle picked up his cartooning pen and drew a bright smiling face on the doll. He dubbed it Raggedy Ann, allegedly from combining the titles of two poems by family friend James Whitcomb Riley, "The Raggedy Man" and "Little Orphan Annie." This account, however, is probably legend, though with elements of truth. Indeed, the

Monument to Johnny Gruelle, the Arcola artist and writer who created Raggedy Ann and Andy —Author's collection

Raggedy Ann stories begin with a little girl named Marcella finding the doll in her grandma's dusty attic. Gruelle's wife, Myrtle, later said that it was her husband, not her daughter, who found the doll in the attic of his parents' home in Indianapolis, and that it happened before Marcella was born. Years later, watching his daughter play, Gruelle remembered the doll and concocted a story about a rag doll that comes to life.

In any case, around 1915, Gruelle did design a rag doll with yarn hair, button eyes, a triangle nose, and a whimsical smile. He received a patent for the doll's design on September 7, 1915; he also trademarked the name Raggedy Ann the same year. In November 1915, however, thirteen-year-old Marcella died from complications following a smallpox vaccine. It is uncertain when Gruelle wrote the first Raggedy Ann stories, but it is possible that, in concurrence with the legend, he made the stories up to entertain Marcella when she was ill and wrote them down after her death. What is certain is that the first stories were published in 1918 by the P. F. Volland Company of Chicago. Shortly after the stories appeared, Gruelle and his family made by hand an unknown number of his dolls to be marketed with the books. The stories soon caught on and demand for the dolls grew, leading the Volland Company to have the Raggedy Ann dolls mass-produced.

By 1920 the stories and the doll had become so popular that Gruelle created another character, Raggedy Andy. Gruelle produced a continuous stream of Raggedy Ann and Raggedy Andy stories until his untimely death from heart failure in 1938, at age forty-two. The enduringly beloved, redheaded dolls continue to be produced to this day, with variations, and vintage Raggedy Ann and Andy dolls are collector's items. Raggedy Ann was inducted into the National Toy Hall of Fame in 2002.

The Raggedy Ann and Andy Museum in Arcola was closed in 2009, with its main pieces donated to the Strong National Museum of Play in Rochester, New York. Its replacement is Marcella's Corner Gift Shop, located in Rockome Gardens.

Hippie Memorial

An unusual tribute to an earlier era stands in downtown Arcola near the old railroad depot. The "Hippie Memorial," created by Arcola artist and iconoclast Bob Moomaw in 1992, is believed to be the only monument of its kind. It is basically a large wall, about sixty feet long by six feet high, comprised of "iron rods, junk parts, and crafted metal." Upon his death in 1998, Moomaw bequeathed his creation to friend and self-described hippie Gus Kelsey. The memorial was dedicated a year later.

The monument spans the years of Moomaw's life, with each foot representing roughly one year. The left side represents Moomaw's early life, beginning in 1936 (the year Moomaw was born) and continuing through the Great Depression, World War II, and the "hypocrisy" of the 1950s. The middle part, taller than either side, represents the peak: the Kennedy years, Vietnam, the hippie movement, Woodstock, and the 1970s. The eighteen feet on the right represent "the return to small-mindedness," starting with the election of Ronald Reagan in 1980 and presumably ending in 1998, the year of Moomaw's death.

Across the street, a new monument, dedicated on Memorial Day 2002, encourages remembrance of Americans killed by war or terrorism. It features a black marble globe with various inscriptions along with two benches—one reads "Always remember Dec. 7, 1941" and the other says "Always remember Sept. 11, 2001."

Arcola resident Bob Moomaw created this "Hippie Memorial" in 1992 to represent his life; it is believed to be the nation's only memorial to hippies and nonconformists. —Author's collection

I-72 and US 45
DECATUR–RANTOUL
62 miles

This tour uses the major highways and passes through Monticello—with its three historic districts, several museums, and huge and gorgeous park—then through the Champaign-Urbana metropolitan area, ending in Rantoul, home of the Octave Chanute Aerospace Museum.

DECATUR
See Region 3

MONTICELLO

It is fitting that the city of Monticello, named after Thomas Jefferson's sprawling Virginia home, neighbors the 1,500-plus-acre Allerton Park and Retreat Center, with its century-old Georgian-style mansion, reflecting pond, formal gardens, and woodlands. The park's main entrance, a few miles west of Monticello, is accessible from I-72 via local roads. Once the private estate of the Allerton family, in 1946 Robert Henry Allerton donated the mansion and its beautiful, sprawling grounds to the University of Illinois at Champaign-Urbana. The school utilizes the park for various educational purposes, but it is also open to the public. The forty-room, 1900 manor house is used as a retreat and conference center for the university and for government and corporate events.

The first settler in what is now the city of Monticello was Quaker George Haworth, who was sent here as a liaison between the federal government and local Indian tribes. Haworth left in 1827, and two years later he sold his log cabin to James A. Piatt, who, along with three other men, founded the town of Monticello in 1837. After Piatt County was established in 1841, Monticello became the county seat, and it was incorporated as a city in 1872, shortly after the arrival of the Monticello Railroad Company, which later became part of the Illinois Central Railroad.

For more than ninety years, beginning in 1893, a major employer in Monticello was the Pepsin Syrup Company, manufacturer of a popular laxative. The medicine was formulated by Dr. William B. Caldwell, who bought a drugstore in Monticello in 1885. A year later, he sold the store but stayed in the building, establishing a medical practice upstairs. After prescribing his own senna pepsin formula for several years, Caldwell authorized two entrepreneurs to manufacture, bottle, and sell the concoction, branded Dr. Caldwell's Syrup Pepsin, in 1892. The Pepsin Syrup Company, formed the following year, grew by leaps and bounds. Through the twentieth century the company was sold and resold several times under various names, but the plant remained in Monticello. The final owner, the Mentholatum Company, bought the rights in 1984 and stopped production, closing the Monticello factory the following year.

The spacious grounds of the Allerton Park and Retreat Center near Monticello offer a bucolic setting for conferences and gatherings. —Author's collection

Abraham Lincoln and U.S. Senator Stephen A. Douglas met at Francis E. Bryant's cottage in Bement on July 29, 1858, to plan their famous debates. —Author's collection

Attesting to Monticello's dedication to historic preservation are its three National Register Historic Districts. The North State Street Historic District, also known as "Millionaires Row," is a six-block-long residential area featuring mansions of various architectural styles. An even broader range of elegant historic homes can be seen just south of downtown, in the three-block neighborhood known as the South Charter Street Historic District. In between is the distinctive Monticello Courthouse Square Historic District, which covers sixteen blocks of mostly commercial structures. Local historical landmarks include the Monticello Depot and the Piatt County Courthouse.

Monticello's historic appeal does not end there. North of the city, visitors may climb aboard a vintage steam-powered passenger train and ride ten miles from the Monticello Railway Museum to downtown Monticello and back again. The museum, founded in 1966 as SPUR (Society for the Perpetuation of Unretired Railfans), is jam-packed with old railroad cars, equipment, and paraphernalia. Seven miles south of Monticello is the Bryant Cottage State Historic Site, where Abraham Lincoln and Stephen A. Douglas met and laid out the format for their famous senatorial debates in 1858. The restored four-room frame house, located in nearby Bement on IL 105, was the home of early Bement settler Francis E. Bryant, a personal friend of Douglas.

CHAMPAIGN-URBANA

Though the twin cities of Champaign and Urbana grew up side by side, Urbana, established in 1833, existed first, while Champaign started out as West Urbana in 1857. Urbana was created to serve as the seat of the newly established Champaign County.

The names for both the county and its seat were chosen by the district's state senator, John W. Vance, after his childhood home of Urbana, Champaign County, Ohio. Urbana was incorporated as a city in 1855.

Urbana grew quickly, but when the Illinois Central Railroad arrived in the area in the mid-1850s, it built its depot, called Urbana Station, several miles west of the city. The area around Urbana Station evolved as a separate community known as West Urbana. Before long, the population of the newer town surpassed that of Urbana, invoking intense rivalry. Interested parties in Urbana attempted to incorporate the two towns into one municipality, but the effort failed. In 1857 West Urbana filed for separate incorporation. Three years later, its name was changed to Champaign, after the county, but Urbana remained the county seat.

Champaign and Urbana are best known for the University of Illinois, which straddles the two cities.

The University of Illinois: Legacy of Agricultural Innovations

Although they remained separate municipalities, Champaign and Urbana jointly established the Illinois Industrial University (predecessor to the University of Illinois) on 625 acres in Urbana. When it opened in 1867, the school had three faculty members, a head farmer, and seventy-seven students. The curriculum focused on agriculture, engineering, home economics, and other subjects pertinent to rural concerns. In 1885 the name was changed to the University of Illinois (UI), and the areas of study expanded to include numerous academic and professional fields, such as agribusiness, veterinary medicine, science, mathematics, fine arts, and others. Today the school has an enrollment of about 35,000.

In the mid-1870s, five acres of the UI campus were set aside as an experimental agronomic field for an ongoing crop study. Charles W. Silver, an agricultural chemist, and Manley Miles, a professor of agriculture, share the credit for founding the project, originally known as "Experiment 23 Rotation Study." It was later named the Morrow Plots, for George E. Morrow, then a professor of agriculture and later Dean of the College of Agriculture. Silver outlined a detailed layout for a long-term field study on corn in 1875. The following year, Miles proposed a concept similar to Silver's, and the two worked together to initiate the project. The object of the study was to determine the long-term effects of crop rotation versus continuous replanting on harvest yields and soil depletion rates.

After approximately twenty years, the data showed that continuous replanting led to nutrient depletion in the soil, while rotating crops retarded such depletion. In spite of this success, by 1903 the Morrow Plots had been dramatically reduced in size to only three one-tenth-acre plots, separated by permanent borders. Furthermore, the program had no specific budget and no one to officially oversee it. Even so, experiments continued for decades, with various faculty members volunteering their time to continue the studies. On September 12, 1968, the Morrow Plots were designated a National Historic Landmark as the oldest agronomic experiment field in the United States. The field is still used for crop studies today.

Around the time that the Morrow Plots were being scaled back, another agricultural innovator arrived on the UI campus and established his own experimental

James H. Petit (left) and Cyril G. Hopkins extract soil samples from the Morrow Plots experimental agriculture field at the University of Illinois.
—Courtesy University of Illinois Archives

agronomy field. Dr. Cyril G. Hopkins joined the university staff in 1894 as a chemist with the Agricultural Experiment Station. In 1900 he began teaching agronomy, and three years later he was named vice director of the Agricultural Experiment Station. In conflict with many of his peers, Hopkins believed that soil would become more productive if fed with nutrients. To conduct his research, he established an experimental field on a small tract of land west of Edgewood, in southern Champaign County. He later set up several similar fields elsewhere in the region.

Hopkins experimented with many fertilizers, including composted crop scraps, limestone, rock phosphate, and potash. Through these experiments, he succeeded in quadrupling crop yields from those of the early 1800s. Hopkins soon became one of the world's foremost authorities on soils, writing three classics of agronomy: *Soil Fertility and Permanent Agriculture* (1910), *The Story of the Soil* (1911), and *The Farm That Won't Wear Out* (1913).

In 1918 Hopkins joined an American Red Cross relief mission to famine-stricken Greece to study and improve their war-ravaged agricultural conditions. En route back to the United States, near Gibraltar, he died from complications of malaria on October 6, 1919. The following year, the Hopkins Memorial Association was founded to further the work that was interrupted by his death and to conduct new investigations in soil fertility.

The University of Illinois today, with the Morrow Plots experimental agriculture field in foreground at bottom —Courtesy University of Illinois Archives

RANTOUL

The first settler in this area, Archa Campbell, arrived by covered wagon in 1848 and started a farm. The Indians called the place *Neipswah*, meaning "mink," and it was known to Euro-Americans as Mink Grove. The area remained sparsely settled until the Illinois Central Railroad established a station here in 1854. The railroad named the stop Rantoul to honor ICRR executive Robert Rantoul, Jr. The depot attracted more settlers, new businesses, and developers. By 1870 the village had a large flour mill, a telegraph office, three churches, and numerous stores.

The biggest change for the community occurred in 1917, when the War Department selected Rantoul as the site for one of the twenty-seven airfields the government was building to train pilots. The town was chosen for its level ground, railroad access, and proximity to the University of Illinois ground school.

Chanute Field, named after civil engineer Octave Chanute, an early proponent of aviation development, was used for pilot training during World War I and for technical training into the early 1930s. The facility was expanded as a Works Progress Administration project in the late 1930s—just in time, it turned out, for World War II. As that war got under way, the number of troops sent to Chanute Field exceeded the facility's housing capacity, and many men had to be sheltered in tents. During the Korean War, the size of the airfield, renamed Chanute Air Force Base, was doubled. Its training courses focused on aircraft maintenance, missile maintenance, military meteorology, and various other specialized fields.

In December of 1993, as part of a government effort to reduce military spending, the Department of Defense closed Chanute Air Force Base, the country's oldest military technical training center. With the base's closure, Rantoul lost its major economic engine. Undaunted, city officials redeveloped parts of the facility into a commercial, recreational, and residential center of the community. The former base now houses shops, restaurants, homes, schools, services, light manufacturing, an airport, and recreational facilities. Of special interest to many visitors is the Octave Chanute Aerospace Museum, the largest aviation museum in Illinois.

Other sites of interest in the Rantoul area include "Gordyville USA," a permanent auction house and flea market, and Hardy's Reindeer Ranch. The latter was created in 1995 by Julie and Mark Hardy when they purchased two live reindeer to promote their Christmas-tree business. In 1997 they went to Alaska and bought thirteen more animals. Today, visitors can view the ranch's sixteen reindeer, shop for Christmas trees, check out the gift shop, or attend an event at the banquet hall.

US 45 and I-57
RANTOUL–KANKAKEE
62 miles

On this stretch, US 45 and I-57 parallel each other, and the stops on this tour may be reached from either highway.

RANTOUL
See previous trip

PAXTON

The Illinois Central Railroad, which figured so prominently in the development of Illinois, no longer stops in Paxton, but the town's old depot preserves the railroad's heritage, serving as the headquarters of the Illinois Central Historical Society, established in 1979. The brick depot, built by the Lake Erie & Western Railroad around 1913, houses the society's archives along with a small museum and gift shop.

The depot is just one of many historic buildings in Paxton, the seat of Ford County. Numerous Victorian homes grace the downtown area, and the city has several buildings on the NRHP, including the 1904 Paxton Carnegie Public Library, the 1897 Dunnan–Hampton House, and the 1857 Paxton First Schoolhouse (a.k.a. Corbett House). Perhaps most distinctive of all is the 1887 brick water tower and pump house, an eighty-foot-tall, Gothic-style structure that now houses the Ford County Historical Society museum.

Both Ford County and its seat were founded in 1859. Before that, Paxton was known as Prospect City, and before that, as Prairie City. Its final, permanent name came from investor Sir Joseph Paxton, a prominent British architect who had envisioned building an English settlement here. As it turned out, the town was developed mostly by Swedes, not Englishmen, but the name was kept.

ONARGA

The story of Onarga's creation is not unlike that of other towns in this region—in 1854, at the site of a small but established farming settlement, a village was laid out as a railroad stop along the route of the Illinois Central, and Onarga became one of many shipping points for area farmers. The community distinguished itself, however, by cultivating a specialty. In addition to raising the usual crops of corn and soybeans, residents established a number of tree and shrub nurseries, growing starter plants for landscapers, orchards, and berry farms. That industry continues today, and Onarga is still known as the "Nursery Capital of the Midwest."

One unexpected aspect of Onarga's history is its association with the famous Allan Pinkerton Detective Agency. In the early days of the agency, founded in Chicago in 1850, Allan Pinkerton hired New York City police officer Timothy Webster to come to Chicago to work for him as a detective. In 1858, at Pinkerton's suggestion, Webster moved his family to Onarga, where it was deemed safer for them.

Just before the Civil War broke out, Pinkerton entered federal service and recruited Webster as a spy for the Union. Sent to infiltrate a Baltimore group that was planning to assassinate Abraham Lincoln, Webster helped foil the scheme. He was later sent to Richmond, where he was able to obtain additional significant information.

In early 1862 Pinkerton received word that Webster had fallen ill, and he sent out two agents to bring him home. The agents were caught en route, however, and they subsequently revealed information that exposed Webster as a spy. Webster was soon caught and hanged by the Confederates. After the war, Webster's widow, Charlotte, asked Pinkerton to recover her husband's remains for reburial in Onarga. He was reinterred at Onarga Cemetery in 1871.

In the meantime, Pinkerton had purchased his own property in Onarga. In 1864 he bought 254 acres and ordered 85,000 larches from his native Scotland to be planted on the estate, which became known as the Larch Farm. He had hoped to sell the lumber for railroad ties, but this did not pan out. A few years after retiring from detective work in 1869, Pinkerton began developing the Larch Farm as a country estate. Among other things, he built a large house, designed to resemble a Scottish mansion from his youth, and dubbed it "the Villa." According to some historians, locals often referred to it as the "Whoopie House," as Pinkerton enjoyed lively entertaining.

Pinkerton died in 1884. Contrary to his wishes, the Larch Farm was not maintained after his death, and the property was sold off over the years. The Villa was allowed to deteriorate and was scheduled for demolition until a private party purchased it in 2011. The new owner is renovating the house, but it will not be open to the public.

KANKAKEE, BRADLEY, AND BOURBONNAIS

The city of Kankakee and the adjacent villages of Bradley and Bourbonnais grew up side by side in this metro area about sixty miles south of Chicago. The first settlement was Bourbonnais, originally known as Bourbonnais Grove, a colony of French Canadian immigrants that was platted in 1832. When Kankakee County, named for the region's Kankakee River, was founded in 1853, a new town, Kankakee City, was created to be the seat. Established south of Bourbonnais along the new Illinois Central Railroad line, Kankakee City soon overshadowed its older neighbor. Within a few decades, the northern part of Kankakee City became a booming industrial district. This area, known as North Kankakee, was incorporated as a separate village in 1892, and four years later it was renamed Bradley, for local industrialist David Bradley.

Visitors to the tri-cities will find much of historical interest. Both Bradley and Bourbonnais have their own historical societies, and the latter is especially proud of its two main historic sites, the LeTourneau Home and Museum and the Perry Farm. The LeTourneau Home was the residence of George R. LeTourneau, Bourbonnais' first mayor. The original part of the Greek Revival house, built about 1837, was expanded in the 1850s and further improved in subsequent decades. It is now a museum and the headquarters of the Bourbonnais Grove Historical Society. The Perry Farm, an 1830s homestead now operated as a recreation area, includes a living-history farm, a nature preserve with "Indian Caves," and a children's museum. The original farmhouse serves as the park's visitor center.

Kankakee, the largest of the three communities, contains a cornucopia of historic sites, including several museums, two homes designed by Frank Lloyd Wright, two National Register Historic Districts, and some of the oldest homes in the county. Kankakee also has the honor of being the only city in Illinois to have produced three governors—Lennington Small (1921–29), Samuel Shapiro (1968–69), and George Ryan (1999–2003).

The oldest standing structure in downtown Kankakee is the Lemuel Milk Carriage House, a.k.a. the Stone Barn, erected in 1860 by prominent early settler Lemuel Milk. Over the years, the carriage house has been used as a stable for fire-department horses, an automotive garage, a hardware warehouse, a bakery, and until recently, the headquarters of the Kankakee County Junior League. In July 2012 it opened as the Kankakee County French Heritage Museum. The museum is one of several operated by the Kankakee County Historical Society. Established in 1906, it is the oldest historical society in Illinois. Its main museum complex, the Kankakee County Museum, stands across the river from downtown.

The focal point of the city is the 1912 Kankakee County Courthouse, which is surrounded by six nineteenth-century churches and other historical structures. Nearby is the still-active 1898 Illinois Central train depot. Now used by Amtrak, the depot also houses the Kankakee Railroad Museum.

Just south of the downtown courthouse area, along the Kankakee River, is the Riverview Historic District, a residential neighborhood with wide, tree-lined boulevards and large Victorian homes. The two most prized buildings in the district are the B. Harley Bradley House and the Warren Hickox House, the first Prairie-style homes ever built by Frank Lloyd Wright; both were constructed in 1900. Kankakee is the only place in the world where two of Wright's designs are located side by side. While the Hickox home is still privately owned, the Bradley house was recently purchased by a nonprofit group called Wright in Kankakee and is open for tours.

While Kankakee has a lot to be proud of, in 1999 it was the recipient of a dubious honor. The city was in a slump when the *Places Rated Almanac* ranked Kankakee County dead last of 354 best metro areas to live. Picking up on the story, late-night TV talk-show host David Letterman announced he wanted to boost the city's image by sending it two prefabricated gazebos, explaining that Kankakee could then bill itself as the "Home of the Twin Gazebos." After this rather embarrassing episode, Kankakee embarked on a massive revitalization project that included erecting new buildings and restoring old ones, pumping up community cultural programs, and installing numerous new recreational facilities. The two gazebos are still standing in Kankakee, one in Cobb Park and the other in front of the Kankakee Railroad Museum.

I-55 (Old Route 66) and IL 53
BLOOMINGTON-NORMAL—WILMINGTON
81 miles

Travelers dedicated to following historic US 66 may trace the entire route by following the historical markers, but it gets a little complicated outside Chicago, so you might want to do your own research. This trip is a simplified version of the section of the route called the "Red Carpet Corridor," presumably so named for its hospitality. Here we follow I-55, which has exits to the famous highway's major stops, up to Gardner; from there we switch to IL 53 to get to Wilmington. Alternatively, various state highways, many of which contain sections of old Route 66, closely parallel the interstate most of the way. Many of the towns on this trip—including Lexington, Pontiac, Odell, Gardner, and Wilmington—have some sort of attraction honoring the Mother Road and its history. Twelve towns between Towanda and Joliet take part in the "Illinois Route 66 Red Carpet Corridor Festival" each May.

The history of this route predates US 66, however. The current interstate runs parallel to the route of the Chicago & Alton Railroad line, built in 1854, and many of the towns along this stretch started as railroad towns. Shortly after the railroad was built, coal was discovered in the northern part of this area, and additional towns, including Braidwood and Coal City, sprung up near the mines. Some of the scarred and barren land the mines left behind was reclaimed and converted to parkland, such as the Mazonia Fish and Wildlife Area near Gardner.

BLOOMINGTON-NORMAL
See Region 3

LEXINGTON

Lexington was one of many towns founded in McLean County by eager developers during the land boom of 1836. In this case the developers were Bloomington banker Asahel Gridley and Kentuckian James Brown. It was the latter who named the city Lexington, after his hometown in Kentucky. Unfortunately for the partners, the real estate bubble burst before Lexington caught on, and the new town was left largely unoccupied until the Chicago & Alton Railroad arrived in 1854. Suddenly Lexington was in a position to grow, and so it did.

Over the years, the railroad brought Lexington not only prosperity but also excitement, including a visit from President-elect Abraham Lincoln in 1860 and from President Theodore Roosevelt in 1902. In between, in 1872, the relationship between Lexington and the Chicago & Alton became the focus of a key legal case.

The 1870 Illinois state constitution included language that allowed the government to regulate the freight industry, but the railroad, which naturally objected to the idea, continued to set shipping rates according to its own needs. Shipping lumber from Chicago to Lexington, for example, cost more than shipping the same amount from Chicago to Bloomington. In 1872 Ruben M. Benjamin, a prominent Bloomington lawyer and author of the disputed provision, prepared to file suit against the railroad, choosing Lexington as his test case. In *The People v. the Chicago & Alton Railroad*, Benjamin argued that it was unfair to small-town residents for the railroad to charge higher fees for shipping a shorter distance. After the lower court ruled in favor of the state, the railroad appealed, and the case made its way to the U.S. Supreme Court. In a landmark decision, the court upheld the lower court's ruling that states did have the right to impose regulations on corporations.

As the railroads, which had brought so much success to Lexington and other towns like it, began to fade, the federal highway system took its place. Beginning in 1915, State Route 4, the "Pontiac Trail" connecting Chicago and Springfield, ran through Lexington, opening the city to highway traffic. In 1926 State Route 4 became US Route 66, and Lexington became a favorite stop for motorists traveling on the legendary Mother Road. The completion of I-55 in 1978 bypassed the city, but nostalgic travelers can still find a one-mile section of the old highway intact in Lexington; it is now a walking trail called "Memory Lane," lined with vintage billboards.

Another historical attraction in Lexington predates Route 66 by nearly a century. The 1829 Patton Cabin is a preserved settler's home from the early days of white settlement in eastern Illinois. It was originally built beside a Kickapoo village a few miles southeast of present Lexington; in fact, the Indians helped the Patton family construct it. The cabin was moved and reassembled in a city park in 1969. After undergoing further restoration, it was listed on the NRHP in 1986. The streets of Lexington also boast a number of well-maintained historic homes, several dating from the 1860s.

PONTIAC

Pontiac sits about halfway between Chicago and Springfield, just east of I-55. Fans of old Route 66 can visit the Old Log Cabin Restaurant, which opened in 1926, the same year the historic highway was commissioned. Built along the original route of US 66, the restaurant was passed by when the highway was realigned in the 1940s, so the owners raised the building on jacks and turned it around to face the highway again. Pontiac is also the home of the Route 66 Association of Illinois Hall of Fame and Museum as well as numerous other museums, historic structures, and sites of interest.

The settlement was platted in 1837 as the seat of the newly created Livingston County, and despite several attempts by rival communities to move it, Pontiac remains the county seat. The current courthouse, built in 1874–75, was the county's third. Installed on an exterior wall of the courthouse is a plaque honoring the Ottawa chief Pontiac, who, according to the plaque, is the city's namesake, so christened by early settler Jesse W. Fell.

Incorporated as a city in 1856, a year after the Illinois Central Railroad arrived, Pontiac was booming by the late 1800s. In 1893 a former boys' reformatory was converted into a state prison. Originally called the State Reformatory, the prison was

Sketch of Ottawa chief Pontiac
—Courtesy Schaumburg Township
District Library, Illinois Collection

renamed the Illinois State Penitentiary-Pontiac Branch in 1933, and forty years later it became known as the Pontiac Correctional Center. The prison suffered two major riots in the 1970s. In the first one, on April 23, 1973, two inmates were killed in a mess-hall melee between rival gangs. Five years later, on July 22, 1978, another riot erupted, this one involving a thousand inmates and causing the death of three prison workers—the deadliest prison riot in Illinois history. Still in use, the Pontiac Correctional Center is a major employer in the county.

In December 1997, *Time* magazine named Pontiac one of the "Ten Best Small Towns" in the United States. The article praised the local rebellion against high-volume discounters and the conversion of the old City Hall into a low-rent business incubator for independent shops. The magazine also noted the city's "brick-paved streets, canoes in the Vermilion River beneath a swinging wooden bridge that leads to the town park . . . and gooseberry pie at the Apple Tree Restaurant."

In 2004 Pontiac became the home of the Route 66 Association of Illinois Hall of Fame and Museum, after the original museum site, Dixie Trucker's Home in McLean, was sold to new owners. Pontiac is also the headquarters of the "Walldogs," a group dedicated to restoring and recreating historic outdoor commercial art. The International Walldog Mural and Sign Art Museum, which opened in 2010, preserves and displays old murals, hand-painted signs, and other outdoor advertising. Other places of interest in Pontiac include the Livingston County War Museum, the Yost Museum and Art Center, the Pontiac Oakland Automobile Museum, three swinging bridges, the striking 1875 Livingston County Courthouse, and several historic homes, as well as the nearby Humiston Woods Nature Center.

DWIGHT

Dwight's residents proudly proclaim that their village is "Not just a bump in the road." Among its treasures are the 1857 Pioneer Gothic Church, a rare example of the Carpenter Gothic style of architecture; the First National Bank building, designed by Frank Lloyd Wright in 1905; the Richardsonian Romanesque Chicago & Alton Railroad Depot, which now serves Amtrak and houses the Dwight Historical Society Museum and the Chamber of Commerce; and Ambler's Texaco station, which served motorists along US Route 66 from 1933 to 1999. The latter, which was the longest-operating gas station on Route 66 before it closed, was restored in 2007 and now houses a Route 66 visitor center. It was added to the NRHP in 2001.

Dwight began in the early 1850s, when several men associated with the Chicago & Mississippi Railroad bought land here and platted a town around a proposed new depot. The station, originally called West New York, was soon renamed for Henry Dwight, a New York capitalist who funded the railroad from Joliet to Bloomington. By 1869 the village had several railroads, and Dwight became a shipping center for local farmers.

Dwight's historic Chicago & Alton Railroad Depot, built in 1891, was designed by Henry Ives Cobb. It now serves as the offices of the Dwight Historical Society and the Dwight Chamber of Commerce. —Photo by Marylin Thorsen, courtesy Dwight Historical Society

On September 22, 1860, the eighteen-year-old Prince of Wales, eldest son of Queen Victoria and Prince Albert, arrived in Dwight during a visit to the United States. He stayed a week, hunting quail and prairie chickens on the open land and attending Sunday services at the Pioneer Gothic Church. Wishing to remain incognito, the prince was introduced to the locals as Baron Renfrew, one of his hereditary titles. Dwight's Renfrew Park was named for the royal visitor. Upon the death of his mother in 1901, the prince became King Edward VII.

In 1903 another high-ranking visitor came to Dwight. President Theodore Roosevelt was on hand at the dedication of the newly rebuilt facilities for the internationally known Keeley Institute, whose original office building had been destroyed in a fire the previous year. The institute, founded by Dr. Leslie E. Keeley and John R. Oughton in 1879, created a sensation as a theraputic community for alcoholics and other addicts. The economic boom the Keeley Institute brought to Dwight during much of the facility's eighty-seven-year existence can hardly be overestimated.

Keeley Institute

In 1879 Dwight physician Dr. Leslie E. Keeley and chemist John R. Oughton created a drug they called the "Double Chloride of Gold Cure" to treat alcoholism. Enlisting financial support from a local merchant, Keeley built a treatment center in Dwight around this medication, which he claimed was a surefire cure for "drunkenness." In addition to dispensing the gold cure, the institute's approach was revolutionary in that it treated alcoholism as a disease rather than a vice.

As word-of-mouth testimonials spread, the institute began to draw attention. In 1891 *Chicago Tribune* publisher Joseph Medill challenged Keeley's claims by sending six hardened drinkers to Dwight for treatment. When they returned reformed, Medill was sold. The subsequent articles lauding the facility created a stampede of patients. Within a few years, the institute had become internationally known, and Keeley eventually opened some two hundred branches in the United States and Europe.

In spite of its success, the institute and its gold cure—whose composition remained a secret—had its share of critics. Many in the medical profession condemned Keeley's practices as quackery, and numerous patients fell off the wagon after leaving the facility. Nevertheless, Keeley maintained that his treatment worked, and the public largely believed it. Effective or not, the gold cure made Dr. Keeley a wealthy man.

The Keeley Institute had an enormous impact on the community of Dwight. James Oughton, Jr., grandson of cofounder John Oughton, worked at the Dwight facility for much of his life. He noted: "Keeley turned the whole town of Dwight into a kind of therapeutic community. Treating alcoholism and other addictions became the town mission. . . . The townspeople of Dwight developed a great sympathy for the distinguished visitors who came to their city for treatment."

Dr. Leslie Keeley died of heart failure in 1900. His body was entombed in a stone mausoleum in Dwight's Oak Lawn Cemetery. The life-size bust that adorned the gravesite was sculpted by Leonard Wells Volk, who cast Abraham Lincoln's death mask and designed the tomb of Sen. Stephen A. Douglas. To safeguard the sculpture, it was moved to the Dwight Historical Museum around 2008.

In 1902 a fire destroyed the Keeley Institute's main building and some of the other structures on the property. Spared was John Oughton's twenty-room, Victorian-style mansion. Built in 1891 as a boardinghouse by Dwight resident Walter T. Scott, the building was moved to the institute's grounds in 1894 to serve as a clubhouse; a year later, it was remodeled and became Oughton's home. After Oughton's death in 1925, the mansion was donated to the institute for patient lodging.

The facility's main building was rebuilt and it reopened in 1903, but by then the institute's popularity had begun to wane. Although the Dwight facility would continue to operate into the mid-twentieth century, most of the institute's structures eventually became vacant. The rebuilt main building, which featured five Tiffany-style stained-glass windows, each depicting one of the five senses, was leased to the Veterans Administration in 1919 for a hospital, and the federal government bought it five years later.

By the 1930s, most of the Keeley Institute branches had closed down, though the facility in Dwight operated until 1965. Later that year, the 1903 main building was sold to the state of Illinois and it reopened as the still-operating William W. Fox Children's Development Center. The stained-glass windows, designed by Louis J. Millet, founder of the Chicago School of Architecture, still grace the entrance.

The still-standing John R. Oughton House and its outbuildings—a carriage house and a five-stories-tall windmill—were added to the NRHP in 1980. Today, the mansion is privately owned and serves as a restaurant, while the carriage house became the Prairie Creek Public Library. The windmill, built in 1896, is owned by the village of Dwight.

GARDNER

Gardner was and remains mostly a farming community, though many residents work in nearby cities such as Joliet or Kankakee. Like many other towns in this area, it started out as a rail stop in the 1850s and was named for a railroad engineer, in this case Henry A. Gardner. In the late 1800s, however, when coal deposits were discovered nearby, Gardner became, for a time, a mining town. Coal production began to decline after only a few decades, and by the early twentieth century the mines had been abandoned. Gardner was resilient, though, and quietly returned to agriculture.

In recent decades, the village has also enjoyed a sideline in tourism. Much of the tourist traffic in Gardner is associated with the same Route 66 nostalgia that draws visitors to the other towns along the old highway. One site promoted along with the Mother Road attractions, although it is actually unrelated to the highway, is Gardner's intact two-cell jail, built in 1906 and used into the 1950s. The limestone-block jail now stands as a mini-museum in a city park.

Unfortunately, the main attraction in Gardner that was connected to the heyday of Route 66 recently burned down. The storied Riviera Restaurant was built in 1928 by South Wilmington businessman James Girot. During Prohibition, the Riviera offered liquor and gambling to discreet travelers. Reportedly among its clientele were movie stars Gene Kelly and Tom Mix, as well as notorious gang boss Al Capone. Even after the demise of Route 66, the restaurant continued to operate into the twenty-first century, enjoying its status as a legendary watering hole before closing in 2008. The building's fate was still uncertain when, in June 2010, the Riviera was completely destroyed by fire. It was a sad blow to the entire community.

Another old Route 66 stop in Gardner, the Streetcar Diner, is still intact. In 1932 local entrepreneur George Kaldem purchased an old horse-drawn streetcar from

Kankakee, moved it to Gardner, and converted it into a cafe. The diner closed in 1939, but in 1955 James Girot's son-in-law bought it and moved it to a spot behind the Riviera, where it served various purposes over the years. In the late 1990s the Route 66 Association of Illinois began restoration work on the diner, which was inducted into the Route 66 Hall of Fame in 2004. When the Riviera burned down in 2010, the neighboring streetcar was not damaged. Later that year, the owners donated it to the city of Gardner, and it was relocated to a new site on a concrete foundation near the two-cell jail. The Route 66 Association of Illinois and volunteers from the community completed the restoration of the diner, and it was rededicated in 2011.

BRAIDWOOD AND VICINITY

The city of Braidwood and its neighbors—including Coal City, Diamond, and Carbon Hill to the west and Godley, Braceville, and Central City to the south—originated as mining boomtowns. Braidwood (named for local mine owner James Braidwood) was established in 1867, and most of the other towns in the area were founded during the same coal boom, in the 1860s and '70s.

Coal had been harvested in northeastern Illinois as early as the 1820s, but it was not until the 1860s, with the discovery of major seams of marketable coal, that commercial coal mining in this region began in earnest. By then the railroad was already in place in the area, making transportation of the product to the vast Chicago market simple and cheap. In addition, the railroad itself was a large consumer of coal. By the mid-1870s, the boom was in full swing. Easterners and European immigrants flocked to the area, turning mining camps into cities.

The Diamond Mine Disaster of 1883 was one of many accidents that highlighted the dangers shaft miners faced. After a heavy snowmelt in the area, the Diamond Mine suddenly flooded and collapsed, causing the deaths of more than seventy workers. A monument now stands at the site in downtown Diamond, Illinois.

These hazardous working conditions, coupled with low pay, long hours, and corporate control of workers' lives, led to a number of labor strikes in Braidwood and elsewhere. Several Braidwood miners emerged as major union leaders, including Dan McLaughlin in the 1870s and William Ryan and John Mitchell in the 1890s. Most of the strikes were unsuccessful, however, and ultimately the coal companies shut down or moved into strip mining, putting most miners in the area out of work by the early twentieth century.

Although the development of strip-mining technology of the 1920s allowed coal companies to increase production at a lower cost, mounting competition from other coal regions and from alternative fuel industries (oil, natural gas, diesel, and later, nuclear) kept the northern Illinois coal industry from fully rebounding. After decades of struggling, the last mining operations in the area shut down in the 1970s. By then, many of the towns in the region had been abandoned or nearly so. Braidwood and a few others survived, however, having developed a manufacturing base; area factories produced everything from cream cheese to chemicals to cigars.

In the meantime, US Route 66 brought automobile traffic through Braidwood, boosting its economy for a few decades. More recently, the city's position on the old highway has given it a modest tourist industry. Its main attraction is the still-operating Polk-a-Dot Drive In restaurant. This eatery started in 1956 as a converted school bus painted with bright, multicolored polka dots. Its décor reflects the 1950s theme, with memorabilia hanging from the walls and lifesize statues of Elvis, Marilyn Monroe, and others standing outside.

In the 1980s, two nuclear power plants were installed in Braidwood, bringing steady income to the entire area. The city's current population is more than 5,000.

WILMINGTON

A good chunk of Wilmington is located in the middle of the Kankakee River, thus it is known as the "Island City." Most of the island is occupied by a large city park, one of many green areas in and around Wilmington. In fact, a dozen nature preserves and parks lie within a few miles of this city of 5,000, making it a recreation and nature lover's paradise.

Wilmington's founder, merchant and entrepreneur Thomas Cox, bought 400 acres of land, including the island, from the government in 1834 and proceeded to build a sawmill, a gristmill, and other services that brought in settlers from miles around. Two years later Cox surveyed lots for a town, originally called Winchester. The lots sold like hotcakes, and within a few years the community had an inn, two stores, and a school as well as a number of large homes, at least one of which sheltered fugitive slaves on the Underground Railroad. Wilmington was incorporated as a village in 1854, the same year the Chicago & Alton Railroad arrived. The railroad spawned even more rapid growth, and Wilmington was incorporated as a city in 1865. Around the same time, the discovery of coal in this region further contributed to Wilmington's prosperity, although it was not a mining town per se.

Today, Wilmington's downtown area is known for its antique shops, and the city boasts several buildings from the mid-1800s, including the 1857 public library, formerly a church, and the old city hall, built in 1879, the current home of the Wilmington Area Historical Society. The main portion of the Eagle Hotel, built around 1838, is the oldest structure in town. It was refurbished in 1982 to accommodate a meeting room and museum for the Wilmington Area Historical Society, but after a fire in 1990 it was abandoned, awaiting repairs. A developer later bought it, but after renovation plans stalled, the partially restored building, listed on the NRHP in 1994, was put up for sale in 2012 and, as of this writing, remains vacant.

Wilmington also has one of the most popular Route 66 attractions on the Red Carpet Corridor: the still-operating Launching Pad Drive-In restaurant, with its kitchy "Gemini Giant." The Launching Pad opened as a hot dog and ice cream place in 1960. The green-clad Gemini Giant, an old fiberglass "muffler man" statue converted into an eye-catching advertisement for the restaurant, wears a space helmet and holds a rocket. Another green fiberglass statue from the Route 66 era, one of the old Sinclair dinosaurs, stands proudly atop a Wilmington tire store.

IL 17, IL 18, I-39/US 51, and IL 71
DWIGHT–STARVED ROCK STATE PARK
54 miles

While the headquarters for Starved Rock State Park is in Utica, on the north bank of the Illinois River, the park itself lies south of the river and Interstate 80, this book's regional boundary. Adjacent to Starved Rock is another state park, Matthiessen State Park, also south of the boundary. Several other nature preserves can be found in the vicinity as well, including the Margery Carlson Nature Preserve and Plum Island Eagle Sanctuary. Besides the parks, this region comprises several interesting places, notably Streator, hometown of Clyde Tombaugh, the man who discovered Pluto (then considered the ninth planet) in 1930, and Oglesby, a major cement-manufacturing center and the site of a frontier fort. Most of the area, however, is rural, dotted with tiny villages, many of them faded railroad or mining towns.

DWIGHT
See previous trip

STREATOR

The city of Streator, population near 14,000, serves as the commercial center for the many small rural communities in the area, known locally as "Streatorland." Settlers came to this area as early as the 1820s, with more arriving after the Illinois & Michigan Canal was built in 1848. The first settler in the place that became Streator was John O'Neil, who opened a store here in 1861. After coal was discovered in the region, the sparse settlement grew into a mining town, originally called Hardscrabble, then Unionville, and finally incorporated as the town of Streator, named for mining investor Worthy S. Streator, in 1868. By 1880 the population had tripled, and Streator incorporated as a city in 1882.

The success of the coal mines spawned other industries, notably glass manufacturing; throughout the twentieth century, Streator was known as the "glass container capital of the world," and the Owens Bottle Company, which opened its factory in Streator in 1916, is still a major employer in the area. Other early factories made brick, tile, and farm equipment.

Streator's primary historic attractions include the 1903 Carnegie Library; the Streatorland Historical Society Museum, housed in a modest brick bungalow built in 1924; the Riverview Cemetery, where tours are available; and the Weber House and Garden, a "storybook Tudor cottage" with an elaborate, two-acre English garden. This property, owned and operated by Chicago media personality Ted Weber, was built by Weber's parents in 1936. Ted, who often interviewed celebrities on his radio show, was called back home in the early 1980s to take care of his terminally ill parents. After their deaths in 1983, he decided to stay, fixing up the house and gardens in the style of the late eighteenth century. He later opened the house and grounds for tours, personally regaling visitors with stories of his famous and infamous acquaintances, such as Eleanor Roosevelt, Myrna Loy, and Richard Nixon, a tradition he continues to this day.

Streator is also notable as the birthplace of astronomer Clyde Tombaugh, who in 1930 discovered what was then considered the ninth planet, Pluto. Recent controversy over Pluto's astronomical status has drawn new attention to Streator and its star-gazing native son.

Clyde Tombaugh and the Dwarf Planet

Clyde Tombaugh was born in Streator in 1906. His family later moved to Kansas, where young Clyde, unable to attend college, built his own homemade telescope and sent his observations to the Lowell Observatory in Flagstaff, Arizona. Impressed, the observatory offered him a job as a research assistant in 1929. It was here that the untrained young astronomer discovered Pluto the following year, an achievement for which he was awarded the Jackson-Gwitt Medal by Great Britain's Royal Astronomical Society in 1931. Tombaugh eventually went to college, earning a master's degree from the University of Kansas in 1938. He went on to discover hundreds of asteroids and variable stars, star clusters, galaxy clusters, comets, and other celestial bodies. He also observed numerous UFOs and was a believer in extraterrestrial life.

Originally designated the ninth planet in our solar system, Pluto was considered a bona fide planet for seventy-six years before its astronomical classification was downgraded to a trans-Neptunian object, or dwarf planet, in 2006. The scientific community revamped its classification system after new technologies led to more sophisticated knowledge about space objects. The decision was controversial, however, especially among laypeople, and most especially among the residents of Streator.

The controversy had already surfaced before Clyde Tombaugh died in 1997 at age ninety. According to his family, Tombaugh resisted the idea of his discovery being reclassified, but he died before all the evidence was in. Family members believe he would ultimately have accepted the change. The public's acceptance of the decision, on the other hand, was a different story. The state legislatures of New Mexico, where Tombaugh lived for many years, and Illinois, the state of his birth and childhood, passed resolutions asserting that the reclassification was unfair. Some people even took to the streets with protest signs.

In 2009 popular science writer Neil DeGrasse Tyson, director of the Hayden Planetarium in New York, wrote a bestselling book about the controversy, *The Pluto Files*, later made into a documentary for PBS. In the TV special, Tyson traveled to Streator to interview the locals, most of whom maintained that Pluto is indeed a planet. Either way, Tombaugh is still Streator's favorite hometown hero. An outdoor mural in downtown Streator commemorates Tombaugh and his discovery, as does a plaque outside City Hall. The Streatorland Historical Society Museum displays one of Tombaugh's telescopes and other artifacts from his life.

As a final tribute to Clyde Tombaugh, some of his ashes were placed aboard the *New Horizons* spacecraft, launched in 2006 and scheduled to reach Pluto's orbit in 2015. It's possible that the information gathered by New Horizons will put the debate to rest one way or the other.

*Astronomer Clyde Tom-
baugh in 1957 with the twin
telescope he built* —Courtesy
Streatorland Historical Society

OGLESBY

The first cement factory in what would become Oglesby opened in 1892, a decade before the town was established. The area had an abundance of natural exposed limestone and coal, as well as two nearby rivers for shipping. Cement was a product much in demand by the turn of the twentieth century, and it was not long before the community was a major producer.

The town was founded in 1902 as Portland, named for England's famous Portland Cement, a product very close to the local cement. In 1913 the city was renamed for Illinois governor Richard J. Oglesby (see under Decatur in Region 3). Until 2008, the Marquette factory (now Buzzi Unicem) still manufactured cement, but economic changes caused the company to shut down its quarry and kiln, and the Oglesby facility is now used for distribution only.

Due to its proximity to historic Starved Rock State Park (see next stop), Oglesby's economy is partly based on tourism. A less well-known historic site in the Oglesby area is the site of Fort Wilbourn, a frontier post built during the Black Hawk War.

Fort Wilbourn

Atop a bluff on the south bank of the Illinois River, on County Road 62 at the northwest end of the campus of Illinois Valley Community College in Oglesby, a marker identifies the site of Fort Wilbourn, a frontier post erected in 1832, at the beginning of the Black Hawk War. The fort was built more or less spontaneously after low water and rapids near the mouth of the Vermilion River prevented a riverboat from proceeding up the Illinois River. The boat stopped, the supplies were unloaded, and a shelter was constructed to protect the provisions. The fort would serve as a supply depot during the sustained offensive against the Sauk and Mesquakie (Fox) Indians, and as a refuge for local farmers seeking to escape Indian raiding parties. Later, in addition to storing supplies, the fort also was used to process and dispatch Illinois militia. The blockhouse and supply depot were completed by mid-May of 1832. The post was originally called Fort Horn, then Fort Deposit, but since most of the construction was done by Capt. John S. Wilbourn's company, the fort was ultimately renamed in his honor.

Fort Wilbourn took on greater importance when Brig. Gen. Henry Atkinson moved his headquarters there. New and expired enlistments of Illinois militia were mustered here, including members of the Third Army of Illinois Volunteers, the outfit in which Abraham Lincoln served. After completing two brief enlistments, Lincoln mustered in for a third time at Fort Wilbourn on June 16, 1832. Although he had earlier been appointed a company captain, he reenlisted as a private in Jacob Early's independent company. Lincoln never saw action during the war.

Fort Wilbourn was eventually abandoned, and local homesteaders reclaimed the wood from the buildings for their own use. Not a trace was left, but a century later, in 1934, the Illinois State Historical Society erected a plaque at the site.

STARVED ROCK STATE PARK

An unusual sandstone rock formation along the Illinois River, just east of present-day Oglesby, commanded the attention of early explorers. The first to notice and record the rock's existence were Père Jacques Marquette and Louis Jolliet in 1673. Nine years later, French explorers René-Robert Cavalier, Sieur de La Salle, and Henri de Tonti built Fort St. Louis atop the wooded butte that would later come to be called Starved Rock. Erected as a defense against British incursions, the fort included a headquarters building, a chapel, a powder magazine, and a barracks, all enclosed within a wooden palisade. The post was abandoned less than a decade later, in 1691, after Iroquois warriors forced settlers out of the area during the French and Indian War; a new Fort St. Louis was then erected in future Peoria (see Peoria in Region 2). The old post was used periodically for various purposes until it burned down in 1720.

According to legend, Starved Rock got its name from a battle in the early 1770s. The dispute started after a Kaskaskia warrior assassinated the Ottawa chief Pontiac in 1769, and the Ottawa and Potawatomi tribes vowed revenge against the Illiniwek Confederation. Soon afterward, Ottawa and Potawatomi warriors cornered about three hundred Illini men, women, and children atop the 136-foot-high sandstone butte. The siege continued for weeks as the Illini defenders slowly died of starvation. Thus the outcropping became known as Starved Rock.

The Starved Rock area was privately owned during the nineteenth and early twentieth centuries. In the 1890s, the owner at the time, Ferdinand Walther, tried to develop his 900-acre property into a resort, but it never took off. In 1911 Walther sold the Starved Rock property to the Illinois State Parks Commission, which operated it as a public park. In the early days, the park was accessible only by ferry. As part of the New Deal in the 1930s, President Franklin Roosevelt established three camps of the Civilian Conservation Corps (CCC) at Starved Rock, where workers built trails, bridges, shelters, benches, cabins, and a parking lot, as well as the rustic Starved Rock Lodge, with its massive stone fireplace.

Starved Rock State Park, now spanning more than 2,800 acres, was designated a National Historic Landmark in 1960. The CCC-built lodge and cabins were added to the NRHP in 1985. Today the park, one of the "Seven Wonders of Illinois," hosts some 2 million visitors each year.

IL 1/US 150
LAWRENCEVILLE–DANVILLE
106 miles

This scenic route begins near Lawrenceville and takes us north to I-74 at Danville. This mostly two-lane section of the highway passes through a number of picturesque rural towns that encompass a surprising amount of history.

LAWRENCEVILLE
See Region 1

PALESTINE

Some believe that this area was settled after French explorer John LaMotte made a wrong turn in 1678, became separated from René-Robert Cavalier, Sieur de La Salle, and found his way to the Wabash River, on which he traveled south to a place he described as "the land of milk and honey," like the Biblical holy land of Palestine. Here he established a trading post and a small settlement by the river.

By the early 1800s, a few white settlers from the East and South had come to the area, built cabins, and begun farming. For protection, in 1811 they erected a stockade around their collection of cabins, calling the fortified settlement Fort LaMotte. The village of Palestine was chartered the same year, making it the oldest town in Illinois still at its original location. One report in 1814 noted that as many as twenty-six families lived inside the stockade, but they never suffered an attack. The presence of a company of rangers, commanded by Capt. Pierce Andrews, at the fort was no doubt a deterrent. A second fort, Fort Foot, was later built nearby.

In 1818 Palestine was named the Crawford County seat, and it remained so until 1843, when the seat was moved to Robinson. By then, however, Palestine had established itself as a port on the Wabash River, and the village continued to grow and thrive. Incorporated in 1855, the community became the "Paris of the Prairie," with fashionable shops and lively entertainment. In the 1870s the Illinois Central Railroad built a repair shop, switching yard, and roundhouse in Palestine, adding to the town's prosperity.

In 1898 Palestine businessman David Fife constructed a three-story building to house a hardware store on the first floor, and on the second floor, the odd combination of opera house and funeral home, the latter located in the rooms behind the auditorium. Performances at the several-hundred-seat opera house ended in 1912, but the hardware and mortuary businesses continued. The building housed various operations until 1989, when the newly formed Palestine Preservation Projects Society purchased the Fife Opera House and began to restore it as a historic museum. The building was placed on the NRHP in 1990.

Other Palestine sites on the NRHP include the Riverton and Swan Island Archaeological Survey Areas, which contain artifacts from the Late Archaic, Woodland, and Mississippian Cultures; the Palestine Commercial Historic District; and the Judge John B. Harper House, built in the 1830s and thought to be the oldest home in Crawford County.

HUTSONVILLE

Among the first settlers in the Crawford County area was Ohio native Isaac Hutson and his family, for whom the town of Hutsonville is named. The Hutsons arrived here in early 1812, building a cabin near the banks of the Wabash River. The family had barely settled in when tragedy struck.

It was a brisk April morning in 1812 when Isaac Hutson left his wife and six children at the cabin while he rode about eight miles south to the mill at Fort LaMotte, near today's Palestine. He returned after dark, and while still a distance away, he noticed a bright light in the direction of his homestead. Alarmed, he galloped ahead to find his home ablaze and his family all dead. They and a neighbor had been attacked and killed by Indians, probably a roving band of Plankeshaws.

Overcome with grief and rage, Hutson swam across the Wabash River to the blockhouse in Turman, Indiana, arriving around midnight. Several days later he went to Fort Harrison, near present Terre Haute, and enlisted in the Indiana Territorial Militia to fight against the Indians. Not long afterward he was killed in a skirmish, never finding the band who murdered his family.

The cabin site and surrounding land were eventually sold to Charlie McCoy. After his death in August 1953, McCoy left an acre of land near the massacre site to be set aside for a memorial to the Hutson family. In 1967 the Hutsonville Historical Society was formed to build the Hutson Memorial Village at the site. The first donation was an 1892 log cabin. The re-created village, completed in 1989, now includes several cabins, a country store and gift shop, a chapel, an inn, and a barbershop, among other buildings. Also in the village is a near-replica of the Hutson cabin, where volunteers reenact the massacre each year. The museum building, made of reclaimed logs, houses local historical artifacts.

MARSHALL AND PARIS

See earlier trips

DANVILLE

Salt deposits along the Vermilion River near the present site of Danville were discovered and highly valued by the Miami, Kickapoo, and Potawatomi Indians for preserving meat. Six years after the Kickapoo ceded their lands to the federal government in 1818, the salt deposits were developed as an industry by Major (honorary rank) John W. Vance. A resident of Urbana, Ohio, Vance moved to Illinois with his brother, Joseph, and obtained a state lease to control and operate the salines. Vance's operation, which produced a hundred bushels of salt weekly, evolved into the community of Salt Springs (or Salt Works), a cluster of twelve cabins and a tavern.

When Vermilion County was established in 1826, Salt Springs was originally named the seat, but due to its low-lying land and saltwater, its selection was rescinded a few weeks later. The new county seat was located several miles east, on one hundred acres of land donated by trader and county surveyor Dan Beckwith. The new town was named Danville in his honor.

Meanwhile, Vance continued to operate the saltworks until 1836, when a decline in salt production, competition from other parts of the country, and the mandated partial sale of the Saline Reservations by the federal government caused Vance to reduce his operations. He lost his remaining 120 acres to foreclosure, although the saltworks continued under different ownership until 1840.

As production in the saltworks waned, a new industry emerged in the region—coal. The resource was discovered near the ground's surface in the mid-1800s. For decades afterward, Vermilion County led the state in coal production, and area strip mines once employed over 4,000 miners, but by the 1940s the mines had all closed. Many of the old mines have since been reclaimed as recreational lands. In 2007, in one of these abandoned coal mines, just southwest of Danville, scientists found an entire fossilized rainforest. The forest, thought to be 300 million years old (Pennsylvanian Epoch), may have been one of the first rainforests on the planet. The Pennsylvanian Mire Forest is the largest fossilized forest ever found, extending about forty square miles.

Over the years, the city of Danville has had many notable residents. Among them was Republican Congressman Joseph G. "Uncle Joe" Cannon. Born in North Carolina in 1836, Cannon came to Illinois in 1859, working as a lawyer in Tuscola. He moved to Danville in 1873 and lived here until his death in 1926. First elected to the U.S. House of Representatives in 1873, the popular politician served almost continuously until 1923. During that tenure, he served as the Speaker of the House from 1903 to 1911. In 1923 he retired to his home in Danville, where he died in his sleep three years later. His modest gravestone may be viewed at Danville's Spring Hill Cemetery.

Later in the twentieth century, Danville was home to several future TV and movie stars, including Donald O'Connor, Dick Van Dyke and his brother Jerry Van Dyke, and Oscar winner Gene Hackman. Singers Bobby Short and Helen Morgan (born Helen Riggins) also hailed from Danville. A mural celebrating these six entertainers graces the outside of a local furniture store.

Of the dozens of historical markers that dot today's Danville, about a third relate to Abraham Lincoln. Lincoln shared a law office in Danville with Ward Hill Lamon, one of the city's leading attorneys, from 1852 to 1856. The future president also campaigned here during his 1858 senatorial race against Stephen A. Douglas, and Danville residents often relate the story of how Lincoln, as a houseguest of William E. Fithian, once climbed shoeless out a second-floor window onto a balcony to give an impromptu campaign speech. The Fithian home now houses the Vermilion County Museum.

One of Danville's most prominent historical markers remembers the 1838 Potawatomi "Trail of Death" that passed through here. This plaque stands in Ellsworth Park.

The Trail of Death

President Andrew Jackson's enactment of the Indian Removal Act on March 28, 1830, gave the federal government legal authority to forcibly relocate all eastern tribes to

Indian Territory west of the Mississippi River. In 1838 the army rounded up the Cherokee people in Georgia and Tennessee and the Potawatomi people in northern Indiana. The horrific forced march of the Cherokee, known later as the Trail of Tears, became infamous (see Region 1). Less well known was the equally terrible march of the Potawatomi through central Illinois.

A few Potawatomi bands resisted the relocation, the largest of which was led by chief Menominee. In August 1838 Maj. Gen. John Tipton and a contingent of Indiana militia rounded up hundreds of tribal members and held them at Menominee's village near Twin Lakes. On September 4, the march of about 860 Potawatomi men, women, and children began. The group would travel 658 miles from their Indiana homeland to Osawatomie, Kansas, passing through central Illinois.

Upon reaching Danville on September 16, the prisoners were turned over to federal authorities. Their meandering 234-mile route across Illinois passed through Homer, Monticello, Decatur, Springfield, Jacksonville, Perry, Liberty, and Quincy, among others, crossing the Mississippi River into Missouri at Palmyra. During their twenty-five day trek through the state, the Potawatomi lost more than twenty children and adults to sickness, malnutrition, exposure, contaminated water, and accidents. On September 21, agent Jesse C. Douglass wrote in his journal, "There are yet fifty sick in camp—three have died since my last. The farther we get into the prairie the scarcer becomes water. . . . A child died since we came into camp. This morning before we left the Encampment of last night, a chief, Muk-kose, a man remarkable for his honesty and integrity, died after a few days sickness."

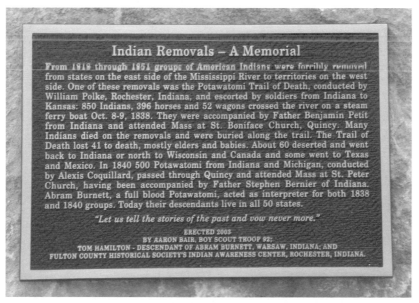

This plaque at Quinsippi Island Park in Quincy, erected in 2003, is one of many memorials along the Trail of Death —Photo by Larry Prichard, courtesy Fulton County, Indiana, Historical Society

About 750 Potawatomi people arrived in Osawatomie on November 10, more than forty having died en route and the rest believed to have escaped. In the late twentieth century—mostly during the 1990s—various groups placed memorial plaques, statues, and markers at certain points along the trail. The one in Danville was installed in 1990. It reads, in part, "This monument is to commemorate the hardships, deaths and humiliation these people suffered during their forced passage. We salute their courage."

In 1994 the four state legislatures cooperated to approve a Regional Historic Trail from Plymouth, Indiana, to Osawatomie, Kansas, to commemorate this heartbreaking episode in American history.

IL 1
DANVILLE–WATSEKA
48 miles

This is another scenic trip on a mostly two-lane road through a quiet rural landscape. North of Danville, IL 1 follows an old north-south trade route originally known as Hubbard's Trace, later called the Vincennes-to-Chicago Road. In the early twentieth century, the road became part of the Dixie Highway, which connected the southern states with the Midwest. Just south of Rossville, eagle-eyed travelers on IL 1 may spot an original stone mile marker from the Vincennes-to-Chicago Road that dates from the 1830s. From Watseka, motorists may continue north on IL 1 to Kankakee and beyond, all the way to Chicago.

DANVILLE
See previous trip

ROSSVILLE

John Liggett, who arrived in this area in 1829, was one of the first settlers to build an inn along Hubbard's Trace, a trade route between Fort Dearborn (Chicago) and Danville that was blazed in the early 1820s by fur trader Gurdon S. Hubbard. The settlement was originally called Liggett's Grove, but a year after Alvan Gilbert purchased Liggett's property in 1838, a post office was established with the name Rossville. The name was chosen because the settlement was the main populated place in the newly formed Ross Township, named in honor of prominent early settler Jacob Ross.

Rossville was incorporated as a village in 1859. It was and has remained an agricultural community, surrounded by farms and agriculture-related industries. The community got along with limited transportation options until the railroad arrived, which did not happen until 1903. The Chicago & Eastern Illinois Railroad (C&EIRR) provided Rossville with passenger and freight service until the 1960s. In 1976 the local chapter of the National Railway Historical Society restored the old C&EIRR depot to its 1950s-era appearance and now operates it as the Rossville Depot Railroad Museum. The museum houses a vast collection of railroad memorabilia, archives, and an operating model railroad. Another place of interest to historical-minded visitors is the Rossville Historical Society Museum, which includes, in addition to general exhibits and archive resources, re-creations of a 1916 library, jail, courtroom, doctor's office, drugstore, and one-room country school.

Rossville, which bills itself as the "Village of Unusual Shops," enjoys a lively retail trade with locals and visitors alike. Sadly, a fire in 2004 destroyed several of Rossville's downtown historic buildings and antique shops. Nevertheless, some stores still stand on Main Street along with a number of Victorian homes, all enhanced by vintage streetlamps.

On the way into town, travelers may want to stop at two other sites of historical interest that lie a few miles south of Rossville just off IL 1. At the intersection of IL 1 and County Road 3200 (Mann's Chapel Road), three and a half miles south of Rossville, is Mann's Chapel. Constructed in 1857, it is the oldest church in Vermilion County, and its congregation continues to meet there today. Just north of the chapel on IL 1 is Milestone 121, an original stone mile marker that stood along the Vincennes-to-Chicago Road. Beneath the weathered old marker, which dates from 1833, is an inscribed granite plaque that identifies it as a historical site. The plaque was installed in 1984 by the local chapter of the Daughters of the American Revolution and the Rossville Historical and Genealogical Society.

HOOPESTON

This little city of about 6,000 residents is known as the "Sweet Corn Capital of the World" for both its corn growing and its corn canning. Vegetable canning was one of Hoopeston's earliest industries. The Illinois Canning Company was built here in 1875; after several name changes and mergers over the years, the company became Hoopeston Foods, which still operates a cannery in this city. In 1925 the American Can Company, which manufactured the cans themselves, opened a plant in Hoopeston. This company too, now called Silgan Containers Corporation, still maintains a factory here, producing metal can lids.

The corn theme pervades Hoopeston's culture. Each year at the National Sweet Corn Festival, the city serves about fifty tons of corn on the cob, and Hoopeston's McFerren Park features a sixteen-foot-tall sculpture of a stalk of corn, placed there in 2004. The high school's athletic teams, as well as their fans, are known as the Cornjerkers (from an old slang term for corn pickers), and their mascot is a corn cob called "Jerky." The region's agricultural heritage may be explored further at the McFarland Early Americana Museum, where exhibits take visitors through decades of American agricultural industry.

Hoopeston's story does not begin with corn, however, but with railroads. Originally called Leeds, Hoopeston was laid out in 1871 at the crossing point for two rail lines, the Lafayette, Bloomington & Western and the Chicago, Danville & Vincennes. The land was donated by several men, including Thomas Hoopes, for whom the community was then renamed. The new town developed quickly, incorporating as a village in 1874 and as a city three years later. At first, saloons proliferated in Hoopeston, but by 1879 alcohol sales were banned within the city limits, and it remained a "temperance town" for decades.

During World War II, Hoopeston became the site of a German prisoner-of-war camp, one of twenty-one such camps in Illinois. The American government set up these temporary prison camps throughout the country, using the internees to provide labor during the wartime shortage of manpower. In Hoopeston, the prisoners helped farmers and the cannery during the harvest and canning season. The Germans were housed in the cannery warehouse and area barns until housing could be built. Shortly after the first group of seventy-five prisoners arrived in April 1944, three of the Germans escaped under a fence, only to be caught a few days later in Indiana. At its peak, the camp held more than 1,200 prisoners.

Today, downtown Hoopeston boasts several historic buildings, including the 1922 Lorraine Theater. Remodeled and updated, the theater still operates, showing movies and live stage shows. Another impressive early-twentieth-century building is Hoopeston's Carnegie Library, built in 1905. Since then, the library has been renovated and expanded numerous times; the latest expansion, which doubled the structure's original size, was completed in 2002.

WATSEKA

Watseka's roots date to the 1820s, when American fur trader and land speculator Gurdon S. Hubbard, one of the early developers of Chicago, established trading posts along Hubbard's Trace, a trade route between Chicago and Vincennes, Indiana. Arriving in future Watseka in 1822, Hubbard lived in an abandoned cabin at the junction of the Iroquois River and Sugar Creek. Between 1824 and 1826, he was married to a Potawatomi woman named Watchekee ("Daughter of the Evening Star"), who helped defend the settlement from a band of Indian raiders. Later, residents would honor her by naming their community Watseka. The first settlement here, however, was called Middleport.

After Iroquois County was created in 1833, a village called Iroquois was platted as the county seat. After several years, no courthouse had been built there, so the seat was relocated to Middleport in 1839, and Iroquois soon faded away. Middleport's first courthouse was completed in 1847. When the Peoria & Oquawka Railroad arrived in the area in 1858, railroad officials wanted Middleport to donate land for a depot, but when town leaders balked, landowners to the southeast stepped in with a land donation for the station, creating South Middleport. In 1865 Middleport and South Middleport were combined and incorporated as a city under a new name, Watseka, which then became the county seat.

The 1847 courthouse in Middleport was destroyed by fire in 1862, and its replacement burned down four years later. Immediately rebuilt in Watseka, the new courthouse served the county for the next hundred years, with occasional expansions. In 1962 a county resident bequeathed $1.5 million to Watseka for a new courthouse. The two-story, Classical Modern structure was completed in 1966. It is the only courthouse in the nation to be built entirely with private funds. The old courthouse, listed on the NRHP in 1975, became the headquarters for the Iroquois County Historical Society.

As stories of the past are told, facts often mix with folklore. One of the best-known tales in Watseka's history concerns two teenage girls with a supernatural connection.

The Roff House and the Watseka Wonder

According to local lore, Wateska was the center of paranormal events in the 1860s and 1870s. Some say the "Watseka Wonder" was the first documented case of spiritual possession in the United States. The bizarre story began with a young girl named Mary Roff, who suffered from an unknown illness that caused seizures and strange behavior.

Mary's first fit came when she was only six months old. As she grew older, the episodes grew more frequent and more violent, and she began to experience severe mood swings, occasionally cutting herself with a knife. She also complained of excruciating headaches. After one extended and exceptionally violent episode in 1864, she was no longer able to identify—or apparently even to see—other people in the room. She began to show uncanny powers, including the ability to read books while totally blindfolded. Finally, on July 5, 1865, at age nineteen, Mary Roff died during one of her seizures.

A year before Mary Roff's death, on April 16, 1864, Mary Lurancy Vennum, called "Rancy" by her family, was born a few miles south of Watseka. In 1871 the Vennum family moved to Watseka, residing in a house not far from the Roff home. In 1877, when Rancy was thirteen years old, she suddenly had a seizure, after which she reported hearing and seeing people who were not there. Over the next few months she fell into a number of trances during which she talked to "angels."

Meanwhile, Mary Roff's father, Asa Roff, heard of young Rancy's affliction and asked to see her. On his visit to the Vennum home, Asa, who had turned to spiritualism after his daughter's mysterious death, brought with him a spiritualist doctor, Elhanan W. Stevens. They observed the girl in one of her spells, during which she claimed to be Mary Roff and asked to be taken home, i.e., to the Roff home. Rancy's parents reluctantly agreed to allow their daughter to stay with the Roffs for a while.

Rancy lived at the Roff home for one hundred days in 1878. From the moment she walked into the front parlor, strange things began to happen. Rancy, who had never been in the house, recognized the piano and sat down to play. She played and sang a number of Mary's favorite tunes. In the days that followed, Rancy expressed intimate knowledge of Roff family history and described people long dead.

On May 21, after asking to say goodbye to her family, the spirit Mary purportedly left Rancy's body, and Rancy returned to her family and resumed her normal, healthy life. She did, however, call on the Roff family several times over the years, supposedly allowing Mary to re-enter her body during the visits. Rancy eventually married and gave birth to thirteen children. She lived to be eighty-eight.

The Roff's Victorian Italianate brick home still stands at its original location in Watseka. After numerous different owners, the house is now owned and occupied by John Wittman, who has restored it and opened most of its rooms to visitors. The house attracts ghost hunters and curiosity seekers from all over the country. Special events, especially at Halloween, play up the home's spooky history.

OTHER COMMUNITIES AND SITES OF INTEREST IN EASTERN ILLINOIS

Georgetown (US 150/IL 1): Incorporated as a city in 1873, Georgetown prospered from area coal mining through the mid-twentieth century, and a few mines remain in operation today. Sites of interest in Georgetown include the Georgetown Public Library, built in 1938 as a New Deal Works Progress Administration project; the Georgetown Historical Society Museum, located in a historic home on Main Street; and the Flag Monument in Patriot Park, dedicated in 2000.

Odell (I-55): Odell was founded in 1855 by three Chicago & Alton Railroad engineers and named after one of them, William H. Odell. In the early twentieth century, the railroad was displaced by the highway that was built along the same route, and Odell prospered as an attractive stop for travelers on this new road, US Route 66. Several classic structures from that era remain, including an impeccably refurbished 1932 Standard Oil Station, designed in the classic house-and-canopy style. After the station closed in 1999, the village purchased the building and restored it. It now serves as a welcome center. Another remnant from Route 66 is the site of an underground walkway that once passed beneath the highway, now marked with a plaque.

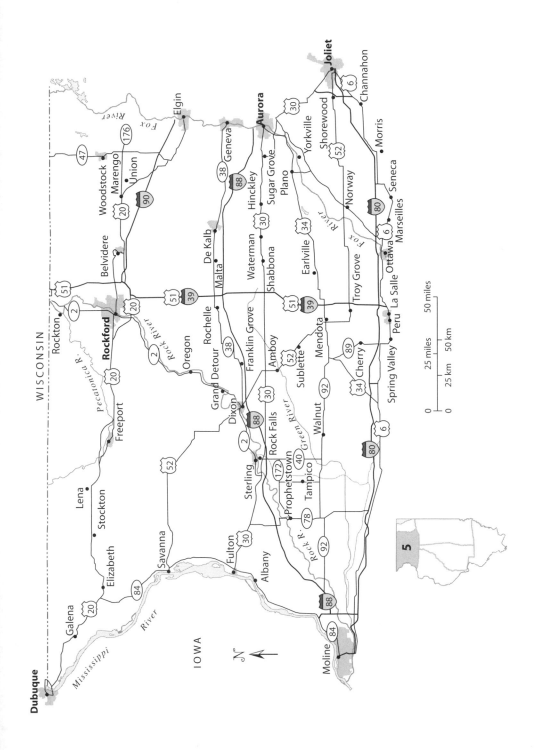

Northern Illinois
ROCK RIVER AND BEYOND

As the Rock River meanders through northern Illinois, it splits the region into two nearly equal sections. Hundreds of thousands of years ago, only the far northwest part of the state was spared the incursion of glaciers, leaving rolling hills and wooded areas extending into the bluffs above the Mississippi River. Of the ten highest peaks in Illinois, nine are in Jo Daviess County, in far northwestern Illinois. Not to say they are towering mountains—they barely exceed 1,000 feet, and they are usually called "mounds," not "mounts" (Charles Mound is the highest, at 1,227 feet elevation); others are simply called hills or knobs. Elsewhere in the region, the pushing and retreating pressure of grinding ice sheets left a relatively level landscape with mineral-rich soil, abundant wildlife, and verdant groves.

The Rock River, geologically older than Lake Michigan, breaks up the rolling prairie of northern Illinois with woodlands along both sides. Much of northern Illinois' early history relates to this river, upon which many of the region's native tribes and early settlers depended. The river has supported human occupation since prehistoric times; burial grounds and other remnants of the ancient Hopewell Indian Culture can still be found along the river's banks and bluffs.

When white settlers began to arrive, they hoped to use the Rock River for transportation, but it proved difficult to navigate. By the mid-1800s, the Illinois & Michigan Canal and the railroad provided for most transportation needs in the region, but the Rock's presence was still vital to the region's development. The river's waterpower was well utilized for early mills and later for electricity. Also of primary importance were the riverside's abundant timber and the fertile soil of the valley. Today, the recreation opportunities offered by the Rock River are a major part of the economic base of surrounding communities.

Discoveries, Difficulties, and Development
The earliest white men in the region were French missionary Père Jacques Marquette and French Canadian explorer Louis Jolliet, who arrived in the region in 1673 and

discovered the Mississippi River. From there they traveled along the Illinois and Des Plaines Rivers to Lake Michigan. Seven years later, René Robert Cavelier, Sieur de La Salle, sought to open new channels of commerce and extended French hegemony throughout the Mississippi River Valley and into the far northwest part of the Illinois Country. In the 1700s France increased its commercial influence by establishing trading posts in the area, but its success was ultimately limited by insufficient markets, military defeats, and Indian resistance. The British who succeeded them ultimately fared no better. When the United States gained Illinois in 1783, the government was already encouraging Americans to settle in the territory.

In the early 1820s, the federal government leased land in northwestern Illinois for lead mining. Later, zinc also was mined and transported for processing in Peru, on the Illinois River. The arrival of the steamboat in 1823 bolstered commerce in the area, and three years later the first major settlement, Galena, was established. Before long, other settlements emerged, scattered throughout this 7,084-square-mile area.

In 1832 the short-lived but fierce Black Hawk War created fear and anxiety among the settlers. The Sauk leader Black Hawk led about 2,500 followers, including about 2,000 women and children, across the Mississippi River from what is now eastern Iowa to Illinois in an attempt to reoccupy northern Illinois, the territory the Sauks had given up according to what Black Hawk considered an unscrupulous 1804 treaty. The resulting four-month conflict led some settlers to erect makeshift forts or to travel to the more secure Fort Dearborn on the Lake Michigan shore. Battles and skirmishes occurred at Stillman's Run in Stillman Valley, Apple River Fort near Elizabeth, and Kellogg's Grove near Kent. Massacres and isolated attacks also took a toll, such as the massacres on Indian Creek, north of Ottawa, and Buffalo Grove, near Polo. The war ended with Black Hawk's capture at the Bad Axe River in present Wisconsin, then part of Michigan Territory.

The end of the Black Hawk War in 1832 was a turning point for settlement in northern Illinois. By 1833 most Indians had been moved west of the Mississippi River, and settlers, no longer afraid of Indian raids, came to the region in waves to farm, open businesses, practice professions, and establish a religious presence.

After settlement, things progressed quickly. In 1837 John Deere introduced his steel plow in Grand Detour; in 1848 the Illinois & Michigan Canal opened, linking Lake Michigan with the Illinois River; railroads were built through the region in the 1850s, '60s, and '70s; in 1874 DeKalb farmer Joseph Glidden patented a new fencing material called barbed wire; and in 1914 in Malta, the first "seedling" mile of concrete was poured for a transcontinental roadway, later known as the Lincoln Highway. In the 1960s, the Dresden Nuclear Generating Station, the first of six nuclear power plants built in northern Illinois, opened near Morris.

Of course, the region's history includes bad times as well as good. In addition to the mayhem of the Black Hawk War, northern Illinois residents have had to contend with everything from mining disasters to tornadoes to marauding desperadoes. From 1837 to 1845, an outlaw gang known as the Banditti of the Prairie robbed, murdered, and wreaked havoc on settlers throughout northern Illinois. In 1909 fires at the Cherry Mine killed 259 workers. And on April 21, 1967, a series of tornadoes in northern Illinois killed dozens and injured more than a thousand. Among the worst hit was Belvidere, where thirteen students were killed at the high school.

Northern Illinois was also home to two U.S. presidents. Ulysses S. Grant was a resident of Galena for a time, and Ronald Reagan was born in Tampico in 1911, and as a youngster, from 1920 to 1932, he lived in Dixon. Reagan was the only native Illinoisan ever to serve in the White House. In 2000 his daughter, Maureen, helped establish the Ronald Reagan Trail, which connects a dozen communities of significance in Reagan's life. Other motorways honoring the "Gipper" include the Ronald Reagan Highway (US 14) and the Ronald Reagan Memorial Tollway, the section of I-88 from Dixon to Chicago.

Great River Road National Scenic Byway (IL 84 and US 20)
MOLINE–GALENA
87 miles

This northern part of the Great River Road National Scenic Byway (IL 84) traces the Mississippi River from the greater Moline area north to US 20, which leads to the lovely and historic town of Galena.

MOLINE
See Region 2

ALBANY

In 1835 two land speculators from Ohio, brothers-in-law David Mitchell and Edward Corbin, purchased land opposite the narrows of the Mississippi River. Eager to make a quick profit, they sold their interests the following year—Mitchell's northern parcel, sold to a pair of Illinoisans, became known as Upper Albany, later called Van Buren. Corbin's southern parcel went to three partners from New York. This settlement was called Lower Albany and then just Albany. The two communities finally united as Albany, which was platted as a village in 1840.

With several good transportation options—ferry service connected the village with Camanche, Iowa; the Frink, Walker & Company stagecoach line provided overland transportation to Galena and Chicago; and steamboats linked it to Galena and St. Louis—Albany's future looked bright. The village reached its zenith in 1854, when the population reached 1,100.

In 1860 the common belief that a tornado will not jump a body of water was disproved here when the Great Tornado of 1860 swept across Camanche, Iowa, and crossed the Mississippi River to strike Albany. In crossing the water, the twister overturned a raft holding twenty-four men, drowning twenty-one of them. It then proceeded into downtown Albany, destroying all but one business and killing five more people and much livestock. The community rebuilt, and in 1869 it was incorporated as a village. Today, Albany is a mostly middle-class community with a population of about 900.

Albany's primary visitor attraction is a site that preceded the village by millennia, the Albany Mounds State Historic Site, one of the most important archaeological sites in Illinois. The area was occupied by the Hopewell Culture more than 2,000 years ago, and evidence of human habitation goes back 10,000 years. The Hopewellians were mostly hunter-gatherers, but they cultivated plants, made pottery, and participated in a wide trading network. The mounds, created for burials, once numbered an estimated ninety-six; thirty-nine survive in good condition. Preservation efforts began in the 1970s, and in the 1990s the site was refurbished with trails, interpretive signs, restrooms, parking lots, and recreation areas. Today Albany Mounds comprises two hundred-plus picturesque acres of restored native prairie and tree-covered hills and includes the mile-long Great River Recreation Trail. The Friends of the Albany Indian Mounds Foundation, established in 1988, maintains the grounds and conducts educational programs.

FULTON

The narrows of the Mississippi River attracted Fulton's first settler, John Baker, in 1835. Baker built a three-room cabin that served as an inn as well as his home. He also opened a flatboat ferry operation, and the settlement became known as Baker's Ferry. In 1840 Baker and about ten other settlers purchased federal land to develop a planned community. Inspired by the sight of majestic steamboats on the Mississippi, one of the settlers suggested naming the village after steamboat inventor Robert Fulton. The first railroad came to Fulton in the 1850s, and three other lines followed, making the town a railroad hub. It was incorporated as a village in 1855 and as a city in 1859.

A strange episode occurred in Fulton in 1875, after local counterfeiter Benjamin Boyd and his accomplice wife were captured by federal agents. When Boyd was sentenced to ten years in the Illinois State Penitentiary, his cohorts devised a scheme to steal Abraham Lincoln's body from its vault in Springfield's Oak Ridge Cemetery and hold it as ransom for Boyd's release. The plot was foiled, the thieves were captured, and Boyd remained in prison.

Although Fulton's prosperity attracted residents of many ethnicities, a large number of Dutch immigrants settled here during the nineteenth century. The first, Thomas Smith, arrived in 1856; by 1900 more than two hundred Dutch families lived in Fulton. The last wave of Dutch immigrants arrived in the 1950s. Today, Fulton holds an annual Dutch Days Festival, in which participants don wooden shoes and traditional costumes. In 2000 residents of Dutch heritage dedicated "De Immigrant Windmill," the only fully operating, authentic Dutch windmill in Illinois. The attraction was enhanced in 2010 with the Windmill Cultural Center, which features displays, educational programs, and a gift shop where visitors can buy, among other things, fresh stone-ground flour.

Both the Lincoln Highway (see Malta on later trip) and the Great River Road pass through Fulton. The Lincoln Highway, in particular, helped Fulton grow, as the town was the location of the highway's bridge over the Mississippi River. The original bridge, opened in 1891 and connected to the Lincoln Highway in 1915, was replaced by a modern one in 1975. Fulton is also the home of one of forty commemorative murals and of one of fifteen interpretive gazebos being installed by the Illinois Lincoln Highway Coalition.

Fulton is also a stop on the Ronald Reagan Trail. Reagan's parents, John Edward (Jack) Reagan and Nelle Wilson, grew up here, and they were married in Immaculate Conception Catholic Church in 1904. In 1906 the Reagans moved to Tampico, where John Neil Reagan and his brother, Ronald Wilson Reagan, were later born.

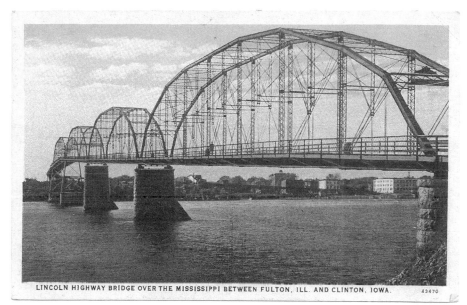

LINCOLN HIGHWAY BRIDGE OVER THE MISSISSIPPI BETWEEN FULTON, ILL. AND CLINTON, IOWA. 43470

The Fulton-Lyons Bridge over the Mississippi River between Fulton, Illinois, and Clinton, Iowa, was part of the historic Lincoln Highway. The bridge was torn down in 1975. —Courtesy Fulton Historical Society

In 1998 Fulton residents Leonard and Maxine Martin donated their two-story, twelve-room antebellum home to the city of Fulton for use as a museum. The Fulton (Martin House) Museum, headquarters of the Fulton Historical Society, includes various artifacts from Fulton's history. The museum also features a Ronald Reagan Room, where exhibits display family photos and information about the Reagan and Wilson families when they lived in Fulton.

SAVANNA

Named for the oak savanna landscape of the valley here, Savanna was settled and grew up as a river town. The first settlers, the Pierce family, arrived in 1828 and, using the area's abundant timber, set up a fuel stop for steamboats on the Mississippi River. The settlement grew very quickly. By the time steamboat traffic died down, the railroads had arrived to keep the town flourishing. Savanna became a city in 1875.

The twentieth century brought more growth to Savanna. In 1917 the U.S. Army built an ordnance depot near the city. After a peacetime lull, Savanna boomed again during World War II. By the 1950s, however, the city's growth had slowed to a halt and the population began to decline. Redevelopment projects in the 1960s and the 1980s saw modest success.

Since the late twentieth century, the Savanna Historical Society and other local preservationists have been actively developing the city's tourism industry. Taking advantage of nearby recreational areas, particularly Mississippi Palisades State Park, and its own naturally beautiful surroundings, Savanna has become a destination town and a "sportsman's paradise." In addition, the city's downtown historic district includes many attractions, including the Savanna Museum and Cultural Center, the Savanna Train Car Museum, and the Pulford Opera House Antique Mall. The Savanna Army Depot, which closed in 2000, is currently under redevelopment.

ELIZABETH

It is uncertain whether the village of Elizabeth was named after Elizabeth Armstrong or Elizabeth Winters. Elizabeth Winters was the wife of John Winters, who owned part of the land on which the village was built, so it is reasonable to believe that Elizabeth was named for her. Elizabeth Armstrong, however, was a local heroine who rallied the defenders of the settlement's fortress, Apple River Fort, to hold off about two hundred Sauk warriors during the Black Hawk War of 1832. The stance that the town's name honors her is equally plausible.

The original settlement was known as Apple River for its location on the river of the same name, a small tributary of the Mississippi River in far northwest Illinois. The first settler here was A. P. Van Matre, who arrived in 1825 after lead deposits were discovered nearby. He built the area's first smelter, which became a successful enterprise, attracting others to come here and establish farms and small businesses.

When the Black Hawk War erupted in May 1832, the miners and settlers in Apple River settlement built a small, hastily constructed log fort lined with parapets and rifle portholes. A few weeks later, word arrived that Black Hawk's band was in the area, and Apple River's approximately forty-five settlers congregated inside and prepared for an assault.

On June 24, Black Hawk and about two hundred warriors did indeed attack Apple River Fort. Farm wife Elizabeth Armstrong is credited with rallying the settlers—especially the women—to the defense. The men poured a steady stream of fire on the Indians, while the women molded shot balls and loaded muskets. After a forty-five-minute battle, Black Hawk retreated. One settler and several Sauk and Mesquakie warriors were killed in the fight. The Black Hawk War ended less than six weeks later. Apple River Fort remained standing for about fifteen years, until its wood was carted off to build new cabins and fences.

After the war, in 1839, Apple River was platted as a village and renamed Elizabeth. The village grew steadily and was incorporated in 1868. Twenty years later, the Chicago Great Western Railroad constructed a depot here as it laid track west to its hub in Oelwein, Iowa. The railroad's presence made Elizabeth a commercial center for the region.

Today Elizabeth is a quiet community of fewer than four hundred residents, but it survives as an appealing stop for tourists. Among its attractions are the 1876 Banwarth House and Museum; the old railroad depot, added to the NRHP in 1996 and now home of the Elizabeth Historical Society; and the Long Hollow Tower, a hundred-foot-tall lookout tower constructed by the U.S. Department of Transportation in the 1980s.

The village's main historic site, that of the old Apple River Fort, was developed in the 1990s. The Apple River Fort Historic Foundation was established in 1995 to identify the fort's original site. The following year, some four hundred volunteers set to work to re-create the fort, splitting logs by hand, digging trenches, and building replica cabins, a blockhouse, and surrounding parapets. An interpretive center was added in 1998, and in 2000 the fort became a state historic site, managed by the Illinois Historic Preservation Agency.

GALENA

In the far northwestern corner of Illinois, Galena is something of an epicenter of northern Illinois history. It was officially established in 1826, making it the oldest city in this part of the state, and eighty-five percent of Galena's buildings are in a National Register Historic District.

The word *galena* is the scientific name of lead sulfide, the primary lead ore mineral, the mining of which was the city's original economic base. Archaeological evidence indicates that small pieces of lead from this area were used as trade items over 5,000 years ago. French explorers reported deposits along the Mississippi River as early as 1687. Following the issuance of the first federal lease to mine lead in 1822, a flood of miners entered the region, and by 1845 steamboats were transporting thousands of tons of lead ore from the Galena area to urban centers. As lead mining reached a high, Galena became the largest port on the Mississippi River north of St. Louis.

The center of commerce in nineteenth-century Galena was the Market House, a Greek Revival building in the center of Market Square, near the riverfront. Here

Galena, 1850s. By this time the city had become the busiest river port between St. Louis and St. Paul. —Courtesy Galena Public Library, Alfred Mueller Photograph Collection

livestock, produce, and general merchandise were bought and sold until the early twentieth century. For a time, the Market House also served as Galena's municipal building and included two jail cells in the basement (once described as a "miserable hole").

Construction of the two-and-a-half-story Market House was completed in 1846, and a two-story addition was built in 1889. Vendors operated from twelve stalls on the first floor, where farmers, Indians, miners, housewives, and well-dressed ladies and gentlemen roamed, haggling over prices and exchanging gossip. Overseeing the trade was the market master, who was paid by the city "to enforce order and decorum, and decide all disputes in the market between the buyer and seller." He was also expected to keep the market clean and tidy. The market master signaled the opening and closing of the market by ringing a bell.

Near the Market House, the five-story DeSoto House rivaled the East's most lavish hotels. Completed in 1855 at a cost of $85,000, the DeSoto House contained more than two hundred rooms, an extravagant entryway, a spacious lobby, an elegant dining room, several ladies' parlors, and five men-only barrooms, with luxurious furnishings throughout. A spiral staircase led to the second-floor balcony that overlooked Main Street. Among the orators to address crowds from this balcony were Abraham Lincoln, Stephen A. Douglas, and Ulysses S. Grant, who lived in Galena before becoming president.

Lincoln and Grant were not the only U.S. presidents who spent time in Galena over the years. The others were Martin Van Buren, Millard Fillmore, William McKinley,

Ulysses S. Grant —From *Frank Leslie's Illustrated History of the Civil War*

Theodore Roosevelt, and Barack Obama. As the region's principal city, Galena hosted many notable visitors in its time, including Joseph Smith, Jefferson Davis, Herman Melville, Mark Twain, William Jennings Bryan, Susan B. Anthony, Elizabeth Cady Stanton, and Booker T. Washington.

For all its prominence and prosperity, Galena did suffer a few dips in its history. The 1860s saw a decline in lead production, causing a corresponding decline in population. Meanwhile the Galena River had become clogged with silt and sediment from mining, smelting, and farming activities, rendering it largely unnavigable. Floods inundated the city in 1870, 1880, 1892, 1916, and 1937, causing further deterioration and loss of population. For decades, Galena stood virtually frozen in time.

Later in the twentieth century, the tourism industry gave Galena new life. The Old Market House was the first historic building to be restored, and it is now a state historic site. The market shut down around 1910, but the city council and fire department continued to use the building until 1938. Nine years later, its ownership was transferred to the state of Illinois, which oversaw its restoration, completed in 1954. Now managed by the Illinois Historic Preservation Agency, the Old Market House State Historic Site serves as a local history museum, a community meeting and events space, and a visitor center for Galena.

The famous DeSoto House Hotel underwent extensive renovations in 1986; only the original stairway and exterior walls were retained. The hotel still lodges guests, making it the oldest continuously operating hotel in Illinois. Besides the Market House and the DeSoto House, Galena's restored historical attractions include the 1843 Elihu B. Washburne House and the former home of President Ulysses S. Grant.

Ulysses S. Grant Home

Ulysses S. Grant, born Hiram Ulysses Simpson Grant in Ohio in 1822, entered West Point Academy at age seventeen. In 1846, three years after his graduation, he served as a lieutenant in the Mexican War. After leaving the army in 1854, Grant lived in St. Louis before moving to Galena in April 1860 to work in his father's tannery. Accompanied by his wife, Julia, and their four children, Grant arrived in Galena aboard the steamboat *Itasca*. The family lived in a rented brick house that is still standing today as a private residence.

After the fall of Fort Sumter in 1861, Grant reenlisted in the army. He was commissioned as a colonel to lead the Twenty-First Infantry Regiment. It was the beginning of a career that culminated four years later, when he was named commander-in-chief of the Union Army.

Grant's triumphant return to Galena on August 18, 1865, was a day of great celebration. More than 10,000 people greeted him at the train and led him in a festive, patriotic procession to the town center. Not adept at public speaking, the general made only a brief statement before being presented with a gift from the residents of Galena—a stylish new home, fully furnished. The Grant family lived in this Italianate-style brick house sporadically over the next few years, staying there during Grant's 1868 presidential campaign. The day after his election on November 3, Grant addressed supporters from the porch, bidding them a heartfelt farewell.

During his administration, Grant sometimes longed for the tranquility of Galena and his many friends there, but he returned only twice as president—on September 28,

1871, and May 1, 1873, staying several days each time. After completing his two terms of office in 1877, Grant visited Galena briefly before embarking on a two-year trip around the world. The Grant family returned to their Galena home off and on between travels in 1879 and 1880, after which time they moved to New York. The Grants made one final overnight visit to Galena in 1883, staying at the DeSoto House. President Grant died in New York in 1885.

In 1904 Grant's children presented the house to the city of Galena, requesting that it be preserved as a memorial to their father. Unable to keep up with the maintenance costs, the city deeded the property to the state of Illinois in 1931. The state undertook a major restoration in 1955, returning the home to its 1860s appearance with many of the original furnishings. Named a National Historic Landmark in 1960, the house is now managed by the Illinois Historic Preservation Agency. The first floor is open for tours, and an adjacent building houses a visitor center and museum.

IL 92, IL 78, IL 172, and IL 40
MOLINE–ROCK FALLS VIA PROPHETSTOWN
67 miles

The four state highways on this trip take us through historic Prophetstown, Tampico—the birthplace of Ronald Reagan, Illinois' only native president—and Rock Falls, where a feeder canal from the Rock River entered the now-obsolete Hennepin Canal, a.k.a. the Illinois & Mississippi Canal (see also Region 2).

MOLINE
See Region 2

PROPHETSTOWN

As many as fourteen Indian villages once stretched along the banks of the beautiful Rock River from Dixon to Rock Island. The most significant was the one occupied by Wa-bo-kie-shiek, also known as the Prophet. Half Winnebago and half Sauk, he served as an adviser to Ma-ka-tai-me-she-kia-kiak, or Black Hawk. Though the Prophet had been friendly with early white settlers, during the 1832 Black Hawk War he stood firm and encouraged Black Hawk to do the same. As U.S. troops and Illinois militia marched northeast from Rock Island along the Rock River, they destroyed the Prophet's village and the villages of other Indians who supported Black Hawk's rebellion. The troops finally drove the insurgent Sauks—including the Prophet and Black Hawk—into Wisconsin, where they were soon captured and sent to reservations in Kansas and Iowa. The Prophet died on a Kansas reservation in 1841.

After the war, white settlers flooded into the Rock River region. A settlement was established at the site of the Prophet's village, and interestingly, the white newcomers named their community in honor of the rebellious warrior. In the early days, the two-story frame home of settler Asa Crook, a Vermont native, served as an inn, a community meeting place, a school, and occasionally a church. In 1838 the village of Prophetstown was platted. Among the village's original landowners was Daniel Webster, the famous

U.S. senator and orator, though Webster sold his interest only a few years later. Prophetstown was incorporated as a city in 1859.

The citizens of Prophetstown have taken care to preserve their history. The site of the original Indian village is now Prophetstown State Park, established in 1947, and Asa Crook's farmhouse is currently being restored by the Prophetstown Area Historical Society. In 1993 the city was chosen to participate in a rural downtown revitalization initiative known as the Illinois Main Street program. As part of the project, Prophetstown High School art students created seven murals around town, each depicting a scene from local history. More murals are planned, and some of the city's boosters hope to tag Prophetstown as the "mural capital of Illinois."

TAMPICO

Tampico, founded in 1858, was a small town when Ronald Reagan was born in 1911, and it remains so today. The only Illinois native to become president, Ronald Wilson Reagan was born to John (Jack) and Nelle Reagan in an apartment over what was then a tavern (now a bank) on Main Street. Jack, a salesman, struggled in his career, so the family moved around a lot when Ron was a child. He was only three when his family left Tampico for Chicago, and two years later the Reagans moved to Galesburg (see Region 2). They briefly returned to Tampico in 1919 before moving to Dixon, where Ron spent most of his youth and which he considered his hometown (see next trip).

Reagan's birthplace, the Graham Building, was added to the NRHP in 1982 as part of the Tampico Main Street Historic District. Tours of the apartment, restored to its 1911 appearance, are available to the public. The H. C. Pitney Variety Store, also part of the historic district, was Jack Reagan's workplace, and the apartment above the store was the Reagan family's home from 1919 to 1920. A Reagan-themed mural graces one of the building's exterior walls.

ROCK FALLS

Rock Falls basically started as an offshoot of its neighbor to the north, Sterling (see next trip). The first settlers here, Isaac Merrill and Edward Atkins, arrived in 1837 and founded Rapids City, named for the nearby section of whitewater in the Rock River. Things did not pan out as expected, however, and the settlement stagnated until the arrival of developer Augustus P. Smith in 1867. A native of New York state, Smith had come to Illinois in 1856, settling in Sterling. Nine years later he bought about sixty-five acres across the river, platted a town, and named it Rock Falls. After purchasing an interest in the Sterling Hydraulic Company, established in 1854, Smith built a race connecting the Sterling dam to Rock Falls, and before long, the city evolved into an industrial town of significant proportions. Within ten years, Rock Falls had some fifteen factories as well as shops, hotels, a bank, and a railroad, the Chicago & Rock Falls (which later became the Chicago, Burlington & Quincy Railroad). A bridge connecting Rock Falls with its twin city, Sterling, was completed in 1878. The rapidly expanding Rock Falls was incorporated as a city in 1889.

In 1906 the Sinnissippi Dam was completed, raising the water level of the Rock River by eleven feet so as to feed into the newly completed Hennepin Canal (see Region 2). Both Rock Falls and Sterling prospered from the canal for a time, though it was eventually made obsolete by railroads and automobile highways. In the meantime, the two cities prospered on their own with industry and other commercial enterprises. The Sinnissippi Dam was restored in 2008 as a historic site with a pedestrian bridge along the river's edge. In the city center, museums include the Rock Falls Fire Department Museum and the Little Red Schoolhouse, a replica of a frontier one-room school.

Ronald Reagan Memorial Highway (I-88)
ROCK FALLS–DEKALB
54 miles

Interstate 88 traverses northern Illinois from Moline to the Chicago suburb of Hillside, running roughly parallel to and just south of the Lincoln Highway National Scenic Byway (see next trip). Shortly after former president Ronald Reagan's death in 2004, I-88, which passes near Reagan's two childhood home sites in Illinois, was dubbed the Ronald Reagan Memorial Tollway.

ROCK FALLS
See previous trip

DIXON

Chippewa, Ottawa, and Potawatomi Indians still roamed northern Illinois when the first settler, Joseph Ogee, a fur trader of mixed French and Indian blood, arrived in the Dixon area in 1828 with his Potawatomi wife. Ogee established a ferry on the Rock River, and a post office was opened the following year. Located along the narrow Galena Trail (a.k.a. the Kellogg Trail), a stage route between Peoria and Galena, Ogee's Settlement was the only river crossing and mail station for many miles in either direction.

In the spring of 1830, John Dixon and his family moved to the settlement and purchased the ferry from Ogee. Dixon became the postmaster, and the post office was renamed Dixon's Ferry. Dixon's cabin served not only as the post office but also as a trading post and an inn. During the 1832 Black Hawk War, the army built an outpost at Dixon's Ferry, on the north side of the river. Fort Dixon, used as a supply base and rendezvous point for U.S. troops and state militia, was the staging area for the fateful Battle of Stillman's Run (see below).

After the war, Dixon's Ferry returned to a more tranquil state. The town of Dixon was platted in 1835 and welcomed arriving settlers. Four years later, the community became the seat of the newly formed Lee County. It was incorporated as a town in 1853 and as a city only six years later.

In 1845 the Dixon Dam & Bridge Company was organized to build a bridge across the Rock River along with a small dam. The latter allowed the residents of Dixon to control flooding and power a sawmill. The dam was replaced by a larger and stronger one in 1851, and additional mills soon followed. As commercial and industrial growth in Dixon continued, the dam was repeatedly improved to keep pace. By the early twentieth century, the dam was generating electric power, which stimulated further growth. In addition to its water power, the Rock River provided Dixon with a number of other enterprises. Fishing and clamming were perennial industries, and in winter, pure ice was cut from the frozen river in chunks and sold throughout the region.

In 1887 a young Charles Walgreen, a native of Knoxville (near Galesburg), moved to Dixon with his parents. As a young man, he became an apprentice pharmacist with a local druggist, and a few years later he moved to Chicago's South Side to work for pharmacist Isaac Blood. In 1901 he bought Blood's drugstore and opened it as his own store—the first Walgreens (see under Bronzeville in Region 7).

Dixon continues to retain its beauty and charm along the Rock River, helped along by the work of the Dixon Men's Club, who in the 1960s planted thousands of petunias to replace trees that had succumbed to Dutch elm disease. The project grew to involve residents, schoolchildren, city employees, and various local organizations. The results earned Dixon the official title of "Petunia City."

Dixon is probably best known as the boyhood home of Ronald Reagan, who considered this city his hometown, and the Reagans' home is now a popular museum (see below). Other attractions in town include the Loveland Museum, the Dixon Historic Center, the Lee County Historical Society, the Old Settlers' Memorial Log Cabin, the Dixon Welcome Center, and Lowell Park, among others.

While there is nothing left of Fort Dixon, a ten-foot-tall bronze statue of Abraham Lincoln, erected in 1930, marks the site. The centerpiece of the Lincoln Monument State Memorial, the statue is the only major sculpture depicting Lincoln as a young, beardless soldier. Nearby is a plaque commemorating the city's founder, John Dixon. Efforts to erect a replica of the fort have yet to materialize, but possiblilities are under discussion.

Fort Dixon and the Battle of Stillman's Run

When the Black Hawk War erupted in April 1832, Dixon's Ferry was chosen as the site for the U.S. Army's central command post, Fort Dixon. The first troops, about nine hundred mounted Illinois riflemen under the command of Brig. Gen. Samuel Whiteside, arrived at Dixon's Ferry in May of 1832 and camped on the south side of the Rock River. Shortly afterward, Brig. Gen. Henry Atkinson and his regular army unit arrived with supplies, supplemented with beef furnished by John Dixon. Atkinson ordered that a fort be constructed on the north side of the river as the base of operations for U.S. Army and Illinois militia troops. The hastily built fortress consisted of two blockhouses—one large and one small—enclosed within a four-foot-high breastworks.

Immediately upon his arrival, Atkinson dispatched scouting parties to find Black Hawk and his warriors. A few days later, seven men under Capt. John Dement returned with news that Black Hawk was camped near Kishwaukee Creek, about thirty miles northeast of Fort Dixon. In the meantime, however, the impetuous Maj. Isaiah Stillman had left the fort with a battalion of inexperienced volunteers "eager to get a shot at an Indian," according to the *History of Lee County*. The ensuing encounter (of which there are conflicting accounts) became known as the Battle of Stillman's Run, a.k.a. the Battle of Old Man's Creek or the Battle of Sycamore Creek.

Stillman and his party followed the river northeast, in the general direction of Black Hawk's suspected whereabouts. On May 14, the approximately 275 militiamen unknowingly camped about five miles from Black Hawk's encampment. Black Hawk's scouts spotted the troops and informed their leader, who sent them back to Stillman's camp to signal for a parley. The attempt at a parley proved futile, however. The soldiers killed one scout and aggressively pursued the others. Though greatly outnumbered, Black Hawk pulled together a counterattack. His fears of defeat were dispelled when he saw Stillman's troops retreat in total disarray. According to one report, the militiamen thought they were being chased by "a thousand savage warriors."

> [T]he flying soldiers rushed through the camp, spreading terror and consternation among their comrades. The wildest confusion ensued, there was mounting in hot haste and the efforts of the officers to rally the troops were without avail. The panic was complete: every man seemed bent upon saving his scalp, and fled, never stopping until they reached Dixon's Ferry, or some other place of safety.

Stillman's troops staggered into the fort throughout the night. The next day, several hundred volunteers marched to the battlefield. What they found there were the bodies of eight soldiers and one government scout, with no trace of the Indians. The volunteers gathered the bodies and buried them in a common grave near the battlefield. Later, another three bodies were found nearby; these were buried where they fell. According to some historians, among the men in the burial party was twenty-three-year-old Capt. Abraham Lincoln. Although Lincoln's presence here is undocumented, the monument at the battlefield proudly asserts the future president's participation in the burial of the dead at Stillman's Run.

Back at Fort Dixon, Atkinson and Whiteside mounted a new offensive against the insurgent Indians. In June the militia engaged Black Hawk and his band at Kellogg's Grove, and on August 2, the troops defeated the Indians at Bad Axe, Wisconsin Territory. Following Black Hawk's surrender on August 27, some troops were discharged on the spot and others were mustered out at Fort Dixon.

The fort's blockhouse disappeared in the mid-1850s, but the Lincoln Monument State Memorial now stands at the site. At the site of the Stillman's Run Battle, in Stillman Valley, about thirty miles north of Dixon, is a plaque listing the twelve Americans killed in the fight. The site was added to the National Register of Historic Places in 1983.

Ronald Reagan in Dixon

In 1920 a nine-year-old boy arrived in Dixon with his family. As an adult, he went on to pursue a career in broadcasting, then movies, and finally politics. In 1980 he was elected to the first of his two terms as president of the United States. Throughout these years, Ronald Reagan returned often to the city of his youth. "All of us have a place to go back to. Dixon is that place for me," he once proclaimed.

The Reagans were a mobile family, having moved about ten times in four cities before coming to Dixon, and while in Dixon they lived at five different addresses. The family occupied their first house in Dixon—now designated the Ronald Reagan Boyhood Home National Historic Site—for less than three years. The Reagans rented this American vernacular–style farmhouse until March of 1923. Ronald, nicknamed "Dutch," and his brother, Neil ("Moon"), raised rabbits in the barn here. Of the other four homes in Dixon where the Reagan family lived, two are now private residences and two were torn down.

For Dutch Reagan, the time he spent in Dixon was perhaps the most satisfying period of his life. Here he attended grade school, middle school, and high school, performed in theatrical productions at school and church, and participated in several sports. Beginning in the summer of his freshman year at North Side High School, Dutch was hired as a lifeguard to patrol the beaches at the 230-acre Lowell Park on the Rock River. For ten to twelve hours a day, seven days a week, he scanned the river for swimmers in trouble. During his seven consecutive summers as a lifeguard, Reagan rescued an estimated seventy-seven people. He was equally active during the school year. In high school he served as an officer of the Dramatics Society, president of his senior class, and art director of the yearbook. He also lettered in football.

After graduating from North Dixon High School in 1928, Ron attended Eureka College, about ninety miles south of Dixon, returning to Dixon during the summer. He received his B.A. from Eureka in 1932, and later that year he moved to Iowa to pursue a job in broadcasting. In the ensuing years, through movie stardom, a governorship, and the presidency, Reagan returned to visit Dixon numerous times, the final one in 1994.

Dixon now contains five official sites on the Ronald Reagan Trail, as well as a few unofficial ones. In addition to the Ronald Reagan Boyhood Home, the sites include his former middle school, now the Dixon Historic Center; the First Christian Church, where he and his mother attended services and taught Sunday School; Lowell Park, where he worked as a lifeguard; and the Wings of Peace and Freedom Park.

ROCHELLE

So many transportation routes pass through Rochelle that it has gained the nickname "the Hub City." With two interstates, two other major highways, and two railroads intersecting there, Rochelle resembles the hub of a wagon wheel. The moniker is so popular that Rochelle High School's sports teams call themselves "the Hubs."

There were a number of homesteads scattered throughout Flagg Township when the sparse settlement of Hickory Grove welcomed the arrival of the Chicago & North Western Railway in 1854, connecting it with Chicago. Railroad officials named the stop Lane Station, honoring Rockford developer Dr. Robert P. Lane. Hickory Grove adopted the name and incorporated as the village of Lane in 1861. Not long afterward, Lane endured a series of fires that consumed most of its downtown buildings. Residents became suspicious after the second fire, and when a third one erupted, a suspect named Thomas Burke was arrested and tried for arson. But before a verdict was reached, the locals took the law into their own hands and hanged Burke in the middle of the town. After the incident, disapproving outsiders began to refer to Lane as "Hangtown" or "Hangman's Town." Unable to shake the epithet, embarrassed Lane residents sought a new name. They came by it in an unlikely way—when a group of local men in a drug store noticed a bottle of the laxative Rochelle Salts on the shelf, they declared that because the city needed "a good cleaning out," it should be called Rochelle. The name change became official in 1866.

Because of the railroad, the city grew quickly, and a second rail line, the Chicago & Iowa, arrived in 1870. By the late 1870s, Rochelle had a number of factories, and by the

1930s, the Stokely-Van Camp and Del Monte companies had both opened canneries here. During hard times, especially the Great Depression, the canneries attracted groups of able-bodied but homeless men who spent the harvest season in Rochelle, erecting several hobo camps at the outskirts of town. To illustrate the realities of that era, a replica of one of these "hobo jungles" was built at Rochelle Railroad Park. This park and open-air museum, dedicated in 1998, honors the city's long association with the railroads and supporting industries. Situated at the crossing of the still-active Union Pacific and Burlington Northern Santa Fe rail lines, the park provides safe viewing areas for train watchers. Nearly a hundred freight trains still pass through Rochelle each day, and park visitors can not only watch the trains but also listen to real-time dispatches to the crews. The facility also includes an original Whitcomb locomotive, manufactured in Rochelle by the Whitcomb Locomotive Works; various displays; and a gift shop.

Rochelle's historical attractions do not end at the Railroad Park. The city's pride in its past is evident in its downtown historic district, several historical museums, and a number of annual festivals that celebrate the region's heritage. The Rochelle Visitor Center is housed in an eye-catching restored 1918 Standard Oil filling station, and the thriving downtown business district, traversed by the Lincoln Highway National Scenic Byway (IL 38), features numerous buildings of historical significance. Among them are the Hub Theatre, still operating as a movie theater since its opening in 1930; the 1912 Andrew Carnegie–funded Flagg Township Public Library; and the 1872, Italianate-style William H. Holcomb House (a.k.a. the Carl Vandre House). The City and Town Hall, built in 1884, is now the home of the Flagg Township Museum. The building and its annexes once housed municipal offices as well as the fire station and the police station, and two of the original jail cells are still intact. Inside, the museum displays the world's only remaining 1915 Partin-Palmer automobile, built at Rochelle's own Whitcomb Locomotive Works. Nearby, the Rochelle Firehouse Museum includes a 1924 American LaFrance fire truck and other antique equipment.

About six miles west of Rochelle, the 320-acre Skare Park offers a variety of recreational activities and the Norman Lincoln Skare Homestead Museum, located in one of the original wood-framed, two-story outbuildings that was part of farmer Norman Skare's forty-acre orchard and fruit farm, believed to have been established in the 1930s. In 1972, Skare donated his land to the Flagg-Rochelle Community Park District "so that people of all ages can enjoy God's handiwork forever."

DEKALB

Settled in 1836 and incorporated forty-one years later, DeKalb was named after the German-born Revolutionary War hero Baron Johann de Kalb. The future city was founded in 1837 by New Yorker Russell Huntley and his brother, Lewis; the original settlement was called Huntley's Grove. In 1853, having paved the way for the Union Pacific Railroad to stop at the site, the brothers platted the village of DeKalb. They set aside land for a public square and donated land for the town's first two churches. DeKalb soon established itself as a budding city, and its economy and population grew steadily.

The founding of Northern Illinois State Normal School in DeKalb in 1895 added to the city's status as well as its economy. Part of the extension of the normal school (teacher's college) system in Normal, the school's name was changed numerous times as its course offerings and degree programs expanded. It is now Northern Illinois University (see below).

DeKalb has preserved its rich history and many of its architecturally interesting buildings, including the famed Egyptian Theatre. This 1929 art deco movie house is the only operating theatre in the Midwest that reflects the Egyptian revival fad of the 1920s that coincided with the discovery of King Tut's tomb. One of the oldest historical buildings in DeKalb is the George H. Gurler House, a two-story Greek Revival home built in 1857.

DeKalb's commitment to farming innovation was evident as early as 1860, when a county society to promote agriculture was organized. The city's reputation for leadership in this field was solidified with the establishment of the DeKalb County Farm Bureau, the first organization of its kind in the nation, in 1912. In the 1930s the DeKalb AgResearch Corporation (now Monsanto) introduced hybrid seed corn. DeKalb's best-known contribution to agriculture, however, is barbed wire.

The Development of Barbed Wire

The movie industry might portray the six-gun and the repeating rifle as the tamers of the Plains, but to a great extent it was barbed wire, first developed and mass produced in DeKalb. In fact, several inventors—four from the DeKalb area—designed early versions of the new fencing material, and all vied to have his design chosen as the favorite. The winner was Joseph F. Glidden.

Although Glidden ultimately came to be known as the "Father of Barbed Wire," his design was not the first. The earliest barbed-wire patent was issued on February 11, 1868, to New York blacksmith Michael Kelly. As Kelly described it, "my invention relates imparting to fences of wire a character approximately to that of a thorn hedge." Errors in the patent's language and poor business practices, some believe, contributed to Kelly never receiving credit for inventing barbed wire.

Five years later at the DeKalb County Fair, Henry Rose, a farmer from nearby Waterman, introduced his wood and metal-barb fencing, receiving a patent on May 13, 1873. Three other local men saw Rose's exhibit and set to work on their own designs. The three were merchant Isaac L. Ellwood, farmer Joseph F. Glidden, and lumberman Jacob Haish.

Ellwood's barbed fence, whose patent was issued on February 24, 1874, proved to be impractical and was never manufactured. Glidden and Haish developed similar double-strand designs, Glidden with a spur-style barb (patent issued on November 24, 1874) and Haish with his special "S" barb (patent issued on August 31, 1875). Glidden and Haish would later charge each other with patent infringements. In the meantime Ellwood, recognizing his own fence's deficiencies, purchased a half interest in Glidden's design in July 1874, and the two formed the Barb Fence Company. The following year they opened their first factory in an unlikely spot—Glidden's barn. The two-story brick barn, built sometime between 1861 and 1871, has been called the most significant barn in the nation.

Although the company did fairly well in its early years, it repeatedly failed to crack the biggest market—Texas. Finally in 1876 the partners hired fellow Illinoisan John W. Gates (a.k.a. "Bet-A-Million" Gates), who proved to be a salesman extraordinaire. With conviction and enthusiasm, Gates conquered the Texas cattlemen's skepticism. Within six years, annual production increased from five to forty tons. In the meantime, however, Glidden, already in his sixties, decided to sell out his half of the company to Washburn & Moen Manufacturing Company, a wire factory in Massachusetts, in 1876. With Ellwood now the sole owner, the Barb Fence Company became the I. L. Ellwood Company. Ellwood's company mostly sold to the Western markets, while Washburn & Moen handled the South and Southwest.

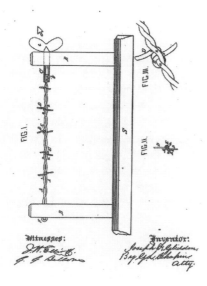

J. F. GLIDDEN.
Wire-Fences.
No.157,124.   Patented Nov. 24, 1874.

Sketch of Joseph F. Glidden's barbed wire design, patent number 157,124, issued November 24, 1874
—Author's collection

J. HAISH.
Wire-Fence Barbs.
No. 167,240.   Patented Aug. 31, 1875.

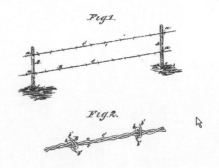

Sketch of Jacob Haish's barbed wire design, patent number 167,240, issued August 31, 1875 —Author's collection

Sketch of Henry Rose's barbed wire design, patent number 138,763, issued May 13, 1873 —Author's collection

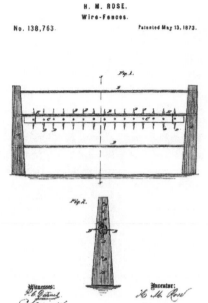

Sketch of Isaac Ellwood's barbed wire design, patent number 147,756, issued February 24, 1874 —Author's collection

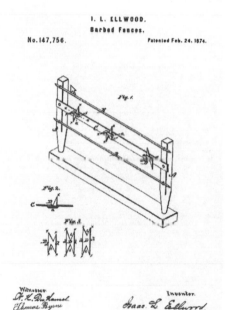

Finally, on December 15, 1880, the courts ruled on the infringement suit between Glidden and Haish, deciding in favor of Glidden. The ruling solidified Glidden's place in western history as the "Father of Barbed Wire." He died a millionaire in 1906, at age ninety-three. Ellwood also did all right for himself. In 1898 he helped establish American Steel & Wire Company, with Gates as its president. American Steel became part of U.S. Steel in 1901, and wire production continued in DeKalb until 1938. Ellwood died in 1910, at age seventy-seven. Both Ellwood and Glidden were generous supporters of their hometown of DeKalb, and both played a key role in establishing Northern Illinois State Normal School, now Northern Illinois University (see below).

Though he lost his patent fight, Jacob Haish continued in the barbed-wire business and made a fortune of his own. Like Ellwood and Glidden, he made significant contributions to NIU, donating books and helping to build the university's library. To the DeKalb community he donated a public library, an opera house, a gymnasium, and an addition to the DeKalb Public Hospital. Haish died in 1926.

Isaac Ellwood's thirty-three-room, 1879 mansion and coachhouse was donated to the city of DeKalb in 1964 and turned into the Ellwood House Museum. A mile west of the Ellwood House, near the campus of NIU, is the Glidden Homestead & Historical Center, which opened in 2006 after extensive restoration. The center comprises Glidden's 1861 two-story brick home and the historic barn where he invented his winning wire design. The barn, which has been carefully preserved and restored, is open for interior viewing only once a year, during its Spring Open House in May.

Joseph F. Glidden, known as the "Father of Barbed Wire" —Author's collection

Barbed wire designer Jacob Haish
—Author's collection

Barbed wire designer Isaac Ellwood
—Author's collection

Northern Illinois University

In 1895 Northern Illinois State Normal School (now Northern Illinois University) was established in DeKalb as a teachers' college. Its first building, the castlelike Altgeld Hall (named for the school's founder, Gov. John P. Altgeld), still stands. Over the years, the school, renamed Northern Illinois University in 1957, has expanded into a full-service liberal arts university with more than 24,000 students. It is now the second-largest university in the state and the DeKalb area's largest employer.

On February 14, 2008, a horrible crime destroyed the serenity of the NIU campus. At about 3 p.m., a mentally unbalanced former student burst into Cole Hall's East Auditorium and fired indiscriminately into a crowd of students attending a lecture, killing five and wounding eighteen before turning the gun on himself. The tragedy sent shock waves through the community and the nation.

The following year, the university created a Memorial Garden near Cole Hall. The garden includes a walking path and a curved memorial wall engraved with the words "Forward, Together Forward," lyrics from the school's fight song that came to symbolize NIU's hopeful spirit. An eighteen-foot-high stainless-steel sculpture honoring the five slain students was unveiled in October 2009.

Meanwhile, Cole Hall was closed for several years while plans for its future were decided and implemented. After it was agreed that the building would be extensively remodeled, the overhaul began in 2010. The renovated and modernized Cole Hall reopened in 2012 with a state-of-the-art collaborative-learning center, an anthropology museum, and a new auditorium.

Lincoln Highway (US 30, IL 2, and IL 38)
FULTON–DEKALB
86 miles

The Lincoln Highway, which ran between New York City and San Francisco, was America's first transcontinental motorway. Going west to east, as we will do here, the Illinois section of the historic highway starts at the Iowa state line near Fulton and goes to the Indiana state line just east of Chicago Heights. The route, marked with red-white-and-blue signs, follows present US 30, IL 2, IL 38, and IL 31, then back on to US 30 near Aurora to Chicago Heights. This trip ends at DeKalb. The Lincoln Highway Association's national headquarters is in Franklin Grove, and the first seedling mile of concrete for the highway was laid in Malta; we will visit both of these towns on this trip.

In 2006 the Illinois Lincoln Highway Coalition (ILHC) launched a project to create historically themed murals in forty communities along the Illinois Lincoln Highway National Scenic Byway. As of 2012, twenty-one have been installed. On this trip, travelers may view ILHC murals in Fulton, Dixon, Rochelle, Malta, and DeKalb. Other murals in this region are located in Byron, Oregon, and Rock Falls.

FULTON
See earlier trip

STERLING

Like other parts of northern Illinois, the Sterling area was settled after the 1832 Black Hawk War ended and all Indians were forced out of the state. The first cabin was built in 1834 by settler Hezekiah Brink; the following year, he brought his family from Indiana to join him here. Other settlers arrived around the same time. Brothers John and Isaac Albertson from New York state settled just east of Brink's homestead, and William Kirkpatrick from Sangamon County built his cabin just west of Brink's place.

In 1836 Brink sold part of his claim to Daniel S. Harris. Together the two men laid out a village called Harrisburgh. The same year, Kirkpatrick founded a town on his property, dubbing it Chatham. Whiteside County had just been established, and the two settlements vied to be named the county seat. Eventually, realizing they'd have a better chance with a larger town, Harrisburgh and Chatham combined as Sterling, named for Black Hawk War hero Maj. James Sterling. Even so, Sterling lost the honor to Lyndon in 1839. Undaunted, Sterling demanded a recount and won. But the battle was not over. Another vote in 1843 placed the seat at Lyndon again. Sterling complained that it had already started building a courthouse, an argument it won in 1849. In the end, however, after yet another vote in 1857, the seat was permanently moved to an upstart called Morrison, a city on US 30 west of Rock Falls, in northern Whiteside County.

In 1854 Sterling Hydraulic was founded, ushering in an era of industry. The company built a one-thousand-foot-long dam across the Rock River to attract factories, even though the dam curtailed the river's navigability. The water power created by the dam brought the young city much growth and prosperity, and the navigability issue soon became moot when the Galena & Chicago Union Railroad arrived in 1856. More than 3,000 people celebrated this event with an old-fashioned barbecue. The following year, Sterling was incorporated as a city.

Over the years, several bridges were built to unite Sterling with its younger neighbor, Rock Falls (see earlier trip). The first one, a wooden structure, was constructed in 1856, but it soon washed out. An iron toll bridge replaced it in 1863, but residents, loathe to pay the tolls, demanded that the city provide a free bridge, which it finally did in 1878. By then, Sterling had three hotels, more than one hundred businesses, and numerous factories.

Among the most prominent manufacturers in Sterling was the Northwestern Barb Wire Company, founded by Washington M. Dillon in 1879. In 1882 Dillon bought the Italianate mansion of Col. Edward N. Kirk, built in 1858. Dillon's son, Paul W. Dillon, was born in the house the following year. After the younger Dillon's death in 1980, the historic home was donated to the Sterling Park District, and it was added to the NRHP the same year. The Sterling-Rock Falls Historical Society Museum took up residence in the carriage house while the main house was converted into the Dillon Home Museum (a.k.a. the Kirk House).

In 2011 another historic home, now called the Lincoln-Manahan Home, opened in Sterling. The one-and-a-half story brick home of Whiteside County sheriff William Manahan, built in 1847, was recently restored to its 1856 appearance, reflecting the time when Abraham Lincoln was an overnight guest there. Purchased by the Sterling-Rock Falls Historical Society in 2007, it is one of the oldest houses in Sterling and is believed to be the only private home in which Lincoln stayed that is still standing on the Lincoln Highway.

In addition to its historic buildings, Sterling boasts nearly twenty murals in the downtown area. The paintings, commissioned by the not-for-profit Sterling Mural Society since 1996, depict significant people, places, and events from the city's past. Among other subjects, the murals portray settler Hezekiah Brink; Sterling's first schoolteacher, Sarah Worthington; the first city hall and fire station; the Sterling Hydraulic Company; and the city's Hispanic community.

DIXON

See previous trip

FRANKLIN GROVE

A smattering of settlers arrived in the Franklin Grove area in 1836, but there was no real effort to form a village until late 1848, when a settlement called Chaplin was platted. In 1853, after residents heard that the Chicago, St. Charles & Mississippi Air Line Railroad would pass through the area, land along the rail line, north and east of Chaplin, was platted as the village of Franklin Grove.

One of the most influential men in Franklin Grove's early days was Massachusetts native Col. Nathan Whitney, who in 1838 built an Italianate-style frame house and a few years later established a commercial nursery and apple orchard. The house, still standing, was added to the NRHP in 1990.

Franklin Grove has had many other noteworthy buildings through the years. In 1860 Henry I. Lincoln, a distant relative of Abraham Lincoln, erected a two-story, native limestone building as a dry-goods store. It later housed the offices of the town news-paper and other enterprises, but it was sitting empty in 1995 when a group of local preservationists bought the building and restored it. This unique structure is now the home of the Lincoln Highway Association National Headquarters and their gift shop. About a mile northwest of town, at the 881-acre Franklin Creek State Natural Area, is a re-created mid-1800s gristmill, whose second floor houses an interpretive center.

Just south of Franklin Grove, visitors can experience nineteenth-century life on the prairie in Chaplin Creek Village, a full-scale historical restoration of a typical northern Illinois settlement. The Franklin Grove Area Historical Society operates the village and hosts a Summer Harvest Festival each August.

ROCHELLE
See previous trip

MALTA

The small agricultural community of Malta, six miles west of DeKalb, is witnessing change. Farms on either side of the town have been purchased for development, and Malta High School is now an experimental elementary school under the auspices of Northern Illinois University. Yet even as the DeKalb area expands, Malta maintains its rural identity.

Malta was founded in the mid-1850s under the name Milton, later changed to Etna and finally to Malta. The village grew in the late 1850s and 1860s, after the Galena & Chicago Union Railroad arrived, but further growth was sporadic. Malta still has fewer than a thousand residents, though its community college, Kishwaukee College, established in 1968, has an enrollment of approximately 10,000 full-time, part-time, and online students.

About twenty inches below the surface of IL 38 near Malta lies the first "seedling" mile of America's first transcontinental highway. The installation of this section of con-crete road on November 12, 1914, gave Malta national historical significance. The Old Town Hall Museum, home of the Malta Historical Society, features a mural, created in 2010, depicting the highway's history.

The idea of building a paved roadway to link the east and west coasts was the brain-child of Carl G. Fisher, an Indiana car-parts manufacturer and a cofounder of the newly built Indianapolis Motor Speedway. Supporting Fisher were Frank A. Seiberling of Goodyear Tire & Rubber Company, Henry B. Joy of the Packard Motor Car Com-pany, Roy Chapin of the Hudson Motor Car Company, William C. Durant of General Motors, and Edsel Ford of the Ford Motor Company, all of whom pledged money for what was originally planned to be a cross-country gravel road. Fisher called the project the "Coast-to-Coast Rock Highway."

The goal was to connect various stagecoach routes, emigrant trails, county and town roads, and city streets into one long east-west highway between New York and San Francisco. To stimulate interest in the project, Joy suggested that the group change the roadway's name to the "Lincoln Highway," believing that the revered president's name would generate support. The Lincoln Highway Association (LHA) formed in 1913. Pledges from private donors put the group close to their $10 million goal with

Beneath this section of IL 38 near Malta is the original "seedling mile" of the Lincoln Highway —Author's collection

little state aid and no federal assistance. Once the final route was announced, however, residents of bypassed towns and states quickly lost interest, funding fell off, and the project stalled.

The highway's planners had intended to use gravel and dirt as the road's primary composition; concrete was a relatively new product. But when backing for the original project faltered, Joy turned to this new material in the hope that it would reinvigorate interest in the highway. His plan was to construct six separate seedling miles of concrete road in locations across the country to demonstrate the wonder of this new road material and convince Americans to support the Lincoln Highway effort. Once again, Joy proved to be right. The Lehigh Portland Cement Company donated 1.5 million barrels of cement, and when Malta was chosen as the site for the first seedling mile, a local supplier donated 8,000 barrels. Other supporters contributed money, equipment, and staff. Construction on the first seedling mile began on September 21, 1914, and it was completed on November 12. Farmers and others in the region immediately saw the benefits of transporting freight and people over a smooth concrete surface.

The demands of World War I delayed further construction, but the need for a national highway system was becoming increasingly apparent to the American public, large and small businesses, and even the U.S. military. After the war, citizens and groups began to pressure Washington to fund such a project. In 1921 Congress passed the Federal Highway Act, and the U.S. government took over the construction of the Lincoln Highway, though with some changes in the route. The highway was never completely finished, but the idea of a government-supported interstate highway system had taken hold.

When Congress instated a number system for government highways a few years later, the connecting roads comprising the Lincoln Highway were individually designated with numbers, diluting the original concept. The Lincoln Highway Association, along with the Boy Scouts of America and other groups, worked to preserve the Lincoln theme; in 1928 the Boy Scouts installed thousands of markers all along the route. Afterward, the LHA disbanded, but some six decades later—in 1992—the group was reorganized to preserve the heritage of the road that was once called the "Main Street Across America."

DEKALB
See previous trip

US 52 and IL 89
DIXON–SPRING VALLEY
56 miles

This route from Dixon follows US 52 southeast through Amboy and Mendota to Troy Grove, the former home of James Butler "Wild Bill" Hickok. From there we veer west to connect with IL 89, on which we head south to Cherry, site of a devastating coal mine disaster, and continue south to Spring Valley.

DIXON
See earlier trip

AMBOY

When the first settlers arrived in 1837, this area was known as Rocky Ford. For years, the settlement consisted of only a few farms and, for a while, a colony founded by a faction of the Church of Jesus Christ of Latter Day Saints (LDS). After the murder of Joseph Smith Jr. in 1844, some Mormons believed that Smith's son, Joseph Smith III, was the rightful successor to lead the church, not Brigham Young. Rather than follow Young west from Nauvoo in 1846, they moved to Rocky Ford, where a small LDS congregation had been established around 1840. The sect, which denounced polygamy and other practices that Young advocated, called itself the Reorganized Church of Jesus Christ of Latter Day Saints. In 1860, by which time Rocky Ford had become the town of Amboy, Joseph Smith III was ordained as president and prophet of the Reorganized Church at Amboy's Goldman's Hall. Six years later, Smith and his followers set up their headquarters in Plano (see later trip). They moved their headquarters to Lamoni, Iowa, in 1881, and to Independence, Missouri, in 1921.

In the meantime, in 1854, the Illinois Central Railroad arrived in the Amboy area, planning to build its Northern Division headquarters here. The railroad recruited more than four hundred workers to build and staff its depot, roundhouse, and repair shops, and within two years, Amboy's population had soared to nearly 2,000. In 1856 community leaders gathered to choose a name for their town and prepare for its incorporation. Agreeing on the name Bath, the settlers submitted the incorporation papers to the county courthouse in Dixon. When the papers came back, however, residents were stunned to see that the town had been incorporated under the name Amboy. How this happened remains a mystery, but the settlers chose not to pursue the matter, and the town remained Amboy.

The same year the railroad arrived, two young entrepreneurs, Samuel Carson and John T. Pirie, arrived here from Ireland and opened a dry-goods business in a former saloon. The store was an immediate success, so much so that it outgrew its original venue within a few months. Setting up a new shop in a nearby building, the Carson & Pirie Company prospered for the next ten years, opening several branches around the region, including one in Chicago in 1864. Later that year, Carson and Pirie moved their headquarters to Chicago, and in 1890 they partnered with brothers George and Robert S. Scott of Scotland and changed the company's name to Carson Pirie Scott & Company. A plaque now stands at the site of the company's original Amboy store.

After Amboy's original 1854 train depot burned down in 1875, the Illinois Central Railroad built the two-story, brick-and-limestone Amboy Depot, completed in 1876. The ticketing station, on the first floor, had separate waiting rooms for men and women; the second floor housed corporate offices. Only eighteen years later, in 1894, the ICRR closed its Amboy headquarters and moved its repair shops to Freeport and Clinton. Part of the Amboy depot's first floor remained in use as a station, while the rest of the rooms downstairs and the rooms on the second floor were leased out for other purposes. The station finally closed completely in 1967, and the building was abandoned. The Amboy ICRR depot was rescued from deterioration in the 1970s and 1980s, and it was listed on the NRHP in 1992. The restored building now serves as a historical museum, opened in 2003.

Other sites of historic interest in Amboy include the 1845 Davis House—the oldest frame home in the city—and a number of prefabricated "kit houses," or "catalog houses," built from mail-order kits from catalogs such as Sears and Montgomery Ward in the early 1900s.

MENDOTA

Mendota is known statewide for its National Sweet Corn Festival, where 100,000 pounds of buttered sweet corn are served free to visitors each August. The annual community event, sponsored by the Del Monte Company, began in 1947 and features a parade, a carnival, live music, and more. But Mendota is about more than just corn. Among its attractions are three museums, two lakes, and a full complement of shops, restaurants, and city parks. Nearby Snyder's Grove Nature Area is a 104-acre preserve with numerous hiking trails.

The settlement's economic launch came with the railroads. The Illinois Central and the Chicago, Burlington & Quincy arrived in 1853 and 1854, respectively. Astute entrepreneurs built a store and several other businesses before the tracks were even laid. Timothy B. Blackstone, a division engineer for the Illinois Central and later president of the Chicago & Alton Railroad, platted the town, initially called Junction. Blackstone later founded the Union Stock Yard in Chicago. When the settlement was incorporated as a village in 1855, the name was changed to its Indian appellation, Mendota, meaning "connection," or "meeting of trails." Twelve years later, Mendota was chartered as a city.

Mendota's economy combined farming and industry. The surrounding fertile croplands produced corn, oats, soybeans, and wheat for both local and distant markets. In the late 1800s, corn industrialist Justus D. Tower built his main factory, which produced high-quality cultivators and other farm machinery, in Mendota. The J. D. Tower & Sons Company became a major part of Mendota's economy almost immediately after it was founded in 1872, and the town grew along with the company.

The large, multifunctional Union Depot was built in 1895 after the original Passenger House burned down. Politicians often stopped in Mendota and gave speeches in front of the depot. The building, which still serves as an Amtrak station, also now houses the Union Depot Railroad Museum. Mendota's other two museums are the Hume-Carnegie Museum, home of the Mendota Historical Society, and the recently built Breaking the Prairie Museum, which comprises a replica barn and chapel.

TROY GROVE

The Little Vermilion River meanders east and south of Troy Grove, providing serene beauty to the flat surrounding prairie. Among the first settlers in the area was Warren Root, who arrived here shortly after the Black Hawk War. He built a cabin near a cluster of trees, which he called Troy Grove after his former home in Troy, New York. In 1836 two men, named Kirtland and Colton (first names unknown), laid out the village of Homer, so named for Colton's hometown of Homer, New York, but the following year the settlement's name was changed back to Troy Grove.

One of the settlement's earliest arrivals was William A. Hickok, who settled here with his family in late 1836 and opened the first store in the village. The following year, James Butler Hickok was born (see below). James would grow up to become one of the best-known and most colorful characters of the Old West, giving his hometown a claim to fame.

Troy Grove's future appeared promising until the 1850s, when the Illinois Central Railroad laid its tracks several miles south of the village, dooming its prospects. The community survives today as a tiny village of about three hundred people. A granite monument in the middle of a state park identifies Hickok's birthplace.

James Butler "Wild Bill" Hickok

"Wild Bill" Hickok was a dead shot, a high-stakes gambler, and a well-respected lawman. His exploits rivaled, to some extent, those of "Buffalo Bill" Cody, minus the longevity—Hickok was only thirty-nine years old when he died, while Cody lived to be seventy-one.

James Butler Hickok was born in Troy Grove on May 27, 1837, the fifth of seven children. Growing up, James helped on the family farm and attended school. His father, an abolitionist, harbored fugitive slaves at his store and helped them get to the next station on the Underground Railroad. James's parents instilled in him a sense of justice and fair play, a trait that remained with him throughout his life. At age eighteen, James left for the western frontier, where he eventually became a legend.

After serving briefly as a constable in Monticello, Kansas, Hickok worked as a teamster for Jones & Cartwright from 1859 to 1861. Contrary to popular belief, he was never a Pony Express rider. When the Civil War broke out, Hickok signed on as a scout, guerrilla fighter, and wagonmaster for the Union Army. While the origin of Hickok's nickname of "Wild Bill" is a subject of debate, Hickok authority Joseph G. Rosa believes he acquired the moniker from his comrades during the war.

After the war, Hickok worked as a deputy U.S. Marshal at Fort Riley, Kansas, where he sometimes scouted for George Armstrong Custer's 7th Cavalry. In 1869 he was elected sheriff of Ellis County, Kansas, and in 1871 he was appointed city marshal of Abilene, Kansas. During his tenure as a lawman, he was involved in a number of gunfights and earned for himself both admirers and detractors. In a February 2003 article in *Wild West* magazine, Joseph G. Rosa maintained that Hickok was in reality "in complete contrast to his newspaper-inspired desperado image. . . . He was gentlemanly, courteous, soft-spoken and graceful in manner, yet left no one in any doubt that . . . if threatened [he] would meet violence with violence. Wild Bill could be generous to a fault, and [was] slow to anger. . . . When angered, however, he . . . faced down those who insulted or challenged him. This man-to-man approach . . . earned him respect among his peers."

In the late spring of 1876, Hickok joined a wagon train headed for the Dakota goldfields. The company arrived in Deadwood, Dakota Territory, in July. On August 2, while Hickok was playing cards at Nuttall & Mann's Saloon No. 10 in Deadwood, twenty-four-year-old frontiersman Jack McCall entered the saloon, walked up behind Wild Bill, and shot him in the back of the head. McCall's motives are uncertain, though during the trial McCall claimed that Hickok had killed his brother. McCall was hanged for the murder on March 1, 1877.

Four of the cards Wild Bill was playing when he was shot—a pair of aces and a pair of eights—later came to be known as the "dead man's hand." Hickok is buried in Deadwood's Mount Moriah Cemetery, where his grave is a tourist attraction.

In Troy Grove, a granite monument in a small park identifies Hickok's birthplace. The house itself was torn down in 1929, and the monument was erected later that year. A new bronze bust was installed at the well-maintained site in 2009.

CHERRY

Built as a company town by the St. Paul Coal Company in 1904, Cherry was named for mine supervisor James Cherry. The coal company was a subsidiary of the Chicago, Milwaukee & St. Paul Railway, and the coal was used primarily to fuel the railroad's steam locomotives. St. Paul Coal erected 125 homes for its workers, and individual families built another 200, as laborers—mostly European immigrants—arrived in the area, eager to obtain a steady job.

The first mine opened in 1905. Only four years later, Cherry became the site of the third deadliest mining accident in U.S. history.

Cherry Mine Disaster

On November 13, 1909, between noon and 1 p.m., six hay bales for the mule stables on the third level were placed in a pit car and left at the shaft entrance. No one is certain how the bales caught fire—perhaps kerosene from a leaky torch dripped down on them and ignited the dry hay. When the fire was discovered, workers pushed the car down the shaft and extinguished the flames on the bales, but the fire had already spread to the shaft's overhead shoring timbers.

Some miners managed to escape via the main hoisting cage before smoke and heat shut off that route. Others clambered through the airshaft, but that passage, too, was soon blocked. Wooden stairs and ladders burned while hundreds of miners were still trapped below. A dozen miners who had escaped went back down repeatedly to aid their fellows.

Six of these attempts were successful; on the seventh trip, however, the rescuers and the men they were trying to save all perished.

Workers labored for more than a week to bring the fire under control. Two shafts were sealed in an attempt to smother the flames, but this further endangered the men below by cutting off their air supply. After eight days, twenty-one miners were miraculously found alive, though one died shortly after being rescued. The mine remained sealed until February 1, 1910, when it was reopened to recover the bodies.

In the end, 259 men and boys died in the disaster. The St. Paul Coal Company helped compensate the families for losses and set aside five acres south of Cherry for a cemetery; others were buried in Ladd. Meanwhile, the Cherry Relief Commission was organized to assist the victims' families. The group raised and distributed $220,000 in public donations and $100,000 in appropriations from the state.

As a result of the tragedy, the Illinois legislature enacted extensive new safety regulations for coal mining in 1910. A year later, the lawmakers passed a liability act that paved the way for the Illinois Workmen's Compensation Act.

On November 13, 1911, the Cherry Mine Disaster monument, erected by the United Mine Workers of America, was unveiled at the Holy Trinity Miners Cemetery, with a number of survivors present. An interpretive plaque was added in 1971 by the state of Illinois, and a second monument was erected in 2009 in honor of the tragedy's centennial. To this day, a commemorative wreath-laying ceremony is held annually at the monument.

SPRING VALLEY

Indians who partook of the cool, clear water of the springs that fed Spring Creek called this area the Valley of the Springs. But water was not all this place had to offer. As it was discovered after the 1860s, Spring Valley lay in the heart of northern Illinois coal country.

In 1884 a private speculator, Henry J. Miller, and his son-in-law, Charles J. Devlin, acquired mineral rights to more than 5,000 acres in the Spring Valley area and bought 500 acres to lay out a town. With financial backing and support from several prominent investors, Miller and Devlin formed the Spring Valley Coal Company and the Spring Valley Townsite Company, spending more than $2.5 million over four years to build the town. Lots were set aside for churches, schools, a library, and various public buildings.

By 1888 four mines were operating and the population had swelled to more than 3,000. The Chicago & North Western Railway extended its line from DeKalb to Spring Valley, and the town's growth was so rapid that it was nicknamed the "Magic City." But trouble was brewing as mine owners and union leaders sparred, leading to a lockout in 1889. Tensions continued to mount for years, and in 1894 Italian immigrant workers, who had originally been brought in as scabs, called their own strike. In response, the mine owners replaced the Italians with black workers from the South. A riot ensued, and Gov. John P. Altgeld called in the state militia to quell the disturbance.

The following year, tensions erupted once more after an Italian immigrant reported that he had been attacked and robbed by a group of black men. After police released the accused for lack of evidence, a mob of European immigrants, many of them miners, raided the black section of Spring Valley, smashing windows, breaking down doors, and burning and looting homes. Although no one was killed, the rioters terrorized women and children and beat many of the men, leaving the black community deeply shaken. The victims took the attackers to court, winning convictions in more than a dozen cases; eight of the rioters were imprisoned. The case led to legislation that prohibited companies from bringing in replacement workers during a strike.

Spring Valley was the longtime home of union leader John Mitchell, who played a part in the strikes and later served as president of the United Mine Workers (UMW) from 1898 to 1908. During his terms as UMW president, Mitchell increased membership and wages, negotiated the eight-hour day, and orchestrated two major miners' strikes in Pennsylvania, in 1900 and 1902.

Eventually, Spring Valley miners ended up out of work anyway. Competition from southern coal mines forced the local mines to close in 1927. In the meantime, however, the town had established itself as a stable community with an emphasis on education, and that stability, along with economic activity from surrounding agriculture, helped Spring Valley survive and continue to thrive.

US 6
SPRING VALLEY–MORRIS
46 miles

This trip roughly follows the Illinois & Michigan Canal State Trail, a nearly fifty-mile-long pedestrian and bicycle trail that follows accessible parts of the canal between Peru-LaSalle and Rockdale, just south of Joliet. The trail is the main section of the ninety-seven-mile long Illinois & Michigan Canal National Heritage Corridor, established by President Ronald Reagan—a native Illinoisan—in 1984. Since we are traveling by car, we will follow US 6, which approximately parallels the trail. I & M Canal visitor centers are located near Utica and in Morris, Channahon, Joliet, and Lockport (see also Region 6).

The I & M Canal, built between 1836 and 1848, connected the South Branch of the Chicago River at Bridgeport with the Illinois River at Peru, creating a water route between the Great Lakes and the Mississippi River. Much of the work on the canal was done by immigrant labor, especially Irish workers. Towns were platted all along the route, but due to overeager speculation, only about half were ever built. Many, however, survived and thrived, including the communities on this trip.

The railroads, built through this area in the 1850s and '60s, supplanted the canal to an extent, but it remained in use through the early twentieth century. In the 1930s, the Civilian Conservation Corps along with the National Park Service began to restore and renovate the canal corridor as a historic-preservation and recreation project. The effort was revived in 1984 when Congress approved funding for development of the National Heritage Corridor.

SPRING VALLEY
See previous trip

PERU

Though many communities along the route of the Illinois & Michigan Canal prospered during its early years of operation, Peru was not among them. First settled by Tennessee farmer John Hays in 1830, the little settlement on the Illinois River was a successful river port until the canal was built in 1848, when neighboring LaSalle, where the steamboat basin was located, eclipsed Peru as a shipping point. In the end, though, it did not matter, as Peru had its own abundant natural resources, including ice, timber, stone, and most profitably, coal.

Peru's coal made the city, incorporated in 1851, a processing center for zinc ore mined in northwestern Illinois. Other thriving industries in Peru included the Maze Lumber and Maze Nail Companies, Star Union Brewery, the Westclock clock company, the Peru Plow & Wheel Company, and Carus Chemical. Both the W. H. Maze Company, opened in 1848, and the Carus Chemical Company, established in 1915, still operate in Peru today. With a current population over 10,000, the city enjoys a healthy economy, as does its slightly smaller twin city, LaSalle (see next stop).

Peru's most famous native is renowned violinist Maud Powell. Powell gained international acclaim as the first American violinist to earn international ranking and the

Maud Powell, violinist from
Peru —Courtesy LaSalle
County Historical Society

first woman to lead a professional string quartet, among many other achievements. Born in Peru in 1867, she first studied violin and piano in Aurora, then in Chicago, and eventually in Europe. At a time when there were few female professional musicians, she toured throughout the world and was among the most respected—as well as the most popular—violinists of her day. She was one of the first musicians to make recordings in the early days of the phonograph, and all her records became bestsellers. With this phenomenon, she almost single-handedly popularized classical music among the general public. She also pioneered the practice of giving benefit concerts for charities and staging goodwill performances at schools and military bases. Her rigorous schedule may have contributed to her early death from a heart attack in 1920. In 1995 the city of Peru launched its annual Maud Powell Music Festival with the unveiling of a bronze statue created in her honor.

LASALLE

A few settlers had already built homes in the LaSalle area when construction on the Illinois & Michigan Canal began in 1836. Many laborers, mostly Irish immigrants, swelled the local population. A post office was established and the town was platted, but funds ran out and canal work stopped the following year. In 1845 the state of Illinois stepped in, arranging for creditors to advance construction funds, with taxes earmarked to repay the debt. Construction resumed, LaSalle was repopulated, and the canal was completed in 1848. In 1852, residents voted to incorporate as a city.

Goods shipped along the Illinois River to and from Chicago were loaded on and off steamboats at LaSalle, near the canal's confluence with the Illinois River. Although the new city prospered, the land was swampy and the infrastructure was slapdash. A historical sketch by the 1952 LaSalle Centennial Committee described 1850s LaSalle:

> *Swamplands were to be found in almost every section of the platted town. Streets were puddles of mud in wet weather and hardened ruts in dry. There were no street-lights. The sidewalks were two narrow strips of planking from which the pedestrians, depending on the time of year, would be splashed with mud or covered with dust by each passing horse and vehicle. Nearly every family kept a cow, a pig, and chickens, and these were frequently found wandering or resting on the streets and sidewalks.*

The Chicago & Rock Island Railroad arrived in LaSalle in 1853, providing east-west transportation; nearly two months later, the Illinois Central Railroad offered north-south service. The railroads directly competed with canal boats for passengers and lighter freight, though shipping bulkier, heavier freight—such as grain, lumber, and stone—by water continued to be more cost-effective for many years, keeping the canal in business. By the early 1900s, however, canal traffic had all but ceased.

Luckily, LaSalle was not completely dependent on the canal for its economic well-being. Area coal mines and farms kept LaSalle going as a shipping center, and zinc from Wisconsin was shipped to LaSalle for smelting. A variety of manufacturers built plants along the river, and supporting businesses expanded as well. Among the best known is Open Court Publishing Company, one of the first academic presses in the nation, founded in 1887 by LaSalle zinc magnate Edward C. Hegeler. Open Court still produces books today, specializing in philosophy, science, and world religion.

Although the heyday of river transportation has passed, strings of barges filled with grain, petroleum, coal, crushed rock, sulfur, and other products still ply the Illinois River daily. Moreover, LaSalle has recently revitalized its business district and expanded its tourism efforts. Among the sites of interest are three historic buildings managed by the Hegeler Carus Foundation, a historic-preservation and educational group formed in 1987. Two of the buildings, the Julius W. Hegeler Home and the Stone Cottage, are still undergoing restoration, but the most impressive of the three, the stunning, fifty-seven-room Hegeler Carus Mansion, built in 1876 by industrialist and publisher Edward C. Hegeler, is open for tours.

LaSalle's main visitor attraction is the Lock 16 Visitor Center, on the Illinois & Michigan Canal National Heritage Corridor. In 2008 mostly private donations funded the LaSalle Canal Boat, a replica mule-powered canal boat that offers tours of the canal during the summer.

OTTAWA

In the 1820s Dr. David Walker and his family, as well as several other families, settled on land that would soon become the village of Ottawa—a name derived from the Algonquin word for "trade." When LaSalle County was organized in 1831, the recently platted Ottawa was named the seat. In the early years, one side of Walker's "saddlebag" cabin served as the county's first courtroom, while Walker and his family lived on the other side.

The 1832 Black Hawk War briefly disrupted Ottawa's development, but nearby Fort Johnson, erected atop a bluff overlooking the Illinois River, protected and sustained the village during the four-month conflict. Originally called Fort Ottawa, it was soon renamed to honor Col. James Johnson, commander of the Fifth Regiment of Illinois Militia (Whiteside's Brigade), who oversaw the fort's construction in the spring of 1832. Fort Johnson served as operational headquarters for enlisting and dispatching troops.

When Capt. Abraham Lincoln completed his first army enlistment on May 27, 1832, he mustered out at Fort Johnson. The same day, he reenlisted as a private for a twenty-day tour with Capt. Elijah Iles's Company. Later Lincoln again reenlisted, this time with Capt. Jacob Early's independent spy company, for his third and final tour. The site of Fort Johnson is now covered by a residential housing development at the north end of South Ottawa. The state of Illinois placed a marker at the site, near the junction of IL 71 and IL 23, in 1934.

After the Black Hawk War, a ferry was built on the Illinois River at Ottawa, enabling stagecoaches from the south to serve the settlement. Construction of the Illinois & Michigan Canal in the 1840s brought an influx of foreign workers to Ottawa and stimulated further growth. The railroad arrived in 1853, the same year that Ottawa incorporated as a city. Five years later, the first of the famed Lincoln–Douglas debates put Ottawa in the spotlight (see below).

During the days of slavery, many Ottawa residents were active in the abolition movement, and the city was a major stop on the Underground Railroad. One of the town's major shelters for runaway slaves was the home of John Hossack, who harbored at least a dozen fugitives there before the Civil War. In 1860 Hossack and two other Ottawans were convicted in federal court for violating the Fugitive Slave Law of 1850.

The slave in question, Jim Gray, was secretly taken from the courtroom in Ottawa by unknown rescuers, who helped him escape to Canada. Hossack's 1855 home was listed on the NRHP in 1972, but it is not open to the public.

One of the major natural resources in the Ottawa area is its plentiful St. Peter sandstone, also called Ottawa sandstone. The silica sand derived from the stone is a primary element in making glass and other products. Ottawan Edmund B. Thornton began mining and processing silica for industrial purposes in 1900. Sandstone is still harvested and processed in Ottawa, and the glass industry remains a staple of the local economy.

Ottawa also has a thriving tourist industry. In addition to the abundant recreational opportunities in the area, the city's own historical sites regularly bring visitors into town. Besides the site of Fort Johnson and the Hossack house is another historic home, the Reddick Mansion. The twenty-two-room Italianate home, built in 1856, has recently undergone renovations and is open to visitors; further restorations are planned. One of the city's most popular attractions is the Ottawa Scouting Museum, which honors the venerable Boy Scouts of America organization as well as its primary founder, Ottawan William Dickson Boyce (see below).

First Lincoln-Douglas Debate (Ottawa, August 21, 1858)

The 1858 Lincoln–Douglas debates are considered classics in political history. The forty-nine-year-old Abraham Lincoln, Republican candidate for the U.S. Senate, was a decided underdog. The campaign of his opponent, Democratic incumbent Stephen A. Douglas, was better organized and much better financed. After considerable prodding by the *Chicago Daily Press and Tribune*, Lincoln challenged Douglas to a series of debates in the state's nine congressional districts. Since both candidates had already spoken in Chicago and Springfield, the debates were scheduled only in the remaining seven districts. The first one would take place in Ottawa on August 21.

Spectators came from nearby communities such as LaSalle and Peru, as well as a significant number from Chicago. Some arrived by train, while others came on foot, on horseback, in carriages and wagons, or on canal boats. On the day of the debate, Ottawa saw a crowd at least twice the size of its own population of approximately 7,000. The day was hot, and planners had not anticipated the large crowd or the circuslike atmosphere that attended it. Marching bands and vendors hawking souvenirs fought to be heard above the noise of the crowd. Storefronts along the main streets were draped with bunting, banners, and flags to celebrate the exciting event.

The two candidates arrived at the debate site, Washington Square, in separate carriages. Most spectators stood throughout the three-hour event, which began at 2:30 p.m., and it is doubtful that many in the crowd actually heard much of the debate, as the remarks of both men were often interrupted by heckling as well as cheering and applause. The bombastic Douglas led off by accusing Lincoln and the Republicans of secretly being radical abolitionists who among other things sought to repeal the Fugitive Slave Law. He followed up with stinging attacks against Lincoln's opposition to the Mexican War and the Dred Scott decision. Douglas concluded by charging that the extremist ideas of Lincoln and the Republicans would incite civil war.

In his response, Lincoln said Douglas misrepresented his views, and he spent the bulk of his time repudiating his rival's remarks. In his conclusions, he maintained that

Douglas and the Democrats wanted to extend slavery into free territories and throughout the nation. After the debate, Democratic newspapers proclaimed Douglas the obvious winner, while Republican papers asserted exactly the opposite.

The debate site, in Ottawa's Washington Square Park, is marked by a bronze plaque, a fountain, and heroic-size bronze statues of Lincoln and Douglas created by Rebecca Childers Caleel.

William Dickson Boyce and the Boy Scouts of America

In 1909 in London, a young lad in a khaki uniform helped a fifty-one-year-old American find an address and refused a tip. The boy remains nameless to history, but the man, William Dickson Boyce, was inspired by this act of kindness to learn more about the organization behind the uniform. The British boys' group known as the Boy Scouts, Boyce discovered, had been founded only two years earlier by Sir Robert Baden-Powell of Brown Sea Island, England. With a mind to establish a similar group across the pond, Boyce visited the scouts' London headquarters to find out more.

Returning to the United States with books, pamphlets, and first-hand information, Boyce, a wealthy newspaper and magazine publisher, set up meetings with several YMCA officials, all of whom supported the idea of a scouting organization for boys but complained that no funding was available. Boyce agreed to contribute $1,000 a month for two years to launch the plan, stipulating that the group be open to all boys, regardless of race or religion. The Boy Scouts of America organization was incorporated on February 8, 1910, in Ottawa, where Boyce maintained his main residence.

Boyce died on June 11, 1929, and is buried at Ottawa Avenue Cemetery. A nearby statue, dedicated in 1941, commemorates his contribution to the now worldwide Scout movement. The privately funded Ottawa Scouting Museum, which opened in 1997, features exhibits outlining the history of scouting, including Boyce's special role in the movement.

SENECA

More than 150 years before Seneca was settled, this spot on the Illinois River was the site of Illinois' first Catholic martyrdom. In 1680 a group of French missionaries that included Père Gabriel de la Ribourde, Henri de Tonti, and Père Zenobius Membre stopped here to repair a canoe. When Père Ribourde left the group to pray, he was ambushed and murdered by a band of Kickapoo Indians, making the good father the first martyr in the future state. In 1856 St. Patrick Church was built near the site, and a wooden cross was placed at the location where the incident is believed to have occurred.

The church was built not long after Irish immigrant Jeremiah Crotty established the settlement of Crotty (a.k.a. Crotty Town or Crotty Village) in 1854. Jeremiah Crotty had arrived a few years earlier as a builder on the Illinois & Michigan Canal and purchased land here, erecting the first house in 1850. When the Chicago & Rock Island Railroad arrived in 1854, the railroad named the train stop Seneca Station, but the post office used the name Crotty, and the village was called Crotty for some time. The post office adopted the name Seneca in 1865, even though the village had been incorporated as Crotty earlier that year. The town gradually became known as Seneca, but the name was not official for nearly a century; it was legally changed in 1957.

In 1879, during the height of Seneca's prosperity, a fire consumed most of the businesses in the village. It was promptly rebuilt, however, and the town prospered into the twentieth century. Two coal mines opened in the early 1900s, creating further growth for a while, but they both closed in the 1920s. Seneca got another boost during World War II. Due to its position on the Illinois River, the village was chosen as a site for a wartime shipyard. In 1942 a private firm, the Chicago Bridge & Iron Company, teamed with the U.S. Navy to construct the two-hundred-acre Seneca Shipyard, which produced 157 Landing Ship Tanks (LSTs) during the war, providing thousands of jobs in the region.

Many of the 327-foot-long LSTs produced at Seneca's "Prairie Shipyard" were used to transport troops and supplies in both the European and Pacific theaters. The dedication and skill of its workers earned the Seneca Shipyard the prestigious Army-Navy "E" Award for outstanding performance in the production of war equipment. In 1961 the Seneca Regional Port District was established at the site of the former shipyard. A monument dedicated to the builders of the LSTs as well as to local war veterans was unveiled in Crotty Park in 2005.

Seneca's other main historic site is the four-story Armour's Warehouse (a.k.a. Seneca Grain Elevator or Hogan's North Elevator), the oldest standing grain elevator along the Illinois & Michigan Canal. Constructed in 1862, the grain elevator and two outbuildings were listed on the NRHP in 1997.

MORRIS

More than a thousand years before settlers arrived in this area along the Illinois River, the land was occupied by a village of about 1,500. Remains of this culture were unearthed during the digging of the Illinois & Michigan Canal in the 1840s, and more were found as the city developed.

John Cryder built the first cabin in future Morris in 1834. A few years later, William E. Armstrong and John P. Chapin laid out a town called Grundy, or Grundyville, and opened the Grundy Hotel. Armstrong lobbied for the creation of Grundy County, hoping his settlement would be named the county seat. To help its prospects, Armstrong and other ambitious residents platted a new, larger municipality that encompassed Grundyville. The new town was named for Isaac N. Morris, a commissioner on the Illinois & Michigan Canal. When the county was established in 1841, Morris indeed became the county seat. To pay for construction of a courthouse, Armstrong again stepped forward. The two-story frame building lasted until 1858, when it was replaced by a stone structure.

Early Morris was accessible by the Frink, Walker & Company stage line between Galena and Chicago. By 1848 the I & M Canal was also serving the town, and in 1853 the Chicago & Rock Island Railroad arrived. Industry blossomed. The first factory, the Morris Plow Factory, opened in 1857, followed by the Gebhard Brewery, Coleman Hardware Company, Woelful Leather Company, Morris Cutlery Company, Morris Oatmeal Company, and many others. Today, the city's Downtown Commercial Historic District contains a treasure trove of historic buildings from the late 1800s and early 1900s. The district, added to the NRHP in 2006, exudes an old-fashioned charm.

Modern Morris is also the site of the Dresden Generating Station, the first nuclear-power plant built in Illinois and the first privately funded plant in the nation. The facility's first reactor began operating in 1960, followed by two more in 1970. The original unit was deactivated in 1978, but the other two continue to provide electricity to Chicago and surrounding communities.

Morris is also known for its connection to the famous Potawatomi chief Shabbona. Once the home of this Native American leader as well as his burial place, Morris is also the trailhead for the Chief Shabbona Historical Trail, a designated section of the I & M Canal National Heritage Corridor trail.

Shabbona, born an Ottawa Indian about 1775, grew up to be a leader of the Potawatomi tribe. Although he fought against the United States in the War of 1812, he became an American ally after the war, having decided resistance was futile. At the start of the Black Hawk War of 1832, Shabbona advised Sauk leader Black Hawk against fighting, and during the conflict he made it a point to warn white settlers of Black Hawk's approach.

In 1829 the U.S. government promised Shabbona a reserve for the Potawatomi near today's Shabbona, Illinois (see later trip), but after the Black Hawk War, the Potawatomi were forced out of Illinois along with all the other tribes. Shabbona himself was later able to return to Illinois, however, spending his final years in Morris, where he died in 1859. His grave in Evergreen Cemetery is marked with a large granite boulder.

In Gebhard Woods State Park, on the southwest edge of Morris, is the trailhead for the Chief Shabbona Historical Trail, a twenty-mile section of the I & M Canal trail between Morris and Joliet. Established in 1960 by Boy Scout Troop 25 of Joliet, the trail follows paths that the great chief once walked. Suitable for walking, cycling, canoeing and kayaking, and even cross-country skiing, the trail is open year-round and has restroom and picnic facilities all along the route.

IL 71, Millbrook Road (County Rte 14), and Fox River Drive (County Rtes 1 and 15)
OTTAWA–PLANO
31 miles

This scenic route on IL 71 passes through the heart of the region settled by Scandinavians in the 1830s through 1850s. In 1975 Gov. Dan Walker presided over the dedication of IL 71 between Yorkville and Ottawa as the Cleng Peerson Memorial Highway, named for the founder of Norway, the first Norwegian settlement in the Midwest.

The road also passes through the 1,350-acre Silver Springs State Park, which includes a large native prairie restoration area. The trip ends in Plano, where historic sites include a glass house designed by famed architect Ludwig Mies van der Rohe.

OTTAWA
See previous trip

NORWAY

The Norwegian migration to the United States began in 1825, when a group of fifty-two "sloopers" left Stavanger, Norway, to escape political and religious persecution. They arrived in New York aboard the ship *Restaurasjonen* (Restoration). Meeting the immigrants in New York was Cleng Peerson, who had traveled ahead to make arrangements for a settlement in today's Kendall, New York, the first Norwegian colony in the United States. Peerson and the sloopers spent eight difficult years in Kendall. In 1834, dreaming of greener pastures, Peerson led most of the colonists west to found a new Norwegian settlement in the Fox River Valley of northern Illinois. Naturally they named their new village Norway, where they settled permanently and where some of their descendants still live. Peerson, meanwhile, moved on to establish Norwegian colonies in Missouri, Iowa, and Texas. He died at his home near Clifton, Texas, on December 16, 1865.

Norway survived a number of challenges, but it never grew into a town. Still, despite the small population, Norway and surrounding communities proudly honor their Scandinavian heritage. In 1934 Norway celebrated the centennial of its founding with the dedication of Norwegian Settlers State Memorial Park, just south of the village. In October of 1975, during Norway's sesquicentennial celebration, King Olav V visited the community; a plaque at the memorial park commemorates this event. And in 1977, the local chapter of the Sons of Norway established the Norsk Scandinavian Museum, housed in the former Norwegian Lutheran Church in Norway.

PLANO

Plano, which means "plains" in Spanish, was laid out along the Chicago & Aurora Railroad line in 1853, but this area along Big Rock Creek, a tributary of the nearby Fox River, had been settled since the 1830s and inhabited by Native Americans for centuries. Both the railroad and the river were significant contributors to Plano's development, and many industries were established there. For nearly sixty years, until 1919, at least five companies developed and manufactured new styles of mechanical harvesters and other farm equipment. Plano was incorporated as a town in 1865 and as a city in 1883.

From 1866 to 1881, Plano was the headquarters of the Reorganized Church of Jesus Christ of Latter Day Saints (today called the Community of Christ). After Mormon Church founder Joseph Smith Jr. was killed in 1844, followers suffered a period of disorganization. While the main body of believers chose to follow Brigham Young, others believed that Smith's rightful successor was his son, Joseph Smith III. But young Joseph was just a boy of eleven at the time of his father's death, so his supporters waited. In 1860 Smith received his calling and took his place as leader of the Reorganized Church of Jesus Christ of Latter Day Saints at a conference in Amboy (see earlier trip). In 1866 Smith moved to Plano, where the church had established its printing operations and oversaw other activities. Upon the completion of the Plano Stone Church in 1868, church leaders moved the headquarters into that building, which still stands. Smith and his church later established the Mormon colony of Lamoni, Iowa, moving the headquarters there in 1881.

The Plano Stone Church was listed on the NRHP in 1990. Other Plano buildings on the NRHP are the 1913 Chicago, Burlington & Quincy Railroad Depot; the 1868

Plano Hotel; the 1881 Albert H. Sears House (a.k.a. Robin's Nest); the 1854 Lewis Steward House (a.k.a. the Homestead); and the 1951 Farnsworth House.

Of all these historic structures, the most distinctive is the Farnsworth House, designed by famed architect Ludwig Mies van der Rohe. Created for Dr. Edith Farnsworth as a country retreat along the Fox River, it is considered one of Mies van der Rohe's most significant works. Supported by steel columns, this one-story modernist structure stands five feet above the ground, and its floor-to ceiling windows on all sides allow nearly unobstructed views of the home's natural surroundings. The Farnsworth House, which has undergone several restorations over the years, is now operated as a museum by the National Trust for Historic Preservation.

This modern one-story country retreat in Plano, known as the Farnsworth House, was built for Dr. Edith Farnsworth in 1951. —Photo by author, courtesy Farnsworth House

US 34, County Rtes 41 and 6, US 30, and I-39/US 51
MENDOTA–ROCHELLE
48 miles

This pleasant drive through a bucolic landscape takes us to the small town of Earlville, which could be called the birthplace of the suffragette movement in Illinois, though it is better known for the nearby site of the Indian Creek Massacre, the worst atrocity of the Black Hawk War of 1832. From there, on our way north to Rochelle, we will pass through picturesque Shabbona Lake State Park and the community of Shabbona, named for the beloved Potawatomi chief.

MENDOTA
See earlier trip

EARLVILLE

Bostonian Charles Sutphen, who arrived in this area in 1834, is considered Earlville's first settler. Beginning in 1847 Sutphen served as postmaster of the first post office in the village, which was named after Sutphen's nephew, Earl. The railroad came through in 1853, and Earlville prospered. It was incorporated as a town ten years later.

In 1855 Alonzo J. Grover, a lawyer and abolitionist, gave a speech in Earlville supporting women's right to vote. The speech inspired another Earlville resident, Susan Hoxie Richardson, a cousin of suffragette Susan B. Anthony. She and Grover's wife, Octavia, formed the Earlville Suffrage Association, the first such group in the state, predating Chicago's Illinois Woman Suffrage Association by fourteen years.

Although Earlville was not established until the 1840s, the surrounding area was inhabited—if sparsely—before the Black Hawk War of 1832. One of the earliest of these settlements was built southeast of Earlville along Indian Creek, which runs between Earlville and the Fox River near Wedron. The massacre there was among the worst of the many depredations that occurred before the Indians were defeated and removed from the region.

Massacre at Indian Creek Settlement

The land along Indian Creek in north-central LaSalle County was an ideal location for the families of William Davis, William Hall, and William Pettigrew to settle. In the fall or early winter of 1831, the John H. Henderson family of Tennessee, along with a hired man named Robert Norris, joined the community. More of Henderson's family arrived the following spring, and the blossoming settlement showed promise.

About ten miles upriver, near Paw Paw Grove, was a Potawatomi village, which depended on Indian Creek for food and water. When the settlers built a dam on the creek to power a mill, the fish were unable to reach the Indians' village upstream. The natives had asked the mill owner, William Davis, several times to remove the dam, but he had refused. For a while the Indians traveled downriver to fish, but one day the settlers noticed that they had stopped coming around. Meanwhile, the Black Hawk War had begun with the Battle of Stillman's Run on May 14, 1832, causing restlessness among the local tribes (see under Dixon on earlier trip). Henderson and Davis, along with two other men, went to the Indian village, only to find it abandoned. Meanwhile

Henderson's father, a cautious old man, persuaded the families at Indian Creek settlement to go to Fort Johnson in nearby Ottawa for safety.

When Davis and company got back to Indian Creek late that night, Davis defiantly stayed behind in his cabin while the other three men went on to Fort Johnson. In the morning, Davis started out on the road to Ottawa, where he overtook the Hall and Pettigrew families as well as his own family and convinced them all to return to their cabins, assuring them there was no danger. Upon reaching Ottawa, Davis tried to persuade the Hendersons to return to Indian Creek as well, but they were skeptical. The elder Henderson proposed that the men go back to work their fields during the day but return to Fort Johnson at night; the women and children would remain at the fort. And so it went, with the Davises, Halls, and Pettigrews going back to their homes while the Hendersons and some others stayed in Ottawa, the men commuting back and forth.

Several days later, on the afternoon of May 21, twenty to forty Potawatomi warriors attacked Indian Creek settlement. It is believed that the friendly Potawatomi chief Shabbona had tried to warn the settlers the day before the attack, but he was ignored. Some of the men in the fields saw the Indians approach, and several fled to Ottawa while a few others rushed to the cabins to try to defend the women and children. Within a few minutes, however, the Indians had slaughtered Mrs. Davis, Mrs. Hall, Mrs. Pettigrew, and most of the children. Davis, William Hall, William Pettigrew, and two other men were killed in their futile attempt to fend off the attackers. In all, fifteen people—five men, three women, and seven children—were murdered that day, and two teenage girls were captured. The girls were later ransomed and released.

*This conceptual illustration depicts the 1832
Indian Creek Massacre.* —Author's collection

The next morning, a company of men returned to the settlement to bury the dead. The scene they found was horrific. According to a letter written by 1st Lt. Reuben Holmes, "The men were mutilated beyond the reach of modest description; the women hung up by the feet, and the most revolting acts of outrage and indecency practiced upon their bodies. The children were literally chopped to pieces, and placed in the most revolting position; the houses were burned, the furniture all destroyed, and the stock killed, even the barnyard fowls." The remains were gathered together and buried in a large common grave.

The Indian Creek Massacre site is commemorated by two monuments in Shabbona County Park near Earlville, the first erected in 1877 and the other in 1905. Also at the site is the mass grave of the victims.

SHABBONA AND SHABBONA GROVE

Shabbona is a village of about nine hundred residents; Shabbona Grove is an unincorporated community about four miles south of Shabbona. In between is the 1,550-acre Shabbona Lake State Park. All of these places were named in honor of the Potawatomi chief who once lived here.

Shabbona Grove was originally a village along the Chicago Road Trail. When the Chicago, Burlington & Quincy Railroad arrived in 1871, the route bypassed Shabbona Grove, so most of its residents moved north to form the new town of Shabbona along the rail line. Shabbona was incorporated as a village in 1875. It remains primarily a farming community today, supported in part by visitors to the state park, which contains a 300-plus-acre lake, trails, and campsites. Also of interest is the Shabbona-Lee-Rollo Historical Museum, which features exhibits and archives related to local history.

Chief Shabbona, often referred to as "the white man's friend," originally fought against the United States during the War of 1812, but after Great Britain's defeat, he transferred his allegiance to the Americans and advocated for peaceful coexistence. Acting as a mediator between whites and Indians, he helped to quell the Winnebago uprising of 1827 and, during the Black Hawk War of 1832, he and his son, Pypeogee, raced through the Illinois and Fox River Valleys alerting white families of impending danger from Black Hawk and his band. He also repeatedly warned settlers, including the families at Indian Creek settlement (see previous stop), about rogue bands of raiders.

After the Black Hawk War, Shabbona was given a reservation at Shabonna Grove, an area he considered home, in appreciation for his role as a peacemaker. Although he lived at Shabbona Grove, he sometimes traveled to Kansas to visit his people on the Potawatomi reservation. During a lengthy absence in the late 1840s, the federal government declared the reservation abandoned and resold it. Upon returning to Illinois, Shabbona found his beloved home occupied by new owners, who drove him off as an intruder. To mitigate the injustice, a sympathetic group of whites bought him a tract of land near Morris, built a cabin for him and his family, and supported him with donations until his death in 1859. He is buried in Morris's Evergreen Cemetery (see Morris on earlier trip).

ROCHELLE
See earlier trip

IL 2
DIXON–ROCKFORD
42 miles

The towns and cities along this route have some of the most varied histories in the region. This trip also traverses some of the territory where the notorious outlaw gang known as the Banditti of the Prairie once rampaged. A marker on IL 2 just south of Byron describes the Banditti's reign of terror.

DIXON
See earlier trip

GRAND DETOUR

Grand Detour, named for a distinctive bend in the Rock River, was settled shortly after the 1832 Black Hawk War ended. Many of the early settlers came from Vermont, including Leonard Andrus, who built the first sawmill here. Although the railroad bypassed Grand Detour in the mid-1800s, the village survived. In the early twentieth century, because of its natural beauty, Grand Detour attracted a number of artists.

Richard Welles, father of legendary filmmaker Orson Welles, ran a hotel in town called the Sheffield House, where the younger Welles—born George Orson Welles in 1915—spent many summers as a boy. But Grand Detour is best known as the home of John Deere, who obtained the first patent for a steel-bladed plow. While Deere is often credited with inventing the steel plow, Will County farmer John Lane created one several years before Deere, but he never applied for a patent (see under Lockport in Region 6). Therefore, it was Deere's design that revolutionized farming, and Deere whose name became synonymous with innovative agricultural machinery and remains so to this day.

John Deere Historic Site

John Deere, whose mechanical genius contributed immensely to agricultural expansion in the Midwest and West, was born on February 7, 1804, in Rutland, Vermont. He grew up there and began his career as a blacksmith. Having tried and failed several times to open his own shop, in November 1836 Deere moved to Grand Detour, where he had heard there was a shortage of blacksmiths. Two days after arriving, he built a forge and opened for business. The following summer, after establishing his blacksmith shop and building a three-room cottage, he sent for his wife and five children to join him.

At the time, most plows had wooden or cast-iron blades, or moldboards, to break through the prairie crust and reach the rich black soil. But these plows did not do their job cleanly. Dirt clung to the moldboard, requiring the operator to stop every several feet and scrape it. Deere decided to use his blacksmith skills to try to solve the problem. Working with old, discarded saw blades, Deere experimented until he came up with a successful design for a "self-polishing" plow in 1837. He produced only ten plows in the first year, most of which he sold to local farmers. By the end of 1842, his output had reached one hundred.

In the spring of 1843, Deere teamed up with a neighbor, fellow Vermonter Leonard Andrus. The partners built a factory on the Rock River and imported special rolled steel from England to produce over 1,000 plows. Deere dissolved the partnership in

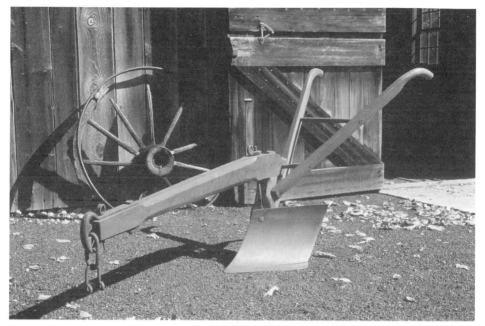

*A replica of the steel plow that John Deere
patented in 1837* —Author's collection

1848, when he moved his operations to Moline, seventy-five miles southwest, where better transportation was available. By that time he had taken on two new partners, John Gould and Robert N. Tate, to form Deere, Tate & Gould. In 1853 Deere bought out his partners, renaming the company John Deere, Manufacturer.

In 1858 Deere transferred his interest in the company to his son, twenty-one-year-old Charles, while remaining the president. The business incorporated ten years later as Deere & Company. Today Deere & Company—better known as John Deere—is the world's largest manufacturer of agricultural and forestry equipment and related products.

John Deere died in Moline on May 17, 1886, at age eighty-two. He was buried at Riverside Cemetery. Deere's 1836 Grand Detour home and replica shop are now open to the public as the John Deere Historic Site.

OREGON

The city of Oregon was first settled in 1835 by Virginia native John Phelps and his family. Originally named Oregon City, the settlement was chosen to be the seat of Ogle County in 1836, and it grew rapidly. For a time the town was called Florence, after the Italian city, but residents changed the name back to Oregon in 1843, and it was incorporated as a city in 1869. After the arrival of the Chicago & Iowa Railroad two years later, Oregon enjoyed a boom of industry that included two grain mills, two furniture factories, and a foundry.

Oregon's first courthouse, erected in 1841, was burned to the ground by outlaws before it was ever used. The current three-story brick courthouse, built in 1892, was the city's third, replacing an 1848 one-story structure at the same site. Still in use, this commanding Romanesque Revival building is the centerpiece of downtown Oregon, added to the NRHP in 1981. After undergoing a series of restorations and renovations in the 1980s, it was opened for public tours. Surrounding features include a pair of Civil War cannons and an 1896 cast-iron fountain familiarly known as "Iron Mike." The courthouse is part of the Oregon Commercial Historic District, which comprises more than a dozen other buildings, among them the city's 1902 Andrew Carnegie library and the 1920 Oregon City Hall.

Other structures of historic interest in Oregon include the 1913 Chicago, Burlington & Quincy Railroad Depot; the 1874 Pinehill Inn Bed and Breakfast; the 1883 Chana School; and the 1878 Nash Home and Museum. The two-room Chana School, which served the nearby community of Chana until 1953, is now an education museum. The schoolhouse was moved to its current location in Oregon in 1997 and refurbished in the late 1990s and early 2000s. The two-story, Prairie-style home of inventor Chester Nash, now headquarters of the Ogle County Historical Society, was restored in 1962. The main rooms serve as a museum that focuses on life in the late nineteenth century.

Just north of town, atop a steep bluff overlooking the Rock River Valley, is one of Oregon's most distinctive landmarks. It is a forty-eight-foot-high concrete monument entitled *The Eternal Indian*, more widely known as the Chief Black Hawk statue, designed by noted sculptor Lorado Taft. The sculpture, completed in 1911, depicts a towering Indian with folded arms surveying the forests, farms, and waterways that lie amid the valley's rolling hills. The Rock River Valley was a revered place for Black Hawk, the Sauk leader who in 1832 led about 2,500 men, women, and children into Illinois to try to reclaim their homeland, spawning the conflict known as the Black Hawk War.

Lorado Taft once lived and worked on the bluff where the statue now stands, after founding an artists' community called Eagle Nest's Art Colony.

Eagle's Nest Art Colony

Noted American sculptor Lorado Taft came to Oregon in 1898 and established a summer haven for his fellow Chicago artists, calling it Eagle's Nest Art Colony. The land was leased from Chicago attorney and arts patron Wallace Heckman, who charged the artists one dollar a year along with a promise to give a free lecture or demonstration in the Ogle County area.

The original eleven colony members set up tents until plans were settled. Later, many of the artists built permanent studios and cottages. Taft's own studio was a converted barn, in which he produced the preliminary models for his sculpture *The Eternal Indian*. Taft also created other works that enhance the local landscape. The *Soldiers' Monument*, which honors veterans of the Civil War and the Spanish-American War, graces the lawn of the Ogle County Courthouse, and a sculpted fountain called *Boys with Fish,* or *The Fish Boys,* stands in downtown Oregon's Mix Park.

The Eagle's Nest colony disbanded after its last member died in 1942. Nine years later, Gov. Adlai Stevenson II transferred most of the colony site, excluding *The Eternal Indian,* to Northern Illinois University along with other acreage. The university restored some of the buildings, though many of them were unsalvageable. Many of the refurbished buildings are currently used as classrooms or meeting rooms. The property, now called the Lorado Taft Field Campus, is open to visitors. In addition, more than fifty paintings produced by members of the art colony are displayed in the second-floor art gallery of the Oregon Public Library.

OGLE COUNTY AND THE BANDITTI OF THE PRAIRIE

Traveling on IL 2 from Oregon to Byron, motorists may see a roadside marker describing the Banditti of the Prairie, a band of outlaws who roamed through northern Illinois in the 1830s and 1840s, stealing horses, robbing travelers, plundering homesteads, and murdering innocent people.

Beginning around 1835, the Banditti, led by John Driscoll and his four sons (William, David, Taylor, and Pierce), terrorized settlers in Ogle County and the surrounding region. The Banditti cabal directed and controlled the movements of their many henchmen, who tore through the countryside raiding and pillaging. The Banditti also maintained a stable of abettors who sheltered, fed, assisted, and covered for the outlaws in exchange for a share in the spoils. Among these accomplices were local law-enforcement officials.

In March 1841 several Banditti members were arrested and jailed in the newly built Ogle County Courthouse in Oregon, Illinois. In an attempt to free them, some of their cohorts set fire to the courthouse. Although the courthouse was destroyed, the adjoining jail was not, and the prisoners did not get away. Three of them were tried and convicted, but they later escaped.

Fed up with the lawlessness, a group of fifteen "fearless and determined" men gathered in a log schoolhouse in White Rock, a now bygone town about fourteen miles south of Rockford, shortly after the courthouse incident. Calling themselves the Ogle County Regulators, they pledged to rid the region of these brutal criminals or die trying. Before long, more than a hundred men had joined the group, who began patrolling Ogle, Lee, DeKalb, Winnebago, and surrounding counties, rooting out the Banditti and sparing none. When they found any known Banditti members, the Regulators dragged them out, whipped them, and ran them out of the area.

In April, Banditti leader William Driscoll sent a threatening letter to Regulator captain John Campbell. In response, a group of nearly two hundred Regulators marched to Driscoll's home in South Grove, some twelve miles east of White Rock in DeKalb County. Driscoll's cronies summoned the sheriff, but he sided with the vigilantes and ordered Driscoll and his family to leave the state within twenty days.

The Driscolls ignored the sheriff's demand, and two months later, in late June, John Campbell was gunned down in his own front yard by Driscoll brothers David and Taylor. The community was enraged. Soon afterward, the Ogle County sheriff and his men arrested patriarch John Driscoll as an accessory to the murder and locked him in the jail in Oregon. A few hours later, the sheriff captured William Driscoll and his younger brother Pierce and brought them to Campbell's place; by then the actual gunmen, David and Taylor, were long gone. After Campbell's wife said that William and Pierce were not the Driscolls who murdered her husband, the brothers were released, but a posse of

Regulators later caught up with them, captured them, and took them to Washington Grove, a few miles southwest of Chana.

Meanwhile, three Regulators rode into Oregon and broke into the jail, abducting John Driscoll and taking him across the Rock River to join his sons in Washington Grove. Soon a crowd of hundreds, including 120 Regulators, had gathered at the grove to conduct a "trial." All but nine of the Regulators formed a circle around the prisoners. After witnesses were questioned and evidence was presented, Pierce was released, but the "jury" of 111 Regulators unanimously found John and William Driscoll guilty of conspiring to murder Campbell. The convicted were sentenced to hang, but at the Driscolls' own request, the method of execution was changed to a firing squad. The 111 Regulators were divided into two squads of riflemen. John Driscoll was executed first, then William. A historical marker now stands near the site of the mob trial, and a boulder marks the execution site.

News of the episode was not received without controversy; many decried it as a lynching and clamored for the Regulators to be brought to justice. In September, all 111 Regulators who participated in the executions were arrested and tried for murder in Oregon. The jurors, however, delivered their verdict of "not guilty" without even leaving their seats.

Southeast of Oregon on South Prairie Road, this plaque memorializes the 1841 execution of bandits John and William Driscoll.—Author's collection

After Campbell's murder, a reward was offered for the capture of David and Taylor Driscoll. Taylor was later caught and tried, but he was eventually acquitted. David left the state and was never captured. About two years after the murder, however, he was reportedly shot dead by a sheriff in Iowa.

Although the deaths of John and William Driscoll broke the back of the Banditti in Ogle County, roving bands of outlaws continued committing crimes in northern Illinois. The final straw was the despicable murder of Col. George Davenport in his home on Rock Island in July 1845 (see under Rock Island in Region 2). After three of the killers were tried and hanged for the crime, the Banditti scattered, and their decade-long reign of terror finally ended.

ROCKFORD

Rockford, the largest city in Illinois outside the Chicago metro area, began as two settlements, one on each side of the Rock River. Both stood at the site of a shallow, stone-bottomed river crossing known as Rock Ford, which had been used by Indians for years. On the west bank was Kentville, settled by Germanicus Kent, Thatcher Blake, and Lewis Lemon, all from Galena, in 1834. The following year, Daniel Shaw Haight and his family arrived from Geneva and established themselves on the east bank, founding Haightville. The two communities combined to form a settlement originally named Midway, so called because it was halfway between Galena and Chicago. Residents officially united the two settlements into one in 1839, incorporating as the village of Rockford. The same year, Rockford was chosen as the seat of Winnebago County.

Rockford was incorporated as a city in 1852, and the Galena & Chicago Union Railroad arrived later that year. The railroad brought a commercial explosion to the town. One of the early major industries was furniture manufacturing. Later manufacturers produced heavy machinery, automotive parts, hardware, and many other products.

The railroad also opened Rockford to new residents. Many Swedes who had immigrated to Chicago via New York were steered to Rockford by local pastors. Within a short time, Swedish immigrants comprised about 25 percent of Rockford's population. Visitors can learn about Rockford's Swedish community at the Erlander Home Museum, headquarters for the Swedish Historical Society. The 1871 brick building was originally the home of Swedish settler John Erlander, born Johannes Jönsson, who came to Rockford in 1855.

During the Civil War, a military training post for new recruits was established in Rockford. Camp Fuller existed between August and December of 1862. Afterward, the pine barracks and other buildings were dismantled and the lumber was auctioned off. Another military post, Camp Grant, was established in Rockford in 1917. It functioned as a processing and training center during World Wars I and II, and during the latter war it was also used as a POW camp. Between the wars, the camp was used by the Illinois National Guard and by the Civilian Conservation Corps. The military facility was closed in 1946, and most of the 1,200-acre site south of the city later became the Chicago-Rockford International Airport. The Camp Grant Museum is housed in the Command Post Restaurant, a former fire station that later served as a military induction and discharge center.

Among Rockford's lesser-known contributions to history was its role in the development of our national pastime. Rockford's original team, the Forest City Base Ball

Club, produced several early baseball legends, and the Rockford Peaches was one of the four original teams that formed the All American Girls Softball League (see below).

After World War II, Rockford experienced another population boom. In the late twentieth century, however, Rockford saw a drastic decline in industry and a deterioration of its economy. Since then, the city has struggled—with some success—to rebuild its economy and its image. Many of these redevelopment efforts have focused on tourism and recreation.

Among the many historical attractions in Rockford are the Midway Village Museum, a collection of early-twentieth-century structures and gardens; the Tinker Swiss Cottage Museum, a restored 1865 Swiss-style cottage; the 1903 Veterans Memorial Hall; and several refurbished hotels, theaters, and historic homes. Nature lovers will enjoy the Klehm Arboretum and Botanical Garden, which contains 150 acres of rare plants; the Anderson Japanese Gardens, designed by renowned landscape architect Hoichi Kurisu; the Burpee Museum of Natural History, home of Jane the Rockford T-rex; and the Discovery Center Museum, an interactive children's science museum.

Another place that played a significant part in the city's past (and present) is Rockford College, founded as Rockford Female Seminary in 1847. Among the school's most notable alumni were three passionate social reformers—Jane Addams, Ellen Gates Starr, and Julia Lathrop, all Illinois natives.

Rockford Female Seminary and Its Distinguished Alumni

Rockford Female Seminary received its charter in 1847. The faculty temporarily held classes in a building that had once been used as the county courthouse. Five years later, Rev. Arastus Kent, brother of Rockford cofounder Germanicus Kent, laid the cornerstone for the school's first building.

In 1882 the school graduated Jane Addams, who in 1931 would make it the only college in Illinois to have a Nobel Peace Prize winner among its alumni. Among her many achievements, Addams founded Hull-House in Chicago in 1889 with fellow Rockford Seminary alumna Ellen Gates Starr (see under Near West Side in Region 7).

Another notable Rockford Female Seminary student was also a native of Rockford. Julia C. Lathrop, the first woman appointee to a federal post, dedicated her life to correcting social injustices. Born in Rockford in 1858 and educated at the seminary and Vassar College, Julia was the daughter of Congressman William Lathrop, for whom she worked as a young woman. In 1890 she visited Addams and Starr at Hull-House; she stayed and worked there for more than two decades. She became head of the Illinois Board of Charities in 1893, and in 1899 she established the first juvenile court in Chicago. In 1912 the Federal Children's Bureau was established to investigate and report "upon all matters pertaining to the welfare of children and child life among all classes of people." Lathrop's reputation as a reformer led President William Howard Taft to name her chief, making her the first woman ever to head a federal agency. Lathrop resigned from the Children's Bureau in 1921 because of ill health and returned to Rockford, but she remained active in social issues until her death in 1932. She was buried at Rockford's Greenwood Cemetery.

The Female Seminary was renamed Rockford College in 1892, and over the years, the school continued to expand its curriculum. It became a coeducational liberal-arts college in the mid-twentieth century.

Baseball Legends

In the latter half of the nineteenth century, Rockford produced a number of baseball pioneers. One of these was Albert Goodwill Spalding, who honed his skills playing for the local team, the Forest City Base Ball Club, from 1866 to 1870. Others included Adrian C. "Cap" Anson, who played for Rockford in 1871, and William A. Hulbert, who jointly founded the National Baseball League with Spalding. All three men were inducted into the National Baseball Hall of Fame in Cooperstown, New York.

Perhaps the best player of the Forest City Base Ball Club was Roscoe (Ross) Barnes. He played for Forest City from 1866 to 1870, later joining the Boston Red Stockings, then the Chicago White Stockings. In 1876, while playing for the latter team, he hit the first home run in the National League and became the league's first batting champion, with a .404 average. Injuries ended his career prematurely in 1881. Though some baseball historians consider him the greatest player of the nineteenth century, Barnes was never inducted into the Baseball Hall of Fame. He died in 1915 and is buried in Greenwood Cemetery in Rockford.

Another piece of baseball history belongs to the Rockford Peaches, one of the four original teams that formed the All American Girls Softball League, organized in 1943 by Chicago Cubs owner Phillip K. Wrigley. The women's league was meant to offset declining national interest in baseball during World War II, when most of the professional (male) players were overseas. Midway through the first season, the league changed its name to the All American Girls Professional Baseball League, as the players mostly followed the rules of major league baseball, not of women's softball. Over the next several years, the league expanded to six teams, then eight, peaking at ten teams in 1948 before decreasing again.

The Rockford Peaches won the league championship four times before the league disbanded in 1954, after the return of men's baseball drained interest away from the women's teams. Beyer Stadium, the home of the Rockford Peaches, was torn down in 1990, leaving only the original ticket booth and a commemorative plaque. A few years later, efforts began to rebuild the field and restore some of its former appearance. The new Beyer Stadium was dedicated on June 5, 2010.

US 20
GALENA–ROCKFORD
77 miles

US 20 from Galena to Freeport is a National Scenic Byway with panoramic views of the countryside. There is even an observation tower between Galena and Elizabeth. From Freeport, the highway heads to Rockford, where travelers can pick up I-39 or I-90, or continue on US 20 into the Chicago suburbs.

An equally scenic alternative route follows the old Stagecoach Trail between Galena and Lena, once part of the Frink, Walker & Company stage line to Chicago. The historic road, marked with signs, passes through the villages of Scales Mound, Apple River, Warren, Nora, and Waddams Grove.

GALENA AND ELIZABETH

See earlier trip

STOCKTON

Stockton's historic downtown district reflects its beginnings as a late-1800s and early-1900s boomtown. Among the vintage structures is a restored 1890s brick commercial building that now houses the Stockton Heritage Museum. The district also contains numerous examples of the ornate cast-iron and sheet-metal storefront facades that were popular in the late nineteenth and early twentieth centuries. Commonly known as Meskers for their main manufacturer, the Mesker Brothers Iron Works, these storefronts can be seen throughout Illinois and across the country. But the centerpiece of downtown Stockton is the Queen Anne–style W. E. White Building. Completed in 1897, a year after a fire destroyed most of the young village, the striking brick structure represented rebirth to the people of Stockton. It was added to the NRHP in 1997.

One of Stockton's oldest residential structures is the Townsend Home, located about three miles northwest of town. The two-story limestone house, built by early settler George Townsend, originally stood on an eight-hundred-acre farm. A native of New York, Townsend settled in Illinois in 1826, but in 1849 he left for the California goldfields. He returned two years later with money in his pocket and built this elegant home. Completed in 1856, the house is an excellent example of Upright and Wing design, prevalent in New England and the Great Lakes region. At least six generations of Townsends have occupied the home, which was listed on the NRHP in 2005.

Stockton's history is relatively short but diverse. The village grew up after the Minnesota & Northwestern Railroad established a depot here amid the hog and cattle farms in 1887. Recognizing an opportunity, two local farmers, Marvin F. Carpenter and Lucius Benton, divided their land into town lots and competed for sales. Benton offered a free lot to merchant Charles Hermann of nearby Pitcherville if he relocated his store, which became the first business in Stockton. Others followed, and a village was founded in 1890.

After recovering from the severe fire of 1896, the village continued its pattern of growth. In 1914 Chicago cheese wholesaler James L. Kraft and his four brothers opened their first cheese factory in Stockton, where they developed and patented a recipe for nonperishable processed cheese, packaged in tin cans. The company flourished during World War I when the army bought the canned cheese for the troops. Kraft Foods sold its Stockton plant in 1998 to the Stockton Cheese Company, which produces cheeses for Kraft.

During World War II, Camp Stockton, a Civilian Conservation Corps government work camp built in the 1930s, was converted into an internment camp for about fourteen Japanese Americans. The detainees voluntarily worked at the nearby Bauch Truck Farm, growing vegetables for army training camps in the area.

A side trip between Stockton and Lena, south of US 20 via county highways and local roads, will take travelers to the tiny unincorporated community of Kent, near the site of the Battle of Kellogg's Grove. The battle, actually two skirmishes, took place in June 1832, near the end of the Black Hawk War in Illinois (though the war continued for another six weeks in what is now southwestern Wisconsin). Three militiamen were killed in the first clash, five in the second, along with at least nine Sauks and Sauk allies.

A monument, surrounded by the graves of the fallen soldiers, stands in Blackhawk Battlefield Park.

LENA

A quiet village of about 3,000 residents, Lena, at the intersection of the National Scenic Byway on US 20 and the equally lovely Stagecoach Trail from Galena, is surrounded by natural beauty. It is surrounded by history as well, which visitors can explore at the Lena Area Historical Museum. The main museum building houses local archives and artifacts, and the complex includes a reconstructed 1849 log schoolhouse, a general store, a blacksmith shop, and a vintage Illinois Central caboose.

Two other sites of historical significance in the village are the 1879 Lena Opera House and the 1896 Lena Water Tower. The opera house, which until 1938 served as a theater and community center, was featured on the History Channel's antique-hunting series *American Pickers* in 2010. The second-floor theater is preserved, while the ground floor now houses a jewelry store. A few blocks north is the still-operating brick-and-limestone water tower, which was listed on the NRHP in 1997.

FREEPORT

The Pecatonica River offered both natural beauty and industrial potential to enterprising settlers, and Indianan William "Tutty" Baker was the first to take advantage of the opportunity. In 1835 he claimed land on the site of future Freeport and built a cabin for his family, a trading post, and a ferry, offering free ferry crossings to help draw travelers to his store. The following year, with the help of investors, Baker established a settlement called Winneshiek, named after a local Winnebago chief. Forming the firm of Baker, Kirkpatrick, Galbraith & Company, the partners laid out a village and sold lots to new settlers. It is said that in 1836 Mrs. Baker, in reference to her husband's overgenerous nature, suggested the town be renamed Free Port, and the name stuck.

In 1837 Freeport, whose supporters put up thousands of dollars for new buildings, was chosen as the seat of the newly created Stephenson County. Connected to Chicago by stagecoach, Freeport had a population of 2,000 by the early 1850s, and it was chartered as a city in 1855. Three years later, it was selected to be the second of seven statewide sites for the public debates between Abraham Lincoln and Stephen A. Douglas (see below).

The debate site is adjacent to the old part of town, Freeport's "Gold Coast," which contains many other historic structures including the city's oldest home, built in 1838, and the 1885 wrought-iron Van Buren Bridge. A few blocks south is the historic Carnegie Library building, the first Carnegie library in Illinois, built in the late 1890s. The library closed in 2003—replaced by a large, modern structure—and the old building was put up for sale. As of this writing, no buyer has been found. Also downtown is the Freeport Art Museum, established in 1975 in a former elementary school.

In the southeastern part of the city are two excellent historical museums. The older one, the Stephenson County Historical Society Museum, is located in the 1857 Oscar Taylor House. Originally the home of banker Oscar Taylor, one of nineteenth-century Freeport's most prominent citizens, this two-story, Italianate-style home was once known as Bohemiana for the artsy leanings of the Taylor family. The family entertained numerous celebrities at the mansion, including Ralph Waldo Emerson, Jane Addams, and Horace Greeley. Many believe the Taylors, who were rabid abolitionists, harbored runaway slaves in their pantry. Donated to the city in 1944, the Taylor property is now a museum complex that includes the Stephenson County Historical Society Museum, the Taylor Arboretum, an old one-room schoolhouse, a farming museum, and an 1840s log cabin known as the Irish Homestead. Near the Taylor House complex is another fine institution, the twenty-eight-room Silver Creek Railroad Museum, located in a former "poor farm" residential building; the museum was established in 1989.

Second Lincoln-Douglas Debate (Freeport, August 27, 1858)

On the day of the debate, a crowd of about 15,000 assembled in Freeport, whose regular population comprised only 5,000 to 7,000 people. Although the debate itself was later described as lackluster, during the proceedings Lincoln posed a critical question to his opponent; Douglas's answer would draw a definitive line between the two candidates and tarnish Douglas's reputation in the eyes of Southern Democrats.

Lincoln's question indirectly referred to the U.S. Supreme Court's recent Dred Scott decision, which maintained that the government had no authority to ban slavery in the territories, overturning the 1850 Missouri Compromise as unconstitutional. Lincoln asked whether or not Douglas believed that the people of a territory had the right to outlaw slavery before the territory became a state. Douglas responded that "the people of a territory can, by lawful means, exclude slavery from their limits prior to the formation of a State Constitution. . . . It matters not what way the Supreme Court may hereafter decide as to the abstract question whether slavery may or may not go into a territory under the constitution, the people have the lawful means to introduce it or exclude it as they please . . . by [way of] the local legislature."

Douglas's statement established the so-called Freeport Doctrine, which Southerners called the "Freeport Heresy." Though Douglas went on to win his reelection bid for the U.S. Senate, his position on this issue angered Dixie Democrats and hampered his career in national politics.

The debate site, "Debate Square," is commemorated by a plaque that was dedicated in 1903 by President Theodore Roosevelt. A life-size statue depicting the event was added in 1992.

ROCKFORD
See previous trip

US 20, IL 176, and IL 47
ROCKFORD–WOODSTOCK
41 miles

Heading east from Rockford, scenic US 20 takes us through Boone County and into McHenry County, where motorists may spot the results of the McHenry County Quilted Barn Program—large paintings done in quilt patterns and displayed on the sides

of barns, silos, and other rural structures. More than a dozen communities in this historically dairy-farming county participate in the program, including Union and Woodstock,
which we visit on this trip.

ROCKFORD
See earlier trip

BELVIDERE

This area's rolling prairie, wooded hills, and abundant waterways enticed a group of
settlers from New York state to establish a community along the Kishwaukee River in
1835. By year's end, the population had grown to thirty-seven. One of the settlers, Dr.
Daniel H. Whitney, wanted to call the community Elysian Fields for its natural beauty.
A few weeks later another man, Ebenezer Peck, purchased a claim in the settlement and
organized a group of investors to develop it. Peck renamed the place Belvidere, which
means "beautiful to see" in Latin, after his hometown of Belvidere, Canada. Peck's development firm, the Belvidere Company, built the settlement's first hotel in 1835, the first
sawmill in 1836, and a gristmill in 1837. In the meantime, the company also persuaded
the Frink, Walker & Company stage line between Galena and Chicago to stop at Belvidere, securing transportation for the fledgling community. When Boone County was
created in 1836, Belvidere was chosen to be the seat.

With so much support, the village grew and thrived. The arrival of the railroad in
the early 1850s encouraged further development. Before the railroad was built, the main
part of Belvidere stood on the north side of the Kishwaukee River, but the tracks ended
up on the south side, causing some businesses and residents to relocate across the river.

During this time, a lawyer named Stephen A. Hurlbut was practicing in Belvi-
dere. He had moved here in 1845, after serving in the Seminole War. Originally from
South Carolina, Hurlbut went on to become one of Belvidere's most prominent citi-
zens, serving as a Union general, a two-term Illinois legislator (1858–64), a two-term
U.S. Congressman (1873–77), and the U.S. Minister to Colombia (1869–72) and later
Peru (1881–82).

Returning to Belvidere after the Civil War, having achieved the rank of major
general, Hurlbut was elected to be the first commander-in-chief of the newly formed
Grand Army of the Republic. At the time, he was also serving his second term in the
state legislature. In 1869 President Ulysses S. Grant appointed Hurlbut U.S. Minister to
Columbia. After returning to Illinois, Hurlbut was twice elected to the U.S. Congress. In
1881 Secretary of State James G. Blaine appointed him U.S. Minister to Peru, a position
he held until his death on March 27, 1882. General Hurlbut was buried in Belvidere
Cemetery.

In 1886 the June Manufacturing Company relocated to Belvidere from Chicago to
avoid labor problems. It later became the National Sewing Machine Company, though
at times the factory also built bicycles and washing machines and assembled automobiles. The company closed in 1963. Within two years, however, the manufacturing vacuum was filled by the Chrysler Corporation's forty-three-acre assembly plant. The first
car to roll off the assembly line was a 1965 Plymouth Fury; the vehicle is now displayed
in the Boone County Historical Museum.

Maj. Gen. Stephen A. Hurlbut, one of Belvidere's most prominent citizens —Courtesy Library of Congress Prints and Photographs Division, Brady-Handy Collection (LC-BH826-2662 A)

During the late nineteenth and early twentieth centuries, businesses often painted advertisements on the sides of buildings and other outdoor spaces. A resurrection of this trend can be seen in Belvidere, which boasts restored and recreated versions of at least eighteen historic commercial murals. The creators of these nostalgic throwbacks are local members of a group called the Letterheads. Their efforts allow Belvidere to promote itself as the "City of Murals."

On a less happy note, the most tragic event in Belvidere's history happened in the spring of 1967, when a severe tornado hit the town, killing twenty-four, thirteen of whom were children and teenagers.

Tornado of 1967

Many Belvidere residents still remember the horrifying tornado that hit their town on the afternoon of April 21, 1967. The twister first touched down at the Chrysler plant, destroying some four hundred cars. It then tore through a residential area, where it demolished or severely damaged hundreds of homes. The worst, however, was yet to come.

School buses already carrying elementary children were in the process of boarding the older students at Belvidere High School when the tornado hit, seemingly out of nowhere. Twelve buses were overturned, crushing some of the passengers, while students standing outside were swept away in the high winds. Thirteen youngsters were killed and approximately three hundred were injured. Elsewhere in town, eleven other residents had also been killed and two hundred injured.

The Belvidere twister was responsible for the sixth-highest number of school fatalities from a tornado in the nation's history. It was one of more than forty funnels that tore through Illinois and adjacent states that day. These tornadoes—some creating winds of over two hundred miles an hour—caused deaths, injuries, and property damage across Illinois, especially in Boone, Lake, and Cook Counties. The total death toll from the outbreak was fifty-eight. A memorial statue was placed in front of Belvidere High School in 2007, on the fortieth anniversary of the tragedy.

UNION

The village of Union began with farmer William Jackson, who, believing that the Galena & Chicago Union Railroad would pass through part of his land, platted a village in 1851 and dubbed it Union. Jackson was correct—the railroad arrived the following year and built a station at the new settlement. Union flourished, and in 1897 it was incorporated as a village. But the twentieth century brought transportation advances that made Union obsolete as a commercial center, and as its economy suffered, its population declined.

The vacuum was filled in the late twentieth century by tourism. Two well regarded museums and a replica frontier town draw visitors from well beyond the Union area. The latter, Donley's Wild West Town, was established in 1970 on fourteen acres south of Union. This living museum portrays life in the Old West with a blacksmith shop, saloon, jail, and even a gold mine. The main museum building houses cowboy artifacts, Civil War items, mining gear, antique phonographs, outlaw death masks, and other cool stuff. Another first-rate historical museum in Union is operated by the McHenry County Historical Society. Since it opened in 1976, the museum has acquired several historic buildings including an 1847 cabin and an 1895 one-room schoolhouse. A refurbished school bus known as "the James" serves as a mobile history museum.

Yet another Union area museum is one of the most popular attractions in McHenry County—the Illinois Railway Museum, the largest railroad museum in the nation. Originally founded as the Illinois Electric Railway Museum in North Chicago in 1953, eleven years later it moved to its current location, a 112-acre site southeast of Union. The museum complex includes hundreds of pieces of rolling stock, including steam and diesel locomotives, freight cars, passenger coaches, and trolley cars, as well as antique railroad paraphernalia such as signals, signs, tools, uniforms, and tickets. The museum's trains have been used in a number of films, TV shows, and commercials. A five-mile rail line encircles the museum grounds; visitors may disembark at any one of several depots, both replica and authentic.

WOODSTOCK

The charming small city of Woodstock attracts visitors from Chicago, Milwaukee, and elsewhere with its farmer's market, antique shops, cultural events, and historic buildings. One of the biggest draws is the Woodstock Opera House, in continual use since 1890 for plays, lectures, theater classes, and other activities. Among those who once performed there were Ann-Margaret, Paul Newman, and Geraldine Page. In 1934 a young Orson Welles, then a student at Woodstock's prestigious Todd School for Boys, starred in several Shakespearean plays at the Opera House.

The first settlers arrived in the Woodstock area in the 1830s. They called their village Centerville to emphasize its central location within McHenry County, formed in 1836, hoping it would help the town to be chosen as the seat. Six years later, that wish was fulfilled. In 1845, Centerville developer Joel Johnson had the town's name changed to Woodstock after his hometown of Woodstock, Vermont. It was incorporated as a city in 1873. The Old McHenry County Courthouse (1857) and adjoining Sheriff's House (1887) are significant landmarks in Woodstock, both listed on the NRHP.

Following the 1894 Pullman railroad strike in Chicago, labor organizer and social reformer Eugene V. Debs was confined to the Woodstock jail for defying a federal strike injunction (see Pullman in Region 7). Debs later helped form the Social Democratic Party, running for president five times in the early 1900s. Two other political activists, radical anarchists Emma Goldman and Alexander Berkman, lived for a time on a commune in Woodstock around the turn of the twentieth century.

One of Woodstock's major industries in the first half of the twentieth century was typewriter manufacturing. Both the Emerson Typewriter Company and Oliver Typewriter had plants there, and for a time, half of the world's typewriters were produced in Woodstock.

The city's most recent brush with fame occurred in 1992, when Woodstock was used as a substitute for Punxsatawney, Pennsylvania, during the filming of *Groundhog Day*. Several sites in town have plaques to commemorate places where the film was shot. Woodstock celebrates the event each year with a Groundhog Days festival, held during the week of February 2.

OTHER COMMUNITIES AND SITES OF INTEREST IN NORTHERN ILLINOIS

Byron (IL 2 and IL 72): Originally called Fairview, this town's name was eventually changed to Byron after the popular poet Lord Byron. The 1843 home of early settler Lucius Read, believed to have been a stop on the Underground Railroad, served as a residence until 1945 and later as a tavern. In 1990 it was restored and converted into the Byron Museum of History. Another historic site in Byron is the Soldier's Monument, a twelve-foot-high marble shaft adorned with an eagle, dedicated in 1866. In 1963 the Byron Women's Club restored the monument, and it was added to the NRHP in 1985.

Cordova (IL 84): A settlement was established in this hilly, wooded area on the banks of the Mississippi River in the mid-1830s, and in 1877 Cordova, named after the city in southern Spain, was incorporated as a village. Since the 1950s, Cordova has been known for Cordova Dragway Park, begun when Moline resident Bob Bartel built a one-quarter-mile auto-racing track in a local cornfield. Now a million-dollar enterprise with seating capacity for 10,000 fans, the facility, the oldest continuously operating drag strip in the nation, hosts dozens of events throughout the year, the best known of which is the World Series of Drag Racing, the oldest annual drag race in the world.

Marengo (US 20): The Indians called this place Thunder Grove, but the first settlers, who arrived in 1835, named it Pleasant Grove, later changed to Marengo. One interesting leftover from the early days of settlement is a bur oak "witness tree" south of Marengo, believed to be the only remaining witness tree in the state. In the first half of the nineteenth century, certain trees were marked to "bear witness" to property lines in land surveys. The witness tree in McHenry County, about fifty feet tall, was given landmark status in 1999. Another historic site in Marengo is the Charles H. Hibbard House, also known as the Cupola House, a station on the Underground Railroad. It is believed that Hibbard harbored runaway slaves in his 1847 Italianate home, which featured a glass-encased octagonal cupola that, when lit, was allegedly used to signal fugitive slaves that it was safe to enter. A hidden dugout leading to the house's lower level was discovered in 1968. The Hibbard House, privately owned but unoccupied, was listed on the NRHP in 1979.

Rockton (IL 2): In 1835 Vermont-born fur trader Stephen Mack Jr. founded Macktown, a trading post and small settlement along the Pecatonica River. Meanwhile, just to the north, New York entrepreneur William Talcott founded Rockton. After numerous ups and downs, Macktown faded away while Rockton continued to grow until it went into a serious decline in the mid-twentieth century. Soon, however, the construction of interstate highways improved access to Rockton, stimulating interest in this town about fifteen miles north of Rockford. Between 1990 and 2010, the population of this appealing community more than doubled. Nearby, at the site of Stephen Mack's original settlement in the Macktown Forest Preserve, is the Stephen Mack Home, the Whitman Trading Post, and the Macktown Living History Education Center, currently under development. Also at the site are the fenced-in graves of Mack and his family.

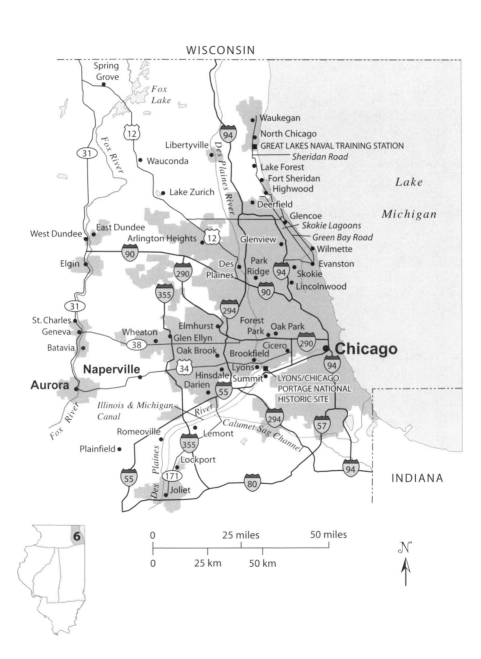

WISCONSIN

Spring
Grove

*Fox
Lake*

Fox River

12

31

Libertyville

Wauconda

Waukegan

North Chicago

94

GREAT LAKES NAVAL TRAINING STATION

Sheridan Road

Lake Forest

Fort Sheridan

Highwood

Lake Zurich

Des Plaines River

Deerfield

Glencoe

Skokie Lagoons

*Lake
Michigan*

West Dundee

East Dundee

Arlington Heights

12

Glenview

Green Bay Road

Wilmette

Elgin

90

Des
Plaines

Park
Ridge

Evanston

290

94

Skokie

90

Lincolnwood

31

355

294

St. Charles

Geneva

Wheaton

Elmhurst

Forest
Park

Oak Park

Batavia

Glen Ellyn

38

Oak Brook

Brookfield

Cicero

290

Chicago

Naperville

34

Hinsdale

Lyons

Summit

94

Aurora

Darien

55

LYONS/CHICAGO
PORTAGE NATIONAL
HISTORIC SITE

*Illinois & Michigan
Canal*

Des Plaines River

294

57

Romeoville

Lemont

Calumet Sag Channel

Plainfield

355

94

Lockport

Des Plaines

55

171

80

INDIANA

Joliet

6

| 0 | | 25 miles | | 50 miles |

| 0 | 25 km | 50 km |

N

Greater Chicagoland
METROPOLITAN DIVERSITY

The residents of suburban Chicago's cities, towns, and villages make up about four-fifths of the population of the greater metropolitan area, affectionately known as Chicagoland. The history of this region is as rich and diverse as that of any other part of the state.

The first settlers in northeastern Illinois were mostly relocating easterners and European immigrants who farmed the rich soil and, as transportation improved, shipped their produce and livestock to the city. They also built mills, inns, stores, and communities. As industry in the region grew, more immigrants flooded in to build railroads and canals, mine coal and limestone, and staff factories. Meanwhile, pockets within the region—especially lakeshore properties—served as country havens for affluent Chicagoans.

By the mid twentieth century, with Chicago burgeoning and middle class families embracing the suburban dream, newly built communities filled in the open space between established towns, creating a forty-mile radius of dense suburban habitat north, west, and south of the city. Today, greater Chicagoland is home to a rich variety of cultures, socioeconomic groups, and ethnicities.

While the landscape of northeastern Illinois is predominantly flat prairie, leveled by receding glaciers thousands of years ago, several natural rivers and abundant woodlands provide topographical variety and beauty. At the time of European contact, the main native tribes here were the Illini, Winnebago, and Miami. Later, during the eighteenth century, nonindigenous peoples migrated to Illinois, displaced by white settlement; these included the Potawatomi, Mesquakie (Fox), Sauk, and Kickapoo Indians, among others.

After the 1832 Black Hawk War ended, the native inhabitants of northern Illinois were sent to reservations in the West and white settlers moved in. Many of these early homesteaders wrote to relatives and friends back East and in Europe about the region's fertile land and abundant economic opportunities, encouraging more settlers to relocate here. Many of the new arrivals abhorred slavery, and northeastern Illinois became a major link in the Underground Railroad. Abolitionists in such towns as Naperville, Wheaton, Glen Ellyn, Downers Grove, Oak Brook, Lake Zurich, and Gurnee used their homes and property to harbor slaves escaping from Missouri and the South.

Construction on the Illinois & Michigan Canal in 1830s and '40s attracted laborers from northern Europe and elsewhere, creating the towns of Summit, Lemont, Lockport, and many others (see also Region 5). Later, the extension of railroads such as the Galena & Chicago Union from Chicago to Elgin increased opportunities and promoted population growth into the new century.

In the early twentieth century, as the villages and towns of northeastern Illinois expanded, wise planners in Cook, DuPage, Kane, Lake, and surrounding counties began to set aside acres of prairie, woods, and wetlands for public use. The extensive Forest Preserve Districts served as barriers to the endless housing and commercial development that came later and ensured natural areas for residents to enjoy picnicking, hiking, and wildlife viewing. The many lakes in the northwestern part of the region, such as those in Chain O'Lakes State Park, offer boatloads of water recreation.

Federal implementation of the interstate highway system in the 1950s, along with state-funded roadway expansion, led to even more development in greater Chicagoland. Clusters of newly constructed homes replaced crop fields, and new roads and highways cut ribbons of concrete through the landscape. The new subdivisions of ranch-style houses stood in contrast to the architecturally distinguished homes of older suburbs such as Evanston, Winnetka, Wheaton, Riverside, and Elgin. During the same mid-century period, Fermilab National Accelerator Laboratory in Batavia and Argonne National Laboratory near Lemont were instrumental in attracting high-tech companies to Chicagoland. By the end of the twentieth century, the farms that were once so prevalent in northwestern Illinois had become as rare as wagons and canal boats.

Stevenson Expressway (I-55) and IL 171
CHICAGO (BRIDGEPORT)–JOLIET
41 miles

The Illinois & Michigan Canal (I & M Canal), completed in 1848, linked the fledgling prairie city of Chicago with waterways to the east, west, and south, spawning the development of cities such as Summit, Lemont, and Lockport while planting the seeds of many other towns in the region. This trip on IL 171 approximately follows the eastern part of the canal route from the Chicago neighborhood of Bridgeport, home of the recently established Canal Origins Park (see Region 7), to Joliet; the rest of the route, which ends just beyond LaSalle-Peru, was described in Region 5. The Illinois & Michigan Canal Museum is in Lockport, which we will visit on this trip.

This trip also follows the route of the Chicago Sanitary & Ship Canal, which was built after the I & M Canal and largely replaced it. Created to improve sanitation in Chicago, the canal reversed the flow of the Chicago River to carry polluted waters away from, rather than into, Lake Michigan. The canal, completed in 1900, started at Lake Michigan in downtown Chicago and ended at Lockport. A later (1907) addition extended the canal to Joliet.

CHICAGO (BRIDGEPORT)
See Region 7

SUMMIT

Just east of the Des Plaines River, atop a ridge about six hundred feet above sea level, sits the village of Summit. This ridge was the first geographical obstacle encountered during the construction of the Illinois & Michigan Canal.

The earliest recorded settler in Summit, originally called Point of Oaks, was Russell Heacock, who arrived in the 1830s to farm. Before long, construction of the canal attracted settlers, primarily Irish laborers, followed shortly thereafter by Germans. By the time the village was founded in 1890, the population included eastern and central Europeans along with a smattering of Mexicans and African Americans. Today Summit is noted as one of the most ethnically diverse towns in Chicagoland.

The area's fertile fields produced a steady stream of produce for Summit farmers, while its quarries furnished much of the stone used to build Chicago's streets. Commerce was well accommodated by the I & M Canal and the railroads, then by the Sanitary & Ship Canal, and eventually by Interstate 55 (Stevenson Expressway).

During the twentieth century, Summit shifted its emphasis to manufacturing. Its biggest employer is nearby Ingredion (formerly Corn Products International), one of the largest corn-processing plants in the world.

Southwest of Summit, adjacent to Willow Springs, the 105-acre Paw Paw Woods Nature Preserve attracts visitors wishing to enjoy year-round recreation. Within the preserve is one of the area's main attractions, the Little Red School House Nature Center, housed in an 1886 one-room country schoolhouse. The school building, relocated from nearby Palos Township to its present location, was refurbished as a nature center in 1955. A new visitor center was added in 2010.

LEMONT

Lemont grew out of two early settlements, Keepataw and Athens, established in the late 1830s. The merged village was incorporated in 1873. During the construction of the I & M Canal, yellow dolomite (a.k.a. Athens Marble, a.k.a. Lemont limestone) was discovered here just beneath the surface, making it easy to extract. The rock was mined extensively for canal construction, as well as for buildings in Lemont's own downtown, and it was also exported.

With the construction of the canal, a large influx of European immigrant workers began to settle in the Lemont area. Irish laborers were followed by Germans, Poles, and Scandinavians, and later, Italians, Czechs, Austrians, and others. When the canal was completed, many of these workers found mining jobs in the limestone quarry and later helped construct the Chicago Sanitary & Ship Canal. After limestone mining declined, primarily due to less expensive stone from Indiana as well as increasing labor conflicts in the area, an eclectic mix of manufacturing filled the void. Following World War II, the creation of the nearby Argonne National Laboratory (see Darien on next trip) brought further demographic changes to the area as this and other high-tech industries displaced manufacturing.

History buffs visiting Lemont will find the Old Stone Church, built of local limestone in 1861, of particular interest. Until 1970, the building served parishioners as the Lemont Methodist Episcopal Church. It is now a museum and the headquarters of the Lemont Area Historical Society.

LOCKPORT

Lockport was founded in 1837 as headquarters for the construction of the Illinois & Michigan Canal. The canal's first lock—which raised and lowered water levels for boats—was built in Lockport, and the town became a bustling port for passenger and freight traffic. The Chicago to Ottawa stagecoach was routed through the town in 1839, the canal was completed in 1848, and Lockport incorporated as a village in 1853. Canal traffic lessened after the railroads arrived in 1854, but despite this competition, the canal continued to thrive for nearly fifty more years. In 1890 the development of another waterway, the Sanitary & Ship Canal, displaced the Illinois & Michigan Canal but kept the town growing. Lockport was incorporated as a city in 1904.

From 1933 to 1942, the Civilian Conservation Corps filled in parts of the obsolete I & M Canal, reducing its width, and developed the old towpaths into hiking trails and picnic areas. Other recreational facilities were also added. Preserved remnants of the canal walls and Lock #1 are still visible along the walking and bike path that now traces the old canal. Various trails, lined with historical markers, lead through downtown Lockport and several city parks.

The canal trail is just the beginning of historic preservation in Lockport, a city proud of its heritage. The entire downtown is a National Register Historic District, as is the Lock #1 area, and several private homes are on the NRHP. The original 1837 I & M Canal headquarters building, at the north end of downtown, is now home to the award-winning Illinois & Michigan Canal Museum and headquarters of the Will County Historical Society.

Near the canal museum is the Gaylord Building National Trust Historic Site. Built in 1838 as a warehouse for canal construction, the three-story limestone structure was sold after the canal was finished to local merchant and grain dealer George Gaylord. Gaylord used the building as a dry-goods store and grain warehouse. Today it serves mainly as a visitor center with several exhibition galleries, while part of the building houses an upscale restaurant.

Like the Gaylord Building, many other major historic buildings in Lockport are made of local limestone. Two are just east of the main downtown historic district—the 1895 Central Square building, originally a school and now used for municipal offices, and the 1839 Congregational Church, today home to the Gladys Fox Museum and Community Center.

Near the canal on the south side of the downtown district is one of Lockport's centerpiece historic structures, the 1850 Norton Building, also made of local limestone. Prominent businessman Hiram Norton built this massive facility as a warehouse for storing and processing grain. The Norton Company once handled hundreds of thousands of bushels of corn, oats, and wheat annually. The restored building now serves multiple functions, with condos, offices, and shops on the upper floors and, on the main floor, the Illinois State Museum's Lockport Gallery, which hosts numerous exhibitions and programs.

As of this writing, plans are under way to relocate and reconstruct another historical attraction, Lockport's Heritage Village, formerly called Pioneer Settlement, a living museum of nineteenth-century buildings. The new site will be north of downtown along the canal trail. A new park called Lincoln Landing was created at the old museum site at the North Public Landing.

In addition to Lockport's founders and early developers, another local resident found a place in history. John Lane, a blacksmith by trade, was an early settler in Runyonstown, the settlement that would soon become Lockport. Lane arrived here in 1833, and within two years he had developed an invention that would revolutionize agriculture—the steel-bladed plow.

John Lane: Inventor of the First Steel Plow

Many people believe that John Deere invented the first steel plow, but historical evidence shows that John Lane, Sr., a Will County blacksmith and farmer, was the true originator, having created a steel-bladed plow several years before Deere received the patent for his own plow design in 1837 (see under Grand Detour in Region 5).

Born in New Hampshire in 1793, Lane migrated to northeastern Illinois at age forty-one, along with his family and a few other settlers, to pursue farming. Like other farmers, Lane used a plow with a wooden blade, or moldboard, which tended to get jammed up with mud and tangled roots and so required frequent scraping with a wooden paddle.

Determined to find a solution to this problem, Lane set up a forge in front of his cabin and began to experiment. He believed that thin sheets of steel fused together, if properly shaped and highly polished, would pass through the ground without muck clinging to the blade. Taking worn or broken saw blades from a nearby sawmill, Lane fused the steel pieces together and cut, shaped, hammered, and polished them into plow blades. He and his neighbors conducted field tests and made adjustments until a working design evolved. He had no interest in obtaining a patent, however; he was satisfied just to be of service to other farmers.

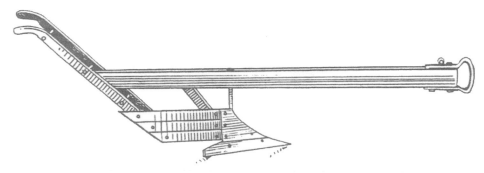

*Sketch of John Lane's steel-bladed plow, from a description
by John Lane, Jr.* —Author's collection

Some reports state that Lane began manufacturing his plow in 1835, but he probably started limited production the year before. After producing about two hundred plows using old saw blades, Lane began buying new sheet steel from Pittsburgh for his plow blades. With demand soon outpacing production, Lane's son, John Jr., opened a factory in Lockport, where he made plows as well as carriages and other equipment. Additional plants were built to fill orders from throughout the nation. After the elder Lane died in 1857, John Jr. successfully continued manufacturing, taking out patents for his own plow designs, including the "soft center" steel plow. At this point he was competing with John Deere, whose name would become synonymous with farm machinery, while his father's name became little more than a historical footnote.

JOLIET

Joliet, originally named Juliet, was founded in 1833 with its first post office. The source of the name Juliet is uncertain; the settlement may have been named for a settler's female relative, or perhaps it was a version of Jolliet, after explorer Louis Jolliet, for whom the village was eventually renamed. In any case, not long after Juliet was established, a nearby settlement decided to make a droll play on its neighbor's name and call itself Romeo. In 1845 the Illinois legislature changed Juliet's name to Joliet (opting for the anglicized spelling of Jolliet), and shortly afterward, Romeo became Romeoville. (See also Romeoville on next trip.)

The two towns grew up together, and in the early days, both economies were based on the same two things: traffic along the Illinois & Michigan Canal and area limestone deposits. The local limestone was used in many major buildings, including the Illinois State Capitol, the Lincoln Monument, Rock Island Arsenal, the U.S. Marine Hospital, the Illinois State Penitentiary, and numerous others. By 1900, however, canal traffic had dropped off, and the demand for limestone dried up soon after that. Romeoville began to fade, while Joliet forged ahead. An abundance of soft coal had been found in the Joliet area, providing perfect conditions for iron and steel manufacturing and spurring further economic growth for the city. Today Joliet has five times the population of Romeoville.

Joliet's first steel mill was built in 1869, and soon the city was as well known for its iron and steel as it was for its limestone. The Joliet Iron & Steel Works was once the second-largest steel mill in the nation, and it was one of the city's major employers for sixty years before closing in the 1930s. Beginning in the 1990s, the Will County Forest Preserve District undertook the challenge of developing the factory ruins as the Joliet Iron Works Historic Site, which opened in 1998. A 1.5-mile walking trail leads through the ruins and interpretive signs describe the factory's historic significance. The trail, which follows part of the I & M Canal, has been further improved in recent years. Additions include restrooms, water fountains, and picnic facilities.

The Iron Works is just one of many historical attractions in Joliet. Others include the 1876 Jacob Henry Mansion, the 1891 Auditorium Building, and the 1926 Rialto Square Theater. Two more recent additions are the Route 66 Visitors Center and the Joliet Area Historical Museum.

Another, more unusual historical site in Joliet is the birthplace of a classic American institution—the Dairy Queen. Few people have heard of John F. McCullough, but millions have enjoyed his creation, "soft-serve" ice cream. In 1938 McCullough approached Kankakee ice cream shop owner Sherwood Dick "Sherb" Noble with his newly concocted treat, and Noble agreed to sell the product on a trial basis. He sold more than 1,600 servings the first day. Noble and McCullough became business partners and opened the first Dairy Queen in Joliet two years later, launching a multimillion dollar business. Today, there are more than 5,900 Dairy Queen locations worldwide. The original shop, a nondescript old storefront now used as a church, was granted historic landmark status in 2011.

Another Joliet landmark is not quite so sweet—the Joliet Correctional Center. When it opened in 1858, it was the largest prison in the nation, and over the years it developed a reputation as one of the toughest. Its notoriety, combined with its distinctive architecture, made it a popular set location for films and television shows. Seven years after its 2002 closure, the city opened Old Joliet Prison Park, an open-air visitor center in the former prison parking lot, but the prison buildings are still closed to the public.

In addition to its historic sites, Joliet has developed a thriving entertainment industry. Two riverboat casinos and two car-racing facilities, the Chicagoland Speedway NASCAR racetracks and the Route 66 Raceway IndyCar tracks, have yielded millions in visitor dollars.

The greater Joliet area offers additional points of interest, such as the site of ancient Joliet Mound, a flat-topped, steep-walled landform that measured about 60 feet high, 1,350 feet long, and 225 feet wide. The mound was mined into oblivion in the late nineteenth and early twentieth centuries; nothing remains.

In nearby Elwood is the former Joliet Arsenal (Joliet Army Ammunition Plant), which closed in 1976. Built in 1940, the arsenal served as an ordnance depot during WWII, the Korean War, and the Vietnam War. In 1993 the property was divided into sections for several different uses—3,000 acres were allocated for two industrial parks; 19,100 acres became the Midewin National Tallgrass Prairie, managed by the U.S. Forest Service; and 455 acres were turned into a landfill. Another 982 acres was set aside to establish the Abraham Lincoln National Veterans Cemetery, which was dedicated in October 1999.

I-55
SUMMIT–PLAINFIELD
26 miles

Following I-55 all the way to Plainfield takes us north of the route of the Illinois & Michigan Canal, along what was once the route of a stagecoach trail. On the previous trip, which follows IL 171 along the canal route itself, we visited many communities that came into being with the construction of the canal. A few towns along this route, including Romeoville, were also established by the canal builders, but many were earlier settlements, such as Darien and Plainfield, that more or less grew on their own. Several, including Countryside and Bolingbrook, remained farmland until the suburban expansion of the mid-twentieth century. The building of modern highways after World War II turned virtually all of these places into suburban communities. Interstate 55, built in the 1970s, displaced much of the traffic from historic US Route 66, of which about 85 percent remains between Chicago and St. Louis.

SUMMIT

See previous trip

DARIEN

Darien was first settled by New Englanders, who established a village called Cass along the old stagecoach trail between Chicago and Plainfield. The settlement's founder, Thomas Andrus, built an inn here that also served as a stage stop and post office. Homes, churches, and schools followed, and later, a cheese factory and other businesses were built. Meanwhile, the village of Lace grew up adjacent to Cass. In 1969, as the region was being transformed into suburbs, the two communities merged as Darien.

The creation of Argonne National Laboratory in the late 1940s brought high-tech jobs and new prosperity to this part of Chicagoland. Established in Palos Hills in 1946, this research facility was moved a few years later to a larger campus (1,700 acres) just south of Darien. In 1951 the lab produced the world's first nuclear-generated electricity, followed by many other developments in physics, chemistry, medicine, and engineering. Its original focus on nuclear energy has been expanded to include other alternative energy sources as well as general scientific research.

ROMEOVILLE

Romeoville was founded as an Illinois & Michigan Canal community in 1835 and somewhat facetiously named Romeo as a counterpoint to nearby Juliet (now Joliet), which was also built as a canal town. Both towns prospered not only from the canal itself but also from their own limestone quarries, as well as from surrounding farms. In 1845 Juliet, perhaps tired of the joke, became Joliet, and Romeo became Romeoville. (See also Joliet on previous trip.)

Both villages prospered until the early twentieth century, when the area's economic mainstays began to fade; the canal became obsolete and concrete replaced limestone as a popular building material. Although advancing industrial development opened new opportunities, Romeoville was not in a position to take advantage of them. Unlike Joliet, whose location in the Des Plaines River Valley was ideal for expansion, Romeoville, situated atop high bluffs, was less accessible and therefore less desirable. The village's population in 1950 was about the same as it had been a century earlier.

Mid-twentieth-century suburban expansion revived Romeoville. New roads and highways brought developers who built affordable housing subdivisions, which in turn attracted associated businesses. The main growth took place not in Romeoville's original downtown area but in the valley below. Later I-55, built in the 1970s just north of Romeoville, kept the flow going. Retail, offices, and light manufacturing took up residence here into the 1990s and beyond.

Those interested in the earlier roots of Romeoville will enjoy a visit to the Isle a la Cache, an island in the Des Plaines River, and its surrounding nature preserve. As early as the seventeenth century, French voyageurs were trading with the local Potawatomi

Indians in this region, and the traders often used this natural river island as a safe storage place for their goods, thus its name. Today the island is part of a 100-acre nature preserve and recreation area. Within the preserve, the recently renovated Isle a la Cache Museum provides a glimpse into fur-trade era Illinois. In addition to numerous exhibits and programs, the museum hosts an Island Rendezvous each June to recreate the traditional annual gathering of trappers, traders, and Native Americans of the 1700s.

PLAINFIELD

Considered to be the oldest community in Will County, Plainfield started out as Walker's Grove, a small settlement established by James Walker and his family in 1828. Walker built a cabin, a sawmill, and a gristmill at the site of an old Potawatomi village on the DuPage River. The mills served early settlements thoughout the region, including the fledgling town of Chicago. In fact, Plainfield regularly provided Chicago with supplies and services of various kinds, leading it to be referred to later as the "Mother of Chicago."

During the Black Hawk War of 1832 (see Region 5), the home of Walker's Grove minister Rev. Stephen R. Beggs was temporarily used as a defensive fort for some 125 area settlers. Beggs's fences, shed, and barn were dismantled to build a breastworks around the main house. Fort Beggs was never attacked, but word of the massacre on Indian Creek in May (see under Earlville in Region 5) sent the inhabitants fleeing to Chicago's Fort Dearborn. The fort at Beggs's place was later torn down. A marker was placed at the site in 1936.

As Walker's Grove flourished, other small settlements sprang up nearby. Plainfield, originally spelled Planefield, was platted next to Walker's Grove in 1834. Eventually Plainfield merged with Walker's Grove and other adjacent settlements, incorporating as Plainfield in 1869.

One of the earliest buildings in the Plainfield settlement was a stage stop, tavern, and post office called Arnold's Tavern, erected in 1834. A few years later, the tavern was sold to Dr. Erastus C. Wight, who expanded it into a full-service inn called Plainfield House, also known as Wight Tavern or Wight House. For all its different names, however, the place was always best known as Halfway House since it was halfway between Chicago and Ottawa on the stage trail. Halfway House was a focal point of the community for many years. During the Civil War, part of the building was used as headquarters for the local militia. Plainfield House operated as an inn until around 1886, and it served as the private home of Wight's descendants until the 1950s. A marker was erected in front of the house, officially called Plainfield Halfway House, in 1969, and it was listed on the NRHP in 1980.

For decades, Plainfield's economy was based on agriculture. Beginning in the 1920s and accelerating throughout the twentieth century, however, new highways opened the village to travelers as well as commuters. After World War II, much farmland was sold to developers for housing subdivisions and commercial enterprises. For a time, both the Lincoln Highway and US Route 66 passed through Plainfield. One remnant of that era is the Standard Oil Gas Station, built in 1928. The station operated until 1984; the building was placed on the NRHP the same year. It has been renovated and is now used for offices.

Ogden Avenue (US 66 and US 34)
I-290 (Chicago)—Aurora
38 miles

Before settlement, an Indian trail stretched between Chicago and Ottawa, mainly following along the Illinois River. After settlement, part of the Ottawa Trail evolved into the Southwestern Plank Road between Chicago and Lyons. This road was later extended to Naperville and eventually to Aurora. The eastern section of the road was renamed Ogden Avenue, for Chicago's first mayor, William B. Ogden, in 1878.

Today, between Chicago and Lyons, Ogden Avenue is also designated as US 66, and at Lyons it becomes US 34. Ogden Avenue ends in Aurora, while US 34 continues west.

CICERO

Founded in 1857 and incorporated in 1869, the town of Cicero originally covered thirty-six square miles, encompassing present-day Oak Park and Berwyn as well as Chicago's Austin neighborhood and other areas. After various splits and annexations in the late 1800s and early 1900s, the town shrunk to less than 20 percent of its original size. Nevertheless, as the nearest suburb to the Chicago Loop, Cicero remained a popular place to live and do business, and the town prospered through the twentieth century.

For eighty years, Cicero's largest employer was a Western Electric factory known as the Hawthorne Works, established in 1904. The plant, which produced telephone equipment and other products, had tens of thousands of employees and helped Cicero's population to quadruple over the next two decades. The Hawthorne Works operated until 1983, after which time it was torn down for a shopping center, though one of the plant's original water towers still stands on Cicero Avenue. The Hawthorne Works Museum at Morton College tells the factory's story, including the *Eastland* disaster, in which an employee outing turned into a tragedy (see under Wacker Drive in Region 7).

Probably the best-known aspect of Cicero's history is its association with notorious mobster Al Capone. At the height of Chicago's gangster era of the 1920s, Cicero served as Capone's headquarters when things got too hot in the city. His main hangout was the now-defunct Hawthorne Inn. For almost a decade, Capone and his cohorts ruled Cicero, controlling most of the town's police and elected officials. Shootouts were so commonplace that there was a saying, "If you smell gunpowder, you're in Cicero." After Capone went to prison for income tax evasion in 1931, the violence died down, but his cronies kept Cicero's corruption going for decades.

Cicero furthered its controversial reputation when a race riot broke out in July 1951. After a black family moved into an all-white neighborhood, a mob of 4,000 whites attacked them in their apartment. Police and National Guard troops battled with the rioters for two days before the disturbance was quelled. No one was killed, but about twenty-three people were injured. Today Cicero has a diverse population, the dominant ethnicity being Hispanic.

Also of historical interest, in nearby Stickney, is the Hawthorne Race Course, one of the oldest horse-racing tracks in America. The track first opened in 1891, but it was forced to close down when horse racing was banned in Chicago in 1905. It reopened legally in 1922 and has operated continuously since. The Hawthorne Race Course is also the home of the Chicagoland Sports Hall of Fame. The museum, which began in a beer trailer in 1979, was relocated several times before it was moved to the racetrack in 2008.

LYONS

What is now the village of Lyons was, in 1673, the spot where the seeds of Chicago were sown. Here existed a muddy half-mile stretch of land between the Des Plaines and Chicago Rivers that indigenous tribes had used for centuries as a portage. When the French explorers Louis Jolliet and Père Jacques Marquette were returning north from their expedition on the Mississippi, the Indians advised them of this portage as a shortcut to Lake Michigan and the waterways leading east. The discovery of *Le Portage* opened a path to what eventually became the great city of Chicago. A century and a half later, the Chicago Portage, which early settlers called Mud Lake, became part of the route of the Illinois & Michigan Canal.

The settlement of Lyons began in the late 1820s, when brothers David and Bernardus Laughton established a trading post and tavern at a shallow crossing of the Des Plaines River near Salt Creek, supplying traders, settlers, and military troops as they made their way west. About a decade later, construction of the I & M Canal brought workers to the area, and a few settlers, most of them German farmers, established homesteads. In 1856 a large brewery began operations, and gradually other businesses and homes emerged in the area. In the early 1880s, a limestone quarry and lime kiln were established, bringing immigrant workers, particularly Poles, to Lyons. The village was incorporated in 1888.

By the turn of the twentieth century, Lyons had gained a rowdy reputation as a hub for saloons and brothels. Despite the efforts of progressive-era reformers, the saloons stayed open even after Prohibition was enacted.

A more family-oriented side of Lyons developed when brewer George Hofmann Jr. opened a recreation and amusement park on the Des Plaines River in 1908. Centered around an eight-story, castlelike concrete tower, the park offered boat rides, games, concerts, dancing, and picnicking. By 1920, however, most of the amusements had closed down due to pollution in the river. The impressive Hofmann Tower still remains as a Lyons landmark. Extensive renovations and restoration work have been done with the goal of turning the tower into a museum, but as of this writing it is still closed to the public.

After World War II, most of the remaining open land in Lyons was utilized for residential developments, but the bars, strip clubs, and organized crime activity remained for several decades. By the 1990s, however, most of the wilder adult entertainments in Lyons had become history, giving way to a more sedate community served by a Metra commuter line.

The portage area called Mud Lake was eventually reclaimed for industrial development and is now the site of the world's largest sewage-treatment plant, but history-minded visitors can explore the Chicago Portage National Historic Site, a small preserved area that straddles the Portage Woods and Ottawa Trail Woods Forest Preserves. Part of the I & M Canal Heritage Corridor, the site, sometimes referred to as "Chicago's Plymouth Rock," is accessible via IL 43 (Harlem Avenue), off Ogden Avenue from the

Hofmann Tower in Lyons is the only structure remaining from Niagara Park, an amusement complex built by brewer George Hofmann, Jr., around 1908.
—Author's collection

Marked by this plaque embedded in a boulder, the Chicago Portage National Historic Site, in the Portage Woods Forest Preserve in Lyons, is often called "Chicago's Plymouth Rock."
—Courtesy Summit Public Library Historical Archives

THE CHICAGO PORTAGE 1673–1836

THIS MARKS THE WEST END OF THE CARRYING OR CONNECTING PLACE UNITING THE WATERS OF THE ST. LAWRENCE RIVER AND THE GREAT LAKES WITH THOSE OF THE MISSISSIPPI RIVER, ITS TRIBUTARIES AND THE GULF OF MEXICO. THE EARLIEST FACTOR IN DETERMINING CHICAGO'S COMMERCIAL SUPREMACY. AN ARTERY OF TRAVEL USED BY THE ABORIGINES IN THEIR MIGRATIONS AND LATER BY JOLIET, MARQUETTE, LA SALLE, TONTI AND THE FUR TRADERS OF NEW FRANCE. AN EARLY STRATEGICAL POINT IN THE WARS INCIDENT TO THE WINNING OF THE NORTH-WEST FOR THE SETTLERS-DISCOVERED BY JOLIET AND MARQUETTE IN 1673.

ERECTED BY THE CHICAGO HISTORICAL SOCIETY IN PURSUANCE OF A PLAN TO GIVE POSTERITY THE FACTS OF CHICAGO'S EARLY HISTORY. A.D.1930.

north or I-55 from the south. A memorial sculpture of Marquette and Jolliet stands near the parking lot, from which a trail leads to the remnants of the western edge of the portage. Plans to build a visitor center are currently under way.

BROOKFIELD

Neighboring Brookfield, home of the Chicago Zoological Park, a.k.a. the Brookfield Zoo, is also worth a stop. The village of Brookfield was founded in 1889 by Samuel E. Gross, who developed a community of affordable housing called Grossdale. He built a railroad station to service his village, which was incorporated in 1893. Residents later had a falling out with their founder and changed the town's name to Brookfield in 1905. The original 1889 train depot, Grossdale Station, is now a historical museum.

In 1919 wealthy philanthropist Edith Rockefeller McCormick, daughter of mogul John D. Rockefeller and daughter-in-law of mogul Cyrus Hall McCormick, donated a tract of land that was eventually developed as the Brookfield Zoo, which opened in 1934. Its design was not only gorgeous but also revolutionary—Brookfield was the first zoo in the world to use natural-style enclosures rather than cages. More innovations followed, including the first exhibit of a giant panda and the first interactive animal exhibits. An example of the latter is the Fragile Kingdom, which features the world's first enclosed rainforest ecosystem. The Chicago Zoological Society, founded at the time of the zoo's premiere, is an international leader in conservation and animal-care research and development.

HINSDALE AND OAK BROOK

The Hinsdale area, including nearby Oak Brook and other neighboring communities, has an extraordinary number of historical sites and museums. The excellent historic preservation in this area is largely due to the efforts of local historical societies. Both the Hinsdale Historical Society and the Oak Brook Historical Society were founded in 1975, and Oak Brook's Fullersburg Historic Foundation was established in 1986 to develop the Fullersburg Historic District. The Hinsdale society's Hinsdale History Museum is housed in a restored 1874 home outfitted with Victorian furnishings, and the Oak Brook Historical Society is currently renovating the 1921 Butler School as the Oak Brook Heritage Center.

Hinsdale and Oak Brook share historical roots. The first settlement in the area, Brush Hill, was established in the 1830s. In 1851 Benjamin Fuller platted the town of Fullersburg at Brush Hill, but when the Chicago, Burlington & Quincy Railroad arrived in the area in 1864, the line was built about a mile south of Fullersburg. Having foreseen this, settler William Robbins had purchased property closer to the tracks, where he platted a new settlement called Hinsdale. The village was incorporated in 1873. Part of Fullersburg was absorbed into Hinsdale, while the remaining area to the north became known as Oak Brook, though the latter was not incorporated as a village until 1958. That same year in Hinsdale, the nation's first health-education center opened. Originally called the Hinsdale Health Museum, the facility was renamed Robert Crown Center for Health Education in 1974.

Hinsdale's entire downtown historic district is listed on the NRHP, as is the village's Robbins Park Historic District, which contains 368 buildings. Several separate Hinsdale buildings are also listed on the NRHP, including four nineteenth-century homes and a former church, the 1900 Immanuel Hall, now home of the Roger and Ruth Anderson Architecture Center. Hinsdale also contains a number of distinctive homes designed by renowned architect R. Harold Zook, including Zook's own 1924 home and studio.

Oak Brook, too, has a number of unique historical sites. At the southern end of town is the Graue Mill and Museum, the only operating water-wheel gristmill in Illinois and a former Underground Railroad station, and the adjacent Ben Fuller Farmhouse, currently undergoing restoration by the Fullersburg Historic Foundation as part of its Fullersburg Historic District project. Oak Brook is also the home of the Czechoslovak Heritage Museum; the NRHP-listed Mayslake Peabody Estate; the 1897, Prairie-style Pleasant Home; and the Oak Brook Historical Society Museum. For popular-culture fans, Oak Brook boasts a landmark, the Ray A. Kroc Museum, housed in the former offices of McDonald's restaurant mogul and Oak Park native Ray Kroc (see also Oak Park and Des Plaines on later trips).

NAPERVILLE

In 1831 Ohio natives Joseph Naper and his brother, John, along with their families, arrived at the DuPage River. Each built a home and a sawmill. Joseph Naper's cabin, near present-day Mill and Jefferson Streets, became the nucleus of Naperville, originally known as Naper's Settlement. The community was well-located at a crossroads: one roadway (Aurora Avenue) led southwest to Ottawa; the other (Galena Road) was the Frink, Walker & Company stage route between Galena and Chicago. But the settlement's growth would be limited until after the Black Hawk War of 1832.

After word of the attack at Indian Creek settlement in May 1832 (see under Earlville in Region 5) reached Naper's Settlement, most of the women and children left for Fort Dearborn in Chicago while the men marched to Fort Johnson, near Ottawa, to request help from Brig. Gen. Henry Atkinson. The general ordered Capt. Morgan L. Payne and his company from Joliet to Naper's Settlement to construct a fort, subsequently named Fort Payne in his honor. The fort, one hundred feet square, was built in June 1832, about half a mile east of the main settlement.

When Fort Payne was completed, the families returned. The fort was never attacked, but during the summer of 1832, raiders had swept through the region, causing significant damage to several emerging communities, including Naper's Settlement. In August 1832, not long after the fort was finished, Black Hawk surrendered and the war ended. Caroline Strong, staying at Fort Payne with her husband, Robert, described the aftermath:

> *People are just beginning to creep out of their hives and tremblingly take a peep at their old homes which, I assure you, do not look as though they had ever been inhabited by human beings. . . .[The contents of the houses were] not carried off or burned, but left in the house to aggravate and distress the now destitute owners. Good furniture, iron ware, crockery smashed; clothing and bedding cut and torn to pieces. Murdered cats, dogs, and hogs lay about the house. . . . I never before realized the importance of living every day as though it were the last to be so spent.*

After the war, Fort Payne was abandoned, and it eventually deteriorated into nothing. A historical marker, now obscured by a dorm building on the North Central College campus, identifies the fort's approximate location. Today's Naper Settlement Museum, a recreated pioneer village, contains a reduced-scale replica of Fort Payne among other structures (see below).

In 1848 the J & N Stenger Brewery opened on the Stenger family farm, producing both ale and lager beer. The brewery soon became the village's largest business. For a short time, one of its foremen was Adolph Coors, who left Stenger to start his own brewery in Golden, Colorado, in 1873. The Stenger Brewery closed in 1893, and its buildings were demolished in 1956. During Naperville's sesquicentennial celebration in 1981, one of Stenger's brews was revived locally as a commemorative by the Joseph Huber Brewing Company of Monroe, Wisconsin.

The arrival of the Chicago, Burlington & Quincy Railroad in the 1850s brought prosperity to Naper's Settlement, which incorporated as the Village of Naperville in 1857. It served as the seat of DuPage County until residents of Wheaton wrested control in 1868 (see Wheaton on later trip). Nevertheless, Naperville kept growing, incorporating as a city in 1890.

Thanks largely to mid- to late-twentieth-century suburban development, Naperville is now the fifth-largest city in Illinois. It is home to eight college and university campuses, including North Central College and satellite campuses for Northern Illinois University, DePaul University, and University of Illinois.

To say Naperville is preservation-minded is an understatement. The city's downtown, which comprises much of the site of the original settlement, became a designated Historic District in 1986. The district contains more than six hundred buildings. In the late 1990s, in celebration of the new century, the city erected the Moser Tower and Millennium Carillon. The carillon contains seventy-two bells; the bells are run by an automated system, but many special events and concerts feature skilled musicians ringing the bells by hand. Tying it all together is the city's beautiful Riverwalk. Created by local volunteers in 1981, the 1.7-mile-long, landscaped trail meanders along the DuPage River.

One of Naperville's most popular heritage sites was conceived in 1969 by the newly formed Naperville Heritage Society. Over the next few years, the group established Naper Settlement, a twelve-acre outdoor history museum complex, which now contains thirty original and recreated historic buildings.

Naper Settlement Museum

Naper Settlement, Naperville's re-created pioneer village, was established in 1969 on land that had been donated to the city by Caroline Martin Mitchell upon her death in 1936. The original Martin Mitchell property contained the family's twelve-room Victorian home, a carriage house, and 200 acres; some of the land was converted, per the donor's request, into a public park called Martin Park. In the 1970s, Martin Park was redeveloped as Naper Settlement. In addition to the 1883 Martin Mitchell Mansion, the first buildings in the museum complex included the 1864 St. John's Episcopal Church, later renamed Century Memorial Chapel.

The Naperville Heritage Society was busy developing the museum throughout the 1970s, adding nine more buildings. Some were relocated original structures and others were replicas, including a reduced-scale reproduction of Fort Payne created in 1979. The 1980s saw several more buildings added, including an old barn, a recreated blacksmith shop, and a replica schoolhouse.

The 1990s were mostly devoted to the reconstruction of the 1830s Pre-Emption House. In the early days of Naperville, travelers passing through the settlement could stop for food and lodging at the Pre-Emption House, named by lawyers who met there to file, or "pre-empt," federal land claims for settlers. The original inn was demolished in 1946, but in the 1990s the Naperville Heritage Society built a replica, and since 1997 it has served as the visitor center at Naper Settlement Museum.

The most extensive work done at the museum in the 2000s was the restoration of the Martin Mitchell Mansion; the project was completed in 2003. Since then, in addition to welcoming 150,000 guests per year, Naper Settlement has continued to look for new acquisitions.

AURORA

In 1834 New Jersey–born brothers Joseph and Samuel McCarty spotted a bend in the swift-running Fox River and, feeling it was an ideal location for a sawmill, they purchased land on both sides of the river. After building a mill on the east side, they sold the land on the west side to another pair of brothers, Theodore and Zaphna Lake, who built a similar sawmill. A friendly competition emerged between the two sides, and eventually two separate villages were founded—East Aurora, incorporated in 1845, and West Aurora, incorporated in 1854.

In 1857, a year after the Chicago, Burlington & Quincy (CB&Q) Railroad built a roundhouse in East Aurora, the two settlements incorporated as the city of Aurora. In a compromise decision, the new city's municipal buildings were constructed on Stolp Island, in the middle of the Fox River.

For more than a century, the CB&Q Railroad was Aurora's largest employer and led to manufacturing and other commercial development, keeping the city economically healthy. In 1881 Aurora became one of the first American cities with electric streetlights, earning it a new nickname, the "City of Lights." The city prospered until the early 1970s, when the railroad shops closed and many industrial jobs disappeared.

The arrival of a riverboat casino, the *Hollywood Casino Aurora*, in 1993 boosted commercial and residential development in the city. Further improvements followed, and today Aurora is the second-largest city in Illinois.

Remnants of the past can be seen throughout Aurora. Downtown, the old Chicago, Burlington & Quincy roundhouse, listed on the NRHP in 1978, is now the Two Brothers Roundhouse and contains a brewpub, restaurant, and museum. Historic homes include the 1912 Greene House, designed by Frank Lloyd Wright, and numerous Sears catalog homes. Aurora also features the popular Phillips Park Zoo. Established in 1915, the zoo once featured exotic animals but it now focuses on animals native to Illinois, including elk, wolves, and mountain lions.

The main historic area in Aurora is Stolp Island, named a National Register Historic District in 1986. A number of the island's forty-one buildings are individually

This brick roundhouse, shown here with an engine and workers of the Chicago & Iowa Railroad (a subsidiary of the Chicago, Burlington & Quincy Railroad) in the 1870s, was part of Aurora's railroad complex until it was demolished in the 1920s.
—Courtesy Aurora Historical Society

listed on the NRHP as well. One of these is the Grand Army of the Republic Hall, built in 1877 as a memorial to Civil War Union veterans and used as a meeting place; it is now part of the David L. Pierce Art and History Center. Several commercial structures on the island are also NRHP buildings, including the 1931 art deco Paramount Theatre, which still hosts live shows.

A side trip on US 30 leads to Sugar Grove, a small village about seven miles west of Aurora. A group of early settlers founded this town in the 1830s at the site of an Indian sugar camp. One of these settlers was Peleg Young Bliss, owner of Sugar Grove's first store. Bliss's one-story home, built in 1838, is now the headquarters of the Sugar Grove Historical Society.

In the early 1970s Sugar Grove faced a shortage of volunteer firefighters. To solve the problem, the Sugar Grove Fire Protection District made the history-making decision to train women for the job. In 1972 thirteen of these local women became the first female firefighters in the Midwest.

In 1972, thirteen women in Sugar Grove (ten of whom are shown here) became the first female volunteer firefighters in the Midwest.
—Courtesy Sugar Grove Historical Society

IL 31
AURORA–WEST DUNDEE
25 miles

The meandering Fox River, which runs from Menomonee Falls, Wisconsin, to Ottawa, Illinois, was once the home to the Potawatomi Indians, who fished its waters and canoed its path, hunting in the nearby woodlands. Today, IL 31 parallels the Fox's western shoreline between Oswego and Algonquin, connecting the many towns that now line the river. We will visit several of those communities on this trip.

AURORA
See previous trip

BATAVIA

From its earliest history, Batavia has been a product of the plentiful natural resources along the Fox River. The first settler, Christopher Payne, arrived around 1833 and built a large cabin for his family that also served as an inn for travelers. Payne called his settlement, near the opening to two groves of heavy timber, "Head of Big Woods." After Payne sold his land to Judge Isaac Wilson and moved west, Wilson, a cavalry captain during the War of 1812 and later a New York state congressman, renamed the settlement Batavia after his hometown in upstate New York.

Although it wasn't incorporated as a village until 1856, Batavia showed industrial potential from the beginning. The Newton Wagon Company, which built Conestoga wagons, established a facility here in 1854, the same year the Chicago, Burlington & Quincy Railroad arrived in town. Two years later, the U.S. Wind Engine & Pump Company, after finding windmills a hard sell in the East, relocated to Batavia from Connecticut. Several decades later, other windmill manufacturers, such as the Challenge

Company, Appleton Manufacturing Company, and a number of others followed, giving the town a new nickname, the "Windmill City."

Nearby limestone quarries also contributed to the growth of Batavia. With a labor force of immigrants from Sweden, England, Ireland, Norway, Germany, and elsewhere, the quarries supplied Niagara limestone for construction projects in the area and, after the Great Fire of 1871, in Chicago. Batavia was incorporated as a city in 1891. With its strong industrial base, Batavia prospered through the end of World War II.

In the later twentieth century, with manufacturing in decline, Batavia entered the field of high-tech physics research when the National Accelerator Laboratory was established here in 1967. The facility, completed in 1974, was renamed Fermi National Accelerator Laboratory (Fermilab) in honor of Enrico Fermi, an Italian–American physicist who was instrumental in discovering nuclear fission, which led to the development of the atomic bomb. Today Fermilab, which continues to conduct research in particle physics, contains the world's second-largest energy particle accelerator.

Despite its association with advanced physics, Batavia remains grounded to its historical roots. The stone building built by the Appleton Manufacturing Company now houses the city's government offices, and the 1854 Chicago, Burlington & Quincy Railroad station is now the Depot Museum, a repository for local historical artifacts.

The pride of the city is the Riverwalk, a broad walking trail that encircles a twelve-acre peninsula in the Fox River. Built largely by local volunteers over a six-year period

Batavia's Riverwalk along the Fox River features many original windmills built by local manufacturers from the mid-1800s to the 1940s. —Author's collection

in the 1990s, the Riverwalk provides an idyllic setting for views of the river, seven original Batavia windmills, and a wealth of historic buildings, as well as the Batavia Dam, built to harness the Fox River in 1916.

While Batavia's existence has been a relatively happy one, it contains one reminder of a particularly sad episode, one of many in the tragic life of Mary Todd Lincoln, widow of President Abraham Lincoln. In 1875 a distraught Mrs. Lincoln was institutionalized for three months at Bellevue Place, a mental hospital for women. Although no longer a hospital, the original limestone building still stands and is listed on the NRHP. Some of Mrs. Lincoln's furnishings are preserved at the Depot Museum.

Bellevue Place

Bellevue Place, built in 1853 as Batavia Institute, a boarding school for teenage girls, in 1867 became a sanitarium for disturbed women. In May 1875 the institution admitted its most famous resident, Mary Todd Lincoln.

After the death of her son Thomas (Tad) in July 1871, having already endured the loss of two other sons and her husband, Mrs. Lincoln exhibited increasingly erratic behavior. After several years of this, upon the recommendations of doctors, Mary's surviving son, Robert, took legal action to institutionalize her. On May 20, 1875, she was admitted into Bellevue Place, operated by Dr. Richard J. Patterson, who believed in "peace, quiet, and gentleness" for the care of the mentally ill.

The former Bellevue Place mental hospital in Batavia. When Mary Todd Lincoln was a resident here in 1875, only the center building existed; the two wings were added around 1885. —Author's collection

This display at the Batavia Historical Society Museum depicts Mary Todd Lincoln's room at Bellevue Place as it looked when she was a resident; most of the furniture is original.
—Author's collection

According to records kept of Mrs. Lincoln's stay at Bellevue Place, she was given more freedom than was typical for patients. She often left the beautifully landscaped grounds, taking carriage rides into town, visiting friends in St. Charles, and even dining with Dr. Patterson's family. Although she did well at Bellevue, she was not happy to be confined. After less than four months and against Dr. Patterson's advice, she was released into the care of her sister, Elizabeth Edwards, in Springfield. Legally declared of sound mind in 1876, Mary began traveling abroad, but eventually her physical health declined, and she returned to her sister's home in 1880. She died two years later, possibly from a stroke, at age sixty-three. She was interred at the Lincoln Tomb in Springfield's Oak Ridge Cemetery.

Bellevue Place remained a sanitarium until 1964, when it became a residential school for unwed pregnant girls. The school relocated in the 1970s, and later, townhouses were built on the grounds. The original hospital was converted into apartments in 1986.

GENEVA

Geneva was first settled in 1833 by Daniel Shaw Haight, who called his homestead "Big Spring." Two years later, Haight sold his claim to James and Charity Herrington, the founders of Geneva. A year after that, Geneva was named the seat of the newly created Kane County. Like Batavia, Geneva was named for a town in New York state.

Due to its status as county seat and its location on the Fox River, the town grew rapidly, especially after the arrival of the Chicago & North Western Railway in 1853. Geneva was incorporated as a village in 1858 and as a city in 1887. By 1900 industry flourished and an influx of Swedish immigrants had swelled the population. Among the major companies in town were the Butter & Cheese Manufacturing Company (later Geneva Rock Springs Creamery), the Bennett Mill, and the Geneva Grape Sugar Company (later the Charles Pope Glucose Company).

An unusual development began in 1905, when millionaire Col. George Fabyan and his wife, Nelle, began to accumulate what became a 350-acre estate near Geneva. Riverbank, as the Fabyans called their place, eventually contained an eclectic mix of sculptures, greenhouses, cows and chickens, an elaborate Japanese garden, an old lighthouse, a Roman-style swimming pool, and even zoo animals. In 1907 the Fabyans hired famous architect Frank Lloyd Wright to refurbish the old farmhouse that stood on the property into a luxury home they called the Villa. This house is now the Fabyan Villa Museum. Around 1914 Fabyan purchased an 1850s windmill from Elmhurst and moved it to the estate for restoration. The still-operating windmill, added to the NRHP in 1979, is a cherished local landmark.

George Fabyan's contribution to Geneva did not stop with his home. Among his many varied interests was an obsession with proving that Francis Bacon was the real author of many of William Shakespeare's plays. In 1912 he gathered a group of expert cryptographers and established a laboratory on his estate for the sole purpose of confirming his theory. Riverbank Laboratories, the first privately owned research facility in the United States, would soon expand beyond this esoteric pursuit. Within a few years, Fabyan's researchers were experimenting in fields as diverse as acoustics and genetic engineering of crops.

These activities were put aside, however, when the United States entered World War I in 1917. Needing cryptographers to decode German messages, the federal government turned to Fabyan. By 1918 the U.S. Army had established a Department of Codes and Ciphers at Riverbank Laboratories, often seen as the forerunner of the

The Fabyan house, redesigned by Frank Lloyd Wright —Author's collection

The grounds of the Fabyan estate
—Author's collection

Historic windmill on the Fabyan estate
—Author's collection

National Security Agency and the Central Intelligence Agency. In addition, the lab conducted research in explosives and trench fighting. Further code work was done here during World War II. Later, Riverbank's findings contributed to such medical advances as hearing aids and radiation therapy for cancer. Today, Riverbank Laboratories continues its research in acoustical engineering. The Riverbank Estate, including the Villa, the windmill, the laboratory, and other buildings, is a National Historic District.

Central Geneva is also a National Historic District. It contains a cornucopia of historic architecture, including mid-1800s Greek Revival, Italianate, and neoclassical homes as well as the Frank Lloyd Wright–designed P. D. Hoyt House, built in 1906. Another interesting historic building in Geneva is the 1936 Campana Factory, a former hand-lotion manufacturing plant, now a costume shop.

ST. CHARLES

Two years after the Black Hawk War ended, Evan Shelby and William Franklin purchased government land on the east side of the Fox River. Together with subsequent settlers, they built a dam, bridge, gristmill, and sawmill, and Shelby donated land to plat the settlement, calling it Charleston. Shelby, who died in 1837, witnessed the development of his village, but the name was changed to St. Charles in 1839—a Charleston already existed in southern Illinois.

The Fox River's water power made St. Charles a magnet for industry, and a wave of Irish and Swedish immigrants came to settle there in the 1840s and '50s. The arrival of the Chicago & North Western Railway in 1871 connected St. Charles with Chicago.

The Hotel Baker in St. Charles, late 1920s
—Courtesy St. Charles Heritage Center

The same year, Mary Todd Lincoln, grieving over the loss of her husband and three sons, came to the Howard House Hotel in St. Charles to seek the psychic powers of Caroline Howard. Checking in under the pseudonym of Mrs. May, Mrs. Lincoln wanted to connect with her deceased family members. Four years later, her son Robert would have her institutionalized at the Bellevue Place mental asylum in Batavia (see under Batavia).

In 1874 St. Charles was incorporated as a city, and within twenty-five years its economy was booming, attracting many eastern European immigrants. In the 1920s, Edward Baker and Dellora Angell, heirs to the fortune of John "Bet-A-Million" Gates (see under DeKalb in Region 5), built two lavish attractions, and the city became something of a resort town. Baker's contribution was the Hotel Baker, built in 1928 on the west side of the Fox River. Featuring a two-story oval ballroom with a lighted dance floor, the hotel drew first-class entertainers. Three Venetian gondolas provided nightly rides on the river. Across the river, Angell and her husband, Lester Norris, built the Arcada Theatre, presenting vaudeville shows and nationally known entertainers.

ELGIN

Founded in 1835 by James T. Gifford, Elgin was a small stop on an old trail between Chicago and the thriving lead mines in Galena. Benjamin W. Raymond, the third mayor of Chicago, saw potential in the settlement, invested some resources, and convinced the Galena & Chicago Union Railroad to extend their line there in 1850. Incorporated as a city in 1854, Elgin became the home to the Borden Condensed Milk Company and the Elgin National Watch Company.

East coast dairyman Gail Borden invented the process for canning milk and obtained a patent in 1856. During the Civil War, condensed milk was a popular staple in the Union military. When the war ended, Borden built a new condensed-milk plant in Elgin, and the company became one of the nation's largest producers of canned milk, as well as processing other food products.

The Elgin National Watch Company, founded in 1864, produced fine-jeweled pocket watches. Within three years, in addition to its factory of more than 4,000 employees, the company operated a large boardinghouse, a watch-repair school, and an observatory to time its watches by the stars. Over the decades, however, market changes forced the company into the red. After a hundred years of creating world-famous watches, the Elgin Watch Company ceased operations. In 1966 the company's crowning symbol—a tower clock—was dynamited, ending the corporation that shared its name with the city.

Many of Elgin's cobblestone streets and Victorian homes are preserved in the Elgin Historic District, the Spring-Douglas Historic District, and the Elgin National Watch Historic District. These and other civic improvements are partly funded by revenue from the *Grand Victoria* Riverboat Casino on the Fox River. Also of interest is Lord's Park, established in Elgin by the Lord family in 1892. This lovely, 108-acre park includes the Elgin Public Museum, a historic 1898 pavilion, an aquatic center, a small zoo, and numerous recreational facilities.

EAST AND WEST DUNDEE

In the fall of 1834, settlers Jesse Newman and Joseph Russell staked land claims along the Fox River. Russell's property was on the east bank and Newman's was on the west, atop a bluff. Both settlements grew and eventually incorporated—West Dundee in 1867 and East Dundee in 1871. Many historians believe the Dundees were named after Dundee, Scotland.

The Chicago & North Western Railway arrived in 1854 in East Dundee. Through the late nineteenth and early twentieth centuries, cattle from nearby farms were herded through downtown West Dundee and across the river to the station. Later, a streetcar provided commuters with north-south transportation between Elgin and Carpentersville.

In 1871 David Haeger, a German immigrant who operated a grain elevator near Barrington, bought the Dundee Brick Company in East Dundee. After the Great Chicago Fire, the factory produced the majority of bricks used to rebuild Chicago. In 1914 Haeger's son Edmund introduced ceramic art to their product line and Dundee Brick Company became Haeger Potteries, which gained worldwide recognition. The original factory is now one of dozens of historic buildings in the Dundee Township Historic District, which comprises parts of East and West Dundee as well as neighboring Carpentersville. The district includes many commercial buildings along with churches, government buildings, schools, and private homes.

West Dundee was the birthplace of Helen Thompson "Ma" Sunday, wife of baseball player turned temperance preacher Billy Sunday, and the couple had a farm here in the early 1900s. The farm no longer exists, and most of the land was developed for single-family housing in the early 2000s. A historical plaque marks the site of the Sundays' farm.

Another West Dundee resident of note was famous detective Allan Pinkerton, whose fortuitous start in law enforcement began with the discovery of a gang of counterfeiters on an island in the Fox River in the 1840s.

Allan Pinkerton

A cooper by trade, Allan Pinkerton stumbled upon his future career after he moved to West Dundee. The Scottish-born Pinkerton had settled in Chicago with his new wife,

Joan Carfrae, in 1842. About a year later, upon learning that Dundee, forty miles north-west of Chicago, had a large concentration of Scots and also needed a cooper, Pinkerton relocated and opened a barrel-making shop near the Fox River.

Pinkerton took advantage of a free wood supply for barrel hoops from the forests along the Fox River. One day in 1847, while searching for wood, he rowed out to an uninhabited island and found remnants of a fire and some suspicious materials. After reporting his findings to Kane County sheriff Bartholomew C. Yates, Yates deputized Pinkerton, and together they caught nearly a dozen counterfeiters trying to cache their phony cash on the island.

Local merchants and the town council wanted Pinkerton to find the people who were passing the bogus banknotes. He tracked down the ringleader, John Craig, and, supported by local police, arrested the man in the Sauganash Hotel in Chicago. After this success, Pinkerton later wrote, "I suddenly found myself called upon from every quarter to undertake matters requiring detective skill."

In the late 1840s or early 1850s, Pinkerton accepted a position as a Cook County deputy sheriff and moved his wife and children back to Chicago. He was appointed Chicago's first detective and amassed a number of celebrated arrests while there. In 1855, tired of police work, Pinkerton opened Pinkerton National Detective Agency. As his agency broke open cases and collared crooks, his reputation mushroomed.

Pinkerton developed a code of conduct for his staff and insisted upon honesty and integrity as well as thoroughness. His procedures laid the groundwork for organizing other law enforcement agencies. Pinkerton also hired the nation's first woman detective, Kate Warne. During his tenure, Pinkerton uncovered a plot to assassinate President-elect Abraham Lincoln in Baltimore, and after the Civil War began, Maj. Gen. George B. McClellan asked Pinkerton to organize a secret service for the president.

After the war, Pinkerton resumed his private detective work, joined by his two sons, William and Robert. During a coal miners' dispute in eastern Pennsylvania, he squelched a secret labor society known as the Molly Maquires, further enhancing his national reputation. Out West, the Reno brothers, Jesse James's gang, Butch Cassidy's Wild Bunch, and countless others felt the heat of "a Pinkerton on their tail."

Allan Pinkerton died in 1884 and is buried in Graceland Cemetery in Chicago. Sons William and Robert ran the agency until their deaths, followed by other family members. After Robert Pinkerton II, a great-grandson of the founder, died in 1967, the company became a public corporation, and in 1999 it merged with Securitas AB, headquartered in Stockholm, Sweden. A historical marker now identifies the site of Pinkerton's home in West Dundee.

Eisenhower Expressway (I-290) and Roosevelt Road (IL 38)
CHICAGO (LOOP)–WHEATON
25 miles

This trip takes motorists through some of the most interesting towns in Chicago-land, from Oak Park, former home of architect Frank Lloyd Wright and author Ernest Hemingway, through Forest Park, site of the Haymarket Martyr's Monument, to Wheaton, the DuPage County seat and hometown of the comic Belushi brothers and the football-playing Grange brothers. Travelers may pick up IL 38 from I-290 at the Elmhurst interchange.

CHICAGO (LOOP)
See Region 7

OAK PARK

Oak Park, originally part of Cicero (see Cicero on earlier trip), became its own municipality in 1902. The first settlers in what became the village of Oak Park were Joseph and Betty Kettlestrings of Yorkshire, England, who moved here in 1837. The Kettlestrings, whose property bordered the Frink, Walker & Company stage line between Chicago and Galena, used their home as a tavern for travelers and farmers.

The arrival of the Galena & Chicago Union Railroad in 1848 brought an influx of settlers to the area, then known as Oak Ridge. The Kettlestrings saw an opportunity to subdivide their farm and sell lots to the new arrivals. They were selective about whom they sold to, however, offering lots only to "good people who were against saloons and for good schools and churches." In the 1850s Oak Ridge became part of Cicero.

The Great Chicago Fire of 1871 brought more newcomers to Oak Ridge, renamed Oak Park the same year. The village was one of many Chicago-area communities to ban alcohol sales, even before national Prohibition was enacted, and Oak Park remained "dry" until the 1970s. In 1901 the Chicago Transit Authority built an "L" station in Oak Park, attracting early commuters. The community was incorporated as a village the following year. Today Oak Park, known for its historic preservation and its range of architecture, has three National Historic Districts.

An impressive number of prominent individuals are associated with Oak Park. Dozens of scientists, writers, artists, entertainers, athletes, and business leaders hail from this village, including McDonald's corporation founder Ray Kroc, comic actors Bob Newhart and Betty White, and *Tarzan* creator Edgar Rice Burroughs. Sears, Roebuck & Company founder Richard Sears lived in Oak Park for many years, as did James Dewar, inventor of the Hostess Twinkie. Illinois governor Pat Quinn attended high school here. In spite of its long list of notable citizens, Oak Park is mostly known for two men—architect Frank Lloyd Wright and author Ernest Hemingway.

Frank Lloyd Wright, a native of Wisconsin, lived and worked in Oak Park from 1889 to 1909. Developing a philosophy he called "organic architecture," Wright founded the Prairie School of design and came to be considered by many to be the greatest American architect of all time. Visitors from all over the globe flock to Oak Park to see the town's two dozen Wright-designed structures, especially the Frank Lloyd Wright Home and Studio, now a museum. The Frank Lloyd Wright–Prairie School of Architecture Historic District, one of three National Historic Districts in Oak Park, contains numerous private homes designed by the famous architect. In addition, Wright's Unity Temple is a National Historic Landmark.

Ernest Hemingway, born in Oak Park in 1899, graduated from Oak Park and River Forest Township High School in 1917. After a brief stint reporting for the *Kansas City Star*, he volunteered with the Red Cross and served as an ambulance driver in Italy during World War I. Returning home in 1919, he resumed his career as a journalist in Toronto, Canada, and in Chicago.

In 1921 Hemingway returned to Europe, where he soon took up fiction writing, publishing his first book of fiction in 1923. Hemingway went on to become one of the most acclaimed American novelists in literary history. He traveled extensively and lived, among other places, in France, Florida, Spain, Cuba, and Idaho. In 1953 he won the Pulitzer Prize for fiction, and in 1954 he received the Nobel Prize in Literature. He commited suicide at his home in Ketchum, Idaho, in 1961.

The Ernest Hemingway Foundation of Oak Park manages two museums related to the great writer, the Ernest Hemingway Museum, housed in the Oak Park Arts Center, and the Hemingway Birthplace Museum. The foundation no longer owns the author's boyhood home; it was recently purchased by a private buyer.

Another notable, if less well known, Oak Park resident was chemist Percy Julian, who moved to the village with his wife and children in 1951. The Julians were the first African American family to live in Oak Park, and their arrival proved to be a turning point in the community. After their home was firebombed twice, townspeople rallied to their defense. The village adopted an Open Housing Ordinance in 1968 and later proclaimed that "diversity is Oak Park's strength."

FOREST PARK

The earliest inhabitants of today's Forest Park were the Potawatomi Indians, as evidenced by the two mounds, skeletons, and artifacts discovered in the town's Forest

Ernest Hemingway returned to his boyhood home in Oak Park after World War I to recuperate from his wounds. —Courtesy JFK Presidential Library & Museum, National Archives and Records Administration

Home Cemetery in 1900. A historical marker identifies the site of the ancient Indian village and burial ground. Interestingly, Forest Park is known not only for these early burial grounds but also for later ones—the community contains five cemeteries, several of which date to the 1870s. It is often said that Forest Park contains thirty times more dead "residents" than living ones.

The village's first settler was French trader Leon Bourassa, who built a cabin here in 1839. Seventeen years later, the Galena & Chicago Union Railroad established a shop and roundhouse here, bringing in about twenty-five workers and their families. Recognizing an opportunity, area settler John Henry Quick purchased a large tract of land the same year and platted a town, naming it Harlem after his New York hometown, which later became part of New York City. The village grew, incorporating in 1884. Harlem was renamed Forest Park—a combination of the names of its two neighboring villages, River Forest and Oak Park—in 1907.

Even before it was incorporated, Forest Park had more than its share of cemeteries. Chicago began running out of suitable land for burial in the 1860s, and Harlem landowner Ferdinand Haase saw a chance to establish a profitable industry. The land had good drainage and the village was accessible by train. By 1876 Forest Park had four cemeteries, and by 1912 it had six; many of their names reflect the community's German heritage—Jewish Waldheim (1870), Concordia (1872), German Waldheim (1873), Forest Home (1876), Altenheim (1885), and Woodlawn (1912). Forest Home merged with adjacent German Waldheim in 1968. Several of these cemeteries have interesting histories of their own (see below).

Perhaps to balance out its plethora of graveyards, Forest Park had, over the years, several recreational attractions. In the late 1800s, a small excursion boat took visitors up and down the Des Plaines River, docking at the well-appointed Haase Park. A thoroughbred horse-racing track was built 1894 and lasted until 1904, when a fire destroyed most of the structures. Next came a popular amusement park, opened in 1907. The Forest Park Amusement Park featured a ballroom, a casino, a beer garden, a swimming pool, a skating rink, and one of the largest roller coasters in the nation at the time. In 1922 it too burned down. The world-class Harlem Golf Course was created on the racetrack site in 1912. It closed in 1938, and a mall now stands at the location.

Today, Forest Park's blend of industrial, commercial, and residential properties has attracted new growth. The village now comprises a diverse population of commuters, local workers, and retirees (in addition to its deceased "residents").

Forest Home Cemetery and Haymarket Martyrs' Monument

Forest Park's largest cemetery is the nondenominational Forest Home, established in 1876 on the site of an Indian burial ground. In addition to the Indian burials are the graves of several prominent Illinoisans, including Charles Chamberlin, who wrote the lyrics to the Illinois state song; evangelist Billy Sunday and his wife, Helen; anarchist activist Emma Goldman; and Chicago radio personality Paul Harvey. Adjacent German Waldheim Cemetery became part of Forest Home in 1968.

The memorial that attracts the most interest at Forest Home is the Haymarket Martyrs' Monument, designed by sculptor Albert Weinert and unveiled on June 25, 1893. Although the Haymarket Square Riot took place miles away in Chicago, Forest

Home was chosen as the burial site for the Haymarket martyrs, the four labor activists who were hanged for their alleged role in the riot, and for the monument to them. The monument was designated a National Historic Landmark in 1997.

During the 1880s, Chicago was a hotbed for anarchists, socialists, and social reformers. Among other things, these organizers lobbied for better conditions for factory workers, seeking an eight-hour work day, increased workplace safety, and other improvements. After an ongoing strike at the McCormick Harvesting Machine Company factory in Chicago (see under Lower West Side and Pilsen in Region 7) erupted into a violent clash between strikebreakers and demonstrators on May 3, 1886, in which two protesters were killed, one of the organizers, August Spies, called for an outdoor rally in Haymarket Square the following evening.

Of the anticipated 20,000 attendees, fewer than 3,000 actually turned out, while more than 150 armed police officers stood ready to quell any disturbance. The rally was nearly over and the crowd was already dispersing when the police advanced on the crowd. An unknown person threw an explosive device into the line of police, killing seven officers and injuring many more. In the ensuing gunfire, four protesters were killed and at least fifty were wounded. Afterward, nearly all press reports sided with the police. A monument to the seven slain policemen was erected in Haymarket Square in 1889. It now stands in front of the Chicago Police Headquarters (see under Douglas in Region 7).

Although the bomb thrower was never identified, police later arrested about a dozen anarchist activists, most of whom were not even at the rally when the bomb

August Spies, editor of the Chicago Anarchist, *was one of the four anarchists hanged for his role in the 1886 Haymarket Square bombing in Chicago. This sketch appeared in* Frank Leslie's Illustrated Newspaper, *May 15, 1886.* —Author's collection

was thrown. One man, Albert Parsons, turned himself in, in solidarity with the accused. Some of those arrested were released, but eight of them—Parsons, George Engel, Samuel Fielden, Adolph Fischer, Louis Lingg, Oscar Neebe, Michael Schwab, and August Spies—were indicted as accessories to murder. At the trial, all eight defendants were found guilty. Seven were sentenced to hang, while one, Neebe, received a fifteen-year prison term. Appeals were heard by the Illinois Supreme Court and later by the U.S. Supreme Court, but the verdicts were upheld in all cases.

The day before the hanging, Gov. Richard Oglesby granted clemency to Fielden and Schwab, whose sentences were commuted to life imprisonment. That night, one of the condemned prisoners, Louis Lingg, committed suicide in his cell. The next morning, November 11, 1887, Engel, Fischer, Parsons, and Spies were hanged. They were buried at German Waldheim (now Forest Home) Cemetery. Seven years after the incident, Gov. John P. Altgeld denounced the judge for conducting an unfair trial and pardoned Neebe, Fielden, and Schwab.

In 1893 the Haymarket Martyrs' Monument was erected near the graves of the four executed men. It is engraved with part of the final statement of Albert Parsons, who spoke these prophetic words as the noose was placed around his neck: "The day will come when our silence will be more powerful than the voices you are throttling today."

Other Cemeteries

The first cemetery established in Forest Park was Jewish Waldheim, built in 1870; its first burial took place in 1873. Made up of 250 sections, it is the largest Jewish cemetery complex in the Chicago metro area. Among its most famous gravesites is that of movie producer Michael Todd, third husband of actress Elizabeth Taylor. Todd was killed in a plane crash in 1958 and interred here under his real name, Avrom Hirsch Goldbogen. Two decades later, in 1977, grave robbers unearthed his body looking for a diamond ring rumored to have been buried with him. Finding no ring, the robbers left the body in some brush, where police found it two days later.

Concordia Cemetery is a lovely and well-kept burial ground, noted for its obelisks and marble angel sculptures. Notably, it is the burial place of about twenty-three of the victims of Chicago's 1915 *Eastland* boating disaster (see under Wacker Drive in Region 7).

Altenheim Cemetery, a small graveyard adjacent to Concordia, was established shortly after the opening of Altenheim German Old People's Home in 1885 as a burial place for the home's residents when they died. The nursing home operated for more than a century before it closed in 2000, and the Victorian building was converted into apartments for independent seniors. The grounds have been subdivided for various uses, including a small community farm and a military helicopter training field; plans for a high school football stadium and a privately operated ice rink are under consideration at the time of this writing.

The nondenominational Woodlawn Cemetery, established in 1912, is best known for its Showmen's Rest section, the burial place of hundreds of circus folk, including nearly sixty of the victims of a 1918 circus-train wreck. The five life-size elephant statues that surround Showmen's Rest make it a local landmark.

Showmen's Rest had actually been created two years before the wreck as a cemetery for circus and road-show performers, established by Buffalo Bill Cody and the

Showmen's League of America. On June 22, 1918, a horrific tragedy occurred that would soon make use of the graveyard. In the early morning hours, a twenty-six-car Hagenbeck-Wallace Circus train on its way to Hammond, Indiana, stalled on the tracks. In spite of warning signals, the driver of an empty train, asleep at the wheel, slammed into it from behind. The crash killed dozens of the passengers, and a subsequent fire killed several more. The final death toll was eighty-six. The grave markers show that about forty of the victims' names were unknown, while several others were known only by their stage names.

WHEATON

Sometime in the 1830s, brothers Jesse and Warren Wheaton arrived in Illinois from Connecticut and purchased about 1,000 acres of the land that now encompasses downtown Wheaton. In 1849 the Galena & Chicago Union Railroad built a station on land donated by the Wheatons and others, naming the stop Wheaton. A town was soon platted around the depot, and Wheaton was incorporated as a city in 1859. The following year, after Warren Wheaton donated some money and land to Illinois Institute, founded in 1853, the school was renamed Wheaton College in his honor. From its founding, the college served as a refuge on the Underground Railroad.

In 1857 Wheaton boosters began to lobby the state legislature to hold an election to move the DuPage County seat from Naperville to their city. Wheaton lost its first bid, but ten years later, after a very close vote, the county seat was moved to Wheaton. The city immediately built a courthouse, but over the next few decades the county

The second DuPage County Courthouse in Wheaton,
early 1900s —Courtesy Center for History, Wheaton, Illinois

government outgrew this space, and a new courthouse was erected in 1896. This still-standing structure served DuPage County until 1990, when a third courthouse replaced it. The old courthouse, used for classrooms for a time and now converted to condominiums, was listed on the NRHP in 1978.

In 1894 Wheaton became the site of the first eighteen-hole golf course in the United States, the Chicago Golf Club. The city became a magnet for golfers as well as equipment manufacturers and stores, instructors, greenskeepers, and the like. Chicago Golf Club founder Charles B. Macdonald (1855–1939), sometimes referred to as the "Father of Golf Architecture" in America, was inducted into the World Golf Hall of Fame in 2007. The course still exists as the oldest (and among the most exclusive) in the nation.

Historical museums in Wheaton include the DuPage County Historical Museum, the DuPage Heritage Gallery, the Robert R. McCormick Museum, the First Division Museum (honoring the First Infantry Division of World War I) and the Wheaton History Center (two locations). Wheaton was once the home of a number of celebrities, including legendary comic actor John Belushi and his brother, James, as well as journalist Bob Woodward of Watergate fame, football great Red Grange and his brother Garland, and astronomer Edwin Hubble. The Wheaton National Baseball Hall of Fame honors a dozen natives and former residents of Wheaton who played in the Major League.

I-294 (Tri-State Tollway) and US 14/IL 58 (Dempster Street)
I-290 (ELMHURST)–SKOKIE
24 miles

This trip takes us north from Elmhurst, in DuPage County, past O'Hare Airport (see Region 7) to Des Plaines, then east on Dempster Street to Skokie.

ELMHURST

Before the first settlers arrived in this area around 1836, Potawatomi Indians camped along Salt Creek near the future city of Elmhurst. In 1843 settler Gerry Bates opened an inn called the Cottage Hill Tavern; two years later, the settlement of Cottage Hill was founded. The Galena & Chicago Union Railroad came through Cottage Hill in 1849. The settlement was renamed Elmhurst twenty years later. It was incorporated as a village in 1882 and reorganized as a city in 1910.

One noteworthy resident of Elmhurst was poet Carl Sandburg. Born in Galesburg in 1878, Sandburg moved to Elmhurst in 1919 and lived here until 1930. The house he occupied no longer exists. (See also under Galesburg in Region 2.)

From 1914 to 1928 Elmhurst was home to the Lindlahr Sanitarium, founded by Dr. Henry Lindlahr. The doctor, believing in the theraputic value of fresh air and exercise, developed what he called the "nature cure" for depressed or anxious patients, as opposed to using drugs, surgery, and other conventional treatments. The sanitarium's most famous patient was labor union leader Eugene Debs, who died of heart failure there in 1926, at age seventy, a few weeks after being admitted.

Like Forest Park (see previous trip), Elmhurst has five major cemeteries. The most notable is Mount Emblem Cemetery, established in 1925. Mount Emblem is known for its Old Dutch Windmill, a.k.a. the Fischer Windmill, constructed at this site in 1850. The windmill is the only remaining structure from the farm on which the cemetery was built.

A more uplifting place to visit than a cemetery is the art deco York Theatre, continuously operating as a movie house since 1924. On the second floor of the York is the headquarters of the Theatre Historical Society of America, a movie theater preservation group founded in 1969, as well as the society's American Movie Palace Museum.

Visitors may delve further into Elmhurst's history at the Elmhurst Historical Museum, located in the 1874 Glos Mansion. In addition to this museum, the Elmhurst Historical Society manages the restored 1846 Churchville Schoolhouse, listed on the National Register of Historic Places in 1999. The city also boasts several homes on the NRHP.

PARK RIDGE

Park Ridge has had more than its share of famous and distinguished residents. Two of the biggest are Hillary Rodham Clinton and Harrison Ford, both of whom grew up here. Movie star Harrison (then called Harry) Ford graduated from Maine East High School in 1960, while Clinton, who would later become the First Lady of the United States, a U.S. senator, and Secretary of State, graduated from Maine South High School in 1965. Besides Ford, other well-known actors from Park Ridge include Karen Black, Carrie Snodgress, and Gary Cole.

Park Ridge, in Maine Township, began as Pennyville. In the early 1850s, shortly after the railroad arrived in this area, enterprising brickmaker George Penny found clay deposits in the soil here and partnered with fellow businessman Robert Meacham to establish the Penny & Meacham Brickworks in 1854. Three years later, the partners subdivided the property surrounding their factory and changed the community's name to Brickton. The village was incorporated under its current name in 1873. The brick factory closed around 1880, having exhausted the clay deposits.

In 1910 Park Ridge, wanting to remain independent from Chicago, incorporated as a city, but it saw little growth until the 1950s. The completion of nearby O'Hare International Airport in 1955 and of the Northwest (Kennedy) Expressway in 1960, among other developments, made Park Ridge a convenient location for raising a family. Today it has a population of more than 37,000.

During much of the twentieth century, Park Ridge was something of a mecca for artists as the home of a well-known artists' colony. The Kalo Arts and Crafts Community House, which operated from 1900 to 1970, trained artists and craftspeople for careers in the arts, particularly in silversmithing and jewelry making. Among those artists who worked at the Park Ridge colony were Grant Wood, best known for his painting *American Gothic*, and sculptor and industrial designer Alfonso Iannelli. In 2011 the Kalo Foundation acquired Iannelli's former home and studio with plans to restore and renovate the building as a museum and educational center.

While living in Park Ridge, Iannelli helped design the city's art deco Pickwick Theatre movie palace. Built in 1928 with a distinctive marquee and a one-hundred-foot-high tower, the iconic theater was added to the NRHP in 1975. The Pickwick and the Iannelli studio are two of seven recognized local landmark structures in Park Ridge. Other historical buildings here include dozens of Sears catalog houses and other mail-order kit homes. Manufactured and sold in the early twentieth century, the house kits helped families on a budget to have their own homes.

DES PLAINES

The Des Plaines River attracted settlers to this area beginning in the 1830s, and the next several decades brought an influx of German immigrants. In 1852 a sawmill was built here to provide lumber for construction of the Illinois & Wisconsin Railway, which arrived in 1854. Three years later, after the Chicago, St. Paul & Fond du Lac Railroad bought out the Illinois & Wisconsin, the community of Rand, named after early set-tler Socrates Rand, was platted. In 1859 the railroad, now called the Chicago & North Western Railway, changed the station's name to Des Plaines, after the nearby river. A decade later, the vicinity of the train station, including Rand, incorporated as the village of Des Plaines.

In 1867 a group of Chicago Methodist ministers established the Des Plaines Meth-odist Camp Ground as an outdoor Christian meeting place, later adding indoor-assembly buildings and, eventually, more than a hundred cottages. The facility, which has remained in continuous operation since its founding, was listed on the NRHP in 2005.

Des Plaines grew steadily, and in 1925 it was incorporated as a city. In 1934, dur-ing the Great Depression, the Civilian Conservation Corps built a work camp near the river. The CCC occupied the camp until World War II, when it became a prisoner-of-war camp. Camp Pine housed about two hundred prisoners, who were sent to work on nearby farms. After the war, Boy Scout and Girl Scout troops used the camp's buildings.

Des Plaines saw major growth in the 1950s with the opening of O'Hare Interna-tional Airport (see Region 7) to commercial flights in 1955 and the construction of two interstate highways a few years later.

The 1950s also brought to Des Plaines what would become an integral part of American popular culture—the first McDonald's franchise restaurant. On April 15, 1955, future McDonald's CEO Ray Kroc, a native of Oak Park, opened the first restau-rant established under the McDonald's Systems franchise company. Sales on the first day totaled less than four hundred dollars, but Kroc would eventually become a billionaire.

Although the original building was torn down in 1984, the company later created a replica restaurant using the McDonald brothers' original blueprints. The McDonald's First Store Museum features original equipment and mannequins dressed in 1955 uni-forms. The inside is not open to the public; the museum grounds, where visitors may look into the windows, are open seasonally.

Exhibits from the city's colorful past are displayed at the Des Plaines History Cen-ter, located in a former savings and loan building, and at the restored 1907 Kinder House next door.

SKOKIE

Part of Niles Township, established in 1850, Skokie was incorporated as the village of Niles Centre (later spelled Center) in 1888. By this time, the area was already well settled by immigrant farmers from Germany and Luxembourg. Due to its proximity to Chicago, Niles Center became urbanized more quickly than other farming communities in the region; by the 1910s the village had paved roads, sewers, and telephone service. The community experienced a housing boom in the 1920s, after the Chicago Rapid Transit Company extended its "L" line to Niles Center. In 1940, to avoid confusion with nearby Niles, the village changed its name to Skokie.

The construction of the Edens Expressway and other improvements in the 1950s brought so much growth to Skokie that by 1962 it had become the nation's most populated community organized as a village, and for many years it promoted itself as "the world's largest village." During this period of growth, demographic changes in adjacent Chicago led to a particularly large influx of Jewish residents and the construction of many synagogues and Jewish schools in Skokie. By the mid-1960s, Skokie's population was 40 percent Jewish, the largest percentage of Jewish residents in Chicagoland. Later, Asian Americans, African Americans, and Hispanics added to the population. This diversity has, over the years, made Skokie a target for racist hate groups. The best-known example of this is the attempted Nazi rally of 1977.

In 1977 the National Socialist Party of America (NSPA), a branch of the American Nazi Party, sought to hold a rally and parade in Skokie, igniting a firestorm of

This German railcar, on permanent display at the Illinois Holocaust Museum, is the kind used by the Nazis to transport Jews to death camps in Poland.
—Courtesy Illinois Holocause Museum & Education Center, Skokie

controversy. After a county court issued an injunction to stop the march, the American Civil Liberties Union took up the case as a free-speech issue. A circuit court ultimately upheld the NSPA's right to march in Skokie, but by that time the Nazis had already held their demonstration in Chicago, so a Skokie rally never took place.

This controversy was not the only racist episode in Skokie's recent history. In 1999 an African American Skokie resident was killed in a three-day shooting spree by white supremacist Benjamin Smith, who also murdered a Korean student in Indiana and wounded nine Orthodox Jews in Chicago. A year and a half later, the Ku Klux Klan held a rally in Skokie; the demonstrators were pelted with snowballs. In 2009 neo-Nazis demonstrated at the opening of the Illinois Holocaust Museum and Education Center in Skokie.

The holocaust museum began as a response to the 1977 Nazi march debate. The Holocaust Memorial Foundation of Illinois opened its first museum in a small Skokie storefront in 1981. After years of fundraising and planning, the new center opened in April 2009. One of its primary exhibits is an original boxcar used to transport Jewish prisoners to Nazi concentration camps during World War II.

On a lighter note, Skokie has served as a filming location for many motion pictures, beginning in the silent era and especially in the 1980s, when *The Blues Brothers*, *Risky Business*, and *The Breakfast Club* were filmed here. More of the area's history can be explored at the Skokie Heritage Museum complex, which includes a historic firehouse and an 1847 log cabin.

I-94
SKOKIE—LIBERTYVILLE
29 miles

On this trip we follow I-94 north to a number of interesting sites, including the famed Chicago Botanic Garden in Glencoe. Most of the way, I-94 is called the Edens Expressway, merging with US 41 (Skokie Highway) between northern Wilmette and the botanic garden, then veering west to hook up with I-294 (the Tri-State Tollway) north to Libertyville. This stretch of the interstate passes by an astounding number of golf courses and country clubs, attesting to the affluence of Chicago's northern suburbs.

SKOKIE
See previous trip

GLENVIEW

When Northfield Township was established in 1850, the area later known as Glenview was called South Northfield. After the Great Chicago Fire in 1871, the Milwaukee & St. Paul Railway ran a single track through this area, primarily to transport supplies for rebuilding Chicago. The station at South Northfield was built in 1872.

In 1878 the community changed its name to Oak Glen, but since the railroad had an Oak Glen station elsewhere, it renamed the South Northfield station Barr. In 1895, because of the other Oak Glen, the post office, too, insisted on a new name. When residents chose the name Glenview for the post office, they also renamed the rail depot. Glenview was incorporated as a village in 1899.

In the meantime, around 1893, members of the Swedenborgian Church purchased forty acres nearby and built a small cluster of homes along with a church, school, and clubhouse. When Glenview was organized as a village, the Swedenborgian community, known as The Park, was included within its borders.

Shortly after its incorporation, Glenview was modernized with roads, sidewalks, streetlights, and public water and sewer systems. Even more advanced technology came to the village in 1929, when Curtiss Flying Service opened a large airfield, Curtiss-Reynolds Field, northwest of town. The four-hundred-plus-acre airfield was intended as an alternative to Chicago's Midway Airport, but when the stock market crashed, those plans were shelved and the half-finished facility was used as a flight-training school. Air races were held there in 1930 and again in 1933, the latter in conjunction with the Chicago Century of Progress. Shortly after that, Curtiss Flying Service merged with Wright Aeronautical to become the Curtiss-Wright Corporation.

In 1937 the U.S. Navy, in need of more space, leased part of the Curtiss-Wright facility, calling their half the Naval Reserve Aviation Base Glenview. During World War II, the Navy purchased the entire airfield and expanded it extensively. Renamed Naval Air Station Glenview, the base became the primary training facility for aircraft-carrier pilots. It was later used by the Army and Navy Reserves and the Coast Guard.

After the base was closed in 1995, the village of Glenview oversaw the property's redevelopment into homes, golf courses, public parks, offices, and commercial space. The revamped 1.5-square-mile district was dubbed The Glen. Hangar One, which includes the control tower, was listed on the NRHP in 1998. The Naval Air Station Museum Glenview, which originally occupied a space at The Glen, moved into a new building nearby in 2006.

The old air base is not the only historical site preserved in Glenview. Another major landmark—much older than the airfield—is The Grove, former home of Dr. John Kennicott, one of Glenview's earliest settlers.

Dr. Kennicott, originally from New Orleans, moved to the area that would become Glenview and built his estate, The Grove, in 1836. He was the first professionally trained physician in the Glenview area, and his brother, William, was the first dentist. In addition to practicing medicine, Dr. Kennicott focused a good deal of his attention to agriculture at The Grove. His son, Robert, grew up to be a prominent scientist and in 1856 helped found the Academy of Natural Sciences (later the Chicago Academy of Sciences) in Chicago, among other accomplishments. In May 1866, while on an expedition in Alaska, Robert Kennicott died of heart failure at age thirty. His body was returned to Illinois, and he was buried at The Grove.

The Kennicotts' 123-acre farm, designated a National Historic Landmark in 1976, has been developed into an outdoor nature and history museum. The complex includes the Kennicotts' 1856 house, an interpretive center, several replica buildings, and other structures as well as extensive walking trails through the park's prairies, forests, and wetlands.

Another outdoor museum, the Wagner Farm, represents early agrarian life in Glenview. The original farm, established in the 1850s, was much larger, but it dwindled over

Robert Kennicott, explorer and naturalist —Courtesy The Grove National Historic Landmark, Glenview Park District

the years to less than twenty acres. The Glenview Park District bought the remaining land in 1998 and developed it into a living-history museum. The Wagner Farm Heritage Center was added in 2006.

In addition to all these sites is the Glenview History Center, which includes a museum and an archive library operated by the Glenview Historical Society. The museum is housed in a restored 1864 farmhouse, and the library occupies a newer building designed to resemble a Victorian coachhouse.

SKOKIE LAGOONS AND CHICAGO BOTANIC GARDEN

As I-94 heads north from Glenview to Deerfield, it passes the 190-acre Skokie Lagoons reservoir and nature preserve. Originally a marsh, it presented a flooding problem to farmers who settled in the area. In the 1930s the Civilian Conservation Corps transformed the giant bog into seven interconnected lagoons suitable for recreation and wildlife viewing. Over the years, however, the shorelines became degraded, so in the 1990s the Chicago Audubon Society and the Cook County Forest Preserve District began an extensive restoration program to stabilize erosion and clear out invasive plant species.

Although the lagoons preserve is managed by the county, its main address is Glencoe. Our next stop, the delightful Chicago Botanic Garden, is also in Glencoe. This

This scene of tranquil beauty is one of many that beckons tourists to the Chicago Botanic Garden in Glencoe. —Author's collection

world-class public botanical garden, established in 1972, covers 385 acres and contains 2.4 million plant species. Managed by the Chicago Horticultural Society, the site is divided into nine islands with twenty-four display gardens surrounded by four natural habitats—lake, river, prairie, and woodland.

The Chicago Botanic Garden is dedicated to plant conservation, public education, and botanical and environmental research. Among the institutions based here are the Joseph Regenstein Jr. School of the Chicago Botanic Garden and the recently built Daniel F. and Ada L. Rice Plant Conservation Science Center. The school, which began in 1990, offers degree programs in various plant-related subjects. The conservation center, opened in 2009, features labs and teaching facilities for scientists, land managers, and students.

DEERFIELD

Deerfield's story is a mixed bag of preservation and progress. Located near both the Des Plaines River and the North Branch of the Chicago River, the settlement attracted farmers in the nineteenth century and industry in the twentieth. Today, numerous corporations, including Walgreens and Baxter Healthcare International, have their headquarters here, keeping the economy humming in the new millennium. At the same time, the community values historic preservation, supporting the Deerfield Historic Village, the Edward L. Ryerson Historic District and Conservation Area, the 1917 train depot, and even a three-hundred-year-old tree that was used as a landmark by Native Americans and early settlers.

In its infancy Deerfield was known as Cadwell's Corner, for early settler Jacob Cadwell, who homesteaded here in 1835. In 1840 the settlement was called Le Clair, and ten years later it was rechristened Deerfield. It was incorporated as a village in 1903, but it remained a small agricultural community until the 1950s, when better roads and highways attracted commuters and modern industries. Today's Deerfield is more than a suburban bedroom community for Chicago commuters; many of the village's 18,000 residents are employed locally, and the community takes pride in preserving its own heritage.

The town's main historical attraction is the Deerfield Historic Village, an outdoor museum and headquarters of the Deerfield Area Historical Society. The oldest of the museum's three restored buildings is the Caspar Ott Cabin, built in 1837. The others are the 1847 George Luther House and the 1854 Bartle Sacker Farmhouse. In addition, the village has two replica structures, a carriage house and a one-room schoolhouse.

Just west of Deerfield, the Edward L. Ryerson Conservation Area (a.k.a. Ryerson Woods), a five-hundred-plus-acre nature preserve, features the Greek Revival mansion known as Brushwood, former home of the Ryerson family. Steel magnate Edward L. Ryerson built the estate in 1942, and in the 1960s he began to donate much of his Deerfield-area property to the Lake County Forest Preserve District.

LIBERTYVILLE

In 1835 settler George Vardin purchased a large tract of land, built a cabin, and platted a small settlement he called Vardin's Grove. He left a year later, but the settlement remained. In 1837 a post office was established there under the name Independence Grove, later changed to Libertyville. Libertyville got a boost when the Chicago-Milwaukee stage line came through in 1863, and the arrival of the Chicago, Milwaukee & St. Paul Railway seventeen years later helped the community grow even more. These improvements led Libertyville to incorporate as a village in 1882.

A devastating fire in 1895 destroyed many of the village's wooden buildings downtown, though one frame house, a two-story summer home built by Ansel Cook in 1879, survived the blaze. The home was later deeded to the village for a public library; it now serves as the headquarters for the Libertyville-Mundelein Historical Society.

In 1906 Samuel Insull, founder of Commonwealth Edison, purchased the first 160 acres of what would become his 4,000-plus-acre property, dubbed Hawthorne-Melody Farms, south of Libertyville. But the Great Depression ruined him, and he sold off the farm. In 1935 part of it was sold to prominent Chicago attorney and future Illinois governor Adlai E. Stevenson II, who lived at the estate for the next twenty-seven years. The house he built in 1938 still stands and is open for tours. The building also houses the Adlai E. Stevenson Center on Democracy, which "seeks to enhance the global understanding and practice of democracy."

Off I-94 just east of Libertyville is Lambs Farm, a highly regarded facility for people with developmental disabilities. The organization originally started in 1961 as Lambs Pet Shop in Chicago in 1961. Four years later, philanthropist W. Clement Stone bought and donated a seventy-acre farm in Libertyville to help expand the program. Lambs Farm now houses more than 250 residents and provides training and support services for the developmentally disabled throughout the region. It raises most of its funds from its tourist attractions, which include a pet shop, a petting zoo, amusement rides, a gift shop, a thrift store, and a restaurant.

A little farther east, in the unincorporated community of Rondout, a historical marker on IL 176 (Rockland Road) describes the 1924 Rondout Train Robbery, which at the time was the largest train robbery in United States history in terms of amount stolen.

The Great Train Robbery

On the night of June 12, 1924, a Chicago, Milwaukee & St. Paul train was on its way to Milwaukee from Chicago carrying about $3 million in cash, bonds, and jewels. Unbeknownst to the crew, two members of a band of outlaws known as the Newton Gang had boarded the train disguised as crewmen. Their accomplice was Chicago postal inspector William J. Fahy, who provided inside information about the shipment.

The train was passing the remote rail crossing at Rondout when Jess and Willis Newton pulled out guns and forced the engineer to halt the train. Waiting about two miles up the track were several gang members, armed with pistols and sawed-off shotguns, and four getaway cars. After shooting through the windows, the bandits forced the guards to open the door of the mail car, drag the sacks of money across the tracks, and load them into the waiting automobiles. Amid the darkness and confusion, Brent Glasscock mistook his comrade Wylie Newton for a guard and shot him several times. The gangsters put the wounded man into one of the cars before speeding off, marring a clean getaway.

The car carrying the wounded man eventually headed back to Chicago to hole up in a friend's apartment and find a doctor. Police were tipped off and raided the place, apprehending the wounded Wylie and two of his brothers. Jess Newton and Glasscock evaded capture for a while, hiding much of the loot, but eventually all eight of the conspirators were caught and arrested. All were convicted in federal court later that year, receiving various sentences. Most of the money was recovered, but about $1 million was never found.

US 12 (Rand Road)
DES PLAINES–SPRING GROVE
38 miles

This trip passes through what has historically been a recreational region of lakeside resorts, nature preserves, golf courses, and a major racetrack.

DES PLAINES
See previous trip

ARLINGTON HEIGHTS

In 1853 early settler William Dunton founded the rail stop of Dunton, which evolved into Arlington Heights, incorporated as a village in 1887. Since 1927, the town has been home of the internationally recognized Arlington Park Racetrack, established on former farmland by millionaire California horse breeder Harry D. "Curley" Brown. A fire in 1985 burned part of the facility, including the grandstand. A new six-story grandstand was completed in 1989.

Horses enter the first turn at Arlington Park during this early 1970s race. The grandstand was destroyed by a fire in 1985; the park re-opened in 1989 as Arlington International Racecourse.
—Courtesy Arlington Heights Historical Society

Worth a visit is the Arlington Heights Historical Museum complex, which contains several historic structures, including a 1906 soda pop factory. Nearby, the Arlington Heights Memorial Library has one of the most extensive genealogy and local history collections in the state.

LAKE ZURICH

To the Potawatomi and early French trappers, Lake Zurich, originally called Cedar Lake, brought comfort and sustenance. In the 1830s, Vermont native Seth Paine moved from Chicago to Cedar Lake and opened Union Store, a trading center. In 1841 he changed the lake's name to Lake Zurich because its beauty reminded him of Zurich, Switzerland. A dedicated idealist, Paine built a three-story meeting hall with a store, a meeting room, a small school, and living quarters for needy people. He called it the Stable of Humanity. It is believed that Paine, an abolitionist, used the building's basement as a stop on the Underground Railroad. In 1868 he returned to Chicago, where he died three years later.

Lake Zurich was incorporated as a village in 1896. Beginning in the 1920s, it was a popular summer resort town. Over the years, residential development increased the village's permanent population. In 2006 it was named one of the top one hundred places to raise a family and one of the top twenty-five affordable places to live.

Main Street, Lake Zurich, 1930s —Courtesy Ela Historical Society

WAUCONDA

The 380-acre Bangs Lake was an unnamed body of water when Justus Bangs and Elihu Hubbard arrived in 1836, both building cabins along its shoreline. The settlement that grew up around the lake was dubbed Wauconda, a Winnebago word that means "spirit water." It was incorporated as a village in 1877.

Wauconda was one of many stops on the Janesville, Wisconsin, to Chicago stage route, but a century after its founding, the population was still less than 1,000. After World War II, many Chicagoans, who began to see Wauconda and Bangs Lake as a respite from the rigors of urban congestion, built cottages along the lakeshore. Now a popular suburb, Wauconda currently has more than 13,000 residents.

Wauconda's highlight attraction is the Lake County Discovery Museum, an interactive museum of history, art, and culture established in the 1970s. The museum is notable for the Curt Teich Postcard Archives, the nation's largest permanent exhibition on the history and significance of postcards. Also of interest is the Wauconda Bog Nature Preserve, named a National Natural Landmark in 1972.

SPRING GROVE

The village of Spring Grove, named for the area's natural springs and groves of trees, was settled in the 1830s as a farming community called English Prairie. The most notable historical event in this village was the invention of the vertical grain silo.

In 1873 area dairy farmer Fred Hatch, a graduate of Illinois Industrial University (now the University of Illinois), constructed North America's first tower-style silo. Hatch built the sixteen-foot-high wooden structure atop a rock-and-mortar foundation as a way to keep his cow feed drier and more easily accessible than with underground storage pits, bins, or grain houses. The idea caught on. Later silos improved on Hatch's design, using cylindrical shapes and new materials such as steel and concrete.

Hatch's silo was used until 1919. Although only the foundation remains today, a replica of it was erected in Spring Grove's Lyle Thomas Park in 1984, and the original site was designated a Historic Landmark of Agricultural Engineering by the American Society of Agricultural Engineers.

While industry now plays a significant part in the local economy, Spring Grove is still a quiet community with a rural feel. The village also reaps recreation and tourism dollars as the home of Chain O'Lakes State Park.

Sheridan Road
CHICAGO (ROGERS PARK)–WAUKEGAN
35 miles

This scenic route follows Sheridan Road, which hugs the Lake Michigan shoreline most of the way from the far north Chicago neighborhood of Rogers Park to Wisconsin, becoming IL 137 in suburban North Chicago. Those in a hurry may hop onto the roughly parallel US 41 (Skokie Highway) to reach the same destinations.

Another alternative route, Green Bay Road, which closely parallels Sheridan Road between Evanston and North Chicago, follows the most historic path, but modern development has broken up the original military road, which went from Fort Dearborn in downtown Chicago (now Clark Street; see Region 7) to Fort Howard in Green Bay, Wisconsin, 250 miles north. The original pathway was formed by large mammals such as woolly mammoths that followed the high ridges along the lakeshore during their seasonal migrations. Later, the trail was used by Indians, and later still by white traders and settlers. In 1832 Congress established the Green Bay Trail as an official military road. For those who want to leave their car, a parallel recreation trail now runs between Wilmette and Highland Park.

No matter which route you choose, this trip traverses Chicago's North Shore, which comprises some of the wealthiest communities in the Midwest: Wilmette, Winnetka, Glencoe, Highland Park, and Lake Forest among others. Most of these towns began as farming communities in the mid-1800s and expanded as the real estate was developed. Due to their affluence, North Shore residents hired some of the world's premier architects—including Frank Lloyd Wright, David Adler, Howard Van Doren Shaw, and others—to design their homes, making this tour an architecture lover's dream.

CHICAGO (ROGERS PARK)
See Region 7

EVANSTON

Early French traders knew this area as Grosse Pointe, so called for the large tip of land that jutted out into Lake Michigan here. Among the first settlers at Grosse Pointe was New Jersey native Maj. Edward H. Mulford, who purchased 160 acres in 1836 and built a cabin, later erecting a tavern along the Green Bay Trail. The tavern, called Ten-Mile House, was also used as a post office and a courtroom; Mulford served as postmaster and justice of the peace. Before long, a number of others settled in the Grosse Pointe area, and a small community known as Ridgeville evolved.

The face of Ridgeville changed forever in 1855, after nine Methodist Church leaders founded a new university on a 379-acre farm facing Lake Michigan. They platted the land for the school as well as for a surrounding town, which they named Evanston after one of the nine founders, Dr. John Evans. Northwestern University opened in November 1855. Its first building, later called Old College, contained a chapel, two meeting rooms, several classrooms, and a few attic spaces that served as dorm rooms. Over the next 150-plus years, the school became one of the most respected research universities in the nation. Also built on the campus was a Methodist seminary, Garrett Biblical Institute, now called Garrett-Evangelical Theological Seminary, established in 1853.

With the success of the university and seminary, Evanston grew. It was incorporated as a town in 1863 and as a city in 1872. Because the school's charter stipulated that no liquor be sold within a four-mile radius of the campus, Evanston remained "dry" for more than a century. Local laws prohibited alcohol until 1972, when the sale of spirits was allowed in restaurants; the sale of packaged liquor was permitted eleven years later.

Evanston's blue laws went so far as to forbid the selling of ice cream sodas on the Sabbath. This fact gave rise to the claim that the ice cream sundae—an ice cream soda without the soda, with the spelling of Sunday altered to avoid offending the pious—was invented in Evanston in 1890. Several other American towns also claim the distinction of being the birthplace of the sundae, however, and Evanston's story is undocumented, so the debate rages on.

Because of its rocky coast, Evanston was never a port city. Ships on Lake Michigan had to navigate past the hazardous shoals along the city's shoreline to enter the narrow

Officers of the World's Woman Christian Temperance Union with their president, Frances E. Willard (center)
—Author's collection

channel that led to the harbor at Chicago. After nearly thirty shipwrecks occurred here, including the 1860 collision of the freighter *Augusta* with the passenger steamer *Lady Elgin*, in which more than four hundred lives were lost, the public clamored for a lighthouse to be built to warn ships of the danger. Finally, in the 1870s, the Grosse Pointe Lighthouse was built. The structure, which soon became an Evanston icon, operated well into the twentieth century and still functions as a secondary navigational aid. It was named a National Historic Landmark in 1999. The *Lady Elgin* shipwreck site, near Highwood, was placed on the NRHP the same year.

Evanston has had more than its share of notable residents. Among them was women's rights and temperance crusader Frances E. Willard, who lived in Evanston from 1857 until her death in 1898. After she died, her Evanston home served as headquarters for the Woman's Christian Temperance Union. The house, built in 1865 and expanded in 1878, was declared a National Historic Landmark in 1965. Today it is the Frances Willard House Museum and archive library.

Another world-renowned Evanston resident was Charles Gates Dawes, Calvin Coolidge's vice president and recipient of the 1925 Nobel Peace Prize. The prize was awarded to Dawes for the Dawes Plan, devised to reorganize the German fiscal system after World War I. Dawes's 1894 home, in which he lived from 1909 to 1951, was declared a National Historic Landmark in 1976. It now houses the Evanston History Center.

Evanston nurtured a large number of celebrities in the modern era as well, especially in the entertainment industry. To name only a few, actors born and/or raised in Evanston include John and Joan Cusack, Elizabeth McGovern, and Jeremy Piven. The city even has ties to screen legends Charlton Heston, born in Evanston and graduated from Northwestern University, and Marlon Brando, who lived here for a few years as a child. Rock stars born in Evanston include Grace Slick and Eddie Vedder. In addition, Northwestern University has produced scores of prominent statesmen, educators, scientists, business leaders, journalists, artists, and entertainers.

Over the years, Evanston has evolved as an epicenter of not only education but also culture, dining, shopping, and architecture. The city's tree-lined streets abound with historic buildings. Besides the Grosse Pointe Lighthouse, the Frances Willard House, and the Charles Gates Dawes House, Evanston contains more than fifty other sites on the NRHP and four National Register Historic Districts.

WILMETTE

French Canadian fur trader Antoine Ouilmette and his Potawatomi wife, Archange, did not live to see their namesake town come to be. In fact, they left their 1,280-acre property here—awarded to them for their part in facilitating the 1829 Treaty of Prairie du Chien—in 1838 and moved to Iowa, where both of them died a few years later. In 1848 the Ouilmette children sold the family's lakeside land to developers, and a settlement quickly sprang up. In 1872 the village of Wilmette (an anglicized spelling of Ouilmette) was incorporated.

One of Wilmette's most identifiable landmarks is the Baha'i House of Worship, the first Baha'i temple constructed in the Western Hemisphere, the second in the world, and the oldest still standing. Known as the "Mother Temple of the West," this 135-foot-tall,

The pure white temple of the National Spiritual Assembly of the Baha'i of the United States rises majestically above the village of Wilmette. —Photo by author, courtesy National Spiritual Assembly of the Baha'i of the United States

all-white, nine-sided building with an intricate domed top stands surrounded by gorgeous gardens and numerous fountains.

The building's groundbreaking and blessing was held on May 1, 1912, with Abdu'l-Baha, son of the Baha'i religion's founder, in attendance, though construction did not begin until 1920, and it was not completed and formally dedicated until 1953. Named one of the Seven Wonders of Illinois in 2007, the temple is open every day of the year.

Another point of interest is the Wilmette Historical Museum, housed in the former Gross Point Village Hall, built in 1896. Gross Point, a small farming community north of Evanston, was annexed to Wilmette in 1924. Its old village hall was restored in the 1990s and later expanded into a large museum and research complex. Wilmette has several buildings and two historic districts listed on the NRHP.

HIGHWOOD AND FORT SHERIDAN

The Highwood area was only sparsely occupied by European immigrant farmers and settlers until the construction of the Chicago & Milwaukee Railroad in the early 1850s, which attracted an influx of laborers to the vicinity. In 1868 Baptist minister William Wallace Everts and attorney Elisha Ashley Mears partnered to plat a village, but it was not until the building of nearby Fort Sheridan in 1887 that Highwood really developed.

The stories of Highwood and Fort Sheridan are intertwined, and even their names, for a time, were interchangable. The village of Highwood was incorporated in 1887, and

Fort Sheridan opened the same year as Camp Highwood. The following year, however, both the village and the army post were renamed Fort Sheridan, after Lt. Gen. Philip H. Sheridan, who had close ties to Chicago. The community was incorporated in 1902 as the City of Fort Sheridan, but two years later it was reincorporated as the City of Highwood.

Before the post of Fort Sheridan was established, the closest military installation to Chicago was Fort Leavenworth, Kansas. In 1886 a small group of wealthy Chicagoans donated a 632.5-acre parcel twenty-five miles north of the city for the construction of an army post. The first troops arrived in November 1887, living in tents until funding for permanent buildings was approved. Upon its completion in 1889, Fort Sheridan housed six companies of infantry and four of cavalry. Shortly after the Wounded Knee massacre of December 29, 1890, nineteen Sioux prisoners were transported from the Pine Ridge Reservation in South Dakota to Fort Sheridan and held there for a few weeks; most of the Indians were released after agreeing to join Buffalo Bill's Wild West Show.

The village took advantage of the fort's proximity to make a few bucks, establishing a plethora of saloons and gambling houses, plus a brothel or two, to serve restless soldiers. During most of the 1890s, Fort Sheridan was the only "wet" town on the railroad line between Chicago and the Wisconsin border, earning it the nickname "Whiskey Junction." In 1899 the Chicago & Milwaukee Electric Railroad created Fort Sheridan Park, a summer recreation area that featured not only picnic areas and playgrounds but also vaudeville shows and concerts at which wine was served. All this activity drew disapproval from the sober residents of neighboring communities, but efforts to clean up Highwood mostly failed until Prohibition was enacted in 1919.

Nineteen Sioux warriors taken prisoner at Wounded Knee, South Dakota, in 1890 were brought to Fort Sheridan. —Photo by E. Spencer, courtesy Lake County Discovery Museum, Lake County History Archivves

The 3rd Field Artillery passes in review on the parade ground at Fort Sheridan,
1920s —Courtesy Lake County Discovery Museum, Lake County History Archives

During the Spanish-American War, Fort Sheridan was used as a mobilization center, and during World War I as a training camp. In the 1930s it served as a staging area
for Civilian Conservation Corps workers. When World War II erupted, the post became
a training facility for anti-aircraft artillery units and later a recruitment center. It continued to be used as an administrative and logistics facility during the Korean and Vietnam
Wars, and in its later years it functioned as a reservist training center.

After Fort Sheridan was decommissioned in 1993, about 750 acres of the fort
property was annexed to Highwood, doubling the city's geographic area. Another section of the original fort grounds was used for military family housing for the nearby
Great Lakes Naval Station, and 90 acres still operate as the Sheridan Reserve Center.
The remainder of the land was allocated between Highwood, Highland Park, and Lake
Forest. The fort's 110-acre historic district was designated a National Historic Landmark
in 1984.

NORTH CHICAGO

The city of North Chicago was founded in the early 1890s as South Waukegan, a
planned community created by a group of land developers from Chicago and Detroit.
So ardent were these investors in their belief in the potential of this attractive lakeside
acreage south of Waukegan that they offered local farmers up to $1,000 an acre for their
properties, more than ten times the going price. The partners divided the land into lots
and promoted their new town as ideal for manufacturing, with its location near the lake,
its accessibility to railroad transportation, and the availability of a sizable workforce of
eastern Europeans in the area. South Waukegan would also be perfect for families, they

claimed, as no saloons would be allowed in the village. The Woman's Land Syndicate, an affiliate of the Woman's Christian Temperance Union, portrayed the area as "a dry utopia."

By 1892 South Waukegan had a train depot and had attracted its first factory, that of barbed-wire maker Washburn & Moen Manufacturing Company (later called American Steel & Wire Company). The community was incorporated as the village of South Waukegan in 1895 and reincorporated as the city of North Chicago six years later. By the end of its second decade, North Chicago had at least fifteen factories.

As manufacturing expanded, local workers, who saw the city's alcohol ban as an unwelcome restriction, demanded change. Soon North Chicago had more than twenty-five saloons, each paying a substantial license fee. When the Naval Training Station Great Lakes opened in 1911, government requirements prohibited liquor sales within two miles of the installation. Some North Chicago saloons relocated or closed, but most continued to operate regardless.

In 1920 Abbott Alkaloidal Company (now called Abbott Laboratories) relocated its headquarters to North Chicago. The pharmaceutical and medical-supply company, founded in Chicago in 1888 by Dr. Wallace Calvin Abbott, became one of the area's biggest employers. The city continued to attract industry and new residents through the mid-twentieth century. The Naval Training Station Great Lakes was annexed to the city in the 1960s, expanding North Chicago geographically as well as demographically. The population peaked in 1970, at more than 47,000 residents.

The boom did not last, however. The 1970s saw a major decline in American manufacturing, and North Chicago was hit hard. The closing or relocation of many factories, a lack of new development, and the departure of many middle-class residents led to a dwindling tax base. As home prices dropped, less affluent newcomers moved in. Within the Chicago metropolitan area, North Chicago's per capita income was near the bottom by 1990.

Though it was down on its luck, the city was not defeated. The Rosalind Franklin University of Medicine and Science, which includes the Chicago Medical School and the Dr. William M. Scholl College of Podiatric Medicine, moved to North Chicago in 1980, creating economic opportunities for the depressed city.

The military helped keep North Chicago afloat as well. When the U.S. Navy closed two of its three training facilities in 1993, the Naval Training Center Great Lakes was the one that remained open.

Great Lakes Naval Training Center

In 1902, after the Spanish-American War, President Theodore Roosevelt recognized the need for a major naval training facility. A special committee created to research potential sites ultimately recommended a spot north of Chicago on Lake Michigan, a thousand miles away from the nearest ocean. By 1905 private investors from Chicago had raised enough money to buy 172 acres, and construction of the facility began soon afterward. Thirty-nine buildings were erected during a six-year period, at a cost of $3.5 million. The installation included a recruit processing center, a training camp, barracks, a hospital, and a detention facility. Many of the buildings were designed by prominent Chicago architect Jarvis Hunt. The Naval Training Center Great Lakes opened on July 1, 1911.

After the United States declared war on Germany in April 1917, Great Lakes was overwhelmed with recruits. Tents and makeshift wooden barracks were erected to house the overflow. By the end of World War I, 45,000 sailors had been trained at the Great Lakes station.

During peacetime, the facility became a school for radio and telegraph operators as well as for navy pilots. After war was declared on Japan in December 1941, the base was again inundated. During the war, 25 percent of the American naval force—nearly a million men—were processed and trained here.

Six months after World War II began, the Navy began accepting African American recruits, but they were segregated in a separate facility called Camp Robert Smalls. Later, responding to pressure from the White House, the Navy opened its V-12 officer-training program to black enlistees in 1944. Of the sixteen black men selected for the program, thirteen received commissions as ensigns upon completion. Nicknamed the "Golden Thirteen," they were the first black naval officers in U.S. history.

The Great Lakes base was condensed after the Second World War, but it was expanded again during the Korean War. Following the Vietnam War, the installation faced deep budget cuts, but it remained in operation. After the Pentagon closed its naval training facilities in California and Florida in 1993, Great Lakes became the U.S. Navy's only training center. Since then, the base has been expanded and numerous upgrades have been made.

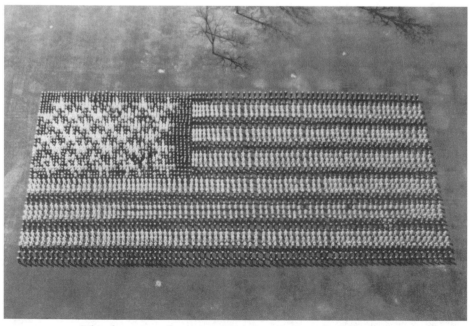

This formation of recruits on the Parade Ground of the Great Lakes Naval Training Station in 1918 depicts the American flag. —Courtesy Great Lakes Naval Museum

The Navy's first black commissioned officers, later known as
the "Golden Thirteen," received their assignments in 1944.
—Courtesy Great Lakes Naval Museum

The Naval Training Center Great Lakes (now called Naval Station Great Lakes) was designated a National Historic District in 1986. A naval museum opened at the facility in 2009. In addition, a new military hospital, the Captain James A. Lovell Federal Health Care Center, opened in 2010.

WAUKEGAN

The first settlement at the future site of Waukegan was a French trading post known as Little Fort, established near Lake Michigan around 1725. By 1760, however, the post was gone and the area was left to the Potawatomi until 1829, when the tribe ceded the land to the U.S. government. In 1835 the first settler, Thomas Jenkins, built a two-story home and store at the Little Fort site, and before long, other settlers arrived.

In 1841 Little Fort was incorporated as a town. Due to its waterfront location and growing population, it was immediately named the county seat. The harbor handled about 1,000 ships per year, and industry soon developed along the lake. After a while, some residents, feeling that the meek-sounding word "little" no longer fit, suggested the name be changed, so in 1849 the town was rechristened Waukegan, the Potawatomi word for fort. It was incorporated as a city in 1852.

Thanks largely to industry, Waukegan continued to grow and develop over the next century and a half. After the first railroad arrived in 1855, the city expanded even more, and there was no end in sight. Between 1890 and 1900, Waukegan's population nearly doubled. In the twentieth century, Waukegan's industrial and commercial enterprises continued to thrive even as the community became more residential. The population kept swelling, more than tripling to 33,500 by 1930. By 1990 the count was over 69,000, and by 2000 it was 88,000. Today the city has an ethnically diverse population of 92,000.

Waukegan's Near North Historic District was placed on the NRHP in 1978. The city's other heritage area, the Shimer Historic District, contains five buildings ranging from the 1840s to the 1940s. The Waukegan Historical Society has also designated eleven individual homes as city landmarks. The society's headquarters and the Waukegan History Museum are housed in the 1843 home of John C. Haines, who was the mayor of Chicago from 1858 to 1860.

Prominent Waukegan natives include mid-twentieth-century comedian Jack Benny (born Benjamin Kubelsky in 1894) and the late science fiction writer Ray Bradbury. Both of these men and several others are honored in Waukegan's Walk of Stars Park. Jack Benny is particularly revered in Waukegan. A statue of the great comedian stands near the Genesee Theatre in downtown Waukegan, and the Jack Benny Center for the Arts stands as an active tribute. Of Benny's boyhood homes in Waukegan, the only one that still exists is a house the Kubelsky family rented between 1909 and 1910, known as the Jack Benny House, designated a city landmark in 2006.

OTHER COMMUNITIES AND SITES OF INTEREST IN GREATER CHICAGOLAND

Downers Grove (US 34): Settled in 1832, Downers Grove was a stop on the Chicago, Burlington & Quincy Railroad line between Chicago and Aurora; the first train arrived in 1864. Historical sites include the Downers Grove Historical Society Museum, the Beller Museum, and the 1846 Blodgett House.

Lisle (I-88 and I-355): Like its neighbor Downers Grove, Lisle was first settled in 1832 and later became a stop on the Chicago, Burlington & Quincy Railroad. The village's 1875 depot is now part of a museum village known as Lisle Station Park. Other sites of interest include the Jurica-Suchy Nature Museum, on the Benedictine University campus, and Morton Arboretum.

Lombard and Glen Ellyn (I-355): The adjacent villages of Lombard and Glen Ellyn began as Babcock's Grove, settled in 1834. Over time, Lombard developed on the east side of the settlement and Glen Ellyn on the west. In 1846 early settler Moses Stacy opened a large guesthouse called the Wayside Inn, later known as Stacy's Tavern, in future Glen Ellyn. Listed on the NRHP in 1974, Stacy's Tavern is now a museum. In Lombard is the home of artist Sheldon Peck, once used as an Underground Railroad station and now a museum, and the 1882 Victorian Cottage, which houses the Lombard History Museum.

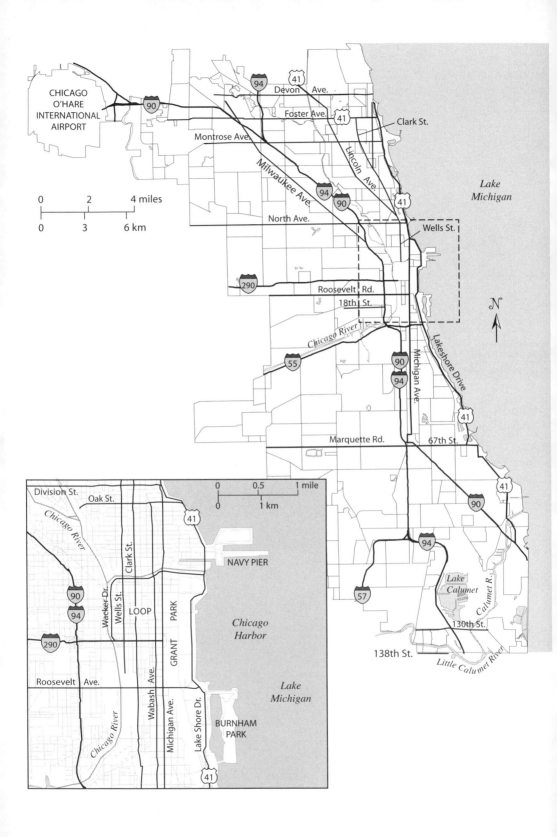

CHICAGO
O'HARE
INTERNATIONAL
AIRPORT

90

94 41
Devon   Ave.

Foster Ave. 41

Clark St.

Montrose Ave.

Milwaukee Ave.

Lincoln Ave.

94
90

41

North Ave.

Wells St.

0   2   4 miles

0   3   6 km

290

Roosevelt Rd.
18th St.

Chicago River

55

90
94

Michigan Ave.

Lakeshore Drive

Lake
Michigan

N

Marquette Rd.

67th St.

41

90

94

57

Lake
Calumet

Calumet R.

130th St.

138th St.

Little Calumet River

Division St.

Oak St.

41

Chicago River

Clark St.

Wacker Dr.

Wells St.

90
94

290

LOOP

GRANT   PARK

NAVY PIER

Chicago
Harbor

0   0.5   1 mile

0   1 km

Roosevelt   Ave.

Chicago River

Wabash Ave.

Michigan Ave.

Lake Shore Dr.

BURNHAM
PARK

Lake
Michigan

41

Chicago
CITY OF NEIGHBORHOODS

In its nearly two-hundred-year history, Chicago has acquired many nicknames: the Windy City, the Second City, Chi-Town, the City of the Big Shoulders, and others. Few know that the name *Chicago* itself came from the foul-smelling vegetation the Miami Indians called *Chicagoua*, a wild garlic plant that grew in the future city's beds of clay. But of all of Chicago's monikers, perhaps the most apt is City of Neighborhoods. The expanse of marshy swampland and muddy shorelines that once covered the area between the Des Plaines River and the South Branch of the Chicago River has been replaced by more than two hundred urban neighborhoods, whose boundaries are forever fluctuating according to significant events, ethnic influxes, and structural changes. Place names like Bronzeville, Little Italy, Greektown, Ukrainian Village, Chinatown, and the Gold Coast attest to Chicago's patchwork heritage.

The genesis for this thriving metropolis began with the Treaty of Greenville in 1795, when Indians ceded to the U.S. government six square miles of land at the mouth of the Chicago River. The early settlers never imagined that this section of land would evolve into a world-class city covering 212.8 square miles. The Treaty of Chicago thirty-eight years later ended native occupation and led to the incorporation of Chicago as a town.

Many of Chicago's major streets began as trails used by Indians and traders and later by settlers, farmers, and stagecoach lines. Most were spokes of a wagon wheel that emanated from the hub at Fort Dearborn and usually traversed ridges of higher ground surrounding the swamps of Chicagoua. As the population increased and more farms and towns were established, the original trails sprouted branches as shortcuts to reduce travel time. A number of the city's existing streets and avenues, including Clark Street, Lincoln Avenue, and State Street, trace the path of these early trails. Most are diagonal streets, outside the grid pattern that was later imposed on the city, and so are easily recognizable.

Chicago's emergence as a community started around 1833 with scattered small buildings and several hundred people. Most of the early settlers were immigrants, primarily western Europeans who settled among their own, bonded by ethnicity, lan-

This map shows the growth of Chicago in the mid-1800s; the center right square indicates the boundaries of the original town, incorporated in 1833; the extension surrounding it on three sides was added when Chicago incorporated as a city in 1837; and additional parcels were annexed in 1847, 1853, 1863, and 1869.
—Author's collection

guage, religion, and customs. African Americans migrated here, too, primarily from the South. Before the Civil War, runaway slaves made their dangerous way to Chicago along the Underground Railroad; after Reconstruction, newly emancipated black men and women came here seeking employment. As more immigrants arrived throughout the nineteenth and twentieth centuries, they often squeezed out previous groups. The constant churn of ethnic immigration fostered Chicago's tradition of urban reform.

Today Chicago has seventy-seven official community areas, further subdivided—mostly unofficially—into some 228 named neighborhoods. Local understandings of community borders don't always agree with the official boundaries, but even out-of-towners are familiar with some of these neighborhoods, such as the Loop, the Gold Coast, Lincoln Park, Wrigleyville, Hyde Park, and the Magnificent Mile. In the early days, Chicago residents often lived, worked, shopped, worshipped, and educated their children within the same area. In many cases, church parishes were the social center of the neighborhood, and many Chicagoans still refer to their home neighborhoods by parish.

A Brief History of Chicago

While Père Jacques Marquette and Louis Jolliet were the first known Europeans to paddle the waters of the Chicago River in 1673, it was French Jesuit priest Père Pierre François Pinet who established the first European settlement, the Mission of the Guardian

Angel, built in 1696 to serve and convert the local Miami Indians. The exact site of the mission is unknown, but many historians believe it may have been located on the main stem of the Chicago River, near present downtown Chicago. The mission lasted until 1701, when the Miami began to move east. Père Pinet then went to work with the Illiniwek in the Cahokia area, where he died the following year.

Trader Jean Baptiste Point de Sable, Chicago's first permanent non-Indian resident, arrived around 1779. The U.S. Army built Fort Dearborn in 1803, and the following year John Kinzie opened a trading post near the fort. The massacre at Fort Dearborn (see Battle of Fort Dearborn under Prairie Avenue Historic District on first trip) in 1812 all but erased the outpost, but not for long. Four years later, Americans rebuilt the fort, which became the commercial and cultural foundation of the future city.

Telegraph service reached the city in 1848, and the Illinois & Michigan Canal was completed later that year. The 1850s saw the formation of the Chicago Historical Society, the Academy of Sciences, the Chicago Relief and Aid Society, Rush Medical College, and other civic institutions.

Chicago played a major role in the antislavery movement. The city held many stations on the Underground Railroad, a network of safe houses for fugitive slaves escaping to freedom and safety in the North. Among them were the home of pharmacist Philo Carpenter, owner of Chicago's first drugstore; the shop and home of John Jones, a wealthy black tailor; the Tremont House, a saloon and boardinghouse; and a number of churches.

In 1840 a group of abolitionists formed the Chicago Anti-Slavery Society. One of its founding members was Rev. Flavel Bascom, pastor of the First Presbyterian Church,

Artist's perception of Jean Baptiste Point de Sable, the first permanent non-Indian settler in the Chicago area. —Author's collection

which functioned as an Underground Railroad clearinghouse. Another society founder was Dr. Charles V. Dyer, president of the Chicago, Burlington & Quincy Railroad, who secretly used the railroad for transporting runaway slaves, earning him the sobriquet "President of the Underground Railroad."

After the Civil War, Chicago became a major transportation and economic center for the nation. As a primary railroad hub, a slaughtering and meat-processing center, and a nucleus for manufacturing, Chicago had become the second-largest city in the country by 1870. But the young metropolis was caught by surprise when, after several hot, dry October nights in 1871, the Great Chicago Fire ignited and roared through town, consuming about one-third of the city. As Chicago rebuilt, its railroad lines extended to many of the nearby villages and outlying towns that would soon make up the Chicago metropolitan area, known familiarly as "Chicagoland."

As the city grew, in addition to the railroad, Chicago developed its own metropolitan public-transportation systems. The first elevated train, known as the "L," opened on the South Side in 1892, just in time for the World's Columbian Exposition. The first "L" trains ran on steam along conventional tracks, like regular railroad trains; the third-rail electrical system was established in 1898. The "L" lines were expanded and modernized throughout the twentieth century. The Chicago Transit Authority (CTA) was created in 1947 to coordinate and maintain the "L" system as well as city bus lines. Today, the Chicago "L" is second only to the New York City subway in distance served.

The "L" system was only one of many improvements made to the city in preparation for the 1893 World's Columbian Exposition. Chicago beat out New York and other major cities to become the host of this event, the national commemoration of the four-hundredth anniversary of Christopher Columbus's arrival in America. Braggadocio by Chicago's campaign committee inspired the town's famous nickname, "the Windy City." The exposition brought worldwide attention to Chicago, and its success brought the city a much-needed economic boost. The fair is also credited with introducing the public to such American classics as the hamburger, ragtime jazz, picture postcards, and the Ferris Wheel; it also spawned the "City Beautiful" movement in architecture and urban planning.

The *Plan of Chicago*, coauthored by Daniel H. Burnham and Edward H. Bennett and published in 1909, was one of the first urban development plans in the United States. The extensive plan influenced not only the development of modern Chicago but the field of city planning itself. The plan called for wider streets, expanded rail services, civic buildings, numerous municipal parks, and especially extensive development of the lakefront as public space. While only parts of the plan were directly implemented, its ideas inspired the creation of Northerly Island, Navy Pier, the Field Museum of Natural History, Soldier Field, and many other civic improvements. Burnham's vision also directed the expansion of Grant Park and the construction or redesign of many city streets, including Michigan Avenue's Magnificent Mile.

The late nineteenth century witnessed the birth of the labor movement in the United States. Chicago contributed to the cause in blood when labor organizers clashed with police in Haymarket Square in 1886, and in 1894, when federal troops prevented labor protesters from disrupting mail service at Pullman, on Chicago's South Side. The city was a center of union activity and conflict well into the twentieth century. In May

1937, city police killed ten strikers and wounded thirty at the Republic Steel plant, on the Southeast Side, in an incident known as the "Memorial Day Massacre." Chicago played midwife to other social movements as well. Near the turn of the twentieth century, activists like Jane Addams called attention to intolerable working conditions, public health deficiencies, and inadequate education in Chicago and throughout the nation.

The new century brought further growth and fresh challenges to Chicago as new waves of immigrants added to the city's melting pot and social reforms took root. In the early decades of the 1900s, Evangelist Billy Sunday preached against society's sins, helping to usher in the Eighteenth Amendment, a.k.a. Prohibition, which ironically spawned more sin in the form of bootlegging, speakeasies, and gangster violence. Through most of the 1920s and early 1930s, noted Chicago mobster Al Capone controlled bookie joints, breweries, distilleries, gambling, nightclubs, and racetracks throughout the region. Meanwhile, Franklin Roosevelt's Civilian Conservation Corps and Works Projects Administration added trails, walkways, parks, and public art to the urban landscape. Despite the Great Depression, Chicago showed the world its strength with its 1933–34 Century of Progress exhibition, which attracted nearly 40 million people.

Chicago also made unique contributions to popular culture, particularly in the areas of music, theater, sports, and food. According to legend, the Chicago-style hot dog debuted at the World's Columbian Exposition, but it gained popularity during the Great Depression, when hot dog carts provided a quick, cheap, and tasty meal—Chicago's own Vienna Beef frankfurter on a poppy-seed bun and a "salad on top" that includes, among other things, fresh chopped onions, tomato wedges, a pickle spear, and a dash of celery salt. Chicago's famous deep-dish pizza was created in 1943 by Texan Ike Sewell, who opened Pizzeria Uno on Chicago's Near North Side. The pizza featured an outer crust nearly two inches high, instead of the crisp, flat New York version. Today more than two thousand pizzerias across Chicagoland copy Sewell's creation.

After World War II, returning veterans came to the Chicago area seeking urban jobs and suburban homes, triggering a housing boom. In the 1950s, a small airfield on Chicago's far northwest side became O'Hare International Airport, laying the groundwork for an economic renaissance.

This period of explosive growth was overseen by Mayor Richard J. Daley, elected in 1955. During his twenty-one-year reign, Daley amassed unprecedented power over Chicago politics and civic affairs. While the ethics of the Daley Machine's near-total control of Chicago has been questioned, Richard J. Daley is nonetheless credited with saving his city from the urban blight that other major American metropolises suffered in the 1960s and '70s.

Daley's son, Richard M. Daley, enjoyed the longest tenure of any Chicago mayor, serving from 1989 to 2011. Like his father, the junior Daley was criticized for his strong-arm methods, but his administration's power did not approach that of his father's "machine."

By the end of the twentieth century, Chicago's population hovered just below 3 million, and its impact was nationwide. The city's jazzy, electrified version of the blues, which began in the speakeasies of the 1920s, had spread throughout the country, influencing rock, jazz, folk forms such as zydeco, and later, hip-hop. Chicago, with its famous Second City troupe and others, fostered the development of improvisational theater into a theatrical form in its own right. And in the world of sports, Mike Ditka coached the Chicago Bears to a 1985 Super Bowl victory, and the Chicago Bulls, led by superstar Michael Jordan, won six NBA championships during the 1990s.

The Chicago municipal flag, a popular symbol of this great city, shows two blue bands and four red stars on a white field. The original flag, adopted in 1917, had two stars; additional stars were added in 1933 and 1939. Each star signifies a pivotal event in the city's history. From left to right, the stars represent the Battle of Fort Dearborn, the 1871 Great Chicago Fire, the 1893 World's Columbian Exposition, and the 1933–34 Century of Progress Exposition.

South Lake Shore Drive (US 41)
ROOSEVELT ROAD–67TH STREET
7 miles

There are few if any city streets that rival Chicago's Lake Shore Drive. The freeway, sometimes called by its initials, LSD, runs from Hollywood Avenue on the north to Marquette Drive on the south. About midway are some of Chicago's biggest attractions, including Navy Pier, Grant Park, Chicago Harbor, and Burnham Park. To the north, the Drive passes many lakeside parks, beaches, and marinas while skirting the upscale neighborhoods of Streeterville, the Gold Coast, and Lincoln Park. This northern part of the LSD will be discussed on a later trip.

Our tour of the south half of Lake Shore Drive begins with the attractively land-scaped Burnham Park and adjacent Northerly Island, which played a significant role in the 1933 Century of Progress exposition. Farther south, the Drive edges the eastern side of several historic neighborhoods, including Hyde Park, Kenwood, and South Shore. The LSD ends at Marquette Drive near 67th Street, about a mile east of Oak Woods Cemetery.

BURNHAM PARK AND NORTHERLY ISLAND

Burnham Park is the physical site of the Shedd Aquarium, the Field Museum of Natural History, and Soldier Field, home of the Chicago Bears; adjacent Northerly Island is the site of the Adler Planetarium. Technically, however, the three museums were annexed to Grant Park in the 1990s. Burnham Park still contains Soldier Field as well as the McCormick Place convention center. Northerly Island was the home of the former Meigs Field airstrip, which was demolished in 2003 and made into a park.

Northerly Island, completed in 1925, was one of several man-made islands proposed in Daniel H. Burnham and Edward H. Bennett's 1909 *Plan of Chicago* (often called the Burnham Plan), but it was the only one that was actually built. It was constructed as an island, but the causeway that replaced the original bridge in the 1930s turned it into a peninsula. The lakeside Burnham Park, also inspired by the Burnham Plan, was created in 1927. Both parts of the park complex were built in anticipation of the 1933 Century of Progress.

This aerial view of Northerly Island shows a squadron of seaplanes arriving at the Century of Progress in 1933. —Courtesy Lake County Discovery Museum, Lake County History Archives

Chicago's 1933–34 Century of Progress

Despite the Great Depression, Chicago was determined to celebrate the one-hundredth anniversary of its 1833 founding with a world's fair. The Century of Progress International Exposition Chicago would tout the city's advances in agriculture, construction, manufacturing, and transportation. The planning corporation for the fair got to work on January 5, 1928, in expectation of millions of visitors.

Plans for the Century of Progress built on some of the successes from the 1893 World's Columbian Exposition (see under Hyde Park later on this trip). The organizers brought in nationally recognized architects to design the exposition space, which featured multicolored buildings and neon lights. Promoters billed it as the "Rainbow City," analogous to the World's Columbian Exposition's "White City."

The centerpiece of the 424-acre, lakefront fair site was Northerly Island, created in the 1920s using sand dredged from Lake Michigan's shores. Attractions on the island included the Terrazzo Esplanade, the Hall of States, Enchanted Island for children, the Hollywood Pavilion, a number of science buildings, and many others. Temporary constructions housed pavilions for the fourteen foreign nations that officially participated and thirteen other countries represented by vendors or displays. One of the few buildings constructed on Northerly Island as a permanent structure was the Adler Planetarium, built in 1930.

The most prominent and most popular fair attraction was the Sky Ride, which transported visitors between Northerly Island and the mainland aboard a high tramway that ran along steel cables between two 628-foot towers. Observation decks atop the towers provided a spectacular view of the fairgrounds and the surrounding country, including parts of Indiana, Michigan, and Wisconsin. Another noteworthy exhibit was a full-scale replica of old Fort Dearborn, which featured a number of buildings and a seventy-foot-high flagpole.

The fair opened on May 27, 1933, and was scheduled to close five months later. The event was so successful, however, that the trustees chose to repeat it in 1934. With the income from the second year, the city was able to recoup its original investment and repay all its loans. Total attendance over the two years exceeded 48 million people.

The success of the fair in the midst of the Depression brought the hope of a prosperous future to the people of Chicago and the entire nation.

PRAIRIE AVENUE HISTORIC DISTRICT

Today's Prairie Avenue Historic District was once Chicago's most fashionable neighborhood. From the 1870s to the early 1900s, the mansions of Philip Armour, Marshall Field, John J. Glessner, William W. Kimball, George Pullman, and others lined the wide boulevard, often called "Millionaire's Row." In the early twentieth century, however, railroads came through the vicinity and disturbed the serenity of the neighborhood, while an expanding vice district crept into the area, compelling most of its wealthy residents to move to quieter and more respectable environs.

In the 1970s, during Mayor Richard J. Daley's administration, the city took stock of its historic buildings. In 1977 the 1836 Henry B. Clarke House, thought to be the oldest building in Chicago, was moved from its South Wabash location and placed on a modern foundation within what would soon be designated the Prairie Avenue Historic District. After undergoing a five-year restoration, the Greek Revival–style home opened in 1982 as the Clarke House Museum. The stunning 1887 John J. Glessner home, designed by noted architect Henry Hobson Richardson, is also a museum.

The historic district encompasses not only Gilded Age mansions but also a landmark of Chicago musical history—the Blues Heaven Foundation, located in the former headquarters of Chess Records. From 1957 to 1967, this building housed the studio where dozens of legendary blues and rock musicians once recorded, including Muddy Waters, Chuck Berry, Etta James, Buddy Guy, Aretha Franklin, and many others. Grammy-winning blues artist Willie Dixon recorded there and acted as a producer for many of the label's records. In 1993 Willie's widow, Marie Dixon, bought the studio building and donated it to house the Willie Dixon Blues Heaven Foundation, which offers educational programs for children, students, musicians, and music lovers.

Another major historic site in the Prairie Avenue District is that of the 1812 Fort Dearborn Massacre (a.k.a. Battle of Fort Dearborn), commemorated by a small park.

Battle of Fort Dearborn (Fort Dearborn Massacre)

During the War of 1812, Fort Dearborn (see also Fort Dearborn Historic Site on later trip) was exposed to attacks from Indians loyal to the British, and in August 1812, Gen. William Hull ordered the fort to be evacuated. The post's commander, Capt. Nathan Heald, led a column of three officers, fifty-four regulars, and twelve militiamen out of Fort Dearborn on August 15, along with twenty-seven women and children and a few sick men in wagons. The group plodded south along the lakeshore toward Fort Wayne,

Indiana, accompanied by an escort of fifteen to twenty Miami Indians from Fort Wayne. The escort party's leader, Capt. William Wells, split his men between the advance and rear of the column.

The company had traveled less than two miles when scouts sighted more than five hundred Potawatomi and allied warriors near the dunes, watching them. Wells shouted for the troops to form a line and charge the sand hills. The men moved forward and forced the Indians out onto the prairie, only to find themselves nearly surrounded. While most of the troops were fighting on the dunes, a detachment of Indians attacked the wagons, killing the outnumbered guards and many of the women and children.

Wells died in the battle along with more than forty soldiers and more than a dozen women and children; Heald survived. The Indian attackers lost only about fifteen men. About forty whites—including troopers, women, and children—were taken prisoner but were later released.

Back at Fort Dearborn, the Indians plundered the unprotected post, shot the cattle, and set the whole thing on fire. Only the powder magazine, built of stone, remained standing. At the battle site, the bones of the dead lay unburied on the beach for more than a year.

Years later, the battle and its participants were memorialized in several ways. In 1893 industrialist George M. Pullman, who lived close to the massacre site on Prairie Avenue, commissioned a sculpture portraying a scene from the battle, which he placed near his home. The statue was later moved to the Chicago Historical Society (now the Chicago History Museum), but after some Native Americans protested the work's depiction of the battle, it ended up in a city storage unit. A more recent memorial is Battle of Fort Dearborn Park, at 18th Street and Calumet Avenue. The park was dedicated in 2009, on the 197th anniversary of the battle.

DOUGLAS

Among the properties that U.S. Senator Stephen A. Douglas once owned in Chicago was a fifty-acre lakefront parcel on the South Side, an estate he named Oakenwald. He bought the land in 1852. For several years he lived in a modest house among a stand of trees at the south end of the estate, a section he dubbed Cottage Grove. After his death in 1861, he left part of his Oakenwald property to the federal government, which developed it as Camp Douglas. During the Civil War, Camp Douglas was used as a training facility for Union soldiers and as a Confederate prison (see Camp Douglas below). Douglas was buried on his property, and in 1881 an elaborate monument was completed at the burial site, now known as the Douglas Tomb Historic Site (see below).

Ever since the community's early days, Douglas residents have represented a mixture of ethnicities. Some parts of the area were settled by the Irish, many of whom were employed at the Union Stock Yard, with the railroads, or in the local breweries. Jewish families also settled in Douglas, mostly on the eastern side. The southwest side of Douglas, historically occupied by African Americans, eventually became known as Bronzeville (see Bronzeville on later trip). In the mid-twentieth century, Douglas was the focus of several urban-renewal projects, which saw mixed success.

Northeast of Bronzeville, Douglas comprises the neighborhoods of Lake Meadows, Prairie Shores, South Commons, and Groveland Park, all residential areas. Groveland

Park, built around the large oval park of the same name, is a unique niche in the Douglas community. The park is the only surviving remnant of Stephen Douglas's original development. Groveland Park's large houses made it a popular neighborhood for wealthy Chicagoans, including Joy Morton of Morton Salt. Some of the mansions remain today, providing a glimpse into late-1800s gracious living in Chicago.

Prairie Shores is the site of the recently demolished Michael Reese Hospital, once a major research and teaching hospital. The hospital campus itself contained the site of the Farragut Boat Club, torn down in 1949. It was in the gymnasium of the boat club that the game of softball was invented in 1887.

On November 24, Thanksgiving Day, George Hancock, a young reporter for the Chicago Board of Trade, was horsing around with a group of friends at the club when one of them tossed a boxing glove at another young man, who deflected the assault with a broomstick. Inspired, Hancock made up a game, "indoor baseball," on the spot. He fashioned the boxing glove into a ball by binding it up with its laces, chalked out a small baseball diamond on the floor of the gym, organized the group into two teams, and commenced the game. Thus the sport of softball was born. Hancock later wrote down the rules and created a soft, oversize ball and rubber-tipped bat that could be used indoors. A monument commemorating the event now stands near the site of the boat club.

Also in the Douglas area is the Chicago Police Headquarters, noteworthy for the Haymarket Memorial statue. The nine-foot-tall bronze sculpture honors the seven police officers who were killed during the 1886 Haymarket Square riot. (For more details about the riot, see under Forest Park in Region 6.) The original statue, which portrays a policeman holding his hand up, was erected in Haymarket Square, at Randolph and Desplaines Streets, in 1889, but it did not stay there. Deemed a traffic hazard in 1900, the monument was moved to Union Park, where it got smashed by a runaway streetcar. It was restored and later moved back to the riot site, where vandals dynamited it in 1969. Again it was restored, only to be blown up again a few months later.

It was moved again in 1972, then once more in 1976, this time to the Chicago Police Academy, where it was kept out of public view for three decades. Finally, in 2007, the statue was refurbished and rededicated at what is expected to be its permanent home, at the Chicago Police Headquarters on Michigan Avenue at 35th Street. Haymarket Square itself now features a new memorial, dedicated to labor activists (see under Near West Side on later trip). The main memorial, the Haymarket Martyrs' Monument, is at Forest Home Cemetery in suburban Forest Park, where the remains of the four protesters who were tried and executed—many feel unjustly—for inciting the riot are interred (see under Forest Park in Region 6).

Douglas Tomb Historic Site

Although he was only about five feet tall, Stephen A. Douglas was a giant in Illinois. Born of humble means in Brandon, Vermont, Douglas moved to Illinois at the age of twenty and became involved in Democratic Party politics. Throughout his career, he held numerous local, state, and national offices. He moved to Chicago in 1847, shortly after his election to the U.S. Senate.

Douglas is probably best known for his landmark 1858 senatorial campaign debates with Abraham Lincoln. During the Lincoln-Douglas debates, Douglas advocated

U.S. Sen. Stephen A. Douglas, the "Little Giant" —Author's collection

"popular sovereignty"—leaving the question of slavery up to each state—as a solution to the slavery issue and won the 1858 election. He failed to win the Democratic Party presidential nominations in 1852 and 1856, however, and in 1860 he ran as an Independent, splitting the Democratic vote and enabling Lincoln to win the presidency. Douglas died of typhoid fever on June 3, 1861, and was buried on his property at a site near the lake.

After Douglas's death, the state of Illinois bought his burial site and laid the cornerstone for an elaborate tomb over his grave. Prominent Chicago sculptor Leonard Wells Volk, a personal friend of Douglas, was commissioned to build a monument to the senator at the tomb site. Volk had met Douglas in 1852, and Douglas later subsidized Volk's studies in Rome. Volk's monument to Douglas, completed in 1881, consists of a four-pillared mausoleum, above which a forty-six-foot-high, white marble column stands, topped by a ten-foot-tall bronze statue of the statesman. Surrounded by a beautifully landscaped park, the tomb was designated a Chicago Landmark in 1977.

Camp Douglas

Camp Douglas was built on land donated to the U.S. government by Stephen A. Douglas upon his death in 1861. About four miles south of what was then Chicago's city limits, the post site was near Lake Michigan and surrounded by open prairie. The U.S. Army built Camp Douglas at the start of the Civil War as a recruiting and training base for volunteers. The post was converted to a prison camp the following year, and it continued to serve as a prison for the rest of the war.

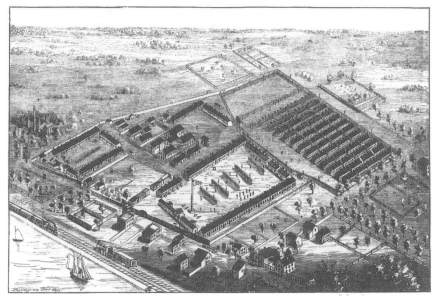

A conceptual aerial illustration of Camp Douglas; in the center is the parade ground, with the cemetery to the left, the hospital above, and the main prison quarters to the right. —Author's collection

During its lifetime, Camp Douglas overflowed with Confederate soldiers captured from battlefields throughout the Mississippi River Valley and northern Tennessee. Before long, the camp had become filthy and was wracked with infectious diseases, earning it the nickname "Eighty Acres of Hell." By the end of the war, more than 4,000 of the camp's 26,000 Confederate prisoners had died.

There were no barracks when the first contingent of more than 4,000 prisoners from Tennessee battlefields, guarded by about 450 Union men, arrived at Camp Douglas in February 1862. Nor were there medical facilities for the sick or wounded. Conditions did not improve during the war as the camp became increasingly overcrowded. The post had been established on low, wet land, which could not absorb the amounts of waste produced by the prisoners, soldiers, and animals. Frequent flooding turned the grounds into muddy sludge and produced pools of stagnant, contaminated water.

In the summer of 1862, U.S. Sanitation Commissioner Henry W. Bellows concluded that:

> . . . the amount of standing water, of un-policed grounds, of foul sinks, of unventilated and crowded barracks, of general disorder, of soil reeking with miasmatic accretions, of rotten bones and the emptying of camp-kettles is enough to drive a sanitarian to despair. . . . I do not believe that any amount of drainage would purge that soil loaded with accumulated filth or those barracks fetid with two stories of vermin and animal exhalations.

Even as conditions worsened, the army was slow to approve building improvements. Furthermore, security was lax, and prisoners began to escape in alarming numbers.

The bitter winter of 1863–64 took the highest toll at Camp Douglas. Although sanitation had improved somewhat by then, inadequate clothing and blankets as well as malnutrition led to more deaths. By spring 1864, more than a thousand prisoners had died from exposure or disease. Burials were practically random; many bodies were thrown into shallow mass graves, and a large number were reportedly dumped into Lake Michigan. The majority of the 4,000 dead Confederates ended up buried in the pauper's section of Chicago City Cemetery (which later became part of Lincoln Park); most of those bodies were later reinterred at Oak Woods Cemetery, where a monument to them was erected in 1895 (see under South Shore later on this trip).

Camp Douglas went down in history as the deadliest prison camp in the North. The camp closed in July 1865. By the end of the summer, most of the buildings had been sold, and by the end of the year, all traces of the camp were gone. Today, condominium complexes, apartment buildings, businesses, playgrounds, and parking lots cover the site. In 2012, however, an archaeological dig began at Lake Meadows Park (believed to be atop part of the prison grounds) to locate artifacts and remnants of the buildings' limestone footings.

KENWOOD

The community of Kenwood lies adjacent to the south end of Burnham Park. Once one of the wealthiest neighborhoods in the city, Kenwood underwent significant changes in the twentieth century. Two historic districts attest to Kenwood's opulent past, and recent redevelopment has brought parts of Kenwood back to their former glory.

An affluent residential community was already forming when the Illinois Central railroad established a depot at 47th Street in the 1850s. The railroad called its new station Kenwood, the name that prosperous dentist Jonathan A. Kennicott had given his nearby estate, after his family home in Scotland. Among those drawn to the area during this period of rapid growth were U.S. Senator Lyman Trumbull, Ambassador Norman Judd, and mapmaker William Rand. Later, lumber tycoon Martin Ryerson, meatpacking magnate Gustavus Swift, and Sears, Roebuck executive Julius Rosenwald also built mansions here.

With the arrival of the "L" in the early 1900s, a different class of people began streaming into Kenwood. Office workers, salesclerks, and other middle-class commuters found the community to be a convenient and wholesome place to live. As the common folk moved in, the elite moved out. To meet the needs of the new population, developers added walk-up apartment buildings and, later, converted some of the older mansions into apartment buildings and boardinghouses. With the community in flux, warehouses and factories began to encroach into the area.

Over the years, many beautiful mansions were allowed to decay and vacant lots multiplied. The deterioration continued until the late 1970s, when historic preservation districts were established in Hyde Park–Kenwood, Kenwood, and North Kenwood. Most of the vintage homes and mansions in these districts are privately owned, but a stroll down the streets offers outside views of Tudor, Classical Revival, Queen Anne, Prairie School, and other style homes, as well as distinctive mosques, synagogues, and churches. One of Kenwood's most recent attractions is the private home of President Barack Obama.

Barack Obama in Chicago

The Hawaiian-born Barack Obama spent less than half his life in Chicago, but his ties to the city run deep. From 1997 to early 2004, only a smattering of people in his South Side senatorial district knew the name of this energetic and charismatic young politician. After winning a seat in the U.S. Senate in 2004, Obama exploded onto the national scene with a strikingly eloquent keynote address at the 2004 Democratic National Convention in Boston. Four years later, he was elected president of the United States.

Obama first moved to Chicago in 1985, after graduating from Columbia University and a short stint working in New York. Hired as director of the Developing Communities Project, he received his first taste of community activism and local politics in the Windy City. Assigned to the Roseland, West Pullman, and Riverdale community areas, Obama oversaw job-training programs, college preparatory classes, and a tenants' rights group at Altgeld Gardens (see under Riverdale on later trip). In 1988 he entered Harvard Law School, where he became president of the prestigious *Harvard Law Review*. While a student at Harvard, he spent his summers in Chicago working as a law clerk.

In 1989 Obama took a summer internship with the law firm of Sidley & Austin, where his supervisor was an attractive young lawyer named Michelle Robinson. The two eventually began dating. After receiving his law degree in 1991, Obama, newly engaged to Robinson, again returned to the South Side when he accepted a fellowship at the University of Chicago, where he would go on to teach constitutional law. He and Michelle, married on October 3, 1992, first lived in an apartment in Hyde Park. During this busy period Obama also began work on his first book, published in 1995 as *Dreams From My Father*; directed Illinois' 1992 Project Vote, which registered hundreds of thousands of black voters across the state; and practiced law at a prominent Chicago firm. In 1997 he began serving the first of his three terms in the Illinois Senate.

In 2005 the Obamas, now with two young daughters, purchased a 1910 Georgian Revival house on Greenwood Avenue in Kenwood. Since Barack Obama became president, security is extremely tight for several blocks surrounding the home, especially when the family is in Chicago. The president's association with Kenwood has created a cottage industry for souvenir hawkers, bus-tour operators, paparazzi, and others. Even the real estate industry has profited from Kenwood and Hyde Park's sudden vogue.

The president's old barbershop (Hyde Park Hair Salon & Barber Shop), favorite bookstore (57th Street Books), favorite restaurants, and other places associated with him and the first lady abound for the inquisitive visitor. But access to the block on which the Obamas live is severely restricted.

HYDE PARK

Sometime in the mid-1850s Paul Cornell, a New York lawyer and shrewd investor, purchased three hundred acres of lakefront property between what are now 51st and 55th Streets, deeding sixty acres to the Illinois Central Railroad for a train station. The easy access drew other residents to the area, and for the next thirty years, the community expanded at a steady pace. The township of Hyde Park, incorporated in 1861, was annexed to Chicago in 1889. Before and during the Civil War, Cornell, a committed abolitionist, and some of his associates used their Hyde Park homes as Underground Railroad havens. In 1869 Cornell built the community's two stunning public parks—Jackson and Washington—as well as the Midway Plaisance, which connected the two.

Several events in the early 1890s put Hyde Park in the spotlight: in 1892 the University of Chicago was completed, and the following year the World's Columbian Exposition took place (see below). Two years after the exposition, on November 28 (Thanksgiving Day), 1895, another notable event took place in this neighborhood—the first automobile race in the United States. Sponsored by the *Chicago Times-Herald,* the race followed a primitive fifty-four-mile round-trip route between Chicago and Evanston, starting and finishing at the Palace of Fine Arts building (now the Museum of Science and Industry) in Jackson Park. Commercial production of autos had not yet begun, so all of the vehicles in the race were privately built cars and motorcycles; of the dozens of initial entries, only six contestants showed up with vehicles that were viable to race. The course took the winner nearly eight hours to complete, and the second racer arrived an hour and a half later. The other four were unable to finish the race.

With all this development, the neighborhood began to attract Chicago's elite. In the late 1800s and early 1900s, several wealthy Hyde Park residents hired prominent architects to design their homes. The most famous of these architects was Frank Lloyd Wright, who created the Isidore H. Heller house in 1897 and the Frederick C. Robie house in 1910. The latter, now a museum, is a classic example of Wright's Prairie School design and is considered a masterpiece of modern architecture. Later in the twentieth century, I. M. Pei, Ludwig Mies van der Rohe, and Eero Saarinen added their own landmark buildings to the community.

As a center of arts, culture, architecture, and history, Hyde Park has been home at various times to national luminaries such as author Saul Bellow, poet Carl Sandburg, physicist Enrico Fermi, economist Milton Friedman, poet Gwendolyn Brooks, President Barack Obama, Mayor Harold Washington, and many others. Near the west side of Jackson Park, edging the Midway Plaisance, was the home of famed attorney Clarence Darrow (1857–1938). Darrow moved to Chicago in 1887 and spent the rest of his life here. Among his best-known cases was the Scopes "Monkey Trial" of 1925 (see under Salem in Region 1). Another famed resident—though he lived here only from ages three to four—was Pres. Ronald Reagan. His boyhood home—a little-known site that the University of Chicago purchased along with the area around it in 2004—was demolished amid protests in 2013.

University of Chicago

In 1892 oil magnate and philanthropist John D. Rockefeller established the University of Chicago, built on ten acres of land donated by fellow tycoon-philanthropist Marshall Field. Noted architect Henry Ives Cobb designed the school's buildings in Gothic Revival style and laid the campus out in quadrangles, modeled after the campuses of Cambridge and Oxford Universities in England. The university's trustees hoped to assemble a "community of scholars."

Although affiliated with the Baptist Church, the university was founded as a secular, coeducational institution. William Rainey Harper, the university's first president, hired some of the best minds in their fields to establish the school's philosophy, sociology, and science departments. The business school was added in 1898, and the law school opened in 1902.

In the mid-twentieth century, the school's fifth president, Robert Maynard Hutchins, launched a number of innovative programs that further elevated the university's position and prestige. Beginning in the 1920s, with its pioneering research on community studies, immigration, race, and ethnicity, the work of the University of Chicago's sociology department became known as the "Chicago School." Similarly, in the 1950s the university produced the Chicago School of economics. In 1942 physicist Enrico Fermi produced the world's first nuclear reaction on this campus.

One of the most respected institutions of higher learning in the world, the University of Chicago continues to expand. Since its founding, the school has produced hundreds of internationally renowned scholars. Alumni include dozens of Fulbright Award recipients and Rhodes Scholars, as well as more than eighty-five Nobel Prize winners. Other graduates became world-recognized statesmen, scientists, business executives, federal justices, physicians, writers, entertainers, athletes, educators, and scholars. Counted among the faculty have been such notables as T. S. Eliot, Hannah Arendt, John Dewey, Daniel Boorstin, Thorton Wilder, Antonin Scalia, Bertrand Russell, Milton Friedman, and Barack Obama.

World's Columbian Exposition of 1893

Eighteen years after the Great Fire, Chicago prepared to reassert itself on the world stage. In its bid for the 1893 World's Columbian Exposition, Chicago beat out St. Louis, Washington, D.C., and its toughest rival, New York City. The fair was conceived to celebrate the four-hundredth anniversary of the 1492 arrival of Christopher Columbus in the New World, as well as to showcase artistic and industrial advancements in the United States and various other countries. For its own part, Chicago wanted to display its progress since the fire and to advance the city's physical and economic recovery.

Famous landscape architect Frederick Law Olmsted recommended Jackson Park, in the city's Hyde Park neighborhood, for the fair site. The final exposition area, which included Jackson Park and the Midway Plaisance, covered more than six hundred acres. A team of world-renowned architects led the two-and-a-half-year effort to design the exposition: Daniel H. Burnham was named chief of construction, John Root was the supervising architect, and Olmsted and Henry B. Codman were the supervising landscape architects. At one planning session, sculpture consultant Augustus Saint Gaudens proclaimed, "Do you realize that this is the greatest meeting of artists since the fifteenth century?"

To help pay for the endeavor, Congress authorized the minting and sale of commemorative Columbian half-dollars, as well as special quarters, for 1892 and 1893—the first commemorative coins minted by the United States. Sale of the coins raised about $2.5 million. Private contributors to the fair's funding included bankers, industrialists, railroad executives, and many others in Chicago and nationwide.

President Grover Cleveland participated in the fair's opening ceremonies, held on May 1, 1893, in the Court of Honor. The exposition's main buildings were clustered in this courtyard, surrounded by pavilions representing different states, territories, and foreign countries. Electric lights illuminated the Court of Honor's elegant, neoclassical structures of white stucco, creating a dazzling glow that awed fairgoers and inspired the exposition's affectionate nickname, "The White City."

The Ferris Wheel, designed by George Washington Gale Ferris, was a feature attraction at the World's Columbian Exposition of 1893. —Courtesy Chicago Public Library, Special Collections and Preservation Division

The six-hundred-foot-wide, one-mile-long Midway Plaisance was lined with sideshows, rides, food and souvenir vendors, displays, and street performers, creating a carnival atmosphere that some described as bawdy. Anchoring the Midway was an extraordinary new structure, the Ferris Wheel, created by Galesburg native George Washington Gale Ferris (see also Galesburg in Region 2). During preparations for the fair, planner Daniel Burnham had challenged civil engineers to design something sensational for the event, and Ferris's invention was selected. The 264-foot-high wheel, turned by a huge steel axle, accommodated more than 2,000 riders at a time. By the end of the fair, about 1.5 million passengers had enjoyed the thrilling ride, which provided a panorama of the White City and its environs.

Buffalo Bill Cody's "Wild West Show and Congress of Rough Riders of the World" performed in an arena just outside the fairgrounds. Not an official part of the exposition, Cody set up his show and camp near the fair's west entrances at Jackson Park and kept all his own profits. During the six-month engagement, Cody and his entourage gave 318 performances to audiences that averaged about 12,000 patrons per show, netting $1 million. An additional attraction was Cody's "Great Cowboy Race of 1893." The race started in Chadron, Nebraska, on June 13 and ended two weeks and 1,000 miles later in front of Cody's tent in Chicago. Prizes included cash purses as well as items such as guns and saddles. Organizers expected dozens, if not hundreds, of riders to sign up, but only nine did. Of the nine contestants, ranging in age from fourteen to fifty-eight, eight finished the race. All of the finishers received prizes.

In all, more than 26 million people from around the world attended the World's Columbian Exposition, which closed on October 30, 1893. But a pall was cast over the closing celebration. Two days before the fair closed, a disappointed office seeker named Patrick Eugene Prendergast shot and killed Chicago's beloved mayor, Carter Harrison, in Harrison's own home. The elaborate and joyous concluding ceremonies that had been planned were turned into a somber memorial. Attendees solemnly filed out of Festival Hall to the sounds of Beethoven's Funeral March. Prendergast was later hanged for the murder.

With the closing of the exposition, the White City's life was over. Shortly after the fair ended, a fire swept through the area, destroying at least ten of the exposition buildings. A few buildings were purchased by private interests and moved to other cities. Most of the rest were left to salvage companies. Only two buildings, the Palace of Fine Arts and the World's Congress Auxiliary Building, survived into the new century. The former now houses the Museum of Science and Industry, and the latter became the Art Institute of Chicago. The Ferris Wheel, disassembled after the fair ended, was later reconstructed at the 1904 St. Louis World's Fair.

Although the White City was temporary, it left a permanent legacy. For one thing, the fairgrounds' inspired design spawned the nationwide "City Beautiful" movement that influenced urban planning for the next forty years. Many major U.S. cities borrowed elements of the fair's plans in designing new public buildings, parks, plazas, and boulevards. The exposition also left permanent improvements in Chicago itself, including the "L" tracks and the beautification of Jackson Park.

Shortly after the World's Columbian Exposition closed in 1893, a fire broke out and destroyed many of the buildings, including the Electricity Building (left). —Courtesy Chicago Public Library, Special Collections and Preservation

The Fine Arts Building was the only remaining structure on the original grounds of the World's Columbian Exposition of 1893; it now houses the Museum of Science and Industry. —Courtesy Chicago Public Library, Special Collections and Preservation

SOUTH SHORE

Until the 1920s, the community now called South Shore was part of Hyde Park, which was annexed to Chicago in 1889. The area was originally a smattering of small settlements—Bryn Mawr, Cheltenham Beach, Essex, Parkside, and Windsor Park—mostly inhabited by middle-class British immigrants who worked for the Illinois Central Railroad or at nearby steel mills.

The 1893 World's Columbian Exposition spurred a building boom in the neighborhoods around the fairgrounds in Jackson Park. In 1905 the more affluent residents of the area built Jackson Park Highlands, an exclusive community just south of Jackson Park that featured fine homes on large lots, underground utilities, and the sixty-seven-acre South Shore Country Club. The restricted club included a private beach, horse stables, tennis courts, and a golf course. Residential construction in South Shore continued through the 1920s, including high-rise apartment houses and single-family bungalows in the area south of Jackson Park Highlands, inviting a more diverse population. Chicagoans of Irish, German, Scandinavian, and Jewish heritage established middle-class neighborhoods in this part of South Shore, building churches, synagogues, and community centers.

As the middle-class neighborhoods to the south were expanding, however, posh Jackson Park Highlands experienced a population decline beginning in the 1940s. Eventually many of the neighborhood's historic homes were threatened with demolition, and the South Shore Country Club began to deteriorate, finally closing in 1974. The following year, the Chicago Park District bought the club property and restored it to much of its former grandeur. Renamed the South Shore Cultural Center, it was opened to the public as a recreational and cultural center for the community. The center's renovation, together with the designation of Jackson Park Highlands as a Chicago Landmark historic district in 1989, spawned a rebirth of the entire neighborhood. In 1992 Barack and Michelle Obama held their wedding reception at the South Shore Cultural Center.

The rest of South Shore also saw ups and downs. In the 1960s, poor African Americans began moving into the area, causing an economic shift in the community. By the early 1970s, in spite of "managed integration" efforts, most white residents had left, and the community fell into decline. Soon, however, commercial and residential rehabilitation projects in the 1970s and '80s helped revitalize many neighborhoods in South Shore, and today it is a stable, middle-class community of primarily African American families. Michelle Robinson Obama grew up in one of these South Shore neighborhoods, in a modest apartment on Euclid Avenue.

Oak Woods Cemetery

At the western edge of the South Shore community area is Oak Woods Cemetery, the final resting place of many Chicago luminaries, including baseball great Cap Anson, physicist Enrico Fermi, Bishop Louis Henry Ford, Olympic gold medalist Jesse Owens, and former Chicago mayor Harold Washington. Also interred here are several thousand Confederate prisoners of war who died at Camp Douglas (see under Douglas earlier on this trip). Many of these men were originally buried in the City Cemetery in what is now Lincoln Park. After the Civil War, fearing that the graves' proximity to Lake Michigan might contaminate Chicago's water supply, city officials closed the City Cemetery in 1870 and moved most of the bodies to other cemeteries, one of which was Oak Woods. Unfortunately, Oak Woods was built on a site that was nearly as swampy as the City Cemetery had been, causing similar problems before landscape engineers redesigned the grounds.

In 1893 a group of mostly private interests erected a forty-six-foot-tall monument to the Confederate dead at Oak Woods. The monument, known as Confederate Mound, was dedicated on May 30, 1895. Among those present at the ceremony were President Grover Cleveland, several members of his cabinet, and a large number of Civil War veterans from both sides. In 1911 bronze panels listing the names, units, and home states of the 4,234 Confederate soldiers buried here were installed at the base of the monument.

North Lake Shore Drive (US 41) and Sheridan Road
ROOSEVELT ROAD—DEVON AVENUE
10 miles

In the summer along North Lake Shore Drive, the lakefront abounds with sailboats and powercraft from the marinas at Diversey Harbor, Belmont Harbor, and Montrose Harbor. Motorists traveling north on the freeway from Roosevelt Road will pass Grant Park, the Loop, Chicago Harbor, Navy Pier, and many of the major lakeside parks and beaches while edging a number of upscale North Side neighborhoods, several of which we will explore on this trip. At its northern end, the LSD terminates at Hollywood

Avenue, where it connects with Sheridan Road. Continuing on Sheridan, we end our tour at Loyola University in Rogers Park.

CHICAGO HARBOR

East of Grant Park across Lake Shore Drive is Chicago Harbor, the city's first and main port on Lake Michigan. Now used mostly as a marina for pleasure craft, the harbor was established in 1833 as a shipping wharf, the basis for the development of the city. The harbor was carved out of the giant sandbar that originally blocked access to the Chicago River. A few years later, the Illinois & Michigan Canal was completed, connecting the lake to the Mississippi River. The Port of Chicago was born.

The Chicago Harbor Lighthouse (a.k.a the Chicago Breakwater Light) was built in 1893 for the World's Columbian Exposition (see under Hyde Park on previous trip). It was moved to its present location in 1919. Still an active aid to navigation, the lighthouse is not accessible to the public, but it is a delightful sight on Lake Michigan boat tours. It was listed on the NRHP in 1984 and was designated a Chicago Landmark in 2003. Ownership was transferred from the U.S. Coast Guard to the City of Chicago in 2009.

NAVY PIER

Lake Shore Drive borders the city's most visited attraction, Navy Pier. Lined with shops, eateries, museums, parks, and pavilions, the pier was not an obsolete industrial wharf converted into a tourist attraction—it was originally conceived as an amusement promenade, at least in part.

Municipal Pier #2 was completed in 1916 as part of Burnham and Bennett's 1909 *Plan of Chicago*; the name was changed to Navy Pier in 1927 to honor World War I Navy veterans. From the beginning, the 3,000-foot-long extension into Lake Michigan served as both a commercial shipping dock and a venue for public entertainment and cultural facilities.

During the two World Wars, the U.S. Navy secured the pier for military purposes. The buildings and other facilities were used for housing troops and, during the second war, for training pilots. After that, the pier continued its role as a commercial landing while also serving as a venue for trade exhibitions and cultural events, as a branch campus of the University of Illinois, and for a variety of other purposes before falling into disuse during the 1970s.

In 1989 the newly created Metropolitan Pier and Exposition Authority began a five-year, $200 million renovation that transformed the aging pier into one of the city's most spectacular attractions. Of particular interest is the renowned Chicago Children's Museum, founded in 1982 at the Chicago Public Library (now the Chicago Cultural Center) and established at its Navy Pier facility in 1995.

NEAR NORTH SIDE: GOLD COAST

As its name implies, the Near North community area is immediately north of the Loop. It comprises about eleven different named neighborhoods, many of which are discussed on other trips—Streeterville, Washington Square, River North, and Old Town. On this tour we explore the exclusive neighborhood known as the Gold Coast. Dominated by luxury brownstones and high-rise apartments, the Gold Coast is a vibrant area for upscale shopping, entertainment, and dining. It is also an official historic district.

In the northern part of the district, the area along Astor Street is a designated Chicago Landmark for its elegant late-nineteenth- and early-twentieth-century residential architecture. During that time, the lakefront property in this part of town was home to some of the wealthiest families in Chicago, including Cyrus Hall McCormick, Potter Palmer, and John Wellborn Root. The district still quarters many of the city's most elite residents, including the Catholic Archbishop of Chicago, who lives in the same mansion that was built for the first Archbishop of Chicago, Patrick Feehan, in 1885.

Amid the high-rises along the Gold Coast lakefront is the 1917 mansion built for heiress Eleanor Robinson Countiss and her family. Designed by noted architect Howard Van Doren Shaw, the interior of the house features eight marble fireplaces and a gilded grand staircase. In 1950 Dr. Max Thorek purchased the mansion for the sole purpose of establishing the International Museum of Surgical Science. After nearly twenty years of collecting and sorting papers, artifacts, and artworks, Dr. Thorek opened the museum, the only one of its kind, in 1954. Displays range from marble busts to antique surgical kits to perforated human skulls and trays full of mummified kidney stones. Paintings depicting medical procedures through the ages adorn walls throughout the building. These and other exhibits ensure that visitors to the Museum of Surgical Science will have a memorable, if rather disturbing, experience.

Another historic site in this neighborhood, though unmarked, is the location of Brand's Hall (now a Walgreens store), where the Industrial Workers of the World (IWW, a.k.a. the "Wobblies") was founded in the summer of 1905. As the American labor movement pursued parity with capitalists, some charged that the American Federation of Labor was not a working-class movement. For nearly two weeks, beginning on June 27, 1905, more than two hundred Socialists and labor leaders from across the country met at Brand's Hall, on the southeast corner of Clark and Erie Streets, to form one large union to "combat with the financial powers that now exist." By the time the convention ended on July 8, the delegates, among whom were Eugene V. Debs, Lucy E. Parsons, and Mary Harris "Mother" Jones, had formed the IWW, whose sole purpose was "to bring the workers of this country into the possession of the full value of the product of their toil." The IWW is still based in Chicago, with its general headquarters on Montrose Avenue.

In 1959 *Playboy* magazine mogul Hugh Hefner purchased the 1899 former home of a wealthy Chicago doctor and began renovating it as a hedonistic palace, the original Playboy Mansion. A native Chicagoan, Hefner was living in Hyde Park when he published the first issue of *Playboy* in 1953, and within a few years, he was a millionaire and a legend. Hefner's first Playboy Club, opened in 1960, was conveniently located a few blocks away on East Walton Street. When Hefner moved permanently to Los Angeles in 1974, he donated the mansion to the Chicago Art Institute; the building was later sold to developers, who converted it into seven exclusive single-family condominiums. The original Playboy Club closed in 1986; the building still stands as One Magnificent Mile, a mixed-use high-rise.

LINCOLN PARK (THE PARK)

Chicago's largest public park lies all along the lakeshore from Ohio Street Beach in Streeterville to Ardmore Avenue in Edgewater. Created in 1860 as Lake Park, it was renamed for President Abraham Lincoln after his assassination. The community area called Lincoln Park, which extends west of the park, will be discussed on later trips.

The oldest part of the 1,208-acre park was once Chicago City Cemetery, which dates back to 1843. Around 1870 local residents, believing the proximity of the graves to Lake Michigan risked contaminating the water supply, persuaded the city to close the cemetery and exhume the remains. Most of the interred were reburied at cemeteries outside the city limits. The body of former mayor James Curtiss, however, was lost during the removal, and his remains along with others that were inadvertently left behind still lie beneath the parkland.

One grave left in the park was that of David Kennison, who moved to Chicago in the late 1840s and claimed, among other things, to have been born in 1736 and that he was a participant in the Boston Tea Party. At the time of his death in 1852, he was supposedly 115 years old and was a Chicago legend. The city paid for his funeral, an elaborate military pageant attended by thousands. Most of the stories he told about his life—including his age—were later debunked. His supposed grave, near Wisconsin Avenue and Clark Street, is marked with a plaque on a large boulder, placed there in 1903.

Over time, Lincoln Park was chosen as the site of many prominent institutions, including the Peggy Notebaert Nature Museum and Museum of the Chicago Academy of Sciences, the Chicago History Museum, the Lincoln Park Conservatory, and the world-renowned Lincoln Park Zoo. The latter, founded in 1868, is one of the country's oldest zoos. The history museum, formerly known as the Chicago Historical Society, opened in Lincoln Park in 1932. Among the thousands of manuscripts and artifacts obtained in 1920 from the estate of Charles F. Gunther was the bed on which Abraham Lincoln died. Other exhibits include treasures of fine, decorative, and industrial arts.

Lincoln Park also comprises seven miles of public beaches, including those at Ohio Street, Oak Street, North Avenue, Foster Avenue, and Montrose Avenue (the largest). Amenities vary, but all of these beaches are developed and maintained for public swimming and recreation. Chicago's first public beach opened in Lincoln Park in 1885. Burnham and Bennett's 1909 *Plan of Chicago*, which encouraged lakefront development, led to the creation of additional public beaches, which were further expanded through the second half of the twentieth century.

EDGEWATER

Like many lakefront areas, Edgewater was developed as a residential community for wealthy Chicagoans in the 1880s. Before that, the area was dominated by woodland dotted with small farms and orchards. Edgewater was originally part of Lake View Township, which was annexed to the city in 1889. Over the decades the community continued to grow, incorporating the adjacent Swedish village to the southwest, known as Andersonville. Today the Andersonville Commercial Historic District is one of three historic districts in Edgewater. The two others are the Lakewood Balmoral and Bryn Mawr Historic Districts, the former famous for its brick row houses and the latter for its historic hotels and apartment buildings.

ROGERS PARK

Phillip Rogers was an early settler in this area, where two major Indian trails intersected and where family bands from regional tribes seasonally camped. Rogers originally set up shop here to trade with the local Indians, but as more whites arrived, he began to buy up land for a settlement. Many of the early arrivals to the village were from Luxembourg and Germany; later, English, Irish, and Jewish immigrants joined them. Rogers Park was annexed to Chicago in 1893.

Architecture fans will find much to love in Rogers Park, especially the Frank Lloyd Wright–designed Emil Bach House, built in 1915. It was deemed a Chicago Landmark in 1977 and was added to the NRHP two years later.

Today Rogers Park is one of the most culturally diverse communities in the nation. Rogers Park Baptist Church, founded in 1891, conducts Sunday services in three languages. Students, faculty, and staff from Loyola University and nearby Northwestern University contribute to the community's vitality and multiculturalism.

Loyola University

While the main campus of Loyola University Chicago is in Rogers Park, the university comprises twelve schools and colleges on six campuses. This private research institution, founded by the Society of Jesus (the Jesuits) in 1870 as St. Ignatius College, is now the largest Jesuit university in the United States. The school moved its main campus (now the College of Arts and Sciences) from downtown Chicago to Rogers Park in 1912. In addition to its four other Chicagoland campuses, the university maintains a campus in Rome, Italy. The John Felice Rome Center, established in 1962, offers programs for students from Loyola and other schools wishing to study abroad.

Michigan Avenue
WACKER DRIVE–ROOSEVELT ROAD
1.5 miles

Although this trip is short in distance, it is jam-packed with Chicago history and culture. Just south of the Magnificent Mile and across the DuSable Bridge we find the site of Fort Dearborn, the seed from which Chicago grew. Continuing south, Michigan Avenue fronts Grant Park, arguably the heart of the entire city. The stretch of Michigan across from the park, known as the Michigan Avenue Streetwall, comprises the Historic Michigan Boulevard District, which contains some of the city's most important buildings. And representing twenty-first-century Chicago is the eye-popping Millennium Park, at the north end of Grant Park, completed in 2004.

FORT DEARBORN HISTORIC SITE

An outline embedded in the street at the intersection of Wacker Drive and Michigan Avenue shows the approximate location of Fort Dearborn, the first permanent military stockade and first settlement in Chicago. The fort site is on the south end of the Michigan-Wacker Historic District, the main part of which will be discussed on a later trip.

Fort Dearborn stood near the mouth of the Chicago River on part of a six-square-mile tract that Indian tribes ceded to the U.S. government in the Treaty of Greenville on August 23, 1795. The property was a prime spot to protect the Chicago Portage, which connected Lake Michigan with the Illinois River via the Des Plaines and Chicago Rivers.

In the spring of 1803, Capt. John Whistler and six men arrived here, under the orders of Secretary of War Henry Dearborn, to survey the area for a site to build a fort. In August troops began construction on the post, which would be named after the secretary. For the buildings, hand-hewn logs cut from a nearby forested area were placed horizontally and chinked with clay, hay, and moss. A double stockade of vertical logs enclosed the grounds.

The following year, fur trader John Kinzie set up shop near the newly finished fort. His trading post attracted the local Indians as well as some early settlers, and a small village developed. By then, many of the area tribes had aligned themselves with the British, who promised to end American expansionism and return their land. Main Poc, a Potawatomi chief with a large village on the Kankakee River, spoke openly of attacking Fort Dearborn in 1808 and again in 1810, after Capt. Nathan Heald replaced Whistler as the fort's commander.

The War of 1812 against England heightened unrest in the Illinois Territory. Indian war parties attacked isolated cabins and farms throughout the state. Fort Dearborn, the westernmost outpost at this time, fell under the jurisdiction of Brig. Gen. William Hull, governor of the Michigan Territory, stationed in Detroit. Hull had enjoyed a distinguished career during the Revolutionary War, but he was past his prime and an inveterate drunk. In early August 1812, after Indians attacked Detroit, the general ordered Fort Dearborn's evacuation.

This sketch depicts early Fort Dearborn, built in 1803. —Author's collection

Sketch of the blockhouse and lighthouse at Fort Dearborn,
all that remained of the fort in 1857 —Author's collection

On August 8, Heald received Hull's message, which instructed him to distribute the fort's property among the local Indians, evacuate the post, and march overland to Fort Wayne. Heald vacillated for six days before acting. Although he distributed blankets, pots, and similar items, he withheld the fort's surplus arms, ammunition, and whiskey, angering many young warriors. On August 15, Capt. William Wells arrived from Fort Wayne with a small party of troops and Indian guides to escort the evacuation. After traveling about a mile and a half, the caravan was attacked and overwhelmed by Potawatomi warriors in a battle known as the Fort Dearborn Massacre, a.k.a. the Battle of Fort Dearborn (see earlier trip). Back at the fort, other Indians plundered the unprotected buildings and shot the cattle. The next day they set the fort on fire. Only the stone-walled powder magazine remained standing.

Following the 1814 Treaty of Ghent that ended the war, the fort was rebuilt. Its troops saw action in the 1827 Winnebago War and again in the 1832 Black Hawk War. In 1839 the fort property was divided into lots and sold. By 1860, most of the buildings had been demolished. The rest were destroyed in the Great Fire of 1871. The site of Fort Dearborn was dedicated as a Chicago Landmark in 1971.

GRANT PARK

The beautifully landscaped open space of Grant Park, "Chicago's front yard," rests atop residue from the Great Fire of 1871. Chicago's 1837 city charter proclaimed that this section of the lakefront, then called Lake Park, would always be open and free of buildings, but in 1901, with the transfer of the park to the city park commission, civic planners proposed that a number of public buildings be erected within the park, which they had renamed for President Ulysses S. Grant.

One of the biggest boosters of the open-space plan for the park was Aaron Montgomery Ward, of catalog fame (see also Near North Side: Washington Square Park on later trip). In the early 1900s, he twice sued developers for violating the charter's open-space provision, launching a decade-long battle between conflicting visions. Ward won his suit in 1911, but in the end, the park reflected an unofficial compromise as developers expanded the lakefront south of the original park and built the Field Museum and other structures. Ward himself agreed to exempt the Art Institute, built in 1893 (see below).

The traditional focal point of the park is the Clarence Buckingham Memorial Fountain, commissioned by philanthropist Kate Buckingham in 1927 to honor her brother. Its design is reminiscent of a fountain at the Palace at Versailles, with three tiers of basins, representing Lake Michigan, and four pairs of bronze seahorses, representing the four states that border the lake. Jets of water shoot up every twenty minutes, illuminated by colored lights after dark in the summer. The fountain remains one of Chicago's most popular attractions.

In addition to Buckingham Fountain and the Art Institute, the 319-acre park also comprises the Petrillo Music Shell, Daley Bicentennial Plaza, and Hutchinson Field, as well as innumerable monuments and sculptures, walking trails, marinas, playing fields, and special gardens. The Museum Campus, annexed to Grant Park in 1998, contains the Field Museum of Natural History (established in 1893), the Adler Planetarium, and the Shedd Aquarium (both established in 1930). In the late 1990s, the city began plans to extend the park to the north. The eventual result was today's stunning Millennium Park (see below).

Art Institute of Chicago

At the western edge of the park, on Michigan Avenue, is the world-renowned Art Institute of Chicago, the second-largest art museum in the nation and the third most visited. The institute building, constructed during the 1893 World's Columbian Exposition, is the only building in the Historic Michigan Boulevard District on the east (park) side of the avenue; it was the lone exception to the city's policy of allowing no buildings in Grant Park. During the fair, it served as the World's Congress Auxiliary Building, where such luminaries as Susan B. Anthony and Frederick Douglass spoke.

The Art Institute offers one of the finest collections of impressionist paintings in the country, as well as ancient artifacts and examples of Asian art, African American art, photography, and American decorative art. The museum building also houses the School of the Art Institute of Chicago, established in 1866 as the Chicago Academy of Design, later called the Chicago Academy of Fine Arts. After the World's Columbian Exposition, the Art Institute received the beautiful Michigan Avenue building that became its permanent home. The two bronze lions guarding the entrance steps were created by Edward Kemeys, a former Illinois resident.

Police Riot of 1968

Grant Park has its own claims to history. Perhaps the most widely known episode was the infamous 1968 riot, in which city police clashed violently with antiwar demonstrators during the Democratic National Convention. That turbulent year saw a hundred riots throughout the United States, many triggered by the assassinations of Dr. Martin Luther King Jr. and Robert F. Kennedy, and protests against the Vietnam War were reaching their peak. In August Mayor Richard J. Daley, determined to have an orderly convention week, brought in extra security and delivered stern warnings to would-be troublemakers.

During the convention, a number of protests sprang up around the city, and the various conflicts that occurred between protesters and police created escalating tension. The largest gathering, comprising some 10,000 people, legally assembled in Grant Park on August 28. When officers attacked a teenage boy as he pulled down an American flag, the crowd responded by throwing food and rocks at the cops, who in turn opened up with tear gas and billy clubs. Television crews captured much of the chaos as the crowd chanted, "The whole world is watching." Seven police officers were indicted on charges of civil rights violations, but all were acquitted.

The following year, eight protest leaders, the "Chicago Eight," were indicted for conspiracy and intent to incite a riot. When the judge separated one of them, Bobby Seale, from the case due to his unruly behavior, the remaining defendants became the Chicago Seven. In the controversial, widely publicized trial, the defendants' repeated outbursts added contempt of court citations to their charges. The trial ended with the conviction of five of the defendants for intent to incite a riot (later reversed on appeal), and the acquittals of all seven on the conspiracy charges. The judge also sentenced all seven defendants, plus two of their lawyers, to prison for more than 150 incidents of criminal contempt during the trial. This ruling was also reversed on appeal.

The bad feelings generated by the riots created deeper divisions within the Democratic Party and among the American public in general, ultimately leading to the election of Republican Richard Nixon as president in November.

Millennium Park

Since its establishment in 1901, Grant Park has seen countless additions and improvements. The latest is the twenty-five-acre Millennium Park, Chicago's tribute to the new century, at the northwest corner of Grant Park. Built between 1998 and 2004, the expansion of parkland attractively covered unsightly commuter railroad tracks and parking lots.

Among the new park's myriad features are the Jay Pritzker Pavilion, an ultramodern outdoor concert area; the Joan W. and Irving B. Harris Theater for Music and Dance, an indoor theater and concert hall; McCormick Tribune Plaza and Ice Rink, a multipurpose recreational space; the Park Grill, Millennium Park's only restaurant, which boasts the largest outdoor dining area in the city; the 2.5-acre Lurie Garden; the McDonald's Cycle Center, a large indoor bicycle station; and the winding, 925-foot-long BP Pedestrian Bridge, which connects Millennium Park with Daley Bicentennial Plaza. Major public artworks in the park include the Crown Fountain, composed of two fifty-foot-tall glass-block towers that project changing video images beneath a cascade of water; the Cloud Gate sculpture, a highly polished bean-shaped structure; and the Millennium Monument, a forty-foot-high Doric column.

The park opened in 2004, years behind schedule, way over budget, and amid controversy over wasteful spending and cronyism. Nevertheless, the result has drawn accolades around the world for its beauty, innovation, accessibility, and environmental friendliness.

HISTORIC MICHIGAN BOULEVARD DISTRICT

More than forty buildings grace the Historic Michigan Boulevard District, across the avenue from Grant Park. Many of these structures played a memorable part in the city's history. Among them are the ornate 1897 Chicago Cultural Center, the city's official reception venue and free exhibition and events space (see below); the distinctive 1924 Metropolitan Tower, built as the headquarters for investment firm S. W. Straus & Company and now housing mostly high-rise condominiums; and the legendary 1910 Blackstone Hotel (see below).

Another landmark building, at Jackson Boulevard, is the Motorola Building, originally known as the Railway Exchange Building and later as the Santa Fe Building, designed by Daniel H. Burnham. Burnham and his partner, Edward H. Bennett, used a small enclosed penthouse on the roof as an auxiliary office, which provided them with a spectacular view of the lakefront while they were drafting their *Plan of Chicago.*

At Madison Street and South Michigan Avenue is a high-rise luxury condo building formerly known as the Montgomery Ward Tower. Built by catalog king Aaron Montgomery Ward (see also Near North Side: Washington Square Park on later trip), it was the tallest building in Chicago when it was erected in 1898. Sadly, its original architectural highlight, a ten-story tower with a three-story pyramid, was dismantled for safety reasons in 1947.

Architects Daniel H. Burnham and Edward H. Bennett created their Plan of Chicago *from a small enclosed office on the roof of what is now the Motorola Building; the space has since been renovated.* —Author's collection

The district also contains two major museums. The Museum of Contemporary Photography, part of Columbia College Chicago, was founded in 1984 as the only museum in the Midwest exclusively devoted to photography. The Spertus Museum, dedicated to Jewish history and culture, is located on the ninth and tenth floors of the ultramodern Spertus Institute for Jewish Learning and Leadership, which also houses the esteemed Spertus Institute for Jewish Studies.

Also of note, a marker at Michigan Avenue and Adams Street identifies the starting point of historic US Route 66, though the actual departure point was at Jackson Street and Lake Shore Drive.

Chicago Cultural Center

The magnificent Chicago Cultural Center, nicknamed the "People's Palace," is renowned for both its free public events and its architectural splendor. Originally built as a public library, the facility opened to great fanfare in October 1897. Chicagoans and visitors marveled at the building's neoclassical limestone and granite façade, two Tiffany stained-glass domes, marble stairways, and mosaic-covered walls—as indeed they still do.

As the library expanded in the early decades of the twentieth century, it began to outgrow its Michigan Avenue facility. Some of the collections were housed elsewhere while the building's fate remained in limbo for decades. It was not until the 1980s that a new library, the Harold Washington Library Center, was designed. In the meantime, preservationists lobbied to keep and restore the original building on Michigan Avenue. With the new library's completion in 1991, plans to renovate the old structure as a free public museum and cultural center began in earnest. The new Chicago Cultural Center opened in 1994. Today the center attracts thousands each year, and the building is a treasured showpiece of downtown Chicago.

Blackstone Hotel

The twenty-three-story Blackstone Hotel and the adjacent Blackstone Theatre (now the Merle Reskin Theatre) were built in 1910 by John and Tracy Drake, sons of hotel magnate John Drake. The hotel site was purchased from the widow of Timothy B. Blackstone, a prominent railroad executive who was once a business partner of the elder John Drake. The Blackstones' once-opulent 1860s mansion was among the last private residences in the area to be razed to make way for new commercial development. To honor the site's history, the Drake brothers named their new Beaux Arts hotel for Blackstone. The Drakes would later build the famous Drake Hotel on North Michigan Avenue.

The recently renovated Blackstone, now called the Renaissance Blackstone Hotel, more than earned its historic landmark status for having hosted innumerable public figures including U.S. presidents, movie stars, and gangsters. It was in one of the hotel's suites that Warren G. Harding, in a backdoor meeting, was chosen as the Republican nominee in the 1920 presidential election. Afterward, a reporter coined the phrase "smoke-filled room" to describe the shady proceedings. It was also at the Blackstone that John F. Kennedy took the call informing him of the Cuban Missile Crisis in 1962.

Wabash Avenue, Van Buren Street, and Wacker Drive
THE LOOP
2 miles

The Loop, Chicago's business and cultural core, got its name from the circular route of the streetcars, and later the "L" trains, in this part of town. To many people, the Loop's skyscrapers, street-level cafes and shops, and profusion of public art encapsulate the essence of a major urban center. From the Sears Tower to Daley Plaza to the Harold Washington Library, its attractions are many and various.

Two major streets that traverse the Loop, State Street and Lake Street, were originally settlers' trails. State Street heads south from downtown Chicago to the Calumet River; along with Vincennes Avenue, State Street formed the northern part of the Vincennes Trail (or Trace), which stretched from the fledgling town of Chicago to Vincennes, Indiana. Likewise, Lake Street, once called Lake Trail, connected Fort Dearborn and Chicago with several towns and farming communities to the west, including Oak Ridge (now Oak Park), Cottage Hill (now Elmhurst), Addison, and Elgin.

While the Loop community area encompasses everything between Lake Shore Drive and the South Branch of the Chicago River on the east and west, respectively, and between the main river and Roosevelt Road on the north and south, we will focus on the vicinity around the loop of the "L" tracks, the neighborhood commonly referred to as the Loop.

Our tour of the Loop is itself a loop. It follows Wabash Avenue south to Van Buren Street, which leads west to Wacker Drive. Wacker takes us north then east to complete the loop near the Wabash Avenue (Irv Kupcinet) Bridge. While this route will take you around the Loop's perimeter by car, completing this tour requires traveling on foot, not only because the traffic is daunting, but because these sites are worth more than a drive-by glance.

INSIDE THE LOOP

Within the Loop are several loosely defined districts devoted to government, finance, theater, and retail. The Loop is also dotted with plazas and other open spaces, along with numerous public artworks. Among these are sculptures by Marc Chagall, Joan Miró, Henry Moore, Pablo Picasso, and Lorado Taft.

Beginning with the northeastern corner of the Loop, just south of the Fort Dearborn site, we will tour the theater and retail districts and the southeastern part of the Loop. Moving west, we'll explore the government district with its famous public art. Finally we'll check out the financial district in the southwestern part of the Loop.

North Loop Theater District

Chicago's main theater district, in the northern part of the Loop, contains four historic theaters—the Cadillac Palace Theatre, the Goodman Theatre, the Ford Center for the Performing Arts (formerly the Oriental Theatre), and the world-renowned Chicago Theatre. A few blocks south is the Bank of America Theatre, better known by its former name, the Shubert Theatre. The other major historic downtown theater, the Auditorium Theatre, stands in the far southeast corner of the Loop. Five of these six structures were restored in the 1980s, 1990s, and early 2000s.

The Chicago Theatre, with its iconic vertical lighted sign, is among the best known of Chicago's historic theaters. Opened as a movie house and live theater in 1921, it still contains its original Wurlitzer pipe organ. The building deteriorated over the years and the theater closed briefly in 1985, but volunteers restored it, and it reopened less than a year later. Tours are available.

Just southwest of the Chicago Theatre is the Oriental Theatre, named for its Far East design, which opened as a movie house in 1926. The venue also held live shows, including performances by major stars such as Al Jolson, Fanny Brice, Judy Garland, and later, Little Richard and Stevie Wonder. The Oriental was built at the site of the Iroquois Theatre, which burned down on December 30, 1903. This devastating fire occurred during a matinee performance and claimed 602 lives. The alley behind the theater is believed to be haunted. During the later twentieth century, the Oriental building fell into disrepair and was threatened with demolition, but with public and private funding it was finally restored in 1998, reopening as the Ford Center for the Performing Arts.

Nearby, the Goodman Theatre, founded in 1922, the original Goodman, which included a drama school, opened its doors in 1925 at Monroe Street and Columbus Drive. It was moved to its current spot in 2000. Two blocks west is the Cadillac Palace Theatre, which opened as the Palace Theatre in 1926. Elegantly designed and lushly furnished, it was the main venue for the big vaudeville acts, including Jimmy Durante, Mae West, and Jack Benny. Renovated in 1999, it reopened as the Cadillac Palace Theatre.

A few blocks south of the main theater district is the oldest of these historic venues, the Bank of America Theatre, originally called the Majestic Theatre and best known as the Shubert Theatre. The Majestic opened in 1906 as a vaudeville house. At the time, it was the tallest building in the city. Closed down during the Great Depression, it reopened as the Sam Shubert Theatre in 1945. It was restored and became the LaSalle Bank Theatre in 2006. It was renamed for the Bank of America in 2008, after the latter bank bought out the former.

Loop Retail Historic District

The Loop Retail Historic District runs along both Wabash and State Streets between Lake and Van Buren. The Loop emerged as a major shopping area when the city was still young. After the Great Fire of 1871, many of the retailers rebuilt with bigger and better stores, ushering in the era of the modern department store. Chicago was in the vanguard of this development in retail shopping, led by innovative merchant Marshall Field.

Before the advent of the suburban shopping center in the 1970s, most extra-urban residents traveled to the nearest city to shop for items beyond what was stocked in their local general store or dry-goods store. In the late nineteenth century, Marshall Field and others envisioned creating a new kind of urban shopping experience, providing not only a plethora of goods but also customer-oriented amenities such as attractive surroundings, personal attention, merchandise delivery, and unconditional refunds. By the turn of the century, the Loop had several major department stores housed in grand, multilevel buildings along State Street.

The heyday of the Loop shopping district lasted from about 1912 to the early 1950s, when development of the Magnificent Mile drew shoppers to North Michigan Avenue. With the explosive growth of far-flung malls in the 1970s and '80s, downtown stores in Chicago and other big cities floundered. By the mid-1980s, all but a few of the original big department stores in the Loop were gone, leaving mostly office buildings, eateries, and some hotels. Over the years, however, new retailers, along with restaurants and specialty shops, have moved into the Loop near State Street, gradually putting a new face on this historic retail district.

A number of historic department-store buildings still stand in the Loop, though only one of them—the Marshall Field building—still comprises a single department store. The former flagship store of Marshall Field's, on State Street between Randolph and Washington, is now home to Macy's, which bought out Field's in 2005. On the seventh floor of this gorgeous turn-of-the-twentieth-century building is a visitor center, where various displays examine Chicago's retail history.

Another big department store in Chicago, Carson Pirie Scott, originally operated out of what is now the Sullivan Center, at State and Madison Streets. The building, with its distinctive rounded corner, was designed by legendary architect Louis Sullivan in 1899. After more than a century in that location, Carson Pirie Scott closed its doors in 2007. A full renovation of the building for mixed use was completed in 2011.

In addition to its retail buildings, the district contains a number of historic hotels, including the 1925 Palmer House (now the Palmer House Hilton) at State and Monroe Streets. The first Palmer House burned down in the Great Chicago Fire, only two weeks after it opened its doors in 1871. Immediately rebuilt in iron and brick, the new fireproof hotel reopened in 1875. It boasted the city's first elevator, first electric lights, and first telephones. In 1879 the hotel was the venue for the Military Court of Inquiry of Maj. Marcus A. Reno, 7th U.S. Cavalry, held to investigate his conduct at the 1876 Battle of the Little Bighorn River in eastern Montana Territory.

The Palmer's third incarnation, an expansion erected on the same site, was an elegant, twenty-five-story structure advertised as the largest hotel in the world. Still housed in this 1925 building, the Palmer House is the oldest continuously running major hotel in North America. The structure underwent an extensive restoration between 2007 and 2009.

Southeastern Loop

At Wabash Avenue and Congress Parkway is the recently renovated, acoustically perfect 1889 Auditorium Theatre Building, which has hosted everything from operas to political party conventions to rock concerts. Northwest of the theater is the Harold Washington Library, the largest public library in the world. Named for Chicago's first African American mayor, who was also the chief booster for the new building, it was completed in 1991. Also in this area is DePaul University's downtown campus.

Government District

The central part of the Loop, between LaSalle and Dearborn Streets from Lake Street to Jackson Boulevard, is the seat of Chicago's municipal, state, and federal government buildings. Among them are the James R. Thompson State of Illinois Center, which houses state government offices; the 1911 City Hall and the adjacent Cook County Building; the Richard J. Daley Center, which houses municipal and county courtrooms and offices as well as the Cook County Law Library; and the Chicago Federal Center, which includes the Everett M. Dirksen United States Courthouse and the John C. Kluczynski Federal Building, both designed by Ludwig Mies van der Rohe.

A southbound stroll down Clark Street takes pedestrians past many of the city's major public sculptures, beginning with Jean Dubuffet's *Monument with Standing Beast* at the State of Illinois Center and ending with Alexander Calder's *Flamingo* in Federal Plaza. In between are three other famous statues—Pablo Picasso's untitled sculpture in Daley Plaza; Joan Miro's *Chicago* in Brunswick Plaza; and Marc Chagall's *Four Seasons* mosaic in Chase Tower Plaza.

Just west of Clark, at Adams and LaSalle Streets, is another iconic structure, though it's not a government building. The Rookery, designed by Daniel Burnham and John Root and completed in 1888, is considered an architectural masterpiece. The lobby of this majestic twelve-story office building was redesigned in 1905 by Frank Lloyd Wright. The Rookery was named a Chicago Landmark in 1972 and a National Historic Landmark in 1975.

Also on LaSalle Street, just across Adams Street from the Rookery, is the site of the Home Insurance Building, widely considered the world's first skyscraper. Designed by William Le Baron Jenney and completed in 1885, the ten-story building (two more stories were added in 1890) was the first to use a frame of structural steel. This remarkable piece of architectural history was demolished in 1931; a bank building now stands at the location. A plaque in the lobby describes the former structure and its significance.

Built in 1885, the Home Insurance Building in Chicago, designed by William Le Baron Jenny, was the world's first skyscraper.
—Author's collection

Financial District

The main structure in this southwestern Loop district is the Chicago Board of Trade Building. A National Historic Landmark as well as an official Chicago Landmark, this art deco skyscraper originally housed the Chicago Board of Trade, now merged with the Chicago Mercantile Exchange as the CME Group. Built in 1930 on LaSalle Street at Jackson Boulevard, it was the third headquarters of the Chicago Board of Trade, founded in 1848. (See also Chicago Mercantile Exchange Center below.) In 2011 the CME Group announced its plans to sell the historic building as the company adapts global economic changes as well as technological changes in the financial world.

WACKER DRIVE

L-shaped Wacker Drive, which edges the Chicago River, forms the western and northern borders of the Loop. Here visitors can view some of the most famous structures in the city as well as a few lesser-known historical sites.

Willis Tower (Sears Tower)

Renamed Willis Tower in 2009, the former Sears Tower is often still called by its familiar original name. At 1,450 feet, it remains the tallest building in the United States and the fifth-tallest building in the world. From the Skydeck, a 1,353-foot-high observation area, visitors may see forty or fifty miles out if the day is clear.

Construction on this building, commissioned by Sears, Roebuck & Company, began in 1971 and was completed two years later. Over the next few years, however, the Sears company's growth projections fell short, and much of the building was rented out to other interests. When London-based insurance broker Willis Group Holdings became the tower's major tenant in 2009, the company was granted naming rights to the building as part of the deal.

Chicago Mercantile Exchange Center

The Chicago Mercantile Exchange, a.k.a. the "Merc," was founded in 1898 as the Chicago Butter and Egg Board, which traded contracts for only two products—butter and eggs. In 1919 the company, now expanded to include other products, was reorganized as the Chicago Mercantile Exchange (CME).

The first forty-story tower of the two-towered Chicago Mercantile Exchange Center on South Wacker Drive was built in 1983; the adjacent tower, also forty stories tall, was added in 1987. The structure opened as the fifth headquarters building for the Chicago Mercantile Exchange; when the exchange merged with the Chicago Board of Trade in 2007, its trading floor was moved to the historic Board of Trade Building. The CME still keeps offices here while the rest of the building is rented to other entities for various purposes.

Civic Opera House

Opened in 1929, the Civic Opera House is the second-largest opera auditorium in the country. Chicago business tycoon and avid arts patron Samuel Insull built the hall for the benefit of the Chicago Civic Opera. The shape is thought to resemble a large chair, or throne. The forty-five-story office tower depicts the chair's back, flanked by two twenty-two-story wings representing the armrests. Legend has it that the building was designed in this manner in honor of Insull's wife, Gladys Wallis, an aspiring singer-actress who had been rejected by the New York Metropolitan Opera—the back of the "throne" faces east, expressing disdain for New York's rebuff of Gladys. Now occupied by the Lyric Opera of Chicago, the building underwent a major restoration in 1996.

Site of the First Wigwam

For the Algonquian Indians, a wigwam was a temporary dwelling constructed of tree branches and bark. In Chicago, a wigwam was a place for choosing presidential candidates. The first and most famous Wigwam was constructed at the southeast corner of Lake Street and Market Street (now Wacker Drive), near the Chicago River. It housed the second Republican National Convention—the first political party convention held in Chicago—in May 1860.

The original Wigwam, built in just five weeks, was a temporary, two-story wooden building nearly a block long. Though simple in design, it did boast twenty-foot-high arched entrances, tall rectangular windows for air circulation, and square turrets at each corner. The building cost $5,000 to construct; each attendee was charged a twenty-five-cent admission fee to offset the expense.

The week of the convention, attendees poured into Chicago by train. Ten thousand delegates gathered inside the building, sitting on chairs borrowed from local residents. An equal number stood outside to follow the proceedings. Shouters relayed information to those who were too far away to hear.

This sketch from Harper's Weekly, *May 12, 1860, shows the Wigwam of 1860, the scene of the Republican National Convention in which Abraham Lincoln was nominated for president.* —Author's collection

This sketch by L. Braunhold shows the Sauganash Hotel, the first hotel in Chicago; the structure, which began as a small log tavern, reopened as a hotel in 1831, after owner Mark Beaubien built an addition. —Author's collection

New York senator William H. Seward was the favorite candidate. His supporters already had one-third of the delegates locked up. Twelve other men were also in the running. One of the hopefuls, Abraham Lincoln, was considered a dark horse. But Lincoln's supporters had a plan. The night before the final day of balloting, Ward H. Lamon, a Springfield friend and former law partner of Lincoln, and others printed counterfeit tickets and distributed them to Lincoln supporters, instructing them to arrive early. Lincoln's backers packed the convention, and by the time Seward's delegates arrived, they were barely able to find a seat. Abe's faction also assigned men to lead loud cheers, drowning out the words of the other delegates. The scheme worked. Lincoln's side created a groundswell of support that won him the nomination on the third ballot.

After the convention, the Wigwam was used for meetings and rallies; part of it was used as retail space. Sometime between 1867 and 1871, the building was destroyed. It may have been razed by the city, or it may have burned down. Some believe the building burned in 1867; others maintain that it was a victim of the 1871 Great Fire. Two other wigwams were later constructed in Chicago for national conventions, in 1864 and 1892, both of them hosting the Democratic Party.

The site of the first Wigwam, today marked by a plaque as a Chicago Landmark, was thirty years earlier the location of Chicago's first hotel, the Sauganash Hotel. Early settler Mark Beaubien built a tavern, the Eagle Exchange Tavern, here in 1829, and two years later he expanded it into a two-story hotel. The Sauganash served as a community meeting place and, for a time, as a theater—the first in Chicago—before burning down in 1851.

Site of the Eastland Disaster and Chicago Riverwalk

On what is now West Wacker Drive between LaSalle and Clark Streets, near the present-day Marshall Suloway (LaSalle Street) Bridge, is the site of the worst boat accident in Great Lakes history. On July 24, 1915, several thousand employees of the Western Electric Company in Cicero (see Cicero in Region 6) gathered at what was then an open dock on the Chicago River for their annual company outing, a daylong boat excursion across Lake Michigan from Chicago to Michigan City, Indiana, and back. Three steamer ships—the *SS Eastland*, the *SS Theodore Roosevelt*, and the *SS Petoskey*—had been chartered for the trip.

Boarding started at 6:30 a.m., and within an hour, the 269-foot *SS Eastland* had reached its capacity of 2,500 people. The passengers were not assigned seats, so some went below deck while many others stayed atop to wave to onlookers. Most of them were standing on the starboard side to face the crowd on the wharf, causing the steamer to list to starboard. The crew compensated for this by adding ballast to the port side. The ship steadied briefly but then listed ten degrees to port, so the crew filled the starboard ballast tanks.

Meanwhile, passengers moved freely from one side of the ship to the other, thinking little of the wobbling. Suddenly, for reasons that are still uncertain, the ship leaned sharply to port, causing water to pour in through the portholes and gangways. Within a few minutes, the ship had capsized and sunk to the river bottom. The passengers

Onlookers gather along both sides of the Chicago River while rescuers scramble to pull trapped passengers from the capsized Eastland —Courtesy
Eastland Disaster Historical Society

standing below deck became trapped. Heavy furniture crashed into some of these unfortunates and crushed them; other passengers were crushed against one another.

Hundreds of rescuers responded. A nearby tugboat, the *Kenosha*, pulled alongside the *Eastland* and helped victims scramble aboard. Bodies were taken in commandeered vehicles to a makeshift morgue at the 2nd Regiment Armory on Washington Boulevard (now Oprah Winfrey's Harpo Studios). Identification of the dead took several days. A total of 844 people lost their lives that day, including twenty-two entire families.

Three weeks after the accident, the *Eastland* disaster was removed from the Chicago River and recommissioned as a navy vessel, renamed the *USS Wilmette*. The ship was decommissioned in 1945 and scrapped two years later. A plaque near the LaSalle Street Bridge, dedicated in 1989, marked the site of the tragedy until it disappeared (presumably stolen) in 2000. The city of Chicago installed a temporary replacement later that year. Plans for a permanent exhibit at the site are currently under way as part of the new Chicago Riverwalk along Wacker Drive.

Also part of the Riverwalk, four blocks east of the *Eastland* disaster site, is the new Vietnam Veterans Memorial Plaza, completed in 2005 near the Wabash Avenue Bridge (Irv Kupcinet Bridge). Nearby is the Heald Square Monument, designed by Lorado Taft in 1936.

Michigan Avenue
WACKER DRIVE–OAK STREET
1 mile

The section of North Michigan Avenue known as the "Magnificent Mile" blends the historic, such as the Old Water Tower near the north end, with the ultramodern, such as the skyscraping Trump International Hotel and Tower near the south end. Lined with department stores, specialty shops, boutiques, and restaurants, the Magnificent Mile— a nickname created in the 1940s by urban developer Arthur Rubloff—is a world-renowned shopping mecca. On this short trip, we will explore the Mag Mile as well as the surrounding area.

According to most local definitions, the Mag Mile is the western boundary of the Near North Side neighborhood known as Streeterville, a mix of restaurants, hospitals, high-rise condominiums, and commercial offices on some of the most expensive real estate in the city. Within the Streeterville area are three designated historic districts— the Michigan-Wacker Historic District, the Old Water Tower District, and the East Lake Shore Drive Historic District—each of which we will visit below. Just west of Streeterville is Rush Street, a famed grownup playground lined with nightclubs, bars, restaurants, shops, day spas, and hotels.

NEAR NORTH SIDE: STREETERVILLE

The history of the Near North neighborhood known as Streeterville—roughly bounded by Michigan Avenue on the west, Lake Michigan on the north and east, and the Chicago River on the south—is a unique story. George Streeter, who was basically a squatter and a con artist, eventually lost his claim to this land in court, but the neighborhood nonetheless still carries his name.

Over the first fifty years of his life, Michigan-born George Wellington "Cap" Streeter was a Union Army soldier, trapper, logger, ice cutter, steamship captain, and circus owner. In 1886 Streeter took his new steamship for a test run on Lake Michigan. Due to what Streeter claimed was a bad storm, he ran aground near Chicago's shoreline on what was locally called "the sands," an accumulation of sand and silt that collected around a large pier just west of present-day Michigan Avenue and created a sandbar of partially usable land. The city had encouraged construction sites to dump their debris onto the sandbar to build up and stabilize the land for building. Upon his arrival here, Streeter proclaimed that the land was beyond the Illinois border, called it the "District of Lake Michigan," and laid claim to the entire area.

Influential city leaders and property owners maintained that Streeter was a squatter and that his claim to the land was entirely fraudulent. Streeter countered that as a Civil War veteran, he was entitled to a homestead. The city made numerous attempts to oust Streeter and to arrest him for various charges—including murder—but time after time, he was acquitted. Although Streeter lost his land case in 1918, he continued to fight the decision until his death in 1921. Litigation filed by his alleged heirs continued until 1940, when the last suit was finally dismissed.

MICHIGAN-WACKER HISTORIC DISTRICT

Michigan Avenue on both sides of the Chicago River contains some of the most significant landmarks and historic sites in Chicago, including the DuSable (Michigan Avenue) Bridge, the Wrigley Building, and Tribune Tower, as well as the site of Fort Dearborn (see previous trip). Together these structures and others comprise the Michigan-Wacker Historic District. Here we will explore the bridge itself and points north, all of which are within the boundaries of Streeterville.

DuSable (Michigan Avenue) Bridge

For nearly a hundred years, Chicago residents crossed the Chicago River by canoe or rowboat. A wooden bridge was built at Rush Street in 1857 and rebuilt several times. Other small bridges appeared on the river over the years, but it was not until Daniel H. Burnham and Edward H. Bennett published their *Plan of Chicago* in 1909 that an elaborate permanent bridge was designed. Construction on the Michigan Avenue Bridge (officially DuSable Bridge) began in 1917 and was completed three years later. Prominently featured on the four corner bridge houses are striking bas-relief panels sculpted by James Earle Fraser and Henry Hering, each depicting a theme from the city's early history.

Now a designated Chicago Landmark, the bridge received a makeover in 2009, when the railings were replaced with a near-replica of the original 1920s design. Visitors to the McCormick Tribune Bridgehouse and Chicago River Museum, on the southwest corner, can get a closer look at the structure's history, mechanics, and significance.

Pioneer Court

Anchoring the south end of the Magnificent Mile is Pioneer Court, which contains several historic landmarks including the site of the home and trading post of early settler Jean Baptiste Point de Sable, later occupied by settler John Kinzie, and the site of Chicago's first post office, established in 1831 and operated by fur trader Jonathan Bailey.

Sketch of the cabin and trading post in which Jean Baptiste Point de Sable and his wife lived in the late 1700s; the site is now known as Pioneer Court. —Author's collection

The identity of Chicago's first non-Indian settler is an oft-debated issue, but the title of first permanent non-native resident belongs to trader and farmer Jean Baptiste Point de Sable. Most likely the name Point de Sable (French for "sand point") was not his real surname but one he gave himself.

While little is known about Point de Sable's early life, most historians agree that by 1788, he was firmly entrenched at Chicagoua, and evidence suggests that Point de Sable's operation was not simply a trading post but an extensive farm, now covered by Pioneer Court. In 1800 Point de Sable sold his farm to John La Lime; three years later, John Kinzie purchased the property from La Lime and took over the trading post and the farm operations, going on to become a key player in the city's development. The Jean Baptiste Point de Sable Home Site in Pioneer Plaza was named a National Historic Landmark in 1976, with a bronze plaque and porcelain placard added in 1977.

Landmark Skyscrapers

Near Pioneer Court are two iconic Chicago buildings, the Wrigley Building and the Chicago Tribune Tower. These and other neighboring structures were created during the downtown construction boom that followed the 1920 completion of the Michigan Avenue Bridge. The historic Wrigley Building, which still serves as headquarters for the Wrigley chewing gum company, was designed to resemble the Giralda Tower in Seville, Spain. It consists of two towers (one built in 1920 and the other in 1924) connected by walkways. But its most striking feature is probably the four-faced clock tower that graces the top of the south building. The Wrigley Building was designated a Chicago Landmark in 2012.

Across Michigan Avenue is another official Chicago Landmark, the Chicago Tribune Tower, completed in 1925. How its neo-Gothic design came to be is an unusual story. In 1922 the newspaper sponsored an international design competition to create the "most beautiful and distinctive office building in the world." The winners, out of more than 260 entries, were John Mead Howells and Raymond Hood of New York.

Among the building's unique features is an assemblage of bricks, stones, and fragments gathered from historic sites around the world and imbedded into the walls along Michigan Avenue and Illinois Street. The relics were collected by the *Chicago Tribune*'s own correspondents at the request of the paper's owner, "Colonel" Robert R. McCormick.

OLD CHICAGO WATER TOWER HISTORIC DISTRICT AND JOHN HANCOCK OBSERVATORY

The Old Chicago Water Tower is a symbol of the city's indestructibility. The Water Tower and Pumping Station, built in 1869, were the only public buildings in the lakefront area to survive the Great Chicago Fire of 1871. Furthermore, during the first half of the twentieth century, at least three attempts were made to have the complex demolished, and all failed.

Designed by architect William W. Boyington, the Greek Revival water tower, built of Joliet limestone, originally housed a 138-foot standpipe that held water and regulated pressure. The adjacent Pumping Station provided the city with clean water from Lake Michigan. The functions of both buildings were obsolete by the early 1900s. The tower building now houses a gallery of photographic displays of Chicago by local photographers. In 2003 and 2004 the Pumping Station was extensively renovated for multiple uses.

The Old Water Tower District covers a fairly small area, bound by Pearson Street and Chicago Avenue on the north and south, respectively, and by North Michigan Avenue and Mies Van Der Rohe Way on the east and west. Within this area is the Museum of Contemporary Art, which began in 1967 in a small space on East Ontario Street and eventually grew into the world's largest institution devoted to visual art created after 1945. The museum has been at its current location on East Chicago Avenue since 1996.

A block north of Water Tower Place, the John Hancock Observatory is technically outside the Water Tower historic district, but it is definitely a Magnificent Mile landmark. The one-hundred-story building was erected in 1969 as part of a downtown construction boom that started in the 1960s and has continued into the twenty-first century. A major feat of engineering in its time, requiring some 5,000,000 man-hours, the John Hancock Observatory is considered a prime example of "structural expressionism." It also offers a stunning view of the city and the lake, as well as glimpses of surrounding states.

EAST LAKE SHORE DRIVE HISTORIC DISTRICT

In northern Streeterville, just east of the north end of the Magnificent Mile, is another small but architecturally significant neighborhood. The East Lake Shore Drive Historic District comprises seven luxury high-rise apartment buildings and the legendary Drake Hotel.

The Italian Renaissance–style Drake Hotel, built in 1920, is notable for both its architecture and its history. Among the many prominent people who have stayed at the Drake over the years were Winston Churchill, Judy Garland, Elizabeth Taylor, Marilyn Monroe, and Frank Sinatra, as well as numerous heads of state and other major celebrities. Princess Diana visited the hotel about a year before her death, and President-elect Barack Obama held press conferences there in 2008.

Clark Street
OAK STREET–FOSTER AVENUE
6 miles

While not as famous as Lake Shore Drive or Michigan Avenue, Clark Street is a history buff's delight. It began as an old Indian trail, which later became part of the Green Bay Trail, a major military roadway from Fort Dearborn to Fort Howard in Green Bay, Wisconsin. Named for Revolutionary War hero George Rogers Clark, brother of Corps of Discovery leader William Clark, it was one of the streets on the city's original 1830 plat. Today Clark Street passes through many of Chicago's most popular neighborhoods, several of which we will visit on this trip.

Our trip begins at Washington Square Park, across from the famous Newberry Library, and heads north to Lincoln Park. At North Avenue, Clark becomes a diagonal street, passing through the Lincoln Park community area to Lakeview, home of Wrigley Field, then Uptown, where we will find the gates to Graceland Cemetery.

NEAR NORTH SIDE: WASHINGTON SQUARE PARK (BUGHOUSE SQUARE)

For many years, this one-square-block park on Chicago's Near North Side attracted crowds of people, gathered to hear speakers espouse their causes, recite poetry, and rant about the issues of the day. The park was informally known as Bughouse Square, "bughouse" being slang for insane asylum, as a sly commentary on the speakers' ravings.

The three-acre parcel of land was given to the city in 1842 by the American Land Company. In the 1870s and 1880s, the park was improved with diagonal walkways, picket fencing, and a Victorian fountain. But within a couple of decades, however, the park had deteriorated from neglect. In 1906 Alderman Robert R. McCormick (who later became publisher of the *Chicago Tribune*) donated his own salary to make improvements, and the city contributed another $10,000.

Among the "soapboxers" of the 1920s and 1930s were feminist Martha Biegler, labor activist John Loughman, socialist Frank Midney, anarchist Lucy Parsons, "hobo doctor" Ben Reitman, and poet Bill Zavatsky. The tradition continues with the Newberry Library's Bughouse Square Debates, a free-speech gathering held each July in conjunction with the library's annual book sale.

In 1990 Bughouse Square, along with the Newberry Library and several area residences, was incorporated into the Washington Square Chicago Landmark District. The park underwent a restoration in the 1990s, and it remains a popular tourist attraction.

One unmarked historic site in this neighborhood, outside the historic district, is now a parking lot. In the 1870s, however, an office building stood on Clark Street just north of Chicago Avenue. It was in this building that Aaron Montgomery Ward launched his mail-order catalog business.

Aaron Montgomery Ward, born in New Jersey in 1843, came to Chicago in 1865. Seven years later, ready to start his own business, he rented an office and shipping room on Clark Street and produced the first Montgomery Ward catalog. After achieving phenomenal success, in 1898 he built the spectacular Montgomery Ward Tower on Michigan Avenue (see Historic Michigan Boulevard District on earlier trip). In 1906 the company moved its warehouse and distribution operations to a still-standing building on Chicago Avenue near the Chicago River, in today's River North neighborhood (see under Near North Side on next trip). In addition to his triumphs as a retailer, Ward was instrumental in keeping open space in Grant Park (see Grant Park on earlier trip). He died in Chicago in 1913.

LINCOLN PARK: MID-NORTH AND PARK WEST

Like virtually all of the community areas in Chicago, Lincoln Park is made up of several named neighborhoods, in addition to the main part of the park itself. From North Avenue, Clark Street passes through the eastern part of the Lincoln Park community area—including the Mid-North and Park West neighborhoods—before continuing north to the Wrigleyville and "Boystown" areas of Lakeview. The western part of the Lincoln Park community area, commonly known as the DePaul area, will be discussed on the next trip, and the park itself was described on an earlier trip.

The two neighborhoods bisected by Clark Street, both immediately west of the park, are sometimes called Mid-North and Park West. Both were historically affluent, mostly residential areas and remain so. Park West is the home of the National Shrine of Saint Frances Xavier Cabrini (see below), and Mid-North, just south of Park West, contains a historic district noted for its lovely architecture. It also contains the site of the infamous 1929 St. Valentine's Day Massacre.

St. Valentine's Day Massacre Site

Although the building at 2122 North Clark Street (across the street from Chicago Pizza & Oven Grinder restaurant) no longer exists, in 1929 it was the site of one of the most shocking episodes of Chicago's gangster era—the St. Valentine's Day Massacre.

The 1919 Volstead Act, a.k.a. Prohibition, spawned a wave of criminal activity and violence, especially in Chicago. Here, Al Capone was the kingpin of a consortium of illegal operations in the city and its nearby suburbs. The Near North Side, however, was the domain of rival gang leader George "Bugs" Moran, and Capone had his eye on Moran's territory.

Capone was in Florida on February 14, 1929, when it is alleged that he sent a "red hot valentine" to Moran. But the message—a dose of lead—never reached Moran himself. About midmorning, several of Moran's minions were gathered at the garage of the S-M-C Cartage Company, possibly waiting for a shipment of liquor. Moran was expected but had not yet arrived when a black Cadillac pulled up in front of the building. At least four men—two dressed as police officers—stepped out and entered the

This was the grisly scene that greeted police when they entered the garage of Chicago's S-M-C Cartage Co. on February 14, 1929, an event that became known as the St. Valentine's Day Massacre. —Courtesy William J. Helmer Collection

garage, where they found seven men and a dog. Five of the men were part of Moran's gang, while the other two were unlucky hangers-on.

The visitors lined the seven occupants against a wall and unloaded two Thompson submachine guns at point-blank range. The bodies were found after a neighbor complained of loud noises and a howling dog. One of Moran's men survived the assault but died in the hospital a few hours later, after refusing to answer police questions. Following the incident, Moran was said to exclaim, "Only Al Capone kills like that." Although the machine guns were found in the home of one of the gang members, no conclusive evidence ever was produced to tie Capone's men to the crime.

National Shrine of Saint Frances Xavier Cabrini
Unveiled in the fall of 2012, the new National Shrine of Saint Frances Xavier Cabrini was built at the site of the original shrine, where the chapel of the old Columbus Hospital once stood. The first shrine, dedicated in 1955, remained at the Columbus Hospital chapel until the hospital was torn down in 2002 to make way for condominiums. The shrine was closed to the public and carefully preserved until a new sanctuary was installed a decade later. The lovely new space, a block east of Clark Street on Lakeview Avenue, includes landscaped gardens, a marble statue of Mother Cabrini, and a small chapel.

Francesca Cabrini was born in 1850 in Lombardy, Italy. She took her vows as a Roman Catholic nun in 1877, and three years later she founded the Missionary Sisters of the Sacred Heart of Jesus. In 1889 she asked for papal permission to go to China to set up missions there; instead, Pope Leo XIII sent her and six other nuns to New York City to help Italian immigrant families. Her first accomplishment was establishing an orphanage in Ulster County, New York. She went on to found sixty-six more institutions in the United States, Central and South America, and Europe.

Beginning in 1899, Chicago became a hub of Mother Cabrini's work when she established the Assumption School, the first Italian immigrant school in the city. It remained open until 1945. In 1903, with the help of some wealthy benefactors, she purchased the old North Shore Hotel in the Lincoln Park area and transformed it into Columbus Hospital. A few years later she established the Columbus Extension Hospital (later renamed St. Cabrini Hospital) in Little Italy. Neither institution exists today: St. Cabrini Hospital closed in 1996, and Columbus Hospital was torn down in 2002.

Mother Cabrini became an American citizen in 1909. She continued to travel throughout the United States and abroad, visiting Rome for the last time in 1912. Finally, with her health failing, she returned to Chicago in April 1917. On December 22, 1917, while in her quarters at Columbus Hospital preparing for a children's Christmas party, she died of a sudden heart attack. Her body was moved to West Park, New York, for interment. In 1933 her remains were exhumed and moved to the chapel at Mother Cabrini High School in New York City. Later, as part of the canonization process, her body was examined by church officials and subsequently enshrined at the school chapel.

On July 7, 1946, only twenty-nine years after her death, Frances Xavier Cabrini was canonized by Pope Pius XII, making her the first American to be declared a Catholic saint. Because of her life's work in America, she is known as the patron saint of immigrants.

LAKEVIEW

Looking at the neighborhood around Wrigley Field today, it is difficult to imagine the celery farms of immigrants from Switzerland, Germany, Luxembourg, and Sweden. One of the area's first permanent structures, Hotel Lake View, or Lakeview House, was built in 1853. The hotel and its pastoral surroundings attracted wealthy Chicagoans who wanted to escape the city's heat, crowds, and dirty conditions. Shortly after the hotel opened, a cholera epidemic in the city impelled droves of Chicago residents to resettle in Lakeview, which incorporated as an independent township in 1857. It became part of Chicago in 1889.

During the Civil War, a military post called Camp Fry stood at the intersection of Broadway, Clark Street, and Diversey Parkway. Opened in 1864 as a volunteer training camp, it later served as a prison camp for captured rebels.

Lakeview comprises several smaller, unofficial neighborhoods: Lakeview East (a.k.a. New Town, a.k.a. Boystown), West Lakeview, and Wrigleyville. Lakeview East is often referred to as Boystown for its gay residents. It was the first gay community ever officially recognized as such by a municipality. In 1970 Lakeview residents marched in the first Chicago Gay Pride Parade, an annual event that continues today.

West of Lakeview East is Wrigleyville, nickname for the area around Wrigley Field, home of the Chicago Cubs baseball team. On game days, the neighborhood's bars are overrun with fans, and some residents can see games from their rooftops and even catch an occasional fly ball.

Within Wrigleyville is the block-long historic district called Alta Vista Terrace, made up of forty single-family row houses. Modeled after Mayfair, a famous row-house neighborhood in London, it was built in the early twentieth century by Chicago realtor and builder Samuel Eberly Gross. Sometimes called the "Street of Forty Doors," Alta Vista was designated a Chicago Landmark District in 1971.

Wrigley Field

A true icon of both Chicago and of baseball itself, Wrigley Field has been the home stadium of the Chicago Cubs since 1916. To baseball fans, this ballpark offers a nostalgic experience, with its natural grass, ivy-covered outfield wall, and hand-turned score-board. It is the oldest active National League stadium and the second-oldest active major league stadium, after Boston's Fenway Park.

Built in 1914 for the short-lived Federal League's Chicago Whales, the stadium was originally named Weeghman Park for owner Charles Weeghman. After the Federal League failed in 1916, Weeghman bought the Chicago Cubs and moved the team from its West Side Park location, a site now occupied by the University of Illinois Medical Center. In 1920 Weeghman sold the team to chewing-gum magnate William Wrigley, Jr., who made improvements and renamed the stadium Cubs Park. Wrigley put his own name on the park in 1926.

Over the years, the park has hosted All-Star games three times and the World Series six times, though the Cubs have not won a world championship since they've been at Wrigley Field (the last Cubs World Series win was in 1908, while the team was still at West Side Park). On August 8, 1988, seven years after Wrigley Field and the Cubs were sold to the Tribune Company, the stadium's first night game was played under lights, ending a seventy-two-year tradition of day games only.

Wrigley Field has also been used for events other than baseball. From 1921 to 1970, the Chicago Bears played there, as did the Chicago Sting soccer team, and in 2009 the park hosted the National Hockey League's Winter Classic. From time to time, concerts are held there as well.

Although it has been more than a century since the Cubs have won a World Series, Wrigley Field continues to attract crowds in record numbers, attesting to both the loyalty of Cubs fans and the unique charm of this historic urban ballpark.

UPTOWN

The remnants of Uptown's glory days as a vibrant entertainment mecca of the early twentieth century can still be seen in this lakeside area north of Irving Park Road and south of Foster Avenue. Still operating are the legendary Green Mill jazz club (opened 1907), the Riviera Theatre (1917), and the stately Aragon Ballroom (1926).

John Lewis Cochran, a Philadelphia land speculator and developer, arrived in Chicago around 1885 and began buying land in what is now the Uptown area for a planned community. Around 1886 he enticed the Chicago, Milwaukee & St. Paul Railroad to stop at Bryn Mawr Avenue, then proceeded to build mansions on the east side, near the lake, and multifamily housing to the west. Many of these homes still stand, and a few, including the former homes of poet and Lincoln biographer Carl Sandburg and avant-garde publisher Margaret Anderson, are open for tours.

Eventually, Uptown was divided into two communities. The northern half became Edgewater while southern half remained Uptown. Comprising some nine neighborhoods, Uptown has several historic districts, including Uptown Square, West Argyle Street ("Little Vietnam"), Buena Park, and Sheridan Park.

A large section of Uptown—more than 120 acres—is taken up by Graceland Cemetery, a historic 1860 necropolis containing the remains of many of the city's early settlers and prominent citizens. Dotting the beautifully landscaped grounds are distinctive tombs, mausoleums, headstones, and sculptures—two of which were designed by noted artist Lorado Taft. Here lie the graves of two Illinois governors (John P. Altgeld and Frank O. Lowden); ten Chicago mayors; numerous celebrated architects including David Adler, Daniel Burnham, Ludwig Mies van der Rohe, and Louis Sullivan; famous detective Allan Pinkerton; inventor Cyrus Hall McCormick; boxer Jack Johnson, the first black heavyweight champion; industrialist George Pullman; and early Chicago settler John Kinzie.

North of the cemetery, on the campus of St. Augustine College (the first bilingual college in Illinois), is the site of the former Essanay Studios, 1345 W. Argyle Street, a landmark of early American film history. From 1907 to 1917, Chicagoan George K. Spoor, acclaimed as the "father of the motion picture industry," and his partner Gilbert M. ("Bronco Billy") Anderson nurtured the likes of Charlie Chaplin, Harold Lloyd, Gloria Swanson, and other stars of the silent era. When the movie industry moved to California in the late 1910s, Spoor remained in Chicago to experiment with "natural vision" (widescreen) pictures and other innovations (see under North Center and Roscoe Village on next trip). He died in Chicago in 1953.

North Wells Street and Lincoln Avenue
WELLS STREET BRIDGE–DEVON AVENUE
9.5 miles

This trip begins at the Merchandise Mart, at the north end of the Wells Street Bridge across the Chicago River from the Loop. We will follow Wells Street north, through the Near North Side neighborhoods of River North and Old Town, to the community of Lincoln Park, where Wells intersects with the south end of Lincoln Avenue. Turning onto Lincoln Avenue, which slices diagonally through the Lincoln Park area to points north, we continue through North Center, Lincoln Square, and West Ridge (a.k.a. North Town) to the northern edge of the city limits.

Lincoln Avenue was once known as Little Fort Trail because it connected Fort Dearborn to Little Fort, near present-day Waukegan. The trail began close to where modern Lincoln Avenue begins and continued into what are now the northern suburbs. Today's Lincoln Avenue ends at Dempster Street in Morton Grove, many miles south of the trail's original endpoint.

NEAR NORTH SIDE: RIVER NORTH AND OLD TOWN

The two Near North neighborhoods that Wells Street passes through are River North and Old Town. The latter, just west of the Gold Coast area, contains most of the few still-standing buildings that survived the Great Fire of 1871. The former, River North, encompasses the stately Merchandise Mart, the Gallery District, and various residential developments.

River North Gallery District

In the early twentieth century, the area now known as River North was called Smokey Hollow because of its numerous factories. It was here that nine-year-old Louis Terkel moved with his family from New York in 1922. His parents operated a boardinghouse on Wells Street and Grand Avenue, where the boy, later known as Studs Terkel, learned about the denizens of his new hometown. He lived in Chicago for the rest of his life, writing and speaking extensively about the city and its people. Author of numerous histories and other nonfiction books, Terkel won the Pulitzer Prize for general nonfiction in 1985 for his World War II history, *The Good War.* He died in Chicago in 2008, at age ninety-six.

Before the mid-1970s, the River North area was mostly commercial and industrial; crime and poverty had consumed the residential neighborhoods. Beginning in 1974, developer Albert Friedman bought up property here and revamped it, dubbing his chic new development "River North" to attract art galleries, design companies, and similar artsy enterprises. Today the River North Gallery District contains the highest concentration of art galleries in the nation outside of New York City. The neighborhood also contains trendy shops, restaurants, nightclubs, and entertainment venues as well as upscale high-rise condos. A recent addition to the River North area is the Museum of Broadcast Communications. The original museum opened in 1987 in the South Loop; after several moves, it reopened in this new North State Street building in 2012. The museum collects, preserves, and displays historic broadcast content and maintains a digitized library of more than 8,500 television and radio programs.

Another major landmark in River North is the Merchandise Mart. As one can infer from its name, Merchandise Mart was created as a space for wholesale showrooms and warehouses. Built by Marshall Field & Company, it was designed to consolidate the nation's wholesale goods and vendors under one roof. At the time it was erected, in 1930, the Merchandise Mart was the world's largest building. Even though it has since been expanded into a massive complex of buildings, plazas, and walkways, it long ago lost its status as the largest building in the world—it is not even the largest building in Chicago anymore. It is, however, one of the largest and finest art deco structures in the city. Today the complex includes numerous retail stores and professional offices as well as wholesale space.

In 1906 mail-order retail giant Montgomery Ward & Company, founded by Aaron Montgomery Ward in 1872, moved its warehouse and distribution operations to a building near the Chicago River on West Chicago Avenue at North Larrabee Street. The company closed permanently in 2000, but the building still stands as an architectural treasure, converted into condominiums and commercial spaces. A city park named for A. Montgomery Ward was recently established nearby. (See also Near North Side: Washington Square Park on previous trip.)

Continuing north from River North, Wells Street traverses the Washington Square neighborhood (see previous trip), passing Moody Bible Institute, a Christian college established in 1886 by evangelist Dwight L. Moody. To the west is Cabrini-Green, formerly the site of a notorious 1960s public-housing project. Redeveloped in the 1990s and early 2000s, the neighborhood is now primarily made up of mixed-income high-rise apartment buildings and row houses. At Division Street, Wells enters the part of Chicago known as Old Town.

Old Town

In the heart of the fashionable shopping and residential area known as Old Town is St. Michael's Church, built in 1869. Constructed of brick, it was one of the few buildings to survive the Great Chicago Fire. Other buildings in the area also predate the fire, and in the 1960s, area shops began to promote the neighborhood as Old Town.

Old Town straddles two community areas, the Near North Side south of North Avenue, and Lincoln Park north of North Avenue. From the late 1920s, the neighborhood has been associated with artistic and cultural movements. In the 1930s, sculptors Sol Kogen and Edgar Miller managed an artists' residence known as Carl Street Studios. Soon other artists moved into the area, and Old Town became a thriving arts community. In the 1960s it evolved into a haven for hippies, homosexuals, and others who lived outside the mainstream culture.

By the 1950s, Old Town had also become an epicenter for American folk music, with many popular nightclubs and coffeehouses as well as the original Old Town School of Folk Music, founded in 1957. In 1968 the school moved out of Old Town into a building near Oz Park, in the Lincoln Park community area (see next stop). In 1998 the school opened a second location, some five miles north of its original site, and in 2012 it moved into a new $17 million building across the street in Lincoln Square. The new facility, Old Town School East, now serves as the venerable institution's main location (see Lincoln Square later on this trip).

Today, trendy boutiques and entertainment venues line the streets of Old Town, including the famed Second City improvisation venue, which opened in 1959. For those who want to see the "old" in Old Town, the Old Town Triangle Historic District, north of North Avenue, south of Armitage Avenue, and west of Clark Street, contains the largest concentration of buildings that survived the 1871 fire.

LINCOLN PARK: DEPAUL AREA

While Lincoln Park is divided into some eight named neighborhoods, those west of Halsted Street are often collectively referred to as the DePaul area, named, of course, after DePaul University, whose main campus lies along Fullerton Avenue between Halsted and Racine Streets.

The community of Lincoln Park, named for the park on its eastern side (see earlier trip), was originally swampland. In 1824 the U.S. Army established a small outpost at what is now the intersection of Clybourn and Armitage Avenues. At the time, the post was surrounded by Indian camps along present-day Fullerton Avenue and Halsted Street. The first white settlers were German farmers; one early nickname for the area was the "cabbage patch." The first part to be developed was the south end, now labeled the Old Town Triangle, in the Near North community (see previous stop).

Aside from the surviving buildings concentrated in Old Town, the Great Chicago Fire of 1871 nearly destroyed the entire Lincoln Park community. Changes took place as it rebuilt. To the west rose various industries that used the Chicago River for transportation. Italian and eastern European immigrants worked in the riverside factories and lived nearby on the community's western side, while the wealthy built luxurious homes facing the park on the eastern side.

The beating heart of Lincoln Park is the intersection of Lincoln Avenue, Fullerton Avenue, and Halsted Street, where visitors will find a cluster of popular entertainment venues, shops, and restaurants. A famous historic site in the area is the still-standing Biograph Theater, built in 1914. It was near here that gangster John Dillinger met his end at the hands of the FBI in 1934.

Also nearby is Oz Park, named in honor of *Wonderful Wizard of Oz* author L. Frank Baum, who once lived in the neighborhood. Oz Park contains various tributes to the author and his famous book, which was first published in 1900. Not far from Oz Park is the Old Town School of Folk Music. Founded in 1957, the school moved to this location in 1968. Thirty years later it opened a second facility, Old Town School East, in

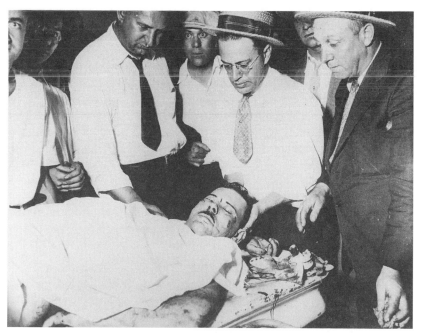

The body of John Dillinger, killed by federal agents outside the Biograph Theater in July 1934, is viewed by police and curious onlookers at the county morgue. —Courtesy William J. Helmer Collection

Lincoln Square, discussed later on this trip. Although over the years the school has seen good times and bad, it has survived and, in the long run, thrived. Today it offers more than 700 courses in international music, dance, theater, and visual arts and operates several concert halls, two music stores, and a large public resource center.

Another major part of the Lincoln Park community is the main campus of DePaul University, the largest private university in Illinois and the largest Catholic university in the nation.

DePaul University

Founded in 1898 as St. Vincent's College (named for St. Vincent DePaul) at the site of a former Presbyterian Seminary, DePaul was established to educate the children of Roman Catholic immigrants. It was rechartered as DePaul University, which was open to students of all religions, in 1907, and the school began admitting women in 1911.

Today the university comprises eleven undergraduate colleges and graduate schools on six campuses throughout Chicagoland. Among its illustrious alumni are mayors Richard J. and Richard M. Daley, Pulitzer Prize–winning composer George Perle, NBA All-Star George Mikan, and actors Joe Mantegna and John C. Reilly.

NORTH CENTER AND ROSCOE VILLAGE

The North Center community area comprises four neighborhoods: Northcenter (named for the community area but spelled as one word), Roscoe Village (named for its main drag, Roscoe Street), St. Ben's (named for the Catholic parish), and Hamlin Park (named for the park).

The best known of these neighborhoods is Roscoe Village, between Belmont Avenue and Addison Street, originally the site of a large amusement park called Riverview Park, which opened in 1904; expansions and improvements to the park followed throughout the first half of the century, but it finally closed down in 1967. In the meantime, businesses and residences had grown up around the park, and after the park closed, the structures stayed.

Through most of the twentieth century, Roscoe Village was a quiet residential area with the same ups and downs as other older Chicago neighborhoods. The last few decades of the century brought renewal to the area, thanks in large part to community organizations such as Roscoe Village Neighbors (originally called Riverview Neighbors). Today it is a popular place to live for families and young professionals.

A lesser known historic site in North Center is the former Selig Studios building. Few people realize that Chicago, not Hollywood, was the birthplace of the motion picture industry.

Birth of the Film Industry

The movie industry owes its start in the late 1890s to two Midwesterners, William Nicholas Selig and George K. Spoor. Spoor was the founder of Essanay Studios in 1907 (see under Uptown on previous trip). Selig, however, created his studio, the Selig Polyscope Company, eleven years earlier.

Established in 1896 on a lot at Byron Street and Claremont Avenue, near present-day Revere Park, Selig Polyscope focused primarily on short films, though it later produced some longer features. Among its first productions was *The Tramp and the Dog*, a short narrative comedy filmed in Chicago. The film was well received in local vaudeville houses and went on to greater success at showings in major cities. Further Selig productions also proved profitable. William Selig is often credited as being the inventor of the cliffhanger, based on his 1913 film series *The Adventures of Kathlyn*.

Around 1906 Max Aronson, star of Thomas Edison's first feature, *The Great Train Robbery*, left Edison's New Jersey studio to join Selig in Chicago as an actor and director. Changing his name to Gilbert Anderson, Aronson later joined forces with Spoor at Essanay Studios. Both companies eventually left Chicago in favor of the West Coast. Selig stopped producing movies in 1918. As is the case with most early movies, only a handful of prints of Selig's films have survived.

Other movie pioneers worked in Chicago during its filmmaking heyday, among them two African Americans: William Foster, founder of Foster Photoplay Company, the first African American film production company, and Illinois native Oscar Micheaux of Micheaux Film & Book Company, which produced *The Homesteader* in 1919 and *Within Our Gates* in 1920. (See also under Metropolis in Region 1.) Foster Photoplay, founded in 1919, lasted only four years. Micheaux was more successful; he transferred his operations to New York shortly after establishing the company, closing his Chicago office in 1926.

The entrance to the condominium building on the northwest corner of Byron and Claremont (now called St. Ben's Lofts, 3900 N. Claremont Avenue) is still emblazoned with the "S" trademark of the Selig Polyscope Company, a reminder of Chicago's role in motion-picture history.

LINCOLN SQUARE

Within the community area of Lincoln Square is the neighborhood of Lincoln Square, both named for the commercial plaza called Lincoln Square, at the intersection of Lincoln, Lawrence, and Western Avenues. Other named neighborhoods in the community area include Bowmanville, Budlong Woods, Ravenswood, and Ravenswood Gardens.

The attractive Lincoln Square community is known not only for its wide variety of shops and restaurants but also for its abundance of public art, especially murals. The Old Town School of Folk Music has its main facility in this community, though it's a long way from Old Town; the school also maintains its older location in Lincoln Park, discussed earlier on this trip.

The first settlers in the Lincoln Square area were German farmers and merchants, and the German influence can still be seen today in the area's architecture, shops, and restaurants, which stand side-by-side with Thai, Middle Eastern, Greek, and Italian eateries. The Dank Haus German Cultural Center sits right in the center of Lincoln Square plaza. One unusual monument to the area's German heritage is a thirty-foot-tall Maypole. Another is the Berlin Wall monument, erected in 2008. The entire Lincoln Square neighborhood and much of the adjacent Ravenswood neighborhood are considered historic districts.

A major point of historic interest in the Lincoln Square community is the 1864 Rosehill Cemetery, the largest cemetery in Chicago, whose majestic main entrance was listed in the NRHP in 1975. The name Rosehill was a clerical error; the actual name was Roe's Hill, named for farmer Hiram Roe, who sold part of his property for the cemetery on the condition that it would be named for him. Graves include those of Civil War generals, former governors and mayors, and prominent athletes, entertainers, architects, and industrialists.

NORTH PARK AND WEST RIDGE

North Park was once a largely Swedish community and later became a haven for Orthodox Jews. Today it has a multicultural population. The establishment of Bohemian National Cemetery in 1877 drew in a number of Czechs, though they did not stay in the area. On the west side of the Bohemian Cemetery is Montrose Cemetery and Crematorium, and to the east is the main campus of Northeastern Illinois University (NEIU). In addition to NEIU, North Park is home to a number of other institutions of higher learning, including North Park University, North Park Theological Seminary, and the Telshe Yeshiva rabbinical school. Near the campus of North Park University is one of the area's most interesting features—Chicago's only natural waterfall, which spills into the North Shore Channel.

East of North Park, across the North Branch of the Chicago River, is the community area of West Ridge, a.k.a. North Town, a.k.a. West Rogers Park. Once part of Roger's Park, the community split in the 1890s after a conflict known as the "Cabbage War," in which people on the east side of the community taunted the farmers on the west side as "cabbage heads." The "war" started over a disagreement about taxation and the creation of Chicago park districts; the west side won, and most public parks were developed in this area, while Rogers Park contains relatively few to this day.

In the center of West Ridge is the Talman West Ridge Bungalow Historic District, birthplace of the Chicago bungalow, which evolved here in the 1920s. Another historic neighborhood here is familiarly known as the "Golden Ghetto," so named around the 1930s for its large population of Hasidic Jews. While the area's demographic makeup is now more diverse, West Ridge still contains the largest Hasidic community in the Midwest. Another notable ethnic presence is Pakistani and East Indian; this community, centered along Devon Avenue between Western and California Avenues, is sometimes referred to as "Little India."

JFK Expressway and Dan Ryan Expressway (I-90/I-94)
KINZIE STREET–GARFIELD BOULEVARD
8 miles

This section of I-90/94 (called the Kennedy Expressway north of I-290 and the Dan Ryan Expressway south of there) slices through a number of community areas. When it was completed in the early 1960s, the interstate obliterated sections of neighborhoods, especially on the Near West Side, which contains many Chicago landmarks, including Greektown, the University of Illinois at Chicago and Jane Addams's Hull-House, Little Italy, and the Maxwell Street Market.

Traveling to the South Side, we find a part of Chicago originally settled in the mid-1800s by wealthier Chicagoans wishing to live away from urban congestion but still have easy access to town. After the Civil War, industry began moving south of downtown, and the factories, steel mills, and meatpacking plants spawned working-class ethnic neighborhoods like the Back-of-the-Yards, Canaryville, Armour Square, Bronzeville, and others. In the later decades of the twentieth century, the Union Stock Yard and many other industrial enterprises closed or relocated, and the area's economic base shifted and changed.

Today, all of these historic communities have evolved into a remarkably diverse and vibrant mixture of wealthy, middle-income, working-class, and poor residential neighborhoods along with commercial and industrial areas and abundant cultural facilities.

NEAR WEST SIDE

Near West Side community area, across the Chicago River west of the Loop, contains a wide range of neighborhoods settled by various immigrant groups, as indicated by the presence of Greektown and Little Italy. It is also the location of the Hull-House settlement house, a social-reform institution created in 1889 to help poor immigrants in the area. Around the same time, several health colleges were established in this part of town, all of which were incorporated by the University of Illinois at Chicago (UIC) in 1913, though the main UIC campus was not built here until the 1960s.

Diagonally bisecting this part of Chicago is Ogden Avenue, once an Indian trail called the Ottawa Trail, which led from Fort Dearborn southwest to Ottawa, Illinois. When this part of the trail was improved with wooden planks in 1848, it was renamed Southwestern Plank Road, along which many taverns, trading posts, and other business sprang up to accommodate travelers and area settlers. The road was later paved and renamed for Chicago's first mayor, William B. Ogden.

The various neighborhoods of the Near West Side are generally identified as the Maxwell Street area, University Village/Little Italy, the Illinois Medical District, Tri-Taylor, the West Loop, and the United Center area. The areas on the eastern side, along the interstate, are the best known and include Greektown and the Fulton River District. On the western side is the Illinois Medical District, the site of Cook County Hospital, Rush University Medical Center, the UIC Medical Center, and the UIC Colleges of Medicine, Dentistry, and Pharmacy, among many other facilities.

Just west of the medical district is the Tri-Taylor residential neighborhood, once an extension of Little Italy but now home to a widely diverse population. To the north is the United Center, the home arena for the Chicago Bulls basketball team and the Chicago Blackhawks hockey team. United Center was built in 1994 to replace Chicago Stadium. The neighborhood surrounding the arena is sometimes called United Park.

West Loop, Greektown, and the Fulton River District

Although specific boundaries are debatable, the West Loop area contains several smaller neighborhoods, including Greektown and the Fulton River District. As its name indicates, the West Loop is the section of the Near West Side that lies just west of the Loop, north of the UIC campus complex. The best-known feature in the West Loop is Union Station, built in 1925. At one time, six railroad stations accommodated intercity rail transportation to and from Chicago, but today, the majestic, neoclassical Union Station is the only one that is still active.

The Fulton River District, once an industrial area but now largely residential, is one of Chicago's up-and-coming neighborhoods. The district contains several historical sites. At Fulton and Desplaines Streets, for example, Sears & Roebuck established their first mail-order warehouse. The biggest historical site in the neighborhood is that of the 1886 Haymarket Square riot, where violence erupted during a labor demonstration at Haymarket Square, a commercial center at Randolph and DesPlaines Streets. During the melee, an unidentified anarchist lit a dynamite bomb, killing eight police officers and wounding dozens. (The riot is described further under Forest Park in Region 6, where the Haymarket Martyrs' Monument stands over the graves of the four protesters who were hanged for supposedly instigating the deadly incident.)

A statue honoring the fallen officers was erected at the riot site in 1889, but it was moved a number of times due to vandalism. A restored version now stands at the Chicago Police Headquarters on Michigan Avenue at 35th Street (see under Douglas on earlier trip). In 2004 a new memorial sculpture was unveiled at Haymarket Square, this one honoring the labor activists.

Just west of the Fulton River District, on Halsted Street between Van Buren and Madison Streets, is Greektown, essentially a long row of Greek restaurants. The original Greek neighborhood, known as "the Delta," was near Little Italy but was displaced, along with many other ethnic neighborhoods, when UIC was built in the 1960s. Most of the residents moved elsewhere in the city or to the suburbs, but some Greek

Sketch showing the aftermath of the 1886 labor riot
in Chicago's Haymarket Square —Author's collection

restaurateurs and merchants shifted their businesses north to the West Loop. It remains a popular spot for authentic Greek cuisine.

A few blocks west of Greektown is Harpo Studios, established by actress and talk-show queen Oprah Winfrey in the mid-1980s. Born into poverty in rural Mississippi in 1954, Winfrey moved to Chicago in 1983 to pursue a career in broadcasting. To say she was successful is an understatement—today she is a billionaire and one of the most influential women in the world. Winfrey bought and renovated the building on Washington Boulevard and Carpenter Street to film and produce her now legendary television program, *The Oprah Winfrey Show*, which ran from 1986 to 2011. Harpo Studios is part of Harpo Productions, a major multimedia corporation.

The building in which Harpo Studios operates has an interesting history of its own. It was originally the armory for the 2nd Regiment of the Illinois National Guard. In 1915 the armory served as a makeshift morgue for victims of the *SS Eastland* disaster (see under Wacker Drive on earlier trip). In the 1940s and early '50s, the building housed a roller-skating rink, and from the late 1950s through the early 1980s, it served as a movie studio. Rumor has it that the building is haunted by the ghosts of victims of the *Eastland* wreck.

Hull-House and the University of Illinois at Chicago

Jane Addams and Ellen Gates Starr, both Illinois natives, founded Hull-House in 1889. It was Chicago's first "settlement house," created to house social workers within the community they served. In this neighborhood of poor immigrants, Addams, Starr, and their associates provided educational, social, and cultural opportunities for struggling local residents and newcomers. The house soon expanded into a complex of some fourteen buildings, including a summer camp called the Bowen Country Club.

Jane Addams was born in Cedarville, a few miles north of Freeport, on September 6, 1860; Starr was born in 1859 in Laona Township, in far northern Winnebago County. Both women attended Rockford Female Seminary, where they met (see also Rockford in Region 5). The two friends traveled widely in Europe, where they visited Toynbee Hall, the original settlement house in London, and returned to America with visions of a better life for the poor.

Addams and Starr moved to Chicago in January 1889, occupying the former home of Charles J. Hull on Halsted Street, in which Hull allowed them to live rent-free. The two women and their associates established a kindergarten, homemakers' clubs, and social activities in the house and invited unions and social-service organizations to meet there. In addition, Addams and Starr dedicated themselves to political reform, leading the fight for child-labor and compulsory-education laws at the state and national levels. Addams was also a prolific writer and lecturer, authoring eleven books and numerous articles and delivering speeches worldwide.

When World War I broke out, Addams, a dedicated pacifist, gave antiwar speeches across the country. In 1915 she helped establish the Woman's Peace Party and organized and presided over the International Congress of Women at The Hague, Netherlands. Four years later she founded the Women's International League for Peace and Freedom, which she led for ten years. She also helped found the American Civil Liberties Union and the National Association for the Advancement of Colored People. The international

*Jane Addams comforts a child
at Hull-House in Chicago*
—Courtesy Chicago Public
Library, Special Collections and
Preservation Division

impact of her contributions earned her the Nobel Peace Prize in 1931. Jane Addams served with Hull-House until her death on May 21, 1935, and was buried in Cedarville Cemetery.

The site of the Hull-House complex was designated a Chicago Landmark in 1974. Today, the original Hull-House and the residents' dining hall are the only two buildings that still stand after years of expansions by the University of Illinois at Chicago (UIC). The university acquired much of the Hull-House property in 1963 to build its campus, and over the ensuing decades the school proceeded to tear down most of the Hull-House structures, along with large swaths of the Little Italy and Maxwell Street neighborhoods, to make way for new facilities. The house, however, still serves the community as a museum and cultural center.

After UIC moved in and dismantled the original complex, the nonprofit umbrella organization Jane Addams Hull House Association (not affiliated with the Hull-House Museum) took over Hull-House's social-welfare functions, providing services at various locations throughout Chicago. In 2012, however, the association filed for bankruptcy and closed its doors, ending 123 years of helping Chicago's needy.

University Village and Little Italy

The residential and shopping area surrounding the University of Illinois at Chicago was dubbed University Village rather recently, but the neighborhood's history dates from the late nineteenth century. Known as Little Italy, it was actually a neighborhood of mixed ethnicities, but Italian culture dominated in the area's restaurants, grocery stores, and shops. The section between the university and Illinois Medical District is still referred to as Little Italy, though the population is largely gentrified. The area around Halsted and Taylor Streets still contains a sizeable population of Italian Americans, but much of Little Italy is now part of UIC.

Maxwell Street

The Maxwell Street Market no longer takes place on Maxwell Street. The market was moved after 120 years at its original location at Maxwell and Halsted Streets, now part of the UIC campus. Some of the original buildings still stand, thanks to preservationists, but the market was moved to Canal Street in 1994, then moved again, to its current location along Desplaines Street at Roosevelt Road, in 2008.

Beginning in the 1870s, Maxwell Street was an entry point for new immigrants to Chicago; it was sometimes called the "Ellis Island of the Midwest." The area residents were Irish, Greek, Italian, German, Russian, and other ethnicities. Most of the neighborhood survived the Great Fire of 1871, and immigrants continued to settle here, especially Eastern European Jews. Later, African Americans from the South added to the community, and after that, Mexican immigrants.

The legendary open-air market sprang up shortly after the Great Fire of 1871. For more than a century, merchants, street vendors, and Chicago residents with junk to sell hawked their wares here. Beginning in the 1930s, street musicians, especially black musicians from the South, performed at the market and developed a new style of amplified music known as the blues. Thus Maxwell Street is often identified as the birthplace of the blues.

The market continues today, every Sunday, as the New Maxwell Street Market, and in spite of all the changes, it remains a Chicago tradition. Meanwhile, preservation-minded groups are still fighting to save the last remnants of the old neighborhood.

Another place of significant historical interest in this area, a mere block away from the new marketplace, is the site where the Great Chicago Fire originated. On October 8, 1871, a blaze started in the twenty-by-sixteen-foot wooden barn of Patrick and Catherine O'Leary at 137 De Koven Street and spread for several days until about a third of the city was in flames. Today the Chicago Fire Academy stands where the home was, now numbered 558 De Koven Street, and a bronze sculpture was erected near the entrance in 1961 as a monument to the Great Fire.

Site of the Great Chicago Fire

No other event in Chicago history has generated more interest and myth than the Great Fire of 1871. Legend has it that the conflagration started when Mrs. O'Leary's cow kicked over a lantern. The cow herself was eventually exonerated, but to this day, no one knows for sure how the blaze began. An official investigation begun November 23, 1871, resulted in "no definitive conclusion." Over the decades, investigators and historians looking into the matter have come to the same nonconclusion.

What is known is the place and time. Around 9:00 on the evening of Sunday, October 8, 1871, a fire started in the barn at the O'Leary home on De Koven Street. The blaze spread quickly to neighboring buildings, although the O'Leary home, adjacent to the barn, was incredibly spared.

Very little rain had fallen in the months preceding the fire, and the city's wooden structures were unusually dry. On the day the disaster began, area firefighters were already exhausted from battling a stubborn seventeen-hour fire they had finally conquered that very morning. Within thirty minutes, the fire on De Koven Street was out of control. Fanned by high winds, it spread for miles, jumping the river and continuing northward. The blaze became so hot that even supposedly fireproof buildings collapsed from the flames.

While the fire raged, Lt. Gen. Philip Sheridan gathered food from St. Louis, Missouri, tents from Jeffersonville, Indiana, and infantry troops from Fort Omaha, Nebraska, and Fort Leavenworth, Kansas, to come to Chicago's aid. Army troops and state militia maintained martial law in the city for weeks after the fire stopped.

By the time rains came and assisted in subjugating the last of the blaze in the early hours of Tuesday, October 10, more than 3.5 square miles of the city was destroyed. About 300 people were killed, and at least 100,000 people were left homeless. Property loss was estimated at $192 million.

Some residents left the city, believing it would never recover. But Marshall Field, Potter Palmer, Cyrus Hall McCormick, George Pullman, and others saw it differently. They immediately began rebuilding the city to be bigger than before and structurally sturdier, using brick and other fireproof materials. *Chicago Tribune* editor Joseph Medill's prediction—"CHICAGO SHALL RISE AGAIN"—was achieved.

Sketch of the Great Chicago Fire of 1871, which engulfed about one-third of the city —Author's collection

*The first building erected in Chicago after the Great Fire of
1871 was a real estate office.* —Author's collection

LOWER WEST SIDE AND PILSEN

Like most other neighborhoods in Chicago, the Lower West Side and Pilsen were settled
by European immigrants in the mid-1800s. The first residents were German and Irish,
but later in the nineteenth century, Czechs and other eastern Europeans began moving
in. Pilsen was largely an industrial area, with lumber mills, rail yards, and factories. For
decades, from the 1870s to the 1950s, the biggest employer on the Lower West Side
was the McCormick Harvesting Machine Company plant at Blue Island and Western
Avenues.

McCormick Harvesting Machine Company Factory

Cyrus Hall McCormick was one of the many industrialists to contribute to Chicago's
development as a world-class city. His great-nephew, Robert R. "Colonel" McCormick
(for whom McCormick Place was named), also became a major player in Chicago as
publisher of the *Chicago Tribune* from the 1920s to the 1950s.

Born in 1809, Cyrus Hall McCormick grew up on a farm in Virginia, where his
father, Robert McCormick, tinkered with designing a mechanical reaper. By the age of
twenty-two, Cyrus had improved upon his father's invention, and three years later he
patented it. Seeking to manufacture and sell the machine to local farmers but meeting
with little success, the younger McCormick moved west in 1845. After two years in
Cincinnati, he moved to Chicago, where he opened a three-story brick factory on the
north bank of the Chicago River, just east of what is now the Michigan Avenue Bridge.

The McCormick Harvesting Machine Company proved a great success. For the
next twenty-plus years, sales steadily increased, but the Great Fire of 1871 destroyed

the plant. Undaunted, McCormick bought 130 acres on the city's Lower West Side and built a much larger facility along the South Branch of the Chicago River, in what is now known as Pilsen.

Cyrus Hall McCormick, inventor of the mechanical reaper, was a Chicago mogul. —Author's collection

Cyrus Hall McCormick patented his mechanical reaper, shown in this sketch, in 1834; many believe the revolutionary machine was actually invented by his father, Robert McCormick, as early as 1831. —Author's collection

This sketch by A. A. Fasel depicts the McCormick Harvesting Machine Company factory on Chicago's Lower West Side; the plant was rebuilt in 1873, after the original downtown facility was destroyed in the Great Fire of 1871. —Author's collection

Upon his death in 1884, McCormick passed the business to his son, Cyrus Hall McCormick, Jr., who two years later would be faced with labor unrest that culminated in the Haymarket Square riot (see under Near West Side on earlier trip; see also under Forest Park in Region 6). In 1902 the McCormick company merged with competitor Deering Harvester Company and several smaller manufacturers to form International Harvester (now Navistar International). The plant closed down in the 1950s, when International Harvester moved its operations to less expensive locations outside the city.

ARMOUR SQUARE AND BRIDGEPORT

Armour Square, a sliver of land wedged between Bronzeville on the east and Bridgeport on the west, is a historically working-class area. Its early residents—mostly European immigrants—moved south of the city limits because they were unable to afford to build the brick homes the city mandated after the Great Chicago Fire. The community was named after its centerpiece, Armour Square Park, designed in 1905 by Daniel Burnham and John and Frederick Olmsted. The park's name honors meat mogul Philip Armour, who in 1867 formed Armour & Company in Chicago and went on to contribute much to the development of the city. At the northern end of Armour Square is Chinatown, and near the south end is US Cellular Field, home of the Chicago White Sox.

Adjacent Bridgeport was settled earlier than Armour Square, mainly by Irish immigrants, many of whom came to Chicago to work on the Illinois & Michigan Canal in the 1830s and '40s. The starting point of the canal, Bridgeport is now the home of

Canal Origins Park, created in 2004. (For more about the canal, see Regions 5 and 6.) The Irish were soon joined by Lithuanians, Italians, Poles, and other immigrant groups.

Until 1836, Bridgeport was called Hardscrabble, a tribute to its working-class milieu. The community was annexed to Chicago in 1863. Interestingly, Bridgeport was the home community of five Chicago mayors, including Richard J. and Richard M. Daley. Today, both Bridgeport and Armour Square are counted among the most ethnically diverse communities in Chicago.

Chinatown

Chinatown, at the north end of the Armour Square community, is one of Chicago's most popular tourist destinations. A colorful arched gate, stretched across Wentworth Avenue at Cermak Road, welcomes visitors. The neighborhood's three-block business district contains more than sixty restaurants along with the landmark On Leong Merchants Association Building, known locally as Chinese City Hall.

It was the On Leong Merchants Association that spearheaded the establishment of Chinatown in Armour Square in 1912. The first influx of Chinese Americans arrived in Chicago in the 1870s to escape severe racism in California. They first settled in the Loop, establishing businesses along South Clark Street between Van Buren and Harrison Streets. As downtown rents increased, On Leong Merchants built a headquarters on Cermak Road, some four miles south of the Loop, and urged Chinese Chicagoans to move into the area. By the late 1920s, the association had a new, Oriental-style headquarters and the neighborhood had developed into a vibrant Little China. The 1980s brought further expansion with Chinatown Square mall and several new residential complexes.

U.S. Cellular Field and Old Comiskey Park

The original White Sox baseball team, organized as the White Stockings in 1900, played its early seasons at South Side Park, near today's South Wentworth Avenue and Pershing Road. In 1910, owner Charles A. Comiskey built a new ballpark for his team—its name now shortened to White Sox—a few blocks north at 35th Street and Shields Avenue. The 29,000-seat, steel-and-concrete Comiskey Park, constructed atop a former city dump, lasted for eighty-one years before being replaced with the current stadium, the 40,000-seat U.S. Cellular Field (originally called New Comiskey Park), in 1991. The old Comiskey Park site, directly across the street from the new stadium, is now a parking lot marked with a marble plaque.

The end of the 1919 baseball season was a nadir for the White Sox franchise, in spite of its success on the field. The team was favored to win the upcoming World Series against the Cincinnati Reds, yet they won only three games in the best-of-nine series, losing the world championship in Game 8. Afterward, rumors began circulating that the series had been rigged, leading to what was soon dubbed the "Black Sox" scandal. It was later revealed that the rumors were true: eight players confessed to intentionally losing the series in a gambling conspiracy. Although the players were acquitted in court, all eight were expelled from professional baseball for life.

BRONZEVILLE

The historic neighborhood known as Bronzeville, sometimes called the "Black Metropolis," straddles two official Chicago community areas, Douglas (see earlier trip) and Grand Boulevard. Bronzeville is more or less synonymous with an area once known as "the Black Belt," approximately bordered by 26th and 63rd Streets on the north and south, respectively, and Wentworth and Cottage Grove Avenues on the east and west, respectively. For the first half of the twentieth century, this part of Chicago was a segregated area; by local covenant, African Americans were not allowed to buy or rent property in most other sections of the city.

Bronzeville developed between the late 1800s and the 1940s, during the "Great Migration" of southern black workers seeking opportunities in northern cities. The community's early population was a mixture of both black and white and represented a broad range of incomes. But a race riot in Bronzeville in the summer of 1919, which left thirty-eight dead and hundreds injured, brought negative attention to the community and drove many white residents away. The neighborhood soon bounced back as an African American enclave, emerging as a thriving "Black Metropolis" of black culture and black-owned businesses.

In its early-twentieth-century heyday, Bronzeville was a mecca of African American culture and entertainment, similar to New York's Harlem. The community was home to such luminaries as Pulitzer Prize–winning poet Gwendolyn Brooks; Negro National Baseball League founder Andrew "Rube" Foster; Ida B. Wells, a founding member of the NAACP; and many others. The jazz and blues clubs that once lined 35th and 47th Streets fostered countless musicians, including Louis Armstrong, Duke Ellington, Count Basie, Nat King Cole, Buddy Guy, and Muddy Waters.

The name "Bronzeville," a reference to the skin tone of the residents, was coined by James J. Gentry, an editor at the black-owned newspaper the *Chicago Bee*, in 1930. The

Chicago Bee (founded 1926) and the *Chicago Defender* (founded 1905) were two influential newspapers of the city's black community. The *Bee* shut down in the 1940s, but the *Defender* is still a going concern. The three-story, art deco Chicago Bee Building, listed on the NRHP in 1986 and named a Chicago Landmark in 1998, now houses a branch of the Chicago Public Library.

When segregation policies were lifted in the late 1940s, many middle-class and affluent black residents moved out of Bronzeville, leaving the community to its fate. The public-housing projects of the 1960s, such as the Robert Taylor Homes complex, were meant to help low-income residents but proved to be massive failures, and by the 1970s much of Bronzeville was dilapidated and crime-ridden.

Renewed interest in the area beginning in the 1990s has revitalized many parts of the community, and Bronzeville is once again emerging as a vibrant urban center. Murals and other public art abound throughout the community, and in the evenings, music venues both new and old draw increasingly large crowds of locals and visitors.

Highlights of the Bronzeville neighborhood include the South Side Community Arts Center, the DuSable Museum of African-American History, the Walk of Fame on Martin Luther King Drive, and the Bronzeville Visitor Information Center, as well as the beautiful, 372-acre Washington Park and several other city parks. Also among Bronzeville's attractions are the former homes of numerous Chicago notables, both black and white, such as Daniel Burnham, Ida B. Wells, Louis Armstrong, Bessie Coleman, and the Marx Brothers. Due to the area's importance in African American and Chicago history, efforts are currently under way to establish and develop the Black Metropolis National Heritage Area, which encompasses Bronzeville and some adjacent neighborhoods.

On East 51st Street, the northern border of Washington Park, is Provident Hospital of Cook County, which opened in 1891 as Provident Hospital and Training School, the nation's first African American–owned hospital, the first racially integrated hospital in Chicago, and the first nurse training program for black women in the United States. Provident's founder, Daniel Hale Williams, was not only the first black cardiologist in America but also performed in 1883 the world's first successful open-heart surgery. The hospital closed in 1987 but reopened six years later as Provident Hospital of Cook County.

Near the border of Bronzeville and neighboring Oakland, on South Cottage Grove Avenue, is the site of the nation's first Walgreens drugstore. Native Illinoisan Charles Walgreen moved from Dixon to Chicago in 1893 to work for pharmacist Isaac Blood. When Blood retired in 1901, Walgreen bought his store and opened it as Walgreens. The innovative store included a wide selection of nondrug items, and Walgreen later added a lunch bar with hot food and milkshakes. Fifteen years later, after opening eight more branches, he founded Walgreens Company, which is today the largest retail drug chain in the United States. The company's current headquarters is located in Deerfield.

NEW CITY

Little of New City is new. The community grew around the Union Stock Yard (the Yard), which opened on Christmas Day, 1865, and became the nation's center of the meatpacking industry for the better part of a century. New City comprises the site of the former Union Stock Yard and two adjacent neighborhoods, Back of the Yards on the west side and Canaryville on the east.

Back of the Yards, its name a reflection of its origins, began as a neighborhood of Irish and German immigrants employed at the Union Stock Yard. Later, Poles and other eastern Europeans arrived to live and work there. Canaryville, too, was settled by Irish workers at the Yard, but unlike its neighbor, Canaryville retained much of its largely Irish American population over the years. The name is thought to have come from the sparrows that fed on the trash and spilled grain at the stockyard. Because workers at the Yard were mostly unskilled immigrants, they were paid little money, and living conditions in both Back of the Yards and Canaryville were often shabby, unsanitary, and unsafe. Throughout the late nineteenth and most of the twentieth centuries, Canaryville was considered one of the toughest parts of the city as Irish youth gangs ran roughshod over the neighborhood.

When the stockyard closed in 1971, the community's economy changed dramatically, and many of the original residents left the area. As housing costs fell, immigrants from Mexico as well as low-income African Americans from bordering neighborhoods began moving in, though a number of the original Irish neighborhoods remain ethnically intact.

Union Stock Yard

As the nation expanded west, increased demands for fresh meat created a burgeoning industry in the fledgling settlement of Chicago. The town's first meatpacker was former fur trader Gurdon Saltonstall Hubbard, who in the late 1820s began butchering cattle and hogs and delivering the meat to troops stationed at Fort Dearborn. In 1834 he constructed a large brick warehouse by the Chicago River, in what is now the Loop, to store processed meat. Skeptics, doubting the business would succeed, referred to it as "Hubbard's Folly." When the railroad came to the city, however, Hubbard enjoyed the last laugh. His business exploded, and it wasn't long before others entered the meatpacking game. Although a series of misfortunes, capped off with the Great Chicago Fire, financially destroyed Hubbard, the industry he started permanently transformed Chicago's economy and culture.

In 1864 independent stockyard owner John B. Sherman convinced several railroad companies to support the construction of a large central facility to consolidate the resources of various meatpackers and streamline operations. Eleven railroads and eight meatpacking companies signed on to be part of the project. The Union Stock Yard & Transit Company of Chicago was incorporated on February 13, 1865, and the facility, at the far south end of town, opened on December 25, 1865.

The stockyard had fifteen miles of railroad tracks, five hundred animal pens, and two thoroughfares for moving cattle from the train cars to the pens. The meatpacking industry continued to expand into the twentieth century as new technologies, such as refrigerated rail cars, made operations easier and more efficient. The Yard eventually covered more than one square mile, while meatpackers such as Gustavus Swift, Philip Armour, and Nelson Morris became millionaires.

Due largely to the Union Stock Yard, Chicago became the meatpacking center of the country, supplying 82 percent of the nation's meat by 1880. At its peak, the stockyard

Sketch of the Union Stock Yard, opened in 1865 —Courtesy
Schaumburg Township District Library, Illinois Collection

employed as many as 47,000 workers. But the poor sanitation and working conditions in the Yard were gaining notoriety, as exposed by Upton Sinclair in his 1906 novel *The Jungle*, leading to tighter federal inspection standards in the meatpacking industry. Working conditions at the stockyard remained rough, however.

Employees—mostly poor immigrants and African Americans—worked in round-the-clock shifts. Most lived nearby, creating the neighborhoods of Bridgeport, McKinley Park, Back of the Yards, and Canaryville. Workers were not well paid, and the meatpacking companies considered most of them dispensable. Eventually stockyard employees began to organize for better pay, shorter hours, and safer conditions. Labor struggles began with an unsuccessful strike in 1894 and continued with mixed results into the mid-twentieth century. Stockyard workers were finally fully unionized in 1943, with the formation of the United Packinghouse Workers of America. Within a decade or so, however, the industry was in decline.

By the 1950s, changes in the industry caused many meatpacking companies to move elsewhere, including both Swift & Company and Armour & Company. On July 31, 1971, after 106 years, the Union Stock Yard officially closed. Today, it is a modern industrial park. Standing as a lone reminder of the Yard's former dominance is the original arched limestone entrance gate at Exchange Avenue and Peoria Street. The gate is designated as both a Chicago Landmark and a National Historic Landmark.

Dan Ryan Expressway and Bishop Ford Freeway (I-94)
GARFIELD BOULEVARD–130TH STREET
12 miles

For most of its way through Chicago, I-94 overlaps with I-90. South of I-290 (Eisenhower Expressway), I-90/94 is called the Dan Ryan Expressway; the highway splits at 66th Street, in the Englewood community area on the city's South Side; here I-90 becomes the Chicago Skyway while I-94 continues as the Dan Ryan until 95th Street, where its name changes to the Bishop Ford Freeway, named for Chicago clergyman and civil-rights activist Bishop Louis Henry Ford. On this trip we will travel the interstate from Englewood to the Chicago city limit in Riverdale.

ENGLEWOOD

Prior to 1850, today's Englewood community was little more than oak forests and swamps. After the arrival of nearly ten railroads in the early 1850s, the area grew into a town known as Junction Grove. Most of the early settlers were German and Irish immigrants who held jobs on outlying farms or with the railroads, or later, at the Union Stock Yard. Scottish and Swedish immigrants followed. In 1868 the name Junction Grove was changed to Englewood.

After the Great Fire of 1871, Chicagoans began moving farther away from downtown. With its easy access by train, Englewood became a popular community, and its population mushroomed. It was annexed to the city in 1889. Over the second half of the twentieth century, more and more African Americans moved into the area, while residents of Irish, German, and Swedish heritage moved to other parts of town. By 1970, 96 percent of Englewood's residents were black, and many lived below the poverty line. The next few decades saw rapid deterioration alternating with urban-renewal efforts. Today, Englewood and West Englewood still struggle with crime, crumbling infrastructure, inadequate medical and social services, a depressed local economy, and a general lack of resources. Nevertheless, changes—albeit gradual ones—have come to the community, and many residents are hopeful about the future.

One fascinating—if grim—part of Englewood's history took place during the 1893 World's Columbian Exhibition. Lurking among the throngs of celebrants, it was later discovered, was a homicidal maniac.

Henry Holmes: Serial Killer

In 1886 Herman Webster Mudgett, a graduate of the University of Michigan Medical School, arrived in Chicago, settling on the South Side. Introducing himself as Dr. Henry Howard Holmes, he befriended local drugstore owner Dr. E. S. Holton and his wife. Because Dr. Holton was dying of cancer, Mrs. Holton ran the drugstore herself. To ease her burden, she hired the charming Dr. Holmes as a prescription clerk. Dr. Holton died within a year, and Holmes soon convinced the widow to sell him the drugstore. Immediately afterward, she mysteriously vanished. Holmes claimed she had moved to California leaving no forwarding address.

In 1889 Holmes acquired land across the street from the drugstore, on 63rd Street and Wallace Avenue, where he built a three-story hotel and a number of shops for the thousands of expected visitors to the 1893 World's Columbian Exposition, which planners were building nearby. The hotel was so grand that neighbors dubbed it the "Castle." In addition to some seventy guest rooms, the hotel contained, it was eventually discovered, numerous secret passageways, trapdoors, sliding panels, chutes, and other architectural oddities.

When the fair arrived, the Holmes Castle enjoyed a booming business. Some of the guests, however, never returned home. The fair had attracted its share of crime, including a number of disappearances, but police never suspected the seemingly upstanding Dr. Holmes.

It turned out that Holmes was a professional criminal, specializing in insurance fraud. In medical school, he had perfected a scheme in which he purchased life insurance in the name of cadavers, then reported their deaths and collected the money. Later he took the scam a step further—taking out policies on selected victims then murdering them.

Holmes left Chicago shortly after the fair and hit the road. In 1894 he recruited an accomplice in St. Louis to help with a scheme to fake his own death and collect the insurance money as someone else. When Holmes cheated his partner out of his share, the accomplice ratted him out to police. Soon the authorities were on Holmes's trail, and eventually they found that their suspect had committed more than mere fraud. Detectives discovered the first two bodies in Toronto, Canada, then another in Indianapolis. Police then obtained a warrant to search Holmes's hotel in Chicago, where they found the gruesome mother lode: torture devises, bottles of poison, a dissection table, a gas chamber, an acid tank, and a crematorium with the charred remains of an indeterminate number of victims.

Afterward, Holmes confessed to twenty-seven murders, but some believe he may have killed more than two hundred. Less than a year after Holmes's arrest, the Castle burned to the ground from unknown causes. Henry H. Holmes, America's first major serial killer, was hanged on May 7, 1896, in Philadelphia. His story was told in the 2003 bestseller *Devil in the White City* by Erik Larson. Today, at the site of the "Murder Castle" stands a post office, which some say is haunted.

PULLMAN

Pullman was one of the nation's first planned communities, built as a self-contained industrial village, or company town. Entrepreneurial visionary George M. Pullman, owner of the Pullman Palace Car Company, established Pullman as an ideal living environment for his employees and their families. But what started as an experiment in capitalist paternalism eventually drove the workers to revolt.

Pullman formed his luxury railcar manufacturing company in 1867. Because Chicago, the railroad center of the country, was the perfect place for his national headquarters, he acquired some 4,000 acres south of the city in 1879, setting aside six hundred acres for housing, stores, and recreational facilities for his employees. Construction of the town, designed with attractive Victorian architecture and verdant landscaping, began on May 25, 1880. The first residents, the Edwin A. Benson family, moved in on January 1, 1881.

The community of Pullman, which featured such amenities as gas lighting, indoor plumbing, and a sewer system, was one of the most technically advanced towns in the country. It had its own market, restaurants, hospital, bank, church, library, theater, and more, including a three-acre manmade lake called Lake Vista. The Pullman Company

Inventor and industrialist George M. Pullman, who founded the town of Pullman
—Courtesy Chicago Public Library, Special Collections and Preservation Division

The Pullman Palace Car Company's administration building and factory front the bygone Lake Vista, which was used as a cooling pond. —Courtesy Chicago Public Library, Special Collections and Preservation Division

provided its workers with decent wages and a pleasant, stable living environment—revolutionary for its time. By 1883 the town had 4,512 residents, and within two years, that number had nearly doubled. It hit its peak around 1892, when the population reached 14,702.

After a few years, however, employees began to balk at George Pullman's near-total control over their lives. The unrest escalated during the 1893 economic depression, when the company closed shops, laid off workers, and reduced wages while rent and utilities—automatically deducted from workers' paychecks—remained the same, creating severe hardships for families solely dependent on the boss.

Before long, national labor leader Eugene V. Debs stepped into the fray, organizing the Pullman employees and pressing for wage increases and rent reductions. When Pullman refused the demands, Debs called a strike, which began on May 10, 1894. A month later, in sympathy, American Railway Union members boycotted Pullman cars, creating transportation havoc and disrupting mail service.

In July, in an unprecedented move, President Grover Cleveland sent thousands of federal troops to Chicago to put down the strike. Violence erupted. A series of riots led to the death of at least twelve strikers, dozens of injuries, and hundreds of thousands of dollars in property damage. By early August, the strike had broken down and workers returned to their posts with nothing to show for it. Debs was imprisoned for six months in the McHenry County Jail (see under Woodstock in Region 5) for violating a federal injunction against the strike.

The Hotel Florence opened in the Pullman community in 1881; George Pullman
used it as a gathering place for friends, visiting dignitaries, and clients.
—Courtesy Schaumburg Township District Library, Illinois Collection

George Pullman, embittered by his workers' ingratitude, died of a heart attack in 1897. His family, fearing his body would be stolen or desecrated, buried him under eight feet of concrete at Chicago's Graceland Cemetery. Shortly after Pullman's death, the U.S. Supreme Court ruled that all of the Pullman Company's nonindustrial property had to be sold to private interests.

The community got along for several more decades, but the Great Depression triggered a decline that continued into the 1960s, when historical preservationists stepped in to save the Pullman neighborhood from demolition. Pullman was designated an Illinois Landmark in 1969, a National Historic Landmark District in 1971, and a City of Chicago Landmark in 1972.

The posh, sixty-five-room Hotel Florence, built in 1881 as the showpiece of Pullman's utopia, is now a public museum. Other highlights of the Pullman Historic District include the former Administration Building, with its striking Clock Tower (heavily damaged by a 1998 arson fire); the former Greenstone Church; and the elegant row houses that still line the neighborhood's quiet streets.

SOUTH DEERING AND VICINITY

The Far Southeast Side of Chicago, including South Deering and its adjacent communities, developed from one industry—steel.

South Deering, the largest of Chicago's seventy-seven community areas, began as Brown's Mill, a neighborhood in what was then the independent municipality of Hyde Park. Brown's Mill was created after the Joseph H. Brown Iron & Steel Company was founded here in 1875. The company employed almost a thousand men and women—mostly Irish, German, and Scandinavian immigrants—and the community grew. In 1882 Brown's Mill was renamed Cummings, but as industry expanded, it soon became known as Irondale. In 1889 Irondale, along with the rest of Hyde Park, was annexed to Chicago.

In 1902 International Harvester Company bought the Brown Iron & Steel Company and built Wisconsin Steel Works in the Irondale neighborhood. The following year, Irondale was renamed after Wisconsin Steel cofounder William Deering. As industry boomed and more immigrant workers arrived, many from Italy and Eastern Europe, several working-class communities emerged alongside South Deering, including East Side, Hegewisch, and Riverdale. Later in the twentieth century, Mexicans and African Americans began moving into the vicinity, inciting a number of racial conflicts.

In addition to Wisconsin Steel, other major steel manufacturers in this area included U.S. Steel and Republic Steel. While the factories employed thousands, plant workers were not always treated well, and in 1935 the Steel Workers Organization Committee (SWOC) was formed to negotiate for better pay, shorter hours, and healthier working conditions. Two years later, while U.S. Steel agreed to pay increases and other provisions, other nearby steel plants refused to go along. The SWOC called a strike at Republic Steel and some of the other intractable mills. Republic countered by hiring off-duty police officers as strikebreakers.

On May 30 (Memorial Day), 1937, hundreds of strikers and supporters staged a nonviolent demonstration, marching from the SWOC headquarters at Sam's Place, a former dancehall near today's Rowan Park in East Side, to the mill. Outside the plant, Chicago

Police gathered to block the marchers' path, and an argument erupted. Police fired into the crowd, killing ten unarmed demonstrators and wounding about thirty. Many other protesters, including women, were beaten with clubs. The incident broke the strike, but within a few years Republic Steel was pressured into signing a contract with the United Steelworkers union. A plaque near Rowan Park honors the victims of the "Memorial Day Massacre."

Steel remained the Far Southeast Side's economic mainstay until the 1970s, when the industry suffered a decline. Wisconsin Steel closed its plant in 1982, and U.S. Steel departed in 1992. Much of the area deteriorated during this period, and most middle-class residents left. Today, however, many of these communities are under redevelopment as residential neighborhoods for commuters. Eggers Grove Forest Preserve, Calumet Park and Beach, and numerous other public parks provide recreation and natural beauty for area residents.

The darkest episode in South Deering's history was a horrifying crime that stunned the nation. In the early morning hours of July 14, 1966, in the Jeffrey Manor neighborhood, a psychopath named Richard Speck brutally murdered eight female student nurses in their residence. A ninth woman, unseen by the maniac, hid under a bed during the bloody rampage, and she was later able to identify Speck and testify against him. He was convicted and sentenced to death, but in 1972 the Illinois Supreme Court declared the death penalty unconstitutional, so Speck's execution was never carried out. He died in prison in 1991.

RIVERDALE

The first settlement in the community area now known as Riverdale was a ferry crossing on the Little Calumet River called Riverdale Crossing, established around 1836. Other settlements also grew up in the area, and in 1852 the Illinois Central Railroad built a station called Calumet Junction to serve these communities. A settlement called Kensington grew up around the depot, which was soon also known as Kensington.

In 1880, when George Pullman began building his model town (see Pullman earlier on this trip), Kensington's saloons served the influx of immigrants who came to work in Pullman. The rowdiness of these drunken patrons earned Kensington the nickname of "Bumtown." In 1889 the entire area was annexed to the city of Chicago, and part of Kensington became Riverdale.

Completion of the Cal-Sag Channel in 1922, along with work on other nearby waterways, fostered further industrial development in the area, and more workers poured into Riverdale as large manufacturers moved to the Far South Side. Also in 1922, the Metropolitan Sanitary District (now the Metropolitan Water Reclamation District) constructed a sewage treatment plant here. Around the same time, Cook County acquired 135 acres at the southeastern edge of Riverdale for the Beaubien Woods Forest Preserve. With its vast grasslands, oak forests, and the large Flatfoot Lake, Beaubien Woods remains a popular recreational spot for South Side residents.

Until World War II, Riverdale was mostly industrial property, with few residential areas. In the 1940s and '50s, the federal government and the city of Chicago built several public and low-income housing projects on the South Side for black veterans returning from World War II. The first of these projects was called Altgeld Gardens, constructed in

1945. The complex comprised a total of 1,498 apartments in a 130-block maze of two-story brick buildings in the southern part of Riverdale.

The housing projects ended up overtaxing Riverdale's community services and left residents floundering. Since most government-housing residents were black, racial tensions added to the community's struggle for stability. At the same time, economic conditions on the Far South Side deteriorated as manufacturers began shutting their doors. By the 1980s, most of the jobs in the area had evaporated, and many residents left. Of those remaining in Riverdale, more than half lived in poverty.

Beginning in the 1980s, Altgeld Gardens became the focus of an urban-recovery campaign led by future president Barack Obama. The efforts were only partially successful, however. While crime is not as prevalent here as in some other public-housing projects, many Altgeld Gardens residents still live in substandard housing, and the complex remains isolated from community resources such as schools, hospitals, libraries, and even grocery stores.

As one of the first public-housing developments in the country, Altgeld Gardens is considered a historic landmark, and Barack Obama's work in the community heightened its historical interest. Efforts to revitalize the neighborhood continue, including a new "urban farm" established by Altgeld residents in 2010 to provide fresh organic produce for the community.

Milwaukee Avenue
KINZIE STREET—MONTROSE AVENUE
8 miles

Milwaukee Avenue was once a trail leading from Chicago to Milwaukee, Wisconsin. North of Harlem Avenue, it is also designated Illinois Route 21. Traveling northwest, Milwaukee Avenue starts at Kinzie Street and cuts diagonally through the River West community area. Other community areas on or adjacent to this section of Milwaukee Avenue include Logan Square, Avondale, and Irving Park. The heritages of residents in these areas include Polish, Italian, Ukrainian, German, Puerto Rican, Mexican, and others.

WEST TOWN

The vicinity north of the Near West Side and west of the Chicago River is called West Town, part of which dates to the city's incorporation in 1837. In the mid-nineteenth century, railroad tracks and factories sprouted up along the river, spawning first construction jobs, then manufacturing work, for new immigrants. Germans and Scandinavians settled in the north and northwest parts of the area, while Poles gravitated to the core of West Town, often called the "Polish Triangle." Russian Jews settled to the west, in the area called Humboldt Park, while Italians and Sicilians concentrated in the southeast, around Smith Park. Ukrainian immigrants clustered north of Garfield Park in a neighborhood known as Ukrainian Village.

Most of these neighborhoods remain, though over the years the traditional ethnic flavor has been diluted with diversity. In the latter half of the twentieth century,

Puerto Ricans moved into Humboldt Park and Mexicans into Ukrainian Village. These changes, along with recent gentrification all along Milwaukee Avenue, have altered the face of West Town.

River West and Noble Square

The neighborhood called River West is in the southeast corner of West Town. Previously an industrial area, River West is now mostly residential, with many of the old warehouses having been converted to lofts and condos beginning in the 1980s. Adjacent Noble Square is a small residential section of West Town.

The "Noble" in Noble Square comes from Noble Street, which borders a one-block-square park, from which the "square" part comes. Like nearby Pulaski Park and Wicker Park, Noble Square was traditionally a Polish neighborhood, but today many residents are arty types or young professionals. The Polish influence can still be found in the area's churches, shops, and restaurants, and explored further at the Polish Museum of America, established in 1935.

A notable resident of this community was Walt Disney, born in Hermosa in 1901 (see Logan Square and Hermosa below). Although the Disney family moved out of Illinois when Walt was a small child, they returned to Chicago in 1917, residing in the Noble Square area. Here the teenage Walt attended McKinley High School and took night classes at the now-defunct Chicago Academy of Fine Arts. Though Walt Disney did not remain in Illinois, he was undoubtedly influenced by what he saw, heard, and did here.

Ukrainian Village and East Village

Although Ukrainian Village and East Ukrainian Village are considered separate neighborhoods, divided by Damen Avenue, the two adjacent "villages" share a common history. Both areas were once farmland, and most of the early settlers were German. In the late 1800s, Slavic immigrants began to move in. The western half eventually became known as Ukrainian Village. Ethnic cultural institutions still in existence here include the Ukrainian Institute of Modern Art and the Ukrainian National Museum, as well as several churches.

While the west side was populated by Ukrainians, the east side was mostly Polish, especially after World War II. After the construction of the Northwest (JFK) Expressway in the 1960s, these two neighborhoods, like Wicker Park to the north, saw an influx of displaced Hispanics. Also like Wicker Park, the twin Ukrainian Villages became more gentrified in the last couple of decades of the twentieth century. Both neighborhoods contain Chicago Landmark Districts to help preserve their heritage.

Wicker Park and Pulaski Park

The adjacent neighborhoods of Wicker Park and Pulaski Park, west of the JFK Expressway between Division Street and North Avenue, were traditionally Polish communities. This part of West Town was called Chicago's "Polish Downtown," and the intersection of Division Street, Milwaukee Avenue, and Ashland Avenue was known as the "Polish Triangle" (or Polonia Triangle, a.k.a. "Kostkaville"). At this junction stands a fountain dedicated to renowned Chicago writer Nelson Algren (1909–81), who was not himself Polish but who lived in this area and had a Polish wife. The controversial but locally beloved Algren, who grew up on the North Side, won the National Book Award in 1950 for his novel *The Man with the Golden Arm*, which was set in Polonia.

The first Polish settlers arrived in this area in the 1850s, and Polish immigrants continued to populate the area well into the twentieth century. It became Wicker Park after Charles and Joe Wicker bought eighty acres here in 1870. Parts of Wicker Park, especially the streets near the park itself, were wealthy areas occupied by Germans, Scandinavians, and other northern Europeans. Some of their mansions still stand. One distinctive Wicker Park landmark is the Flat Iron Building, erected in 1930 and now used as artist studios.

During the 1960s and '70s, Puerto Ricans and other Hispanics, displaced by gentrification in Lincoln Park and elsewhere, began moving into the area, while much of the Polish population left for the suburbs. By the late 1980s, Wicker Park had become a popular area for musicians, artists, and students, who lived side-by-side with the Hispanic residents until the late 1990s, when more affluent people moved in and gentrified much of the neighborhood.

LOGAN SQUARE AND HERMOSA

The Logan Square community area, west of the Chicago River and north of West Town, is so called for its public square at Kedzie and Logan Boulevards and Milwaukee Avenue. The square itself was named for Civil War general and politician John A. Logan. Once a predominately Norwegian neighborhood, Logan Square saw a surge in immigrants from eastern Europe, especially Poland. The community now has residents representing a multiplicity of backgrounds, including Hispanic, black, and Polish Americans. Logan Square Boulevards Historic District, named an official Chicago Landmark District in 2005, includes Logan Square and the Victorian buildings along Logan, Kedzie, and Humboldt Boulevards.

Logan Square was the home neighborhood of iconic Chicago columnist Mike Royko, born here in 1932. Royko was born and grew up in an apartment above his father's tavern, the Blue Sky Lounge, on Milwaukee Avenue. He lived in Chicago his entire life, working as a reporter and columnist for all three daily papers, the *Daily News*, the *Sun-Times*, and the *Tribune*. In 1972, while working at the *Daily News*, he won the Pulitzer Prize for commentary. The city lost a cherished local voice when Mike Royko died in 1997.

The neighborhood known as Bucktown, in the eastern part of Logan Square, was originally settled by Polish farmers who raised goats; the nickname came from this, as male goats were called bucks. Bucktown, like adjacent Wicker Park, is a haven for artists, but, also like Wicker Park, parts of the neighborhood have been gentrified, and trendy shops, cafes, and bars now line its major streets.

The Hermosa community area, a formerly unincorporated subdivision annexed to Chicago in 1889, is just west of Logan Square. In 1890 Elias Disney, a carpenter originally from Canada, was among the thousands of workers who poured into Chicago to work on the 1893 World's Columbian Exposition. Disney built a frame house in Hermosa, and it was in this house that his son, Walter, was born in 1901. Although the house still stands, it is privately owned and unmarked. The Disney family moved to Missouri a few years later, but they returned to Chicago in 1917, moving to the West Town area (see under West Town: River West and Noble Square above).

AVONDALE

The community area known as Avondale began as a suburb called Jefferson, which was annexed to the city in 1889. The early settlers were immigrants from Germany, Poland, and Scandinavia who came to work in the factories that lined the railroad tracks. The population is now largely Hispanic, but along Milwaukee Avenue, Avondale's Polish neighborhoods, collectively known as "Polish Village," still thrive. Polish immigrants gathered in Avondale around the turn of the twentieth century and again during the political turmoil of the 1980s and 1990s.

Avondale was once the home of a popular park complex, the Olson Park and Waterfall. When the park opened in 1935, the land was symbolically deeded back to the local Indian tribes in an elaborate ceremony. The twenty-two-acre park and its thirty-five-foot-high artificial waterfall were a cherished Avondale institution until the place was closed down in the 1970s to make way for the parking lot that occupies the site today.

IRVING PARK

Like most areas outlying the original city of Chicago, Irving Park was originally settled as farmland. In 1869 a group of New York developers, in concert with the Chicago & North Western Railway, built a depot and a subdivision they called Irvington, after author Washington Irving, later changed to Irving Park. The developers built a number of mansions, all of which are now gone.

After the Great Chicago Fire, new residents moved in and built somewhat more modest homes. Many of these survive in Irving Park neighborhoods, one of which, known as the Villa District, is an official Chicago Landmark District. Buildings in a number of other Irving Park neighborhoods are currently being preserved and renovated.

Shortly after Irving Park was annexed to Chicago in 1889, multifamily housing was added to accommodate the influx of Germans and Swedes, followed later by Poles and Russians. Near the end of the twentieth century, Hispanics moved into the area and now make up more than forty percent of the community's population.

PORTAGE PARK

The community area of Portage Park is known for its namesake park as well as for the Six Corners shopping district, at the intersection of Irving Park Road, Cicero Avenue, and Milwaukee Avenue. The name Portage Park refers to its origin as a swampland portage between the Des Plaines and Chicago Rivers.

European immigrants began to occupy the area in the early twentieth century. Originally the residents were of mixed ethnicity, but it soon became a largely Polish community and remains so today. Among the Polish institutions in Portage Park are the Polish American Association, the Polish Jesuit Millennium Center, and the Polish Army Veterans Association, as well as many Polish Catholic churches, a number of which are historic. A major landmark in the area is the restored Portage Theater performing arts center, originally built in 1920 as a movie house and renovated in 2006.

JFK Expressway (I-90)
MONTROSE AVENUE—O'HARE INTERNATIONAL AIRPORT
9 miles

This part of the JFK Expressway takes commuters and travelers through the far northwestern sections of Chicago, where visitors can find a surprising number of historically and architecturally interesting places, including "Koreatown," Ravenswood Manor Historic District, and the Noble-Seymour-Crippen House in Norwood Park.

ALBANY PARK

Although originally settled by Scandinavians, Albany Park is today one of the most ethnically diverse community areas in Chicago. While many of its current residents are Hispanic, Albany Park is also home to a significant number of people of Asian, Pacific Island, Middle Eastern, Eastern European, and Scandinavian descent. Part of Albany Park is popularly known as "Koreatown," and the section of Lawrence Avenue between Kedzie and Pulaski Avenues is called "Seoul Drive" for its Korean shops and restaurants.

In the first half of the twentieth century, Albany Park had a largely Jewish population due to the influx of Russian Jews moving into the area to escape overcrowding in other parts of the city. After World War II, many Jewish families left for nearby suburbs such as Skokie and Lincolnwood, leaving Albany Park to deteriorate. Redevelopment projects in the 1980s and 1990s brought the area back to life, and immigrants from all over the world moved in to occupy Albany Park's revitalized middle-class homes.

Besides Koreatown, Albany Park's other named neighborhoods include Mayfair, North Mayfair, and Ravenswood Manor. The Ravenswood Manor Historic District is especially famous for its historic bungalows and is listed on the NRHP, as is the entire neighborhood of North Mayfair.

JEFFERSON PARK AND FOREST GLEN

Jefferson Park is sometimes referred to as the "Gateway to Chicago." In the early days, the Chicago-to-Milwaukee Road (now Milwaukee Avenue) crossed through this area, bringing a steady movement of hunters, traders, and settlers. In the 1830s John Kinzie Clark built the area's first cabin here, making him Jefferson Township's first resident. Another settler, Elijah Wentworth, arrived shortly afterward and built a tavern on the Milwaukee Road near present-day Lawrence Avenue. A small settlement grew up around the tavern, and in 1850 it became part of Jefferson Township. By the time Jefferson was annexed to Chicago in 1889, the older part of the community, where Wentworth had his farm, had become known as Jefferson Park.

Like many other communities on the Far Northwest Side, Jefferson Park attracted a large Polish population from the late nineteenth through the late twentieth century. By the early 1900s, newcomers from Germany, Russia, Italy, and Eastern Europe had also begun to settle here. Later in the century, people of Asian and Hispanic heritage added to the mix.

Today, Jefferson Park's population is more ethnically diverse than ever, though residents of Polish descent still maintain a strong presence in the community. The

Copernicus Foundation, established in 1971 and named for Polish scientist Nicolaus Copernicus, opened a Polish cultural center in Jefferson Park in 1982. The historic Gateway Theater, the first Chicago movie house built for the "talkies," was preserved as part of the Copernicus complex. A "Solidarity Tower," a scale replica of the clock tower that adorns the Royal Castle in Warsaw, was added in 1985. The venue hosts a variety of programs for Polish Americans and other ethnic groups.

The adjacent Forest Glen community area includes the Old Edgebrook Historic District, a residential area built in 1894. This neighborhood was designated a Chicago Landmark in 1988.

NORWOOD PARK

Between Jefferson Park and O'Hare Airport, the JFK Expressway skirts the community of Norwood Park. In 1868 a development group, the Norwood Land & Building Association, designed an elegant suburban community with curved streets, Victorian homes on large lots, a luxurious resort hotel, and a small man-made lake. The developers took the name Norwood from the 1868 Henry Ward Beecher novel *Norwood: Or, Village Life in New England*, at the suggestion of one of the trustees, and set out "to translate the poetry of Beecher's prose into a picturesque Illinois village." The word *park* was added to the name when the post office was established. In 1853 the Illinois & Wisconsin Railroad passed through Norwood Park, and a train station was added in 1870, attracting more visitors and new residents. In 1874 Norwood Park was incorporated as a village; nineteen years later it was annexed to the city.

Around 1906, to accent the community's elegant homes, the Chicago Special Parks Commission hired noted landscape architect Jens Jensen to upgrade some of Norwood Park's public spaces, including Norwood Circle Park, Myrtle Grove Park, and the grounds of the Chicago & North Western Railway station. Jensen called his design for the latter the "Railway Garden Park."

Many nice turn-of-the-twentieth-century homes still stand near Circle Avenue, the circular street in the heart of the community. After World War I, middle-class bungalows sprung up in many Norwood Park neighborhoods, and following World War II, ranch-style homes became popular. More recently, new, larger homes were added, and the community remains a mixed-income residential area today. The Norwood Park community area encompasses several named neighborhoods, including Oriole Park, Big Oaks, and Union Ridge.

Beginning in the 1980s, Norwood Park stepped up efforts to preserve its heritage. In 2002 part of the community was placed on the NRHP. The historic area comprises, among other sites, Norwood Circle Park, the 1907 train station and the Railway Garden Park, Mulberry Point Park (Chicago's smallest park), William Howard Taft High School (see below), and the Noble-Seymour-Crippen House, the oldest home in Chicago.

Noble-Seymour-Crippen House

A wealthy Englishman named Mark Noble, along with his family, arrived in Chicago in August 1831. The Nobles originally lived in the dilapidated former home of Jean Baptiste Point de Sable in what is now downtown Chicago's Pioneer Court. Two years

A winding gravel driveway leads to the Noble-Seymour-Crippen House, the oldest house in Chicago, located in the Norwood Park community. —Author's collection

later Noble purchased several hundred acres of prairie and timberland northwest of the city. Here he built a sturdy frame farmhouse on a high ridge.

In 1868 New York native Thomas H. Seymour bought Noble's farmhouse along with sixty-eight acres, on which he planted about 1,000 cherry and apple trees and 2,000 grapevines, and raised a small herd of shorthorn cattle. To accommodate their large family of seven children, Seymour and his wife built an Italianate-style wing to the north side of the farmhouse and expanded the loft area into a second floor. They also added a front porch and twin porticos for the two front entrances.

After Seymour died in 1915, his heirs sold the house and about two acres of land to the Stuart Crippen family, who added indoor plumbing and electricity and a number of other improvements. In 1987 Crippen's descendants sold the home—widely accepted as the oldest house in Chicago—to the Norwood Park Historical Society, which made the property its headquarters. A state grant in 1997 funded the home's extensive restoration to its 1915 appearance. The Noble-Seymour-Crippen House was designated a Chicago Landmark in 1988 and placed on the NRHP in 2000.

Taft High School
An unlikely historic site in Norwood Park is William Howard Taft High School. In addition to the school's unusually high number of famous (and at least one infamous) alumni, it is well known as the model for the hit musical *Grease*. The show's co-creator, Jim Jacobs, graduated from Taft in June 1960.

Jacobs was a part-time actor and an office boy at the *Chicago Tribune* when he met New York native Warren Casey in the 1960s. Inspired by the rock 'n' roll music of their high school days, the pair came up with the idea of a musical about teenagers in the 1950s. The show, which they titled *Greased Lightning,* portrayed people and places from Jacob's old neighborhood, featuring such hangouts as Superdawg, Canale's Pizza Parlor, Skips Drive-In, and the Hub Roller Rink. In the show, Taft High School was called Rydell High in honor of singer Bobby Rydell.

Greased Lightning opened on February 5, 1971, at the Kingston Mines Theatre on North Halsted Street. Two New York producers, Ken Waissman and Maxine Fox, saw the show and asked Jacobs and Casey to rewrite it as a full-scale musical production. The new show, retitled *Grease,* opened on February 14, 1972, at the off-Broadway Eden Theater in lower Manhattan. As *Grease* gained popularity, it moved to Broadway, where it ran for years; revivals in 1994 and 2007 were also very successful both critically and commercially. The original script, which had much vulgar dialogue and a grittier theme, was cleaned up for publication. A sanitized script was also used for Paramount Pictures' 1978 movie version, and the setting was moved from Chicago to southern California. In 2011 the original script was used in a production called *The Original Grease,* presented by Chicago's American Theater Company.

Other famous Taft High alumni include actress Donna Mills; 1960s NFL running back Jim Grabowski; longtime Chicago Bulls manager Jerry Krause; and Terry Kath, guitarist for the band Chicago. The school is not so proud of its alumnus Robert Hanssen, an FBI agent who in 2001 was discovered to have been a spy for the Soviet and Russian governments since 1979. Hanssen is now serving a life sentence in a maximum-security prison in Florence, Colorado. Several films, including the 2007 movie *Breach,* have portrayed Hanssen's shady career and the events leading to his capture.

O'HARE (COMMUNITY AREA) AND O'HARE INTERNATIONAL AIRPORT

The land on which O'Hare now sits was part of the 1829 Treaty of Prairie du Chien. The treaty awarded two square miles of land adjacent to the Des Plaines River to Scottish-Ottawa interpreter and Potawatomi chief Alexander Robinson (Che-che-Pin-Qua) as a reward for his role in aiding white victims of the 1812 Battle of Fort Dearborn and in negotiating several treaties. Today a stone monument marks his approximate burial site in the Robinson Woods Forest Preserve, just southeast of the airport.

In the 1840s, German immigrants and other settlers established a few farms near the Robinson property, and the area became known as Orchard Place. In 1887 a Wisconsin Central Railroad depot was built at Orchard Place, but the area remained sparsely populated through the mid-twentieth century. An effort to create a subdivision there in the 1930s drew little interest.

In 1942, at the beginning of World War II, the Army Air Corps bought up much of the property in Orchard Place, including Orchard Field, one of several small local airfields. Here, Douglas Aircraft built a manufacturing and assembly facility, which produced C-54 Skymaster cargo planes for the war effort. After the war, Douglas, which had decided to move most of its operations to the West Coast, left their two-million-square-foot factory behind, along with four runways. With the air traffic at the Midway municipal airport rapidly increasing, the city seized the opportunity to use the Douglas site for a new international airport. Originally called Orchard Field Airport, in 1949 it was renamed for Edward H. "Butch" O'Hare, a World War II naval flying ace and recipient of the Congressional Medal of Honor who died in action in the South Pacific.

With the airport established, the surrounding area soon developed into a major economic base as corporations established offices, hotels were erected, and residences went up for employees of the airport and the nearby businesses. In 1956 the city of Chicago annexed the airport and vicinity as the O'Hare community area, the seventy-sixth of what are today seventy-seven official community areas; part of the Cook County Forest Preserve was annexed into the community in 1958, providing residents with several hundred acres of open green spaces.

After handling limited air traffic in its first few years, during which time improvements were made to the facilities, O'Hare began serving commercial passenger flights in 1955. In 1962, with the completion of O'Hare's international terminal, nearly all the flights served by Midway Airport were transferred to O'Hare, making the latter the instant recipient of Midway's title as the "World's Busiest Airport." O'Hare held this distinction until 1998, when the Hartsfield-Jackson Airport in Atlanta, Georgia, surpassed O'Hare's record for number of passengers served annually.

The O'Hare community has become a popular place to live in recent years, and the airport has received a number of further expansions and improvements to keep pace with traffic and technology. The latest modernization project, approved in 2005, is currently under way.

About two miles east of O'Hare International Airport, in an unincorporated part of Norwood Park Township, an episode occurred that many locals wish they could forget. In December of 1978, residents of Chicago's far northwest side and the near northwest suburbs were horrified to learn that a seemingly upstanding member of the community—John Wayne Gacy—was a sadistic serial killer. Police found the remains of a large number of murder victims at Gacy's home, and Gacy later confessed to killing dozens of teenage boys; he made the confession, he said, in order to give his victims "a proper burial." Soon after the investigation was completed, Gacy's house was demolished. He was convicted in 1980 and sentenced to death; the sentence was carried out in 1994.

OTHER COMMUNITIES AND SITES OF INTEREST IN CHICAGO

Edison Park (West of IL 43/N. Harlem Avenue between JFK Expressway and Howard Street): Originally called Canfield, this community was renamed for Thomas Alva Edison in 1893, after local developers installed six electric streetlights and promoted it as an "electric suburb." It was annexed to Chicago in 1910. The community expanded after World War II with the construction of nearby O'Hare International Airport and the Northwest (now John F. Kennedy) Expressway. A reminder of the many farms that once dotted the landscape here is the 1854 John Wingert farmhouse, designated a Chicago Landmark in 1990.

Goose Island (East of JFK Expressway at Division Street): The only island on the Chicago River, Goose Island is mostly industrial. It is a man-made island, although originally there was a small natural island nearby, seasonally inhabited by geese and other migrating birds, which is where the name probably came from. After the North Branch Canal was built in 1853, the natural island was dredged out and the new one was created. Irish immigrants, Poles, and Germans settled on the island, which was also known as Kilgubbin, but in the late nineteenth century the residents were displaced by incoming industry.

Printers Row and Dearborn Station (S. Dearborn Street and W. Polk Street, South Loop): The Printing House Row District was named a National Historic District in 1976 and a Chicago Landmark in 1996. The adjacent South Loop Printing House District is also a National Historic District, so designated in 1978. Many of the buildings that once housed printing and publishing companies were converted into residential lofts in the 1980s and '90s. Among the numerous historic structures in the neighborhood is Dearborn Station, built in 1883. The large brick terminal, with its distinctive twelve-story clock tower, closed as a train depot in 1971 and now houses offices and retail shops.

Acknowledgements

The writing of this history of Illinois required an extensive amount of research and personal contact with archivists, authors, chambers of commerce, historians, historical societies, libraries, local history buffs, museum staffs, tourism offices, and other experts knowledgeable about the myriad details related to our state's historical development. Although the list is lengthy, I believe it is important to acknowledge the contributions of the many individuals who gave their time to verify facts, review individual pieces, debunk myths, offer suggestions, and provide details that are occasionally overlooked in a book of this nature. They are the ones who handled my numerous e-mails, phone calls, letters, and personal visits about the people and events they, as locals, know so well. To each of them, I am profoundly grateful.

Among those I want to thank are:

Rich Aarstad, Montana Historical Society

Alberta Adamson, president, Wheaton Center for History

Anna Adermann, director, Assumption Public Library

Regina Agnew, reference librarian, East St. Louis Public Library

Elmer C. Alft, author

Donnie Allen, vice president, Williamson County Historical Society

Marylou Anderson, director, Streatorland Historical Society Museum

Meredith Anderson, librarian, Geneva Public Library

Roger Anderson and Ron Anderson, Cumberland County Genealogical and Historical Society

Chris Ashmore, adult services director, Jacksonville Public Library

Mayor Judy Askew, city of Brookport

Laurie Austin, archive specialist, National Archives and Records Administration

MSgt. Jason Axberg, historian, 375th Airlift Wing, Scott Air Force Base

Julia Bachrach, historian and planning supervisor, Chicago Park District

Bill Bailey, board member, Ogle County Historical Society

Richard F. Bales, author

Linda Banks, history librarian, Herrin City Library

Kim Bauer, Lincoln curator, Abraham Lincoln Presidential Library and Museum

Rev. Roy Bauer (Ret.), Quincy

Rose Marie Benedetti, commissioner, Lyons Historical Commission

Gilda Bennett, secretary, St. Philip Neri Catholic Church

Kristina Benson, director, Du Quoin Public Library

Arnie Bernstein, author

Patsy Berry, Edgar County Historical Society

Phil Bertoni, Mount Pulaski 175th Anniversary Committee

Bruce Beveridge, local historian, Summit Public Library

Deb Bier, reference librarian, Peoria Public Library

Kelly Bischof, publicity and special events coordinator, Carson Pirie Scott & Co.

LaVerne Bloemker, archival research assistant, Madison County Archival Library

Harold Boyles, Marion County Historical Society

Gerald Brauer, executive director, Ellwood House Museum

Sue Breese, Joiner History Room, Sycamore Public Library

Mark Brown, district forester, Illinois Department of Natural Resources

Steven E. Brown, head of Quaternary and Engineering, Illinois State Geological Survey

Kathy Bruski, assistant to department head of adult services, Schaumburg Township District Library

Rose Bucciferro, director, Will County Historical Society

Terence Buckaloo, director and curator, Sterling-Rock Falls Historical Society

Donna Buckley, Treasurer, Village of Minooka

Linda Bullen, curator, Pullman State Historic Site

Henry Burgweger, Kirkland

Margaret Bush, librarian, Tazewell County Genealogical and Historical Society

George Bushnell, author

Kathy Butcher, research coordinator, Illiana Genealogical and Historical Society

Barbara Call, volunteer, Brookport Public Library

Tacie Campbell, curator, National Mississippi River Museum and Aquarium

Gayle A. Carr, director, Greenup Township Public Library

Jan Carter, Local History and Genealogy Room, Rockford Public Library

Elizabeth A. Carvey, assistant site manager, Black Hawk State Historic Site

Bill Case, curator, Funks Grove

Magdaleno Castaneda, volunteer, Cicero Public Library and library science student, Dominican University

Ramon J. Castro, art teacher, Freeport High School

Lisa Cervac, president, Highwood Historical Society

Robert Chambers, Glen Ellyn Historical Society

Elwyn Cheatum, former mayor, Kinmundy

Harold Chisamore, Ela Historical Society

Fred Christensen, Urbana

Harry Church, Lebanon Historical Society

Ralph Church, director, Mound City National Cemetery

Alice Cisna, director, Arthur Public Library District

J. Rolland Clark, Brown County Historical Society

Beth E. Clausen, Government Publications and Maps, Northwestern University Library

Nancy Claypool, director, Marshall Public Library

Liora Cobin, Evanston Historical Society

Loretta Cohen, research chairperson, Illiana Genealogical and Historical Society

Mary Cole, site superintendent, Vandalia Statehouse State Historic Site

Barbara Collins, director, Moweaqua Public Library

Margaret Collins, patent and trademark librarian, Illinois State Library

Raymond Collins, reference librarian, Illinois State Library

Patricia Conroy, reference librarian, Cicero Public Library

Pat Cooper, executive secretary, Greater Fairfield Area Chamber of Commerce

Sarah Cooper, archivist, Bureau County Historical Society

Andrew Cooperman, library assistant for genealogy and local history, Morrison-Talbott Library, Waterloo

Charlene Copeland, Rushville Public Library

Mary Lou Cornelison, executive director, Marshall Area Chamber of Commerce

James M. Cornelius, Ph.D., curator, Lincoln Collection, Abraham Lincoln Presidential Library and Museum

Sister Joaquina Costa, Missionary Sisters of the Sacred Heart of Jesus

Robert Cowan, Stacy's Tavern

Jody Crago, executive director, DuPage County Historical Museum

Margaret Crane, director, Woodstock Public Library

John H. Croessman, publisher, Du Quoin *Evening Call*

Sue Cunnea, Grundy County Historical Society

Linda Dahl, adult services librarian, Fondulac District Library, East Peoria

Neil Dahlstrom, reference archivist, Deere & Company World Headquarters

Steve Dancey, curator, Mendota Museum and Historical Society

Claudia Dant, president, Wabash County Museum

Carl P. Daw, Jr., executive director, The Hymn Society in the United States and Canada

Beverly Dawson, librarian, Glenview Area Historical Society

Dora Dawson, Meredosia

Daniel Deck, Olney

Clari Dees, library assistant, Pittsfield Public Library

Sue Degges, Naper Settlement, Naperville

Mary DeMoss, media librarian, Lumpkin Library, Blackburn College

Kim Denny, library clerk, Dillon Public Library, Montana

Shirley DeWeese

Otto Dick, former president, Ogle County Historical Society

Elizabeth Doetsch, library assistant, University of Illinois Undergraduate Library

Susan Donahue, museum coordinator, Lemont Area Historical Society

James Dowd, author

Nancy Drago, research associate, Naperville Public Library–Nichols Library

Bernie Drake, executive director, Peoria Historical Society

Diana Dretske, collections coordinator, Lake County Discovery Museum

Anneta Drilling-Sowa, lead paraprofessional, information services, Joliet Public Library

Darrell Duensing, site manager, Fort de Chartres State Historic Site

Robert Dunker, Ph.D., agronomist and superintendent, Department of Crop Sciences, University of Illinois

Kim S. Dunnigan, office manager, Dickson Mounds Museum

Marge Edwards, program coordinator, Dundee Township Historical Society

Phyllis M. Ellin, executive director, Illinois & Michigan Canal National Heritage Corridor Commission

G. Howard and Florence Eltrevoog, Norsk Museum

Karen Erbach, information services, Arlington Heights Memorial Library

Betty Estes, director, Pontiac Office of Tourism

Dal Estes, assistant tourism director, Pontiac Office of Tourism

Bonnie Estrada, director, Talcott Free Library, Rockton

Betty Eutsler, head librarian, Kinmundy Public Library

Toni Evans, director, Plainfield Historical Society Museum

Karen Everingham, assistant division manager, Illinois Historic Preservation Agency

Sarah Faford, Curator of Collections, Kankakee County Museum

Kathy Farren, editor, *Kendall County Record*

Judy Ficke, director, Iroquois County Historical Society

Nancy Fike, director, McHenry County Historical Society

Anita Fisk, president, Prophetstown Main Street Program

Kristian Flanders, public service librarian, Concordia University

Jean Forness, director, Williamsville Public Library

George Forston, former mayor of Moweaqua

Elaine Foster, Carmi Public Library

Bruce Fox, branch librarian, Carl B. Roden Branch, Chicago Public Library

Judith Franke, Ph.D., Lewistown

Eric French, Smithsonian Institution Libraries

Sandra Fritz, Reference Department, Illinois State Library

Debby Funk, Funks Grove Pure Maple Sirup

Natalie Gacek, director, St. Charles Heritage Center

Roger Gambrel, associate librarian, Joliet Public Library

Audrey Garbe, genealogist, Effingham County Genealogical and Historical Society

William A. Gardner, Ashland

Linda Garvert, librarian, Lincoln Library Sangamon Valley Collection, Springfield Public Library

Char Giardina, historical interpreter, Illinois & Michigan Canal Visitor Center

Betty Gibboney, Lewistown Society for Historical Preservation

Robert Gibler, president, Lee County Historical Society

Robert Gillfillan, president, Onarga Military School Alumni Association

Anthony R. Glass, technical services librarian and college archivist, Eureka College

Nancy Glick, director, Havana Public Library

Kathy Goleman, librarian, Divernon Township Library

Therese Gonzalez, museum staff, Naval Training Center at Great Lakes

Dan Goodwin, Glencoe Historical Society

Chris Gordy, executive director, Stephenson County Historical Society

Susan Gordy, site manager, Apple River Fort State Historic Site

Lee C. Grady, archivist, McCormick-International Harvester Collection, Wisconsin Historical Society

Cathy Grafton, director, Odell Public Library

Joe Graham, editor, *American Bee Journal*

Robert Greene, assessor, Oregon–Nashua Township, Ogle County

Charles E. Gregersen, architect and historian

Nevin Grigsby, executive vice president, Farmers State Bank, Pittsfield

Debbie Grinnell, director of preservation services, Naper Settlement

Stella Grobe, treasurer, Lee County Historical Society

Maryrose Grossman, archive specialist, National Archives and Records Administration

Sharon Gums, reference librarian, Chicago Public Library

Gary Hacker, Johnson County Genealogical and Historical Society

Nancy Hackett, president, Romeoville Area Historical Society

Mary Hale, manager, Boone County Historical Museum

Karen Hallam, Jonesboro Public Library

Andrew Hamilton, Carl B. Roden Branch, Chicago Public Library

Joyce Hanna, volunteer, Rock Island County Historical Library

Martha Hansen, reference librarian, Woodstock Public Library

Amanda Hanson, facility manager, Skokie Heritage Museum

Carol Hanson, director, Pankhurst Memorial Library, Amboy

Joan Hardekopf, treasurer, Sandwich Historical Society

Alan Harn, curator, Dickson Mounds Museum

Gwen Harrison, reference librarian, Illinois State Library

Dan Hauter, president, Macoupin County Historical Society

Randy Hawkins, site superintendent, Lincoln Trail Homestead State Memorial

Heather Hayes, photographer, Illinois Secretary of State

Nadine Hayward, Williamsville Historical Museum

Betty Head, Shawneetown

Melody Heidenreich, Stockton Heritage Museum

William J. Helmer, Boerne, Texas

Bill Hendron, volunteer, DuPage County Genealogical Society

Nancy Henry, Mattoon Public Library

Judy Herder, president, Frankfort Area Historical Society of Will County

Joan Herrick, Kewanee Historical Society

Jan Heuer, secretary, Lexington Genealogical and Historical Society

Jan Hickox, librarian, Casey Township Library

Carol Johnson Hicks, president, Hoopeston Historical Society

Janet Hicks, director, Carnegie-Schuyler Public Library, Pana

Connie Hill, City of Monmouth

Janet Hill, Robinson Public Library District

Michael Hillmer, reference department, Six Mile Regional Library District, Granite City

Ruth Ann Hobrock, Beardstown Houston Memorial Library

Bruce Hodgdon, public information officer, Forest Preserve District of Will County

Kenneth A. Holder, artist, Bloomington

Glenn Holmes, Delavan

Lynda Hoornbeek, Glen Ellyn Historical Society

Sarah Horn, director, Lyons Public Library

Mickey Horndasch, museum curator, Arlington Heights Historical Museum

Lecta Hortin, White County Historical Society

Gerald Hulslander, board member, LaSalle County Historical Society

Paul Idleman, director, Champaign County Historical Museum

Gail Inman, head of adult services, Lincolnwood Public Library

William R. Iseminger, public relations director, Cahokia Mounds State Historic Site

Judi Jacksohn, interpretive site program coordinator, Hennepin Canal Parkway

Bobbi Jackson, Rock Island County Historical Society

Marguerite Jackson, vice president, Assumption Historical Society

Kim Jacobs, commissioner, Riverside Historical Commission

Janice Jamison, executive director, Beardstown Chamber of Commerce

Jack Janik, president, National Flag Day Foundation

John Jaros, executive director, Aurora Historical Society

Dave Joens, director, Illinois State Archives

Terry Johnson, site superintendent, Fort Massac State Park

Chuck Jolicoeur, assessor, Pine Rock Township, Ogle County

Jim Jones, tour director, Route 66 Association of Illinois Hall of Fame and Museum

P. Michael Jones, director, General John A. Logan Museum

Sue Jones, secretary, Clark County Historical Society

William Jones, manager, Ronald Reagan Boyhood Home

Tom Joyce, Rare Books, Chicago

Theodore Karamanski, Ph.D., History Department, Loyola University

Fran Kasten, president, Seneca Parks and Recreation

Wallace Kautz, site superintendent, Mount Pulaski Courthouse

Jean Kay, librarian, Historical Society of Quincy and Adams County

Ann Durkin Keating, Ph.D., C. Frederick Toenniges Professor of History, North Central College

Ellen Keith, Chicago History Museum Research Center

Jason King, director of research, Center for American Archaeology

Phyllis King, librarian, Golconda Public Library

Ruth Kinney, Warren County Genealogical Society

Michelle Knight, assessor, Scott/White Rock Township, Ogle County

Harry Koepp, assistant curator, Stockton Heritage Museum

Carolyn Koetters, office manager, Historical Society of Quincy

Nancy Kolk, Fulton

Greg Koos, executive director, McLean County Historical Society

Katy Kraushaar, reference librarian, Quincy Public Library

Barbara Krehbiel, genealogist, Charleston Carnegie Public Library

Susan J. Kroll, Norwood Park Historical Society

Robin S. Krone, library director, Prairie Skies Public Library District

Rosemary Kurtz, Paxton Carnegie Library

Gloria H. LaHood, local history specialist, Peoria

John M. Lamb, I & M Canal Collection, Lewis University

Judy Wright Landeck, Tuscola

J. Gregory Langan, Lee County Historical Society

Pamela Lange, museum director, Bureau County Historical Society

Dean G. Larson, Libertyville-Mundelein Historical Society

Janice Lauritzen, program manager, Dwight Main Street

Merrilee S. Lee, assistant director, Galena/Jo Daviess County Historical Society and Museum

Kris Leinicke, director, Rock Island Arsenal Museum

Cheryl Lennox, head librarian, Cordova District Library

Phil Lewis, president, Effingham County and National Road Museum Association

Taran Ley, library specialist, Illinois State Library

Vanda Liesman, librarian, Elkhart Public Library

Richard C. Lindberg, author

Alice Lintereur, Shabbona-Lee-Rollo Historical Museum

Lisa Livesay, director, Stinson Memorial Library

Larry Lock, president, Kewanee Historical Society

Lois Lock, historian and genealogist, Jersey County Historical Society Research Center

Katie Lockwood, tourism manager, Southern Illinois Tourism Office

Brenda Logan, Baxter's Vineyards, Nauvoo

Mary Logan, Nauvoo

Anne Lunde, local historian, Norwood Park Historical Society

Emily Lyons, curator, Randolph County Archives and Museum

Jean H. Lythgoe, librarian assistant, Rockford Public Library

Shirley MacDavid, Fairfield

Eleanor Macey, Marshall

Lydia Macklin, administrative assistant, Quinn Chapel A.M.E. Church

Sandy Madsen, assistant district librarian, Illinois Prairie District Public Library

Olivia Mahoney, Chicago History Museum

Marcia Mahood, CEO, Norwood Life Care Foundation

Ed Maldonado, curator, Clarke House Museum

Diane Mallstrom, reference librarian, Public Library of Cincinnati & Hamilton County

Curtis Mann, manager, Sangamon Valley Collection, Lincoln Library

Delores Mark, president, Ela Historical Society

Sherrie Martin, Waterman Area Heritage Society

Sue Martyn, office manager, LaSalle County Historical Society

Jennifer Masengarb, Chicago Architecture Foundation

Barbara Mask, president, Fulton Historical Society

Cathy Masterson, assistant asset manager, Hamilton Partners, Inc.

Jim McAffee, Rockton

Janet McBride, president, Mount Greenwood Historical Society

Lori McCaffrey, Sugar Grove Historical Society

Mildred B. McCormick, researcher, Pope County Historical Society

Patrick McDaniel, executive director, Macon County Historical Society

Sarah McGann, reference library assistant, Massachusetts Historical Society

Beth McGlasson, webmaster, Jersey County Historical Society

Steph McGrath, senior curator, DuPage County Historical Museum

Sue McHugh, secretary, The Grove National Historic Landmark, Glenview

Hearshal McKinney, research assistant, Jersey County Historical Society Research Center

Ralph McTall, Irvington

Robert Meginnes, trustee, Secor Village

Dan Melone, archaeologist

James L. Miessen, Stillman Valley

William Millsap, Robinson

John Molyneaux, Ph.D., historian, Local History Department, Rockford Public Library

Raymond H. and Alia Anna Montgomery, author-historians

Linda Moore, Office of the City Clerk, Jacksonville

Robert Morefield, photo collection chairman, Jackson County Historical Society

Barbara A. Morrell, museum administrator, Macon County Historical Society Museum Complex

Steve Moser, site manager, Hennepin Canal Parkway

David Motley, director of public relations and marketing, City of Waukegan

Norm Mueller, president, and Ione Mueller, corresponding secretary, Plainfield Historical Society

Vicky Mundwiler, tourism associate, Knox County Historical Museum

Carol Murdoch, reference services librarian, Oesterle Library, North Central College

Carolyn Murphy, reference librarian, Illinois State Library

Jean Myers, curator, Metamora Courthouse State Historic Site

James M. Neal, president, Lawrence County Historical Society

Bette Nelson, National Trust for Historic Preservation

Iris Nelson, reference librarian, local history, Quincy Public Library

Carey Lucas Nikonchuk, research consultant, South Carolina Historical Society

Ellen O'Brien, Municipal Reference Collection, Chicago Public Library

Charlotte O'Dea, DeWitt County Genealogical Society

Bryan Ogg, assistant curator, Naper Settlement

Jared Olar, assistant librarian, Pekin Public Library

Ellen Olson, Reference Department, Rockford Public Library

Greg Olson, *Jacksonville-Journal Courier*

Maurice O'Neal, trustee, Village of Royal Lakes

Lauren Ottlinger, assistant director, The Grove National Historic Landmark, Glenview

Sam Park, president, Church of Jesus Christ of Latter Day Saints, Nauvoo

Don Parker, Hancock County Historical Society

Daniela Parish, director, Warsaw Public Library

Barbara A. Paul, administrative librarian, Chicago Heights Free Public Library

Lucille Pech, museum curator, Atlanta Library and Museum

Taylor Pensoneau, author

Mollie Perrot, Ottawa Scouting Museum

Jarrod Peters, site manager, Pierre Menard Home State Historic Site

Paul W. Petraitis, historian

Debora Pfeiffer, office manager and reference specialist, University of Illinois Archives

Michelle Pfister, director, Yorkville Public Library

Tom Phillips, publisher, *Pana News-Palladium*

Leroy K. Pickett, Downers Grove

Joe Piersen, Chicago and North Western Historical Society Archives

Shirley Pierson, administrative assistant, Mendota Museum and Historical Society

Mary Pirkl, Center for American Archeology

Amanda Pope

Dena Porter, supervisor for operations, Marion Carnegie Library

Tony Powers, branch librarian, Austin-Irving Branch, Chicago Public Library

Ivan E. Prall, Malta

Hershel Price, superintendent, Trail of Tears State Park (Missouri)

Bill Provis, Harold Washington Library Center

Welton Pryor, Jr., manager, Tract Book Department, Property Insight

Jennifer Putzier, curator, Aurora Historical Society

Patrick M. Quinn, Ph.D., university archivist, Northwestern University

Cheryl Rabe, president, Onarga Historical Society

Jeff Rankin, director of communications, Monmouth College

Gillette Ransom, Elkhart Historical Society

Julie Rash, *Hardin County Independent*

Robert Rea, Benton

Josephine Remling, former president, Macoupin County Historical Society

John Renshaw, executive director, Coles County Historical Society

Steve Repp, Galena Public Library

Sheila Richey, site interpreter, Fort Massac State Park

Susan Richter, director, Vermilion County Museum

Misty Riutzel, Quincy Public Library

John E. L. Robertson, professor emeritus, University of Kentucky

Ernestine Robey, Greenup

Bob Robinson, public affairs officer, VA Illiana Health Care System

Kathy Robinson, reference librarian, Lincoln Library

Junius Rodriguez, Ph.D., Associate Professor of History, Eureka College

Harriet Roll, director, Harvard Diggins Library

Jantha Rollings, Arcola

Emil Romano, reference specialist, North Chicago Public Library

Joseph G. Rosa, author

Kathy Rosa, Ed.D., library services coordinator, Marion Carnegie Library

Kurt A. Rosentrater, Ph.D., assistant professor, Engineering and Industrial Technology, Northern Illinois University

Kenneth Ross, reference librarian, Presbyterian Church (U.S.A.)

Nathan N. Rothschild, president, Centralia Area Historical Society

Monna Milton Rowley, Lockport

Jane Rozek, Illinois Collection Librarian, Schaumburg Township District Library

Amber Sabin, public information officer, City Water, Power & Light, Springfield

James D. Sanderson

Dean C. Sandstrom

Bruce Sarver, president, Moweaqua Coal Mine Museum

Jeff Saulsbery, assistant site manager, David Davis Mansion State Historic Site

R. Craig Sautter, author

Kim Scace, library director, Stockton Township Public Library

Wanda Schaller, State Historian, Daughters of the American Revolution

Kevin Schnetzler, assessor, South Grove/Mayfield Township, DeKalb County

Catherine Schrimpf, assistant director of library services, Hayner Public Library District, Alton

Bob Sear, Livingston County Historical Society

Roger A. Seifert, Moweaqua

Ken Sereno, board member, Grundy County Historical Society

Kathleen Seusy, Rock Island Historical Society

William H. Shannon, Chatham

Joyce A. Shireman, Ph.D., site coordinator, Joseph Smith Historic Site

Jennifer L. O. Sigmond, Chicago

Beth Simeone, curator, Ogle County Historical Society

Brenda Simms, Mount Carmel Public Library

Robert Sloane, Art Information Center, Chicago Public Library

David Slocum, president, Brown County Historical Society

Ernie Slottag, City Water, Power & Light, Springfield

Dorene Smith, volunteer, Mount Pulaski Courthouse

Monica Smith, director, Cairo Public Library

Angela Snook, curator and director, Geneseo Historical Museum

Susan Soenksen, reference librarian, Niles Public Library

Diane Soffietti, reference librarian, Fondulac District Library, East Peoria

Elizabeth M. Sosa, superintendent of recreation, Flagg-Rochelle Community Park District

Verlyn "Buzz" Spreeman, historian

Linda Stahnke, archival operations and reference specialist, University Archives, University of Illinois

Susan Staley, Illinois General Assembly

Charles H. Stats, Oak Park

Laurie Stein, curator, Lake Forest-Lake Bluff Historical Society

Elaine Steingrubey, director, Morrison-Talbott Library, Waterloo

Carole Stern, librarian, Annawan-Alba Township Library

Jim Stewart, head of social sciences and history, Harold Washington Library Center

Dennis Stiegemeier, City Clerk, Staunton

Ann Stoddard, Montgomery County Historical Society

Michael Stout, lead interpreter, Lewis and Clark State Historic Site

Peg Strobel, director, Hull-House Museum

Hovie Stunson, assistant genealogist, Harrisburg Public Library

David Sullivan, City of Pontiac

Richard M. Sumrall, library director, Lincoln Public Library

Bernard J. Sundstedt, Assistant Vice President for Advancement, Rockford College

Stephan J. Swanson, director, The Grove National Historic Landmark

John F. Swenson

Terry Tatum, coordinating planner, Commission on Chicago Landmarks/Department of Housing and Economic Development

Meredith Tausig, Chicago Landmarks Commission

Marge Teiwes, Glen Ellyn Historical Society

Wayne C. Temple, Ph.D., chief deputy director, Illinois State Archives

Jean Thode, president, Willow Springs Historical Society

Bill Thomas, trustee, Atlanta Public Library

Marylin Thorsen, genealogical researcher, Dwight Historical Society

Lynn Timmerman, site manager, John Deere Historic Site

Patricia Tomczak, dean of library and information resources, Brenner Library, Quincy University

Mary C. Toraason, director, LaSalle County Historical Society

Rick Trahan, site coordinator and blacksmith, John Deere Historic Site

Barbara Traver, Village Clerk, West Dundee

Glennette Tilley Turner, author

Alice Uphouse, State Historian, Daughters of the American Revolution

Gerald and Marilyn Urban, Marengo

William L. Urban, Ph.D., History Department, Monmouth College

Jeanne Valentine, adult services manager, Plano Community Library District

Jerry VanMatre, Ash Grove Christian Church, Windsor

Sandy Vasko, president, Will County Historical Society

Cynthia Vickery, librarian, Shawneetown Public Library

Sherman Virtue, Pearl City

Mike Wagenbach, site superintendent, Pullman State Historic Site

Christopher Walls, executive director, Murphysboro Chamber of Commerce

Daryl Watson, director, Galena/Jo Daviess County Historical Society and Museum

John Watson, Villa Ridge

Eric Wayda, computer consultant

Marsha Kaye Webb, genealogist, Moultrie County Historical and Genealogical Society

Mark R. Weber, Robinson

Arielle Weininger, curator of collections and exhibitions, Illinois Holocaust Museum and Education Center

Rebecca Weinstock, director, Flagg Township Museum

Susan Weller, D.D.S., Jacksonville

Jack and Nancy Wendt, museum cochairs, Dundee Township Historical Society

Charles Werner, treasurer, Illinois Central Railroad Historical Society

Andy West, site superintendent, Trail of Tears State Forest

Mary T. Westerhold, assistant librarian, Madison County Historical Museum and Archival Library

Greg Weydert, director, Creve Coeur Public Library District

Kathleen Whildin, president, Sugar Grove Historical Society

Julie White, office manager, Kankakee County Museum

Kami Whitehurst, IRAD intern, Illinois Regional Archives Depository at Southern Illinois University

Michael Wiant, Ph.D., museum director, Dickson Mounds Museum

Michael Wickens, site superintendent, Jim Edgar Panther Creek State Fish and Wildlife Area

Jane Wiles, manager of operations and user services, Agriculture Consumer Environmental Sciences Library, University of Illinois

Shirley Wilhelmsen, director, Squaw Grove Public Library District

Shirley Willard, president, Fulton County Historical Society, Indiana

Scarlett Williamson, Hutsonville

Tom Wilson, Galesburg

Brad Winn, site superintendent, Lewis and Clark State Historic Site

Daniel Winningham, reporter, *Macoupin County Enquirer-Democrat*

Chris Winter, curator, Batavia Depot Museum

Lisa Winters, director, Allerton Public Library District

Tom Wise, mayor, Village of Gardner

Vada Wood, Ogle County Historical Society

Paula Woods, vice chair, Old Lincoln Courthouse and Museum Commission

Dolores Wright, volunteer, Rock Island County Historical Library

Sonia Yaco, reference archivist, McCormick-International Harvester Collection, Wisconsin Historical Society

David M. Young, author

Marcia Young, Ph.D., site manager, David Davis State Historic Site

Marie Zamberletti, recreation therapy supervisor, VA Illiana Health Care System

Dave Zielinski, president, Wilmington Area Historical Society

Kathy Zimmerman, Pittsfield

Sara Zumwalt, director, Litchfield Public Library

Staff, Bishop Hill State Historic Site
Staff, Eastland Disaster Historical Society
Staff, Hawaii State Department of Health
Staff, Helen M. Plum Memorial Library
Staff, Mississippi Department of Archives and History
Staff, Municipal Reference Collection, Chicago Public Library
Staff, Newberry Library, Chicago

Staff, Shelby County Historical Society & Genealogical Society, Shelbyville
Staff, Tazewell County Genealogical & History Society, Ehrlicher Research Center, Pekin
Staff, Ulysses S. Grant Association, Southern Illinois University
Staff, Willow Springs Historical Society

I want to express a special thank you to the staff of the Schaumburg Township District Library, who continue to assemble and maintain an outstanding Illinois Collection of county histories, which were of inestimable value in my research. Without this collection, my work would have been far more difficult.

I would also like to add a few last-minute thanks to: Barbara Chambers of the Peter Cartwright United Methodist Church; George J. McShan, historian at Quinn Chapel A. M. E. Church in Brooklyn; Fr. Carroll Mizicko, pastor of St. Augustine Catholic Church in East St. Louis; and Leah Nelson of Veterans Memorial Hall.

My very close personal friend and mentor, the late Dee Brown, deserves special thanks for his early guidance and encouragement. His special introduction to this book was the last professional writing he produced from his manual typewriter. He succumbed to failing health in December 2002. It is my hope that I have measured up to his high standards of keen research and informative writing.

I am deeply grateful to my editor, Gwen McKenna, for her unlimited patience, steadfast guidance, and ongoing professional assistance. She turned a very lengthy manuscript into a tight and readable history that will guide readers along the highways and byways of the Land of Lincoln. Her professional skills and talent as an editor make her truly a "miracle worker" within the publishing industry.

And to my wife, Laura, goes my eternal thanks for tolerating my many idiosyncrasies, especially my habit of using the kitchen table as a collection place for newspaper clippings, books, manuscript pages, and other ephemera. She can now have the kitchen table back for its intended purpose, dining interspersed with the lively art of conversation.

Bibliography

BOOKS AND PERIODICALS

Achilles, Rolf. *Made in Illinois*. Chicago: Illinois Manufacturers Assn., 1993.

Addams, Jane. *My Friend, Julia Lathrop*. New York: Macmillan Co., 1935.

————. *Twenty Years at Hull House*. Urbana: University of Illinois Press, 1990.

Adelman, William J. *Haymarket Revisited*. Chicago: Illinois Labor History Society, 1976.

Albers, Adelaide, Virginia Van Pappelendam, and Marie Worthen, comp. *History of Warsaw*. Warsaw, Ill.: Warsaw Bulletin, 1960. Reprint, Warsaw, Ill.: Warsaw Historical Society, 1999.

Aleo, Philip A. *Dundee Township: Moments Frozen in Time*. Carpentersville, Ill.: Carlith Printing Co., 2002.

Allen, John W. *It Happened in Southern Illinois*. Carbondale: Southern Illinois University, 1968.

————. *Legends and Lore of Southern Illinois*. Carbondale: Southern Illinois University, 1963.

Ambrose, Stephen E. *Undaunted Courage*. New York: Simon & Schuster, 1996.

Angle, Paul M. *Bloody Williamson*. New York: Alfred A. Knopf, 1977.

Applebaum, Stanley. *The Chicago World's Fair of 1893: A Photographic Record*. New York: Dover Publications, 1980.

Atwood, J. A. *The Story of the Battle of Stillman's Run*. Stillman Valley, Ill., 1904.

Bach, Ira J. *A Guide to Chicago's Historic Suburbs*. Chicago and Athens, Ohio: Swallow Press and Ohio University Press, 1981.

Badger, R. Reid. *The Great American Fair: The World's Columbian Exposition and American Culture*. Chicago: Nelson Hall, 1979.

Baldwin, Elmer. *History of La Salle County, Illinois*. Chicago: Rand McNally, 1877.

Bales, Richard F. "Did the Cow Do It? A New Look at the Cause of the Great Chicago Fire." *Illinois Historical Journal* 90, no. 1 (Spring 1997).

Banash, Stan, ed. *Dee Brown's Civil War Anthology*. Santa Fe: Clear Light Publishers, 1998.

Barnes, Siley. "George Ferris' Wheel: The Great Attraction of the Midway Plaisance." *Chicago History*, Fall 1977.

Bartlett, Charles. *Chicago Golf Club Diamond Jubilee 1892–1967*. Chicago: privately published, 1967.

Basler, Roy P., ed. *Abraham Lincoln: His Speeches and Writings*. Cleveland: World Publishing Co., 1946.

————, ed. *The Collected Works of Abraham Lincoln, 1809–1865*. New Brunswick, NJ: Rutgers University Press, 1953–55.

Bateman, Newton, and Paul Selby, eds. *Historical Encyclopedia of Illinois*. 1908. Reprint, Astoria, Ill.: Stevens Publishing Co., 1970.

————, eds. *Historical Encyclopedia of Illinois and History of Sangamon County*. Chicago: Munsell Publishing Co., 1912.

Bateman, Newton, and Paul Selby, eds., *Historical Encyclopedia of Illinois and History of Tazewell County*. Chicago: Munsell Publishing Co., 1905.

———, eds. *Illinois Historical and Effingham County Biographical*. Chicago: Munsell Publishing Co., 1910.

———, eds. *Illinois Historical Wabash County Biographical*. Chicago: Munsell Publishing Co., 1911.

Bauer, K. Jack. *Zachary Taylor*. Newtown, Conn.: American Political Biography Press, 1994.

Baxter, James, and Federal Writers' Project [Illinois]. *Cairo Guide*. N.p.: Works Progress Administration, 1938.

Beath, Robert B. *History of the Grand Army of the Republic*. New York: Bryan, Taylor & Co., 1888.

Beberdick, Frank, and the Historic Pullman Foundation. *Chicago's Historic Pullman District*. Charleston, S.C.: Arcadia Publishing, 1998.

Becker, Anthony J. *The Biography of a Country Town, U.S.A.* N.p.: Spencer-Walker Press, 1954.

Beckwith, H. W. *History of Vermilion County*. Chicago: H. H. Hill & Co., 1879.

Beecher, W. J. "Chicago's First Naturalist: Robert Kennicott." *Field Museum of Natural History Bulletin*, Sept. 1973.

Bent, Charles, ed. *History of Whiteside County, Illinois*. Morrison, Ill., 1877.

Bernstein, Arnie. *Hollywood on Lake Michigan: One Hundred Years of Chicago and the Movies*. Chicago: Lake Claremont Press, 1998.

Beveridge, Albert J. *Abraham Lincoln 1809–1858*. Vol. 1. Boston: Houghton Mifflin, 1928. Reprint, St. Clair Shores, Mich.: Scholarly Press, 1971.

Birkbeck, Morris. *Notes on a Journey in America from the Coast of Virginia to the Territory of Illinois*. Reprint, New York: Augustus M. Kelley, 1971.

Black, Arthur D., ed. *Exhibit for Dentistry at a Century of Progress International Exposition, Chicago*. Chicago: R. R. Donnelley & Sons, n.d.

Black, Bessie M. "Greene Vardiman Black, 1836–1915." In *Transactions of the Illinois State Historical Society for the Year 1931*. Springfield: Illinois State Historical Society, 1931.

Blanchard, Rufus. *History of Du Page County*. Chicago: D. L. Baskin & Co., 1882.

Boies, Henry L. *History of DeKalb County, Illinois*. Evansville, Ind.: Unigraphic, 1973.

Bolotin, Norman, and Christine Laing. *The World's Columbian Exposition: The Chicago World's Fair of 1893*. Urbana: University of Illinois Press, 2002.

Boone, L. V. "The Morrow Plots: A National Historic Landmark." *Illinois Research*, Fall 1968.

Bordner, Marjorie Rich, ed. *Fulton County Heritage*. Dallas: Curtis Media Corporation, 1986.

Bradsby, John. *History of Bureau County, Illinois*. Chicago: World Publishing Co., 1885.

Brevet's Illinois Historical Markers and Sites. Sioux Falls, S.D.: Brevet Press, 1976.

Brinkerhoff, J. H. G. *Brinkerhoff's History of Marion County, Illinois*. Indianapolis: B. F. Bowen & Co., 1909.

Browning, Clyde. *Amish in Illinois*. N.p., 1971.

Brusca, Frank. "Our National Road." *American Road*, Autumn 2004.

Buchbinder-Green, Barbara J. *Evanston: A Pictorial History*. St. Louis: G. Bradley Publishing, 1989.

Buisseret, David. *Historic Illinois from the Air*. Chicago: University of Chicago Press, 1990.

Burg, David F. *Chicago's White City of 1893*. Lexington: University Press of Kentucky, 1976.

Burke, Edward M., and R. Craig Sautter. *Inside the Wigwam: Chicago Presidential Conventions, 1860–1996.* Chicago: Wild Onion Books, 1996.

Bushnell, George D. *Wilmette: A History.* Wilmette, Ill.: Village of Wilmette, 1984.

Call, Keith. *Wheaton.* Charleston, S.C.: Arcadia Publishing, 2006.

Cavanagh, Helen M. *Funk of Funk's Grove.* Springfield: Illinois State Historical Society, 1968.

———. *A Guided Tour of Prairie Home: Lafayette Funk Residence at Shirley, Illinois, 1865–1919.* N.p.: privately published, n.d.

———. *Seed, Soil, and Science: The Story of Eugene D. Funk.* Chicago: Lakeside Press, 1959.

A Century of Progress, 1934: Chicago World's Fair. Chicago: Weyburne-Douglas Co., n.d.

Cha-Jua, Sundiata Keita. *America's First Black Town: Brooklyn, Illinois, 1830–1915.* Urbana and Chicago: University of Illinois Press, 2000.

Champagne, Duane, ed. *The Native North American Almanac.* Vol. 1. Detroit: Gale Research, 1994.

Chanute, C. E. O. *Progress in Flying Machines.* New York: American Engineer and Railroad Journal, 1894.

Chase, Audrie Alspaugh, ed. *The Story of an Old Town: Glen Ellyn.* N.p.: Glen News Printing Co., 1928.

Chicago: A Century of Progress, 1833–1933. Chicago: Marquette Publishing Co., 1934.

Chicago and the World's Fair of 1933. Chicago: F. Husum Publishing Co., 1933.

Chicago City Directory, 1861–62 and 1862–63. Chicago: Halpin & Bailey, 1861 and 1862.

Chicago's Century of Progress. Chicago: Rand McNally, 1933.

Clarahan, Donald. *The Great Rondout Train Robbery.* Bloomington, Ill.: Norfolk-Hall, 1980.

Clark, Helen Hollandsworth, ed. *A History of Fulton County, Illinois, in Spoon River Country.* Astoria, Ill.: Stevens Publishing Co., 1969.

Cochrane, Joseph. *Centennial History of Mason County, Illinois.* Springfield, Ill.: Rokker's Steam Printing House, 1876. Reprint, Havana, Ill.: Church of Jesus Christ of Latter Day Saints, 1986.

Coggeshall, William Turner. *Lincoln Memorial: The Journeys of Abraham Lincoln from Springfield to Washington, 1861, as President Elect; and from Washington to Springfield, 1865, as President Martyred . . . .* Columbus, Ohio: [Columbus] *State Journal,* 1865.

Cohen, Adam, and Elizabeth Taylor. *American Pharaoh: Mayor Richard J. Daley—His Battle for Chicago and the Nation.* New York: Little, Brown & Co., 2000.

Collins, David R., B. J. Elsner, Rich J. Johnson, and Bessie J. Pierce. *Rock Island: All American City.* Charleston, S.C.: Arcadia Publishing, 1999.

Collins, David R., Rich J. Johnson, and Bessie J. Pierce. *Moline: City of Mills.* Charleston, S.C.: Arcadia Publishing, 1999.

Combined History of Edwards, Lawrence, and Wabash Counties, Illinois. Philadelphia: J. L. McDonough & Co., 1883.

Combined History of Randolph, Monroe, and Perry Counties, Illinois. Philadelphia: J. L. McDonough & Co., 1883.

Commission on Chicago Landmarks. *Clark House.* Chicago: Commission on Chicago Landmarks, 1996.

Conley, Walter F. *W. D. Boyce: Honoring the Man Who Brought Scouting to America.* 2nd ed. Ottawa, Ill.: privately published, 1985.

Counties of Cumberland, Jasper, and Richland, Illinois. Chicago: F. A. Battey & Co., 1884.

Cremin, Dennis H., and Charlene Giardina. *Starved Rock State Park: The Work of the CCC Along the I & M Canal.* Chicago: Arcadia Publishing, 2002.

Cunningham, Pat. *Rockford: Big Town, Little City.* Rockford, Ill.: Rockford Newspapers, 2000.

Danckers, Ulrich, and Jane Meredith. *A Compendium of the Early History of Chicago to the Year 1835 When the Indians Left.* River Forest, Ill.: Early Chicago, 2000.

Davis, James E. *Frontier Illinois.* Bloomington: Indiana University Press, 1998.

Davis, William C. *Jefferson Davis: The Man and His Hour.* New York: Harper Collins, 1991.

Davis, William W. *History of Whiteside County, Illinois.* Vol. 1. Chicago: Pioneer Publishing Co., 1908.

Deppermann, W. H. "Two Cents an Acre." *North American Review*, Spring 1938.

Derleth, August. *The Milwaukee Road: Its First Hundred Years.* New York: Creative Age Press, 1948.

Dickens, Charles. *American Notes for General Circulation.* Edited by John S. Whitley and Arnold Goldman. Middlesex, England: Penguin Books, 1972.

Dickinson, Burrus. *History of Eureka, Illinois.* Eureka, Ill.: privately published, 1985.

Dyba, Thomas J., and George L. Painter. *Seventeen Years at Eighth and Jackson.* 2nd edition. Lisle, Ill.: IBC Publications, 1985.

Ebner, Michael H. *Creating Chicago's North Shore: A Suburban History.* Chicago: University of Chicago Press, 1988.

Edwards, Wynette. *St. Charles, Illinois.* Charleston, S.C.: Arcadia Publishing, 1999.

Ehresmann, Julia M., ed. *Geneva, Illinois: A History of Its Times and Places.* Geneva, Ill.: Geneva Public Library District, 1977.

Ellman, Richard, ed. *The New Oxford Book of American Verse.* New York: Oxford University Press, 1976.

England, Otis Bryan. *A Short History of the Rock Island Prison Barracks.* Rock Island, Ill.: U.S. Army Armament, Munitions, and Chemical Command, 1985.

Erwin, Milo. *The History of Williamson County, Illinois.* Marion, Ill.: Williamson County Historical Society, 1876.

Farrar, William G., and JoAnn S. Farrar. Edited by Brent Locke. *Historic Profiles of Fort Massac.* Carbondale: Southern Illinois University, 1977.

Federal Writers' Project [Illinois]. *Delavan 1837–1937: A Chronicle of 100 Years.* Delavan, Ill.: City of Delavan, 1937.

———. *Galena Guide.* N.p.: Works Progress Administration, 1937.

———. *The WPA Guide to Historic Illinois.* Reprint, New York: Pantheon Books, 1983.

Feldhake, Hilda Engbring, ed. *Effingham County, Illinois: Past and Present.* Effingham, Ill.: Effingham Regional Historical Society, 1968.

Ferguson, Gillum. "The Cache River Massacre in Context." *Springhouse* 21, nos. 1, 2, 3 (2004–5).

Fishback, Woodson W. *A History of Murphysboro, Illinois, 1843–1982.* Brandon, Miss.: Quail Ridge Press, 1982.

Flagler, D. W. *A History of the Rock Island Arsenal . . . and of the Island of Rock Island . . . from 1804 to 1863.* Washington, D.C.: Government Printing Office, 1877.

Ford, Thomas. *A History of Illinois.* Edited by Milo Milton Quaife. 2 vols. Chicago: R. R. Donnelley & Sons, 1945.

Fricke, Charles W., ed. *Mount Pulaski, Illinois, 1836–1986: 150 Years of Memories.* Mt. Pulaski, Ill.: C. Fricke, 1986.

Fulton County Historical and Genealogical Society. *Fulton County Heritage*. Edited by Marjorie R. Bodner. Dallas: Curtis Media Corporation, 1988.

Fulwider, Addison L. *History of Stephenson County, Illinois*. 2 vols. Chicago: S. J. Clarke Publishing, 1910.

Gaines, Duane. "The History of Crawford County." *Robinson (Ill.) Argus*, Jan. 14, 1914.

———. "Mystery Woman Faces Execution for Murder." *Mid-West Story Magazine*, Sept. 1932.

Gersbacher, Eva Oxford. "Hotel on the Ohio." *Egyptian Key*, Dec. 1945.

Gilbert, Paul, and Charles Lee Bryson. *Chicago and Its Makers*. Chicago: Felix Mendelsohn, 1929.

Gorecki, Meg. "Legal Pioneers: Four of Illinois' First Women Lawyers." *Illinois Bar Journal*, Oct. 1990.

Grant, H. Roger. *The North Western: A History of the Chicago & North Western Railway System*. DeKalb: Northern Illinois University Press, 1996.

Gregg, Thomas. *History of Hancock County, Illinois*. Chicago: C. C. Chapman, 1880.

Gregory, Ruth W., ed. *Waukegan, Illinois: Its Past, Its Present*. 3rd ed. Waukegan, Ill.: League of Women Voters of Waukegan and City of Waukegan, 1967.

Hair, James T. *Gazetteer of Madison County*. Alton, Ill.: J. T. Hair, 1866. Reprint, Evansville, Ind.: Unigraphic, 1973.

Hallwas, John E. *Macomb: A Pictorial History*. St. Louis: G. Bradley Publishing, 1990.

Halsey, John J., ed. *A History of Lake County, Illinois*. N.p.: Roy S. Bates, 1912.

Harper, Terry L., ed. *History of Edwards County, Illinois*. Dallas: Curtis Media Corporation, 1993.

Harris, Neil, Wim de Wit, James Gilbert, and Robert W. Rydell. *Grand Illusions: Chicago's World's Fair of 1893*. Chicago: Chicago Historical Society, 1993.

Harris, Norman Dwight. *The History of Negro Servitude in Illinois, and of the Slavery Agitation in that State, 1719–1864*. Chicago: A. C. McClurg & Co., 1904. Reprint, Ann Arbor, Mich.: University Microfilms, 1968.

Hayes, Jo. *Kane County Celebrates Illinois Sesquicentennial 1818–1968*. Privately published, n.d.

Heath, Caroline R., ed. *Four Days in May: Lincoln Returns to Springfield*. Springfield: Sangamon County Historical Society and Illinois State Historical Society, 1965.

Helm, Linai T. *The Fort Dearborn Massacre*. Edited by Nelly Kinzie Gordon. Chicago: Rand McNally, 1912.

Herath, Jean L. *Indians and Pioneers*. Hinckley, Ill.: Hinckley Review, 1975.

Hicken, Victor, and M. G. Bodine. "Western Illinois Factbook." *Western Illinois University Bulletin* 47, no. 4 (May 1968).

Hickey, James T. *Springfield, May 1865*. Springfield: Civil War Centennial Commission of Illinois, 1965.

Higley, William Kerr. "The Chicago Academy of Sciences: Historical Sketch of the Academy." *Chicago Academy of Sciences*, special pub. no. 1 (Jan. 1, 1902).

Hilton, Suzanne. *Here Today and Gone Tomorrow*. Philadelphia: Westminster Press, 1978.

Historic Rock Island County. Rock Island, Ill.: Kramer & Co., 1908.

History and Families of Gallatin County, Illinois. Paducah, Ky.: Turner Publishing, 1988.

History of Christian County, Illinois. Philadelphia: Brink, McDonough & Co., 1880.

History of Fulton County, Illinois. Peoria: Charles C. Chapman & Co., 1879.

The History of Henry County, Illinois. Chicago: H. F. Kett & Co., 1877.

The History of Jo Daviess County, Illinois. Chicago: H. F. Kett & Co., 1878.

History of Knox County, Illinois. Peoria: Charles C. Chapman & Co., 1878.

History of Lee County. Chicago: H. H. Hill & Co., 1881.

History of Livingston County, Illinois. Chicago: William LeBaron, Jr. & Co., 1878.

History of Logan County, Illinois. Chicago: Donnelley, Loyd & Co., 1878.

History of Madison County, Illinois. Edwardsville, Ill.: W. R. Brink & Co., 1882.

History of McDonough County, Illinois. Springfield, Ill.: Continental Historical Co., 1885.

History of McLean County, Illinois. Chicago: William LeBaron, Jr. & Co., 1879.

History of Morgan County, Illinois. Chicago: Donnelley, Loyd & Co., 1878.

History of Ogle County, Illinois. Chicago: H. F. Kett & Co., 1878.

History of Peoria County, Illinois. Chicago: Johnson & Co., 1880.

History of Pike County, Illinois. Chicago: Charles C. Chapman, 1880.

History of Sangamon County, Illinois. Chicago: Interstate Publishing Co., 1881.

History of Stephenson County, Illinois. Chicago: Western Historical Co., 1880.

History of Tazewell County, Illinois. Chicago: Charles C. Chapman & Co., 1879.

History of Wayne & Clay Counties, Illinois. Chicago: Globe Publishing Co., 1884.

History of Will County, Illinois. Chicago: William LeBaron, Jr. & Co., 1878.

History of Winnebago County, Illinois: Its Past and Present. Chicago: H. F. Kett & Co., 1877. Reprint, Bowie, Md: Heritage Books, 1990.

Holzer, Harold, ed. *The Lincoln-Douglas Debates.* New York: Harper Collins, 1993.

House, R. C. "The Great Cowboy Race of 1893." *Tombstone Epitaph,* Nov. 2001.

Howard, Robert P. *Illinois: A History of the Prairie State.* Grand Rapids, Mich.: William B. Eerdsman Publishing Co., 1972.

————. *Mostly Good and Competent Men.* 2nd ed. Springfield: Institute for Public Affairs, University of Illinois at Springfield, 1999.

Howell, Robert W., and Russell T. Odell. *Department of Agronomy, University of Illinois at Urbana-Champaign: A History 1951–1988.* Urbana, Ill.: Scherer Communications, 1989.

Hoxie, Frederick E., ed. *Encyclopedia of North American Indians.* New York: Houghton, Mifflin, 1996.

Hubbard, Gurdon S. *The Autobiography of Gurdon Saltonstall Hubbard.* Chicago: Lakeside Press, 1911.

Hutchinson, William T. *Cyrus Hall McCormick.* 2 vols. New York: The Century Co., 1930.

Illinois Sesquicentennial Commission. *Illinois Guide & Gazetteer.* Chicago: Rand McNally, 1969.

Illustrated Freeport. 1896. Reprint, Mt. Vernon, Ind.: Windmill Publications, 2000.

In the Foot-Prints of the Pioneers of Stephenson County, Illinois. Freeport, Ill.: The Pioneer Publishing Co., 1900.

Iroquois County History. Watseka, Ill.: Iroquois County Historical Society, 1985.

Jensen, Richard J. *Illinois: A Bicentennial History.* New York: W. W. Norton & Co., 1978.

Keller, Guy, ed. *Elmhurst: Celebrating 150 Colorful Years.* Elmhurst, Ill.: Elmhurst Sesquicentennial Planning and Steering Committee, 1986.

Kern, J. W. *Past and Present of Iroquois County, Illinois.* Chicago: S. J. Clarke Publishing Co., 1907.

Kett, H. F., et al. *The History of Winnebago County, Illinois: Its Past and Present.* Bowie, Md: Heritage Books, 1990.

Kilduff, Dorrell, and C. H. Pygman. *Illinois: History, Government, Geography*. Chicago: Follett Publishing Co., 1962.

Klein, Jerry. *Peoria*. Peoria, Ill.: Visual Communications, 1985.

Knight, Robert, and Lucius Zeuch. *Mount Joliet: Its Place in Illinois History and Its Location*. Joliet, Ill.: Will County Historical Society, 1980.

Knox, Samuel F., ed. *The Revised Ordinances of the City of Highwood*. Highwood, Ill.: Fort Sheridan News Print, 1904.

Krause, Susan, Kelley A. Boston, and Daniel W. Stowell. *Now They Belong to the Ages*. Springfield: State of Illinois, 2005.

Kurland, Gerald. *Richard Daley: The Strong Willed Mayor of Chicago*. Charlotteville, N.Y.: Sam Har Press, 1972.

Ladd, Marta Cates, and Constance Schneider Kimball, eds. *History of Coles County, 1876–1976: Coles County, Illinois*. N.p.: Charleston and Mattoon Bicentennial Commission, 1976.

Lagron, Arthur. "Fort Crevecoeur." *Journal of the Illinois State Historical Society*, Jan. 1913.

Lake Zurich. Bloomingdale, Ill.: Progressive Publishing, 1999.

Lamb, George. *Historical Reminiscences*. Dixon, Ill.: P & M Enterprises, 1970.

Lamb, John. *I & M Canal: A Corridor in Time*. Romeoville, Ill.: Lewis University, 1987.

Lansden, John M. *A History of the City of Cairo, Illinois*. Reprint, Carbondale: Southern Illinois University Press, 1976.

La Salle, Illinois: An Historical Sketch. La Salle, Ill.: La Salle Centennial Committee, 1952.

Lawler, Lucille. *Amazing Shawneetown: A Tale of Two Cities*. Ridgway, Ill.: Self-published, 1985.

Leavitt, Fred, and Nancy Miller. *Pullman: Portrait of a Landmark Community*. Chicago: Historic Pullman Foundation, 1981.

Leonard, Doris Parr, ed. *Big Bureau and Bright Prairies*. Moline, Ill.: Desaulniers & Company, 1968.

Leslie, Frank. *Frank Leslie's Illustrated History of the Civil War*. Edited by Louis Shepheard Moat. 1895[?]. Reprint, New York: Fairfax Press, 1977.

Lincoln, Abraham. *Abraham Lincoln: Speeches and Writings, 1832–1858*. New York: Library of America, 1989.

Lindamood, Jean. "The Lincoln Highway." *Automobile Magazine*, Sept. 1989.

Lindberg, Richard. *Return to the Scene of the Crime*. Nashville: Cumberland House, 1999.

Lohr, Lenox R. *Fair Management*. Chicago: Cuneo Press, 1952.

Lossing, Benson J. *Field-Book of the American Revolution*. 2 vols. Reprint, Cottonport, La.: Polyanthos, 1972.

Maas, David E., and Charles W. Weber, eds. *DuPage Discovery, 1776–1976*. N.p.: Columbian Lithographic Co., 1976.

Mahon, John K. *History of the Second Seminole War, 1835–1842*. Rev. ed. Gainesville: University of Florida Press, 1985.

Mahoney, Olivia. *Go West! Chicago and American Expansion*. Chicago: Chicago Historical Society, 1999.

Marquis Who's Who, Inc. *Who Was Who in America*. Vol. 1, 1607–1896. Chicago: A. M. Marquis Co., 1963.

Martin, Jim, and Bette Cooper. *Monmouth-Western Stoneware*. Des Moines: Wallace-Homestead Book Co., 1983.

Masters, Edgar Lee. *The Sangamon.* Urbana and Chicago: University of Illinois Press, 1988.

Matson, N. *Memories of Shaubena.* Chicago: D. B. Cooke & Co., 1878. Reprint, n.p.: Bureau, Grundy, LaSalle, Marshall, Putnam County Historical Societies, 1989.

Maturi, Richard J. "Lincoln Highway." *American History,* Aug. 1994.

May, George W. *Students' History of Peoria County, Illinois.* Galesburg, Ill.: Wagoner Printing Co., 1968.

McCallum, Henry D., and Frances T. *The Wire That Fenced the West.* Norman: University of Oklahoma Press, 1966.

McCormick, Cyrus. *The Century of the Reaper.* Boston: Houghton Mifflin Co., 1931.

———. *McCormick Reaper Centennial.* Chicago: International Harvester Co., 1931.

McGinnis, Ralph Y., and Calvin N. Smith, eds. *Abraham Lincoln and the Western Territories.* Chicago: Nelson-Hall Publishers, 1994.

McHenry County in the Twentieth Century. Union, Ill.: McHenry County Historical Society and Heart Publications, 1994.

Monson, Bill. "The Sheltons: Downstate Gangsters." www.thezephyr.com/monson/sheltons.htm

Moore, Bob. "Pompey's Baptism." *We Proceeded On,* Feb. 2000.

Moore, Frank. *The Civil War in Song and Story.* New York: P. F. Collier, 1889.

Moore, Jean. *A History of Wheaton, Illinois, from Tower to Tower.* Wheaton, Ill.: Gary-Wheaton Bank, 1974.

———. *Wheaton, Illinois: A Pictorial History.* St. Louis: G. Bradley Publishing, 1994.

———, and Hiawatha Bray. *DuPage at 150 and Those Who Shaped Our World.* West Chicago, Ill.: West Chicago Printing Co., 1989.

Morgan, Charles W., ed. *The Story of Oregon, Illinois.* Oregon, Ill.: Book Committee, n.d.

Mount, Mary Ellen. *History of Johnson County, Illinois.* Vienna, Ill.: McDowell Publications, 1992.

Musgrave, Jon, ed. *Handbook of Old Gallatin County and Southeastern Illinois.* Marion, Ill.: IllinoisHistory.com, 2002.

Nagata, Judith A. *Continuity and Chance among the Old Order Amish of Illinois.* New York: AMS Press, 1989.

Nauvoo: "Beautiful Place" Welcomes You. N.p., Nauvoo Area Foundation, 1968.

Neely, Mark E. *The Abraham Lincoln Encyclopedia.* New York: McGraw Hill Book Co., 1982.

Nelson, William E., ed. *City of Decatur and Macon County, Illinois.* Vol. 1. Chicago: Pioneer Publishing Co., 1910.

Newman, Ralph G. *"In This Sad World of Ours, Sorrow Comes to All."* Springfield: Civil War Centennial Commission of Illinois, 1965.

Noble / Seymour / Crippen House. Chicago: Commission on Chicago Landmarks, 1987.

Nore, Ellen, and Dick Norrish. *Edwardsville, Illinois: An Illustrated History.* St. Louis: G. Bradley Publishing, 1996.

Norton, William T., ed. *Centennial History of Madison County, Illinois, and Its People, 1812 to 1912.* 2 vols. Chicago: Lewis Publishing Co., 1912.

———. *Edward Coles, Second Governor of Illinois, 1786–1868.* Philadelphia: J. P. Lippincott & Co., 1911.

Odell, Robert T. "The Morrow Plots: A Century of Learning." Agricultural Experiment Station, College of Agriculture, University of Illinois at Urbana-Champaign, Bulletin 775, 1982.

Official Book of the Fair. 2nd ed. Chicago: A Century of Progress, 1932–33.

Oursler, Will. *The Boy Scout Story*. Garden City, N.Y.: Doubleday & Company, 1955.

Parks, George E. *History of Union County*. Vol. 1. Privately published, 1983.

The Past and Present of La Salle County, Illinois. Chicago: H. F. Kett & Co., 1877.

The Past and Present of Rock Island County, Illinois. Chicago: H. F. Kett & Co., 1877.

The Past and Present of Warren County, Illinois. Chicago: H. F. Kett & Co., 1877.

The Past and Present of Woodford County, Illinois. Chicago: William LeBaron, Jr. & Co., 1878.

Paxton, Patsy Mighell. *Sin-Qua-Sip: Sugar Grove, a History of Sugar Grove Township, Kane County, Illinois*. Sugar Grove, Ill.[?]: self published, 2006[?].

Pearson, Ruth Seen. *Reflections of St. Charles: A History of St. Charles, Illinois, 1833-1976*. St. Charles, Ill.: St. Charles Historical Society, 1976.

Pelland, Maryan and Dan. *McHenry County, Illinois*. Chicago: Arcadia Publishing, 2001.

Perrin, William Henry. *The History of Edgar County, Illinois*. Chicago: William LeBaron, Jr. & Co., 1879. Reprint, Evansville, Ind.: Unigraphic, 1968.

———, ed. *History of Alexander, Union, and Pulaski Counties, Illinois*. Chicago: O. L. Baskin & Co., 1883.

———, ed. *History of Effingham County, Illinois*. Chicago: O. L. Baskin & Co., 1883.

———, et al. *The History of Coles County, Illinois*. Chicago: William LeBaron, Jr. & Co., 1879.

Petterchak, Janice A. *Lone Scout: W. D. Boyce and American Boy Scouting*. Rochester, Ill.: Legacy Press, 2003.

Phillips, Tom, ed. *Pana Illinois Centennial*. Reprint, Pana, Ill.: Pana News Palladium, 1993.

Pierce, Bessie Louise. *From Town to City*. Vol. 2 of *A History of Chicago, 1848–1871*. New York: Alfred A. Knopf, 1940.

Plainfield Bicentennial Commission. *A History of Plainfield "Then and Now."* Plainfield, Ill.: Plainfield Enterprise, 1976.

Portfolio of Photographs of the World's Fair. Chicago: Werner Company, 1893.

Portrait and Biographical Album of Stephenson County, Illinois. Chicago: Chapman Brothers, 1888.

Power, John Carroll, *Abraham Lincoln His Great Funeral Cortege* . . . Springfield, Ill., 1872.

Power, John Carroll, and Mrs. S. A. Power. *History of the Early Settlers of Sangamon County, Illinois*. Springfield, Ill.: Edwin A. Wilson & Co., 1876.

Proceedings of the First Convention of the Industrial Workers of the World: Founded at Chicago June 27–July 8, 1905. New York: Labor News Company, 1905.

Quaife, Milo Milton. *The Early Day of Rock Island and Davenport: The Narratives of J. W. Spencer and J. M. D. Burrows*. Chicago: Lakeside Press, 1942.

Repp, Steve. *Ulysses S. Grant: The Galena Years*. Galena, Ill.: Galena-Jo Daviess County Historical Society, 1994.

Reyman, Jonathan E. "Mt. Carmel Connection." *The Illinois Steward*, Summer 2003.

Reynolds, Robert L. "Seward's Wise Folly." *American Heritage*, Dec. 1960.

Richmond, C. W., and H. F. Vallette. *History of the County of DuPage, Illinois*. Chicago: Scripps, Dross & Spears, 1857.

Roesch, Roberta Fleming. *World's Fairs: Yesterday, Today, Tomorrow*. New York: John Day Co., 1962.

Rosa, Joseph G. *The Gunfighter: Man or Myth?* Norman: University of Oklahoma Press, 1969.

———. *They Called Him Wild Bill*. Norman: University of Oklahoma Press, 1964.

———. *The West of Wild Bill Hickok*. Norman: University of Oklahoma Press, 1982.

Ross, Harvey Lee. *The Early Pioneers and Pioneer Events of the State of Illinois*. 1899. Reprint, Astoria, Ill.: Stevens Publishing Co., 1970.

Russell, Don. *The Lives and Legends of Buffalo Bill*. Norman: University of Oklahoma Press, 1960.

———. *Elmhurst: Trails from Yesterday*. Elmhurst, Ill.: Heritage Committee of the Elmhurst Bicentennial, 1977.

Russell, John. "The Piasa: An Indian Tradition in Illinois." *The Family Magazine (Monthly Abstract of General Knowledge)*, Aug. 1836.

Ryan, George H., ed. *Illinois Blue Book, 1995–1996*. Springfield: State of Illinois, 1996.

Sammon, Paul E. *At Home with General U. S. Grant in Galena, Illinois*. Stockton, Ill.: Beckmon Publishers, n.d.

Sandburg, Carl. *The Prairie Years*. Vol. 1 of *Abraham Lincoln*. New York: Harcourt, Brace & Company, 1926.

Sayler, Carl E. "City of North Chicago." In *A History of Lake County, Illinois*. Edited by John J. Halsey. N.p.: 1912.

Scholl, Edward T. *Seven Miles of Ideal Living*. Berwyn, Ill.: Norman King Co., 1957.

Shea, John Gilmary. *Discovery and Exploration of the Mississippi Valley . . .* New York: Clinton Hall, 1852.

Sifakis, Stewart. *Who Was Who in the Civil War*. New York: Facts on File, 1988.

Slattery, Thomas J. *An Illustrated History of the Rock Island Arsenal and Arsenal Island*. 2 vols. Rock Island, Ill.: Historical Office, U.S. Army Armament, Munitions, and Chemical Command, 1990.

Smith, Henry. *The Expedition Against the Sauk and Fox Indians, 1832*. Fairfield, Wash.: Ye Galleon Press, 1973.

Sorenson, Martha E., and Douglas A. Martz. *View from the Tower: A History of Fort Sheridan, Illinois*. Highwood, Ill.: Tower Enterprises, 1985.

Spencer, Thomas E. *Where They're Buried*. Baltimore: Clearfield Co., 1998.

Steen, Herman. "The Story of America's First Silo." *The Prairie Farmer* 94, no. 4 (January 28, 1922).

Sterling, Robert E. *Joliet: A Pictorial History*. St. Louis: G. Bradley Publishing, 1986.

Stetson, Charlotte. *Alton, Illinois: A Pictorial History*. St. Louis: G. Bradley Publishing, 1986.

Stevens, Frank E. "Illinois in the War of 1812–1814." *Journal of the Transactions of the Illinois State Historical Society* 9 (1904).

Stevens, W. W. *Past and Present of Will County, Illinois*. Chicago: S. J. Clarke Publishing Co., 1907.

Stewart, George R. *Ordeal by Hunger: The Story of the Donner Party*. Lincoln: University of Nebraska Press, 1986.

Stillwell, Paul, ed. *The Golden Thirteen*. Annapolis: Naval Institute Press, 1993.

Stover, John F. *History of the Illinois Central Railroad*. New York: Macmillan Publishing Co., 1975.

Strand, A. E., ed. *A History of the Norwegians of Illinois*. Chicago: John Anderson Publishing Co., 1905.

Straus, Terry, ed. *Indians of the Chicago Area*. 2nd ed. Chicago: NAES College Press, 1990.

Stringer, Lawrence B. *History of Logan County, Illinois*. Vol. 1. Chicago: Pioneer Publishing Co., 1911.

———. *One Hundred Years of Mount Pulaski, Illinois: 1836–1936*. Mt. Pulaski, Ill.: Mt. Pulaski Times-News, 1937.

Sumner, Charles. *His Complete Works*. Vol. 15. Reprint, New York: Negro Universities Press, 1969.

Sunny, Bernard E. *Report of the President of a Century of Progress to the Board of Trustees March 14, 1936*. N.p.: A Century of Progress, 1936.

Sutton, Robert P., ed. *The Prairie State: A Documentary History of Illinois, Colonial Years to 1860.* Grand Rapids, Mich.: William B. Erdmans Publishing Co., 1976.

Swank, George. *Bishop Hill: Showcase of Swedish History.* Rev. ed. Galva, Ill.: Galvaland Magazine, 1978.

Taft, Lorado. *The History of American Sculpture.* New York: Macmillan Co., 1903.

———. "The Monuments of Chicago." *Art and Archaeology* 12, nos. 3–4 (Sept.–Oct. 1921).

Temple, Wayne C. *By Square and Compasses: The Building of Lincoln's Home and Its Saga.* Bloomington, Ill.: Ashlar Press, 1984.

———. *Indian Villages of the Illinois Country: Historic Tribes.* Springfield: Illinois State Museum, 1966.

———. *Lincoln's Connections with the Illinois & Michigan Canal . . .* Springfield, Ill.: Illinois Bell, 1986.

———. "Thomas and Abraham Lincoln as Farmers." *Bulletin of the 55th Annual Meeting of the Lincoln Fellowship of Wisconsin.* No. 53 (April 22, 1995).

Terras, Donald J. *The Grosse Point Lighthouse, Evanston, Illinois: Landmark to Maritime History and Culture.* Evanston, Ill.: Windy City Press, 1995.

Thayer, William Roscoe. *The Life and Letters of John Hay.* Boston: Houghton Mifflin Co., 1915.

Thompson, Richard A., et al. *DuPage Roots.* Wheaton, Ill.: DuPage County Historical Society, 1985.

Tilton, Clint Clay. "The Genesis of Old Vermilion." *Journal of the Illinois State Historical Society* 20, no. 1 (April 1927).

———. "John W. Vance and the Vermilion Salines." *Transactions of the Illinois State Historical Society for the Year 1931.* Springfield: Illinois State Historical Society, 1931.

Towsley, Genevieve. *A View of Historic Naperville.* Naperville, Ill.: Naperville Sun, 1986.

Tweet, Roald. *Quad Cities: An American Mosaic.* Rock Island, Ill.: East Hall Press, 1996.

Union Stock Yard & Transit Company of Chicago. *Annual Live Stock Reports.* Chicago: Union Stock Yard & Transit Company of Chicago, 1869–1948.

U.S. Congress. *Biographical Directory of the United States Congress, 1774–1989.* Bicentennial Edition. Washington, D.C.: Government Printing Office, 1989.

Volk, Leonard. "The Lincoln Mask and How It Was Made." *Century Magazine,* Dec. 1881.

Wabash County, Illinois. Vol. 1. Marion, Ky.: Riverbend Publishing Co., 1993.

Walton, Clyde C. *An Illinois Reader.* DeKalb: Northern Illinois University Press, 1970.

Warner, Ezra J. *Generals in Blue.* Baton Rouge: Louisiana State University Press, 1964.

Wendt, Lloyd, and Herman Kogan. *Bet A Million! The Story of John W. Gates.* Indianapolis: Bobbs-Merrill Co., 1948.

Wheeler, J. E. "Infamous Alton Prison." www.gwheeler.com/alton1.htm.

Whitney, Ellen M., ed. *The Black Hawk War, 1831–1832.* Vols. 35–38 of the Collections of the Illinois State Historical Library. Springfield: Illinois State Historical Library, 1970–78.

Wickstrom, George W., and Charles P. Ainsworth. *Always Lumber: The Story of Dimock, Gould & Co., 1852–1952.* Rock Island, Ill.: Augustana Book Concern, 1953.

Will County Historical Society. *A Guide to Will County Landmarks.* Joliet, Ill.: Will County Historical Society, 1974.

Williamson, William Hay. "David Kennison Spills a Ship of British Tea." *Chicago Today,* Jan. 28, 1928.

Wilson, D. Ray. *Illinois Historical Tour Guide.* Carpentersville, Ill.: Crossroad Communications, 1991.

Wittelle, Marvyn. *Pioneer to Commuter: The Story of Highland Park.* Highland Park, Ill.: Rotary Club of Highland Park, 1958.

Wright, Bob. *Danville: A Pictorial History.* St. Louis: G. Bradley Publishing, 1987.

Young, Alfred E., and Terry J. Fife. *We the People.* Philadelphia: Temple University Press, 1993.

INTERNET SOURCES

"Early Chicago": *http://www.earlychicago.com*

"Encyclopedia of Chicago": *http://www.encyclopedia.chicagohistory.org*

Grimshaw, William A. "History of Pike County, Illinois: A Centennial Address Delivered by Hon. William A. Grimshaw at Pittsfield, Pike County, Illinois: July 4, 1876": *http://archive.org/stream/historyofpikecou01grim#page/n51/mode/2up*

"Harvesting the River": *http://www.museum.state.il.us/RiverWeb/harvesting/*

Luzerne, Frank. *The Lost City!* (ebook): *http://books.google.com/books?id=nX8XUISyq9kC&pg=PP1&lpg=PP1&dq=frank+luzerne+lost+city&source=bl&ots=D4vgCQkBZx&sig=GF8gSy5Ro8tH-ah3-gXGK1Pqri8&hl=en&sa=X&ei=yMxMUb6QBqGYiALQ44GIDg&ved=0CDAQ6AEwAA*

Museum Link Illinois: "Native Americans–Prehistoric": http://www.museum.state.il.us/muslink/nat-amer/pre/index.html

NEWSPAPERS

Belvidere (Ill.) Daily Republican

Chicago Daily Democrat

Chicago Daily Journal

Chicago Democrat

Chicago Evening Journal

Chicago Heights Star

Chicago Journal

Chicago Tribune

Daily Chronicle (DeKalb, Ill.)

Daily Republican-Register (Mount Carmel, Ill.)

Daily Southtown (Chicago)

Dundee (Ill.) Hawkeye

Farm Implement News (Chicago)

Frank Leslie's Illustrated Newspaper

Great Lakes (Ill.) Bulletin

Hardin County Independent

Harper's Weekly

Illinois Intelligencer

Lawrenceville (Ill.) Daily Record

Lebanon (Ill.) Advertiser

MidWeek (DeKalb, Ill.)

Palestine (Ill.) Register

Robinson (Ill.) Daily News

Wheaton Illinoisan

ARCHIVES AND UNPUBLISHED MATERIALS

Applegate, James Bennett. "Frank W. Bradsby and the Louisville Slugger Baseball Bat." 1992. Lebanon Historical Society, Lebanon, Ill.

Central Military Tract Railroad Company. Report of the directors. Printed by Scripps, Bross & Spears, 1856. Archives, Newberry Library, Chicago.

Greene Vardiman Black Biographical File, Northwestern University Archives, Evanston, Ill.

Lewis, Charles Josiah. "David Kennison, the Last Survivor of the Boston Tea Party." Paper presented on July 30, 1914, at a meeting of the Borrowed Time Club in Oak Park, Ill. Chicago History Museum Archives and Manuscripts.

Ping, Jane Ann. *Where Past Meets Present: A History of the Arthur Amish.* Master's thesis, Eastern Illinois University, 1968.

Ormes, A. E. "Chicago's Revolutionary Hero." N.d. Chicago History Museum Archives and Manuscripts.

Schlup, Leonard. "The Political Career of the First Adlai E. Stevenson." Ph.D. dissertation, University of Illinois at Urbana-Champaign, 1973.

Index

Bold entries indicate towns and significant locations.
Italicized page locators indicate images.

About the Author

Stan Banash, a.k.a. "Tex," was born in Chicago and raised in suburban Niles. He received his Bachelor of Philosophy degree in Political Science from Northwestern University in 1968 and his Master of Arts degree in Urban Studies from Roosevelt University in 1972. He has authored numerous feature articles and book reviews for a variety of national magazines, including *The Tombstone Epitaph*, *Wild West* magazine, *Journal of the West*, and *Western Historical Quarterly*. *Roadside History of Illinois* is his third book; the others are *Best of Dee Brown's West* (1998) and *Dee Brown's Civil War Anthology* (1998), both published by Clear Light.

Stan and his wife, Laura, live on Chicago's far northwest side in a rustic, Old West–style home landscaped with native plants from the western plains. Combined, the couple have seven adult children and twelve grandchildren.

—Photo by Dina T. Kwit

The One Year Book
OF
Bible Readings

THE ONE YEAR®

book of

Bible

Readings

TYNDALE HOUSE PUBLISHERS, INC.
WHEATON, ILLINOIS

Visit Tyndale's exciting Web site at www.tyndale.com

The One Year is a registered trademark of Tyndale House Publishers, Inc.

The readings in *The One Year Book of Bible Readings* are taken from *In Touch*, a compilation created by Edythe Draper.

Notes are taken from the *Life Application Bible*. *Life Application* is a registered trademark of Tyndale House Publishers, Inc.

ISBN 0-8423-5387-9

Printed in Italy

05   04   03   02
6   5   4   3   2

PUBLISHER'S NOTE

The One Year Book of Bible Readings has been prepared to help you in the discipline of daily devotional Bible reading. Each day's reading is a short compilation of several topically related Scriptures. The passages included are referenced at the bottom of each page so that favorite verses can be easily located in your Bible.

Each day's reading is introduced by a special thought that speaks to pressing needs and concerns that everyone has experienced. This thought is followed by Scripture passages that speak to these issues, bringing God's perspective and power into the problems, fears, and joys of everyday life. And each reading includes a powerful application note taken from the *Life Application Bible.*

This book will help you get in touch with God, who is able to solve even the deepest of problems. Each reading is filled with the hope, comfort, and wisdom that God offers to all who are willing to look to him for guidance and help. May this year and every year be enriched as you enjoy these daily portions from God's holy Word.

And now, just as you accepted Christ Jesus as your Lord, you must continue to live in obedience to him. Let your roots grow down into him and draw up nourishment from him, so you will grow in faith, strong and vigorous in the truth you were taught. Let your lives overflow with thanksgiving for all he has done.

Colossians 2:6-7

January

All Things New

Another year of promise and of blessings
A year of uncertainties and of unknowns
A year for seeking God's heart

Whether you are looking forward to the excitement
and possibilities of a new job, relationship,
discovery, or any other new event, God desires to
share each step of the way with you. Take his hand,
and begin a new year full of God's abundant life!

January 1

Do not be afraid or discouraged, for the LORD is the one who goes before you. He will be with you; he will neither fail you nor forsake you.

I know, LORD, that a person's life is not his own. No one is able to plan his own course. ❧ If you don't go with us personally, don't let us move a step from this place.

The steps of the godly are directed by the LORD. He delights in every detail of their lives. Though they stumble, they will not fall, for the LORD holds them by the hand.

Yet I still belong to you; you are holding my right hand. You will keep on guiding me with your counsel, leading me to a glorious destiny. ❧ And I am convinced that nothing can ever separate us from his love. Death can't, and life can't. The angels can't, and the demons can't. Our fears for today, our worries about tomorrow, and even the powers of hell can't keep God's love away. Whether we are high above the sky or in the deepest ocean, nothing in all creation will ever be able to separate us from the love of God that is revealed in Christ Jesus our Lord.

The person in whom God delights is one who follows God, trusts him, and tries to do his will. God watches over and makes firm every step that person takes. If you would like to have God direct your way, then seek his advice before you step out. *LAB note for Psalm 37:23-24*

(DEUTERONOMY 31:8) (JEREMIAH 10:23) (EXODUS 33:15) (PSALM 37:23-24) (PSALM 73:23-24) (ROMANS 8:38-39)

January 2

Sing a new song to the LORD! Sing his praises from the ends of the earth!

Sing praises to God, our strength. Sing to the God of Israel. Sing! Beat the tambourine. Play the sweet lyre and harp. ※ He has given me a new song to sing, a hymn of praise to our God. Many will see what he has done and be astounded. They will put their trust in the LORD.

I command you—be strong and courageous! Do not be afraid or discouraged. For the LORD your God is with you wherever you go. ※ The joy of the LORD is your strength! ※ Paul . . . thanked God and took courage.

The night is almost gone; the day of salvation will soon be here. So don't live in darkness. Get rid of your evil deeds. Shed them like dirty clothes. Clothe yourselves with the armor of right living, as those who live in the light. We should be decent and true in everything we do, so that everyone can approve of our behavior. Don't participate in wild parties and getting drunk, or in adultery and immoral living, or in fighting and jealousy. But let the Lord Jesus Christ take control of you, and don't think of ways to indulge your evil desires.

Look at all the Lord will do for us and through us! Majestic works prompt majestic responses. Do you really appreciate the good things that God does for you and through you? If so, let your praise to him reflect how you really feel. *LAB note for Isaiah 42:10*

(ISAIAH 42:10) (PSALM 81:1-2) (PSALM 40:3) (JOSHUA 1:9) (NEHEMIAH 8:10) (ACTS 28:15) (ROMANS 13:12-14)

January 3

I will not fail you or abandon you.

All of the good promises that the LORD had given Israel came true.

God is not a man, that he should lie. He is not a human, that he should change his mind. Has he ever spoken and failed to act? Has he ever promised and not carried it through?

Understand, therefore, that the LORD your God is indeed God. He is the faithful God who keeps his covenant for a thousand generations and constantly loves those who love him and obey his commands. ※ He always remembers his covenant. ※ So don't worry about tomorrow, for tomorrow will bring its own worries. Today's trouble is enough for today.

Can a mother forget her nursing child? Can she feel no love for a child she has borne? But even if that were possible, I would not forget you! See, I have written your name on my hand.

The LORD your God has arrived to live among you. He is a mighty savior. He will rejoice over you with great gladness. With his love, he will calm all your fears. He will exult over you by singing a happy song.

The more we learn of the promises God has fulfilled and continues to fulfill, the easier it is to hope for those yet to come. Sometimes we become impatient, wanting God to act in a certain way now. Instead, we should faithfully do what we know he wants us to do and trust him for the future. *LAB note for Joshua 21:43-45*

(JOSHUA 1:5) (JOSHUA 21:45) (NUMBERS 23:19) (DEUTERONOMY 7:9) (PSALM 111:5) (MATTHEW 6:34) (ISAIAH 49:15-16) (ZEPHANIAH 3:17)

January 4

You will keep in perfect peace all who trust in you, whose thoughts are fixed on you!

Give your burdens to the LORD, and he will take care of you. He will not permit the godly to slip and fall. ⚘ I will trust in him and not be afraid. The LORD God is my strength and my song; he has become my salvation.

Why are you afraid? You have so little faith! ⚘ Don't worry about anything; instead, pray about everything. Tell God what you need, and thank him for all he has done. If you do this, you will experience God's peace, which is far more wonderful than the human mind can understand. His peace will guard your hearts and minds as you live in Christ Jesus. ⚘ In quietness and confidence is your strength.

Righteousness will bring peace. Quietness and confidence will fill the land forever. ⚘ I am leaving you with a gift—peace of mind and heart. And the peace I give isn't like the peace the world gives. So don't be troubled or afraid. ⚘ Grace and peace from the one who is, who always was, and who is still to come.

We can never avoid strife in the world around us, but when we fix our thoughts on God, we can know perfect peace even in turmoil. As we focus our mind on God and his Word, we become steady and stable. Supported by God's unchanging love and mighty power, we are not shaken by the surrounding chaos. *LAB note for Isaiah 26:3*

(ISAIAH 26:3) (PSALM 55:22) (ISAIAH 12:2) (MATTHEW 8:26) (PHILIPPIANS 4:6-7) (ISAIAH 30:15) (ISAIAH 32:17) (JOHN 14:27) (REVELATION 1:4)

January 5

Jesus asked the man, "What do you want me to do for you?" "Lord," he pleaded, "I want to see!"

Open my eyes to see the wonderful truths in your law.

Then he opened their minds to understand these many Scriptures. ✺ When the Father sends the Counselor as my representative—and by the Counselor I mean the Holy Spirit—he will teach you everything and will remind you of everything I myself have told you. ✺ Whatever is good and perfect comes to us from God above, who created all heaven's lights. Unlike them, he never changes or casts shifting shadows.

God, the glorious Father of our Lord Jesus Christ . . . give you spiritual wisdom and understanding, so that you might grow in your knowledge of God. I pray that your hearts will be flooded with light so that you can understand the wonderful future he has promised to those he called. I want you to realize what a rich and glorious inheritance he has given to his people. I pray that you will begin to understand the incredible greatness of his power for us who believe him. This is the same mighty power that raised Christ from the dead and seated him in the place of honor at God's right hand in the heavenly realms.

Most of us chafe under rules, for we think they restrict us from doing what we want. But God's laws were given to free us to be all he wants us to be. They help us follow his path and avoid paths that lead to destruction. *LAB note for Psalm 119:12-24*

(LUKE 18:41) (PSALM 119:18) (LUKE 24:45) (JOHN 14:26) (JAMES 1:17) (EPHESIANS 1:17-20)

January 6

Take control of what I say, O LORD, and keep my lips sealed.

LORD, if you kept a record of our sins, who, O Lord, could ever survive?

You are not defiled by what you eat; you are defiled by what you say and do.

Gossip separates the best of friends. ▨ Some people make cutting remarks, but the words of the wise bring healing. Truth stands the test of time; lies are soon exposed. ▨ No one can tame the tongue. It is an uncontrollable evil, full of deadly poison. Blessing and cursing come pouring out of the same mouth. Surely, my brothers and sisters, this is not right!

Now is the time to get rid of anger, rage, malicious behavior, slander, and dirty language. Don't lie to each other, for you have stripped off your old evil nature and all its wicked deeds. ▨ God wants you to be holy.

Gentle words bring life and health.

Even though we may not achieve perfect control of our tongues, the Holy Spirit will help us learn self-control, giving us increasing power to monitor and control what we say. Then when we are criticized, the Spirit will heal the hurt and help us not to lash out.   *LAB note for James 3:8*

(PSALM 141:3) (PSALM 130:3) (MATTHEW 15:11) (PROVERBS 16:28)
(PROVERBS 12:18-19) (JAMES 3:8, 10) (COLOSSIANS 3:8-9)
(1 THESSALONIANS 4:3) (PROVERBS 15:4)

January 7

You have raised a banner for those who honor you—a rallying point in the face of attack.

The LORD Is My Banner. ❦ They will respect and glorify the name of the LORD throughout the world. For he will come like a flood tide driven by the breath of the LORD.

May we shout for joy when we hear of your victory, flying banners to honor our God. May the LORD answer all your prayers. ❦ The LORD has vindicated us. Come, let us announce in Jerusalem everything the LORD our God has done. ❦ Overwhelming victory is ours through Christ, who loved us. ❦ How we thank God, who gives us victory over sin and death through Jesus Christ our Lord! ❦ Jesus . . . a perfect leader.

Be strong with the Lord's mighty power. ❦ Prove yourself to be a real warrior by fighting the LORD's battles. ❦ Take courage and work, for I am with you, says the LORD Almighty. . . . Do not be afraid. ❦ Look around you! Vast fields are ripening all around us and are ready now for the harvest.

In the Christian life we battle against rulers and authorities. To withstand their attacks, we must depend on God's strength and use every piece of his armor. As you do battle against the "mighty powers of darkness," ask for the Holy Spirit's help in the fight.

LAB note for Ephesians 6:10-17

(PSALM 60:4) (EXODUS 17:15) (ISAIAH 59:19) (PSALM 20:5) (JEREMIAH 51:10)
(ROMANS 8:37) (1 CORINTHIANS 15:57) (HEBREWS 2:10) (EPHESIANS 6:10)
(1 SAMUEL 18:17) (HAGGAI 2:4-5) (JOHN 4:35)

January 8

There is really only one thing worth being concerned about.

Many people say, "Who will show us better times?" Let the smile of your face shine on us, LORD. You have given me greater joy than those who have abundant harvests of grain and wine.

As the deer pants for streams of water, so I long for you, O God. I thirst for God, the living God. ▓ O God, you are my God; I earnestly search for you. My soul thirsts for you; my whole body longs for you in this parched and weary land where there is no water.

"I am the bread of life. No one who comes to me will ever be hungry again. Those who believe in me will never thirst." "Sir . . . give us that bread every day of our lives." ▓ Mary . . . sat at the Lord's feet, listening to what he taught. ▓ The one thing I ask of the LORD—the thing I seek most—is to live in the house of the LORD all the days of my life, delighting in the LORD's perfections and meditating in his Temple. ▓ Surely your goodness and unfailing love will pursue me all the days of my life, and I will live in the house of the LORD forever.

As the life of a deer depends upon water, so our lives depend upon God. Those who seek him and long to understand him find eternal life. When you feel separated from God, you shouldn't rest until you have restored your relationship with God. Your very life depends on it.

LAB note for Psalm 42:1-2

(LUKE 10:42) (PSALM 4:6-7) (PSALM 42:1-2) (PSALM 63:1) (JOHN 6:35, 34)
(LUKE 10:39) (PSALM 27:4) (PSALM 23:6)

January 9

Come quickly, my love! Move like a swift gazelle or a young deer on the mountains of spices. ❧ Even we Christians, although we have the Holy Spirit within us as a foretaste of future glory, also groan to be released from pain and suffering. We, too, wait anxiously for that day when God will give us our full rights as his children, including the new bodies he has promised us. ❧ Bend down the heavens, LORD, and come down. Touch the mountains so they billow smoke.

Jesus has been taken away from you into heaven. And someday . . . he will return. ❧ He will come again but not to deal with our sins again. This time he will bring salvation to all those who are eagerly waiting for him. ❧ In that day the people will proclaim, "This is our God. We trusted in him, and he saved us. This is the LORD, in whom we trusted. Let us rejoice in the salvation he brings!"

He who is the faithful witness to all these things says, "Yes, I am coming soon!" Amen! Come, Lord Jesus! ❧ We look forward to that wonderful event when the glory of our great God and Savior, Jesus Christ, will be revealed. ❧ We are citizens of heaven, where the Lord Jesus Christ lives.

> Because Christ died and rescued us from sin, we are free from sin's control. God gives us the power and understanding to live according to his will and do good. Then we will look forward to Christ's wonderful return with eager expectation and hope.   *LAB note for Titus 2:11-14*

(ISAIAH 64:1) (SONG OF SONGS 8:14) (ROMANS 8:23) (PSALM 144:5) (ACTS 1:11) (HEBREWS 9:28) (ISAIAH 25:9) (REVELATION 22:20) (TITUS 2:13) (PHILIPPIANS 3:20)

January 10

Don't sin by letting anger gain control over you.

"If another believer sins against you, go privately and point out the fault. If the other person listens and confesses it, you have won that person back." "Lord, how often should I forgive someone who sins against me? Seven times?" "No!" Jesus replied, "seventy times seven!"

When you are praying, first forgive anyone you are holding a grudge against, so that your Father in heaven will forgive your sins, too.

Since God chose you to be the holy people whom he loves, you must clothe yourselves with tenderhearted mercy, kindness, humility, gentleness, and patience. You must make allowance for each other's faults and forgive the person who offends you. Remember, the Lord forgave you, so you must forgive others. ⚘ Be kind to each other, tenderhearted, forgiving one another, just as God through Christ has forgiven you.

The key to forgiving others is remembering how much God has forgiven you. Is it difficult for you to forgive someone who has wronged you a little when God has forgiven you so much? Realizing God's infinite love and forgiveness can help you love and forgive others.

LAB note for Colossians 3:13

(EPHESIANS 4:26) (MATTHEW 18:15, 21-22) (MARK 11:25)
(COLOSSIANS 3:12-13) (EPHESIANS 4:32)

January 11

I lie in the dust, completely discouraged; revive me by your word.

Since you have been raised to new life with Christ, set your sights on the realities of heaven, where Christ sits at God's right hand in the place of honor and power. Let heaven fill your thoughts. Do not think only about things down here on earth. For you died when Christ died, and your real life is hidden with Christ in God. ▓ We are citizens of heaven, where the Lord Jesus Christ lives. And we are eagerly waiting for him to return as our Savior. He will take these weak mortal bodies of ours and change them into glorious bodies like his own, using the same mighty power that he will use to conquer everything, everywhere.

The old sinful nature loves to do evil, which is just opposite from what the Holy Spirit wants. ▓ Dear brothers and sisters, you have no obligation whatsoever to do what your sinful nature urges you to do. For if you keep on following it, you will perish. But if through the power of the Holy Spirit you turn from it and its evil deeds, you will live. ▓ You are foreigners and aliens here. So I warn you to keep away from evil desires because they fight against your very souls.

Setting your sights on heaven means striving to put heaven's priorities into daily practice. Letting heaven fill our thoughts means concentrating on the eternal rather than the temporal.

LAB note for Colossians 3:1-2

(Psalm 119:25) (Colossians 3:1-3) (Philippians 3:20-21) (Galatians 5:17) (Romans 8:12-13) (1 Peter 2:11)

January 12

Be honest in your estimate of yourselves, measuring your value by how much faith God has given you.

[He is] weak in faith. ✹ His faith grew stronger, and in this he brought glory to God.

"You don't have much faith," Jesus said. "Why did you doubt me?" ✹ Your faith is great. Your request is granted.

"Do you believe I can make you see?" "Yes, Lord," they told him, "we do." "Because of your faith, it will happen."

We need more faith. ✹ Continue to build your lives on the foundation of your holy faith. ✹ Let your roots grow down into him and draw up nourishment from him, so you will grow in faith, strong and vigorous in the truth you were taught. ✹ It is God who gives us, along with you, the ability to stand firm for Christ. ✹ After you have suffered a little while, he will restore, support, and strengthen you, and he will place you on a firm foundation.

We must be considerate of the doubts and fears of [others]. . . . We should please others. ✹ Don't condemn each other anymore. Decide instead to live in such a way that you will not put an obstacle in another Christian's path.

Although we start out with good intentions, sometimes our faith falters. But we can be afraid and still look to Christ. When you are apprehensive about the troubles around you and doubt Christ's presence or ability to help, remember that he is always with you and is the only one who can really help. *LAB note for Matthew 14:30-31*

(ROMANS 12:3) (ROMANS 14:1) (ROMANS 4:20) (MATTHEW 14:31)
(MATTHEW 15:28) (MATTHEW 9:28-29) (LUKE 17:5) (JUDE 20) (COLOSSIANS 2:7)
(2 CORINTHIANS 1:21) (1 PETER 5:10) (ROMANS 15:1) (ROMANS 14:13)

January 13

You have rescued me from death and have forgiven all my sins.

God showed how much he loved us by sending his only Son into the world so that we might have eternal life through him. This is real love. It is not that we loved God, but that he loved us and sent his Son as a sacrifice to take away our sins.

Where is another God like you, who pardons the sins of the survivors among his people? You cannot stay angry with your people forever, because you delight in showing mercy. Once again you will have compassion on us. You will trample our sins under your feet and throw them into the depths of the ocean! ▓ O LORD my God, I cried out to you for help, and you restored my health. You brought me up from the grave, O LORD. You kept me from falling into the pit of death. ▓ When I had lost all hope, I turned my thoughts once more to the LORD. And my earnest prayer went out to you in your holy Temple. ▓ I waited patiently for the LORD to help me, and he turned to me and heard my cry. He lifted me out of the pit of despair, out of the mud and the mire. He set my feet on solid ground and steadied me as I walked along.

God delights to show mercy! He does not forgive grudgingly but is glad when we repent, and he offers forgiveness to all who come back to him. Today you can confess your sins and receive his loving forgiveness.

LAB note for Micah 7:18

(ISAIAH 38:17) (1 JOHN 4:9-10) (MICAH 7:18-19) (PSALM 30:2-3)
(JONAH 2:7) (PSALM 40:1-2)

January 14

All that I know now is partial and incomplete.

Now we see things imperfectly as in a poor mirror, but then we will see everything with perfect clarity. . . . Then I will know everything completely, just as God knows me now.

We have even greater confidence in the message proclaimed by the prophets. Pay close attention to what they wrote, for their words are like a light shining in a dark place—until the day Christ appears and his brilliant light shines in your hearts. ▨ Your word is a lamp for my feet and a light for my path.

You, my dear friends, must remember what the apostles of our Lord Jesus Christ told you, that in the last times there would be scoffers. ▨ The Holy Spirit tells us clearly that in the last times some will turn away from what we believe; they will follow lying spirits and teachings that come from demons.

Dear children, the last hour is here. ▨ The night is almost gone; the day of salvation will soon be here. . . . Clothe yourselves with the armor of right living, as those who live in the light.

We have the hope that one day we will be complete when we see God face-to-face. This truth should strengthen our faith. We don't have all the answers now, but one day we will. Someday we will meet Christ in person and be able to see with God's perspective.

LAB note for 1 Corinthians 13:12

(1 CORINTHIANS 13:12) (1 CORINTHIANS 13:12) (2 PETER 1:19) (PSALM 119:105) (JUDE 1:17-18) (1 TIMOTHY 4:1) (1 JOHN 2:18) (ROMANS 13:12)

January 15

Serve each other in humility.

Whoever wants to be a leader among you must be your servant, and whoever wants to be first must become your slave. For even I, the Son of Man, came here not to be served but to serve others, and to give up my life as a ransom for many.

If you think you are too important to help someone in need, you are only fooling yourself. You are really a nobody. ❧ As God's messenger, I give each of you this warning: Be honest in your estimate of yourselves, measuring your value by how much faith God has given you. ❧ When you obey me, you should say, "We are not worthy of praise. We are servants who have simply done our duty."

When we are weighed down with troubles, it is for your benefit and salvation! For when God comforts us, it is so that we, in turn, can be an encouragement to you. Then you can patiently endure the same things we suffer. We are confident that as you share in suffering, you will also share God's comfort. ❧ This precious treasure—this light and power that now shine within us—is held in perishable containers, that is, in our weak bodies. So everyone can see that our glorious power is from God and is not our own.

A real leader has a servant's heart. Servant leaders appreciate others' worth and realize that they're not above any job. If you see something that needs to be done, don't wait to be asked. Take the initiative and do it like a faithful servant. *LAB note for Matthew 20:27*

(1 PETER 5:5) (MATTHEW 20:26-28) (GALATIANS 6:3) (ROMANS 12:3) (LUKE 17:10) (2 CORINTHIANS 1:6-7) (2 CORINTHIANS 4:7)

January 16

His special possession.

You belong to Christ, and Christ belongs to God. ❧ I am my lover's, the one he desires. ❧ I am his. ❧ The Son of God . . . loved me and gave himself for me.

You do not belong to yourself, for God bought you with a high price. So you must honor God with your body. ❧ Remember that the LORD rescued you . . . to become his own people and special possession; that is what you are today.

You are God's field, God's building. ❧ But Christ, the faithful Son, was in charge of the entire household. And we are God's household, if we keep up our courage and remain confident in our hope in Christ. ❧ God is building you, as living stones, into his spiritual temple.

"They will be my people," says the LORD Almighty. "On the day when I act, they will be my own special treasure." ❧ And all of them, since they are mine, belong to you; and you have given them back to me, so they are my glory!

What did Paul mean when he said that our body belongs to God? Many people say they have the right to do whatever they want with their own bodies. But when we become Christians, the Holy Spirit comes to live in us. Therefore we no longer own our bodies.

LAB note for 1 Corinthians 6:19-20

(DEUTERONOMY 32:9) (1 CORINTHIANS 3:23) (SONG OF SONGS 7:10)
(SONG OF SONGS 2:16) (GALATIANS 2:20) (1 CORINTHIANS 6:19-20)
(DEUTERONOMY 4:20) (1 CORINTHIANS 3:9) (HEBREWS 3:6) (1 PETER 2:5)
(MALACHI 3:17) (JOHN 17:10)

January 17

He will be like a blazing fire that refines metal or like a strong soap that whitens clothes. He will sit and judge like a refiner of silver, watching closely as the dross is burned away.

We can rejoice, too, when we run into problems and trials, for we know that they are good for us—they help us learn to endure. And endurance develops strength of character in us, and character strengthens our confident expectation of salvation. And this expectation will not disappoint us. For we know how dearly God loves us, because he has given us the Holy Spirit to fill our hearts with his love. ᚷ As you endure this divine discipline, remember that God is treating you as his own children. Whoever heard of a child who was never disciplined? If God doesn't discipline you as he does all of his children, it means that you are illegitimate and are not really his children after all. No discipline is enjoyable while it is happening—it is painful! But afterward there will be a quiet harvest of right living for those who are trained in this way. So take a new grip with your tired hands and stand firm on your shaky legs.

Christ is the vine, and God is the gardener who cares for the branches to make them fruitful. The branches are all those who claim to be followers of Christ. The fruitful branches are true believers who by their living union with Christ produce much fruit.   *LAB note for John 15:1ff.*

(JOHN 15:2) (MALACHI 3:2-3) (ROMANS 5:3-5) (HEBREWS 12:7-8, 11-12)

January 18

He is our God forever and ever, and he will be our guide until we die.

O LORD, I will honor and praise your name, for you are my God. You do such wonderful things! You planned them long ago, and now you have accomplished them. ※ LORD, you alone are my inheritance, my cup of blessing. You guard all that is mine.

He renews my strength. He guides me along right paths, bringing honor to his name. Even when I walk through the dark valley of death, I will not be afraid, for you are close beside me. ※ You are holding my right hand. You will keep on guiding me with your counsel, leading me to a glorious destiny. Whom have I in heaven but you? I desire you more than anything on earth. My health may fail, and my spirit may grow weak, but God remains the strength of my heart; he is mine forever. ※ In him our hearts rejoice, for we are trusting in his holy name. ※ The LORD will work out his plans for my life—for your faithful love, O LORD, endures forever. Don't abandon me, for you made me.

As we struggle with decisions, we need both a map that gives us directions and a constant companion who has an intimate knowledge of the way and will make sure we interpret the map correctly. The Bible is such a map, and the Holy Spirit is our constant companion and guide. As you make your way through life, use both.   *LAB note for Psalm 48:14*

(PSALM 48:14) (ISAIAH 25:1) (PSALM 16:5) (PSALM 23:3-4) (PSALM 73:23-26) (PSALM 33:21) (PSALM 138:8)

January 19

When doubts filled my mind, your comfort gave me renewed hope and cheer.

My heart is overwhelmed. Lead me to the towering rock of safety.

I am in trouble, Lord. Help me! ✶ Give your burdens to the LORD, and he will take care of you. He will not permit the godly to slip and fall.

I am like a little child who doesn't know his way around. ✶ If you want to know what God wants you to do—ask him, and he will gladly tell you.

Who is adequate for such a task? ✶ I am rotten through and through so far as my old sinful nature is concerned. ✶ My gracious favor is all you need. My power works best in your weakness.

"Take heart, son! Your sins are forgiven." "Daughter, be encouraged! Your faith has made you well."

You satisfy me more than the richest of foods. I will praise you with songs of joy. I lie awake thinking of you, meditating on you through the night. I think how much you have helped me; I sing for joy in the shadow of your protecting wings. I follow close behind you; your strong right hand holds me securely.

Who is adequate for the task of representing Christ? Our adequacy is always from God, who has already commissioned and sent us. As we realize that God has equipped us, we can overcome our feelings of inadequacy. Serving Christ, therefore, requires that we focus on what he can do through us, not on what we can't do by ourselves.

LAB note for 2 Corinthians 2:16-17

(Psalm 94:19) (Psalm 61:2) (Isaiah 38:14) (Psalm 55:22) (1 Kings 3:7) (James 1:5) (2 Corinthians 2:16) (Romans 7:18) (2 Corinthians 12:9) (Matthew 9:2, 22) (Psalm 63:5-8)

January 20

The fact that I am still being persecuted proves that I am still preaching salvation through the cross of Christ alone.

If any of you wants to be my follower, you must put aside your selfish ambition, shoulder your cross, and follow me.

Don't you realize that friendship with this world makes you an enemy of God? I say it again, that if your aim is to enjoy this world, you can't be a friend of God. ❈ They must enter into the Kingdom of God through many tribulations.

Anyone who believes in him will not be disappointed. ❈ He is very precious to you who believe.

God forbid that I should boast about anything except the cross of our Lord Jesus Christ. Because of that cross, my interest in this world died long ago, and the world's interest in me is also long dead. ❈ I have been crucified with Christ. ❈ Those who belong to Christ Jesus have nailed the passions and desires of their sinful nature to his cross and crucified them there.

If we endure hardship, we will reign with him. If we deny him, he will deny us.

God is faithful to his children, and although we may suffer great hardships here, God promises that someday we will live eternally with him. Are you facing hardships? Don't turn away from God—he promises you a wonderful future with him. *LAB note for 2 Timothy 2:11-13*

(GALATIANS 5:11) (MATTHEW 16:24) (JAMES 4:4) (ACTS 14:22) (ROMANS 9:33)
(1 PETER 2:7) (GALATIANS 6:14) (GALATIANS 2:19) (GALATIANS 5:24)
(2 TIMOTHY 2:12)

January 21

The Lord is coming soon.

The Lord himself will come down from heaven with a commanding shout, with the call of the archangel, and with the trumpet call of God. First, all the Christians who have died will rise from their graves. Then, together with them, we who are still alive and remain on the earth will be caught up in the clouds to meet the Lord in the air and remain with him forever. So comfort and encourage each other with these words. ❦ He who is the faithful witness to all these things says, "Yes, I am coming soon!" Amen! Come, Lord Jesus!

Dear friends, while you are waiting for these things to happen, make every effort to live a pure and blameless life. And be at peace with God. ❦Keep away from every kind of evil. Now may the God of peace make you holy in every way, and may your whole spirit and soul and body be kept blameless until that day when our Lord Jesus Christ comes again. God, who calls you, is faithful; he will do this.

Be patient. And take courage, for the coming of the Lord is near.

Because Jesus Christ came back to life, so will all believers. All Christians, including those living when Christ returns, will live with Christ forever. All believers throughout history will stand reunited in God's very presence, safe and secure. *LAB note for 1 Thessalonians 4:15–18*

(PHILIPPIANS 4:5) (1 THESSALONIANS 4:16–18) (REVELATION 22:20)
(2 PETER 3:14) (1 THESSALONIANS 5:22–24) (JAMES 5:8)

January 22

A choice vine.

My beloved has a vineyard on a rich and fertile hill. He plowed the land, cleared its stones, and planted it with choice vines. . . . Then he waited for a harvest of sweet grapes, but the grapes that grew were wild and sour. ▨ How could this happen? When I planted you, I chose a vine of the purest stock—the very best. How did you grow into this corrupt wild vine?

When you follow the desires of your sinful nature, your lives will produce these evil results: sexuality immorality, impure thoughts, eagerness for lustful pleasure, . . . envy, drunkenness, wild parties, and other kinds of sin. . . . But when the Holy Spirit controls our lives, he will produce this kind of fruit in us: love, joy, peace, patience, kindness, goodness, faithfulness, gentleness, and self-control.

I am the true vine, and my Father is the gardener. He cuts off every branch that doesn't produce fruit, and he prunes the branches that do bear fruit so they will produce even more. Remain in me, and I will remain in you. My true disciples produce much fruit. This brings great glory to my Father.

Jesus makes a distinction between cutting off and cutting back branches. Fruitful branches are cut back to promote growth (meaning God must sometimes discipline us to strengthen our character and faith). But branches that don't bear fruit are cut off at the trunk (meaning people who don't bear fruit for God or who try to block the efforts of God's followers will be cut off from his life-giving power). *LAB note for John 15:2-3*

(Genesis 49:11) (Isaiah 5:1-2) (Jeremiah 2:21) (Galatians 5:19, 21-23) (John 15:1-2, 4, 8)

January 23

We are made right in God's sight when we trust in Jesus Christ to take away our sins.

For God made Christ, who never sinned, to be the offering for our sin, so that we could be made right with God through Christ. ◙ Christ . . . took upon himself the curse for our wrongdoing. ◙ God alone made it possible for you to be in Christ Jesus. For our benefit God made Christ to be wisdom itself. He is the one who made us acceptable to God. He made us pure and holy, and he gave himself to purchase our freedom. ◙ He saved us, not because of the good things we did, but because of his mercy. He washed away our sins and gave us a new life through the Holy Spirit. He generously poured out the Spirit upon us because of what Jesus Christ our Savior did.

Everything else is worthless when compared with the priceless gain of knowing Christ Jesus my Lord. I have discarded everything else, counting it all as garbage, so that I may have Christ and become one with him. I no longer count on my own goodness or my ability to obey God's law, but I trust Christ to save me. For God's way of making us right with himself depends on faith.

There is a way to be declared not guilty—by trusting Jesus Christ to take away our sins. Trusting means putting our confidence in Christ to forgive our sins, to make us right with God, and to empower us to live the way he taught us. *LAB note for Romans 3:21-29*

(ROMANS 3:22) (2 CORINTHIANS 5:21) (GALATIANS 3:13) (1 CORINTHIANS 1:30)
(TITUS 3:5-6) (PHILIPPIANS 3:8-9)

January 24

Jesus . . . looked up to heaven and said, "Father . . . Holy Father . . . righteous Father." ⚬ Because you Gentiles have become his children, God has sent the Spirit of his Son into your hearts, and now you can call God your dear Father. ⚬ All of us, both Jews and Gentiles, may come to the Father through the same Holy Spirit because of what Christ has done for us. So now you Gentiles are no longer strangers and foreigners. You are citizens along with all of God's holy people. You are members of God's family.

I will go home to my father and say, "Father, I have sinned against both heaven and you, and I am no longer worthy of being called your son. Please take me on as a hired man." So he returned home to his father. And while he was still a long distance away, his father saw him coming. Filled with love and compassion, he ran to his son, embraced him, and kissed him.

Surely you are still our Father! . . . You are our Redeemer from ages past.

As adopted children of God, we share with Jesus all rights to God's resources. As God's heirs, we can claim what he has provided for us—our full identity as his children. *LAB note for Galatians 4:5-7*

(ROMANS 8:15) (JOHN 17:1, 11, 25) (GALATIANS 4:6) (EPHESIANS 2:18-19) (LUKE 15:18-20) (ISAIAH 63:16)

January 25

Let us go out to him outside the camp and bear the disgrace he bore. For this world is not our home; we are looking forward to our city in heaven, which is yet to come.

Dear friends, don't be surprised at the fiery trials you are going through, as if something strange were happening to you. Instead, be very glad—because these trials will make you partners with Christ in his suffering, and afterward you will have the wonderful joy of sharing his glory when it is displayed to all the world. ▩ We are confident that as you share in suffering, you will also share God's comfort.

Be happy if you are insulted for being a Christian, for then the glorious Spirit of God will come upon you.

The apostles left the high council rejoicing that God had counted them worthy to suffer dishonor for the name of Jesus. ▩ Moses . . . chose to share the oppression of God's people instead of enjoying the fleeting pleasures of sin. He thought it was better to suffer for the sake of the Messiah than to own the treasures of Egypt, for he was looking ahead to the great reward that God would give him.

It is easy to be deceived by the temporary benefits of wealth, popularity, status, and achievement, and to be blind to the long-range benefits of God's Kingdom. Faith helps us look beyond the world's value system to see the eternal values of God's Kingdom.

LAB note for Hebrews 11:24-28

(HEBREWS 13:13-14) (1 PETER 4:12-13) (2 CORINTHIANS 1:7) (1 PETER 4:14) (ACTS 5:41) (HEBREWS 11:24-26)

January 26

When you are arrested and stand trial, don't worry about what to say in your defense. Just say what God tells you to. Then it is not you who will be speaking, but the Holy Spirit. ✹ Don't worry about tomorrow, for tomorrow will bring its own worries. Today's trouble is enough for today.

The God of Israel gives power and strength to his people. Praise be to God! ✹ He gives power to those who are tired and worn out; he offers strength to the weak.

"My gracious favor is all you need. My power works best in your weakness." So now I am glad to boast about my weaknesses, so that the power of Christ may work through me. Since I know it is all for Christ's good, I am quite content with my weaknesses and with insults, hardships, persecutions, and calamities. For when I am weak, then I am strong. ✹ For I can do everything with the help of Christ who gives me the strength I need. ✹ March on, my soul, with courage!

The fact that God's power is displayed in our weaknesses should give us courage and hope. As we recognize our limitations, we will depend more on God for our effectiveness rather than on our own energy, effort, or talent. *LAB note for 2 Corinthians 12:9*

(DEUTERONOMY 33:25) (MARK 13:11) (MATTHEW 6:34) (PSALM 68:35) (ISAIAH 40:29) (2 CORINTHIANS 12:9-10) (PHILIPPIANS 4:13) (JUDGES 5:21)

January 27

Don't be discouraged when he corrects you.

No discipline is enjoyable while it is happening—it is painful! But afterward there will be a quiet harvest of right living for those who are trained in this way. ※ The Holy Spirit . . . will produce fruit in us.

The LORD is like a father to his children, tender and compassionate to those who fear him.

Though our bodies are dying, our spirits are being renewed every day. For our present troubles are quite small and won't last very long. Yet they produce for us an immeasurably great glory that will last forever! So we don't look at the troubles we can see right now; rather, we look forward to what we have not yet seen. For the troubles we see will soon be over, but the joys to come will last forever.

Even though Jesus was God's Son, he learned obedience from the things he suffered. ※ He faced all of the same temptations we do, yet he did not sin.

We may respond to discipline in several ways: (1) We can accept it with resignation; (2) we can accept it with self-pity, thinking we really don't deserve it; (3) we can be angry and resentful toward God; or (4) we can accept it gratefully, as the appropriate response we owe a loving Father.

LAB note for Hebrews 12:11

(PROVERBS 3:11) (HEBREWS 12:11) (GALATIANS 5:22) (PSALM 103:13) (2 CORINTHIANS 4:16-18) (HEBREWS 5:8) (HEBREWS 4:15)

January 28

The God who sees me.

O LORD, you have examined my heart and know everything about me. You know when I sit down or stand up. You know my every thought when far away. You chart the path ahead of me and tell me where to stop and rest. Every moment you know where I am. You know what I am going to say even before I say it, LORD. Such knowledge is too wonderful for me, too great for me to know! I can never escape from your spirit! I can never get away from your presence!

The LORD is watching everywhere, keeping his eye on both the evil and the good. 🕮 For the LORD sees clearly what a man does, examining every path he takes. 🕮 You like to look good in public, but God knows your evil hearts. What this world honors is an abomination in the sight of God. 🕮 The eyes of the LORD search the whole earth in order to strengthen those whose hearts are fully committed to him.

Jesus . . . knew what people were really like. No one needed to tell him about human nature. 🕮 Lord, you know everything. 🕮 You know I love you.

God already knows everything about us, and still he accepts and loves us. He is with us through every situation, in every trial—protecting, loving, guiding. He knows and loves us completely. *LAB note for Psalm 139:1–5*

(GENESIS 16:13) (PSALM 139:1–4, 6–7) (PROVERBS 15:3) (PROVERBS 5:21)
(LUKE 16:15) (2 CHRONICLES 16:9) (JOHN 2:24–25) (JOHN 21:17) (JOHN 21:16)

January 29

When the Holy Spirit controls our lives, he will produce . . .
self-control.

All athletes practice strict self-control. They do it to win a prize
that will fade away, but we do it for an eternal prize. So I run
straight to the goal with purpose in every step. I am not like a boxer
who misses his punches. I discipline my body like an athlete,
training it to do what it should. Otherwise, I fear that after
preaching to others I myself might be disqualified.

Don't be drunk with wine, because that will ruin your life.
Instead, let the Holy Spirit fill and control you.

If any of you wants to be my follower, you must put aside your
selfish ambition, shoulder your cross, and follow me.

Be on your guard, not asleep like the others. Stay alert and be
sober. Night is the time for sleep and the time when people get
drunk. But let us who live in the light think clearly. We are
instructed to turn from godless living and sinful pleasures. We
should live in this evil world with self-control, right conduct, and
devotion to God.

At times we must even give up something good in order to do
what God wants. Without a goal, discipline is nothing but
self-punishment. With the goal of pleasing God, our denial seems like
nothing compared to the eternal imperishable reward that will be ours.

LAB note for 1 Corinthians 9:25

(GALATIANS 5:22-23) (1 CORINTHIANS 9:25-27) (EPHESIANS 5:18)
(MATTHEW 16:24) (1 THESSALONIANS 5:6-8) (TITUS 2:12)

January 30

Let us run with endurance the race that God has set before us. We do this by keeping our eyes on Jesus, on whom our faith depends from start to finish.

If any of you wants to be my follower, you must put aside your selfish ambition, shoulder your cross daily, and follow me. ❈ No one can become my disciple without giving up everything for me. ❈ Don't live in darkness. Get rid of your evil deeds.

All athletes practice strict self-control. They do it to win a prize that will fade away, but we do it for an eternal prize. I discipline my body like an athlete, training it to do what it should. ❈ I am still not all I should be, but I am focusing all my energies on this one thing: Forgetting the past and looking forward to what lies ahead, I strain to reach the end of the race and receive the prize for which God, through Christ Jesus, is calling us up to heaven. ❈ Oh, that we might know the LORD! Let us press on to know him! Then he will respond to us as surely as the arrival of dawn or the coming of rains in early spring.

The Christian life involves hard work. It requires us to give up whatever endangers our relationship with God, to run patiently, and to struggle against sin with the power of the Holy Spirit. To live effectively, we must keep our eyes on Jesus. *LAB note for Hebrews 12:1-4*

(HEBREWS 12:1-2) (LUKE 9:23) (LUKE 14:33) (ROMANS 13:12)
(1 CORINTHIANS 9:25, 27) (PHILIPPIANS 3:13-14) (HOSEA 6:3)

January 31

It is good for the young to submit to the yoke of his discipline.

Teach your children to choose the right path, and when they are older, they will remain upon it.

Since we respect our earthly fathers who disciplined us, should we not all the more cheerfully submit to the discipline of our heavenly Father and live forever? For our earthly fathers disciplined us for a few years, doing the best they knew how. But God's discipline is always right and good for us because it means we will share in his holiness.

LORD, in distress we searched for you. We were bowed beneath the burden of your discipline. ◎ I used to wander off until you disciplined me; but now I closely follow your word. The suffering you sent was good for me, for it taught me to pay attention to your principles.

"I know the plans I have for you," says the LORD. "They are plans for good and not for disaster, to give you a future and a hope." ◎ Humble yourselves under the mighty power of God, and in his good time he will honor you.

When parents teach a child how to make decisions, they don't have to watch every step he or she takes. They know their children will remain on the right path because they have made the choice themselves.

LAB note for Proverbs 22:6

(LAMENTATIONS 3:27) (PROVERBS 22:6) (HEBREWS 12:9-10) (ISAIAH 26:16) (PSALM 119:67, 71) (JEREMIAH 29:11) (1 PETER 5:6)

February

Above All . . . Love

Love speaks honestly and pardons graciously.
Love rejoices in victories and comforts in sorrows.
Love overcomes circumstances.

God is the giver of true love. He created it, and he
rejoices in seeing us learn it from him. May you
experience more of God's perfect love this year so
that your peace and joy will inspire others.

February 1

How kind and gracious the Lord was! He filled me completely
with faith and the love of Christ Jesus.

You know how full of love and kindness our Lord Jesus Christ
was. Though he was very rich, yet for your sakes he became poor, so
that by his poverty he could make you rich. ▓ As people sinned
more and more, God's wonderful kindness became more
abundant.

God saved you by his special favor when you believed. And you
can't take credit for this; it is a gift from God. Salvation is not a
reward for the good things we have done, so none of us can boast
about it. ▓ We have believed in Christ Jesus, that we might be
accepted by God because of our faith in Christ—and not because we
have obeyed the law. For no one will ever be saved by obeying the
law. ▓ He saved us, not because of the good things we did, but
because of his mercy. He washed away our sins and gave us a new life
through the Holy Spirit. He generously poured out the Spirit upon
us because of what Jesus Christ our Savior did.

Jesus did not give up his eternal power when he became human,
but he did set aside his glory and his rights. He became "poor" when he
became human because he set aside so much. Yet by doing so, he made us
"rich" because we received salvation and eternal life.

LAB note for 2 Corinthians 8:9

(1 Timothy 1:14) (2 Corinthians 8:9) (Romans 5:20) (Ephesians 2:8-9)
(Galatians 2:16) (Titus 3:5-6)

February 2

If someone sins against another person, God can mediate for the guilty party. But if someone sins against the LORD, who can intercede?

If you do sin, there is someone to plead for you before the Father. He is Jesus Christ, the one who pleases God completely. He is the sacrifice for our sins. He takes away not only our sins but the sins of all the world. ✎ For God sent Jesus to take the punishment for our sins and to satisfy God's anger against us. We are made right with God when we believe that Jesus shed his blood, sacrificing his life for us. God was being entirely fair and just when he did not punish those who sinned in former times. And he is entirely fair and just in this present time when he declares sinners to be right in his sight because they believe in Jesus.

What can we say about such wonderful things as these? If God is for us, who can ever be against us? Who dares accuse us whom God has chosen for his own? Will God? No! He is the one who has given us right standing with himself. Who then will condemn us? Will Christ Jesus? No, for he is the one who died for us and was raised to life for us and is sitting at the place of highest honor next to God, pleading for us.

When you feel guilty and condemned, don't give up hope—the best defense attorney in the universe is pleading your case. Jesus Christ, your defender, has already suffered your penalty in your place. You can't be tried for a case that is no longer on the docket.   *LAB note for 1 John 2:1-2*

(1 SAMUEL 2:25) (1 JOHN 2:1-2) (ROMANS 3:25-26) (ROMANS 8:31, 33-34)

February 3

The stars differ from each other in their beauty and brightness.

They had been arguing about which one of them was the greatest. He sat down and called the twelve disciples over to him. Then he said, "Anyone who wants to be the first must take last place and be the servant of everyone else." ▧ Serve each other in humility, for "God sets himself against the proud, but he shows favor to the humble." So humble yourselves under the mighty power of God, and in his good time he will honor you.

Your attitude should be the same that Christ Jesus had. Though he was God . . . he took the humble position of a slave and appeared in human form. Because of this, God raised him up to the heights of heaven and gave him a name that is above every other name, so that at the name of Jesus every knee will bow, in heaven and on earth and under the earth, and every tongue will confess that Jesus Christ is Lord, to the glory of God the Father.

Those who are wise will shine as bright as the sky, and those who turn many to righteousness will shine like stars forever.

If we say we follow Christ, we must also say we want to live as he lived. We should develop his attitude of humility as we serve, even when we are not likely to get recognition for our efforts. Are you selfishly clinging to your rights, or are you willing to serve?   *LAB note for Philippians 2:5-11*

(1 Corinthians 15:41) (Mark 9:34-35) (1 Peter 5:5-6) (Philippians 2:5-7, 9-10) (Daniel 12:3)

February 4

Take courage and work, for I am with you, says the LORD Almighty.

I am the vine; you are the branches. Those who remain in me, and I in them, will produce much fruit. For apart from me you can do nothing. ※ I can do everything with the help of Christ who gives me the strength I need. ※ Be strong with the Lord's mighty power. ※ The joy of the LORD is your strength!

This is what the LORD Almighty says: "Take heart and finish the task! You have heard what the prophets have been saying." ※ Strengthen those who have tired hands, and encourage those who have weak knees. Say to those who are afraid, "Be strong, and do not fear, for your God is coming to destroy your enemies. He is coming to save you." ※ The LORD . . . said, "Go with the strength you have."

If God is for us, who can ever be against us? ※ And so, since God in his mercy has given us this wonderful ministry [of telling his Good News to others], we never give up.

So don't get tired of doing what is good. Don't get discouraged and give up, for we will reap a harvest of blessing at the appropriate time. ※ How we thank God, who gives us victory over sin and death through Jesus Christ our Lord!

It is discouraging to continue to do right and receive no word of thanks or see any tangible results. But we must keep on doing good and trust God for the results. In due time we will reap a harvest of blessing.

LAB note for Galatians 6:9-10

(HAGGAI 2:4) (JOHN 15:5) (PHILIPPIANS 4:13) (EPHESIANS 6:10) (NEHEMIAH 8:10) (ZECHARIAH 8:9) (ISAIAH 35:3-4) (JUDGES 6:14) (ROMANS 8:31) (2 CORINTHIANS 4:1) (GALATIANS 6:9) (1 CORINTHIANS 15:57)

February 5

Even in darkness I cannot hide from you.

God carefully watches the way people live; he sees everything they do. No darkness is thick enough to hide the wicked from his eyes. ▨ Can anyone hide from me? Am I not everywhere in all the heavens and the earth?

Do not be afraid of the terrors of the night, nor fear the dangers of the day, nor dread the plague that stalks in darkness, nor the disaster that strikes at midday. If you make the LORD your refuge, if you make the Most High your shelter, no evil will conquer you; no plague will come near your dwelling. ▨ He will not let you stumble and fall; the one who watches over you will not sleep.

The LORD himself watches over you! The LORD stands beside you as your protective shade. The sun will not hurt you by day, nor the moon at night. The LORD keeps you from all evil and preserves your life.

Even though I walk through the dark valley of death, I will not be afraid, for you are close beside me. Your rod and your staff protect and comfort me.

We should never trust a lesser power than God himself. Not only is he all-powerful, he also watches over us. Nothing diverts or deters him. We are safe. We never outgrow our need for God's untiring watch over our life. *LAB note for Psalm 121:1ff.*

(PSALM 139:12) (JOB 34:21–22) (JEREMIAH 23:24) (PSALM 91:5–6, 9–10) (PSALM 121:3) (PSALM 121:5–7) (PSALM 23:4)

February 6

Never return.

If they had meant the country they came from, they would have found a way to go back. But they were looking for a better place, a heavenly homeland. Moses . . . chose to share the oppression of God's people instead of enjoying the fleeting pleasures of sin. He thought it was better to suffer for the sake of the Messiah than to own the treasures of Egypt. ☸ A righteous person will live by faith. But I will have no pleasure in anyone who turns away. ☸ Anyone who puts a hand to the plow and then looks back is not fit for the Kingdom of God.

God forbid that I should boast about anything except the cross of our Lord Jesus Christ. Because of that cross, my interest in this world died long ago, and the world's interest in me is also long dead. ☸ Therefore come out from them and separate yourselves from them, says the Lord. Don't touch their filthy things, and I will welcome you.

I am sure that God, who began the good work within you, will continue his work until it is finally finished on that day when Christ Jesus comes back again.

What does Jesus want from us? Total dedication, not halfhearted commitment. We can't pick and choose among Jesus' ideas and follow him selectively; we have to accept the cross along with the crown, judgment as well as mercy.   *LAB note for Luke 9:62*

(DEUTERONOMY 17:16) (HEBREWS 11:15-16, 24-26) (HEBREWS 10:38)
(LUKE 9:62) (GALATIANS 6:14) (2 CORINTHIANS 6:17) (PHLIPPIANS 1:6)

February 7

My purpose is to give life in all its fullness.

The wages of sin is death, but the free gift of God is eternal life through Christ Jesus our Lord. ▒ The sin of this one man, Adam, caused death to rule over us, but all who receive God's wonderful, gracious gift of righteousness will live in triumph over sin and death through this one man, Jesus Christ. ▒ Just as death came into the world through a man, Adam, now the resurrection from the dead has begun through another man, Christ. Everyone dies because all of us are related to Adam, the first man. But all who are related to Christ, the other man, will be given new life. ▒ Christ Jesus, our Savior . . . broke the power of death and showed us the way to everlasting life through the Good News.

And this is what God has testified: He has given us eternal life, and this life is in his Son. So whoever has God's Son has life; whoever does not have his Son does not have life. ▒ God did not send his Son into the world to condemn it, but to save it.

The life Jesus gives right now is abundantly rich and full. It is eternal, yet it begins immediately. Life in Christ is lived on a higher plane because of his overflowing forgiveness, love, and guidance. Have you taken Christ's offer of life? *LAB note for John 10:10*

(JOHN 10:10) (ROMANS 6:23) (ROMANS 5:17) (1 CORINTHIANS 15:21-22)
(2 TIMOTHY 1:10) (1 JOHN 5:11-12) (JOHN 3:17)

February 8

If you fail to drive out the people who live in the land, those who remain will be like splinters in your eyes and thorns in your sides.

Fight the good fight for what we believe. ▩ We use God's mighty weapons, not mere worldly weapons, to knock down the Devil's strongholds. With these weapons we break down every proud argument that keeps people from knowing God. With these weapons we conquer their rebellious ideas, and we teach them to obey Christ.

Dear brothers and sisters, you have no obligation whatsoever to do what your sinful nature urges you to do. For if you keep on following it, you will perish. But if through the power of the Holy Spirit you turn from it and its evil deeds, you will live.

The old sinful nature loves to do evil, which is just opposite from what the Holy Spirit wants. And the Spirit gives us desires that are opposite from what the sinful nature desires. These two forces are constantly fighting each other, and your choices are never free from this conflict. ▩ But there is another law at work within me that is at war with my mind. ▩ Despite all these things, overwhelming victory is ours through Christ, who loved us.

Some think Christianity is a passive religion that advocates waiting for God to act. On the contrary, we must have an active faith, obeying God with courage and doing what we know is right. Is it time for action on your part? Don't wait—get going! *LAB note for 1 Timothy 6:11-12*

(NUMBERS 33:55) (1 TIMOTHY 6:12) (2 CORINTHIANS 10:4-5) (ROMANS 8:12-13)
(GALATIANS 5:17) (ROMANS 7:23) (ROMANS 8:37)

February 9

When you have eaten your fill, praise the LORD your God for the good land he has given you.

Beware that in your plenty you do not forget the LORD your God. ▨ One of them, when he saw that he was healed, came back to Jesus, shouting, "Praise God, I'm healed!" He fell face down on the ground at Jesus' feet, thanking him for what he had done. This man was a Samaritan. Jesus asked, "Didn't I heal ten men? Where are the other nine? Does only this foreigner return to give glory to God?"

Since everything God created is good, we should not reject any of it. We may receive it gladly, with thankful hearts. For it is made holy by the word of God and prayer. ▨ The blessing of the LORD makes a person rich, and he adds no sorrow with it.

Praise the LORD, I tell myself; with my whole heart, I will praise his holy name. Praise the LORD, I tell myself, and never forget the good things he does for me. He forgives all my sins and heals all my diseases. He ransoms me from death and surrounds me with love and tender mercies. He fills my life with good things. My youth is renewed like the eagle's!

It is easy to get so busy collecting and managing wealth that we push God right out of our lives. But it is God who gives us everything we have, and it is God who asks us to manage it for him.

LAB note for Deuteronomy 8:11-20

(DEUTERONOMY 8:10) (DEUTERONOMY 8:11) (LUKE 17:15-18)
(1 TIMOTHY 4:4-5) (PROVERBS 10:22) (PSALM 103:1-5)

February 10

He had compassion on them.

Jesus Christ is the same yesterday, today, and forever. ❧ We have a High Priest who has gone to heaven, Jesus the Son of God. Let us cling to him and never stop trusting him. This High Priest of ours understands our weaknesses, for he faced all of the same temptations we do, yet he did not sin. ❧ Because he is human, he is able to deal gently with the people, though they are ignorant and wayward. For he is subject to the same weaknesses they have. ❧ Then he returned and found the disciples asleep. "Simon!" he said to Peter. "Are you asleep? Couldn't you stay awake and watch with me even one hour? Keep alert and pray. Overwise temptation will overpower you. For though the spirit is willing enough, the body is weak."

The LORD is like a father to his children, tender and compassionate to those who fear him. For he understands how weak we are; he knows we are only dust.

You, O Lord, are a merciful and gracious God, slow to get angry, full of unfailing love and truth. Look down and have mercy on me. Give strength to your servant; yes, save me, for I am your servant.

Jesus is like us because he experienced a full range of temptations throughout his life as a human being. We can be comforted, knowing that Jesus faced temptation—he can sympathize with us. We can be encouraged, knowing that Jesus faced temptation without giving in to sin.

LAB note for Hebrews 4:15

(MATTHEW 14:14) (HEBREWS 13:8) (HEBREWS 4:14-15) (HEBREWS 5:2)
(MARK 14:37-38) (PSALM 103:13-14) (PSALM 86:15-16)

February 11

Your eye is a lamp for your body. A pure eye lets sunshine into your soul.

People who aren't Christians can't understand these truths from God's Spirit. It all sounds foolish to them because only those who have the Spirit understand what the Spirit means. ▓ Open my eyes to see the wonderful truths in your law.

I am the light of the world. If you follow me, you won't be stumbling through the darkness, because you will have the light that leads to life. ▓ All of us have had that veil removed so that we can be mirrors that brightly reflect the glory of the Lord. And as the Spirit of the Lord works within us, we become more and more like him and reflect his glory even more. ▓ For God, who said, "Let there be light in the darkness," has made us understand that this light is the brightness of the glory of God that is seen in the face of Jesus Christ.

God, the glorious Father of our Lord Jesus Christ, . . . give you spiritual wisdom and understanding, so that you might grow in your knowledge of God . . . [and] understand the wonderful future he has promised to those he called.

Jesus Christ is the Creator of life, and his life brings light to humankind. In his light we see ourselves as we really are (sinners in need of a Savior). When we follow Jesus, he lights the path ahead of us so we can see how to live. He removes the darkness of sin from our lives.

LAB note for John 1:4-5

(LUKE 11:34) (1 CORINTHIANS 2:14) (PSALM 119:18) (JOHN 8:12)
(2 CORINTHIANS 3:18) (2 CORINTHIANS 4:6) (EPHESIANS 1:17-18)

February 12

Who can say, "I have cleansed my heart; I am pure and free from sin"?

The LORD looks down from heaven on the entire human race; he looks to see if there is even one with real understanding, one who seeks for God. But no, all have turned away from God; all have become corrupt. ※ Those who are still under the control of their sinful nature can never please God.

I know I am rotten through and through so far as my old sinful nature is concerned. No matter which way I turn, I can't make myself do right. I want to, but I can't. ※ We are all infected and impure with sin. When we proudly display our righteous deeds, we find they are but filthy rags.

If the law could have given us new life, we could have been made right with God by obeying. But the Scriptures have declared that we are all prisoners of sin, so the only way to receive God's promise is to believe in Jesus Christ. ※ For God was in Christ, reconciling the world to himself, no longer counting people's sins against them.

If we say we have no sin, we are only fooling ourselves and refusing to accept the truth. But if we confess our sins to him, he is faithful and just to forgive us and to cleanse us from every wrong.

No one is without sin. We all need ongoing cleansing, moment by moment. Thank God he provides forgiveness by his mercy when we ask for it. Make confession and repentance a regular part of your talks with God. Rely on him moment by moment for the cleansing you need.

LAB note for Proverbs 20:9

(PROVERBS 20:9) (PSALM 14:2-3) (ROMANS 8:8) (ROMANS 7:18) (ISAIAH 64:6) (GALATIANS 3:22) (2 CORINTHIANS 5:19) (1 JOHN 1:8-9)

February 13

Whom have I in heaven but you? I desire you more than anything on earth. My health may fail, and my spirit may grow weak, but God remains the strength of my heart; he is mine forever. ❧ LORD, you alone are my inheritance, my cup of blessing. You guard all that is mine. The land you have given me is a pleasant land. What a wonderful inheritance!

I say to myself, "The LORD is my inheritance; therefore, I will hope in him!"

Your decrees are my treasure; they are truly my heart's delight.

O God, you are my God; I earnestly search for you. My soul thirsts for you; my whole body longs for you in this parched and weary land where there is no water. You satisfy me more than the richest of foods. I will praise you with songs of joy. I lie awake thinking of you, meditating on you through the night. I think how much you have helped me; I sing for joy in the shadow of your protecting wings.

My lover is mine, and I am his.

If you are lonely or thirsty for something lasting in your life, remember David's prayer: "O God . . . my soul thirsts for you . . . in this parched and weary land." God alone can satisfy our deepest longings!

LAB note for Psalm 63:1-5

(NUMBERS 18:20) (PSALM 73:25-26) (PSALM 16:5-6) (LAMENTATIONS 3:24) (PSALM 119:111) (PSALM 63:1, 5-7) (SONG OF SONGS 2:16)

February 14

Those who feared the LORD spoke with each other, and the LORD listened to what they said. In his presence, a scroll of remembrance was written to record the names of those who feared him and loved to think about him.

Suddenly, Jesus himself came along and joined them and began walking beside them. ❧ For where two or three gather together because they are mine, I am there among them.

Let the words of Christ, in all their richness, live in your hearts and make you wise. Use his words to teach and counsel each other. Sing psalms and hymns and spiritual songs to God with thankful hearts. ❧ You must warn each other every day, as long as it is called "today," so that none of you will be deceived by sin and hardened against God. ❧ Talk about [God's Word] when you are at home and when you are away on a journey, when you are lying down and when you are getting up again.

I tell you this, that you must give an account on judgment day of every idle word you speak. The words you say now reflect your fate then; either you will be justified by them or you will be condemned.

I will tell about your righteous deeds all day long.

What kinds of words come from your mouth? That is an indication of what is in your heart. You can't solve your heart problem, however, just by cleaning up your speech. You must allow the Holy Spirit to fill you with new attitudes and motives.   *LAB note for Matthew 12:34-36*

(MALACHI 3:16) (LUKE 24:15) (MATTHEW 18:20) (COLOSSIANS 3:16)
(HEBREWS 3:13) (DEUTERONOMY 6:7) (MATTHEW 12:36-37) (PSALM 71:24)

February 15

The mighty oceans have roared, O LORD.

Mightier than the violent raging of the seas, mightier than the breakers on the shore—the LORD above is mightier than these! O LORD God Almighty! Where is there anyone as mighty as you, LORD? Faithfulness is your very character. You are the one who rules the oceans. When their waves rise in fearful storms, you subdue them.

Do you have no respect for me? Why do you not tremble in my presence? I, the LORD, am the one who defines the ocean's sandy shoreline, an everlasting boundary that the waters cannot cross. The waves may toss and roar, but they can never pass the bounds I set.

When you go through deep waters and great trouble, I will be with you. When you go through rivers of difficulty, you will not drown!

Peter went over the side of the boat and walked on the water toward Jesus. But when he looked around at the high waves, he was terrified and began to sink. "Save me, Lord!" he shouted. Instantly Jesus reached out his hand and grabbed him. "You don't have much faith," Jesus said. "Why did you doubt me?"

When I am afraid, I put my trust in you.

What is your attitude when you come into God's presence? We should come with respect and trembling because God sets the boundaries of the roaring seas and sends the rain, assuring us of plentiful harvests.

LAB note for Jeremiah 5:22-24

(PSALM 93:3) (PSALM 93:4) (PSALM 89:8-9) (JEREMIAH 5:22) (ISAIAH 43:2)
(MATTHEW 14:29-31) (PSALM 56:3)

February 16

How fragrant your cologne, and how pleasing your name!

Christ . . . loved you and gave himself as a sacrifice to take away your sins. And God was pleased, because that sacrifice was like sweet perfume to him. ❧ He is very precious to you who believe. ❧ God raised him up to the heights of heaven and gave him a name that is above every other name, so that at the name of Jesus every knee will bow, in heaven and on earth and under the earth. ❧ For in Christ the fullness of God lives in a human body.

If you love me, obey my commandments. ❧ We know how dearly God loves us, because he has given us the Holy Spirit to fill our hearts with his love. ❧ Our lives are a fragrance presented by Christ to God. But this fragrance is perceived differently by those being saved and by those perishing.

O LORD, our Lord, the majesty of your name fills the earth! Your glory is higher than the heavens. ❧ Immanuel . . . God is with us. ❧ These will be his royal titles: Wonderful Counselor, Mighty God, Everlasting Father, Prince of Peace. ❧ The LORD is a strong fortress; the godly run to him and are safe.

Just as children imitate their parents, we should follow God's example. His great love for us led him to sacrifice himself so that we might live. Our love for others should be of the same kind—a love that goes beyond affection to self-sacrificing service.   *LAB note for Ephesians 5:1-2*

(SONG OF SONGS 1:3) (EPHESIANS 5:2) (1 PETER 2:7) (PHILIPPIANS 2:9-10) (COLOSSIANS 2:9) (JOHN 14:15) (ROMANS 5:5) (2 CORINTHIANS 2:15) (PSALM 8:1) (MATTHEW 1:23) (ISAIAH 9:6) (PROVERBS 18:10)

February 17

LORD, do not desert me now! You alone are my hope.

Many people say, "Who will show us better times?" Let the smile of your face shine on us, LORD. ❦ I will sing about your power. I will shout with joy each morning because of your unfailing love. For you have been my refuge, a place of safety in the day of distress.

When I was prosperous I said, "Nothing can stop me now!" Your favor, O LORD, made me as secure as a mountain. Then you turned away from me, and I was shattered. I cried out to you, O LORD. I begged the Lord for mercy, saying, "What will you gain if I die, if I sink down into the grave? Can my dust praise you from the grave? Can it tell the world of your faithfulness? Hear me, LORD, and have mercy on me. Help me, O LORD."

"For a brief moment I abandoned you, but with great compassion I will take you back. In a moment of anger I turned my face away for a little while. But with everlasting love I will have compassion on you," says the LORD, your Redeemer. ❦ Your grief will suddenly turn to wonderful joy. ❦ Weeping may go on all night, but joy comes with the morning.

The God we serve is holy, and he cannot tolerate sin. But if we confess our sin and repent, then God will forgive us. Have you ever been separated from a loved one and then experienced joy when that person returned? That is like the joy God experiences when you repent and return to him. *LAB note for Isaiah 54:6-8*

(JEREMIAH 17:17) (PSALM 4:6) (PSALM 59:16) (PSALM 30:6-10) (ISAIAH 54:7-8) (JOHN 16:20) (PSALM 30:5)

February 18

God's law was given so that all people could see how sinful they were.

Who can create purity in one born impure? ▨ For I was born a sinner—yes, from the moment my mother conceived me.

Once you were dead, doomed forever because of your many sins. We were born with an evil nature, and we were under God's anger just like everyone else. ▨ I don't understand myself at all, for I really want to do what is right, but I don't do it. Instead, I do the very thing I hate. I know I am rotten through and through so far as my old sinful nature is concerned. No matter which way I turn, I can't make myself do right.

When Adam sinned, sin entered the entire human race. Adam's sin brought death, so death spread to everyone, for everyone sinned. What a contrast between Adam and Christ, who was yet to come! This other man, Jesus Christ, brought forgiveness to many through God's bountiful gift. Because one person disobeyed God, many people became sinners. But because one other person obeyed God, many people will be made right in God's sight.

For the power of the life-giving Spirit has freed you through Christ Jesus from the power of sin that leads to death.

How we thank God, who gives us victory over sin and death through Jesus Christ our Lord!

As a sinner separated from God, you see his law from below, as a ladder to be climbed to get to God. What relief it is to see Jesus' open arms offering to lift you above the ladder of the law and take you directly to God! *LAB note for Romans 5:20*

(ROMANS 5:20) (JOB 14:4) (PSALM 51:5) (EPHESIANS 2:1, 3) (ROMANS 7:15, 18) (ROMANS 5:12, 14-15, 19) (ROMANS 8:2) (1 CORINTHIANS 15:57)

February 19

The LORD grants wisdom! From his mouth come knowledge and understanding.

Trust in the LORD with all your heart; do not depend on your own understanding. ❧ If you need wisdom—if you want to know what God wants you to do—ask him, and he will gladly tell you. He will not resent your asking. ❧ God is far wiser than the wisest of human plans, and God's weakness is far stronger than the greatest of human strength. God chose things despised by the world, things counted as nothing at all, and used them to bring to nothing what the world considers important, so that no one can ever boast in the presence of God.

As your words are taught, they give light; even the simple can understand them. ❧ I have hidden your word in my heart, that I might not sin against you.

All who were there spoke well of him and were amazed by the gracious words that fell from his lips. ❧ We have never heard anyone talk like this! ❧ God alone made it possible for you to be in Christ Jesus.

Wisdom comes in two ways: It is a God-given gift and also the result of an energetic search. Wisdom's starting point is God and his revealed Word, the source of "knowledge and understanding."

LAB note for Proverbs 2:3-6

(PROVERBS 2:6) (PROVERBS 3:5) (JAMES 1:5) (1 CORINTHIANS 1:25, 28-29)
(PSALM 119:130) (PSALM 119:11) (LUKE 4:22) (JOHN 7:46) (1 CORINTHIANS 1:30)

February 20

Don't harden your hearts against him as Israel did when they rebelled, when they tested God's patience in the wilderness.

In the wilderness, their desires ran wild, testing God's patience in that dry land.

Jesus, full of the Holy Spirit, left the Jordan River. He was led by the Spirit to go out into the wilderness, where the Devil tempted him for forty days. He ate nothing all that time and was very hungry. Then the Devil said to him, "If you are the Son of God, change this stone into a loaf of bread." But Jesus told him, "No! The Scriptures say, 'People need more than bread for their life.'"

No one who wants to do wrong should ever say, "God is tempting me." God is never tempted to do wrong, and he never tempts anyone else either. Temptation comes from the lure of our own evil desires. These evil desires lead to evil actions, and evil actions lead to death.

Since he himself has gone through suffering and temptation, he is able to help us when we are being tempted. Simon, Simon, Satan has asked to have all of you, to sift you like wheat. But I have pleaded in prayer for you, Simon, that your faith should not fail.

In many places the Bible warns us not to "harden" our hearts. This means stubbornly setting ourselves against God so that we are no longer able to turn to him for forgiveness. Be careful to obey God's Word, and do not allow your heart to become hardened.   *LAB note for Exodus 3:7-15*

(Hebrews 3:8) (Psalm 106:14) (Luke 4:1-4) (James 1:13-15) (Hebrews 2:18) (Luke 22:31-32)

February 21

Those who plant in tears will harvest with shouts of joy. They weep as they go to plant their seed, but they sing as they return with the harvest. ❧ Plant the good seeds of righteousness, and you will harvest a crop of my love.

All honor to the God and Father of our Lord Jesus Christ, for it is by his boundless mercy that God has given us the privilege of being born again. Now we live with a wonderful expectation because Jesus Christ rose again from the dead. So be truly glad! There is wonderful joy ahead, even though it is necessary for you to endure many trials for a while. These trials are only to test your faith, to show that it is strong and pure. It is being tested as fire tests and purifies gold—and your faith is far more precious to God than mere gold. So if your faith remains strong after being tried by fiery trials, it will bring you much praise and glory and honor on the day when Jesus Christ is revealed to the whole world.

Don't get discouraged and give up, for we will reap a harvest of blessing at the appropriate time.

God's ability to restore life is beyond our understanding. Our tears can be seeds that will grow into a harvest of joy because God is able to bring good out of tragedy. When burdened by sorrow, know that your times of grief will end and you will again find God's harvest of joy.

LAB note for Psalm 126:5-6

(PSALM 97:11) (PSALM 126:5-6) (HOSEA 10:12) (1 PETER 1:3, 6-7) (GALATIANS 6:9)

February 22

Who are those who fear the LORD? He will show them the path they should choose.

The LORD guided them by a pillar of cloud during the day and a pillar of fire at night.

Your word is a lamp for my feet and a light for my path. ❧ You will hear a voice say, "This is the way; turn around and walk here." ❧ The LORD says, "I will guide you along the best pathway for your life. I will advise you and watch over you. Do not be like a senseless horse or mule that needs a bit and bridle to keep it under control." Many sorrows come to the wicked, but unfailing love surrounds those who trust the LORD. So rejoice in the LORD and be glad, all you who obey him! ❧ The LORD leads with unfailing love and faithfulness all those who keep his covenant and obey his decrees.

I know, LORD, that a person's life is not his own. No one is able to plan his own course. ❧ Show me the path where I should walk, O LORD; point out the right road for me to follow.

To fear the Lord is to recognize God's attributes: He is holy, almighty, righteous, pure, all-knowing, all-powerful, and all-wise. When we recognize who God is and who we are, we will fall at his feet in humble respect. Only then will he show us how to choose his way.

LAB note for Psalm 25:12

(PSALM 25:12) (EXODUS 13:21) (PSALM 119:105) (ISAIAH 30:21) (PSALM 32:8-11) (PSALM 25:10) (JEREMIAH 10:23) (PSALM 25:4)

February 23

Soon a fierce storm arose. High waves began to break into the boat until it was nearly full of water. Jesus was sleeping at the back of the boat with his head on a cushion.

Don't worry about anything; instead, pray about everything. Tell God what you need, and thank him for all he has done. If you do this, you will experience God's peace, which is far more wonderful than the human mind can understand. His peace will guard your hearts and minds as you live in Christ Jesus.

I will lie down in peace and sleep, for you alone, O LORD, will keep me safe. ❊ God gives rest to his loved ones.

As they stoned him, Stephen prayed, "Lord Jesus, receive my spirit." And he fell to his knees, shouting, "Lord, don't charge them with this sin!" And with that, he died. ❊ We are fully confident, and we would rather be away from these bodies, for then we will be at home with the Lord.

Imagine never worrying about anything! It seems like an impossibility; we all have worries on the job, in our homes, at school. But if you want to worry less, pray more! Whenever you start to worry, stop and pray. *LAB note for Philippians 4:6-7*

(PROVERBS 3:24) (MARK 4:37-38) (PHILIPPIANS 4:6-7) (PSALM 4:8) (PSALM 127:2) (ACTS 7:59-60) (2 CORINTHIANS 5:8)

February 24

Who can comprehend the power of your anger?

At noon, darkness fell across the whole land until three o'clock. At about three o'clock, Jesus called out with a loud voice, "Eli, Eli, lema sabachthani?" which means, "My God, my God, why have you forsaken me?" ❧ The LORD laid on him the guilt and sins of us all.

So now there is no condemnation for those who belong to Christ Jesus. ❧ Since we have been made right in God's sight by faith, we have peace with God because of what Jesus Christ our Lord has done for us. ❧ Christ has rescued us from the curse pronounced by the law. When he was hung on the cross, he took upon himself the curse for our wrongdoing.

God showed how much he loved us by sending his only Son into the world so that we might have eternal life through him. This is real love. It is not that we loved God, but that he loved us and sent his Son as a sacrifice to take away our sins. ❧ He declares sinners to be right in his sight because they believe in Jesus.

"Not guilty; let him go free." What would those words mean to you if you were on death row? The whole human race is on death row, justly condemned for repeatedly breaking God's holy law. But thank God! He has declared us not guilty and has offered us freedom from sin and power to do his will. *LAB note for Romans 8:1*

(PSALM 90:11) (MATTHEW 27:45-46) (ISAIAH 53:6) (ROMANS 8:1) (ROMANS 5:1) (GALATIANS 3:13) (1 JOHN 4:9-10) (ROMANS 3:26)

February 25

The Sovereign LORD says, I am ready to hear . . . and . . . grant them their requests.

The reason you don't have what you want is that you don't ask God for it.

Keep on asking, and you will be given what you ask for. Keep on looking, and you will find. Keep on knocking, and the door will be opened. For everyone who asks, receives. Everyone who seeks, finds. And the door is opened to everyone who knocks. ※ We can be confident that he will listen to us whenever we ask him for anything in line with his will. And if we know he is listening when we make our requests, we can be sure that he will give us what we ask for. ※ If you need wisdom—if you want to know what God wants you to do—ask him, and he will gladly tell you. He will not resent your asking.

The eyes of the LORD watch over those who do right; his ears are open to their cries for help. The LORD hears his people when they call to him for help. He rescues them from all their troubles.

Ask in my name. I'm not saying I will ask the Father on your behalf, for the Father himself loves you dearly because you love me.

When you talk to God, what do you talk about? Do you ask only to satisfy your desires? Do you seek God's approval for what you already plan to do? Your prayers will become powerful when you allow God to change your desires so that they perfectly correspond to his will for you.

LAB note for James 4:2-3

(EZEKIEL 36:37) (JAMES 4:2) (MATTHEW 7:7-8) (1 JOHN 5:14-15) (JAMES 1:5)
(PSALM 34:15, 17) (JOHN 16:26-27)

February 26

Should we accept only good things from the hand of God and never anything bad?

I know, O LORD, that your decisions are fair; you disciplined me because I needed it. ❧ LORD, you are our Father. We are the clay, and you are the potter. We are all formed by your hand. ❧ It is the LORD's will. . . . Let him do what he thinks best.

He will sit and judge like a refiner of silver, watching closely as the dross is burned away. ❧ For the Lord disciplines those he loves, and he punishes those he accepts as his children. ❧ The student shares the teacher's fate. The servant shares the master's fate. ❧ Even though Jesus was God's Son, he learned obedience from the things he suffered.

Be very glad—because these trials will make you partners with Christ in his suffering, and afterward you will have the wonderful joy of sharing his glory when it is displayed to all the world. ❧ He said to me, "These are the ones coming out of the great tribulation. They washed their robes in the blood of the Lamb and made them white."

Many people think that believing in God protects them from trouble, so when calamity comes, they question God's goodness and justice. But you should not give up on God because he allows you to have bad experiences. God is capable of rescuing us from suffering, but he may also allow suffering to come for reasons we cannot understand.

LAB note for Job 2:10

(JOB 2:10) (PSALM 119:75) (ISAIAH 64:8) (1 SAMUEL 3:18) (MALACHI 3:3) (HEBREWS 12:6) (MATTHEW 10:25) (HEBREWS 5:8) (1 PETER 4:13) (REVELATION 7:14)

February 27

Resist the Devil, and he will flee from you.

"Get out of here, Satan," Jesus told him. "For the Scriptures say, 'You must worship the Lord your God; serve only him.'" Then the Devil went away, and angels came and cared for Jesus.

Be strong with the Lord's mighty power. Put on all of God's armor so that you will be able to stand firm against all strategies and tricks of the Devil. ※ Take no part in the worthless deeds of evil and darkness; instead, rebuke and expose them. ※ Satan will not outsmart us. For we are very familiar with his evil schemes. ※ Be careful! Watch out for attacks from the Devil, your great enemy. He prowls around like a roaring lion, looking for some victim to devour. Take a firm stand against him, and be strong in your faith. Remember that your Christian brothers and sisters all over the world are going through the same kind of suffering you are. ※ Every child of God defeats this evil world by trusting Christ to give the victory.

I am convinced that nothing can ever separate us from his love. Death can't, and life can't. The angels can't, and the demons can't. . . . Even the powers of hell can't keep God's love away.

Although God and the Devil are at war, we don't have to wait until the end to see who will win. God has already defeated Satan, and when Christ returns, the Devil and all he stands for will be eliminated forever. With the Holy Spirit's power we can resist the Devil, and he will flee from us. *LAB note for James 4:7*

(James 4:7) (Matthew 4:10–11) (Ephesians 6:10–11) (Ephesians 5:11)
(2 Corinthians 2:11) (1 Peter 5:8–9) (1 John 5:4) (Romans 8:38)

February 28

The glow of an emerald circled his throne like a rainbow.

I am giving you a sign as evidence of my eternal covenant with you and all living creatures. I have placed my rainbow in the clouds. It is the sign of my permanent promise to you and to all the earth. When I see the rainbow in the clouds, I will remember the eternal covenant between God and every living creature on earth. ▨ An everlasting covenant . . . eternal, final, sealed. ▨ God has given us both his promise and his oath. These two things are unchangeable because it is impossible for God to lie. Therefore, we who have fled to him for refuge can take new courage, for we can hold on to his promise with confidence. This confidence is like a strong and trustworthy anchor for our souls. It leads us through the curtain of heaven into God's inner sanctuary. Jesus has already gone in there for us. He has become our eternal High Priest in the line of Melchizedek. ▨ In this man Jesus there is forgiveness for your sins. Everyone who believes in him is freed from all guilt and declared right with God.

Jesus Christ is the same yesterday, today, and forever.

Because God is truth, you can be secure in his promises; you don't need to wonder if he will change his plans. Our hope is secure and immovable, anchored in God. This truth should give you encouragement, assurance, and confidence. *LAB note for Hebrews 6:18-19*

(Revelation 4:3) (Genesis 9:12-13, 16) (2 Samuel 23:5) (Hebrews 6:18-20) (Acts 13:38-39) (Hebrews 13:8)

February 29

God . . . always does just what he says, and he is the one who invited you into this wonderful friendship with his Son, Jesus Christ our Lord.

Without wavering, let us hold tightly to the hope we say we have, for God can be trusted to keep his promise. ❧ We are the temple of the living God. As God said: "I will live in them and walk among them. I will be their God, and they will be my people." ❧ You may have fellowship with us. And our fellowship is with the Father and with his Son, Jesus Christ. ❧ Be very glad—because these trials will make you partners with Christ in his suffering, and afterward you will have the wonderful joy of sharing his glory when it is displayed to all the world.

I pray that Christ will be more and more at home in your hearts as you trust in him. May your roots go down deep into the soil of God's marvelous love. And may you have the power to understand, as all God's people should, how wide, how long, how high, and how deep his love really is. May you experience the love of Christ, though it is so great you will never fully understand it. Then you will be filled with the fullness of life and power that comes from God.

We have significant privileges associated with our new life in Christ: (1) we have personal access to God through Christ; (2) we may grow in faith, overcome doubts and questions, and deepen our relationship with him; (3) we may enjoy encouragement from one another; (4) we may worship together.   *LAB note for Hebrews 10:22-25*

(1 CORINTHIANS 1:9) (HEBREWS 10:23) (2 CORINTHIANS 6:16) (1 JOHN 1:3)
(1 PETER 4:13) (EPHESIANS 3:17-19)

March

New Life in Spring

Abundant life and new beginnings
Warm sunny days and cool rainy evenings
Spring brings a sense of refreshment and peace.

Take a moment each morning to pause outside your
door and breathe deeply of the scent of fresh air and
new life. Listen for the chirping of birds, and revel
in the gift of the season.

March 1

The LORD made the heavens, the earth, the sea, and everything in them.

The heavens tell of the glory of God. The skies display his marvelous craftsmanship. ❧ The LORD merely spoke, and the heavens were created. He breathed the word, and all the stars were born. He gave the sea its boundaries and locked the oceans in vast reservoirs. When he spoke, the world began! It appeared at his command. ❧ All the nations of the world are nothing in comparison with him. They are but a drop in the bucket, dust on the scales. He picks up the islands as though they had no weight at all.

Who else has held the oceans in his hand? Who has measured off the heavens with his fingers? Who else knows the weight of the earth or has weighed out the mountains and the hills?

By faith we understand that the entire universe was formed at God's command, that what we now see did not come from anything that can be seen.

When I look at the night sky and see the work of your fingers—the moon and the stars you have set in place—what are mortals that you should think of us, mere humans that you should care for us?

As God reveals himself through nature, we learn about his power and our finiteness. As God reveals himself through Scripture, we learn about his holiness and our sinfulness. As God reveals himself through daily experiences, we learn about his gracious forgiveness that frees us from guilt. *LAB note for Psalm 19:1ff.*

(EXODUS 20:11) (PSALM 19:1) (PSALM 33:6-7, 9) (ISAIAH 40:15) (ISAIAH 40:12) (HEBREWS 11:3) (PSALM 8:3-4)

March 2

Don't brag about tomorrow, since you don't know what the day will bring.

At just the right time, I heard you. On the day of salvation, I helped you. 🕊 My light will shine out for you just a little while longer. Walk in it while you can, so you will not stumble when the darkness falls. If you walk in the darkness, you cannot see where you are going. Believe in the light while there is still time; then you will become children of the light.

Whatever you do, do well. For when you go to the grave, there will be no work or planning or knowledge or wisdom.

And I'll sit back and say to myself, "My friend, you have enough stored away for years to come. Now take it easy! Eat, drink, and be merry!" But God said to him, "You fool! You will die this very night. Then who will get it all?" Yes, a person is a fool to store up earthly wealth but not have a rich relationship with God.

Your life is like the morning fog—it's here a little while, then it's gone. 🕊 This world is fading away, along with everything it craves. But if you do the will of God, you will live forever.

Life is short, no matter how many years we live. Don't be deceived into thinking that you have lots of remaining time to live for Christ, to enjoy your loved ones, or to do what you know you should. Live for God today! Then no matter when your life ends, you will have fulfilled God's plan for you.   *LAB note for James 4:14*

(PROVERBS 27:1) (2 CORINTHIANS 6:2) (JOHN 12:35-36) (ECCLESIASTES 9:10) (LUKE 12:19-21) (JAMES 4:14) (1 JOHN 2:17)

March 3

You are always the same; your years never end.

Before the mountains were created, before you made the earth and the world, you are God, without beginning or end.

I am the LORD, and I do not change. That is why you descendants of Jacob are not already completely destroyed. ❧ Jesus Christ is the same yesterday, today, and forever.

Whatever is good and perfect comes to us from God above, who created all heaven's lights. Unlike them, he never changes or casts shifting shadows. ❧ God's gifts and his call can never be withdrawn.

God is not a man, that he should lie. He is not a human, that he should change his mind. ❧ The unfailing love of the LORD never ends! By his mercies we have been kept from complete destruction.

Jesus remains a priest forever; his priesthood will never end. Therefore he is able, once and forever, to save everyone who comes to God through him. He lives forever to plead with God on their behalf. ❧ Don't be afraid! I am the First and the Last.

Though human leaders have much to offer, we must keep our eyes on Christ, our ultimate leader. Unlike any human leaders, he will never change. Christ has been and will be the same forever. In a changing world we can trust our unchanging Lord.   *LAB note for Hebrews 13:8*

(PSALM 102:27) (PSALM 90:2) (MALACHI 3:6) (HEBREWS 13:8) (JAMES 1:17) (ROMANS 11:29) (NUMBERS 23:19) (LAMENTATIONS 3:22) (HEBREWS 7:24-25) (REVELATION 1:17)

March 4

If God is for us, who can ever be against us? ✺ The LORD is for me, so I will not be afraid. What can mere mortals do to me?

You have raised a banner for those who honor you—a rallying point in the face of attack.

The LORD is my light and my salvation—so why should I be afraid? The LORD protects me from danger—so why should I tremble? Though a mighty army surrounds me, my heart will know no fear. Even if they attack me, I remain confident.

God is with us. He is our leader. ✺ The LORD Almighty is here among us; the God of Israel is our fortress.

They will wage war against the Lamb, but the Lamb will defeat them.

Why do the nations rage? Why do the people waste their time with futile plans? The one who rules in heaven laughs. The Lord scoffs at them. ✺ Call your councils of war, develop your strategies, prepare your plans of attack—and then die! For God is with us!

We can conquer fear by using the bright liberating light of the Lord, who brings salvation. If we want to dispel the darkness of fear, let us remember with the psalmist that "the LORD is my light and my salvation."

LAB note for Psalm 27:1

(EXODUS 17:15) (ROMANS 8:31) (PSALM 118:6) (PSALM 60:4) (PSALM 27:1, 3) (2 CHRONICLES 13:12) (PSALM 46:7) (REVELATION 17:14) (PSALM 2:1, 4) (ISAIAH 8:10)

March 5

Trust in the LORD with all your heart; do not depend on your own understanding.

Seek his will in all you do, and he will direct your paths. ✳ O my people, trust in him at all times. Pour out your heart to him, for God is our refuge.

The LORD says, "I will guide you along the best pathway for your life. I will advise you and watch over you. Do not be like a senseless horse or mule that needs a bit and bridle to keep it under control." Many sorrows come to the wicked, but unfailing love surrounds those who trust the LORD. ✳ You will hear a voice say, "This is the way; turn around and walk here." ✳ The LORD will guide you continually, watering your life when you are dry and keeping you healthy, too. You will be like a well-watered garden, like an ever-flowing spring.

I know, LORD, that a person's life is not his own. No one is able to plan his own course. ✳ If you don't go with us personally, don't let us move a step from this place.

When we have an important decision to make, we sometimes feel that we can't trust anyone—not even God. But God knows what is best for us. He is a better judge of what we want than we are! We must trust him completely in every choice we make. *LAB note for Proverbs 3:5-6*

(PROVERBS 3:5) (PROVERBS 3:6) (PSALM 32:8-10) (ISAIAH 30:21) (ISAIAH 58:11) (JEREMIAH 10:23) (EXODUS 33:15)

March 6

The prize for which God, through Christ Jesus, is calling us up to heaven.

You will have treasure in heaven. . . . Come, follow me. ✻ Your reward will be great.

The master was full of praise. "Well done, my good and faithful servant. You have been faithful in handling this small amount, so now I will give you many more responsibilities. Let's celebrate together!" ✻ They will reign forever and ever.

Your reward will be a never-ending share in his glory and honor. ✻ [You] will receive the crown of life. ✻ An eternal prize.

Father, I want these whom you've given me to be with me, so they can see my glory. You gave me the glory because you loved me even before the world began! ✻ We who are still alive . . . will be caught up in the clouds . . . and remain with him forever.

What we suffer now is nothing compared to the glory he will give us later.

"No eye has seen, no ear has heard, and no mind has imagined what God has prepared for those who love him." But we know these things because God has revealed them to us by his Spirit.

God's crown of life is not glory and honor here on earth but the reward of eternal life—living with God forever. The way to be in God's winners' circle is by loving him and staying faithful even under pressure.

LAB note for James 1:12

(PHILIPPIANS 3:14) (MATTHEW 19:21) (GENESIS 15:1) (MATTHEW 25:21) (REVELATION 22:5) (1 PETER 5:4) (JAMES 1:12) (1 CORINTHIANS 9:25) (JOHN 17:24) (1 THESSALONIANS 4:17) (ROMANS 8:18) (1 CORINTHIANS 2:9-10)

March 7

He will bend his shoulder to the task.

For examples of patience in suffering, dear brothers and sisters, look at the prophets who spoke in the name of the Lord. ❧ All these events happened to them as examples for us. They were written down to warn us, who live at the time when this age is drawing to a close.

Should we accept only good things from the hand of God and never anything bad? ❧ Job is an example of a man who endured patiently. From his experience we see how the Lord's plan finally ended in good, for he is full of tenderness and mercy. ❧ It is the LORD's will. . . . Let him do what he thinks best.

Give your burdens to the LORD, and he will take care of you. He will not permit the godly to slip and fall. ❧ It was our weaknesses he carried; it was our sorrows that weighed him down.

Come to me, all of you who are weary and carry heavy burdens, and I will give you rest. Take my yoke upon you. Let me teach you, because I am humble and gentle, and you will find rest for your souls. For my yoke fits perfectly, and the burden I give you is light.

Jesus frees people from burdens. The rest that Jesus promises is love, healing, and peace with God, not the end of all labor. A relationship with God changes meaningless, wearisome toil into spiritual productivity and purpose. *LAB note for Matthew 11:28-30*

(GENESIS 49:15) (JAMES 5:10) (1 CORINTHIANS 10:11) (JOB 2:10) (JAMES 5:11)
(1 SAMUEL 3:18) (PSALM 55:22) (ISAIAH 53:4) (MATTHEW 11:28-30)

March 8

I am in trouble, Lord. Help me!

I lift my eyes to you, O God, enthroned in heaven. We look to the LORD our God for his mercy, just as servants keep their eyes on their master, as a slave girl watches her mistress for the slightest signal. ❧ O God, listen to my cry! Hear my prayer! From the ends of the earth, I will cry to you for help, for my heart is overwhelmed. Lead me to the towering rock of safety, for you are my safe refuge, a fortress where my enemies cannot reach me. Let me live forever in your sanctuary, safe beneath the shelter of your wings! ❧ To the poor, O LORD, you are a refuge from the storm. To the needy in distress, you are a shelter from the rain and the heat.

Christ, who suffered for you, is your example. Follow in his steps. He never sinned, and he never deceived anyone. He did not retaliate when he was insulted. When he suffered, he did not threaten to get even. He left his case in the hands of God, who always judges fairly. ❧ This High Priest of ours understands our weaknesses, for he faced all of the same temptations we do, yet he did not sin. So let us come boldly to the throne of our gracious God. There we will receive his mercy, and we will find grace to help us when we need it.

The psalmist lifted his eyes to God, waiting and watching for God to send his mercy. The more he waited, the more he cried out to God, because he knew that the evil and proud offered no help—they had only contempt for God. *LAB note for Psalm 123:1ff.*

(ISAIAH 38:14) (PSALM 123:1-2) (PSALM 61:1-4) (ISAIAH 25:4) (1 PETER 2:21-23) (HEBREWS 4:15-16)

March 9

Fight the good fight.

Outside there was conflict from every direction, and inside there was fear. ▓ Don't be afraid! . . . For there are more on our side than on theirs! ▓ Be strong with the Lord's mighty power.

You come to me with sword, spear, and javelin, but I come to you in the name of the LORD Almighty—the God of the armies of Israel, whom you have defied. ▓ God is my strong fortress. . . . He prepares me for battle; he strengthens me to draw a bow of bronze. ▓ Our only power and success come from God.

The angel of the LORD guards all who fear him, and he rescues them. ▓ "O LORD, open his eyes and let him see!" The LORD opened his servant's eyes, and when he looked up, he saw that the hillside around Elisha was filled with horses and chariots of fire.

How much more do I need to say? It would take too long to recount the stories. . . . By faith these people overthrew kingdoms. . . . Their weakness was turned to strength. They became strong in battle and put whole armies to flight.

When you face difficulties that seem insurmountable, remember that spiritual resources are there even if you can't see them. Look through the eyes of faith, and let God show you his resources.   *LAB note for 2 Kings 6:16*

(1 TIMOTHY 6:12) (2 CORINTHIANS 7:5) (2 KINGS 6:16) (EPHESIANS 6:10)
(1 SAMUEL 17:45) (2 SAMUEL 22:33, 35) (2 CORINTHIANS 3:5) (PSALM 34:7)
(2 KINGS 6:17) (HEBREWS 11:32-34)

March 10

He guards the paths of justice and protects those who are faithful to him.

The LORD your God . . . goes before you looking for the best places to camp, guiding you by a pillar of fire at night and a pillar of cloud by day. ❦ Like an eagle that rouses her chicks and hovers over her young, so he spread his wings to take them in and carried them aloft on his pinions. The LORD alone guided them. ❦ The steps of the godly are directed by the LORD. He delights in every detail of their lives. Though they stumble, they will not fall, for the LORD holds them by the hand. ❦ The righteous face many troubles, but the LORD rescues them from each and every one. ❦ For the LORD watches over the path of the godly, but the path of the wicked leads to destruction. ❦ And we know that God causes everything to work together for the good of those who love God and are called according to his purpose for them. ❦ We have the LORD our God to help us and to fight our battles for us!

The LORD your God has arrived to live among you. He is a mighty savior. He will rejoice over you with great gladness.

The Israelites had no excuse for abandoning God. He had been the encircling protector, like a mother eagle who protects her young. The Lord alone had led them. And he alone leads us. Let us remember to trust in him. *LAB note for Deuteronomy 32:10-11*

(PROVERBS 2:8) (DEUTERONOMY 1:32-33) (DEUTERONOMY 32:11-12) (PSALM 37:23-24) (PSALM 34:19) (PSALM 1:6) (ROMANS 8:28) (2 CHRONICLES 32:8) (ZEPHANIAH 3:17)

March 11

You . . . have forgiven all my sins.

Where is another God like you, who pardons the sins of the survivors among his people? You cannot stay angry with your people forever, because you delight in showing mercy. Once again you will have compassion on us. You will trample our sins under your feet and throw them into the depths of the ocean!

"For a brief moment I abandoned you, but with great compassion I will take you back. In a moment of anger I turned my face away for a little while. But with everlasting love I will have compassion on you," says the LORD, your Redeemer. ※ I will forgive their wickedness and will never again remember their sins.

Oh, what joy for those whose rebellion is forgiven, whose sin is put out of sight! Yes, what joy for those whose record the LORD has cleared of sin, whose lives are lived in complete honesty! ※ The blood of Jesus, his Son, cleanses us from every sin. If we say we have no sin, we are only fooling ourselves and refusing to accept the truth. But if we confess our sins to him, he is faithful and just to forgive us and to cleanse us from every wrong.

Prayer brings deliverance, forgiveness, and good from even a bitter experience. The next time you have difficult struggles, pray for God's help to gain something beneficial from them.

LAB note for Isaiah 38:16–18

(ISAIAH 38:17) (MICAH 7:18-19) (ISAIAH 54:7-8) (JEREMIAH 31:34) (PSALM 32:1-2) (1 JOHN 1:7-9)

March 12

I know the one in whom I trust, and I am sure that he is able to guard what I have entrusted to him until the day of his return.

He is able to accomplish infinitely more than we would ever dare to ask or hope.

God will generously provide all you need. Then you will always have everything you need and plenty left over to share with others.

He is able to help us when we are being tempted.

He is able, once and forever, to save everyone who comes to God through him. He lives forever to plead with God on their behalf.

God . . . is able to keep you from stumbling, and . . . will bring you into his glorious presence innocent of sin and with great joy.

He is able to guard what I have entrusted to him until the day of his return.

He will take these weak mortal bodies of ours and change them into glorious bodies like his own, using the same mighty power that he will use to conquer everything, everywhere.

"Do you believe?" . . . "Yes, Lord," they told him, "we do." . . . "Because of your faith, it will happen!"

Even in prison, the apostle Paul knew that God was still in control. No matter what setbacks or problems we face, we can trust fully in God.   *LAB note for 2 Timothy 1:12*

(2 TIMOTHY 1:12) (EPHESIANS 3:20) (2 CORINTHIANS 9:8) (HEBREWS 2:18) (HEBREWS 7:25) (JUDE 1:24) (2 TIMOTHY 1:12) (PHILIPPIANS 3:21) (MATTHEW 9:28-29)

March 13

The LORD Will Provide.

I trust in you, my God! Do not let me be disgraced, or let my enemies rejoice in my defeat.

The LORD is not too weak to save you, and he is not becoming deaf. He can hear you when you call. A Deliverer will come from Jerusalem.

Happy are those who have the God of Israel as their helper, whose hope is in the LORD their God. The LORD watches over those who fear him, those who rely on his unfailing love. He rescues them from death and keeps them alive in times of famine.

This same God who takes care of me will supply all your needs from his glorious riches, which have been given to us in Christ Jesus. For God has said, "I will never fail you. I will never forsake you." That is why we can say with confidence, "The Lord is my helper, so I will not be afraid. What can mere mortals do to me?" The LORD is my strength, my shield from every danger. I trust in him with all my heart. He helps me, and my heart is filled with joy. I burst out in songs of thanksgiving. The LORD protects his people.

We do not have an ironclad guarantee that all believers will be delivered from death and starvation. God can (and often does) miraculously deliver his followers from pain and death; although sometimes, for purposes known only to him, he chooses not to.

LAB note for Psalm 33:18–19

(GENESIS 22:14) (PSALM 25:2) (ISAIAH 59:1) (ROMANS 11:26) (PSALM 146:5)
(PSALM 33:18-19) (PHILIPPIANS 4:19) (HEBREWS 13:5-6) (PSALM 28:7-8)

March 14

The things that please him.

It is impossible to please God without faith. ❧ Those who are still under the control of their sinful nature can never please God. ❧ The LORD delights in his people; he crowns the humble with salvation.

God is pleased with you when, for the sake of your conscience, you patiently endure unfair treatment. Of course, you get no credit for being patient if you are beaten for doing wrong. But if you suffer for doing right and are patient beneath the blows, God is pleased with you. ❧ You should be known for the beauty that comes from within, the unfading beauty of a gentle and quiet spirit, which is so precious to God.

Giving thanks is a sacrifice that truly honors me. If you keep to my path, I will reveal to you the salvation of God. ❧ Then I will praise God's name with singing, and I will honor him with thanksgiving. For this will please the LORD more than sacrificing an ox or presenting a bull with its horns and hooves.

Dear brothers and sisters, I plead with you to give your bodies to God. Let them be a living and holy sacrifice—the kind he will accept. When you think of what he has done for you, is this too much to ask?

God wants us to offer ourselves as living sacrifices—daily laying aside our own desires to follow him, putting all our energy and resources at his disposal, and trusting him to guide us. We do this out of gratitude that our sins have been forgiven. *LAB note for Romans 12:1*

(1 JOHN 3:22) (HEBREWS 11:6) (ROMANS 8:8) (PSALM 149:4) (1 PETER 2:19-20) (1 PETER 3:4) (PSALM 50:23) (PSALM 69:30-31) (ROMANS 12:1)

March 15

I am deeply discouraged.

You will keep in perfect peace all who trust in you, whose thoughts are fixed on you! Trust in the LORD always, for the LORD GOD is the eternal Rock.

Give your burdens to the LORD, and he will take care of you. He will not permit the godly to slip and fall. ❦ He has not ignored the suffering of the needy. He has not turned and walked away. He has listened to their cries for help. ❦ Are any among you suffering? They should keep praying about it.

Don't be troubled or afraid. ❦ Don't worry about everyday life—whether you have enough food, drink, and clothes. Doesn't life consist of more than food and clothing? Look at the birds. They don't need to plant or harvest or put food in barns because your heavenly Father feeds them. And you are far more valuable to him than they are. Can all your worries add a single moment to your life? Of course not. And why worry about your clothes? Look at the lilies and how they grow. They don't work or make their clothing, yet Solomon in all his glory was not dressed as beautifully as they are. And if God cares so wonderfully for flowers that are here today and gone tomorrow, won't he more surely care for you? ❦ Don't be faithless any longer. Believe! ❦ I am with you always.

Sin, fear, uncertainty, doubt, and numerous other forces are at war within us. The peace of God moves into our hearts and lives to restrain these hostile forces and offer comfort in place of conflict. Jesus says he will give us that peace if we are willing to accept it from him.

LAB note for John 14:27-29

(PSALM 42:6) (ISAIAH 26:3-4) (PSALM 55:22) (PSALM 22:24) (JAMES 5:13) (JOHN 14:27) (MATTHEW 6:25-30) (JOHN 20:27) (MATTHEW 28:20)

March 16

Don't hide your light under a basket! Instead, put it on a stand and let it shine for all. In the same way, let your good deeds shine out for all to see, so that everyone will praise your heavenly Father.

Live in a manner worthy of the Good News about Christ, as citizens of heaven. ▧ Keep away from every kind of evil. ▧ Be happy if you are insulted for being a Christian, for then the glorious Spirit of God will come upon you. If you suffer, however, it must not be for murder, stealing, making trouble, or prying into other people's affairs. ▧ In everything you do, stay away from complaining and arguing, so that no one can speak a word of blame against you. You are to live clean, innocent lives as children of God in a dark world full of crooked and perverse people. Let your lives shine brightly before them. ▧ Make the teaching about God our Savior attractive in every way.

Never let loyalty and kindness get away from you! Wear them like a necklace; write them deep within your heart. Then you will find favor with both God and people, and you will gain a good reputation. Trust in the LORD with all your heart; do not depend on your own understanding. ▧ Fix your thoughts on what is true and honorable and right. Think about things that are pure and lovely and admirable. Think about things that are excellent and worthy of praise.

Can you hide a city that is sitting on top of a mountain? Its light at night can be seen for miles. If we live for Christ, we will glow like lights, showing others what Christ is like. Be a beacon of truth—don't shut your light off from the rest of the world. *LAB note for Matthew 5:14-16*

(MATTHEW 5:15-16) (PHILIPPIANS 1:27) (1 THESSALONIANS 5:22)
(1 PETER 4:14-15) (PHILIPPIANS 2:14-15) (TITUS 2:10) (PROVERBS 3:3-5)
(PHILIPPIANS 4:8)

March 17

We are all infected and impure with sin. When we proudly display our righteous deeds, we find they are but filthy rags.

I will praise your mighty deeds, O Sovereign LORD. I will tell everyone that you alone are just and good. ▧ I am overwhelmed with joy in the LORD my God! For he has dressed me with the clothing of salvation and draped me in a robe of righteousness. I am like a bridegroom in his wedding suit or a bride with her jewels.

Bring the finest robe in the house and put it on. ▧ Wear the finest white linen. (Fine linen represents the good deeds done by the people of God.)

Everything else is worthless when compared with the priceless gain of knowing Christ Jesus my Lord. I have discarded everything else, counting it all as garbage, so that I may have Christ and become one with him. I no longer count on my own goodness or my ability to obey God's law, but I trust Christ to save me. For God's way of making us right with himself depends on faith.

Sin makes us unclean so that we cannot approach God any more than a beggar in filthy rags could dine at a king's table. Our best efforts are still infected with sin. Our only hope, therefore, is faith in Jesus Christ, who can cleanse us and bring us into God's presence. *LAB note for Isaiah 64:6*

(JEREMIAH 23:6) (ISAIAH 64:6) (PSALM 71:16) (ISAIAH 61:10) (LUKE 15:22) (REVELATION 19:8) (PHILIPPIANS 3:8-9)

March 18

Through the suffering of Jesus, God made him a perfect leader.

"My soul is crushed with grief to the point of death. Stay here and watch with me." He went on a little farther and fell face down on the ground, praying, "My Father! If it is possible, let this cup of suffering be taken away from me. Yet I want your will, not mine." He prayed more fervently, and he was in such agony of spirit that his sweat fell to the ground like great drops of blood.

Death had its hands around my throat; the terrors of the grave overtook me. I saw only trouble and sorrow. Their insults have broken my heart, and I am in despair. If only one person would show some pity; if only one would turn and comfort me. No one gives me a passing thought! No one will help me; no one cares a bit what happens to me.

He was despised and rejected—a man of sorrows, acquainted with bitterest grief. We turned our backs on him and looked the other way when he went by. He was despised, and we did not care. But he was wounded and crushed for our sins. He was beaten that we might have peace. He was whipped, and we were healed! He was oppressed and treated harshly, yet he never said a word.

I will give him the honors of one who is mighty and great, because he exposed himself to death.

The man of sorrows was despised and rejected by those around him, and he is still despised and rejected by many today. Some reject Christ by standing against him. Others despise Christ and his great gift of forgiveness. Do you despise him, reject him, or accept him?

LAB note for Isaiah 53:3

(HEBREWS 2:10) (MATTHEW 26:38–39) (LUKE 22:44) (PSALM 116:3) (PSALM 69:20) (PSALM 142:4) (ISAIAH 53:3, 5, 7) (ISAIAH 53:12)

March 19

The LORD's searchlight penetrates the human spirit, exposing every hidden motive.

"All right, stone her. But let those who have never sinned throw the first stones!" When the accusers heard this, they slipped away one by one, beginning with the oldest.

"Who told you that you were naked?" the LORD God asked. "Have you eaten the fruit I commanded you not to eat?"

It is sin to know what you ought to do and then not do it.

We will be confident when we stand before the Lord, even if our hearts condemn us. For God is greater than our hearts, and he knows everything. Dear friends, if our conscience is clear, we can come to God with bold confidence.

There is nothing wrong with these things in themselves. But it is wrong to eat anything if it makes another person stumble. Blessed are those who do not condemn themselves by doing something they know is all right.

Search me, O God, and know my heart; test me and know my thoughts. Point out anything in me that offends you, and lead me along the path of everlasting life.

We tend to think that doing wrong is sin. But sin is also not doing right. If God has directed you to do a kind act, to render a service, or to restore a relationship, do it. You will experience a renewed vitality in your Christian faith. *LAB note for James 4:17*

(PROVERBS 20:27) (JOHN 8:7, 9) (GENESIS 3:11) (JAMES 4:17) (1 JOHN 3:19-21) (ROMANS 14:20, 22) (PSALM 139:23-24)

March 20

I will pray in the spirit, and I will pray in words I understand. I will sing in the spirit, and I will sing in words I understand.

Let the Holy Spirit fill and control you. Then you will sing psalms and hymns and spiritual songs among yourselves, making music to the Lord in your hearts. ❧ Let the words of Christ, in all their richness, live in your hearts and make you wise. Use his words to teach and counsel each other. Sing psalms and hymns and spiritual songs to God with thankful hearts.

I will praise the LORD, and everyone on earth will bless his holy name forever and forever.

How good it is to sing praises to our God! How delightful and how right! Sing out your thanks to the LORD; sing praises to our God, accompanied by harps.

I heard a sound from heaven like the roaring of a great waterfall or the rolling of mighty thunder. It was like the sound of many harpists playing together. ❧ Then I saw in heaven another significant event. . . . They were all holding harps that God had given them. And they were singing the song of Moses, the servant of God, and the song of the Lamb: "Great and marvelous are your actions, Lord God Almighty. Just and true are your ways, O King of the nations."

In praying and singing, both the mind and the spirit are to be fully engaged. When we sing, we should also think about the meaning of the words. When we pour out our feelings to God in prayer, we should not turn off our capacity to think. *LAB note for 1 Corinthians 14:15*

(1 CORINTHIANS 14:15) (EPHESIANS 5:18-19) (COLOSSIANS 3:16) (PSALM 145:21) (PSALM 147:1, 7) (REVELATION 14:2) (REVELATION 15:1-3)

March 21

God in all his fullness was pleased to live in Christ.

The Father loves his Son, and he has given him authority over everything. ❧ God raised him up to the heights of heaven and gave him a name that is above every other name, so that at the name of Jesus every knee will bow, in heaven and on earth and under the earth, and every tongue will confess that Jesus Christ is Lord, to the glory of God the Father. ❧ Now he is far above any ruler or authority or power or leader or anything else in this world or in the world to come. ❧ Christ is the one through whom God created everything in heaven and earth. He made the things we can see and the things we can't see—kings, kingdoms, rulers, and authorities. Everything has been created through him and for him.

Christ died and rose again for this very purpose, so that he might be Lord of those who are alive and of those who have died. ❧ You are complete through your union with Christ. He is the Lord over every ruler and authority in the universe. ❧ We have all benefited from the rich blessings he brought to us—one gracious blessing after another.

Christ was fully human; he was also fully divine. Christ has always been God and always will be God. When we have Christ, we have all of God in human form. Don't diminish any aspect of Christ—either his humanity or his divinity. *LAB note for Colossians 1:19*

(COLOSSIANS 1:19) (JOHN 3:35) (PHILIPPIANS 2:9-11) (EPHESIANS 1:21)
(COLOSSIANS 1:16) (ROMANS 14:9) (COLOSSIANS 2:10) (JOHN 1:16)

March 22

He faced all of the same temptations we do, yet he did not sin.

The fruit looked so fresh and delicious, and it would make her so wise! So she ate some of the fruit. She also gave some to her husband, who was with her. Then he ate it, too. ▓ Stop loving this evil world and all that it offers you, for when you love the world, you show that you do not have the love of the Father in you.

Then the Devil came and said to him, "If you are the Son of God, change these stones into loaves of bread." But Jesus told him, "No! The Scriptures say, 'People need more than bread for their life; they must feed on every word of God.'" Next the Devil took him to the peak of a very high mountain and showed him the nations of the world and all their glory. "I will give it all to you," he said, "if you will only kneel down and worship me." "Get out of here, Satan," Jesus told him. ▓ The world offers only the lust for physical pleasure, the lust for everything we see, and pride in our posessions. These are not from the Father. They are from this evil world.

Since he himself has gone through suffering and temptation, he is able to help us when we are being tempted.

God blesses the people who patiently endure testing.

Prepare yourself for the attractive temptations that may come your way. We cannot always prevent temptation, but there is always a way of escape. Use God's Word and God's people to help you stand against it.

LAB note for Genesis 3:6

(HEBREWS 4:15) (GENESIS 3:6) (1 JOHN 2:15) (MATTHEW 4:3-4, 8-10)
(1 JOHN 2:16) (HEBREWS 2:18) (JAMES 1:12)

March 23

My eyes grew tired of looking to heaven for help.

Have compassion on me, LORD, for I am weak. Heal me, LORD, for my body is in agony. I am sick at heart. How long, O LORD, until you restore me? Return, O LORD, and rescue me. Save me because of your unfailing love. ✺ My heart is in anguish. The terror of death overpowers me. Fear and trembling overwhelm me. I can't stop shaking. Oh, how I wish I had wings like a dove; then I would fly away and rest!

Patient endurance is what you need now, so you will continue to do God's will. ✺ Don't get tired of doing what is good. Don't get discouraged and give up, for we will reap a harvest of blessing at the appropriate time.

As they were straining their eyes to see him, two white-robed men suddenly stood there among them. They said, "Men of Galilee, why are you standing here staring at the sky? Jesus has been taken away from you into heaven. And someday, just as you saw him go, he will return!" ✺ We are citizens of heaven, where the Lord Jesus Christ lives. And we are eagerly waiting for him to return as our Savior. ✺ We look forward to that wonderful event when the glory of our great God and Savior, Jesus Christ, will be revealed.

Don't abandon your faith in times of persecution, but show by your endurance that your faith is real. Faith means resting in what Christ has done for us in the past, but it also means trusting him for what he will do for us in the present and in the future.   *LAB note for Hebrews 10:35-38*

(ISAIAH 38:14) (PSALM 6:2-4) (PSALM 55:4-6) (HEBREWS 10:36) (GALATIANS 6:9) (ACTS 1:10-11) (PHILIPPIANS 3:20) (TITUS 2:13)

March 24

When God raised up his servant, he sent him . . . to bless you by turning each of you back from your sinful ways.

All honor to the God and Father of our Lord Jesus Christ, for it is by his boundless mercy that God has given us the privilege of being born again. Now we live with a wonderful expectation because Jesus Christ rose again from the dead.

Our great God and Savior, Jesus Christ . . . gave his life to free us from every kind of sin, to cleanse us, and to make us his very own people, totally committed to doing what is right. ❧ Be holy in everything you do, just as God—who chose you to be his children—is holy. For he himself has said, "You must be holy because I am holy."

God, the Father of our Lord Jesus Christ . . . has blessed us with every spiritual blessing in the heavenly realms because we belong to Christ. ❧ For in Christ the fullness of God lives in a human body, and you are complete through your union with Christ. ❧ We have all benefited from the rich blessings he brought to us—one gracious blessing after another.

Since God did not spare even his own Son but gave him up for us all, won't God, who gave us Christ, also give us everything else?

Christ's freeing us from sin opens the way for him to purify us. He freed us from sin (redeemed us) by purchasing our release from the captivity of sin with a ransom. We are not only free from the sentence of death for our sin, but we are also purified from sin's influence as we grow in Christ.   *LAB note for Titus 2:14*

(ACTS 3:26) (1 PETER 1:3) (TITUS 2:13-14) (1 PETER 1:15-16) (EPHESIANS 1:3) (COLOSSIANS 2:9-10) (JOHN 1:16) (ROMANS 8:32)

March 25

Encourage me by your word.

Remember your promise to me, for it is my only hope. ❖ I am in trouble, Lord. Help me!

Heaven and earth will disappear, but my words will remain forever. ❖ Deep in your hearts you know that every promise of the LORD your God has come true.

Don't be afraid, for I am with you. Do not be dismayed, for I am your God. I will strengthen you. I will help you. I will uphold you with my victorious right hand. ❖ Take courage and work, for I am with you, says the LORD Almighty. ❖ Not by force nor by strength, but by my Spirit, says the LORD Almighty. ❖ Study this Book of the Law continually. Meditate on it day and night so you may be sure to obey all that is written in it. Only then will you succeed. I command you—be strong and courageous! Do not be afraid or discouraged. For the LORD your God is with you wherever you go.

Be strong with the Lord's mighty power.

To succeed you must (1) be strong and courageous, (2) obey God's law, and (3) constantly read and study God's Word. You may not succeed by the world's standards, but you will be a success in God's eyes—and his opinion lasts forever. *LAB note for Joshua 1:6-8*

(PSALM 119:28) (PSALM 119:49) (ISAIAH 38:14) (LUKE 21:33) (JOSHUA 23:14) (ISAIAH 41:10) (HAGGAI 2:4) (ZECHARIAH 4:6) (JOSHUA 1:8-9) (EPHESIANS 6:10)

March 26

Wake up! Strengthen what little remains, for even what is left is at the point of death.

The end of the world is coming soon. Therefore, be earnest and disciplined in your prayers. Be careful! Watch out for attacks from the Devil, your great enemy. He prowls around like a roaring lion, looking for some victim to devour. Watch out! Be very careful never to forget what you have seen the LORD do for you. Do not let these things escape from your mind as long as you live! A righteous person will live by faith. But I will have no pleasure in anyone who turns away. . . . We have faith that assures our salvation.

Keep a sharp lookout! For you do not know when the homeowner will return—at evening, midnight, early dawn, or late daybreak. Don't let him find you sleeping when he arrives without warning. What I say to you I say to everyone: Watch for his return!

Don't be afraid, for I am with you. Do not be dismayed, for I am your God. I will strengthen you. I will help you. I will uphold you with my victorious right hand. I am holding you by your right hand—I, the LORD your God. And I say to you, "Do not be afraid. I am here to help you."

We should live expectantly because Christ is coming soon. Getting ready to meet Christ involves continually growing in love for God and for others. It is important to pray regularly and to reach out to needy people. Invest your time and talents where they will make an eternal difference. *LAB note for 1 Peter 4:7-9*

(Revelation 3:2) (1 Peter 4:7) (1 Peter 5:8) (Deuteronomoy 4:9)
(Hebrews 10:38-39) (Mark 13:35-37) (Isaiah 41:10, 13)

March 27

Is his unfailing love gone forever?

He remembered our utter weakness. His faithful love endures forever. ▨ The LORD is slow to anger and rich in unfailing love, forgiving every kind of sin and rebellion. ▨ Where is another God like you, who pardons the sins of the survivors among his people? You cannot stay angry with your people forever, because you delight in showing mercy. Once again you will have compassion on us. You will trample our sins under your feet and throw them into the depths of the ocean! ▨ He saved us, not because of the good things we did, but because of his mercy. He washed away our sins and gave us a new life through the Holy Spirit.

All praise to the God and Father of our Lord Jesus Christ. He is the source of every mercy and the God who comforts us. He comforts us in all our troubles.

Our merciful and faithful High Priest before God . . . could offer a sacrifice that would take away the sins of the people. Since he himself has gone through suffering and temptation, he is able to help us when we are being tempted.

> Here are several unchanging characteristics of God we can rely on: (1) God is immensely patient; (2) God's love is one promise we can always count on; (3) God forgives again and again; (4) God is merciful, listening to and answering our requests.   *LAB note for Micah 14:17-20*

(PSALM 77:8) (PSALM 136:23) (NUMBERS 14:18) (MICAH 7:18-19) (TITUS 3:5)
(2 CORINTHIANS 1:3-4) (HEBREWS 2:17-18)

March 28

Lot took a long look at the fertile plains of the Jordan Valley in the direction of Zoar. The whole area was well watered everywhere, like the garden of the LORD or the beautiful land of Egypt. (This was before the LORD had destroyed Sodom and Gomorrah.) Lot chose that land for himself—the Jordan Valley to the east of them.

Lot . . . was a good man.

Don't be misled. Remember that you can't ignore God and get away with it. You will always reap what you sow! ※ Remember what happened to Lot's wife!

Don't team up with those who are unbelievers. How can goodness be a partner with wickedness? How can light live with darkness? Therefore, come out from them and separate yourselves from them, says the Lord. Don't touch their filthy things, and I will welcome you. ※ Don't participate in the things these people do. For though your hearts were once full of darkness, now you are full of light from the Lord, and your behavior should show it! Try to find out what is pleasing to the Lord. Take no part in the worthless deeds of evil and darkness; instead, rebuke and expose them. ※ Knowing God leads to self-control. Self-control leads to patient endurance, and patient endurance leads to godliness. The more you grow like this, the more you will become productive and useful in your knowledge of our Lord Jesus Christ.

Just as God rescued Lot from Sodom, so he is able to rescue us from the temptations and trials we face in a wicked world. Lot was not sinless, but he put his trust in God and was spared when Sodom was destroyed. *LAB note for 2 Peter 2:7-9*

(GENESIS 13:10-11) (2 PETER 2:7) (GALATIANS 6:7) (LUKE 17:32)
(2 CORINTHIANS 6:14, 17) (EPHESIANS 5:7-8, 10-11) (2 PETER 1:6, 8)

March 29

Holy, holy, holy is the Lord God Almighty.

The praises of Israel surround your throne. ❧ "Do not come any closer," God told him. "Take off your sandals, for you are standing on holy ground." Then he said, "I am the God of your ancestors—the God of Abraham, the God of Isaac, and the God of Jacob." When Moses heard this, he hid his face in his hands because he was afraid to look at God. ❧ "To whom will you compare me? Who is my equal?" asks the Holy One. ❧ I am the LORD, your God, the Holy One of Israel, your Savior. There is no other God.

Now you must be holy in everything you do, just as God—who chose you to be his children—is holy. For he himself has said, "You must be holy because I am holy." ❧ Don't you know that your body is the temple of the Holy Spirit, who lives in you and was given to you by God? You do not belong to yourself.

And so . . . I plead with you to give your bodies to God. Let them be a living and holy sacrifice—the kind he will accept. When you think of what he has done for you, is this too much to ask?

God is our friend, but he is also our sovereign Lord. To approach him frivolously shows a lack of respect and sincerity. When you come to God in worship, do you approach him casually, or do you come as though you were an invited guest before a king?   *LAB note for Exodus 3:5-6*

(REVELATION 4:8) (PSALM 22:3) (EXODUS 3:5-6) (ISAIAH 40:25) (ISAIAH 43:3, 10)
(1 PETER 1:15-16) (1 CORINTHIANS 6:19) (ROMANS 12:1)

March 30

I will never fail you. I will never forsake you.

That is why we can say with confidence, "The Lord is my helper, so I will not be afraid. What can mere mortals do to me?"

I will be with you, and I will protect you wherever you go. I will someday bring you safely back to this land. I will be with you constantly until I have finished giving you everything I have promised. ❧ Be strong and courageous! Do not be afraid of them! The LORD your God will go ahead of you. He will neither fail you nor forsake you.

Demas has deserted me because he loves the things of this life. The first time I was brought before the judge, no one was with me. Everyone had abandoned me. I hope it will not be counted against them. But the Lord stood with me and gave me strength, that I might preach the Good News in all its fullness for all the Gentiles to hear. ❧ Even if my father and mother abandon me, the LORD will hold me close.

I am with you always, even to the end of the age. ❧ I am the living one who died. Look, I am alive forever and ever! ❧ I will not abandon you as orphans—I will come to you. ❧ I am leaving you with a gift—peace of mind and heart.

When Jesus said, "I will come to you," he meant it. Although Jesus ascended to heaven, he sent the Holy Spirit to live in believers, and to have the Holy Spirit is to have Jesus himself.   *LAB note for John 14:18*

(HEBREWS 13:5) (HEBREWS 13:6) (GENESIS 28:15) (DEUTERONOMY 31:6)
(2 TIMOTHY 4:10, 16-17) (PSALM 27:10) (MATTHEW 28:20) (REVELATION 1:18)
(JOHN 14:18) (JOHN 14:27)

March 31

The Kingdom of Heaven can be illustrated by the story of a man going on a trip. He called together his servants and gave them money to invest for him while he was gone . . . dividing it in proportion to their abilities.

Don't you realize that whatever you choose to obey becomes your master? You can choose sin, which leads to death, or you can choose to obey God and receive his approval.

It is the one and only Holy Spirit who distributes these gifts. He alone decides which gift each person should have. A spiritual gift is given to each of us as a means of helping the entire church. God has given gifts to each of you from his great variety of spiritual gifts. Manage them well so that God's generosity can flow through you. A person who is put in charge as a manager must be faithful. Much is required from those to whom much is given, and much more is required from those to whom much more is given.

Who is adequate for such a task as this? I can do everything with the help of Christ who gives me the strength I need.

God gives us time, gifts, and other resources according to our abilities, and he expects us to invest them wisely until he returns. We are responsible to use well what God has given us. The issue is not how much we have but how well we use what we have. *LAB note for Matthew 25:15*

(MATTHEW 25:14-15) (ROMANS 6:16) (1 CORINTHIANS 12:11, 7) (1 PETER 4:10) (1 CORINTHIANS 4:2) (LUKE 12:48) (2 CORINTHIANS 2:16) (PHILIPPIANS 4:13)

April

One Sunday Morning

One of a kind, timeless significance
From devastating tragedy to extraordinary blessing
No other day means more than this one.

This Easter season may you gain a fresh awareness of
God's wondrous plan offered for you! Such
enormous grace shown to imperfect people—that is
treasure beyond words.

April 1

When the Holy Spirit controls our lives, he will produce . . . love.

We know how much God loves us, and we have put our trust in him. ❧ How dearly God loves us, because he has given us the Holy Spirit to fill our hearts with his love. ❧ He is very precious to you who believe. ❧ We love each other as a result of his loving us first. ❧ Whatever we do, it is because Christ's love controls us. Since we believe that Christ died for everyone, we also believe that we have all died to the old life we used to live. He died for everyone so that those who receive his new life will no longer live to please themselves. Instead, they will live to please Christ, who died and was raised for them.

God himself has taught you to love one another. ❧ I command you to love each other in the same way that I love you. ❧ Most important of all, continue to show deep love for each other, for love covers a multitude of sins. ❧ Live a life filled with love for others, following the example of Christ, who loved you and gave himself as a sacrifice to take away your sins. And God was pleased, because that sacrifice was like sweet perfume to him.

Since Christ's love controls our lives and he died for us, we are dead to our old life. We should no longer live to please ourselves; we should spend our life pleasing Christ, who died for us and rose again from the grave. *LAB note for 2 Corinthians 5:13-15*

(GALATIANS 5:22) (1 JOHN 4:16) (ROMANS 5:5) (1 PETER 2:7) (1 JOHN 4:19) (2 CORINTHIANS 5:14-15) (1 THESSALONIANS 4:9) (JOHN 15:12) (1 PETER 4:8) (EPHESIANS 5:2)

April 2

The reward of the godly will last.

After a long time their master returned from his trip and called them to give an account of how they had used his money. The servant to whom he had entrusted the five bags of gold said, "Sir, you gave me five bags of gold to invest, and I have doubled the amount." The master was full of praise. "Well done, my good and faithful servant. You have been faithful in handling this small amount, so now I will give you many more responsibilities. Let's celebrate together!"

We must all stand before Christ to be judged. We will each receive whatever we deserve for the good or evil we have done in our bodies.

I have fought a good fight, I have finished the race, and I have remained faithful. And now the prize awaits me—the crown of righteousness that the Lord, the righteous Judge, will give me on that great day of his return. And the prize is not just for me but for all who eagerly look forward to his glorious return.

I am coming quickly. Hold on to what you have, so that no one will take away your crown.

While eternal life is a free gift given on the basis of God's grace, each of us will still be judged by Christ. All Christians must give account on the day of judgment, and Christ will reward us for how we have lived.

LAB note for 2 Corinthians 5:9-10

(PROVERBS 11:18) (MATTHEW 25:19-21) (2 CORINTHIANS 5:10)
(2 TIMOTHY 4:7-8) (REVELATION 3:11)

April 3

God is faithful.

God is not a man, that he should lie. He is not a human, that he should change his mind. . . . Has he ever promised and not carried it through? ▧ The Lord has taken an oath and will not break his vow.

God also bound himself with an oath, so that those who received the promise could be perfectly sure that he would never change his mind. So God has given us both his promise and his oath. These two things are unchangeable because it is impossible for God to lie. Therefore, we who have fled to him for refuge can take new courage, for we can hold on to his promise with confidence. ▧ So if you are suffering according to God's will, keep on doing what is right, and trust yourself to the God who made you, for he will never fail you.

I know the one in whom I trust, and I am sure that he is able to guard what I have entrusted to him until the day of his return. ▧ God, who calls you, is faithful; he will do this. ▧ All of God's promises have been fulfilled in him. That is why we say "Amen" when we give glory to God through Christ.

All of God's promises of what the Messiah would be like are fulfilled in Christ. Jesus was completely faithful in his ministry; he never sinned; he faithfully died for us; and now he faithfully intercedes for us.

LAB note for 2 Corinthians 1:19-20

(1 Corinthians 10:13) (Numbers 23:19) (Hebrews 7:21) (Hebrews 6:17-18)
(1 Peter 4:19) (2 Timothy 1:12) (1 Thessalonians 5:24) (2 Corinthians 1:20)

April 4

Be strong and courageous!

The LORD is my light and my salvation—so why should I be afraid? ❧ He gives power to those who are tired and worn out; he offers strength to the weak. Even youths will become exhausted, and young men will give up. But those who wait on the LORD will find new strength. They will fly high on wings like eagles. They will run and not grow weary. They will walk and not faint. ❧ My health may fail, and my spirit may grow weak, but God remains the strength of my heart; he is mine forever.

What can we say about such wonderful things as these? If God is for us, who can ever be against us? Since God did not spare even his own Son but gave him up for us all, won't God, who gave us Christ, also give us everything else? ❧ The LORD is for me, so I will not be afraid. What can mere mortals do to me? ❧ Only by your power can we push back our enemies; only in your name can we trample our foes. ❧ Overwhelming victory is ours through Christ, who loved us.

May the LORD be with you and give you success. Be strong and courageous; do not be afraid or lose heart!

When God commissioned Joshua, he was told three times to be strong and courageous! Apparently he took God's message to heart. The next time you are afraid to do what you know is right, remember that strength and courage are readily available from God.   *LAB note for Joshua 1:18*

(JOSHUA 1:18) (PSALM 27:1) (ISAIAH 40:29-31) (PSALM 73:26) (ROMANS 8:31-32) (PSALM 118:6) (PSALM 44:5) (ROMANS 8:37) (1 CHRONICLES 22:11, 13)

April 5

Riches don't last forever, and the crown might not be secure for the next generation.

We are merely moving shadows, and all our busy rushing ends in nothing. We heap up wealth for someone else to spend. ❧ Let heaven fill your thoughts. Do not think only about things down here on earth. ❧ Don't store up treasures here on earth, where they can be eaten by moths and get rusty, and where thieves break in and steal. Store your treasures in heaven, where they will never become moth-eaten or rusty and where they will be safe from thieves. Wherever your treasure is, there your heart and thoughts will be also.

All athletes practice strict self-control. They do it to win a prize that will fade away, but we do it for an eternal prize. ❧ So we don't look at the troubles we can see right now; rather, we look forward to what we have not yet seen. ❧ The reward of the godly will last. ❧ Now the prize awaits me—the crown of righteousness that the Lord, the righteous Judge, will give me on that great day of his return. And the prize is not just for me but for all who eagerly look forward to his glorious return. ❧ Your reward will be a never-ending share in his glory and honor.

Because life is uncertain, we should be all the more diligent in preparing for the future. We should act with foresight, giving responsible attention to our home, our family, and our career. Thinking ahead is a duty, not an option, for God's people. *LAB note for Proverbs 27:23-27*

(PROVERBS 27:24) (PSALM 39:6) (COLOSSIANS 3:2) (MATTHEW 6:19-21)
(1 CORINTHIANS 9:25) (2 CORINTHIANS 4:18) (PROVERBS 11:18) (2 TIMOTHY 4:8)
(1 PETER 5:4)

April 6

Isaac . . . was taking a walk out in the fields, meditating.

May the words of my mouth and the thoughts of my heart be pleasing to you, O LORD, my rock and my redeemer.

When I look at the night sky and see the work of your fingers—the moon and the stars you have set in place—what are mortals that you should think of us, mere humans that you should care for us? ❧ I will thank the LORD with all my heart as I meet with his godly people. How amazing are the deeds of the LORD! All who delight in him should ponder them.

Oh, the joys of those who do not follow the advice of the wicked, or stand around with sinners, or join in with scoffers. But they delight in doing everything the LORD wants; day and night they think about his law. ❧ Study this Book of the Law continually. Meditate on it day and night so you may be sure to obey all that is written in it. ❧ I will praise you with songs of joy. I lie awake thinking of you, meditating on you through the night. I think how much you have helped me; I sing for joy in the shadow of your protecting wings. I follow close behind you; your strong right hand holds me securely.

Would you change the way you live if you knew that every word and thought would be examined by God first? As you begin each day, determine that God's love will guide what you say and how you think.

LAB note for Psalm 19:14

(GENESIS 24:62-63) (PSALM 19:14) (PSALM 8:3-4) (PSALM 111:1-2)
(PSALM 1:1-2) (JOSHUA 1:8) (PSALM 63:5-8)

April 7

O LORD, how long will you forget me? Forever? How long will you look the other way?

Whatever is good and perfect comes to us from God above, who created all heaven's lights. Unlike them, he never changes or casts shifting shadows. ▨ Yet Jerusalem says, "The LORD has deserted us; the Lord has forgotten us." "Never! Can a mother forget her nursing child? Can she feel no love for a child she has borne? But even if that were possible, I would not forget you!"

I will not forget to help you. I have swept away your sins like the morning mists.

Although Jesus loved Martha, Mary, and Lazarus, he stayed where he was for the next two days and did not go to them. ▨ A Gentile woman . . . came to him, pleading, "Have mercy on me, O Lord, Son of David! . . ." But Jesus gave her no reply—not even a word.

These trials are only to test your faith, to show that it is strong and pure. It is being tested as fire tests and purifies gold—and your faith is far more precious to God than mere gold. So if your faith remains strong after being tried by fiery trials, it will bring you much praise and glory and honor on the day when Jesus Christ is revealed to the whole world.

Why is God sometimes slow to act? Why does he allow evil and suffering to go seemingly unchecked? The psalmist David affirmed that he would continue to trust God, no matter how long he had to wait for God's justice to be realized. When you feel impatient, remember David's steadfast faith in God's unfailing love.   *LAB note for Psalm 13:1-5*

(PSALM 13:1) (JAMES 1:17) (ISAIAH 49:14-15) (ISAIAH 44:21-22) (JOHN 11:5-6) (MATTHEW 15:22-23) (1 PETER 1:7)

April 8

This same God who takes care of me will supply all your needs from his glorious riches, which have been given to us in Christ Jesus.

Your heavenly Father already knows all your needs, and he will give you all you need from day to day if you live for him and make the Kingdom of God your primary concern. ※ Since God did not spare even his own Son but gave him up for us all, won't God, who gave us Christ, also give us everything else? ※ Everything belongs to you: . . . the whole world and life and death; the present and the future. Everything belongs to you, and you belong to Christ, and Christ belongs to God. ※ We own nothing, and yet we have everything.

The LORD is my shepherd; I have everything I need. ※ For the LORD God is our light and protector. He gives us grace and glory. No good thing will the LORD withhold from those who do what is right. ※ The living God . . . richly gives us all we need for our enjoyment. ※ God will generously provide all you need. Then you will always have everything you need and plenty left over to share with others.

God will always meet our needs. However, there is a difference between wants and needs. Most people want to feel good and avoid pain. We may not get all that we want. But by trusting in Christ, our attitudes and appetites can change from wanting everything to accepting his provision and power to live in him.   *LAB note for Philippians 4:19*

(PHILIPPIANS 4:19) (MATTHEW 6:32-33) (ROMANS 8:32) (1 CORINTHIANS 3:21-23) (2 CORINTHIANS 6:10) (PSALM 23:1) (PSALM 84:11) (1 TIMOTHY 6:17) (2 CORINTHIANS 9:8)

April 9

How can goodness be a partner with wickedness?

They loved the darkness more than the light, for their actions were evil. ❧ You are all children of the light and of the day; we don't belong to darkness and night.

Your word is a lamp for my feet and a light for my path.

The land is full of darkness and violence! ❧ Love comes from God. Anyone who loves is born of God and knows God. But anyone who does not love does not know God—for God is love.

The way of the wicked is like complete darkness. The way of the righteous is like the first gleam of dawn, which shines ever brighter until the full light of day.

I have come as a light to shine in this dark world, so that all who put their trust in me will no longer remain in the darkness. ❧ Though your hearts were once full of darkness, now you are full of light from the Lord, and your behavior should show it! For this light within you produces only what is good and right and true. Try to find out what is pleasing to the Lord.

For those who have discovered God's light, there can be no fellowship or compromise with darkness. Does your behavior shine like a light in the darkness, or is it being obscured by the darkness around you?

LAB note for 2 Corinthians 6:14–15

(2 Corinthians 6:14) (John 3:19) (1 Thessalonians 5:5) (Psalm 119:105) (Psalm 74:20) (1 John 4:7–8) (Proverbs 4:19, 18) (John 12:46) (Ephesians 5:8–10)

April 10

If you are really serious about wanting to return to the LORD, get rid of your foreign gods and your images of Ashtoreth. Determine to obey only the LORD.

Dear children, keep away from anything that might take God's place in your hearts. ❧ Therefore come out from them and separate yourselves from them, says the Lord. Don't touch their filthy things, and I will welcome you. And I will be your Father, and you will be my sons and daughters, says the Lord Almighty. ❧ You cannot serve both God and money.

You must worship no other gods, but only the LORD, for he is a God who is passionate about his relationship with you. ❧ Worship and serve him with your whole heart and with a willing mind. For the LORD sees every heart and understands and knows every plan and thought.

You desire honesty from the heart, so you can teach me to be wise in my inmost being. ❧ People judge by outward appearance, but the LORD looks at a person's thoughts and intentions. ❧ Dear friends, if our conscience is clear, we can come to God with bold confidence. ❧ Cling tightly to your faith in Christ, and always keep your conscience clear.

Do you ever feel as if God has abandoned you? Check to see if there is anything he has already told you to do. You may not receive new guidance from God until you have acted on his previous directions. How easy it is for us to complain about our problems, even to God, while we refuse to act, change, and do what he requires!   *LAB note for 1 Samuel 7:2-3*

(1 SAMUEL 7:3) (1 JOHN 5:21) (2 CORINTHIANS 6:17-18) (MATTHEW 6:24) (EXODUS 34:14) (1 CHRONICLES 28:9) (PSALM 51:6) (1 SAMUEL 16:7) (1 JOHN 3:21) (1 TIMOTHY 1:19)

April 11

You must not forget, dear friends, that a day is like a thousand years to the Lord, and a thousand years is like a day.

"My thoughts are completely different from yours," says the LORD. "And my ways are far beyond anything you could imagine. For just as the heavens are higher than the earth, so are my ways higher than your ways and my thoughts higher than your thoughts. The rain and snow come down from the heavens and stay on the ground to water the earth. . . . It is the same with my word. I send it out, and it always produces fruit. It will accomplish all I want it to, and it will prosper everywhere I send it."

God has imprisoned all people in their own disobedience so he could have mercy on everyone. Oh, what a wonderful God we have! How great are his riches and wisdom and knowledge! How impossible it is for us to understand his decisions and his methods! For who can know what the Lord is thinking? Who knows enough to be his counselor? And who could ever give him so much that he would have to pay it back? For everything comes from him; everything exists by his power and is intended for his glory. To him be glory evermore.

So be on your guard, not asleep like the others. Stay alert and be sober. No matter what happens, always be thankful, for this is God's will for you who belong to Christ Jesus.

No one has fully understood the mind of the Lord. No one has been his counselor. And God owes nothing to any one of us. God alone is the possessor of absolute power and absolute wisdom.

LAB note for Romans 11:34-35

(2 Peter 3:8) (Isaiah 55:8-11) (Romans 11:32-36) (1 Thessalonians 5:6, 18)

April 12

Lead me to the towering rock of safety.

Don't worry about anything; instead, pray about everything. Tell God what you need, and thank him for all he has done. If you do this, you will experience God's peace, which is far more wonderful than the human mind can understand. His peace will guard your hearts and minds as you live in Christ Jesus.

I am overwhelmed, and you alone know the way I should turn. ✺ He knows where I am going. And when he has tested me like gold in a fire, he will pronounce me innocent. ✺ Lord, through all the generations you have been our home! ✺ To the poor, O LORD, you are a refuge from the storm. To the needy in distress, you are a shelter from the rain and the heat.

For who is God except the LORD? Who but our God is a solid rock? ✺ They will never perish. No one will snatch them away from me. ✺ Lord, sustain me as you promised, that I may live! Do not let my hope be crushed. ✺ This confidence is like a strong and trustworthy anchor for our souls. It leads us through the curtain of heaven into God's inner sanctuary.

God is concerned for the poor and is a refuge for them. When we are disadvantaged or oppressed, we can turn to God for comfort and help. Jesus said that the Kingdom of God belongs to the poor.

LAB note for Isaiah 25:4

(PSALM 61:2) (PHILIPPIANS 4:6-7) (PSALM 142:3) (JOB 23:10) (PSALM 90:1)
(ISAIAH 25:4) (PSALM 18:31) (JOHN 10:28) (PSALM 119:116) (HEBREWS 6:19)

April 13

My future is in your hands.

Your holy ones are in your hands. ❧ Then the LORD said to Elijah, "Go to the east and hide by Kerith Brook at a place east of where it enters the Jordan River. Drink from the brook and eat what the ravens bring you, for I have commanded them to bring you food." Then the LORD said to Elijah, "Go and live in the village of Zarephath, near the city of Sidon. There is a widow there who will feed you. I have given her my instructions."

Don't worry about everyday life—whether you have enough food, drink, and clothes. Doesn't life consist of more than food and clothing? Your heavenly Father already knows all your needs, and he will give you all you need from day to day if you live for him and make the Kingdom of God your primary concern. So don't worry about tomorrow, for tomorrow will bring its own worries. Today's trouble is enough for today.

Trust in the LORD with all your heart; do not depend on your own understanding. Seek his will in all you do, and he will direct your paths. ❧ Give all your worries and cares to God, for he cares about what happens to you.

In saying, "My future is in your hands," David was expressing his belief that all of life's circumstances are under God's control. Knowing that God loves and cares for us enables us to keep steady in our faith, regardless of our circumstances. *LAB note for Psalm 31:14-15*

(PSALM 31:15) (DEUTERONOMY 33:3) (1 KINGS 17:2-4, 8-9) (MATTHEW 6:25, 32-34)
(PROVERBS 3:5-6) (1 PETER 5:7)

April 14

He is able, once and forever, to save everyone who comes to God through him. He lives forever to plead with God on their behalf.

Who then will condemn us? Will Christ Jesus? No, for he is the one who died for us . . . and is sitting at the place of highest honor next to God, pleading for us. ❧ Christ has entered into heaven itself to appear now before God as our Advocate.

If you do sin, there is someone to plead for you before the Father. He is Jesus Christ, the one who pleases God completely. ❧ There is only one God and one Mediator who can reconcile God and people. He is the man Christ Jesus.

We have a great High Priest who has gone to heaven, Jesus the Son of God. Let us cling to him and never stop trusting him. This High Priest of ours understands our weaknesses, for he faced all of the same temptations we do, yet he did not sin. So let us come boldly to the throne of our gracious God. There we will receive his mercy, and we will find grace to help us when we need it.

All of us . . . may come to the Father through the same Holy Spirit because of what Christ has done for us.

As our High Priest, Christ is our Advocate, the mediator between us and God. He looks after our interests and intercedes for us with God. Christ's continual presence with the Father in heaven assures us that our sins have been paid for and forgiven. *LAB note for Hebrews 7:25*

(HEBREWS 7:25) (ROMANS 8:34) (HEBREWS 9:24) (1 JOHN 2:1) (1 TIMOTHY 2:5)
(HEBREWS 4:14-16) (EPHESIANS 2:18)

April 15

Those who know your name trust in you, for you, O LORD, have never abandoned anyone who searches for you.

This is his name: "The LORD Is Our Righteousness." ❧ I will praise your mighty deeds, O Sovereign LORD. I will tell everyone that you alone are just and good.

His royal titles: Wonderful Counselor. ❧ I know, LORD, that a person's life is not his own. No one is able to plan his own course.

Mighty God, Everlasting Father. ❧ I know the one in whom I trust, and I am sure that he is able to guard what I have entrusted to him until the day of his return.

Prince of Peace. ❧ Christ himself has made peace between us. ❧ Since we have been made right in God's sight by faith, we have peace with God because of what Jesus Christ our Lord has done for us.

The name of the LORD is a strong fortress; the godly run to him and are safe. ❧ Destruction is certain for those who look to Egypt for help, trusting their cavalry and chariots instead of looking to the LORD, the Holy One of Israel. ❧ There is no one like the God of Israel. He rides across the heavens to help you, across the skies in majestic splendor. The eternal God is your refuge, and his everlasting arms are under you.

God will never abandon those who seek him. God's promise does not mean that if we trust in him we will escape loss or suffering; it means that God himself will never leave us no matter what we face.

LAB note for Psalm 9:10

(PSALM 9:10) (JEREMIAH 23:6) (PSALM 71:16) (ISAIAH 9:6) (JEREMIAH 10:23)
(ISAIAH 9:6) (2 TIMOTHY 1:12) (ISAIAH 9:6) (EPHESIANS 2:14) (ROMANS 5:1)
(PROVERBS 18:10) (ISAIAH 31:1) (DEUTERONOMY 33:26-27)

April 16

Let us . . . work toward complete purity because we fear God.

Let us cleanse ourselves from everything that can defile our body or spirit.

You desire honesty from the heart, so you can teach me to be wise in my inmost being. ✻ We are instructed to turn from godless living and sinful pleasures. We should live in this evil world with self-control, right conduct, and devotion to God. ✻ Don't hide your light under a basket! Instead, put it on a stand and let it shine for all. In the same way, let your good deeds shine out for all to see, so that everyone will praise your heavenly Father. ✻ I don't mean to say that I have already achieved these things or that I have already reached perfection!

When he comes we will be like him, for we will see him as he really is. And all who believe this will keep themselves pure, just as Christ is pure.

God himself has prepared us for this, and as a guarantee he has given us his Holy Spirit. ✻ He is the one who gave these gifts to the church. . . . Their responsibility is to equip God's people to do his work and build up the church, the body of Christ, until we come to such unity in our faith and knowledge of God's Son that we will be mature and full grown in the Lord, measuring up to the full stature of Christ.

Cleansing is a twofold action: turning away from sin and turning toward God. Have nothing to do with paganism. Make a clean break with your past and give yourself to God alone. *LAB note for 2 Corinthians 7:1*

(2 Corinthians 7:1) (2 Corinthians 7:1) (Psalm 51:6) (Titus 2:12) (Matthew 5:15-16) (Philippians 3:12) (1 John 3:2-3) (2 Corinthians 5:5) (Ephesians 4:11-13)

April 17

He has enriched your church.

When we were utterly helpless, Christ came at just the right time and died for us sinners. ❧ Since God did not spare even his own Son but gave him up for us all, won't God, who gave us Christ, also give us everything else?

In Christ the fullness of God lives in a human body, and you are complete through your union with Christ. He is the Lord over every ruler and authority in the universe.

Remain in me, and I will remain in you. For a branch cannot produce fruit if it is severed from the vine, and you cannot be fruitful apart from me. Yes, I am the vine; you are the branches. Those who remain in me, and I in them, will produce much fruit. For apart from me you can do nothing. ❧ He has given each one of us a special gift according to the generosity of Christ.

If you stay joined to me and my words remain in you, you may ask any request you like, and it will be granted! ❧ Let the words of Christ, in all their richness, live in your hearts and make you wise.

"In Christ the fullness of God lives in a human body" means that all of God was in Christ's human body. When we have Christ, we have everything we need for salvation and right living.   *LAB note for Colossians 2:9*

(1 Corinthians 1:5) (Romans 5:6) (Romans 8:32) (Colossians 2:9-10)
(John 15:4-5) (Ephesians 4:7) (John 15:7) (Colossians 3:16)

April 18

I will tell of the LORD's unfailing love. I will praise the LORD for all he has done. I will rejoice in his great goodness.

He lifted me out of the pit of despair, out of the mud and the mire. He set my feet on solid ground and steadied me as I walked along. ❧ The Son of God . . . loved me and gave himself for me. ❧ Since God did not spare even his own Son but gave him up for us all, won't God, who gave us Christ, also give us everything else? ❧ God showed his great love for us by sending Christ to die for us while we were still sinners.

He has identified us as his own by placing the Holy Spirit in our hearts as the first installment of everything he will give us. ❧ The Spirit is God's guarantee that he will give us everything he promised and that he has purchased us to be his own people.

God is so rich in mercy, and he loved us so very much, that even while we were dead because of our sins, he gave us life when he raised Christ from the dead. (It is only by God's special favor that you have been saved!) For he raised us from the dead along with Christ, and we are seated with him in the heavenly realms—all because we are one with Christ Jesus.

Through faith in Christ we stand acquitted, or not guilty, before God. But God does not take us out of the world or make us robots—we will still feel like sinning, and sometimes we will sin. The difference is that before we became Christians, we were dead in sin and were slaves to our sinful nature. But now we are alive in Christ.   *LAB note for Ephesians 2:4-5*

(ISAIAH 63:7) (PSALM 40:2) (GALATIANS 2:20) (ROMANS 8:32) (ROMANS 5:8)
(2 CORINTHIANS 1:22) (EPHESIANS 1:14) (EPHESIANS 2:4-6)

April 19

Don't talk too much, for it fosters sin. Be sensible and turn off the flow!

Dear brothers and sisters, be quick to listen, slow to speak, and slow to get angry. ❦ It is better to be patient than powerful; it is better to have self-control than to conquer a city. ❦ Those who control their tongues can also control themselves in every other way. ❦ The words you say now reflect your fate then; either you will be justified by them or you will be condemned. ❦ Take control of what I say, O LORD, and keep my lips sealed.

Christ, who suffered for you, is your example. Follow in his steps. He never sinned, and he never deceived anyone. He did not retaliate when he was insulted. When he suffered, he did not threaten to get even. He left his case in the hands of God, who always judges fairly. ❦ Think about all he endured when sinful people did such terrible things to him, so that you don't become weary and give up. ❦ Gentle words bring life and health.

No falsehood can be charged against them; they are blameless.

When we talk too much and listen too little, we communicate to others that we think our ideas are much more important than theirs. Instead, reverse the process. Put a mental stopwatch on your conversations, and keep track of how much you talk and how much you listen.

LAB note for James 1:19

(PROVERBS 10:19) (JAMES 1:19) (PROVERBS 16:32) (JAMES 3:2) (MATTHEW 12:37) (PSALM 141:3) (1 PETER 2:21-23) (HEBREWS 12:3) (PROVERBS 15:4) (REVELATION 14:5)

April 20

Teach me how to live, O LORD.

The LORD says, "I will guide you along the best pathway for your life. I will advise you and watch over you." ▩ The LORD is good and does what is right; he shows the proper path to those who go astray. He leads the humble in what is right, teaching them his way.

Yes, I am the gate. Those who come in through me will be saved. Wherever they go, they will find green pastures.

Jesus told him, "I am the way, the truth, and the life. No one can come to the Father except through me." ▩ We can boldly enter heaven's Most Holy Place because of the blood of Jesus. This is the new, life-giving way that Christ has opened up for us through the sacred curtain, by means of his death for us. And since we have a great High Priest who rules over God's people, let us go right into the presence of God, with true hearts fully trusting him.

Oh, that we might know the LORD! Let us press on to know him! ▩ The LORD leads with unfailing love and faithfulness all those who keep his covenant and obey his decrees.

We are bombarded today with relentless appeals to go in various directions. Add to that the dozens of decisions we must make concerning our job, our family, our money, and our society, and we become desperate for someone to show us the right way. If you find yourself pulled in several directions, remember that God teaches the humble his way.

LAB note for Psalm 25:8-11

(PSALM 27:11) (PSALM 32:8) (PSALM 25:8-9) (JOHN 10:9) (JOHN 14:6)
(HEBREWS 10:19-22) (HOSEA 6:3) (PSALM 25:10)

April 21

When God's children are in need, be the one to help them out.

One day David began wondering if anyone in Saul's family was still alive, for he had promised Jonathan that he would show kindness to them.

Come, you who are blessed by my Father, inherit the Kingdom prepared for you from the foundation of the world. For I was hungry, and you fed me. I was thirsty, and you gave me a drink. I was a stranger, and you invited me into your home. I was naked, and you gave me clothing. I was sick, and you cared for me. I was in prison, and you visited me. When you did it to one of the least of these my brothers and sisters, you were doing it to me! And if you give even a cup of cold water to one of the least of my followers, you will surely be rewarded.

Don't forget to do good and to share what you have with those in need, for such sacrifices are very pleasing to God. For God is not unfair. He will not forget how hard you have worked for him and how you have shown your love to him by caring for other Christians, as you still do. Our great desire is that you will keep right on loving others as long as life lasts, in order to make certain that what you hope for will come true.

Entertaining focuses on the host and setting; Christian hospitality focuses on the guests' needs. It can happen around a dinner table where the main dish is canned soup. Don't hesitate to offer hospitality just because you are too tired, too busy, or not wealthy enough to entertain. *LAB note for Romans 12:13*

(ROMANS 12:13) (2 SAMUEL 9:1) (MATTHEW 25:34-36, 40) (MATTHEW 10:42) (HEBREWS 13:16) (HEBREWS 6:10-11)

April 22

Are you seeking great things for yourself? Don't do it!

Take my yoke upon you. Let me teach you, because I am humble and gentle, and you will find rest for your souls. ▧ Your attitude should be the same that Christ Jesus had. Though he was God, he did not demand and cling to his rights as God. He made himself nothing; he took the humble position of a slave and appeared in human form. And in human form he obediently humbled himself even further by dying a criminal's death on a cross.

If you refuse to take up your cross and follow me, you are not worthy of being mine. ▧ Christ, who suffered for you, is your example. Follow in his steps. ▧ Many who seem to be important now will be the least important then, and those who are considered least here will be the greatest then.

True religion with contentment is great wealth. After all, we didn't bring anything with us when we came into the world, and we certainly cannot carry anything with us when we die. So if we have enough food and clothing, let us be content. ▧ I have learned how to get along happily whether I have much or little.

It is easy to lose the joy of serving God when we take our eyes off him. The more we look away from God's purposes toward our own sacrifices, the more frustrated we will become. As you serve God, look at him rather than at yourself. *LAB note for Jeremiah 45:5*

(JEREMIAH 45:5) (MATTHEW 11:29) (PHILIPPIANS 2:5-8) (MATTHEW 10:38) (1 PETER 2:21) (MATTHEW 19:30) (1 TIMOTHY 6:6-8) (PHILIPPIANS 4:11)

April 23

Stay true to the Lord.

I have stayed in God's paths; I have followed his ways and not turned aside. The LORD loves justice, and he will never abandon the godly. The LORD keeps you from all evil and preserves your life.

A righteous person will live by faith. But I will have no pleasure in anyone who turns away. But we are not like those who turn their backs on God and seal their fate. We have faith that assures our salvation. These people left our churches because they never really belonged with us; otherwise they would have stayed with us. When they left us, it proved that they do not belong with us.

You are truly my disciples if you keep obeying my teachings. Those who endure to the end will be saved. Be on guard. Stand true to what you believe. Be courageous. Be strong. Hold on to what you have, so that no one will take away your crown. All who are victorious will be clothed in white. I will never erase their names from the Book of Life, but I will announce before my Father and his angels that they are mine.

How do we "stay true to the Lord"? The way to stay true is to keep our eyes on Christ, to remember that this world is not our home, and to focus on the fact that Christ will bring everything under his control.

LAB note for Philippians 4:1

(PHILIPPIANS 4:1) (JOB 23:11) (PSALM 37:28) (PSALM 121:7) (HEBREWS 10:38-39)
(1 JOHN 2:19) (JOHN 8:31) (MATTHEW 24:13) (1 CORINTHIANS 16:13)
(REVELATION 3:11) (REVELATION 3:5)

April 24

Our Lord Jesus . . . Though he was very rich, yet for your sakes he became poor, so that by his poverty he could make you rich.

For God in all his fullness was pleased to live in Christ. ❧ The Son reflects God's own glory, and everything about him represents God exactly. He sustains the universe by the mighty power of his command. After he died to cleanse us from the stain of sin, he sat down in the place of honor at the right hand of the majestic God of heaven. This shows that God's Son is far greater than the angels, just as the name God gave him is far greater than their names. ❧ Though he was God, he did not demand and cling to his rights as God. He made himself nothing; he took the humble position of a slave and appeared in human form.

Foxes have dens to live in, and birds have nests, but I, the Son of Man, have no home of my own, not even a place to lay my head.

Everything belongs to you . . . the whole world and life and death; the present and the future. Everything belongs to you, and you belong to Christ, and Christ belongs to God.

Jesus became poor by giving up his rights as God and voluntarily becoming human. In response to the Father's will, he limited his power and knowledge. Yet by doing so, he made us "rich" because we received salvation and eternal life. *LAB note for 2 Corinthians 8:9*

(2 Corinthians 8:9) (Colossians 1:19) (Hebrews 1:3-4) (Philippians 2:6-7) (Matthew 8:20) (1 Corinthians 3:21-23)

April 25

The time that remains is very short.

How frail is humanity! How short is life, and how full of trouble! Like a flower, we blossom for a moment and then wither. Like the shadow of a passing cloud, we quickly disappear. ▧ This world is fading away, along with everything it craves. But if you do the will of God, you will live forever. ▧ Everyone dies because all of us are related to Adam, the first man. But all who are related to Christ, the other man, will be given new life. Death is swallowed up in victory. ▧ While we live, we live to please the Lord. And when we die, we go to be with the Lord. So in life and in death, we belong to the Lord.

For to me, living is for Christ, and dying is even better.

Do not throw away this confident trust in the Lord, no matter what happens. Remember the great reward it brings you! Patient endurance is what you need now, so you will continue to do God's will. Then you will receive all that he has promised. "For in just a little while, the Coming One will come and not delay." ▧ The night is almost gone; the day of salvation will soon be here. So don't live in darkness. Get rid of your evil deeds. Shed them like dirty clothes. Clothe yourselves with the armor of right living, as those who live in the light. ▧ The end of the world is coming soon. Therefore, be earnest and disciplined in your prayers.

All believers should make the most of their time before Christ's return. Every person in every generation should have this sense of urgency about telling the Good News to others. Life is short—there's not much time! *LAB note for 1 Corinthians 7:29*

(1 CORINTHIANS 7:29) (JOB 14:1-2) (1 JOHN 2:17) (1 CORINTHIANS 15:22, 54) (ROMANS 14:8) (PHILIPPIANS 1:21) (HEBREWS 10:35-37) (ROMANS 13:12) (1 PETER 4:7)

April 26

We look forward to that wonderful event when the glory of our great God and Savior, Jesus Christ, will be revealed.

This confidence is like a strong and trustworthy anchor for our souls. It leads us through the curtain of heaven into God's inner sanctuary. Jesus has already gone in there for us. He has become our eternal High Priest in the line of Melchizedek. For he must remain in heaven until the time for the final restoration of all things, as God promised long ago through his prophets. When he comes to receive glory and praise from his holy people.

We know that all creation has been groaning as in the pains of childbirth right up to the present time. And even we Christians . . . also groan to be released from pain and suffering. We, too, wait anxiously for that day when God will give us our full rights as his children, including the new bodies he has promised us. Dear friends, we are already God's children, and we can't even imagine what we will be like when Christ returns. But we do know that when he comes we will be like him, for we will see him as he really is. When Christ, who is your real life, is revealed to the whole world, you will share in all his glory.

"Yes, I am coming soon!" Amen! Come, Lord Jesus!

Christ gives us power to live for him now, and he gives us hope for the future—he will return. Christians should act now in order to be prepared for Christ's return. *LAB note for Colossians 3:4*

(TITUS 2:13) (HEBREWS 6:19-20) (ACTS 3:21) (2 THESSALONIANS 1:10) (ROMANS 8:22-23) (1 JOHN 3:2) (COLOSSIANS 3:4) (REVELATION 22:20)

April 27

Those who obey God's word really do love him.

May the God of peace, who brought again from the dead our Lord Jesus, equip you with all you need for doing his will. May he produce in you, through the power of Jesus Christ, all that is pleasing to him. Jesus is the great Shepherd of the sheep by an everlasting covenant, signed with his blood. To him be glory forever and ever. Amen.

How can we be sure that we belong to him? By obeying his commandments. ※ All those who love me will do what I say. My Father will love them, and we will come to them and live with them. ※ If we continue to live in him, we won't sin either. But those who keep on sinning have never known him or understood who he is. Dear children, don't let anyone deceive you about this: When people do what is right, it is because they are righteous, even as Christ is righteous.

As we live in God, our love grows more perfect. So we will not be afraid on the day of judgment, but we can face him with confidence because we are like Christ here in this world.

How can you be sure that you belong to Christ? If you do what Christ says and live as Christ wants. True Christian faith results in loving behavior; that is why the way we act can give us assurance that we belong to Christ. *LAB note for 1 John 2:3-6*

(1 JOHN 2:5) (HEBREWS 13:20-21) (1 JOHN 2:3) (JOHN 14:23) (1 JOHN 3:6-7) (1 JOHN 4:17)

April 28

Those who control their anger have great understanding.

He passed in front of Moses and said, "I am the LORD, I am the LORD, the merciful and gracious God. I am slow to anger and rich in unfailing love and faithfulness."

Follow God's example in everything you do, because you are his dear children. ❧ When the Holy Spirit controls our lives, he will produce this kind of fruit in us: love, joy, peace, patience, kindness, goodness, faithfulness, gentleness, and self-control. ❧ God is pleased with you when, for the sake of your conscience, you patiently endure unfair treatment. Of course, you get no credit for being patient if you are beaten for doing wrong. But if you suffer for doing right and are patient beneath the blows, God is pleased with you. This suffering is all part of what God has called you to. Christ, who suffered for you, is your example. Follow in his steps. He never sinned, and he never deceived anyone. He did not retaliate when he was insulted. When he suffered, he did not threaten to get even. He left his case in the hands of God, who always judges fairly.

"Don't sin by letting anger gain control over you." Don't let the sun go down while you are still angry, for anger gives a mighty foothold to the Devil.

When you feel yourself getting angry, look for the cause. Are you reacting to an evil situation that you are going to set right? Or are you responding selfishly to a personal insult? Pray that God will help you control a quick temper, channeling your feelings into effective action and conquering selfish anger through humility and repentance.

LAB note for Proverbs 14:29

(PROVERBS 14:29) (EXODUS 34:6) (EPHESIANS 5:1) (GALATIANS 5:22-23)
(1 PETER 2:19-23) (EPHESIANS 4:26)

April 29

The LORD is in this place.

Where two or three gather together because they are mine, I am there among them. ▓ I am with you always, even to the end of the age. ▓ I will personally go with you. . . . I will give you rest—everything will be fine for you.

I can never escape from your spirit! I can never get away from your presence! If I go up to heaven, you are there; if I go down to the place of the dead, you are there. If I ride the wings of the morning, if I dwell by the farthest oceans, even there your hand will guide me, and your strength will support me. I could ask the darkness to hide me and the light around me to become night—but even in darkness I cannot hide from you. To you the night shines as bright as day. ▓ "Am I a God who is only in one place?" asks the LORD. "Do they think I cannot see what they are doing? Can anyone hide from me? Am I not everywhere in all the heavens and earth?"

Will God really live on earth? Why, even the highest heavens cannot contain you. How much less this Temple I have built! ▓ The high and lofty one who inhabits eternity, the Holy One, says this: "I live in that high and holy place with those whose spirits are contrite and humble. I refresh the humble and give new courage to those with repentant hearts."

Jesus looked ahead to a new day when he would be present with his followers, not in body but through his Holy Spirit. In the body of believers (the church) the sincere agreement of two·people in prayer is powerful because Christ's Holy Spirit is with them.

LAB note for Matthew 18:19-20

(GENESIS 28:16) (MATTHEW 18:20) (MATTHEW 28:20) (EXODUS 33:14)
(PSALM 139:7-12) (JEREMIAH 23:23-24) (ISAIAH 57:15)

April 30

Keep away from anything that might take God's place in your hearts.

O my son, give me your heart. May your eyes delight in my ways of wisdom. ❧ Let heaven fill your thoughts. Do not think only about things down here on earth.

Son of man, these leaders have set up idols in their hearts. . . . Why should I let them ask me anything? ❧ Put to death the sinful, earthly things lurking within you. Have nothing to do with sexual sin, impurity, lust, and shameful desires. Don't be greedy for the good things of this life, for that is idolatry. ❧ People who long to be rich fall into temptation and are trapped by many foolish and harmful desires that plunge them into ruin and destruction. For the love of money is at the root of all kinds of evil. And some people, craving money, have wandered from the faith and pierced themselves with many sorrows. But you . . . belong to God; so run from all these evil things, and follow what is right and good. Pursue a godly life, along with faith, love, perseverance, and gentleness. ❧ Don't try to get rich by extortion or robbery. ❧ My gifts are better than the purest gold, my wages better than sterling silver!

Wherever your treasure is, there your heart and thoughts will also be. ❧ The LORD looks at a person's thoughts and intentions.

> Many things can take God's place in our life. This includes anything that substitutes for the true faith, anything that robs Christ of his full deity and humanity, any human idea that claims to be more authoritative than the Bible, or any loyalty that replaces God at the center of our life.
>
> *LAB note for 1 John 5:21*

(1 JOHN 5:21) (PROVERBS 23:26) (COLOSSIANS 3:2) (EZEKIEL 14:3) (COLOSSIANS 3:5) (1 TIMOTHY 6:9-11) (PSALM 62:10) (PROVERBS 8:19) (MATTHEW 6:21) (1 SAMUEL 16:7)

May

Only a Mother's Love

A mother's love is encouraging but not overbearing.

It is both sheltering and freeing.

A mother's love is a reflection of God's character.

It is often said that a mother's work is never done,

and that is true. A mother never forgets her child's

small victories and character-building experiences

that helped mold him or her into a mature adult.

May your heart be filled with the joy and peace

of a mother's love.

May 1

I will comfort you there as a child is comforted by its mother.

Can a mother forget her nursing child? Can she feel no love for a child she has borne? But even if that were possible, I would not forget you!

[I give] the barren woman a home, so that she becomes a happy mother. Praise the Lord! ✻ She extends a helping hand to the poor and opens her arms to the needy. ✻ She is clothed with strength and dignity, and she laughs with no fear of the future. When she speaks, her words are wise, and kindness is the rule when she gives instructions. She carefully watches all that goes on in her household and does not have to bear the consequences of laziness.

Her children stand and bless her. Her husband praises her: "There are many virtuous and capable women in the world, but you surpass them all!"

Charm is deceptive, and beauty does not last; but a woman who fears the Lord will be greatly praised. Reward her for all she has done. Let her deeds publicly declare her praise.

God will never forget you, just as a loving mother would not forget her little child. *adapted from LAB note for Isaiah 49:15*

(ISAIAH 66:13) (ISAIAH 49:15) (PSALM 113:9)
(PROVERBS 31:20) (PROVERBS 31:25-31)

May 2

Thank you for making me so wonderfully complex!

I have stilled and quieted myself, just as a small child is quiet with its mother. Yes, like a small child is my soul within me. ⚘ You have been with me from birth; from my mother's womb you have cared for me. No wonder I am always praising you! ⚘ You made all the delicate, inner parts of my body and knit me together in my mother's womb. Your workmanship is marvelous—and how well I know it. ⚘ You both precede and follow me. You place your hand of blessing on my head. Such knowledge is too wonderful for me, too great for me to know! I can never escape from your spirit! I can never get away from your presence! If I go up to heaven, you are there; if I go down to the place of the dead, you are there. If I ride the wings of the morning, if I dwell by the farthest oceans, even there your hand will guide me, and your strength will support me.

God's character goes into the creation of every person. When you feel worthless or even begin to hate yourself, remember that God's Spirit is ready and willing to work within you.   *LAB note for Psalm 139:13-14*

(PSALM 139:14) (PSALM 131:2) (PSALM 71:6)
(PSALM 139:13-14) (PSALM 139:5-10)

May 3

Keep none of the plunder.

Come out from them and separate yourselves from them, says the Lord. Don't touch their filthy things. ❊ Dear brothers and sisters, you are foreigners and aliens here. So I warn you to keep away from evil desires because they fight against your very souls. ❊ Be careful that you aren't contaminated by their sins.

We are already God's children, and we can't even imagine what we will be like when Christ returns. But we do know that when he comes we will be like him, for we will see him as he really is. And all who believe this will keep themselves pure, just as Christ is pure. ❊ For the grace of God has been revealed, bringing salvation to all people. And we are instructed to turn from godless living and sinful pleasures. We should live in this evil world with self-control, right conduct, and devotion to God, while we look forward to that wonderful event when the glory of our great God and Savior, Jesus Christ, will be revealed. He gave his life to free us from every kind of sin, to cleanse us, and to make us his very own people, totally committed to doing what is right.

Separation from the world involves more than keeping our distance from sinners; it means staying close to God. There is no way to separate ourselves totally from all sinful influences. Nevertheless, we are to resist the sin around us, without either giving up or giving in.

LAB note for 2 Corinthians 6:17

(Deuteronomy 13:17) (2 Corinthians 6:17) (1 Peter 2:11) (Jude 1:23)
(1 John 3:2-3) (Titus 2:11-14)

May 4

The LORD spread out a cloud above them as a covering and gave them a great fire to light the darkness.

The LORD is like a father to his children, tender and compassionate to those who fear him. For he understands how weak we are; he knows we are only dust.

The sun will not hurt you by day, nor the moon at night. ❧ It will be a shelter from daytime heat and a hiding place from storms or rain.

The LORD himself watches over you! The LORD stands beside you as your protective shade. The LORD keeps watch over you as you come and go, both now and forever. ❧ He found them in a desert land, in an empty, howling wasteland. He surrounded them and watched over them; he guarded them as his most precious possession. ❧ In your great mercy you did not abandon them to die in the wilderness. The pillar of cloud still led them forward by day, and the pillar of fire showed them the way through the night. You sent your good Spirit to instruct them, and you did not stop giving them bread from heaven or water for their thirst. For forty years you sustained them in the wilderness. They lacked nothing in all that time. Their clothes did not wear out, and their feet did not swell! ❧ With unfailing love you will lead this people whom you have ransomed. You will guide them in your strength to the place where your holiness dwells.

Jesus Christ is the same yesterday, today, and forever.

Seeing how God continued to be with his people shows that his patience is amazing! In spite of our repeated failings, pride, and stubbornness, he is always ready to pardon, and his Spirit is always ready to instruct.

LAB note for Nehemiah 9:16-21

(PSALM 105:39) (PSALM 103:13-14) (PSALM 121:6) (ISAIAH 4:6) (PSALM 121:5, 8) (DEUTERONOMY 32:10) (NEHEMIAH 9:19-21) (EXODUS 15:13) (HEBREWS 13:8)

May 5

Wars will break out near and far, but don't panic. Yes, these things must come, but the end won't follow immediately.

God is our refuge and strength, always ready to help in times of trouble. So we will not fear, even if earthquakes come and the mountains crumble into the sea. Let the oceans roar and foam. Let the mountains tremble as the waters surge! Go home, my people, and lock your doors! Hide until the LORD's anger against your enemies has passed. Look! The LORD is coming from heaven to punish the people of the earth for their sins. I will hide beneath the shadow of your wings until this violent storm is past. Your real life is hidden with Christ in God.

Happy are those who fear the LORD. Yes, happy are those who delight in doing what he commands. Such people will not be overcome by evil circumstances. Those who are righteous will be long remembered. They do not fear bad news; they confidently trust the LORD to care for them.

I have told you all this so that you may have peace in me. Here on earth you will have many trials and sorrows. But take heart, because I have overcome the world.

It seems impossible to consider the end of the world without becoming consumed by fear, but the Bible is clear—God is our refuge even in the midst of total destruction. He is not merely a temporary retreat; he is our eternal refuge and can provide strength in any circumstance.

LAB note for Psalm 46:1-3

(MATTHEW 24:6) (PSALM 46:1-3) (ISAIAH 26:20-21) (PSALM 57:1)
(COLOSSIANS 3:3) (PSALM 112:1, 6-7) (JOHN 16:33)

May 6

Come to your senses and stop sinning.

You are all children of the light and of the day; we don't belong to darkness and night. So be on your guard, not asleep like the others. Stay alert and be sober.

Another reason for right living is that you know how late it is; time is running out. Wake up, for the coming of our salvation is nearer now than when we first believed. The night is almost gone; the day of salvation will soon be here. So don't live in darkness. Get rid of your evil deeds. Shed them like dirty clothes. Clothe yourselves with the armor of right living, as those who live in the light. ❧ Use every piece of God's armor to resist the enemy in the time of evil, so that after the battle you will still be standing firm. ❧ Turn from your sins! Don't let them destroy you! Put all your rebellion behind you, and get for yourselves a new heart and a new spirit. ❧ Get rid of all the filth and evil in your lives, and humbly accept the message God has planted in your hearts, for it is strong enough to save your souls.

Now, dear children, continue to live in fellowship with Christ so that when he returns, you will be full of courage and not shrink back from him in shame.

If we renounce our life's direction of sin and rebellion and turn to God, he will give us a new direction, a new love, and a new power to change. You can begin by faith, trusting in God's power to change your heart and mind. Then determine to live each day with him in control.

LAB note for Ezekiel 18:30-32

(1 CORINTHIANS 15:34) (1 THESSALONIANS 5:5-6) (ROMANS 13:11-12)
(EPHESIANS 6:13) (EZEKIEL 18:30-31) (JAMES 1:21) (1 JOHN 2:28)

May 7

Their insults have broken my heart.

He's just a carpenter's son. ❧ Nazareth! . . . Can anything good come from there? ❧ He can cast out demons because he is empowered by the prince of demons. ❧ We know Jesus is a sinner. ❧ He's nothing but a fraud, deceiving the people. ❧ Blasphemy! This man talks like he is God! ❧ I, the Son of Man, feast and drink, and you say, "He's a glutton and a drunkard, and a friend of the worst sort of sinners!"

God is pleased with you when, for the sake of your conscience, you patiently endure unfair treatment. Of course, you get no credit for being patient if you are beaten for doing wrong. But if you suffer for doing right and are patient beneath the blows, God is pleased with you. This suffering is all part of what God has called you to. Christ, who suffered for you, is your example. Follow in his steps. He never sinned, and he never deceived anyone. He did not retaliate when he was insulted. When he suffered, he did not threaten to get even. He left his case in the hands of God, who always judges fairly. ❧ Be happy if you are insulted for being a Christian, for then the glorious Spirit of God will come upon you.

The student shares the teacher's fate. The servant shares the master's fate.

Good is sometimes labeled evil. If Jesus, who is perfect, was called evil, his followers should expect that similar accusations will be directed at them. But those who endure will be vindicated.   *LAB note for Matthew 10:25*

(PSALM 69:20) (MATTHEW 13:55) (JOHN 1:46) (MATTHEW 9:34) (JOHN 9:24) (JOHN 7:12) (MATTHEW 9:3) (MATTHEW 11:19) (1 PETER 2:19-23) (1 PETER 4:14) (MATTHEW 10:25)

May 8

I want men to pray with holy hands lifted up to God, free from anger and controversy.

True worshipers will worship the Father in spirit and in truth. The Father is looking for anyone who will worship him that way. For God is Spirit, so those who worship him must worship in spirit and in truth. ❧ When you call, the LORD will answer. "Yes, I am here." ❧ When you are praying, first forgive anyone you are holding a grudge against, so that your Father in heaven will forgive your sins, too.

It is impossible to please God without faith. Anyone who wants to come to him must believe that there is a God and that he rewards those who sincerely seek him. ❧ When you ask him, be sure that you really expect him to answer, for a doubtful mind is as unsettled as a wave of the sea that is driven and tossed by the wind. People like that should not expect to receive anything from the Lord.

If I had not confessed the sin in my heart, my Lord would not have listened. ❧ My dear children, I am writing this to you so that you will not sin. But if you do sin, there is someone to plead for you before the Father. He is Jesus Christ, the one who pleases God completely.

Besides displeasing God, anger and controversy make prayer difficult. That is why Jesus said that we should interrupt our prayers, if necessary, to make peace with others. God wants us to obey him immediately and thoroughly. *LAB note for 1 Timothy 2:8*

(1 TIMOTHY 2:8) (JOHN 4:23-24) (ISAIAH 58:9) (MARK 11:25) (HEBREWS 11:6) (JAMES 1:6-7) (PSALM 66:18) (1 JOHN 2:1)

May 9

My heart beats wildly, my strength fails.

O God, listen to my cry! Hear my prayer! From the ends of the earth, I will cry to you for help, for my heart is overwhelmed. Lead me to the towering rock of safety.

"My gracious favor is all you need. My power works best in your weakness." So now I am glad to boast about my weaknesses, so that the power of Christ may work through me. Since I know it is all for Christ's good, I am quite content with my weaknesses and with insults, hardships, persecutions, and calamities. For when I am weak, then I am strong.

When he [Peter] looked around at the high waves, he was terrified and began to sink. "Save me, Lord!" he shouted. Instantly Jesus reached out his hand and grabbed him. "You don't have much faith," Jesus said. "Why did you doubt me?" ❋ If you fail under pressure, your strength is not very great. ❋ He gives power to those who are tired and worn out; he offers strength to the weak. ❋ The eternal God is your refuge, and his everlasting arms are under you. ❋ We also pray that you will be strengthened with his glorious power so that you will have all the patience and endurance you need.

Even the strongest people get tired at times, but God's power and strength never diminish. He is never too tired or too busy to help and listen. When you feel all of life crushing you and you cannot go another step, remember that you can call upon God to renew your strength.

LAB note for Isaiah 40:29-31

(Psalm 38:10) (Psalm 61:1-2) (2 Corinthians 12:9-10) (Matthew 14:30-31) (Proverbs 24:10) (Isaiah 40:29) (Deuteronomy 33:27) (Colossians 1:11)

May 10

I will bless the LORD who guides me.

Wonderful Counselor. ❧ Good advice and success belong to me. Insight and strength are mine. ❧ Your word is a lamp for my feet and a light for my path. ❧ Trust in the LORD with all your heart; do not depend on your own understanding. Seek his will in all you do, and he will direct your paths.

I know, LORD, that a person's life is not his own. No one is able to plan his own course. ❧ You will hear a voice say, "This is the way; turn around and walk here." ❧ Commit your work to the LORD, and then your plans will succeed. ❧ How can we understand the road we travel? It is the LORD who directs our steps.

You will keep on guiding me with your counsel, leading me to a glorious destiny. ❧ Even when I walk through the dark valley of death, I will not be afraid, for you are close beside me. Your rod and your staff protect and comfort me. ❧ For that is what God is like. He is our God forever and ever, and he will be our guide until we die.

We must not be wise in our own eyes but be willing to listen to and be corrected by God's Word and wise counselors. Bring your decisions to God in prayer; use the Bible as your guide; and then follow God's leading. He will direct your paths by both guiding and protecting you.

LAB note for Proverbs 3:5-6

(PSALM 16:7) (ISAIAH 9:6) (PROVERBS 8:14) (PSALM 119:105) (PROVERBS 3:5-6)
(JEREMIAH 10:23) (ISAIAH 30:21) (PROVERBS 16:3) (PROVERBS 20:24)
(PSALM 73:24) (PSALM 23:4) (PSALM 48:14)

May 11

I am the LORD your God. . . . Follow my laws, pay attention to my instructions.

Now you must be holy in everything you do, just as God—who chose you to be his children—is holy. ※ Those who say they live in God should live their lives as Christ did.

It is not that we think we can do anything of lasting value by ourselves. Our only power and success come from God. ※ Remain in me, and I will remain in you. For a branch cannot produce fruit if it is severed from the vine, and you cannot be fruitful apart from me.

Be even more careful to put into action God's saving work in your lives, obeying God with deep reverence and fear. For God is working in you, giving you the desire to obey him and the power to do what pleases him. ※ May the God of peace, who brought again from the dead our Lord Jesus, equip you with all you need for doing his will. May he produce in you, through the power of Jesus Christ, all that is pleasing to him. Jesus is the great Shepherd of the sheep by an everlasting covenant, signed with his blood.

He is a God of mercy and justice who cares personally for each of his followers. Our holy God expects us to imitate him by following his high moral standards and by being both merciful and just.

LAB note for 1 Peter 1:15

(EZEKIEL 20:19) (1 PETER 1:15) (1 JOHN 2:6) (2 CORINTHIANS 3:5) (JOHN 15:4)
(PHILIPPIANS 2:12-13) (HEBREWS 13:20-21)

May 12

The Father has life in himself, and he has granted his Son to have life in himself.

Christ Jesus, our Savior . . . broke the power of death and showed us the way to everlasting life through the Good News. ❋ I am the resurrection and the life. Those who believe in me, even though they die like everyone else, will live again. ❋ I will live again, and you will, too. ❋ We will share in all that belongs to Christ. ❋ "The first man, Adam, became a living person." But the last Adam—that is, Christ—is a life-giving Spirit. But let me tell you a wonderful secret God has revealed to us. Not all of us will die, but we will all be transformed. It will happen in a moment, in the blinking of an eye, when the last trumpet is blown. For when the trumpet sounds, the Christians who have died will be raised with transformed bodies. And then we who are living will be transformed so that we will never die. For our perishable earthly bodies must be transformed into heavenly bodies that will never die.

Holy, holy, holy is the Lord God Almighty—the one who always was, who is, and who is still to come . . . the one who lives forever and ever. ❋ The blessed and only almighty God, the King of kings and Lord of lords. ❋ Glory and honor to God forever and ever. He is the eternal King, the unseen one who never dies; he alone is God. Amen.

God is the source and Creator of life, for there is no life apart from God, here or hereafter. The life in us is a gift from him. Because Jesus is eternally existent with God, the Creator, he, too, is "the life" through whom we may live eternally. *LAB note for John 5:26*

(JOHN 5:26) (2 TIMOTHY 1:10) (JOHN 11:25) (JOHN 14:19) (HEBREWS 3:14)
(1 CORINTHIANS 15:45, 51-53) (REVELATION 4:8-9) (1 TIMOTHY 6:15)
(1 TIMOTHY 1:17)

May 13

Let us not become conceited, or irritate one another, or be jealous of one another.

Gideon replied, ". . . I have one request. Each of you can give me an earring out of the treasures you collected from your fallen enemies." (The enemies, being Ishmaelites, all wore gold earrings.) "Gladly!" they replied. They spread out a cloak, and each one threw in a gold earring he had gathered. Gideon made a sacred ephod from the gold and put it in Ophrah, his hometown. But soon all the Israelites prostituted themselves by worshiping it, and it became a trap for Gideon and his family.

Are you seeking great things for yourself? Don't do it! ▨ I have received wonderful revelations from God. But to keep me from getting puffed up, I was given a thorn in my flesh, a messenger from Satan to torment me and keep me from getting proud. Now I am glad to boast about my weaknesses, so that the power of Christ may work through me.

Don't be selfish; don't live to make a good impression on others. Be humble, thinking of others as better than yourself. ▨ Love is patient and kind. Love is not jealous or boastful or proud or rude. Love does not demand its own way.

Take my yoke upon you. Let me teach you. . . . For my yoke fits perfectly.

Everyone needs a certain amount of approval from others. But those who go out of their way to secure honors or to win popularity with a lot of people become conceited. Those who look to God for approval won't need to envy others. *LAB note for Galatians 5:26*

(GALATIANS 5:26) (JUDGES 8:23-25, 27) (JEREMIAH 45:5) (2 CORINTHIANS 12:7, 9) (PHILIPPIANS 2:3) (1 CORINTHIANS 13:4-5) (MATTHEW 11:29-30)

May 14

Keep a close watch on yourself and on your teaching.

All athletes practice strict self-control. They do it to win a prize that will fade away, but we do it for an eternal prize. So I run straight to the goal with purpose in every step. I am not like a boxer who misses his punches. I discipline my body like an athlete, training it to do what it should. Otherwise, I fear that after preaching to others I myself might be disqualified.

Put on all of God's armor so that you will be able to stand firm against all strategies and tricks of the Devil. For we are not fighting against people made of flesh and blood, but against the evil rulers and the authorities of the unseen world, against those mighty powers of darkness who rule this world, and against wicked spirits in the heavenly realms.

Those who belong to Christ Jesus have nailed their passions and desires of their sinful nature to his cross and crucified them there. If we are living now by the Holy Spirit, let us follow the Holy Spirit's leading in every part of our lives.

We must be on constant guard against falling into sin, which can so easily destroy us. Yet we must watch what we believe just as closely. Wrong beliefs can quickly lead us into sin and heresy. We should be on guard against those who would persuade us that how we live is more important than what we believe.   *LAB note for 1 Timothy 4:16*

(1 TIMOTHY 4:16) (1 CORINTHIANS 9:25-27) (EPHESIANS 6:11-12)
(GALATIANS 5:24-25)

May 15

The Holy Spirit helps us in our distress.

The Counselor . . . the Holy Spirit. ※ Don't you know that your body is the temple of the Holy Spirit, who lives in you and was given to you by God? ※ God is working in you.

The Holy Spirit helps us in our distress. For we don't even know what we should pray for, nor how we should pray. But the Holy Spirit prays for us with groanings that cannot be expressed in words. And the Father who knows all hearts knows what the Spirit is saying, for the Spirit pleads for us believers in harmony with God's own will.

He knows we are only dust. ※ He will not crush those who are weak or quench the smallest hope.

Though the spirit is willing enough, the body is weak!

The LORD is my shepherd; I have everything I need. He lets me rest in green meadows; he leads me beside peaceful streams. He renews my strength. He guides me along right paths, bringing honor to his name. Even when I walk through the dark valley of death, I will not be afraid, for you are close beside me. Your rod and your staff protect and comfort me.

As a believer, you are not left to your own resources to cope with problems. Even when you don't know the right words to pray, the Holy Spirit prays with and for you, and God answers. So don't be afraid to ask the Holy Spirit to intercede for you "in harmony with God's own will."

LAB note for Romans 8:26-27

(ROMANS 8:26) (JOHN 14:26) (1 CORINTHIANS 6:19) (PHILIPPIANS 2:13) (ROMANS 8:26-27) (PSALM 103:14) (ISAIAH 42:3) (MATTHEW 26:41) (PSALM 23:1-4)

May 16

When they call on me, I will answer; I will be with them in trouble. I will rescue them and honor them.

Jabez . . . prayed to the God of Israel, "Oh, that you would bless me and extend my lands! Please be with me in all that I do, and keep me from all trouble and pain!" And God granted him his request. God appeared to Solomon in a dream and said, "What do you want? Ask, and I will give it to you!" Solomon replied to God, "You have been so faithful and kind to my father, David, and now you have made me king in his place. Give me wisdom and knowledge to rule them properly, for who is able to govern this great nation of yours?" God gave Solomon great wisdom and understanding, and knowledge too vast to be measured. In fact, his wisdom exceeded that of all the wise men of the East and the wise men of Egypt.

Asa deployed his armies for battle. . . . Then Asa cried out to the LORD his God, "O LORD, no one but you can help the powerless against the mighty! Help us, O LORD our God, for we trust in you alone. It is in your name that we have come against this vast horde. O LORD, you are our God; do not let mere men prevail against you!" So the LORD defeated the Ethiopians in the presence of Asa and the army of Judah, and the enemy fled.

You answer our prayers, and to you all people will come.

Jabez is remembered for a prayer request rather than a heroic act. When we pray for God's blessing, we should also ask him to take his rightful position as Lord over our work, our family time, and our recreation. Obeying him in daily responsibilities is heroic living.

LAB note for 1 Chronicles 4:9-10

(PSALM 91:15) (1 CHRONICLES 4:9-10) (2 CHRONICLES 1:7-8, 10) (1 KINGS 4:29-30) (2 CHRONICLES 14:10-12) (PSALM 65:2)

May 17

Clothe yourselves with the armor of right living.

Let the Lord Jesus Christ take control of you. ❧ I have discarded everything else, counting it all as garbage, so that I may have Christ and become one with him. I no longer count on my own goodness or my ability to obey God's law, but I trust Christ to save me. For God's way of making us right with himself depends on faith. ❧ We are made right in God's sight when we trust in Jesus Christ to take away our sins. And we all can be saved in this same way, no matter who we are or what we have done.

He has dressed me with the clothing of salvation and draped me in a robe of righteousness. ❧ I will tell everyone that you alone are just and good.

For though your hearts were once full of darkness, now you are full of light from the Lord, and your behavior should show it! Take no part in the worthless deeds of evil and darkness; instead, rebuke and expose them. But when the light shines on them, it becomes clear how evil these things are. And where your light shines, it will expose their evil deeds. This is why it is said, "Awake, O sleeper, rise up from the dead, and Christ will give you light."

Attitudes are as important as actions. Just as hatred leads to murder, so jealousy leads to strife and lust to adultery. When Christ returns, he wants to find his people clean on the inside as well as on the outside. *LAB note for Romans 13:12-14*

(ROMANS 13:12) (ROMANS 13:14) (PHILIPPIANS 3:8-9) (ROMANS 3:22)
(ISAIAH 61:10) (PSALM 71:16) (EPHESIANS 5:8, 11, 13-15)

May 18

Your goodness is so great! You have stored up great blessings for those who honor you.

Since the world began, no ear has heard, and no eye has seen a God like you, who works for those who wait for him! ❧ No eye has seen, no ear has heard, and no mind has imagined what God has prepared for those who love him. But we know these things because God has revealed them to us by his Spirit, and his Spirit searches out everything and shows us even God's deep secrets. ❧ You will show me the way of life, granting me the joy of your presence and the pleasures of living with you forever.

How precious is your unfailing love, O God! All humanity finds shelter in the shadow of your wings. You feed them from the abundance of your own house, letting them drink from your rivers of delight.

Spend your time and energy in training yourself for spiritual fitness. Physical exercise has some value, but spiritual exercise is much more important, for it promises a reward in both this life and the next.

We cannot imagine all that God has in store for us, both in this life and for eternity. Knowing the wonderful and eternal future that awaits us gives us hope and courage to press on in this life, to endure hardship, and to avoid giving in to temptation. The best is yet to come.

LAB note for 1 Corinthians 2:9

(PSALM 31:19) (ISAIAH 64:4) (1 CORINTHIANS 2:9-10) (PSALM 16:11) (PSALM 36:7-8) (1 TIMOTHY 4:7-8)

May 19

The Son of God, whose eyes are bright like flames of fire.

The human heart is most deceitful and desperately wicked. Who really knows how bad it is? But I know! I, the LORD, search all hearts and examine secret motives. I give all people their due rewards, according to what their actions deserve. ❧ You spread out our sins before you—our secret sins—and you see them all. ❧ The Lord turned and looked at Peter. . . . And Peter left the courtyard, crying bitterly.

Jesus didn't trust them, because he knew what people were really like. No one needed to tell him about human nature. ❧ He knows we are only dust. ❧ He will not crush those who are weak or quench the smallest hope.

The Lord knows those who are his. ❧ I am the good shepherd; I know my own sheep, and they know me. My sheep recognize my voice; I know them, and they follow me. I give them eternal life, and they will never perish. No one will snatch them away from me, for my Father has given them to me, and he is more powerful than anyone else. So no one can take them from me.

God makes it clear why we sin—it's a matter of the heart. Our heart is inclined toward sin from the time we are born. But we can still choose whether or not to continue in sin. We can ask God to help us resist temptation when it comes. *LAB note for Jeremiah 17:9-10*

(REVELATION 2:18) (JEREMIAH 17:9-10) (PSALM 90:8) (LUKE 22:61-62) (JOHN 2:24-25) (PSALM 103:14) (ISAIAH 42:3) (2 TIMOTHY 2:19) (JOHN 10:14, 27-29)

May 20

Jesus is the great Shepherd of the sheep.

The head Shepherd. ✺ I am the good shepherd; I know my own sheep, and they know me. My sheep recognize my voice; I know them, and they follow me. I give them eternal life, and they will never perish. No one will snatch them away from me. I have other sheep, too, that are not in this sheepfold. I must bring them also, and they will listen to my voice.

The LORD is my shepherd; I have everything I need. He lets me rest in green meadows; he leads me beside peaceful streams. He renews my strength. He guides me along right paths, bringing honor to his name.

All of us have strayed away like sheep. We have left God's paths to follow our own. Yet the LORD laid on him the guilt and sins of us all. ✺ I am the good shepherd. The good shepherd lays down his life for the sheep. ✺ I will search for my lost ones who strayed away, and I will bring them safely home again. I will bind up the injured and strengthen the weak. ✺ Once you were wandering like lost sheep. But now you have turned to your Shepherd, the Guardian of your souls.

A hired hand tends the sheep for money, while the shepherd does it out of love. The shepherd owns the sheep and is committed to them. Jesus is not merely doing a job; he is committed to love us and even lay down his life for us.   *LAB note for John 10:11-12*

(HEBREWS 13:20) (1 PETER 5:4) (JOHN 10:14, 27-28, 16) (PSALM 23:1-3)
(ISAIAH 53:6) (JOHN 10:11) (EZEKIEL 34:16) (1 PETER 2:25)

May 21

The city has no need of sun or moon, for the glory of God illuminates the city, and the Lamb is its light.

A light from heaven brighter than the sun shone down on me and my companions. "Who are you, sir?" I asked. And the Lord replied, "I am Jesus, the one you are persecuting." ▓ Jesus took Peter and the two brothers, James and John, and led them up a high mountain. As the men watched, Jesus' appearance changed so that his face shone like the sun, and his clothing beame dazzling white. ▓ No longer will you need the sun or moon to give you light, for the LORD your God will be your everlasting light, and he will be your glory. The sun will never set; the moon will not go down. For the LORD will be your everlasting light. Your days of mourning will come to an end.

After you have suffered a little while, he will restore, support, and strengthen you, and he will place you on a firm foundation. All power is his forever and ever. ▓ So be truly glad! There is wonderful joy ahead, even though it is necessary for you to endure many trials for a while.

The Transfiguration was a vision, a brief glimpse of the true glory of the King. This was a special revelation of Jesus' divinity to three of the disciples, and it was God's divine affirmation of everything Jesus had done and was about to do. *LAB note for Matthew 17:1ff.*

(REVELATION 21:23) (ACTS 26:13, 15) (MATTHEW 17:1-2) (ISAIAH 60:19-20) (1 PETER 5:10-11) (1 PETER 1:6)

May 22

The LORD is good. When trouble comes, he is a strong refuge.
And he knows everyone who trusts in him.

Give thanks to the LORD Almighty, for the LORD is good. His
faithful love endures forever! ❧ God is our refuge and strength,
always ready to help in times of trouble. ❧ This I declare of the
LORD: He alone is my refuge, my place of safety; he is my God, and
I am trusting him. ❧ How blessed you are, O Israel! Who else is like
you, a people saved by the LORD? He is your protecting shield and
your triumphant sword! ❧ As for God, his way is perfect. All the
LORD's promises prove true. He is a shield for all who look to him
for protection. For who is God except the LORD?

The person who loves God is the one God knows and cares for.
❧ God's truth stands firm like a foundation stone with this
inscription: "The Lord knows those who are his," and "Those who
claim they belong to the Lord must turn away from all wickedness."
❧ The LORD watches over the path of the godly, but the path of the
wicked leads to destruction. ❧ You have found favor with me, and
you are my friend.

To people who refuse to believe, God's punishment is like an
angry fire. To those who love him, his mercy is a refuge, providing for all
their needs without diminishing his supply. The relationship we have with
God is up to us. What kind of relationship will you choose?

LAB note for Nahum 1:7

(NAHUM 1:7) (JEREMIAH 33:11) (PSALM 46:1) (PSALM 91:2) (DEUTERONOMY 33:29)
(2 SAMUEL 22:31-32) (1 CORINTHIANS 8:3) (2 TIMOTHY 2:19) (PSALM 1:6)
(EXODUS 33:17)

May 23

I want you to be free from the concerns of this life.

Give all your worries and cares to God, for he cares about what happens to you. ❋ The eyes of the LORD search the whole earth in order to strengthen those whose hearts are fully committed to him.

Taste and see that the LORD is good. Oh, the joys of those who trust in him! Even strong young lions sometimes go hungry, but those who trust in the LORD will never lack any good thing. ❋ Don't worry about everyday life—whether you have enough food, drink, and clothes. Doesn't life consist of more than food and clothing? Look at the birds. They don't need to plant or harvest or put food in barns because your heavenly Father feeds them. And you are far more valuable to him than they are. ❋ Don't worry about anything; instead, pray about everything. Tell God what you need, and thank him for all he has done. If you do this, you will experience God's peace, which is far more wonderful than the human mind can understand. His peace will guard your hearts and minds as you live in Christ Jesus.

How many ill effects of worry are you experiencing? It damages your health, disrupts your productivity, negatively affects the way you treat others, and reduces your ability to trust in God. Here is the difference between worry and genuine concern—worry immobilizes, but concern moves you to action. *LAB note for Matthew 6:25*

(1 CORINTHIANS 7:32) (1 PETER 5:7) (2 CHRONICLES 16:9) (PSALM 34:8, 10) (MATTHEW 6:25-26) (PHILIPPIANS 4:6-7)

May 24

Continue to live in fellowship with Christ.

A doubtful mind is as unsettled as a wave of the sea that is driven and tossed by the wind. People like that should not expect to receive anything from the Lord. They can't make up their minds. They waver back and forth in everything they do.

I am shocked that you are turning away so soon from God, who in his love and mercy called you to share the eternal life he gives through Christ. You are already following a different way.

If you are trying to make yourselves right with God by keeping the law, you have been cut off from Christ! You have fallen away from God's grace. You were getting along so well. Who has interfered with you to hold you back from following the truth?

Remain in me, and I will remain in you. For a branch cannot produce fruit if it is severed from the vine, and you cannot be fruitful apart from me. But if you stay joined to me and my words remain in you, you may ask any request you like, and it will be granted! ▧ For all of God's promises have been fulfilled in him. That is why we say "Amen" when we give glory to God through Christ.

Because true faith always results in good deeds, those who claim to have faith and who consistently do what is right are true believers. Good deeds cannot produce salvation, but they are necessary proof that true faith is actually present. *LAB note for 1 John 2:28-29*

(1 JOHN 2:28) (JAMES 1:6-8) (GALATIANS 1:6) (GALATIANS 5:4, 7) (JOHN 15:4, 7) (2 CORINTHIANS 1:20)

May 25

I am God Almighty; serve me faithfully and live a blameless life.

I [Paul] don't mean to say that I have already achieved these things or that I have already reached perfection! But I keep working toward that day when I will finally be all that Christ Jesus saved me for and wants me to be. No, dear brothers and sisters, I am still not all I should be, but I am focusing all my energies on this one thing: Forgetting the past and looking forward to what lies ahead, I strain to reach the end of the race and receive the prize for which God, through Christ Jesus, is calling us up to heaven.

Grow in the special favor and knowledge of our Lord and Savior Jesus Christ. ▨ All of us have had that veil removed so that we can be mirrors that brightly reflect the glory of the Lord. And as the Spirit of the Lord works within us, we become more and more like him and reflect his glory even more. ▨ The way of the righteous is like the first gleam of dawn, which shines ever brighter until the full light of day.

Jesus . . . looked up to heaven and said, ". . . I'm not asking you to take them out of the world, but to keep them safe from the evil one. I in them and you in me, all being perfected into one."

We are to obey the Lord in every respect because he is God—that is reason enough. If you don't think the benefits of obedience are worth it, consider who God is—the only one with the power and ability to meet your every need. *LAB note for Genesis 17:1*

(Genesis 17:1) (Philippians 3:12-14) (2 Peter 3:18) (2 Corinthians 3:18) (Proverbs 4:18) (John 17:1, 15, 23)

May 26

Do not bring sorrow to God's Holy Spirit by the way you live.

Love . . . given to you by the Holy Spirit. ❧ The Counselor . . . the Holy Spirit. ❧ In all their suffering he also suffered, and he personally rescued them. In his love and mercy he redeemed them. He lifted them up and carried them through all the years.

God has given us his Spirit as proof that we live in him and he in us. ❧ He identified you as his own by giving you the Holy Spirit, whom he promised long ago. The Spirit is God's guarantee that he will give us everything he promised and that he has purchased us to be his own people. This is just one more reason for us to praise our glorious God. ❧ I advise you to live according to your new life in the Holy Spirit. Then you won't be doing what your sinful nature craves. The old sinful nature loves to do evil, which is just opposite from what the Holy Spirit wants. And the Spirit gives us desires that are opposite from what the sinful nature desires.

The Holy Spirit helps us in our distress.

Are you bringing sorrow to God—or pleasing him with your attitudes and actions? Act in love toward your brothers and sisters in Christ, just as Christ acted in love by sending his Son to die for your sins.

LAB note for Ephesians 4:28-32

(EPHESIANS 4:30) (ROMANS 15:30) (JOHN 14:26) (ISAIAH 63:9) (1 JOHN 4:13)
(EPHESIANS 1:13-14) (GALATIANS 5:16-17) (ROMANS 8:26)

May 27

When you obey me, you should say, "We are not worthy of praise. We are servants who have simply done our duty."

Can we boast, then, that we have done anything to be accepted by God? No, because our acquittal is not based on our good deeds. It is based on our faith. ❧ What makes you better than anyone else? What do you have that God hasn't given you? And if all you have is from God, why boast as though you have accomplished something on your own? ❧ God saved you by his special favor when you believed. And you can't take credit for this; it is a gift from God. Salvation is not a reward for the good things we have done, so none of us can boast about it. For we are God's masterpiece. He has created us anew in Christ Jesus, so that we can do the good things he planned for us long ago.

But whatever I am now, it is all because God poured out his special favor on me. ❧ For everything comes from him; everything exists by his power and is intended for his glory. ❧ Everything we have has come from you, and we give you only what you have already given us!

Do you sometimes feel you deserve extra credit for serving God? Obedience is not something extra we do; it is our duty. Jesus is not suggesting our service is meaningless or useless, nor is he advocating doing away with rewards. He is attacking unwarranted self-esteem and spiritual pride.   *LAB note for Luke 17:7-10*

(Luke 17:10) (Romans 3:27) (1 Corinthians 4:7) (Ephesians 2:8-10)
(1 Corinthians 15:10) (Romans 11:36) (1 Chronicles 29:14)

May 28

Forgive all my sins.

"Come now, let us argue this out," says the LORD. "No matter how deep the stain of your sins, I can remove it. I can make you as clean as freshly fallen snow. Even if you are stained as red as crimson, I can make you as white as wool."

Take heart, son! Your sins are forgiven. ❧ I—yes, I alone—am the one who blots out your sins for my own sake and will never think of them again.

He is so rich in kindness that he purchased our freedom through the blood of his Son, and our sins are forgiven. ❧ He saved us, not because of the good things we did, but because of his mercy. He washed away our sins and gave us a new life through the Holy Spirit. He generously poured out the Spirit upon us because of what Jesus Christ our Savior did. ❧ He forgave all our sins. He canceled the record that contained the charges against us. He took it and destroyed it by nailing it to Christ's cross.

Praise the LORD, I tell myself. . . . He forgives all my sins.

The stain of sin seems permanent, but God can remove that stain from our life. We don't have to go through life permanently soiled. God's Word assures us that if we are willing and obedient, Christ will forgive and remove our most indelible stains. *LAB note for Isaiah 1:18*

(PSALM 25:18) (ISAIAH 1:18) (MATTHEW 9:2) (ISAIAH 43:25) (EPHESIANS 1:7) (TITUS 3:5-6) (COLOSSIANS 2:13-14) (PSALM 103:2-3)

May 29

This younger son packed all his belongings and took a trip to a distant land, and there he wasted all his money on wild living.

There was a time when some of you were just like that, but now your sins have been washed away, and you have been set apart for God. You have been made right with God because of what the Lord Jesus Christ and the Spirit of our God have done for you. ▓ All of us used to live that way, following the passions and desires of our evil nature. We were born with an evil nature, and we were under God's anger just like everyone else. But God is so rich in mercy, and he loved us so very much, that even while we were dead because of our sins, he gave us life when he raised Christ from the dead. (It is only by God's special favor that you have been saved!) For he raised us from the dead along with Christ, and we are seated with him in the heavenly realms—all because we are one with Christ Jesus.

This is real love. It is not that we loved God, but that he loved us and sent his Son as a sacrifice to take away our sins. ▓ God showed his great love for us by sending Christ to die for us while we were still sinners. For since we were restored to friendship with God by the death of his Son while we were still his enemies, we will certainly be delivered from eternal punishment by his life.

Nothing sinful or evil can exist in God's presence. He is absolute goodness. He cannot overlook, condone, or excuse sin as though it never happened. He loves us, but his love does not make him morally lax. If we trust in Christ, however, we will be acquitted by his atoning sacrifice.

LAB note for 1 John 4:10

(LUKE 15:13) (1 CORINTHIANS 6:11) (EPHESIANS 2:3-6)
(1 JOHN 4:10) (ROMANS 5:8, 10)

May 30

He returned home to his father. And while he was still a long distance away, his father saw him coming. Filled with love and compassion, he ran to his son, embraced him, and kissed him.

The LORD is merciful and gracious; he is slow to get angry and full of unfailing love. He will not constantly accuse us, nor remain angry forever. He has not punished us for all our sins, nor does he deal with us as we deserve. For his unfailing love toward those who fear him is as great as the height of the heavens above the earth. He has removed our rebellious acts as far away from us as the east is from the west. The LORD is like a father to his children, tender and compassionate to those who fear him.

So you should not be like cowering, fearful slaves. You should behave instead like God's very own children, adopted into his family—calling him "Father, dear Father." For his Holy Spirit speaks to us deep in our hearts and tells us that we are God's children. ▨ Now you belong to Christ Jesus. Though you once were far away from God, now you have been brought near to him because of the blood of Christ. So now you Gentiles are no longer strangers and foreigners. You are citizens along with all of God's holy people. You are members of God's family.

We are fragile, but God's care is eternal. When God examines our lives, he remembers our human condition. But our weakness should never be used as a justification for sin. His mercy takes everything into account. God will deal with you compassionately. Trust him.

LAB note for Psalm 103:13-14

(LUKE 15:20) (PSALM 103:8-13) (ROMANS 8:15-16) (EPHESIANS 2:13, 19)

May 31

Remember, the Lord forgave you, so you must forgive others.

Then Jesus told him this story: "A man loaned money to two people—five hundred pieces of silver to one and fifty pieces to the other. But neither of them could repay him, so he kindly forgave them both, canceling their debts." ✳ I forgave you that tremendous debt because you pleaded with me. Shouldn't you have mercy on your fellow servant, just as I had mercy on you?

But when you are praying, first forgive anyone you are holding a grudge against, so that your Father in heaven will forgive your sins, too. ✳ Since God chose you to be the holy people whom he loves, you must clothe yourselves with tenderhearted mercy, kindness, humility, gentleness, and patience. You must make allowance for each other's faults and forgive the person who offends you.

"Lord, how often should I forgive someone who sins against me? Seven times?" "No!" Jesus replied, "seventy times seven!"

The most important piece of clothing you must wear is love. ✳ Oh, how kind and gracious the Lord was! He filled me completely with faith and the love of Christ Jesus.

The rabbis taught that people should forgive those who offend them—but only three times. But Jesus said, "Seventy times seven," meaning we shouldn't even keep track of how many times we forgive someone. We should always forgive those who are truly repentant, no matter how many times they ask. *LAB note for Matthew 18:22*

(COLOSSIANS 3:13) (LUKE 7:41-42) (MATTHEW 18:32-33) (MARK 11:25)
(COLOSSIANS 3:12-13) (MATTHEW 18:21-22) (COLOSSIANS 3:14)
(1 TIMOTHY 1:14)

June

A Man among Men

Bike rides and baseball games, tree houses
and camping trips
Lighthearted fun times and spontaneous
teaching moments
One can never overestimate the importance
of a father's involvement.

A father is a wonderful balance of security
and patience, wisdom and integrity, encouragement
and inspiration. He has the unique and essential
role of reflecting the heavenly Father's unconditional
love for his children. May you be blessed by
a fatherly man in your life.

June 1

I will be your Father, and you will be my sons and daughters, says the Lord Almighty.

See how very much our heavenly Father loves us, for he allows us to be called his children, and we really are! But the people who belong to this world don't know God, so they don't understand that we are his children. ❦ Everyone who believes that Jesus is the Christ is a child of God. And everyone who loves the Father loves his children, too. ❦ And because you . . . have become his children, God has sent the Spirit of his Son into your hearts, and now you can call God your dear Father. ❦ Now all of us . . . may come to the Father through the same Holy Spirit because of what Christ has done for us. ❦ He said to Jesus: "You are my Son. Today I have become your Father." And again God said, "I will be his Father, and he will be my Son."

As God's heirs, we can claim what he has provided for us—our full identity as his children. *LAB note for Galatians 4:6*

(2 CORINTHIANS 6:18) (1 JOHN 3:1) (1 JOHN 5:1) (GALATIANS 4:6)
(EPHESIANS 2:18) (HEBREWS 1:5)

June 2

Now a word to you fathers. Don't make your children angry by the way you treat them. Rather, bring them up with the discipline and instruction approved by the Lord.

My children, listen to me. Listen to your father's instruction. Pay attention and grow wise, for I am giving you good guidance. Don't turn away from my teaching. For I, too, was once my father's son, tenderly loved by my mother as an only child.

My father told me, Take my words to heart. Follow my instructions and you will live. Learn to be wise, and develop good judgment. Don't forget or turn away from my words. ❧ Let those who are wise listen to these proverbs and become even wiser. And let those who understand receive guidance. ❧ Listen, my child, to what your father teaches you. ❧ For wisdom will enter your heart, and knowledge will fill you with joy. Wise planning will watch over you. Understanding will keep you safe. ❧ The Lord is like a father to his children, tender and compassionate to those who fear him. ❧ The Lord corrects those he loves, just as a father corrects a child in whom he delights. ❧ Now glory be to God our Father forever and ever.

The purpose of parental discipline is to help children grow, not to exasperate and provoke them to anger or discouragement. Parenting is not easy—it takes lots of patience to raise children.   *LAB note for Ephesians 6:4*

(EPHESIANS 6:4) (PROVERBS 4:1-5) (PROVERBS 1:5) (PROVERBS 1:8)
(PROVERBS 2:10-11) (PSALM 103:13) (PROVERBS 3:12) (PHILIPPIANS 4:20)

June 3

I am making all things new!

I assure you, unless you are born again, you can never see the Kingdom of God. ❧ Those who become Christians become new persons. They are not the same anymore, for the old life is gone. A new life has begun!

I will sprinkle clean water on you, and you will be clean. Your filth will be washed away, and you will no longer worship idols. And I will give you a new heart with new and right desires, and I will put a new spirit in you. I will take out your stony heart of sin and give you a new, obedient heart. And I will put my Spirit in you so you will obey my laws and do whatever I command. ❧ You must display a new nature because you are a new person, created in God's likeness—righteous, holy, and true.

The LORD will give you a new name. The LORD will hold you in his hands for all to see—a splendid crown in the hands of God.

I am creating new heavens and a new earth—so wonderful that no one will even think about the old ones anymore. ❧ Since everything around us is going to melt away, what holy, godly lives you should be living!

Christians are brand-new people on the inside. The Holy Spirit gives them new life, and they are not the same anymore. We are not reformed, rehabilitated, or reeducated—we are re-created (new creations), living in vital union with Christ. *LAB note for 2 Corinthians 5:17*

(REVELATION 21:5) (JOHN 3:3) (2 CORINTHIANS 5:17) (EZEKIEL 36:25–27) (EPHESIANS 4:24) (ISAIAH 62:2-3) (ISAIAH 65:17) (2 PETER 3:11)

June 4

We can be dead to sin and live for what is right.

Throw off your old evil nature and your former way of life, which is rotten through and through, full of lust and deception. Instead, there must be a spiritual renewal of your thoughts and attitudes. You must display a new nature because you are a new person, created in God's likeness—righteous, holy, and true.

You died when Christ died, and your real life is hidden with Christ in God. ▨ We died and were buried with Christ by baptism. And just as Christ was raised from the dead by the glorious power of the Father, now we also may live new lives. Our old sinful selves were crucified with Christ so that sin might lose its power in our lives. We are no longer slaves to sin. For when we died with Christ, we were set free from the power of sin. So you should consider yourselves dead to sin and able to live for the glory of God through Christ Jesus. Do not let any part of your body become a tool of wickedness, to be used for sinning. Instead, give yourselves completely to God since you have been given new life. And use your whole body as a tool to do what is right for the glory of God.

Christ died for our sins in our place, so we would not have to suffer the punishment we deserve. This is called "substitionary atonement." Since Christ has done this for us, we must choose to do right daily and to walk in his footsteps. *LAB note for 1 Peter 2:24*

(1 PETER 2:24) (EPHESIANS 4:22-24) (COLOSSIANS 3:3) (ROMANS 6:4, 6-7, 11, 13)

June 5

Remain in me, and I will remain in you.

I have been cruciified with Christ. I myself no longer live, but Christ lives in me. So I live my life in this earthly body by trusting in the Son of God, who loved me and gave himself for me.

I know I am rotten through and through so far as my old sinful nature is concerned. No matter which way I turn, I can't make myself do right. I want to, but I can't. Oh, what a miserable person I am! Who will free me from this life that is dominated by sin? Thank God! The answer is in Jesus Christ our Lord. ▧ Since Christ lives within you, even though your body will die because of sin, your spirit is alive because you have been made right with God. ▧ But you must continue to believe this truth and stand in it firmly. Don't drift away from the assurance you received when you heard the Good News.

And now, dear children, continue to live in fellowship with Christ so that when he returns, you will be full of courage and not shrink back from him in shame. ▧ Those who say they live in God should live their lives as Christ did.

In our daily life we must regularly crucify sinful desires that keep us from following Christ. And yet the focus of Christianity is not dying but living. Because we have been crucified with Christ, we have also been raised with him. *LAB note for Galatians 2:20*

(JOHN 15:4) (GALATIANS 2:20) (ROMANS 7:18, 24–25) (ROMANS 8:10) (COLOSSIANS 1:23) (1 JOHN 2:28) (1 JOHN 2:6)

June 6

Do you believe in the Son of Man?

Who is he, sir?

The Son reflects God's own glory, and everything about him represents God exactly. 🌿 The blessed and only almighty God, the King of kings and Lord of lords. He alone can never die, and he lives in light so brilliant that no human can approach him. No one has ever seen him, nor ever will. To him be honor and power forever. Amen. 🌿 "I am the Alpha and the Omega—the beginning and the end," says the Lord God. "I am the one who is, who always was, and who is still to come, the Almighty One."

Yes, Lord, . . . I believe! 🌿 I know the one in whom I trust, and I am sure that he is able to guard what I have entrusted to him until the day of his return. 🌿 We believe because we have heard him ourselves, not just because of what you told us. He is indeed the Savior of the world.

"I am placing a stone in Jerusalem, a chosen cornerstone, and anyone who believes in him will never be disappointed." Yes, he is very precious to you who believe.

Jesus Christ is the same yesterday, today, and forever.

Alpha and omega are the first and last letters of the Greek alphabet. The Lord God is the beginning and the end. Without him you have nothing that is eternal, nothing that can change your life, nothing that can save you from sin. Is the Lord your Alpha and Omega?

LAB note for Revelation 1:8

(JOHN 9:35) (JOHN 9:36) (HEBREWS 1:3) (1 TIMOTHY 6:15-16) (REVELATION 1:8) (JOHN 9:38) (2 TIMOTHY 1:12) (JOHN 4:42) (1 PETER 2:6-7) (HEBREWS 13:8)

June 7

My dear Martha, you are so upset over all these details!

Look at the ravens. They don't need to plant or harvest or put food in barns because God feeds them. And you are far more valuable to him than any birds! Look at the lilies and how they grow. They don't work or make their clothing. And don't worry about food—what to eat or drink. Don't worry whether God will provide it for you. These things dominate the thoughts of most people, but your Father already knows your needs.

If we have enough food and clothing, let us be content. But people who long to be rich fall into temptation and are trapped by many foolish and harmful desires that plunge them into ruin and destruction. For the love of money is at the root of all kinds of evil. And some people, craving money, have wandered from the faith and pierced themselves with many sorrows.

All too quickly the message is crowded out by the cares of this life, the lure of wealth, and the desire for nice things.

Let us strip off every weight that slows us down, especially the sin that so easily hinders our progress. And let us run with endurance the race that God has set before us.

Jesus commands us not to worry because it's pointless—it can't fill any of our needs. Worry is foolish because the Creator of the universe loves us and knows what we need. He promises to meet all our real needs but not necessarily all our desires. *LAB note for Luke 12:22-34*

(LUKE 10:41) (LUKE 12:24, 27, 29-30) (1 TIMOTHY 6:8-10) (MARK 4:19) (HEBREWS 12:1)

June 8

One day Jesus told his disciples a story to illustrate their need for constant prayer and to show them that they must never give up.

Then, teaching them more about prayer, he used this illustration: "Suppose you went to a friend's house at midnight, wanting to borrow three loaves of bread. You would say to him, 'A friend of mine has just arrived for a visit, and I have nothing for him to eat.' He would call out from his bedroom, 'Don't bother me. The door is locked for the night, and we are all in bed. I can't help you this time.' But I tell you this—though he won't do it as a friend, if you keep knocking long enough, he will get up and give you what you want so his reputation won't be damaged. Pray at all times and on every occasion in the power of the Holy Spirit. Stay alert and be persistent in your prayers for all Christians everywhere.

"I will not let you go unless you bless me." "You have struggled with both God and men and have won." Devote yourselves to prayer with an alert mind and a thankful heart.

Jesus went to a mountain to pray, and he prayed to God all night.

To persist in prayer and not give up does not mean endless repetition or painfully long prayer sessions. Constant prayer means keeping our requests continually before God as we live for him day by day, believing he will answer. As we persist in prayer, we grow in character, faith, and hope. *LAB note for Luke 18:1*

(LUKE 18:1) (LUKE 11:5–8) (EPHESIANS 6:18) (GENESIS 32:26, 28) (COLOSSIANS 4:2) (LUKE 6:12)

June 9

Be careful how you live, not as fools but as those who are wise. Make the most of every opportunity for doing good in these evil days.

Be very careful to obey all the commands. . . . Love the LORD your God, walk in all his ways, obey his commands, be faithful to him, and serve him with all your heart and all your soul. ❧ Live wisely among those who are not Christians, and make the most of every opportunity. Let your conversation be gracious and effective so that you will have the right answer for everyone. ❧ Keep away from every kind of evil.

When the bridegroom was delayed, they all lay down and slept. At midnight they were roused by the shout, "Look, the bridegroom is coming! Come out and welcome him!" So stay awake and be prepared, because you do not know the day or hour of my return.

Work hard to prove that you really are among those God has called and chosen. Doing this, you will never stumble or fall away. And God will open wide the gates of heaven for you to enter into the eternal Kingdom of our Lord and Savior Jesus Christ. ❧ There will be special favor for those who are ready and waiting for his return. You must be ready all the time, for the Son of Man will come when least expected.

By referring to these days as evil, the apostle Paul was communicating his sense of urgency, due to evil's pervasiveness. We need the same sense of urgency because our days are also difficult. We must keep our standards high, act wisely, and do good whenever we can.

LAB note for Ephesians 5:15-16

(EPHESIANS 5:15-16) (JOSHUA 22:5) (COLOSSIANS 4:5-6) (1 THESSALONIANS 5:22) (MATTHEW 25:5-6, 13) (2 PETER 1:10-11) (LUKE 12:37, 40)

June 10

All of your works will thank you, LORD, and your faithful followers will bless you.

Praise the LORD, I tell myself; with my whole heart, I will praise his holy name. Praise the LORD, I tell myself, and never forget the good things he does for me. ❧ I will praise the LORD at all times. I will constantly speak his praises. I will boast only in the LORD. ❧ I will praise you, my God and King, and bless your name forever and ever. I will bless you every day, and I will praise you forever. Great is the LORD! He is most worthy of praise! His greatness is beyond discovery! Let each generation tell its children of your mighty acts. I will meditate on your majestic, glorious splendor and your wonderful miracles. Your awe-inspiring deeds will be on every tongue; I will proclaim your greatness.

Your unfailing love is better to me than life itself; how I praise you! I will honor you as long as I live, lifting up my hands to you in prayer. You satisfy me more than the richest of foods. I will praise you with songs of joy.

Oh, how I praise the Lord. How I rejoice in God my Savior!

You are worthy, O Lord our God, to receive glory and honor and power. For you created everything, and it is for your pleasure that they exist and were created.

We have plenty for which to praise God. He forgives our sins, heals our diseases, redeems us from death, crowns us with love and compassion, satisfies our desires, and gives righteousness and justice. No matter how difficult your life's journey, you can always count your blessings—past, present, and future. *LAB note for Psalm 103:1ff.*

(PSALM 145:10) (PSALM 103:1-2) (PSALM 34:1-2) (PSALM 145:1-6) (PSALM 63:3-5) (LUKE 1:46-47) (REVELATION 4:11)

June 11

Seek to live a clean and holy life, for those who are not holy will not see the Lord.

I assure you, unless you are born again, you can never see the Kingdom of God. ▨ Nothing evil will be allowed to enter—no one who practices shameful idolatry and dishonesty.

You must be holy because I, the LORD your God, am holy. ▨ Obey God because you are his children. Don't slip back into your old ways of doing evil; you didn't know any better then. But now you must be holy in everything you do, just as God—who chose you to be his children—is holy. For he himself has said, "You must be holy because I am holy." And remember the heavenly Father to whom you pray has no favorites when he judges. He will judge or reward you according to what you do. So you must live in reverent fear of him during your time as foreigners here on earth. ▨ Throw off your old evil nature and your former way of life, which is rotten through and through, full of lust and deception. Instead, there must be a spiritual renewal of your thoughts and attitudes. You must display a new nature because you are a new person, created in God's likeness—righteous, holy, and true. ▨ Long ago, even before he made the world, God loved us and chose us in Christ to be holy and without fault in his eyes.

Sin always blocks our vision of God; so if we want to see God, we must renounce sin and obey him. Holiness is coupled with living in peace. A right relationship with God leads to right relationships with fellow believers. *LAB note for Hebrews 12:14*

(HEBREWS 12:14) (JOHN 3:3) (REVELATION 21:27) (LEVITICUS 19:2) (1 PETER 1:14-17) (EPHESIANS 4:22-24) (EPHESIANS 1:4)

June 12

I assure you that everyone who has given up house or brothers or sisters or mother or father or children or property, for my sake and for the Good News, will receive now in return, a hundred times over, houses, brothers, sisters, mothers, children, and property—with persecutions. And in the world to come they will have eternal life.

Don't be surprised at the fiery trials you are going through, as if something strange were happening to you. ※ Be truly glad! There is wonderful joy ahead, even though it is necessary for you to endure many trials for a while. These trials are only to test your faith, to show that it is strong and pure. It is being tested as fire tests and purifies gold—and your faith is far more precious to God than mere gold. So if your faith remains strong after being tried by fiery trials, it will bring you much praise and glory and honor on the day when Jesus Christ is revealed to the whole world.

After you have suffered a little while, he will restore, support, and strengthen you, and he will place you on a firm foundation. ※ Here on earth you will have many trials and sorrows. But take heart, because I have overcome the world.

Anyone who gives up something valuable for Jesus' sake will be repaid a hundred times over in this life, although not necessarily in the same way. Along with these rewards, however, we experience persecution because the world hates God. Jesus emphasized persecution to make sure that we do not selfishly follow him only for the rewards.

LAB note for Mark 10:29-30

(REVELATION 3:18) (MARK 10:29-30) (1 PETER 4:12) (1 PETER 1:6-7) (1 PETER 5:10) (JOHN 16:33)

June 13

Christ . . . is your example. Follow in his steps.

For even I, the Son of Man, came here not to be served but to serve others, and to give my life as a ransom for many. ❧ Whoever wants to be first must be the slave of all. ❧ Though he was God, [Jesus] . . . took the humble position of a slave and appeared in human form.

Jesus went around doing good. ❧ Share each other's troubles and problems, and in this way obey the law of Christ.

I plead with the gentleness and kindness that Christ himself would use. ❧ Be humble, thinking of others as better than yourself.

Father, forgive these people, because they don't know what they are doing. ❧ Be kind to each other, tenderhearted, forgiving one another, just as God through Christ has forgiven you.

Those who say they live in God should live their lives as Christ did. ❧ We do this by keeping our eyes on Jesus, on whom our faith depends from start to finish. He was willing to die a shameful death on the cross because of the joy he knew would be his afterward. Now he is seated in the place of highest honor beside God's throne in heaven.

Businesses, organizations, and institutions measure greatness by personal achievement. In Christ's Kingdom, however, service is the way to get ahead. The desire to be on top will hinder, not help. Look for ways you can minister to the needs of others. *LAB note for Mark 10:42-45*

(1 PETER 2:21) (MARK 10:45) (MARK 10:44) (PHILIPPIANS 2:6-7) (ACTS 10:38) (GALATIANS 6:2) (2 CORINTHIANS 10:1) (PHILIPPIANS 2:3) (LUKE 23:34) (EPHESIANS 4:32) (1 JOHN 2:6) (HEBREWS 12:2)

June 14

I searched for him, but I couldn't find him anywhere. I called to him, but there was no reply.

Lord, what am I to say, now that Israel has fled from its enemies? But the LORD said to Joshua, "Get up! Why are you lying on your face like this? Israel has sinned and broken my covenant! They have stolen the things that I commanded to be set apart for me. And they have not only stolen them; they have also lied about it and hidden the things among their belongings. That is why the Israelites are running from their enemies in defeat. For now Israel has been set apart for destruction. I will not remain with you any longer unless you destroy the things among you that were set apart for destruction."

Listen! The LORD is not too weak to save you, and he is not becoming deaf. He can hear you when you call. But there is a problem—your sins have cut you off from God. Because of your sin, he has turned away and will not listen anymore.

Dear friends, if our conscience is clear, we can come to God with bold confidence. And we receive whatever we request when we obey him and do the things that please him.

God is not content with our doing what is right some of the time. He wants us to do what is right all the time. We are under his orders to eliminate any thoughts, practices, or possessions that hinder our devotion to him.   *LAB note for Joshua 7:10-12*

(SONG OF SONGS 5:6) (JOSHUA 7:8, 10-12) (ISAIAH 59:1-2) (1 JOHN 3:21-22)

June 15

I will ask the Father, and he will give you another Counselor, who will never leave you. He is the Holy Spirit, who leads into all truth.

It is actually best for you that I go away, because if I don't, the Counselor won't come. If I do go away, he will come because I will send him to you.

His Holy Spirit speaks to us deep in our hearts and tells us that we are God's children. ❦ So you should not be like cowering, fearful slaves. You should behave instead like God's very own children, adopted into his family—calling him "Father, dear Father." ❦ The Holy Spirit helps us in our distress. For we don't even know what we should pray for, nor how we should pray. But the Holy Spirit prays for us with groanings that cannot be expressed in words.

I pray that God, who gives you hope, will keep you happy and full of peace as you believe in him. May you overflow with hope through the power of the Holy Spirit. ❦ This expectation will not disappoint us. For we know how dearly God loves us, because he has given us the Holy Spirit to fill our hearts with his love.

The Holy Spirit is the very presence of God within us and all believers, helping us live as God wants and building Christ's church on earth. By faith we can appropriate the Spirit's power each day.

LAB note for John 14:15-16

(JOHN 14:16-17) (JOHN 16:7) (ROMANS 8:16) (ROMANS 8:15)
(ROMANS 8:26) (ROMANS 15:13) (ROMANS 5:5)

June 16

Be still in the presence of the LORD, and wait patiently for him to act.

There is a special rest still waiting for the people of God. ❧ My people will live in safety, quietly at home. ❧ They will rest from all their toils and trials.

Jesus has already gone in there for us. He has become our eternal High Priest in the line of Melchizedek.

Come to me, all of you who are weary and carry heavy burdens, and I will give you rest. Take my yoke upon you. Let me teach you, because I am humble and gentle, and you will find rest for your souls. For my yoke fits perfectly, and the burden I give you is light. ❧ Only in returning to me and waiting for me will you be saved. In quietness and confidence is your strength. ❧ Look for the old, godly way, and walk in it. Travel its path, and you will find rest for your souls.

The LORD is my shepherd; I have everything I need. He lets me rest in green meadows; he leads me beside peaceful streams. ❧ Now I can rest again, for the LORD has been so good to me.

As the Lord is the good shepherd, so we are his sheep—not frightened, passive animals but obedient followers, wise enough to follow one who will lead us in the right places and in right ways. When you recognize the good shepherd, follow him!   *LAB note for Psalm 23:1*

(PSALM 37:7) (HEBREWS 4:9) (ISAIAH 32:18) (REVELATION 14:13)
(HEBREWS 6:20) (MATTHEW 11:28-30) (ISAIAH 30:15) (JEREMIAH 6:16)
(PSALM 23:1-2) (PSALM 116:7)

June 17

Don't worry about tomorrow, for tomorrow will bring its own worries. Today's trouble is enough for today.

My future is in your hands. ❧ He subdues the nations before us, putting our enemies beneath our feet. He chose the Promised Land as our inheritance, the proud possession of Jacob's descendants, whom he loves. ❧ Lead me in the right path, O LORD. . . . Tell me clearly what to do, and show me which way to turn.

Commit everything you do to the LORD. Trust him, and he will help you. ❧ Seek his will in all you do, and he will direct your paths. ❧ You will hear a voice say, "This is the way; turn around and walk here."

The LORD is my shepherd; I have everything I need. He lets me rest in green meadows; he leads me beside peaceful streams. ❧ The LORD is like a father to his children, tender and compassionate to those who fear him. For he understands how weak we are; he knows we are only dust. ❧ Don't worry about having enough food or drink or clothing. Why be like the pagans who are so deeply concerned about these things? Your heavenly Father already knows all your needs. ❧ Give all your worries and cares to God, for he cares about what happens to you.

Planning for tomorrow is time well spent; worrying about tomorrow is time wasted. Worriers are consumed by fear and find it difficult to trust God. They let their plans interfere with their relationship with God. Don't let worries about tomorrow affect your relationship with God today. *LAB note for Matthew 6:34*

(MATTHEW 6:34) (PSALM 31:15) (PSALM 47:3–4) (PSALM 5:8) (PSALM 37:5) (PROVERBS 3:6) (ISAIAH 30:21) (PSALM 23:1–2) (PSALM 103:13–14) (MATTHEW 6:31–32) (1 PETER 5:7)

June 18

When he comes we will be like him, for we will see him as he really is.

To all who believed him and accepted him, he gave the right to become children of God. ※ And by that same mighty power, he has given us all of his rich and wonderful promises. He has promised . . . that you will share in his divine nature.

For since the world began, no ear has heard, and no eye has seen a God like you, who works for those who wait for him!

Now we see things imperfectly as in a poor mirror, but then we will see everything with perfect clarity. All that I know now is partial and imcomplete, but then I will know everything completely, just as God knows me now. ※ Jesus Christ . . . will take these weak mortal bodies of ours and change them into glorious bodies like his own, using the same mighty power that he will use to conquer everything, everywhere. ※ But because I have done what is right, I will see you. When I awake, I will be fully satisfied, for I will see you face to face.

The Christian life is a process of becoming more and more like Christ. The process will not be complete until we see Christ face to face, but knowing that it is our ultimate destiny should motivate us to stay pure.

LAB note for 1 John 3:2-3

(1 John 3:2) (John 1:12) (2 Peter 1:4) (Isaiah 64:4) (1 Corinthians 13:12) (Philippians 3:20-21) (Psalm 17:15)

June 19

Who will be able to endure it when he comes? . . . For he will be like a blazing fire that refines metal or like a strong soap that whitens clothes.

I saw a vast crowd, too great to count, from every nation and tribe and people and language, standing in front of the throne and before the Lamb. They were clothed in white and held palm branches in their hands. "These are the ones coming out of the great tribulation. They washed their robes in the blood of the Lamb and made them white. That is why they are standing in front of the throne of God, serving him day and night in his Temple. And he who sits on the throne will live among them and shelter them. They will never again be hungry or thirsty, and they will be fully protected from the scorching noontime heat. For the Lamb who stands in front of the throne will be their Shepherd. He will lead them to the springs of life-giving water. And God will wipe away all their tears."

Now there is no condemnation for those who belong to Christ Jesus. ▧ So Christ has really set us free. Now make sure that you stay free, and don't get tied up again in slavery to the law.

All who have been faithful through the ages will sing before God's throne. Their tribulations and sorrows will be over: no more tears for sin, for all sins are forgiven; no more tears for suffering, for all suffering is over; no more tears for death, for all believers will have been resurrected to die no more. *LAB note for Revelation 7:17*

(REVELATION 6:17) (MALACHI 3:2) (REVELATION 7:9, 14–17) (ROMANS 8:1) (GALATIANS 5:1)

June 20

Don't bring your servant to trial! Compared to you, no one is perfect.

"Come now, let us argue this out," says the LORD. "No matter how deep the stain of your sins, I can remove it. I can make you as clean as freshly fallen snow. Even if you are stained as red as crimson, I can make you as white as wool."

He forgave all our sins. He canceled the record that contained the charges against us. He took it and destroyed it by nailing it to Christ's cross.

Since we have been made right in God's sight by faith, we have peace with God because of what Jesus Christ our Lord has done for us. ✠ We have believed in Christ Jesus, that we might be accepted by God because of our faith in Christ. ✠ For no one can ever be made right in God's sight by doing what his law commands. For the more we know God's law, the clearer it becomes that we aren't obeying it.

Everyone who believes in him is freed from all guilt and declared right with God. ✠ How we thank God, who gives us victory over sin and death through Jesus Christ our Lord!

Peace with God means we have been reconciled with him. There is no more hostility between us, no sin blocking our relationship. It is possible only because Jesus paid the price for our sins through his death on the cross.   *LAB note for Romans 5:1*

(PSALM 143:2) (ISAIAH 1:18) (COLOSSIANS 2:13–14) (ROMANS 5:1)
(GALATIANS 2:16) (ROMANS 3:20) (ACTS 13:39) (1 CORINTHIANS 15:57)

June 21

The Holy Spirit tells us clearly that in the last times some will turn away from what we believe; they will follow lying spirits and teachings that come from demons.

Be sure to pay attention to what you hear. ❧ Let the words of Christ, in all their richness, live in your hearts and make you wise. ❧ In every battle you will need faith as your shield to stop the fiery arrows aimed at you by Satan.

Those who love your law have great peace and do not stumble. How sweet are your words to my taste; they are sweeter than honey. Your commandments give me understanding; no wonder I hate every false way of life.

Your word is a lamp for my feet and a light for my path. Your commands make me wiser than my enemies, for your commands are my constant guide.

Satan can disguise himself as an angel of light. ❧ Let God's curse fall on anyone, including myself, who preaches any other message than the one we told you about. Even if an angel comes from heaven and preaches any other message, let him be forever cursed.

But as for me, how good it is to be near God! I have made the Sovereign LORD my shelter, and I will tell everyone about the wonderful things you do.

It is not enough that a teacher appears to know what he is talking about, is disciplined and moral, or says that he is speaking for God. If his words contradict the Bible, his teaching is false. We must guard against any teaching that causes believers to dilute or reject any aspect of their faith.

LAB note for 1 Timothy 4:1-2

(1 TIMOTHY 4:1) (LUKE 8:18) (COLOSSIANS 3:16) (EPHESIANS 6:16)
(PSALM 119:165, 103-104) (PSALM 119:105, 98) (2 CORINTHIANS 11:14)
(GALATIANS 1:8) (PSALM 73:28)

June 22

Loving God means keeping his commandments.

It is my Father's will that all who see his Son and believe in him should have eternal life. We can come to God with bold confidence. And we will receive whatever we request because we obey him and do the things that please him.

Take my yoke upon you. Let me teach you, because I am humble and gentle, and you will find rest for your souls. For my yoke fits perfectly, and the burden I give you is light. If you love me, obey my commandments. Those who obey my commandments are the ones who love me. And because they love me, my Father will love them, and I will love them. And I will reveal myself to each one of them.

Happy is the person who finds wisdom and gains understanding. [Wisdom] will guide you down delightful paths; all her ways are satisfying. Those who love your law have great peace and do not stumble. I love God's law with all my heart.

And this is his commandment: We must believe in the name of his Son, Jesus Christ, and love one another. Love does no wrong to anyone, so love satisfies all of God's requirements.

Jesus never promised that obeying him would be easy. But the hard work and self-discipline of serving Christ is no burden to those who love him. And if our load starts to feel heavy, we can always trust Christ to help us bear it. *LAB note for 1 John 5:3*

(1 JOHN 5:3) (JOHN 6:40) (1 JOHN 3:21-22) (MATTHEW 11:29-30) (JOHN 14:15, 21) (PROVERBS 3:13, 17) (PSALM 119:165) (ROMANS 7:22) (1 JOHN 3:23) (ROMANS 13:10)

June 23

Forgive the rebellious sins of my youth.

I have swept away your sins like the morning mists. ❀ I—yes, I alone—am the one who blots out your sins for my own sake and will never think of them again. ❀ "Come now, let us argue this out," says the LORD. "No matter how deep the stain of your sins, I can remove it. I can make you as clean as freshly fallen snow. Even if you are stained as red as crimson, I can make you as white as wool." ❀ I will forgive their wickedness and will never again remember their sins. ❀ You will trample our sins under your feet and throw them into the depths of the ocean!

Yes, it was good for me to suffer this anguish, for you have rescued me from death and have forgiven all my sins. ❀ Where is another God like you, who pardons the sins of the survivors among his people? You cannot stay angry with your people forever, because you delight in showing mercy. ❀ All praise to him who loves us and has freed us from our sins by shedding his blood for us. He has made us his kingdom and his priests who serve before God his Father. Give to him everlasting glory! He rules forever and ever! Amen!

How tempting it is to remind someone of a past offense! But when God forgives our sins, he totally forgets them. We never have to fear that he will remind us of them later. Because God forgives our sins, we need to forgive others. *LAB note for Isaiah 43:25*

(PSALM 25:7) (ISAIAH 44:22) (ISAIAH 43:25) (ISAIAH 1:18) (JEREMIAH 31:34) (MICAH 7:19) (ISAIAH 38:17) (MICAH 7:18) (REVELATION 1:5-6)

June 24

I am the one who corrects and disciplines everyone I love.

My child, don't ignore it when the Lord disciplines you, and don't be discouraged when he corrects you. For the Lord disciplines those he loves, and he punishes those he accepts as his children. ❧ The LORD corrects those he loves, just as a father corrects a child in whom he delights. ❧ For though he wounds, he also bandages. ❧ Humble yourselves under the mighty power of God, and in his good time he will honor you. ❧ I have refined you in the furnace of suffering. ❧ I am the LORD your God, who teaches you what is good and leads you along the paths you should follow.

He does not enjoy hurting people or causing them sorrow. ❧ He has not punished us for all our sins, nor does he deal with us as we deserve. For his unfailing love toward those who fear him is as great as the height of the heavens above the earth. He has removed our rebellious acts as far away from us as the east is from the west. The LORD is like a father to his children, tender and compassionate to those who fear him. For he understands how weak we are; he knows we are only dust.

Are you lukewarm in your devotion to God? God may discipline you to help you out of your uncaring attitude, but he uses only loving discipline. Just as the spark of love can be rekindled in marriage, so the Holy Spirit can reignite our zeal for God when we allow him to work in our heart. *LAB note for Revelation 3:19*

(REVELATION 3:19) (HEBREWS 12:5-6) (PROVERBS 3:12) (JOB 5:18) (1 PETER 5:6) (ISAIAH 48:10) (ISAIAH 48:17) (LAMENTATIONS 3:33) (PSALM 103:10-14)

June 25

He is in heaven, and you are only here on earth. So let your words be few.

When you pray, don't babble on and on as people of other religions do. They think their prayers are answered only by repeating their words again and again. Don't be like them, because your Father knows exactly what you need even before you ask him!

They called on the name of Baal all morning, shouting, "O Baal, answer us!"

Two men went to the Temple to pray. One was a Pharisee, and the other was a dishonest tax collector. The proud Pharisee stood by himself and prayed this prayer: "I thank you, God, that I am not a sinner like everyone else, especially like that tax collector over there! For I never cheat, I don't sin, I don't commit adultery." But the tax collector stood at a distance and dared not even lift his eyes to heaven as he prayed. Instead, he beat his chest in sorrow, saying, "O God, be merciful to me, for I am a sinner." I tell you, this sinner, not the Pharisee, returned home justified before God. For the proud will be humbled, but the humble will be honored.

We don't even know what we should pray for, nor how we should pray. ▧ Lord, teach us to pray.

When we enter the house of God, we should have the attitude of being open and ready to listen to God, not to dictate to him what we think he should do. *LAB note for Ecclesiastes 5:1*

(ECCLESIASTES 5:2) (MATTHEW 6:7-8) (1 KINGS 18:26) (LUKE 18:10-11, 13-14) (ROMANS 8:26) (LUKE 11:1)

June 26

Enoch . . . enjoyed a close relationship with God. ❧ Can two people walk together without agreeing on the direction? ❧ But as for me, how good it is to be near God! I have made the Sovereign LORD my shelter, and I will tell everyone about the wonderful things you do.

The LORD will stay with you as long as you stay with him! Whenever you seek him, you will find him. But if you abandon him, he will abandon you. Whenever you were in distress and turned to the LORD, the God of Israel, and sought him out, you found him.

"I know the plans I have for you," says the LORD. "They are plans for good and not for disaster, to give you a future and a hope. In those days when you pray, I will listen. If you look for me in earnest, you will find me when you seek me."

We can boldly enter heaven's Most Holy Place because of the blood of Jesus. This is the new, life-giving way that Christ has opened up for us through the sacred curtain, by means of his death for us. And since we have a great High Priest who rules over God's people, let us go right into the presence of God, with true hearts fully trusting him.

According to God's wise plan, we are to have a future and a hope; consequently we can call upon him in confidence. If we seek him whole-heartedly, he will be found. Nothing can break our fellowship with God.

LAB note for Jeremiah 29:13

(JAMES 4:8) (GENESIS 5:24) (AMOS 3:3) (PSALM 73:28) (2 CHRONICLES 15:2, 4) (JEREMIAH 29:11-13) (HEBREWS 10:19-22)

June 27

[Jesus] went back to pray a third time.

While Jesus was here on earth, he offered prayers and pleadings, with a loud cry and tears, to the one who could deliver him out of death.

Oh, that we might know the LORD! Let us press on to know him! Then he will respond to us as surely as the arrival of dawn or the coming of rains in early spring. ❧ Be patient in trouble, and always be prayerful. ❧ Pray at all times and on every occasion in the power of the Holy Spirit. Stay alert and be persistent in your prayers for all Christians everywhere. ❧ Don't worry about anything; instead, pray about everything. Tell God what you need, and thank him for all he has done. If you do this, you will experience God's peace, which is far more wonderful than the human mind can understand. His peace will guard your hearts and minds as you live in Christ Jesus.

I want your will, not mine. ❧ We can be confident that he will listen to us whenever we ask him for anything in line with his will. ❧ Take delight in the LORD, and he will give you your heart's desires. Commit everything you do to the LORD. Trust him, and he will help you.

Have you ever felt that God didn't hear your prayers? Be sure you are praying with reverent submission, willing to do what God wants. God responds to his obedient children.   *LAB note for Hebrews 5:7*

(MATTHEW 26:44) (HEBREWS 5:7) (HOSEA 6:3) (ROMANS 12:12) (EPHESIANS 6:18) (PHILIPPIANS 4:6-7) (MATTHEW 26:39) (1 JOHN 5:14) (PSALM 37:4-5)

June 28

Since we are his children, we will share his treasures   for everything God gives to his Son, Christ, is ours, too.

Now that you belong to Christ, you are the true children of Abraham. You are his heirs, and now all the promises God gave to him belong to you.

See how very much our heavenly Father loves us, for he allows us to be called his children, and we really are! ※ Now you are no longer a slave but God's own child. And since you are his child, everything he has belongs to you. ※ His unchanging plan has always been to adopt us into his own family by bringing us to himself through Jesus Christ. And this gave him great pleasure.

Father, I want these whom you've given me to be with me, so they can see my glory. You gave me the glory because you loved me even before the world began!

To all who are victorious, who obey me to the very end, I will give authority over all the nations. They will rule the nations with an iron rod and smash them like clay pots. ※ I will invite everyone who is victorious to sit with me on my throne, just as I was victorious and sat with my Father on his throne.

To live as Jesus did—serving others, giving up one's rights, resisting pressures to conform to the world—always exacts a price. Nothing we suffer, however, can compare to the great price that Jesus paid to save us.

LAB note for Romans 8:17

(ROMANS 8:17) (GALATIANS 3:29) (1 JOHN 3:1) (GALATIANS 4:7) (EPHESIANS 1:5) (JOHN 17:24) (REVELATION 2:26–27) (REVELATION 3:21)

June 29

God chose things despised by the world.

How can this be? . . . These people are all from Galilee, and yet we hear them speaking the languages of the lands where we were born!

Jesus . . . saw two brothers—Simon, also called Peter, and Andrew—fishing with a net, for they were commercial fishermen. Jesus called out to them, "Come, be my disciples, and I will show you how to fish for people!" ▨ The members of the council were amazed when they saw the boldness of Peter and John, for they could see that they were ordinary men who had had no special training. They also recognized them as men who had been with Jesus.

My message and my preaching were very plain. I did not use wise and persuasive speeches, but the Holy Spirit was powerful among you.

You didn't choose me. I chose you. I appointed you to go and produce fruit that will last. Those who remain in me, and I in them, will produce much fruit. For apart from me you can do nothing. ▨ This precious treasure—this light and power that now shine within us—is held in perishable containers, that is, in our weak bodies. So everyone can see that our glorious power is from God and is not our own.

We all need to fish for souls. If we practice Christ's teachings and share the Good News with others, we will be able to draw those around us to Christ like a fisherman who pulls fish into his boat with nets.

LAB note for Matthew 4:18-20

(1 CORINTHIANS 1:28) (ACTS 2:7) (MATTHEW 4:18-19) (ACTS 4:13)
(1 CORINTHIANS 2:4) (JOHN 15:16, 5) (2 CORINTHIANS 4:7)

June 30

Don't try to act important, but enjoy the company of ordinary people.

How can you claim that you have faith in our glorious Lord Jesus Christ if you favor some people more than others? Listen to me, dear brothers and sisters. Hasn't God chosen the poor in this world to be rich in faith? Aren't they the ones who will inherit the kingdom God promised to those who love him?

Don't think only of your own good. Think of other Christians and what is best for them. ❧ If we have enough food and clothing, let us be content. But people who long to be rich fall into temptation and are trapped by many foolish and harmful desires that plunge them into ruin and destruction.

God deliberately chose things the world considers foolish in order to shame those who are powerful. God chose things despised by the world, things counted as nothing at all, and used them to bring to nothing what the world considers important, so that no one can ever boast in the presence of God.

God alone made it possible for you to be in Christ Jesus.

Are you easily impressed by status, wealth, or fame? Are you partial to the "haves" while ignoring the "have nots"? This attitude is sinful. God views all people as equals, and if he favors anyone, it is the poor and the powerless. We should follow his example.

LAB note for James 2:1–7

(Romans 12:16) (James 2:1, 5) (1 Corinthians 10:24) (1 Timothy 6:8–9) (1 Corinthians 1:27–29) (1 Corinthians 1:30)

July

On Freedom's Wings

Courage and integrity, truth and grace
Safe boundaries without divisive barriers
These are the foundation of freedom.

Any government can offer religious freedom, but
only God offers spiritual freedom. During this
independence season, don't miss out on the far
greater treasure that can be found only in God.

July 1

Your love for me is very great. You have rescued me from the depths of death.

Do not be afraid, for I have ransomed you. I have called you by name; you are mine. I am the LORD, and there is no other Savior. I—yes, I alone—am the one who blots out your sins for my sake and will never think of them again. ❧ They trust in their wealth and boast of great riches. Yet they cannot redeem themselves from death by paying a ransom to God. Redemption does not come so easily, for no one can pay enough. ❧ I have found a ransom for his life. ❧ God is so rich in mercy, and he loved us so very much, that even while we were dead because of our sins, he gave us life when he raised Christ from the dead.

There is salvation in no one else! There is no other name in all of heaven for people to call on to save them. ❧ God our Savior . . . wants everyone to be saved and to understand the truth. For there is only one God and one Mediator who can reconcile God and people. He is the man Christ Jesus. He gave his life to purchase freedom for everyone.

Your unfailing love will last forever. Your faithfulness is as enduring as the heavens.

God created the people of Israel, and they were special to him. God redeemed them and called them by name to be those who belong to him. He protected them in times of trouble. We are important to God, too. And if we claim to belong to God, we should never do anything that would bring shame to him. *LAB note for Isaiah 43:1-4*

(PSALM 86:13) (ISAIAH 43:1, 11, 25) (PSALM 49:6-8) (JOB 33:24)
(EPHESIANS 2:4-5) (ACTS 4:12) (1 TIMOTHY 2:3-6) (PSALM 89:2)

July 2

If sinners entice you, turn your back on them! They may say,
"Come and join us."

The woman was convinced . . . it would make her so wise! So she
ate some of the fruit. She also gave some to her husband, who was
with her. Then he ate it, too. ▩ Didn't God punish all the people
of Israel when Achan, a member of the clan of Zerah, sinned by
stealing the things set apart for the LORD?

Do not join a crowd that intends to do evil.

You can enter God's Kingdom only through the narrow gate.
The highway to hell is broad, and its gate is wide for the many who
choose the easy way.

For we are not our own masters when we live or when we die.
▩ You have been called to live in freedom—not freedom to satisfy
your sinful nature, but freedom to serve one another in love. ▩ You
must be careful with this freedom of yours. Do not cause a brother
or sister with a weaker conscience to stumble. You are sinning
against Christ when you sin against other Christians by encouraging
them to do something they believe is wrong.

All of us have strayed away like sheep. We have left God's paths to
follow our own. Yet the LORD laid on him the guilt and sins of us all.

Sin, even when attractive, is deadly. We must learn to make
choices, not on the basis of flashy appeal or short-range pleasure, but in
view of the long-range effects. Sometimes this means steering clear of
people who want to entice us into activities that we know are wrong.

LAB note for Proverbs 1:10

(PROVERBS 1:10) (GENESIS 3:6) (JOSHUA 22:20) (EXODUS 23:2) (MATTHEW 7:13)
(ROMANS 14:7) (GALATIANS 5:13) (1 CORINTHIANS 8:9, 12) (ISAIAH 53:6)

July 3

I am constantly aware of your unfailing love, and I have lived according to your truth.

The LORD is kind and merciful, slow to get angry, full of unfailing love. ❧ Your Father in heaven . . . gives his sunlight to both the evil and the good, and he sends rain on the just and on the unjust, too. ❧ Follow God's example in everything you do, because you are his dear children. Live a life filled with love for others, following the example of Christ, who loved you and gave himself as a sacrifice to take away your sins. And God was pleased, because that sacrifice was like sweet perfume to him. ❧ Be kind to each other, tenderhearted, forgiving one another, just as God through Christ has forgiven you. ❧ Now you can have sincere love for each other as brothers and sisters because you were cleansed from your sins when you accepted the truth of the Good News. So see to it that you really do love each other intensely with all your hearts. ❧ Whatever we do, it is because Christ's love controls us.

Love your enemies! Do good to them! Lend to them! And don't be concerned that they might not repay. Then your reward from heaven will be very great, and you will truly be acting as children of the Most High, for he is kind to the unthankful and to those who are wicked.

"Sincere" love involves selfless giving. God's love and forgiveness free you to take your eyes off yourselves and meet others' needs. By sacrificing his life, Christ showed that he truly loves you. Now you can love others by following his example and giving of yourself sacrificially.

LAB note for 1 Peter 1:22

(PSALM 26:3) (PSALM 145:8) (MATTHEW 5:45) (EPHESIANS 5:1-2)
(EPHESIANS 4:32) (1 PETER 1:22) (2 CORINTHIANS 5:14) (LUKE 6:35)

July 4

Jesus was led out into the wilderness by the Holy Spirit to be tempted there by the Devil.

While Jesus was here on earth, he offered prayers and pleadings, with a loud cry and tears, to the one who could deliver him out of death. And God heard his prayers because of his reverence for God. So even though Jesus was God's Son, he learned obedience from the things he suffered. In this way, God qualified him as a perfect High Priest, and he became the source of eternal salvation for all those who obey him. This High Priest of ours understands our weaknesses, for he faced all of the same temptations we do, yet he did not sin.

The temptations that come into your life are no different from what others experience. And God is faithful. He will keep the temptation from becoming so strong that you can't stand up against it. When you are tempted, he will show you a way out so that you will not give in to it. My gracious favor is all you need. My power works best in your weakness.

A person has not shown true obedience if he or she has never had an opportunity to disobey. When God led Israel into the wilderness to humble and test them, he wanted to see whether or not they would really obey him. We, too, will be tested—and we should be alert and ready for it!

LAB note for Matthew 4:1

(MATTHEW 4:1) (HEBREWS 5:7–9) (HEBREWS 4:15)
(1 CORINTHIANS 10:13) (2 CORINTHIANS 12:9)

July 5

Even I, the Son of Man, came here not to be served but to serve others, and to give my life as a ransom for many.

Under the old system, the blood of goats and bulls and the ashes of a young cow could cleanse people's bodies from ritual defilement. Just think how much more the blood of Christ will purify our hearts from deeds that lead to death so that we can worship the living God. For by the power of the eternal Spirit, Christ offered himself to God as a perfect sacrifice for our sins.

He was led as a lamb to the slaughter. ⬛ I lay down my life for the sheep. No one can take my life from me. I lay down my life voluntarily. For I have the right to lay it down when I want to and also the power to take it again.

The life of any creature is in its blood. I have given you the blood so you can make atonement for your sins. It is the blood, representing life, that brings you atonement. ⬛ Without the shedding of blood, there is no forgiveness of sins.

God showed his great love for us by sending Christ to die for us while we were still sinners. And since we have been made right in God's sight by the blood of Christ, he will certainly save us from God's judgment.

> You cannot work hard to make yourself good enough for God. Rules and rituals have never cleansed people's hearts. Only Jesus' death and what it means for you can heal your conscience and deliver you from the frustration of trying to earn God's favor.   *LAB note for Hebrews 9:12-14*

(MATTHEW 20:28) (HEBREWS 9:13-14) (ISAIAH 53:7) (JOHN 10:15, 18) (LEVITICUS 17:11) (HEBREWS 9:22) (ROMANS 5:8-9)

July 6

If we confess our sins to him, he is faithful and just to forgive us and to cleanse us from every wrong.

Have mercy on me, O God, because of your unfailing love. Because of your great compassion, blot out the stain of my sins. Wash me clean from my guilt. Purify me from my sin. For I recognize my shameful deeds—they haunt me day and night. Against you, and you alone, have I sinned.

He returned home to his father. And while he was still a long distance away, his father saw him coming. Filled with love and compassion, he ran to his son, embraced him, and kissed him. ❧ I have swept away your sins like the morning mists. I have scattered your offenses like the clouds. Oh, return to me, for I have paid the price to set you free. ❧ Your sins have been forgiven because of Jesus. ❧ God through Christ has forgiven you.

I will sprinkle clean water on you, and you will be clean. . . . And I will give you a new heart with new and right desires, and I will put a new spirit in you. I will take out your stony heart of sin and give you a new, obedient heart. And I will put my Spirit in you so you will obey my laws and do whatever I command. ❧ They will walk with me in white, for they are worthy.

When we come to Christ, he forgives all the sins we have committed or will ever commit. We don't need to confess the sins of the past all over again, and we don't need to fear that God will reject us if we don't keep our slate perfectly clean. Our relationship with Christ is secure. *LAB note for 1 John 1:9*

(1 JOHN 1:9) (PSALM 51:1-4) (LUKE 15:20) (ISAIAH 44:22) (1 JOHN 2:12) (EPHESIANS 4:32) (EZEKIEL 36:25-27) (REVELATION 3:4)

July 7

A student is not greater than the teacher.

You call me "Teacher" and "Lord," and you are right, because it is true.

The student shares the teacher's fate. The servant shares the master's fate. ❧ Since they persecuted me, naturally they will persecute you. And if they had listened to me, they would listen to you! ❧ I have given them your word. And the world hates them because they do not belong to the world, just as I do not.

Think about all he endured when sinful people did such terrible things to him, so that you don't become weary and give up. After all, you have not yet given your lives in your struggle against sin.

Let us run with endurance the race that God has set before us. We do this by keeping our eyes on Jesus, on whom our faith depends from start to finish. He was willing to die a shameful death on the cross because of the joy he knew would be his afterward. Now he is seated in the place of highest honor beside God's throne in heaven. ❧ Since Christ suffered physical pain, you must arm yourselves with the same attitude he had, and be ready to suffer, too.

The world hates Christians because Christians' values differ from the world's. Because Christ's followers don't cooperate with the world by joining in their sin, they are living accusations against the world's immorality. The world follows Satan's agenda.   *LAB note for John 17:14*

(MATTHEW 10:24) (JOHN 13:13) (MATTHEW 10:25) (JOHN 15:20) (JOHN 17:14)
(HEBREWS 12:3-4) (HEBREWS 12:1-2) (1 PETER 4:1)

July 8

My son, give me your heart.

Oh, that they would always have hearts like this, that they might fear me and obey all my commands! If they did, they and their descendants would prosper forever.

Your heart is not right before God. ❡ The sinful nature is always hostile to God. It never did obey God's laws, and it never will. That's why those who are still under the control of their sinful nature can never please God.

Their first action was to dedicate themselves to the Lord. ❡ Above all else, guard your heart, for it affects everything you do.

Work hard and cheerfully at whatever you do, as though you were working for the Lord rather than for people. ❡ Work hard, but not just to please your masters when they are watching. As slaves of Christ, do the will of God with all your heart. Work with enthusiasm, as though you were working for the Lord rather than for people.

If you will help me, I will run to follow your commands.

There is a difference between doing something because it is required and doing something because we want to. God is not interested in forced religious exercises and rule keeping. He wants our hearts and lives completely dedicated to him.　　　　　*LAB note for Deuteronomy 5:29*

(PROVERBS 23:26) (DEUTERONOMY 5:29) (ACTS 8:21) (ROMANS 8:7-8)
(2 CORINTHIANS 8:5) (PROVERBS 4:23) (COLOSSIANS 3:23) (EPHESIANS 6:6-7)
(PSALM 119:32)

July 9

Who can snatch the plunder of war from the hands of a warrior? Who can demand that a tyrant let his captives go? But the LORD says, "The captives of warriors will be released, and the plunder of tyrants will be retrieved. For I will fight those who fight you, and I will save your children. I will feed your enemies with their own flesh. They will be drunk with rivers of their own blood. All the world will know that I, the LORD, am your Savior and Redeemer, the Mighty One of Israel." ❧ Don't be afraid, for I am with you. Do not be dismayed, for I am your God. I will strengthen you. I will help you. I will uphold you with my victorious right hand.

This High Priest of ours understands our weaknesses, for he faced all of the same temptations we do, yet he did not sin. ❧ Since he himself has gone through suffering and temptation, he is able to help us when we are being tempted. ❧ The steps of the godly are directed by the LORD. He delights in every detail of their lives. Though they stumble, they will not fall, for the LORD holds them by the hand.

God proved to the world that he is God by doing the impossible—causing warriors to set their captives free and even return the plunder they had taken! Never should we doubt that God will fulfill his promises. He will even do the impossible to make them come true.

Isaiah 49:24-25

(JEREMIAH 15:20) (ISAIAH 49:24-26) (ISAIAH 41:10) (HEBREWS 4:15) (HEBREWS 2:18) (PSALM 37:23-24)

July 10

He satisfies the thirsty and fills the hungry with good things.

You have had a taste of the Lord's kindness.

O God, you are my God; I earnestly search for you. My soul thirsts for you; my whole body longs for you in this parched and weary land where there is no water. I have seen you in your sanctuary and gazed upon your power and glory. Your unfailing love is better to me than life itself; how I praise you! I will honor you as long as I live, lifting up my hands to you in prayer. ❧ I long, yes, I faint with longing to enter the courts of the LORD. ❧ I long to go and be with Christ.

When I awake, I will be fully satisfied, for I will see you face to face. ❧ They will never again be hungry or thirsty, and they will be fully protected from the scorching noontime heat. For the Lamb who stands in front of the throne will be their Shepherd. He will lead them to the springs of life-giving water. And God will wipe away all their tears. ❧ You feed them from the abundance of your own house, letting them drink from your river of delight. ❧ "I will satisfy my people with my bounty. I, the LORD, have spoken!"

Those who recognize their own lostness can receive the offer of Jesus to satisfy their needs. Jesus is the way, the bread from heaven, the living water, and the giver of rest. Have you received his life-giving offer?

LAB note for Psalm 107:4-9

(PSALM 107:9) (1 PETER 2:3) (PSALM 63:1-4) (PSALM 84:2) (PHILIPPIANS 1:23) (PSALM 17:15) (REVELATION 7:16-17) (PSALM 36:8) (JEREMIAH 31:14)

July 11

I will personally go with you. . . . I will give you rest—everything will be fine for you.

Be strong and courageous! Do not be afraid of them! The LORD your God will go ahead of you. He will neither fail you nor forsake you. ▩ I command you—be strong and courageous! Do not be afraid or discouraged. For the LORD your God is with you wherever you go. ▩ You will find favor with both God and people, and you will gain a good reputation. Trust in the LORD with all your heart; do not depend on your own understanding. Seek his will in all you do, and he will direct your paths. ▩ Happy is the person who finds wisdom and gains understanding. For the profit of wisdom is better than silver, and her wages are better than gold. Wisdom is more precious than rubies; nothing you desire can compare with her.

God has said, "I will never fail you. I will never forsake you." That is why we can say with confidence, "The Lord is my helper, so I will not be afraid. What can mere mortals do to me?" ▩ Our only power and success come from God.

I know, LORD, that a person's life is not his own. No one is able to plan his own course.

To receive God's guidance we must seek God's will in all we do. This means turning every area of life over to him. Examine your values and priorities. What is important to you? In what areas have you not acknowledged him? *LAB note for Psalm 3:6*

(EXODUS 33:14) (DEUTERONOMY 31:6, 8) (JOSHUA 1:9) (PROVERBS 3:4-6) (PROVERBS 3:13-15) (HEBREWS 13:5-6) (2 CORINTHIANS 3:5) (JEREMIAH 10:23)

July 12

Think of ways to encourage one another to outbursts of love and good deeds.

Timely advice is as lovely as golden apples in a silver basket.

Those who feared the LORD spoke with each other, and the LORD listened to what they said. In his presence, a scroll of remembrance was written to record the names of those who feared him and loved to think about him. ✳ If two of you agree down here on earth concerning anything you ask, my Father in heaven will do it for you.

The LORD God said, "It is not good for the man to be alone." ✳ Two people can accomplish more than twice as much as one; they get a better return for their labor. If one person falls, the other can reach out and help. But people who are alone when they fall are in real trouble.

Live in such a way that you will not put an obstacle in another Christian's path. If another Christian is distressed by what you eat, you are not acting in love if you eat it. Don't let your eating ruin someone for whom Christ died. Don't tear apart the work of God over what you eat. Remember, there is nothing wrong with these things in themselves. But it is wrong to eat anything if it makes another person stumble. ✳ Share each other's troubles and problems, and in this way obey the law of Christ.

God will remember those who remain faithful to him, and who love, fear, honor, and respect him. Is your name written in the scroll of remembrance? *LAB note for Malachi 3:16*

(HEBREWS 10:24) (PROVERBS 25:11) (MALACHI 3:16) (MATTHEW 18:19)
(GENESIS 2:18) (ECCLESIASTES 4:9–10) (ROMANS 14:13, 15, 20) (GALATIANS 6:2)

July 13

Search the book of the LORD.

Commit yourselves completely to these words of mine. Tie them to your hands as a reminder, and wear them on your forehead. ❧ Study this Book of the Law continually. Meditate on it day and night so you may be sure to obey all that is written in it. Only then will you succeed.

The godly offer good counsel. ❧ I have followed your commands, which have kept me from going along with cruel and evil people. ❧ I had hidden your word in my heart, that I might not sin against you.

Because [we ourselves heard the voice], we have even greater confidence in the message proclaimed by the prophets. Pay close attention to what they wrote, for their words are like a light shining in a dark place—until the day Christ appears and his brilliant light shines in your hearts. ❧ Such things were written in the Scriptures long ago to teach us. They give us hope and encouragement as we wait patiently for God's promises.

Hiding (keeping) God's Word in our heart is a deterrent to sin. This alone should inspire us to memorize Scripture. But memorization alone will not keep us from sin; we must also put God's Word to work in our life, making it a vital guide for everything we do.   *LAB note for Psalm 119:11*

(ISAIAH 34:16) (DEUTERONOMY 11:18) (JOSHUA 1:8) (PSALM 37:30) (PSALM 17:4)
(PSALM 119:11) (2 PETER 1:19) (ROMANS 15:4)

July 14

Whatever is in your heart determines what you say.

Let the words of Christ, in all their richness, live in your hearts and make you wise. ✺ A good person produces good words from a good heart.

Those who love to talk will experience the consequences, for the tongue can kill or nourish life. ✺ A good person produces good deeds from a good heart. . . . Whatever is in your heart determines what you say. ✺ The godly offer good counsel; they know what is right from wrong. ✺ Don't use foul or abusive language. Let everything you say be good and helpful, so that your words will be an encouragement to those who hear them.

You must give an account on judgment day of every idle word you speak. The words you say now reflect your fate then; either you will be justified by them or you will be condemned.

If anyone acknowledges me publicly here on earth, I will openly acknowledge that person before my Father in heaven. ✺ Make the most of every opportunity. Let your conversation be gracious and effective so that you will have the right answer for everyone.

Jesus reminds us that our speech and actions reveal our true underlying beliefs, attitudes, and motivations. The good impressions we try to make cannot last if our heart is deceptive. What is in your heart will come out in your speech and behavior.   *LAB note for Luke 6:45*

(MATTHEW 12:34) (COLOSSIANS 3:16) (MATTHEW 12:35) (PROVERBS 18:21)
(LUKE 6:45) (PSALM 37:30) (EPHESIANS 4:29) (MATTHEW 12:36-37)
(MATTHEW 10:32) (COLOSSIANS 4:5-6)

July 15

We prayed to our God and guarded the city day and night to protect ourselves.

Keep alert and pray. Otherwise temptation will overpower you. Devote yourselves to prayer with an alert mind and a thankful heart. Give all your worries and cares to God, for he cares about what happens to you. Be careful! Watch out for attacks from the Devil, your great enemy. He prowls around like a roaring lion, looking for some victim to devour. Take a firm stand against him, and be strong in your faith.

Why do you call me "Lord," when you won't obey me? It is a message to obey, not just to listen to.

Then the LORD said to Moses, "Why are you crying out to me? Tell the people to get moving!"

Don't worry about anything; instead, pray about everything. Tell God what you need, and thank him for all he has done. If you do this, you will experience God's peace, which is far more wonderful than the human mind can understand. His peace will guard your hearts and minds as you live in Christ Jesus.

The way to overcome temptation is to keep alert and pray. Because temptation strikes where we are most vulnerable, we can't resist it alone. Prayer is essential because God's strength can shore up our defenses and defeat Satan's power. *LAB note for Matthew 26:40-41*

(NEHEMIAH 4:9) (MATTHEW 26:41) (COLOSSIANS 4:2) (1 PETER 5:7-9) (LUKE 6:46) (JAMES 1:22) (EXODUS 14:15) (PHILIPPIANS 4:6-7)

July 16

A gracious and compassionate God, slow to get angry and filled with unfailing love.

Please, Lord, prove that your power is as great as you have claimed it to be. For you said, "The LORD is slow to anger and rich in unfailing love, forgiving every kind of sin and rebellion. Even so he does not leave sin unpunished, but he punishes the children for the sins of their parents to the third and fourth generations."

Oh, do not hold us guilty for our former sins! Let your tenderhearted mercies quickly meet our needs, for we are brought low to the dust. Help us, O God of our salvation! Help us for the honor of your name. Oh, save us and forgive our sins. ❧ LORD, our wickedness has caught up with us. We have sinned against you. So please, help us for the sake of your own reputation. LORD, we confess our wickedness and that of our ancestors, too. ❧ Oh, don't be so angry with us, LORD. Please don't remember our sins forever. Look at us, we pray, and see that we are all your people.

LORD, if you kept a record of our sins, who, O Lord, could ever survive? But you offer forgiveness, that we might learn to fear you.

Jonah didn't want the Ninevites forgiven; he wanted them destroyed. He did not understand that the God of Israel was also the God of the whole world. Are you surprised when some unlikely person turns to God? We must not forget that in reality we do not deserve to be forgiven by God.   *LAB note for Jonah 4:1-2*

(JONAH 4:2) (NUMBERS 14:17-18) (PSALM 79:8-9) (JEREMIAH 14:7, 20) (ISAIAH 64:9) (PSALM 130:3-4)

July 17

She has done what she could.

This poor widow has given more than all the rest of them. ❦ If anyone gives you even a cup of water because you belong to the Messiah, I assure you, that person will be rewarded. ❦ If you are really eager to give, it isn't important how much you are able to give. God wants you to give what you have, not what you don't have.

Let us stop just saying we love each other; let us really show it by our actions. ❦ Suppose you see a brother or sister who needs food or clothing, and you say, "Well, good-bye and God bless you; stay warm and eat well"—but then you don't give that person any food or clothing. What good does that do? ❦ A farmer who plants only a few seeds will get a small crop. But the one who plants generously will get a generous crop. You must each make up your own mind as to how much you should give. Don't give reluctantly or in response to pressure. For God loves the person who gives cheerfully.

When you obey me you should say, "We are not worthy of praise. We are servants who have simply done our duty."

When we consider ourselves generous in giving a small percentage of our income to the Lord, we resemble those who gave "a tiny part of their surplus." As believers we should consider increasing our giving—whether money, time, or talents—to a point beyond mere convenience. *LAB note for Luke 21:1-4*

(MARK 14:8) (LUKE 21:3) (MARK 9:41) (2 CORINTHIANS 8:12) (1 JOHN 3:18) (JAMES 2:15-16) (2 CORINTHIANS 9:6-7) (LUKE 17:10)

July 18

He, the Mighty One, is holy, and he has done great things for me.

Who else among the gods is like you, O LORD? Who is glorious in holiness like you—so awesome in splendor, performing such wonders? ❋ Nowhere among the pagan gods is there a god like you, O Lord. There are no other miracles like yours. ❋ Who will not fear, O Lord, and glorify your name? For you alone are holy. ❋ May your name be honored.

Praise the Lord, the God of Israel, because he has visited his people and redeemed them.

Who is this who comes from Edom, from the city of Bozrah, with his clothing stained red? Who is this in royal robes, marching in the greatness of his strength? "It is I, the LORD, announcing your salvation! It is I, the LORD, who is mighty to save!" ❋ For the LORD your God has arrived to live among you. He is a mighty savior. He will rejoice over you with great gladness.

Now glory be to God! By his mighty power at work within us, he is able to accomplish infinitely more than we would ever dare to ask or hope. May he be given glory in the church and in Christ Jesus forever and ever through endless ages.

The God of the Bible is unique! He is alive and able to do mighty deeds for those who love him. All human-created deities are powerless because they are merely inventions of the mind, not living beings. You need never fear that God is only one among many or that you may be worshiping the wrong God. The Lord alone is God.

LAB note for Psalm 86:8-10

(LUKE 1:49) (EXODUS 15:11) (PSALM 86:8) (REVELATION 15:4) (MATTHEW 6:9)
(LUKE 1:68) (ISAIAH 63:1) (ZEPHANIAH 3:17) (EPHESIANS 3:20-21)

July 19

Whatever you do or say, let it be as a representative of the Lord Jesus.

He was despised and rejected—a man of sorrows, acquainted with bitterest grief. ❧ Here on earth you will have many trials and sorrows. But take heart, because I have overcome the world.

He is the kind of high priest we need because he is holy and blameless, unstained by sin. He has now been set apart from sinners, and he has been given the highest place of honor in heaven. ❧ No one can speak a word of blame against you. You are to live clean, innocent lives as children of God in a dark world full of crooked and perverse people.

Jesus of Nazareth . . . went around doing good and healing all who were oppressed by the Devil, for God was with him. ❧ Whenever we have the opportunity, we should do good to everyone, especially to our Christian brothers and sisters.

The one who is the true light, who gives light to everyone, was going to come into the world. ❧ You are the light of the world—like a city on a mountain, glowing in the night for all to see. Let your good deeds shine out for all to see, so that everyone will praise your heavenly Father.

     As a Christian, you represent Christ at all times—wherever you go and whatever you say. What impression do people have of Christ when they see or talk with you? What changes would you make in your life in order to honor Christ?   *LAB note for Colossians 3:17*

(COLOSSIANS 3:17) (ISAIAH 53:3) (JOHN 16:33) (HEBREWS 7:26) (PHILIPPIANS 2:15) (ACTS 10:38) (GALATIANS 6:10) (JOHN 1:9) (MATTHEW 5:14, 16)

July 20

Live in such a way that God's love can bless you.

Remain in me, and I will remain in you. For a branch cannot produce fruit if it is severed from the vine, and you cannot be fruitful apart from me. Yes, I am the vine; you are the branches. Those who remain in me, and I in them, will produce much fruit. For apart from me you can do nothing.

When the Holy Spirit controls our lives, he will produce . . . love.

My true disciples produce much fruit. This brings great glory to my Father. I have loved you even as the Father has loved me. Remain in my love. When you obey me, you remain in my love, just as I obey my Father and remain in his love. ❦ Those who obey God's word really do love him.

I command you to love each other in the same way that I love you. ❦ God showed his great love for us by sending Christ to die for us while we were still sinners. ❦ We know how much God loves us, and we have put our trust in him. God is love, and all who live in love live in God, and God lives in them.

In order for God's love to bless you, you must live close to God and his people. You must not listen to false teachers—those who would try to pull you away from God. That means you should constantly check what others do and say against the Scriptures.   *LAB note for Jude 1:21*

(JUDE 1:21) (JOHN 15:4-5) (GALATIANS 5:22) (JOHN 15:8-10) (1 JOHN 2:5)
(JOHN 15:12) (ROMANS 5:8) (1 JOHN 4:16)

July 21

Those who listen to my message and believe in God who sent me have eternal life. They will never be condemned for their sins, but they have already passed from death into life. ❧ Whoever has God's Son has life; whoever does not have his Son does not have life.

It is God who gives us, along with you, the ability to stand firm for Christ. He has commissioned us, and he has identified us as his own by placing the Holy Spirit in our hearts as the first installment of everything he will give us. ❧ It is by our actions that we know we are living in the truth, so we will be confident when we stand before the Lord. If our conscience is clear, we can come to God with bold confidence. ❧ We know that we are children of God.

Once you were dead, doomed forever because of your many sins. Even while we were dead because of our sins, he gave us life when he raised Christ from the dead. (It is only by God's special favor that you have been saved!) ❧ He has rescued us from the one who rules in the kingdom of darkness, and he has brought us into the Kingdom of his dear Son.

"Eternal life"—living forever with God—begins when you accept Jesus Christ as Savior. At that moment new life begins in you. It is a completed transaction. You still will face physical death, but when Christ returns again, your body will be resurrected to live forever.

LAB note for John 5:24

(1 JOHN 3:14) (JOHN 5:24) (1 JOHN 5:12) (2 CORINTHIANS 1:21-22)
(1 JOHN 3:19, 21) (1 JOHN 5:19) (EPHESIANS 2:1, 5) (COLOSSIANS 1:13)

July 22

You will show me the way of life, granting me the joy of your presence.

The LORD says: Take your choice of life or death! ❧ I will continue to teach you what is good and right. ❧ I am the way, the truth, and the life. No one can come to the Father except through me. ❧ Come.

There is a path before each person that seems right, but it ends in death. ❧ You can enter God's Kingdom only through the narrow gate. The highway to hell is broad, and its gate is wide for the many who choose the easy way. But the gateway to life is small, and the road is narrow, and only a few ever find it.

A main road will go through that once deserted land. It will be named the Highway of Holiness. Evil-hearted people will never travel on it. It will be only for those who walk in God's ways; fools will never walk there. ❧ Oh, that we might know the LORD! Let us press on to know him!

There are many rooms in my Father's home, and I am going to prepare a place for you.

As the way, Jesus is our path to the Father. As the truth, he is the reality of all God's promises. As the life, he joins his divine life to ours, both now and eternally. *LAB note for John 14:6*

(PSALM 16:11) (JEREMIAH 21:8) (1 SAMUEL 12:23) (JOHN 14:6) (MATTHEW 4:19) (PROVERBS 14:12) (MATTHEW 7:13-14) (ISAIAH 35:8) (HOSEA 6:3) (JOHN 14:2)

July 23

It was by faith that Abraham obeyed when God called him to leave home and go to another land that God would give him as an inheritance.

He chose the Promised Land as our inheritance, the proud possession of Jacob's descendants, whom he loves. ❧ He found them in a desert land, in an empty, howling wasteland. He surrounded them and watched over them; he guarded them as his most precious possession. Like an eagle that rouses her chicks and hovers over her young, so he spread his wings to take them in and carried them aloft on his pinions. The LORD alone guided them; they lived without any foreign gods. He made them ride over the highlands; he let them feast on the crops of the fields.

I am the LORD your God, who teaches you what is good and leads you along the paths you should follow. ❧ Who is a teacher like him?

We live by believing and not by seeing. ❧ For this world is not our home; we are looking forward to our city in heaven, which is yet to come. ❧ Dear brothers and sisters, you are foreigners and aliens here. So I warn you to keep away from evil desires because they fight against your very souls.

Abraham's life was filled with faith. He obeyed God without question—even when it meant going to another land. Do not be surprised if God asks you to give up secure, familiar surroundings in order to carry out his will. *LAB note for Hebrews 11:8-10*

(HEBREWS 11:8) (PSALM 47:4) (DEUTERONOMY 32:10-13) (ISAIAH 48:17) (JOB 36:22) (2 CORINTHIANS 5:7) (HEBREWS 13:14) (1 PETER 2:11)

July 24

Even the heavens cannot be absolutely pure in his sight. How much less pure is a corrupt and sinful person with a thirst for wickedness! ❧ God is so glorious that even the moon and stars scarcely shine compared to him. How much less are mere people, who are but worms in his sight?

Who else among the gods is like you, O LORD? Who is glorious in holiness like you? ❧ Holy, holy, holy is the LORD Almighty!

Now you must be holy in everything you do, just as God—who chose you to be his children—is holy. For he himself has said, "You must be holy because I am holy." ❧ Share in his holiness.

God's temple is holy, and you Christians are that temple. ❧ What holy, godly lives you should be living! Make every effort to live a pure and blameless life. And be at peace with God.

Let everything you say be good and helpful, so that your words will be an encouragement to those who hear them. And do not bring sorrow to God's Holy Spirit by the way you live. Remember, he is the one who has identified you as his own, guaranteeing that you will be saved on the day of redemption.

The God of Israel and of the Christian church is holy—he sets the standard for morality. He is a God of mercy and justice who cares personally for each of his followers. Our holy God expects us to imitate him by following his high moral standards and by being both merciful and just. *LAB note for 1 Peter 1:14-16*

(PSALM 97:12) (JOB 15:15-16) (JOB 25:5-6) (EXODUS 15:11) (ISAIAH 6:3) (1 PETER 1:15-16) (HEBREWS 12:10) (1 CORINTHIANS 3:17) (2 PETER 3:11, 14) (EPHESIANS 4:29-30)

July 25

You have armed me with strength for the battle; you have subdued my enemies under my feet.

When I am weak, then I am strong.

O LORD, no one but you can help the powerless against the mighty! Help us, O LORD our God, for we trust in you alone. It is in your name that we have come against this vast horde. O LORD, you are our God; do not let mere men prevail against you! ⊠ Jehoshaphat cried out to the LORD to save him, and God helped him by turning the attack away from him.

It is better to trust the LORD than to put confidence in people. It is better to trust the LORD than to put confidence in princes. ⊠ The best-equipped army cannot save a king, nor is great strength enough to save a warrior. Don't count on your warhorse to give you victory—for all its strength, it cannot save you.

For we are not fighting against people made of flesh and blood, but against the evil rulers and authorities of the unseen world, against those mighty powers of darkness who rule this world, and against wicked spirits in the heavenly realms.

We face a powerful army whose goal is to defeat Christ's church. When we believe in Christ, these beings become our enemies, and they try every device to turn us away from him and back to sin. We need supernatural power to defeat Satan, and God has provided this by giving us his Holy Spirit within us and his armor surrounding us.

LAB note for Ephesians 6:12

(PSALM 18:39) (2 CORINTHIANS 12:10) (2 CHRONICLES 14:11)
(2 CHRONICLES 18:31) (PSALM 118:8-9) (PSALM 33:16-17) (EPHESIANS 6:12)

July 26

Live a life filled with love.

I am giving you a new commandment: Love each other. Just as I have loved you, you should love each other. ❧ Continue to show deep love for each other, for love covers a multitude of sins. ❧ Love covers all offenses.

When you are praying, first forgive anyone you are holding a grudge against, so that your Father in heaven will forgive your sins, too. ❧ Love your enemies! Do good to them! Lend to them! And don't be concerned that they might not repay. ❧ Do not rejoice when your enemies fall into trouble. Don't be happy when they stumble. ❧ Don't repay evil for evil. Don't retaliate when people say unkind things about you. Instead, pay them back with a blessing. That is what God wants you to do, and he will bless you for it. ❧ Do your part to live in peace with everyone, as much as possible. ❧ Be kind to each other, tenderhearted, forgiving one another, just as God through Christ has forgiven you.

Dear children, let us stop just saying we love each other; let us really show it by our actions. It is by our actions that we know we are living in the truth, so we will be confident when we stand before the Lord.

We are to love others based on Jesus' sacrificial love for us. Such love will not only bring unbelievers to Christ, it will also keep believers strong and united in a world hostile to God. Jesus was a living example of God's love, as we are to be living examples of Jesus' love.

LAB note for John 13:34

(EPHESIANS 5:2) (JOHN 13:34) (1 PETER 4:8) (PROVERBS 10:12) (MARK 11:25) (LUKE 6:35) (PROVERBS 24:17) (1 PETER 3:9) (ROMANS 12:18) (EPHESIANS 4:32) (1 JOHN 3:18-19)

July 27

I will ask the Father, and he will give you another Counselor, who will never leave you. He is the Holy Spirit, who leads into all truth. The world at large cannot receive him, because it isn't looking for him and doesn't recognize him. But you do, because he lives with you now and later will be in you. ❧ He will not be presenting his own ideas; he will be telling you what he has heard. He will bring me glory by revealing to you whatever he receives from me.

We know how dearly God loves us, because he has given us the Holy Spirit to fill our hearts with his love.

The person who is joined to the Lord becomes one spirit with him. Don't you know that your body is the temple of the Holy Spirit, who lives in you and was given to you by God? You do not belong to yourself.

Do not bring sorrow to God's Holy Spirit by the way you live. Remember, he is the one who has identified you as his own, guaranteeing that you will be saved on the day of redemption. ❧ The Holy Spirit helps us in our distress. For we don't even know what we should pray for, nor how we should pray. But the Holy Spirit prays for us with groanings that cannot be expressed in words.

The Holy Spirit has been active among people from the beginning of time, but after Pentecost he came to live in all believers. Many people are unaware of the Holy Spirit's activities, but to those who hear Christ's words and understand the Spirit's power, the Spirit gives a whole new way to look at life. *LAB note for John 14:17ff.*

(2 CORINTHIANS 13:13) (JOHN 14:16-17) (JOHN 16:13-14) (ROMANS 5:5)
(1 CORINTHIANS 6:17, 19) (EPHESIANS 4:30) (ROMANS 8:26)

July 28

The God of peace . . . produce in you, through the power of Jesus Christ, all that is pleasing to him.

Rejoice. Change your ways. Encourage each other. Live in harmony and peace.

God saved you by his special favor when you believed. And you can't take credit for this; it is a gift from God. Salvation is not a reward for the good things we have done, so none of us can boast about it. ⬛ Whatever is good and perfect comes to us from God above, who created all heaven's lights. Unlike them, he never changes or casts shifting shadows.

Be even more careful to put into action God's saving work in your lives, obeying God with deep reverence and fear. For God is working in you, giving you the desire to obey him and the power to do what pleases him. ⬛ Let God transform you into a new person by changing the way you think. Then you will know what God wants you to do, and you will know how good and pleasing and perfect his will really is. ⬛ May you always be filled with the fruit of your salvation—those good things that are produced in your life by Jesus Christ—for this will bring much glory and praise to God.

It is not that we think we can do anything of lasting value by ourselves. Our only power and success come from God.

God works in us to make us the kind of people that would please him, and he equips us to do the kind of work that would please him. Let God change you from within and then use you to help others.

Hebrews 13:20-21

(HEBREWS 13:20-21) (2 CORINTHIANS 13:11) (EPHESIANS 2:8-9) (JAMES 1:17) (PHILIPPIANS 2:12-13) (ROMANS 12:2) (PHILIPPIANS 1:11) (2 CORINTHIANS 3:5)

July 29

The Temple of the LORD must be a magnificent structure, famous and glorious.

Now God is building you, as living stones, into his spiritual temple. ❧ Don't you realize that all of you together are the temple of God and that the Spirit of God lives in you? God will bring ruin upon anyone who ruins this temple. For God's temple is holy, and you Christians are that temple. ❧ Don't you know that your body is the temple of the Holy Spirit, who lives in you and was given to you by God? You do not belong to yourself, for God bought you with a high price. So you must honor God with your body. ❧ What union can there be between God's temple and idols? For we are the temple of the living God. ❧ You are members of God's family. We are his house, built on the foundation of the apostles and the prophets. And the cornerstone is Christ Jesus himself. We who believe are carefully joined together, becoming a holy temple for the Lord. Through him you Gentiles are also joined together as part of this dwelling where God lives by his Spirit.

Just as our bodies are the "temple of the Holy Spirit," the local church or Christian community is God's temple. Just as the Jews' Temple in Jerusalem was not to be destroyed, the church is not to be spoiled and ruined by divisions, controversy, or other sins as members come together to worship God. *LAB note for 1 Corinthians 3:16-17*

(1 CHRONICLES 22:5) (1 PETER 2:5) (1 CORINTHIANS 3:16-17)
(1 CORINTHIANS 6:19-20) (2 CORINTHIANS 6:16) (EPHESIANS 2:19-22)

July 30

God did not abandon us.

Dear friends, don't be surprised at the fiery trials you are going through, as if something strange were happening to you. ❦ As you endure this divine discipline, remember that God is treating you as his own children. Whoever heard of a child who was never disciplined? If God doesn't discipline you as he does all of his children, it means that you are illegitimate and are not really his children after all.

The LORD your God is testing you to see if you love him with all your heart and soul.

The LORD will not abandon his chosen people, for that would dishonor his great name. He made you a special nation for himself. ❦ Can a mother forget her nursing child? Can she feel no love for a child she has borne? But even if that were possible, I would not forget you! ❦ Happy are those who have the God of Israel as their helper, whose hope is in the LORD their God.

Don't you think God will surely give justice to his chosen people who plead with him day and night? Will he keep putting them off? I tell you, he will grant justice to them quickly!

Who loves his child more—the father who allows the child to do what will harm him, or the one who corrects, trains, and even punishes the child to help him learn what is right? It's never pleasant to be corrected and disciplined by God, but his discipline is a sign of his deep love for us.

LAB note for Hebrews 12:5-11

(EZRA 9:9) (1 PETER 4:12) (HEBREWS 12:7-8) (DEUTERONOMY 13:3)
(1 SAMUEL 12:22) (ISAIAH 49:15) (PSALM 146:5) (LUKE 18:7-8)

July 31

My Father! If it is possible, let this cup of suffering be taken away from me. Yet I want your will, not mine.

Now my soul is deeply troubled. Should I pray, "Father, save me from what lies ahead"? But that is the very reason why I came!

I have come down from heaven to do the will of God who sent me, not to do what I want. ❦ He obediently humbled himself even further by dying a criminal's death on a cross. ❦ While Jesus was here on earth, he offered prayers and pleadings, with a loud cry and tears, to the one who could deliver him out of death. And God heard his prayers because of his reverence for God. So even though Jesus was God's Son, he learned obedience from the things he suffered.

Don't you realize that I could ask my Father for thousands of angels to protect us, and he would send them instantly? ❦ Yes, it was written long ago that the Messiah must suffer and die and rise again from the dead on the third day. With my authority, take this message of repentance to all the nations, beginning in Jerusalem: "There is forgiveness of sins for all who turn to me."

Jesus was not rebelling against his Father's will when he asked that the cup be taken away. In fact, he reaffirmed his desire to do God's will. Instead, his prayer reveals his terrible suffering. His agony was worse than death because he paid for all our sin by being separated from God.

LAB note for Matthew 26:39

(MATTHEW 26:39) (JOHN 12:27) (JOHN 6:38) (PHILIPPIANS 2:8) (HEBREWS 5:7-8) (MATTHEW 26:53) (LUKE 24:46-47)

August

Summer's Goodness

Bright sunny days and clear star-filled nights
Nurturing mornings in the garden and
lazy afternoons at the beach
There's nothing quite like a perfect summer day.

Summer is the time to break from the normal rush
of work and busyness. It's the season for refreshment
and relaxation. Make your summer days events to
remember and celebrate the whole year!

August 1

When the Holy Spirit controls our lives, he will produce . . .
goodness.

Follow God's example in everything you do, because you are his dear children. ❧ Love your enemies! Pray for those who persecute you! In that way, you will be acting as true children of your Father in heaven. For he gives his sunlight to both the evil and the good, and he sends rain on the just and on the unjust. ❧ You must be compassionate, just as your Father is compassionate.

For this light within you produces only what is good and right and true.

Then God our Savior showed us his kindness and love. He saved us, not because of the good things we did, but because of his mercy. He washed away our sins and gave us a new life through the Holy Spirit. He generously poured out the Spirit upon us because of what Jesus Christ our Savior did. ❧ The LORD is good to everyone. He showers compassion on all his creation. ❧ Since God did not spare even his own Son but gave him up for us all, won't God, who gave us Christ, also give us everything else?

By telling us not to retaliate, Jesus keeps us from taking the law into our own hands. By loving and praying for our enemies, we can overcome evil with good. If you love your enemies and treat them well, you will truly show that Jesus is Lord of your life. *LAB note for Matthew 5:43-44*

(GALATIANS 5:22) (EPHESIANS 5:1) (MATTHEW 5:44-45) (LUKE 6:36)
(EPHESIANS 5:9) (TITUS 3:4-6) (PSALM 145:9) (ROMANS 8:32)

August 2

You have given me an inheritance reserved for those who fear your name.

No weapon turned against you will succeed. And everyone who tells lies in court will be brought to justice. These benefits are enjoyed by the servants of the LORD; their vindication will come from me. I, the LORD, have spoken! ▨ The angel of the LORD guards all who fear him, and he rescues them. Taste and see that the LORD is good. Oh, the joys of those who trust in him! Let the LORD's people show him reverence, for those who honor him will have all they need. Even strong young lions sometimes go hungry, but those who trust in the LORD will never lack any good thing. ▨ The land you have given me is a pleasant land. What a wonderful inheritance!

For you who fear my name, the Sun of Righteousness will rise with healing in his wings. And you will go free, leaping with joy like calves let out to pasture. ▨ Since God did not spare even his own Son but gave him up for us all, won't God, who gave us Christ, also give us everything else?

If you feel you don't have everything you need, ask: (1) Is this really a need? (2) Is this good for me? (3) Is this the best time for me to have that desire? Even if you answer yes to all three questions, God may want you to learn that you need him more than you need your immediate desires met.   *LAB note for Psalm 34:9-10*

(PSALM 61:5) (ISAIAH 54:17) (PSALM 34:7-10) (PSALM 16:6)
(MALACHI 4:2) (ROMANS 8:32)

August 3

I will praise you with songs of joy.

How precious are your thoughts about me, O God! They are innumerable! I can't even count them; they outnumber the grains of sand! And when I wake up in the morning, you are still with me! ❧ How sweet are your words to my taste; they are sweeter than honey. ❧ Your love is sweeter than wine.

Your unfailing love, O LORD, is as vast as the heavens; your faithfulness reaches beyond the clouds. Your righteousness is like the mighty mountains, your justice like the ocean depths. You care for people and animals alike, O LORD. How precious is your unfailing love, O God! All humanity finds shelter in the shadow of your wings. You feed them from the abundance of your own house, letting them drink from your rivers of delight. ❧ Whom have I in heaven but you? I desire you more than anything on earth. ❧ You will show me the way of life, granting me the joy of your presence and the pleasures of living with you forever.

Oh, what a wonderful God we have! How great are his riches and wisdom and knowledge! How impossible it is for us to understand his decisions and his methods! For everything comes from him; everything exists by his power and is intended for his glory.

God is faithful, righteous, and just. His love is as vast as the heavens; his faithfulness reaches beyond the clouds; his righteousness is as solid as mighty mountains; his judgments are as full of wisdom as the oceans are with water. We need not fear evil people because we know God loves us, judges evil, and will care for us throughout eternity.

LAB note for Psalm 36:5-8

(PSALM 63:5) (PSALM 139:17-18) (PSALM 119:103) (SONG OF SONGS 1:2)
(PSALM 36:5-8) (PSALM 73:25) (PSALM 16:11) (ROMANS 11:33, 36)

August 4

Peter was following far behind. ❧ Many people, including some of the Jewish leaders, believed in him. But they wouldn't admit it to anyone because of their fear that the Pharisees would expel them from the synagogue. For they loved human praise more than the praise of God. ❧ Fearing people is a dangerous trap, but to trust the LORD means safety.

Those the Father has given me will come to me, and I will never reject them. ❧ He will not crush those who are weak or quench the smallest hope. ❧ Faith as small as a mustard seed.

God has not given us a spirit of fear and timidity, but of power, love, and self-discipline. So you must never be ashamed to tell others about our Lord. ❧ And now, dear children, continue to live in fellowship with Christ so that when he returns, you will be full of courage and not shrink back from him in shame. ❧ If anyone acknowledges me publicly here on earth, I will openly acknowledge that person before my Father in heaven.

Since most of the Pharisees hated Jesus and wanted to kill him, Nicodemus risked his reputation and high position when he spoke up for Jesus. His statement was bold, and the Pharisees immediately became suspicious. After Jesus' death Nicodemus brought spices for his body.

LAB note for John 7:50-52

(JOHN 7:50) (MATTHEW 26:58) (JOHN 12:42-43) (PROVERBS 29:25)
(JOHN 6:37) (ISAIAH 42:3) (MATTHEW 17:20) (2 TIMOTHY 1:7-8)
(1 JOHN 2:28) (MATTHEW 10:32)

August 5

Jesus, on whom our faith depends from start to finish. He was willing to die a shameful death on the cross. ✦ It was only right that God—who made everything and for whom everything was made—should bring his many children into glory. Through the suffering of Jesus, God made him a perfect leader, one fit to bring them into their salvation. ✦ They must enter into the Kingdom of God through many tribulations.

For we are not fighting against people made of flesh and blood, but against the evil rulers and authorities of the unseen world, against those mighty powers of darkness who rule this world, and against wicked spirits in the heavenly realms. Use every piece of God's armor. ✦ We are human, but we don't wage war with human plans and methods. We use God's mighty weapons, not mere worldly weapons, to knock down the Devil's strongholds.

In his kindness God called you to his eternal glory by means of Jesus Christ. After you have suffered a little while, he will restore, support, and strengthen you, and he will place you on a firm foundation.

Despite suffering, we must keep going because of the thought of victory, the vision of winning, and the hope of harvest. We will see that our suffering is worthwhile when we achieve our goal of glorifying God, winning people to Christ, and one day living eternally with him.

LAB note for 2 Timothy 2:3–7

(2 TIMOTHY 2:3) (HEBREWS 12:2) (HEBREWS 2:10) (ACTS 14:22)
(EPHESIANS 6:12–13) (2 CORINTHIANS 10:3–4) (1 PETER 5:10)

August 6

The Lord . . . is full of tenderness and mercy.

The LORD is like a father to his children, tender and compassionate to those who fear him. ❧ Who can forget the wonders he performs? How gracious and merciful is our LORD! He gives food to those who trust him; he always remembers his covenant.

He will not let you stumble and fall; the one who watches over you will not sleep. Indeed, he who watches over Israel never tires and never sleeps. ❧ Like an eagle that rouses her chicks and hovers over her young, so he spread his wings to take them in and carried them aloft on his pinions.

The unfailing love of the LORD never ends! By his mercies we have been kept from complete destruction. Great is his faithfulness; his mercies begin afresh each day.

A vast crowd was there as he [Jesus] stepped from the boat, and he had compassion on them and healed their sick. ❧ Jesus Christ is the same yesterday, today, and forever.

Not even a sparrow, worth only half a penny, can fall to the ground without your Father knowing it. And the very hairs on your head are all numbered. So don't be afraid; you are more valuable to him than a whole flock of sparrows.

Perhaps there is some sin in your life that you think God will not forgive. But God willingly responds with help when we ask. His steadfast love and mercy are greater than any sin, and he promises forgiveness.

LAB note for Lamentations 3:21-23

(JAMES 5:11) (PSALM 103:13) (PSALM 111:4-5) (PSALM 121:3-4)
(DEUTERONOMY 32:11) (LAMENTATIONS 3:22-23) (MATTHEW 14:14)
(HEBREWS 13:8) (MATTHEW 10:29-31)

August 7

I have trodden the winepress alone.

Who else among the gods is like you, O LORD? Who is glorious
in holiness like you—so awesome in splendor, performing such
wonders? ✦ He was amazed to see that no one intervened to help the
oppressed. So he himself stepped in to save them with his mighty
power and justice. ✦ He personally carried away our sins in his own
body on the cross so we can be dead to sin and live for what is right.
You have been healed by his wounds!

Sing a new song to the LORD, for he has done wonderful deeds.
He has won a mighty victory by his power and holiness. ✦ God
disarmed the evil rulers and authorities. He shamed them publicly
by his victory over them on the cross of Christ. ✦ When he sees
all that is accomplished by his anguish, he will be satisfied. And
because of what he has experienced, my righteous servant will make
it possible for many to be counted righteous, for he will bear all
their sins.

March on, my soul, with courage! ✦ Overwhelming victory is
ours through Christ, who loved us.

Because redemption is an impossible task for any human, God
himself, as the Messiah, personally stepped in to help. Whether we sin
once or many times, out of rebellion or out of ignorance, our sin
separates us from God and will continue to separate us until God forgives
us and removes it.   *LAB note for Isaiah 59:16-17*

(ISAIAH 63:3) (EXODUS 15:11) (ISAIAH 59:16) (1 PETER 2:24) (PSALM 98:1)
(COLOSSIANS 2:15) (ISAIAH 53:11) (JUDGES 5:21) (ROMANS 8:37)

August 8

For the LORD corrects those he loves, just as a father corrects a child in whom he delights.

There is no god other than me! I am the one who kills and gives life; I am the one who wounds and heals; no one delivers from my power! ❧ "For I know the plans I have for you," says the LORD. "They are plans for good and not for disaster, to give you a future and a hope." ❧ "My thoughts are completely different from yours," says the LORD. "And my ways are far beyond anything you could imagine."

But then I will win her back once again. I will lead her out into the desert and speak tenderly to her there. ❧ So you should realize that just as a parent disciplines a child, the LORD your God disciplines you to help you. ❧ For the Lord disciplines those he loves, and he punishes those he accepts as his children. ❧ No discipline is enjoyable while it is happening—it is painful! But afterward there will be a quiet harvest of right living for those who are trained in this way. ❧ Humble yourselves under the mighty power of God, and in his good time he will honor you.

I know, O LORD, that your decisions are fair; you disciplined me because I needed it.

God doesn't punish us because he enjoys inflicting pain but because he is deeply concerned about our development. He knows that in order to become morally strong and good, we must learn the difference between right and wrong. His loving discipline enables us to do that.

LAB note for Proverbs 3:11-12

(PROVERBS 3:12) (DEUTERONOMY 32:39) (JEREMIAH 29:11) (ISAIAH 55:8) (HOSEA 2:14) (DEUTERONOMY 8:5) (HEBREWS 12:6) (HEBREWS 12:11) (1 PETER 5:6) (PSALM 119:75)

August 9

The earth is the LORD's, and everything in it. The world and all its people belong to him.

She doesn't realize that it was I who gave her everything she has—the grain, the wine, the olive oil. Even the gold and silver she used in worshiping the god Baal were gifts from me! But now I will take back the wine and ripened grain I generously provided each harvest season. I will take away the linen and wool clothing I gave her to cover her nakedness.

Everything we have has come from you, and we give you only what you have already given us! We are here for only a moment, visitors and strangers in the land as our ancestors were before us. Our days on earth are like a shadow, gone so soon without a trace. O LORD our God, even these materials that we have gathered . . . come from you! It all belongs to you! ▨ For everything comes from him; everything exists by his power and is intended for his glory. To him be glory evermore. Amen.

[Our] trust should be in the living God, who richly gives us all we need for our enjoyment.

This same God who takes care of me will supply all your needs from his glorious riches, which have been given to us in Christ Jesus.

> Because "the earth is the LORD's," all of us are stewards, or caretakers. We should be committed to the proper management of this world and its resources, but we are not to become devoted to anything created or act as sole proprietors, because this world will pass away.
>
> *LAB note for Psalm 24:1*

(PSALM 24:1) (HOSEA 2:8-9) (1 CHRONICLES 29:14-16) (ROMANS 11:36) (1 TIMOTHY 6:17) (PHILIPPIANS 4:19)

August 10

They began to talk about construction projects. "Let's build a great city with a tower that reaches to the skies—a monument to our greatness!" The LORD scattered them all over the earth; and that ended the building of the city. ▨ I worked hard to distinguish wisdom from foolishness. But now I realize that even this was like chasing the wind. For the greater my wisdom, the greater my grief. To increase knowledge only increases sorrow. ▨ I also tried to find meaning by building huge homes for myself and by planting beautiful vineyards. I made gardens and parks, filling them with all kinds of fruit trees. I built reservoirs to collect the water to irrigate my many flourishing groves. I collected great sums of silver and gold, the treasure of many kings and provinces. But as I looked at everything I had worked so hard to accomplish, it was all so meaningless. It was like chasing the wind. There was nothing really worthwhile anywhere.

If you are thirsty, come to me! ▨ For he satisfies the thirsty and fills the hungry with good things.

Let heaven fill your thoughts. Do not think only about things down here on earth.

Who would set aside a fountain of living water for a cracked cistern, a pit that collected rainwater but could not hold it? Why should we cling to the broken promises of unstable "cisterns" (money, power, religious systems, or whatever transitory thing we are putting in place of God) when God promises to constantly refresh us with living water?

LAB note for Jeremiah 2:13

(JEREMIAH 2:13) (GENESIS 11:3-4, 8) (ECCLESIASTES 1:17-18)
(ECCLESIASTES 2:4-6, 8, 11) (JOHN 7:37) (PSALM 107:9) (COLOSSIANS 3:2)

August 11

I'm not asking you to take them out of the world, but to keep them safe from the evil one.

Live clean, innocent lives as children of God in a dark world full of crooked and perverse people. Let your lives shine brightly before them. ❧ You are the salt of the earth. . . . You are the light of the world. Let your good deeds shine out for all to see, so that everyone will praise your heavenly Father.

I kept you from sinning against me. ❧ The temptations that come into your life are no different from what others experience. And God is faithful. He will keep the temptation from becoming so strong that you can't stand up against it. When you are tempted, he will show you a way out so that you will not give in to it.

The Lord is faithful; he will make you strong and guard you from the evil one. ❧ He died for our sins, just as God our Father planned, in order to rescue us from this evil world in which we live. ❧ And now, all glory to God, who is able to keep you from stumbling, and who will bring you into his glorious presence innocent of sin and with great joy. All glory to him, who alone is God our Savior, through Jesus Christ our Lord. Yes, glory, majesty, power, and authority belong to him, in the beginning, now, and forevermore. Amen.

Belief in Christ should unite those who trust him. If your church has some members who are always complaining and arguing, it lacks the unifying power of Jesus Christ. If we stop arguing with other Christians or complaining about people and conditions within the church, the world will see Christ.

LAB note for Philippians 2:14-16

(JOHN 17:15) (PHILIPPIANS 2:15) (MATTHEW 5:13-14, 16) (GENESIS 20:6)
(1 CORINTHIANS 10:13) (2 THESSALONIANS 3:3) (GALATIANS 1:4) (JUDE 1:24-25)

August 12

The LORD is very great and lives in heaven. The LORD is high above the nations; his glory is far greater than the heavens. Far below him are the heavens and the earth. He stoops to look, and he lifts the poor from the dirt and the needy from the garbage dump. He sets them among princes.

But God is so rich in mercy, and he loved us so very much, that even while we were dead because of our sins, he gave us life when he raised Christ from the dead. (It is only by God's special favor that you have been saved!) For he raised us from the dead along with Christ, and we are seated with him in the heavenly realms—all because we are one with Christ Jesus.

Since God did not spare even his own Son but gave him up for us all, won't God, who gave us Christ, also give us everything else? And I am convinced that nothing can ever separate us from his love. Death can't, and life can't. The angels can't, and the demons can't. Our fears for today, our worries about tomorrow, and even the powers of hell can't keep God's love away. Whether we are high above the sky or in the deepest ocean, nothing in all creation will ever be able to separate us from the love of God that is revealed in Christ Jesus our Lord.

Fear of people can hamper everything you try to do. By contrast, fear of God—respect, reverence, and trust—is liberating. Why fear people who can do no eternal harm? Instead, trust God who can turn the harm intended by others into good for those who trust him.

LAB note from Proverbs 29:25

(PROVERBS 29:25) (ISAIAH 33:5) (PSALM 113:4, 6–8)
(EPHESIANS 2:4–6) (ROMANS 8:32, 38–39)

August 13

God deliberately chose things the world considers foolish in order to shame those who think they are wise.

When Israel cried out to the LORD for help, the LORD raised up a man to rescue them. His name was Ehud son of Gera, of the tribe of Benjamin, who was left-handed. After Ehud, Shamgar son of Anath rescued Israel. He killed six hundred Philistines with an ox goad.

Then the LORD turned to him [Gideon] and said, "Go with the strength you have and rescue Israel from the Midianites. I am sending you!" "But Lord," Gideon replied, "how can I rescue Israel? My clan is the weakest in the whole tribe of Manasseh, and I am the least in my entire family!"

The LORD said to Gideon, "You have too many warriors with you. If I let all of you fight the Midianites, the Israelites will boast to me that they saved themselves by their own strength."

"It is not by force nor by strength, but by my Spirit," says the LORD Almighty. ▓ Be strong with the Lord's mighty power.

Is Christianity against rational thinking? Christians clearly do believe in using their minds to weigh the evidence and make wise choices. But no amount of human knowledge can replace or bypass Christ's work on the cross.   *LAB note for 1 Corinthians 1:27*

(1 CORINTHIANS 1:27) (JUDGES 3:15, 31) (JUDGES 6:14–15) (JUDGES 7:2)
(ZECHARIAH 4:6) (EPHESIANS 6:10)

August 14

The joy of the LORD is your strength.

Sing for joy, O heavens! Rejoice, O earth! Burst into song, O mountains! For the LORD has comforted his people and will have compassion on them in their sorrow. ※ God has come to save me. I will trust in him and not be afraid. The LORD God is my strength and my song; he has become my salvation. ※ The LORD is my strength, my shield from every danger. I trust in him with all my heart. He helps me, and my heart is filled with joy. I burst out in songs of thanksgiving.

Now we can rejoice in our wonderful new relationship with God—all because of what our Lord Jesus Christ has done for us in making us friends of God. ※ Even though the fig trees have no blossoms, and there are no grapes on the vine; even though the olive crop fails, and the fields lie empty and barren; even though the flocks die in the fields, and the cattle barns are empty, yet I will rejoice in the LORD! I will be joyful in the God of my salvation. The Sovereign LORD is my strength! He will make me as surefooted as a deer and bring me safely over the mountains.

Celebration is not to be self-centered (just when we feel like it). Often when we celebrate and give to others (even when we don't feel like it), we are strengthened spiritually and filled with joy. Enter into celebrations that honor God, and allow him to fill you with his joy!

LAB note for Nehemiah 8:9-10

(NEHEMIAH 8:10) (ISAIAH 49:13) (ISAIAH 12:2) (PSALM 28:7)
(ROMANS 5:11) (HABAKKUK 3:17-19)

August 15

He existed before everything else began.

The faithful and true witness, the ruler of God's creation. ❧ Christ is the Head of the church, which is his body. He is the first of all who will rise from the dead, so he is first in everything.

The LORD formed me from the beginning, before he created anything else. I was appointed in ages past, at the very first, before the earth began. I was there when he established the heavens, when he drew the horizon on the oceans. I was there when he set the clouds above, when he established the deep fountains of the earth. I was there when he set the limits of the seas, so they would not spread beyond their boundaries. And when he marked off the earth's foundations, I was the architect at his side. I was his constant delight, rejoicing always in his presence. ❧ From eternity to eternity I am God.

Jesus, on whom our faith depends from start to finish. He was willing to die a shameful death on the cross because of the joy he knew would be his afterward. Now he is seated in the place of highest honor beside God's throne in heaven.

God is not only the creator of the world but also its sustainer. Because Christ is the sustainer of all life, none of us is independent from him. We are all his servants who must daily trust him to protect us, care for us, and sustain us.   *LAB note for Colossians 1:17*

(COLOSSIANS 1:17) (REVELATION 3:14) (COLOSSIANS 1:18)
(PROVERBS 8:22-23, 27-30) (ISAIAH 43:13) (HEBREWS 12:2)

August 16

Is there any god in heaven or on earth who can perform such great deeds as yours?

Who in all of heaven can compare with the LORD? What mightiest angel is anything like the LORD? O LORD God Almighty! Where is there anyone as mighty as you, LORD? Faithfulness is your very character. ❧ Nowhere among the pagan gods is there a god like you, O Lord. There are no other miracles like yours. ❧ All heaven will praise your miracles, LORD; myriads of angels will praise you for your faithfulness. ❧ For the sake of your promise and according to your will, you have done all these great things and have shown them to me. How great you are, O Sovereign LORD! . . . We have never even heard of another god like you!

"No eye has seen, no ear has heard, and no mind has imagined what God has prepared for those who love him." But we know these things because God has revealed them to us by his Spirit, and his Spirit searches out everything and shows us even God's deep secrets.

Have you never heard or understood? Don't you know that the LORD is the everlasting God, the Creator of all the earth? He never grows faint or weary.

In the courts of heaven, a host of angels praise the Lord. The scene is one of such majesty and grandeur to show that our God is beyond compare. His power and purity place him high above nature and angels.

LAB note for Psalm 89:5

(DEUTERONOMY 3:24) (PSALM 89:6, 8) (PSALM 86:8) (PSALM 89:5)
(2 SAMUEL 7:21-22) (1 CORINTHIANS 2:9-10) (ISAIAH 40:28)

August 17

The person who wishes to boast should boast only of what the Lord has done.

Let not the wise man gloat in his wisdom, or the mighty man in his might, or the rich man in his riches. Let them boast in this alone: that they truly know me and understand that I am the LORD.

Everything else is worthless when compared with the priceless gain of knowing Christ Jesus my Lord. I have discarded everything else, counting it all as garbage, so that I may have Christ. ❊ His unchanging plan has always been to adopt us into his own family by bringing us to himself through Jesus Christ. ❊ I am not ashamed of this Good News about Christ. It is the power of God at work, saving everyone who believes—Jews first and also Gentiles.

Whom have I in heaven but you? I desire you more than anything on earth. ❊ My heart rejoices in the LORD!

Not to us, O LORD, but to you goes all the glory for your unfailing love and faithfulness. ❊ He must become greater and greater, and I must become less and less.

People tend to admire three things about others: wisdom, power (might), and riches. But God puts a higher priority on knowing him personally and living a life that reflects his justice and righteousness. What do you want people to admire most about you?   *LAB note for Jeremiah 9:23-24*

(1 CORINTHIANS 1:31) (JEREMIAH 9:23-24) (PHILIPPIANS 3:8) (EPHESIANS 1:5)
(ROMANS 1:16) (PSALM 73:25) (1 SAMUEL 2:1) (PSALM 115:1) (JOHN 3:30)

August 18

LORD, you are mine!

Everything belongs to you . . . and you belong to Christ, and Christ belongs to God. ❧ Jesus Christ . . . gave his life to free us from every kind of sin, to cleanse us, and to make us his very own people, totally committed to doing what is right. ❧ God has put all things under the authority of Christ, and he gave him this authority for the benefit of the church. ❧ Christ . . . gave up his life for her [the church]. He did this to present her to himself as a glorious church without a spot or wrinkle or any other blemish. Instead, she will be holy and without fault.

I will boast only in the LORD. ❧ I am overwhelmed with joy in the LORD my God! For he has dressed me with the clothing of salvation and draped me in a robe of righteousness.

Whom have I in heaven but you? I desire you more than anything on earth. My health may fail, and my spirit may grow weak, but God remains the strength of my heart; he is mine forever. ❧ I said to the LORD, "You are my Master! All the good things I have are from you." LORD, you alone are my inheritance, my cup of blessing. You guard all that is mine. The land you have given me is a pleasant land. What a wonderful inheritance!

As Christians we can be confident that God has won the final victory and is in control of everything. We need not fear any dictator or nation or even death or Satan himself. The contract has been signed and sealed; we are waiting just a short while for delivery.

LAB note for Ephesians 1:20-22

(PSALM 119:57) (1 CORINTHIANS 3:21, 23) (TITUS 2:13-14) (EPHESIANS 1:22) (EPHESIANS 5:25, 27) (PSALM 34:2) (ISAIAH 61:10) (PSALM 73:25-26) (PSALM 16:2, 5-6)

August 19

There is a path before each person that seems right, but it ends in death.

Trusting oneself is foolish, but those who walk in wisdom are safe.

Your word is a lamp for my feet and a light for my path. I have followed your commands, which have kept me from going along with cruel and evil people.

Suppose there are prophets among you, or those who have dreams about the future, and they promise you signs or miracles, and the predicted signs or miracles take place. If the prophets then say, "Come, let us worship the gods of foreign nations," do not listen to them. The LORD your God is testing you to see if you love him with all your heart and soul. Serve only the LORD your God and fear him alone. Obey his commands, listen to his voice, and cling to him.

The LORD says, "I will guide you along the best pathway for your life. I will advise you and watch over you. Do not be like a senseless horse or mule that needs a bit and bridle to keep it under control." Many sorrows come to the wicked, but unfailing love surrounds those who trust the LORD. So rejoice in the LORD and be glad, all you who obey him! Shout for joy, all you whose hearts are pure!

The "path . . . that seems right" may offer many options and require few sacrifices. But easy choices merit a second look. Is this solution attractive because it allows you to be lazy or not change your lifestyle? because it requires no moral restraints? The right choice often requires hard work and self-sacrifice. *LAB note for Proverbs 14:12*

(PROVERBS 14:12) (PROVERBS 28:26) (PSALM 119:105) (PSALM 17:4)
(DEUTERONOMY 13:1-4) (PSALM 32:8-11)

August 20

God gave Solomon great wisdom and understanding.

Now someone greater than Solomon is here. ▩ Prince of Peace.

No one is likely to die for a good person, though someone might be willing to die for a person who is especially good. But God showed his great love for us in sending Christ to die for us while we were still sinners. ▩ Though [Jesus] was God, he did not demand and cling to his rights as God. He made himself nothing; he took the humble position of a slave and appeared in human form. And in human form he obediently humbled himself even further by dying a criminal's death on a cross. ▩ May you experience the love of Christ, though it is so great you will never fully understand it.

Christ is the mighty power of God and the wonderful wisdom of God. ▩ In him lie hidden all the treasures of wisdom and knowledge. ▩ The endless treasures available . . . in Christ ▩ God alone made it possible for you to be in Christ Jesus. For our benefit God made Christ to be wisdom itself. He is the one who made us acceptable to God. He made us pure and holy, and he gave himself to purchase our freedom.

Even the queen of Sheba recognized the truth about God when it was presented to her—unlike Israel's religious leaders, who ignored the truth even though it stared them in the face. How have you responded to the evidence and truth that you have? *LAB note for Matthew 12:41-42*

(1 KINGS 4:29) (MATTHEW 12:42) (ISAIAH 9:6) (ROMANS 5:7-8)
(PHILIPPIANS 2:5-8) (EPHESIANS 3:19) (1 CORINTHIANS 1:24) (COLOSSIANS 2:3)
(EPHESIANS 3:8) (1 CORINTHIANS 1:30)

August 21

I made you, and I will care for you.

But now, O Israel, the LORD who created you says: "Do not be afraid, for I have ransomed you. I have called you by name; you are mine. When you go through deep waters and great trouble, I will be with you. When you go through rivers of difficulty, you will not drown! When you walk through the fire of oppression, you will not be burned up; the flames will not consume you." ❧ I will be your God throughout your lifetime—until your hair is white with age.

Like an eagle that rouses her chicks and hovers over her young, so he spread his wings to take them in and carried them aloft on his pinions. The LORD alone guided them. ❧ In his love and mercy he redeemed them. He lifted them up and carried them through all the years.

Jesus Christ is the same yesterday, today, and forever. ❧ I am convinced that nothing can ever separate us from . . . the love of God that is revealed in Christ Jesus our Lord.

Can a mother forget her nursing child? Can she feel no love for a child she has borne? But even if that were possible, I would not forget you!

Our great God created us and cares for us. His love is so enduring that he will care for us throughout our lifetime and even through death. Then, if you have accepted Christ as your Savior, you will go to heaven to spend eternity with him! *LAB note for Isaiah 46:1-4*

(ISAIAH 46:4) (ISAIAH 43:1-2) (ISAIAH 46:4) (DEUTERONOMY 32:11-12)
(ISAIAH 63:9) (HEBREWS 13:8) (ROMANS 8:38-39) (ISAIAH 49:15)

August 22

Consider the quarry from which you were mined, the rock from which you were cut!

I was born a sinner—yes, from the moment my mother conceived me. ▨ No one had the slightest interest in you; no one pitied you or cared for you. On the day you were born, you were dumped in a field and left to die, unwanted. But I came by and saw you there, helplessly kicking about in your own blood. As you lay there, I said, "Live!" And I helped you to thrive like a plant in the field.

He lifted me out of the pit of despair, out of the mud and the mire. He set my feet on solid ground and steadied me as I walked along. He has given me a new song to sing, a hymn of praise to our God.

When we were utterly helpless, Christ came at just the right time and died for us sinners. Now, no one is likely to die for a good person, though someone might be willing to die for a person who is especially good. But God showed his great love for us by sending Christ to die for us while we were still sinners. ▨ God is so rich in mercy, and he loved us so very much, that even while we were dead because of our sins, he gave us life when he raised Christ from the dead.

The faithful remnant may have felt alone because they were few. But God reminded them of their spiritual heritage: Abraham was only one person, but much came from his faithfulness. If we Christians, even a faithful few, remain faithful, think what God can do through us!

LAB note for Isaiah 51:1-2

(ISAIAH 51:1) (PSALM 51:5) (EZEKIEL 16:5-6) (PSALM 40:2-3) (ROMANS 5:6-8) (EPHESIANS 2:4-5)

August 23

I am overwhelmed with joy in the LORD my God!

I will praise the LORD at all times. I will constantly speak his praises. I will boast only in the LORD; let all who are discouraged take heart. Come, let us tell of the LORD's greatness; let us exalt his name together. ❧ The LORD our God is our light and protector. He gives us grace and glory. No good thing will the LORD withhold from those who do what is right. O LORD Almighty, happy are those who trust in you. ❧ With my whole heart, I will praise his holy name.

Those who have reason to be thankful should continually sing praises to the Lord. ❧ Let the Holy Spirit fill and control you. Then you will sing psalms and hymns and spiritual songs among yourselves, making music to the Lord in your hearts. And you will always give thanks for everything to God the Father in the name of our Lord Jesus Christ. ❧ Sing psalms and hymns and spiritual songs to God with thankful hearts.

Around midnight, Paul and Silas were praying and singing hymns to God. ❧ Always be full of joy in the Lord. I say it again—rejoice!

God promises great blessings to his people, but many of them require our active participation: We must seek him, cry out to him, trust him, fear him, reverence him, refrain from lying, turn from evil, do good, seek peace, be brokenhearted, and serve him. *LAB note for Psalm 34:1ff.*

(ISAIAH 61:10) (PSALM 34:1-3) (PSALM 84:11-12) (PSALM 103:1) (JAMES 5:13) (EPHESIANS 5:18-20) (COLOSSIANS 3:16) (ACTS 16:25) (PHILIPPIANS 4:4)

August 24

My cup overflows with blessings!

Taste and see that the LORD is good. Oh, the joys of those who trust in him! Let the LORD's people show him reverence, for those who honor him will have all they need. Even strong young lions sometimes go hungry, but those who trust in the LORD will never lack any good thing. ▨ The unfailing love of the LORD never ends! . . . Great is his faithfulness; his mercies begin afresh each day.

LORD, you alone are my inheritance, my cup of blessing. You guard all that is mine. The land you have given me is a pleasant land. What a wonderful inheritance! ▨ The whole world and life and death; the present and the future. Everything belongs to you. ▨ How we praise God, the Father of our Lord Jesus Christ, who has blessed us with every spiritual blessing in the heavenly realms because we belong to Christ.

I have learned how to get along happily whether I have much or little. ▨ True religion with contentment is great wealth. ▨ God . . . will supply all your needs from his glorious riches, which have been given to us in Christ Jesus.

You say you belong to the Lord, but do you show reverence to him? To revere the Lord means to show deep respect and honor to him. We demonstrate true reverence by our humble attitude and genuine worship. *LAB note for Psalm 34:9*

(PSALM 23:5) (PSALM 34:8-10) (LAMENTATIONS 3:22-23) (PSALM 16:5-6)
(1 CORINTHIANS 3:22) (EPHESIANS 1:3) (PHILIPPIANS 4:11)
(1 TIMOTHY 6:6) (PHILIPPIANS 4:19)

August 25

Your word is a lamp for my feet and a light for my path.

Wherever you walk, their counsel can lead you. When you sleep, they will protect you. When you wake up in the morning, they will advise you. For these commands and this teaching are a lamp to light the way ahead of you. The correction of discipline is the way to life. ▩ You will hear a voice say, "This is the way; turn around and walk here."

I am the light of the world. If you follow me, you won't be stumbling through the darkness, because you will have the light that leads to life. ▩ We have . . . confidence in the message proclaimed by the prophets. Pay close attention to what they wrote, for their words are like a light shining in a dark place—until the day Christ appears and his brilliant light shines in your hearts. ▩ Now we see things imperfectly as in a poor mirror, but then we will see everything with perfect clarity. All that I know now is partial and incomplete, but then I will know everything completely, just as God knows me now.

In this life we walk through a dark forest of evil. But the Bible can be our light to show us the way ahead so we won't stumble as we walk. It reveals the entangling roots of false values and philosophies. Study the Bible so you will be able to see your way clear enough to stay on the right path.

LAB note for Psalm 119:105

(PSALM 119:105) (PROVERBS 6:22–23) (ISAIAH 30:21)
(JOHN 8:12) (2 PETER 1:19) (1 CORINTHIANS 13:12)

August 26

Those who trust the LORD will be happy.

Abraham never wavered in believing God's promise. In fact, his faith grew stronger, and in this he brought glory to God. He was absolutely convinced that God was able to do anything he promised. ▓ Judah defeated Israel because they trusted in the LORD, the God of their ancestors.

God is our refuge and strength, always ready to help in times of trouble. So we will not fear, even if earthquakes come and the mountains crumble into the sea. ▓ It is better to trust the LORD than to put confidence in people. It is better to trust the LORD than to put confidence in princes. ▓ The steps of the godly are directed by the LORD. He delights in every detail of their lives. Though they stumble, they will not fall, for the LORD holds them by the hand.

Taste and see that the LORD is good. Oh, the joys of those who trust in him! Let the LORD's people show him reverence, for those who honor him will have all they need.

"Taste and see" does not mean "check out God's credentials." Instead, it is a warm invitation: "Try this; I know you'll like it." When we take that first step of obedience in following God, we cannot help discovering that he is good and kind. *LAB note for Psalm 34:8*

(PROVERBS 16:20) (ROMANS 4:20-21) (2 CHRONICLES 13:18) (PSALM 46:1-2) (PSALM 118:8-9) (PSALM 37:23-24) (PSALM 34:8-9)

August 27

I will lie down in peace and sleep, for you alone, O LORD, will keep me safe.

Do not be afraid of the terrors of the night, nor fear the dangers of the day, nor dread the plague that stalks in darkness, nor the disaster that strikes at midday. He will shield you with his wings. He will shelter you with his feathers. His faithful promises are your armor and protection. 🕮 He will not let you stumble and fall; the one who watches over you will not sleep. Indeed, he who watches over Israel never tires and never sleeps. The LORD himself watches over you! The LORD stands beside you as your protective shade. The sun will not hurt you by day, nor the moon at night. The LORD keeps you from all evil and preserves your life. The LORD keeps watch over you as you come and go, both now and forever.

Let me live forever in your sanctuary, safe beneath the shelter of your wings! 🕮 Even in darkness I cannot hide from you. To you the night shines as bright as day. Darkness and light are both alike to you.

Since God did not spare even his own Son but gave him up for us all, won't God, who gave us Christ, also give us everything else? 🕮 You belong to Christ, and Christ belongs to God. 🕮 I will trust in him and not be afraid.

Do you ever think that because you aren't good enough for God, he will not save you? Because Christ gave his life for you, God isn't going to hold back the gift of salvation! He will not condemn you. And he will not withhold anything you need to live for him.   *LAB note for Romans 8:31-34*

(PSALM 4:8) (PSALM 91:5-6, 4) (PSALM 121:3-8) (PSALM 61:4) (PSALM 139:12) (ROMANS 8:32) (1 CORINTHIANS 3:23) (ISAIAH 12:2)

August 28

If any of you wants to be my follower, you must put aside your selfish ambition, shoulder your cross daily, and follow me.

We serve God whether people honor us or despise us, whether they slander us or praise us. ▧ Everyone who wants to live a godly life in Christ Jesus will suffer persecution. ▧ The fact that I am still being persecuted proves that I am still preaching salvation through the cross of Christ alone.

Be happy if you are insulted for being a Christian, for then the glorious Spirit of God will come upon you. If you suffer, however, it must not be for murder, stealing, making trouble, or prying into other people's affairs. But it is no shame to suffer for being a Christian. Praise God for the privilege of being called by his wonderful name! So if you are suffering according to God's will, keep on doing what is right, and trust yourself to the God who made you.

For you have been given not only the privilege of trusting in Christ but also the privilege of suffering for him. ▧ If we endure hardship, we will reign with him.

Christians follow their Lord by imitating his life and obeying his commands. We must deny our selfish desires to use our time and money our own way and choose our own direction. Following Christ in this life may be costly, but in the long run, it is well worth the pain and effort.

LAB note for Luke 9:23

(LUKE 9:23) (2 CORINTHIANS 6:8) (2 TIMOTHY 3:12) (GALATIANS 5:11)
(1 PETER 4:14-16, 19) (PHILIPPIANS 1:29) (2 TIMOTHY 2:12)

August 29

Wait patiently for the LORD. Be brave and courageous. Yes, wait patiently for the LORD.

Have you never heard or understood? Don't you know that the LORD is the everlasting God, the Creator of all the earth? He never grows faint or weary. . . . He gives power to those who are tired and worn out; he offers strength to the weak. ❧ Don't be afraid, for I am with you. Do not be dismayed, for I am your God. I will strengthen you. I will help you. I will uphold you with my victorious right hand. ❧ To the poor, O LORD, you are a refuge from the storm. To the needy in distress, you are a shelter from the rain and the heat. For the oppressive acts of ruthless people are like a storm beating against a wall.

When your faith is tested, your endurance has a chance to grow. So let it grow, for when your endurance is fully developed, you will be strong in character and ready for anything. ❧ Do not throw away this confident trust in the Lord, no matter what happens. Remember the great reward it brings you! Patient endurance is what you need now, so you will continue to do God's will. Then you will receive all that he has promised. "For in just a little while, the Coming One will come and not delay."

Waiting for God is not easy. Often it seems he isn't answering our prayers or doesn't understand the urgency of our situation. But that kind of thinking implies God is not in control or not fair. God is worth waiting for—and he often uses our times of waiting to refresh, renew, and teach us.   *LAB note for Psalm 27:14*

(PSALM 27:14) (ISAIAH 40:28-29) (ISAIAH 41:10) (ISAIAH 25:4)
(JAMES 1:3-4) (HEBREWS 10:35-37)

August 30

You don't understand now why I am doing it; someday you will.

Remember how the LORD your God led you through the wilderness for forty years, humbling you and testing you to prove your character, and to find out whether or not you would really obey his commands.

I made a covenant with you, says the Sovereign LORD, and you became mine. ❧ The Lord disciplines those he loves.

Dear friends, don't be surprised at the fiery trials you are going through, as if something strange were happening to you. Instead, be very glad—because these trials will make you partners with Christ in his suffering, and afterward you will have the wonderful joy of sharing his glory when it is displayed to all the world. ❧ Our present troubles are quite small and won't last very long. Yet they produce for us an immeasurably great glory that will last forever! So we don't look at the troubles we can see right now; rather, we look forward to what we have not yet seen. For the troubles we see will soon be over, but the joys to come will last forever.

Imagine being Peter and watching Jesus wash the others' feet, all the while moving closer to you. Seeing his Master behave like a slave must have confused Peter. He still did not understand Jesus' teaching that to be a leader, a person must be a servant. How do you treat those who work under you? *LAB note for John 13:6-7*

(JOHN 13:7) (DEUTERONOMY 8:2) (EZEKIEL 16:8) (HEBREWS 12:6)
(1 PETER 4:12-13) (2 CORINTHIANS 4:17-18)

August 31

Let us lift our hearts and hands to God in heaven.

Who can be compared with the LORD our God, who is enthroned on high? Far below him are the heavens and the earth. He stoops to look, and he lifts the poor from the dirt and the needy from the garbage dump. He sets them among princes. ❧ To you, O LORD, I lift up my soul. ❧ I reach out for you. I thirst for you as parched land thirsts for rain. Come quickly, LORD, and answer me, for my depression deepens. Don't turn away from me, or I will die. Let me hear of your unfailing love to me in the morning, for I am trusting you. Show me where to walk, for I have come to you in prayer.

Your unfailing love is better to me than life itself; how I praise you! I will honor you as long as I live, lifting up my hands to you in prayer. ❧ Give me happiness, O Lord, for my life depends on you. O Lord, you are so good, so ready to forgive, so full of unfailing love for all who ask your aid. Listen closely to my prayer, O LORD; hear my urgent cry. I will call to you whenever trouble strikes, and you will answer me.

If our conscience is clear, we can come to God with bold confidence. And we will receive whatever we request because we obey him and do the things that please him.

Sometimes our trouble or pain is so great that all we can do is cry out to God for protection. And often when there is no relief in sight, all we can do is acknowledge the greatness of God and wait for better days. The conviction that God answers prayer will sustain us in such difficult times. *LAB note for Psalm 86:7*

(LAMENTATIONS 3:41) (PSALM 113:5-8) (PSALM 25:1) (PSALM 143:6-8) (PSALM 63:3-4) (PSALM 86:4-7) (1 JOHN 3:21-22)

September

Teachable Moments

Playpens and classrooms
Offices and family rooms
Learning can happen anywhere.

Although September is the traditional month for
school to begin each year, learning is a year-round
activity and a lifelong endeavor. If learning ceases,
growth ends. What has life been teaching you lately?

September 1

I will give them one heart and mind to worship me forever, for their own good and for the good of all their descendants.

I will give you a new heart with new and right desires, and I will put a new spirit in you. I will take out your stony heart of sin and give you a new, obedient heart. ❧ The LORD is good and does what is right; he shows the proper path to those who go astray. He leads the humble in what is right, teaching them his way. The LORD leads with unfailing love and faithfulness all those who keep his covenant and obey his decrees.

That they will be one, just as you and I are one, Father—that just as you are in me and I am in you, so they will be in us, and the world will believe you sent me.

Lead a life worthy of your calling, for you have been called by God. Be humble and gentle. Be patient with each other, making allowance for each other's faults because of your love. Always keep yourselves united in the Holy Spirit, and bind yourselves together with peace. We are all one body, we have the same Spirit, and we have all been called to the same glorious future. There is only one Lord, one faith, one baptism, and there is only one God and Father, who is over us all and in us all and living through us all.

God uses his power to accomplish his purposes through his people. God doesn't give you power to be all you want to be, but the power to be all he wants you to be. We must develop "one heart" toward him, loving God above everything else.   *LAB note for Jeremiah 32:36-42*

(JEREMIAH 32:39) (EZEKIEL 36:26) (PSALM 25:8-10)
(JOHN 17:21) (EPHESIANS 4:1-6)

September 2

Watchman . . . when will the night be over?

Time is running out. Wake up, for the coming of our salvation is nearer now than when we first believed. The night is almost gone; the day of salvation will soon be here. So don't live in darkness. Get rid of your evil deeds. Shed them like dirty clothes. Clothe yourselves with the armor of right living, as those who live in the light.

Now learn a lesson from the fig tree. When its buds become tender and its leaves begin to sprout, you know without being told that summer is near. Just so, when you see the events I've described beginning to happen, you can know his return is very near, right at the door. Heaven and earth will disappear, but my words will remain forever.

I am counting on the LORD; yes, I am counting on him. I have put my hope in his word. I long for the Lord more than sentries long for the dawn, yes, more than sentries long for the dawn.

He who is the faithful witness to all these things says, "Yes, I am coming soon!" Amen! Come, Lord Jesus!

So stay awake and be prepared, because you do not know the day or hour of my return.

We don't know the day or the hour, but Jesus is coming soon and unexpectedly. This is good news to those who trust him but a terrible message for those who have rejected him. Soon means "at any moment," and we must be ready for him. *LAB note for Revelation 22:20*

(ISAIAH 21:11) (ROMANS 13:11-12) (MATTHEW 24:32-33, 35) (PSALM 130:5-6)
(REVELATION 22:20) (MATTHEW 25:13)

September 3

Don't copy the behavior and customs of this world, but let God transform you into a new person by changing the way you think.

Don't you realize that friendship with this world makes you an enemy of God? I say it again, that if your aim is to enjoy this world, you can't be a friend of God.

Don't team up with those who are unbelievers. How can goodness be a partner with wickedness? How can light live with darkness? What harmony can there be between Christ and the Devil? How can a believer be a partner with an unbeliever? ❦ Stop loving this evil world and all that it offers you, for when you love the world, you show that you do not have the love of the Father in you. This world is fading away, along with everything it craves. But if you do the will of God, you will live forever.

You used to live just like the rest of the world, full of sin, obeying Satan, the mighty prince of the power of the air. ❦ That isn't what you were taught when you learned about Christ. Since you have heard all about him and have learned the truth that is in Jesus, throw off your old evil nature.

God has good, pleasing, and perfect plans for his children. He wants us to be transformed people with renewed minds, living to honor and obey him. Because he wants only what is best for us and gave his Son to make our new life possible, we should joyfully give ourselves as living sacrifices for his service. *LAB note for Romans 12:1-2*

(ROMANS 12:2) (JAMES 4:4) (2 CORINTHIANS 6:14-15) (1 JOHN 2:15, 17)
(EPHESIANS 2:2) (EPHESIANS 4:20-22)

September 4

The Lord is thinking about me right now.

"For I know the plans I have for you," says the LORD. "They are plans for good and not for disaster, to give you a future and a hope." ⬛ "My thoughts are completely different from yours," says the LORD. "And my ways are far beyond anything you could imagine. For just as the heavens are higher than the earth, so are my ways higher than your ways and my thoughts higher than your thoughts."

How precious are your thoughts about me, O God! They are innumerable! I can't even count them; they outnumber the grains of sand! And when I wake up in the morning, you are still with me! ⬛ O LORD, what great miracles you do! And how deep are your thoughts. ⬛ O LORD my God, you have done many miracles for us. Your plans for us are too numerous to list.

Few of you were wise in the world's eyes, or powerful, or wealthy when God called you. ⬛ Hasn't God chosen the poor in this world to be rich in faith? Aren't they the ones who will inherit the kingdom God promised to those who love him? ⬛ Our hearts ache, but we always have joy. ⬛ The endless treasures available . . . in Christ.

God knows the future, and his plans for us are good and full of hope. As long as God, who knows the future, provides our agenda, and goes with us as we fulfill his mission, we can have boundless hope—even in times of pain, suffering, or hardship. *LAB note for Jeremiah 29:11*

(PSALM 40:17) (JEREMIAH 29:11) (ISAIAH 55:8-9) (PSALM 139:17-18)
(PSALM 92:5) (PSALM 40:5) (1 CORINTHIANS 1:26) (JAMES 2:5)
(2 CORINTHIANS 6:10) (EPHESIANS 3:8)

September 5

My feet were slipping, and I was almost gone.

I cried out, "I'm slipping!" and your unfailing love, O LORD, supported me. ▦ Simon, Simon, Satan has asked to have all of you, to sift you like wheat. But I have pleaded in prayer for you, Simon, that your faith should not fail.

They may trip seven times, but each time they will rise again. ▦ Though they stumble, they will not fall, for the LORD holds them by the hand.

Do not gloat over me, my enemies! For though I fall, I will rise again. Though I sit in darkness, the LORD himself will be my light.

He will rescue you again and again so that no evil can touch you.

If you do sin, there is someone to plead for you before the Father. He is Jesus Christ, the one who pleases God completely. ▦ He is able, once and forever, to save everyone who comes to God through him. He lives forever to plead with God on their behalf.

Satan wanted to crush Simon Peter and the other disciples like grains of wheat. He hoped to find only chaff and blow it away. But Jesus assured Peter that his faith, although it would falter, would not be destroyed. It would be renewed, and Peter would become a powerful leader. *LAB note for Luke 22:31-32*

(PSALM 73:2) (PSALM 94:18) (LUKE 22:31-32) (PROVERBS 24:16) (PSALM 37:24) (MICAH 7:8) (JOB 5:19) (1 JOHN 2:1) (HEBREWS 7:25)

September 6

When the Holy Spirit controls our lives, he will produce . . . faithfulness.

God saved you by his special favor when you believed. And you can't take credit for this; it is a gift from God. ❧ It is impossible to please God without faith. Anyone who wants to come to him must believe that there is a God and that he rewards those who sincerely seek him. ❧ There is no judgment awaiting those who trust him. But those who do not trust him have already been judged for not believing in the only Son of God. ❧ I do believe, but help me not to doubt!

Those who obey God's word really do love him. That is the way to know whether or not we live in him.

That is why we live by believing and not by seeing. ❧ I have been crucified with Christ. I myself no longer live, but Christ lives in me. So I live my life in this earthly body by trusting in the Son of God, who loved me and gave himself for me. ❧ You love him even though you have never seen him. Though you do not see him, you trust him; and even now you are happy with a glorious, inexpressible joy.

When someone gives you a gift, do you say, "That's very nice—now how much do I owe you?" No, the appropriate response is "Thank you." Yet how often Christians feel obligated to try to work their way to God. Instead, we should respond with gratitude, praise, and joy.

LAB note for Ephesians 2:8-9

(GALATIANS 5:22) (EPHESIANS 2:8) (HEBREWS 11:6) (JOHN 3:18) (MARK 9:24)
(1 JOHN 2:5) (2 CORINTHIANS 5:7) (GALATIANS 2:19-20) (1 PETER 1:8)

September 7

When I am weak, then I am strong. ✹ My God has given me strength. ✹ "My gracious favor is all you need. My power works best in your weakness." So now I am glad to boast about my weaknesses, so that the power of Christ may work through me. ✹ Trust in the LORD always, for the LORD God is the eternal Rock.

Give your burdens to the LORD, and he will take care of you. He will not permit the godly to slip and fall. ✹ His arms were strengthened by the Mighty One of Jacob, the Shepherd, the Rock of Israel.

You come to me with sword, spear, and javelin, but I come to you in the name of the LORD Almighty—the God of the armies of Israel, whom you have defied. ✹ I will rejoice in the LORD. I will be glad because he rescues me. I will praise him from the bottom of my heart: "LORD, who can compare with you? Who else rescues the weak and helpless from the strong?"

Waiting on the Lord is the patient expectation that God will fulfill his promises in his Word and strengthen us to rise above life's difficulties. It means to completely trust in God.   *LAB note for Isaiah 40*

(ISAIAH 40:31) (2 CORINTHIANS 12:10) (ISAIAH 49:5) (2 CORINTHIANS 12:9)
(ISAIAH 26:4) (PSALM 55:22) (GENESIS 49:24) (1 SAMUEL 17:45) (PSALM 35:9-10)

September 8

Be glad for all God is planning for you.

You are looking forward to the joys of heaven. ❧ If we have hope in Christ only for this life, we are the most miserable people in the world. ❧ They must enter into the Kingdom of God through many tribulations. ❧ You cannot be my disciple if you do not carry your own cross and follow me. ❧ You know that such troubles are going to happen to us Christians.

Always be full of joy in the Lord. I say it again—rejoice! ❧ I pray that God, who gives you hope, will keep you happy and full of peace as you believe in him. ❧ All honor to the God and Father of our Lord Jesus Christ, for it is by his boundless mercy that God has given us the privilege of being born again. Now we live with a wonderful expectation because Jesus Christ rose again from the dead. ❧ You love him even though you have never seen him. Though you do not see him, you trust him; and even now you are happy with a glorious, inexpressible joy. ❧ Because of our faith, Christ has brought us into this place of highest privilege where we now stand, and we confidently and joyfully look forward to sharing God's glory.

When Paul says that we look forward to the joys of heaven, he is emphasizing the security of the believer. Because we know our future destination and salvation are sure, we are free to live for Christ and love others. *LAB note for Colossians 1:5*

(Romans 12:12) (Colossians 1:5) (1 Corinthians 15:19) (Acts 14:22)
(Luke 14:27) (1 Thessalonians 3:3) (Philippians 4:4) (Romans 15:13)
(1 Peter 1:3) (1 Peter 1:8) (Romans 5:2)

September 9

The LORD is for me; he will help me.

In times of trouble, may the LORD respond to your cry. May the God of Israel keep you safe from all harm. May he send you help from his sanctuary and strengthen you from Jerusalem. May we shout for joy when we hear of your victory, flying banners to honor our God. May the LORD answer all your prayers. Some nations boast of their armies and weapons, but we boast in the LORD our God. Those nations will fall down and collapse, but we will rise up and stand firm.

He will come like a flood tide driven by the breath of the LORD. ▨ Remember that the temptations that come into your life are no different from what others experience. And God is faithful. He will keep the temptation from becoming so strong that you can't stand up against it. When you are tempted, he will show you a way out so that you will not give in to it.

If God is for us, who can ever be against us? ▨ The LORD is for me, so I will not be afraid. What can mere mortals do to me?

The God whom we serve is able to save us. He will rescue us from your power.

As long as there have been armies and weapons, nations have boasted of their power, but such power does not last. True might is in God's power. Because God alone can preserve a nation or an individual, be sure your confidence is in God, who gives eternal victory.

LAB note for Psalm 20:6-8

(PSALM 118:7) (PSALM 20:1-2, 5, 7-8) (ISAIAH 59:19) (1 CORINTHIANS 10:13) (ROMANS 8:31) (PSALM 118:6) (DANIEL 3:17)

September 10

You should be known for the beauty that comes from within, the unfading beauty of a gentle and quiet spirit, which is so precious to God. ❧ For you have been born again. Your new life did not come from your earthly parents because the life they gave you will end in death. But this new life will last forever because it comes from the eternal, living word of God. Those who believe in me, even though they die like everyone else, will live again. ❧ They are children of God raised up to new life. ❧ The glorious, ever-living God.

(Those who do not have the Spirit of Christ living in them are not Christians at all.) Since Christ lives within you, even though your body will die because of sin, your spirit is alive because you have been made right with God. The Spirit of God, who raised Jesus from the dead, lives in you. And just as he raised Christ from the dead, he will give life to your mortal body by this same Spirit living within you. ❧ Our earthly bodies, which die and decay, will be different when they are resurrected, for they will never die.

Salt is good for seasoning. But if it loses its flavor, how do you make it salty again? You must have the qualities of salt among yourselves and live in peace with each other.

> If a seasoning has no flavor, it has no value. If Christians make no effort to affect the world around them, they are of little value to God. If we are too much like the world, we are worthless. Instead, we should affect others positively, just as seasoning brings out the best flavor in food.
>
> *LAB note for Matthew 5:13*

(MATTHEW 5:13) (1 PETER 3:4) (1 PETER 1:23) (JOHN 11:25) (LUKE 20:36)
(ROMANS 1:23) (ROMANS 8:9–11) (1 CORINTHIANS 15:42) (MARK 9:50)

September 11

All praise to the God and Father of our Lord Jesus Christ. He is the source of every mercy and the God who comforts us. He comforts us in all our troubles so that we can comfort others. When others are troubled, we will be able to give them the same comfort God has given us. ❦ The LORD is like a father to his children, tender and compassionate to those who fear him. For he knows how weak we are; he knows we are only dust. ❦ I will comfort you there as a child is comforted by its mother. ❦ Give all your worries and cares to God, for he cares about what happens to you.

But you, O Lord, are a merciful and gracious God, slow to get angry, full of unfailing love and truth.

He will give you another Counselor . . . the Holy Spirit, who leads into all truth. ❦ The Holy Spirit helps us in our distress.

He will remove all of their sorrows, and there will be no more death or sorrow or crying or pain. For the old world and its evils are gone forever.

Many think that when God comforts us, our troubles should go away. But being "comforted" can also mean receiving strength, encouragement, and hope to deal with our troubles. The more we suffer, the more comfort God gives us. If you are feeling overwhelmed, allow God to comfort you. *LAB note for 2 Corinthians 1:3–5*

(ISAIAH 51:12) (2 CORINTHIANS 1:3–4) (PSALM 103:13–14) (ISAIAH 66:13)
(1 PETER 5:7) (PSALM 86:15) (JOHN 14:16–17) (ROMANS 8:26) (REVELATION 21:4)

September 12

A doubtful mind is as unsettled as a wave of the sea that is driven and tossed by the wind.

Anyone who puts a hand to the plow and then looks back is not fit for the Kingdom of God.

It is impossible to please God without faith. Anyone who wants to come to him must believe that there is a God and that he rewards those who sincerely seek him. ❧ When you ask him, be sure that you really expect him to answer, for a doubtful mind is as unsettled as a wave of the sea that is driven and tossed by the wind. People like that should not expect to receive anything from the Lord. ❧ You can pray for anything, and if you believe, you will have it.

Then we will no longer be like children, forever changing our minds about what we believe because someone has told us something different or because someone has cleverly lied to us and made the lie sound like the truth. Instead, we will hold to the truth in love, becoming more and more in every way like Christ, who is the head of his body, the church.

Remain in me. ❧ Be strong and steady, always enthusiastic about the Lord's work, for you know that nothing you do for the Lord is ever useless.

Doubt leaves a person as unsettled as restless waves. If you want to stop being tossed about, rely on God to show you what is best for you. Ask him for wisdom, and trust that he will give it to you. Then your decisions will be sure and solid. *LAB note for James 1:6-8*

(JAMES 1:6) (LUKE 9:62) (HEBREWS 11:6) (JAMES 1:6-7) (MARK 11:24) (EPHESIANS 4:14-15) (JOHN 15:4) (1 CORINTHIANS 15:58)

September 13

Weeping may go on all night, but joy comes with the morning.

Such troubles are going to happen to us Christians. Even while we were with you, we warned you that troubles would soon come—and they did, as you well know. ❧ I have told you all this so that you may have peace in me. Here on earth you will have many trials and sorrows. But take heart, because I have overcome the world.

When I awake, I will be fully satisfied, for I will see you face to face. ❧ The night is almost gone; the day of salvation will soon be here.

He is like the light of the morning, like the sunrise bursting forth in a cloudless sky, like the refreshing rains that bring tender grass from the earth.

He will swallow up death forever! The Sovereign LORD will wipe away all tears. ❧ He will remove all of their sorrows, and there will be no more death or sorrow or crying or pain. For the old world and its evils are gone forever. ❧ We who are still alive and remain on the earth will be caught up in the clouds to meet the Lord in the air and remain with him forever. So comfort and encourage each other with these words.

Some think that troubles are always caused by sin or a lack of faith. Trials may be a part of God's plan for believers, building character, perseverance, and sensitivity toward others who also face trouble. Your troubles may be a sign of effective Christian living.

LAB note for 1 Thessalonians 3:1-3

(PSALM 30:5) (1 THESSALONIANS 3:3-4) (JOHN 16:33) (PSALM 17:15)
(ROMANS 13:12) (2 SAMUEL 23:4) (ISAIAH 25:8) (REVELATION 21:4)
(1 THESSALONIANS 4:17-18)

September 14

He will not crush those who are weak.

The sacrifice you want is a broken spirit. A broken and repentant heart, O God, you will not despise. ❧ He heals the brokenhearted, binding up their wounds. ❧ The high and lofty one who inhabits eternity, the Holy One, says this: "I live in that high and holy place with those whose spirits are contrite and humble. I refresh the humble and give new courage to those with repentant hearts. For I will not fight against you forever; I will not always show my anger. If I did, all people would pass away—all the souls I have made."

I will search for my lost ones who strayed away, and I will bring them safely home again. I will bind up the injured and strengthen the weak. ❧ When they walk through the Valley of Weeping, it will become a place of refreshing springs, where pools of blessing collect after the rains! ❧ So take a new grip with your tired hands and stand firm on your shaky legs. Mark out a straight path for your feet. Then those who follow you, though they are weak and lame, will not stumble and fall but will become strong. ❧ Your God . . . is coming to save you.

God wants a broken spirit and a broken and repentant heart. You can never please God by outward actions—no matter how good—if your heart attitude is not right. Are you sorry for your sin? Do you genuinely intend to stop? God is pleased by this kind of repentance.

LAB note for Psalm 51:17

(MATTHEW 12:20) (PSALM 51:17) (PSALM 147:3) (ISAIAH 57:15-16)
(EZEKIEL 34:16) (PSALM 84:6) (HEBREWS 12:12-13) (ISAIAH 35:4)

September 15

He opened their minds to understand these many Scriptures. Then he explained to them, "You have been permitted to understand the secrets of the Kingdom of Heaven, but others have not. Then Jesus prayed this prayer: "O Father, Lord of heaven and earth, thank you for hiding the truth from those who think themselves so wise and clever, and for revealing it to the childlike. Yes, Father, it pleased you to do it this way! And God has actually given us his Spirit (not the world's spirit) so we can know the wonderful things God has freely given us. How precious are your thoughts about me, O God! They are innumerable! I can't even count them; they outnumber the grains of sand! And when I wake up in the morning, you are still with me! Oh, what a wonderful God we have! How great are his riches and wisdom and knowledge! How impossible it is for us to understand his decisions and his methods! For who can know what the Lord is thinking? Who knows enough to be his counselor? For everything comes from him; everything exists by his power and is intended for his glory. To him be glory evermore. Amen.

Have you ever wondered how to understand a difficult Bible passage? Besides reading surrounding passages, asking other people, and consulting reference works, pray that the Holy Spirit will open your mind to understand, giving you the needed insight to put God's Word into action in your life. *LAB note for Luke 24:45*

(PSALM 119:18) (LUKE 24:45) (MATTHEW 13:11) (MATTHEW 11:25-26)
(1 CORINTHIANS 2:12) (PSALM 139:17-18) (ROMANS 11:33-34, 36)

September 16

"The Spring of the One Who Cried Out."

If you only knew the gift God has for you and who I am, you would ask me, and I would give you living water. ※ "If you are thirsty, come to me!" (When he said "living water," he was speaking of the Spirit, who would be given to everyone believing in him.)

"Bring all the tithes into the storehouse so there will be enough food in my Temple. If you do," says the LORD Almighty, "I will open the windows of heaven for you. I will pour out a blessing so great that you won't have enough room to take it in. Try it! Let me prove it to you!" ※ If you sinful people know how to give good gifts to your children, how much more will your heavenly Father give the Holy Spirit to those who ask him. ※ Keep on asking, and you will be given what you ask for. Keep on looking, and you will find.

Because you Gentiles have become his children, God has sent the Spirit of his Son into your hearts, and now you can call God your dear Father. ※ So you should not be like cowering, fearful slaves. You should behave instead like God's very own children, adopted into his family—calling him "Father, dear Father."

What did Jesus mean by "living water"? God is called the fountain of living water. In saying he would bring living water that could forever quench a person's thirst for God, Jesus was claiming to be the Messiah. Only the Messiah could give this gift that satisfies the soul's desire.

LAB note for John 4:10

(JUDGES 15:19) (JOHN 4:10) (JOHN 7:37, 39) (MALACHI 3:10) (LUKE 11:13) (LUKE 11:9) (GALATIANS 4:6) (ROMANS 8:15)

September 17

In his kindness God called you to his eternal glory by means of Jesus Christ.

I will make all my goodness pass before you, and I will call out my name, "the LORD," to you. I will show kindness to anyone I choose, and I will show mercy to anyone I choose. ※ God will be gracious and say, "Set him free. Do not make him die, for I have found a ransom for his life." ※ Yet now God in his gracious kindness declares us not guilty. He has done this through Christ Jesus, who has freed us by taking away our sins. For God sent Jesus to take the punishment for our sins and to satisfy God's anger against us. We are made right with God when we believe that Jesus shed his blood, sacrificing his life for us. God was being entirely fair and just when he did not punish those who sinned in former times. And he is entirely fair and just in this present time when he declares sinners to be right in his sight because they believe in Jesus. ※ God's unfailing love and faithfulness came through Jesus Christ.

God saved you by his special favor when you believed. And you can't take credit for this; it is a gift from God. ※ May God our Father and Christ Jesus our Lord give you grace, mercy, and peace. ※ God has given gifts to each of you from his great variety of spiritual gifts. Manage them well so that God's generosity can flow through you. ※ He gives us more and more strength.

When a judge in a court of law declares the defendant not guilty, all the charges are removed from his record. Legally, it is as if the person had never been accused. When God forgives our sins, our record is wiped clean. From his perspective, it is as though we had never sinned.

LAB note for Romans 3:24

(1 PETER 5:10) (EXODUS 33:19) (JOB 33:24) (ROMANS 3:24-26) (JOHN 1:17) (EPHESIANS 2:8) (1 TIMOTHY 1:2) (1 PETER 4:10) (JAMES 4:6)

September 18

I look up to the mountains—does my help come from there? My help comes from the LORD, who made the heavens and the earth!

Just as the mountains surround and protect Jerusalem, so the LORD surrounds and protects his people. ※ The sun will not hurt you by day, nor the moon at night. The LORD keeps you from all evil and preserves your life. The LORD keeps watch over you as you come and go, both now and forever.

I lift my eyes to you, O God, enthroned in heaven. We look to the LORD our God for his mercy, just as servants keep their eyes on their master, as a slave girl watches her mistress for the slightest signal. ※ I think how much you have helped me; I sing for joy in the shadow of your protecting wings.

O our God, won't you stop them? We are powerless against this mighty army that is about to attack us. We do not know what to do, but we are looking to you for help. ※ Help us, O LORD our God, for we trust in you alone. It is in your name that we have come against this vast horde. ※ My eyes are always looking to the LORD for help, for he alone can rescue me from the traps of my enemies. ※ Our help is from the LORD, who made the heavens and the earth.

If you are facing battles you feel you can't possibly win, don't give up. The secret of victory is first to admit the futility of unaided human effort and then trust God to save. His power works best through those who recognize their limitations. *LAB note for 2 Chronicles 14:11*

(PSALM 121:1-2) (PSALM 125:2) (PSALM 121:6-8) (PSALM 123:1-2) (PSALM 63:7) (2 CHRONICLES 20:12) (2 CHRONICLES 14:11) (PSALM 25:15) (PSALM 124:8)

September 19

But as for me, how good it is to be near God!

I love your sanctuary, LORD, the place where your glory shines. ❧ A single day in your courts is better than a thousand anywhere else! I would rather be a gatekeeper in the house of my God than live the good life in the homes of the wicked. ❧ What joy for those you choose to bring near, those who live in your holy courts. What joy awaits us inside your holy Temple.

The LORD is wonderfully good to those who wait for him and seek him. ❧ The LORD still waits for you to come to him so he can show you his love and compassion. For the LORD is a faithful God. Blessed are those who wait for him to help them.

And so, dear brothers and sisters, we can boldly enter heaven's Most Holy Place because of the blood of Jesus. This is the new, life-giving way that Christ has opened up for us through the sacred curtain, by means of his death for us. Let us go right into the presence of God, with true hearts fully trusting him. For our evil consciences have been sprinkled with Christ's blood to make us clean, and our bodies have been washed with pure water.

Access to God, the joy of living in the Temple courts, was a great honor. God had chosen a special group of Israelites from the tribe of Levi to serve as priests, and they were the only ones who could enter the sacred rooms where God's presence resided. Because of Jesus' death on the cross, believers today have access to God's presence in every place and at any time.   *LAB note for Psalm 65:4*

(PSALM 73:28) (PSALM 26:8) (PSALM 84:10) (PSALM 65:4) (LAMENTATIONS 3:25)
(ISAIAH 30:18) (HEBREWS 10:19-20, 22)

September 20

Let it grow, for when your endurance is fully developed, you will be strong in character and ready for anything.

There is wonderful joy ahead, even though it is necessary for you to endure many trials for a while. These trials are only to test your faith, to show that it is strong and pure. It is being tested as fire tests and purifies gold—and your faith is far more precious to God than mere gold. So if your faith remains strong after being tried by fiery trials, it will bring you much praise and glory and honor on the day when Jesus Christ is revealed to the whole world. We can rejoice, too, when we run into problems and trials, for we know that they are good for us—they help us learn to endure. And endurance develops strength of character in us, and character strengthens our confident expectation of salvation.

It is good to wait quietly for salvation from the LORD. When all you owned was taken from you, you accepted it with joy. You knew you had better things waiting for you in eternity. Do not throw away this confident trust in the Lord, no matter what happens. Remember the great reward it brings you! Patient endurance is what you need now, so you will continue to do God's will. Then you will receive all that he has promised.

Instead of complaining about our struggles, we should see them as opportunities for growth. Thank God for promising to be with you in rough times. Ask him to help you solve your problems or to give you the strength to endure them. Then be patient. God will stay close and help you grow.   *LAB note for James 1:2-4*

(JAMES 1:4) (1 PETER 1:6-7) (ROMANS 5:3-4) (LAMENTATIONS 3:26)
(HEBREWS 10:34-36)

September 21

Humble yourselves under the mighty power of God, and in his good time he will honor you.

The LORD despises pride; be assured that the proud will be punished.

And yet, LORD, you are our Father. We are the clay, and you are the potter. We are all formed by your hand. Oh, don't be so angry with us, LORD. Please don't remember our sins forever. Look at us, we pray, and see that we are all your people. ✿ You disciplined me severely, but I deserved it. I was like a calf that needed to be trained for the yoke and plow. Turn me again to you and restore me, for you alone are the Lord my God. I turned away from God, but then I was sorry. I kicked myself for my stupidity! I was thoroughly ashamed of all I did in my younger days. ✿ It is good for the young to submit to the yoke of his discipline. Let them sit alone in silence beneath the LORD's demands. Let them lie face down in the dust; then at last there is hope for them.

Evil does not spring from the soil, and trouble does not sprout from the earth. People are born for trouble as predictably as sparks fly upward from a fire. ✿ Though he brings grief, he also shows compassion according to the greatness of his unfailing love. For he does not enjoy hurting people or causing them sorrow.

We often worry about our position and status, hoping to get proper recognition for what we do. But God's recognition counts more than human praise. God is able and willing to bless us according to his timing. Humbly obey God regardless of present circumstances, and in his good time—either in this life or in the next—he will honor you.

LAB note for 1 Peter 5:6

(1 PETER 5:6) (PROVERBS 16:5) (ISAIAH 64:8-9) (JEREMIAH 31:18-19)
(LAMENTATIONS 3:27-29) (JOB 5:6-7) (LAMENTATIONS 3:32-33)

September 22

The heavens tell of the glory of God. The skies display his marvelous craftsmanship.

From the time the world was created, people have seen the earth and sky and all that God made. They can clearly see his invisible qualities—his eternal power and divine nature. ▥ He never left himself without a witness. ▥ Day after day they continue to speak; night after night they make him known. They speak without a sound or a word; their voice is silent in the skies.

When I look at the night sky and see the work of your fingers—the moon and the stars you have set in place—what are mortals that you should think of us, mere humans that you should care for us?

The sun has one kind of glory, while the moon and stars each have another kind. And even the stars differ from each other in their beauty and brightness. It is the same way for the resurrection of the dead. Our earthly bodies, which die and decay, will be different when they are resurrected, for they will never die. ▥ Those who are wise will shine as bright as the sky, and those who turn many to righteousness will shine like stars forever.

To say that the universe happened by chance is absurd. Its design, intricacy, and orderliness point to a personally involved Creator. As you look at God's handiwork in nature and the heavens, thank him for such magnificent beauty and the truth it reveals about the Creator.

LAB note for Psalm 19:1-6

(PSALM 19:1) (ROMANS 1:20) (ACTS 14:17) (PSALM 19:2-3) (PSALM 8:3-4)
(1 CORINTHIANS 15:41-42) (DANIEL 12:3)

September 23

The Son can do nothing by himself. He does only what he sees the Father doing. Whatever the Father does, the Son also does.

The LORD grants wisdom! From his mouth come knowledge and understanding. He grants a treasure of good sense to the godly. He is their shield, protecting those who walk with integrity. He guards the paths of justice and protects those who are faithful to him. ❈ I will give you the right words and such wisdom that none of your opponents will be able to reply!

Wait patiently for the LORD. Be brave and courageous. Yes, wait patiently for the LORD. ❈ My gracious favor is all you need. My power works best in your weakness.

Called to live in the love of God the Father and the care of Jesus Christ. ❈ Jesus and the ones he makes holy have the same Father. That is why Jesus is not ashamed to call them his brothers and sisters.

Am I not everywhere in all the heavens and earth? ❈ And the church is his body; it is filled by Christ, who fills everything everywhere with his presence.

I am the LORD, and there is no other Savior. ❈ He is indeed the Savior of the world.

May God the Father and Christ Jesus our Savior give you grace and peace.

Because of his unity with God, Jesus lived as God wanted him to live. Because of our identification with Jesus, we must honor him and live as he wants us to live. The questions "What would Jesus do?" and "What would Jesus have me do?" may help us make the right choices.

LAB note for John 5:19-23

(JOHN 5:19) (PROVERBS 2:6-8) (LUKE 21:15) (PSALM 27:14) (2 CORINTHIANS 12:9) (JUDE 1:1) (HEBREWS 2:11) (JEREMIAH 23:24) (EPHESIANS 1:23) (ISAIAH 43:11) (JOHN 4:42) (TITUS 1:4)

September 24

Show me the path where I should walk, O LORD; point out the right road for me to follow.

Moses said to the LORD, ". . . You call me by name and tell me I have found favor with you. Please, if this is really so, show me your intentions so I will understand you more fully and do exactly what you want me to do. . . ." And the LORD replied, "I will personally go with you, Moses. I will give you rest—everything will be fine for you." ▧ He revealed his character to Moses and his deeds to the people of Israel.

He leads the humble in what is right, teaching them his way. Who are those who fear the LORD? He will show them the path they should choose. ▧ Trust in the LORD with all your heart; do not depend on your own understanding. Seek his will in all you do, and he will direct your paths.

You will show me the way of life, granting me the joy of your presence and the pleasures of living with you forever. ▧ The LORD says, "I will guide you along the best pathway for your life. I will advise you and watch over you." ▧ The way of the righteous is like the first gleam of dawn, which shines ever brighter until the full light of day.

How do we receive God's guidance? The first step is to want to be guided and to realize that God's primary guidance system is in his Word, the Bible. By reading it and constantly learning from it, we will gain the wisdom to perceive God's direction for our lives.   *LAB note for Psalm 25:4*

(PSALM 25:4) (EXODUS 33:12-14) (PSALM 103:7) (PSALM 25:9, 12)
(PROVERBS 3:5-6) (PSALM 16:11) (PSALM 32:8) (PROVERBS 4:18)

September 25

What makes you better than anyone else? What do you have that God hasn't given you? And if all you have is from God, why boast as though you have accomplished something on your own?

Whatever I am now, it is all because God poured out his special favor on me—and not without results. ▓ In his goodness he chose to make us his own children by giving us his true word. ▓ Receiving God's promise is not up to us. We can't get it by choosing it or working hard for it. God will show mercy to anyone he chooses! ▓ Can we boast, then, that we have done anything to be accepted by God? No. ▓ God alone made it possible for you to be in Christ Jesus. For our benefit God made Christ to be wisdom itself. . . . "The person who wishes to boast should boast only of what the Lord has done."

Once you were dead, doomed forever because of your many sins. You used to live just like the rest of the world, full of sin, obeying Satan, the mighty prince of the power of the air. He is the spirit at work in the hearts of those who refuse to obey God. All of us used to live that way, following the passions and desires of our evil nature. We were born with an evil nature, and we were under God's anger just like everyone else. ▓ Now your sins have been washed away, and you have been set apart for God. You have been made right with God because of what the Lord Jesus Christ and the Spirit of our God have done for you.

Don't let your loyalty to church leaders cause strife, slander, or broken relationships. Make sure that your deepest loyalties are to Christ and not to his human agents. Those who spend more time in debating church leadership than in declaring Christ's message don't have the mind of Christ. *LAB note for 1 Corinthians 4:6-7*

(1 CORINTHIANS 4:7) (1 CORINTHIANS 15:10) (JAMES 1:18) (ROMANS 9:16)
(ROMANS 3:27) (1 CORINTHIANS 1:30-31) (EPHESIANS 2:1-3) (1 CORINTHIANS 6:11)

September 26

All praise to him who loves us and has freed us from our sins by shedding his blood for us.

Many waters cannot quench love, neither can rivers drown it. Love is as strong as death. ❧ The greatest love is shown when people lay down their lives for their friends.

He personally carried away our sins in his own body on the cross so we can be dead to sin and live for what is right. You have been healed by his wounds! ❧ He is so rich in kindness that he purchased our freedom through the blood of his Son, and our sins are forgiven.

Your sins have been washed away, and you have been set apart for God. You have been made right with God because of what the Lord Jesus Christ and the Spirit of our God have done for you. ❧ You are a chosen people. You are a kingdom of priests, God's holy nation, his very own possession. This is so you can show others the goodness of God, for he called you out of the darkness into his wonderful light. ❧ I plead with you to give your bodies to God. Let them be a living and holy sacrifice—the kind he will accept. When you think of what he has done for you, is this too much to ask?

We are to love each other as Jesus loved us, and he loved us enough to give his life for us. We may not have to die for someone, but there are other ways to practice sacrificial love: listening, helping, encouraging, giving. Think of someone in particular who needs this kind of love today—and give it! *LAB note for John 15:12-13*

(Revelation 1:5) (Song of Songs 8:7, 6) (John 15:13) (1 Peter 2:24) (Ephesians 1:7) (1 Corinthians 6:11) (1 Peter 2:9) (Romans 12:1)

September 27

There are different kinds of service in the church, but it is the same Lord we are serving.

Azmaveth son of Adiel was in charge of the palace treasuries. Jonathan son of Uzziah was in charge of the regional treasuries throughout the towns, villages, and fortresses of Israel. Ezri son of Kelub was in charge of the field workers who farmed the king's lands. Shimei from Ramah was in charge of the king's vineyards. Zabdi from Shepham was responsible for the grapes and the supplies of wine. All these officials were overseers of King David's property.

Here is a list of some of the members that God has placed in the body of Christ: first are apostles, second are prophets, third are teachers, then those who do miracles, those who have the gift of healing, those who can help others, those who can get others to work together, those who speak in unknown languages.

God has given gifts to each of you from his great variety of spiritual gifts. Manage them well so that God's generosity can flow through you. Are you called to be a speaker? Then speak as though God himself were speaking through you. Are you called to help others? Do it with all the strength and energy that God supplies. Then God will be given glory in everything through Jesus Christ. All glory and power belong to him forever and ever. Amen.

Some people, well aware of their abilities, believe that they have the right to use their abilities as they please. Others feel they have no special talents at all. But everyone has some gifts; find yours and use them. All our abilities should be used in serving others; none are for our own exclusive enjoyment.   *LAB note for 1 Peter 4:10–11*

(1 CORINTHIANS 12:5) (1 CHRONICLES 27:25–27, 31)
(1 CORINTHIANS 12:28) (1 PETER 4:10–11)

September 28

When Moses came down the mountain carrying the stone tablets inscribed with the terms of the covenant, he wasn't aware that his face glowed because he had spoken to the LORD face to face.

To you goes all the glory for your unfailing love and faithfulness. ❧ Lord, when did we ever see you hungry and feed you? Or thirsty and give you something to drink? ❧ When you did it to one of the least of these my brothers and sisters, you were doing it to me! ❧ Be humble, thinking of others as better than yourself. ❧ Serve each other in humility.

Jesus' appearance changed so that his face shone like the sun, and his clothing became dazzling white. ❧ Everyone in the council stared at Stephen because his face became as bright as an angel's. ❧ Glorify your Son so he can give glory back to you. ❧ All of us have had that veil removed so that we can be mirrors that brightly reflect the glory of the Lord. And as the Spirit of the Lord works within us, we become more and more like him and reflect his glory even more.

You are the light of the world—like a city on a mountain, glowing in the night for all to see. Don't hide your light under a basket! ❧ Let your lives shine brightly before them. Hold tightly to the word of life.

Moses' face glowed after he spent time with God. The people could clearly see God's presence in him. How often do you spend time alone with God? Although your face may not light up a room, time spent in prayer, reading the Bible, and meditating should have such an effect on your life that people will know you have been with God.

LAB note for Exodus 34:28-35

(Exodus 34:29) (Psalm 115:1) (Matthew 25:37) (Matthew 25:40)
(Philippians 2:3) (1 Peter 5:5) (Matthew 17:2) (Acts 6:15) (John 17:22)
(2 Corinthians 3:18) (Matthew 5:14-15) (Philippians 2:15-16)

September 29

There are different ways God works in our lives, but it is the same God who does the work through all of us.

Some men from Manasseh defected from the Israelite army and joined David. They were all brave and able warriors who became commanders in his army. ✺ A spiritual gift is given to each of us as a means of helping the entire church.

From the tribe of Issachar, there were 200 leaders of the tribe with their relatives. All these men understood the temper of the times and knew the best course for Israel to take. ✺ To one person the Spirit gives the ability to give wise advice; to another he gives the gift of special knowledge.

From the tribe of Zebulun, there were 50,000 skilled warriors. They were fully armed and prepared for battle and completely loyal to David. ✺ I take joy in doing your will, my God, for your law is written on my heart.

God made our bodies with many parts, and he has put each part just where he wants it. If one part suffers, all the parts suffer with it, and if one part is honored, all the parts are glad.

One Lord, one faith, one baptism.

People are often drawn to a great cause and the brave determined people who support it. As believers, we have the greatest cause—the salvation of people. If we are brave, determined, and faithful, others will be drawn to work with us.   *LAB note for 1 Chronicles 12:22*

(1 CORINTHIANS 12:6) (1 CHRONICLES 12:19, 21) (1 CORINTHIANS 12:7)
(1 CHRONICLES 12:32) (1 CORINTHIANS 12:8) (1 CHRONICLES 12:33)
(PSALM 40:8) (1 CORINTHIANS 12:18, 26) (EPHESIANS 4:5)

September 30

The Coming One will come and not delay.

Write my answer in large, clear letters on a tablet, so that a runner can read it and tell everyone else. But these things I plan won't happen right away. Slowly, steadily, surely, the time approaches when the vision will be fulfilled. If it seems slow, wait patiently, for it will surely take place. It will not be delayed.

You must not forget, dear friends, that a day is like a thousand years to the Lord, and a thousand years is like a day. The Lord isn't really being slow about his promise to return, as some people think. No, he is being patient for your sake. He does not want anyone to perish, so he is giving more time for everyone to repent. You, O Lord, are a merciful and gracious God, slow to get angry, full of unfailing love and truth. Oh, that you would burst from the heavens and come down! How the mountains would quake in your presence! For since the world began, no ear has heard, and no eye has seen a God like you, who works for those who wait for him!

It isn't easy to be patient when evil and injustice seem to have the upper hand in the world. But it helps to remember that God hates sin even more than we do. Punishment of sin will certainly come. We must wait patiently, trusting God even when we don't understand why events occur as they do.   *LAB note for Habakkuk 2:3*

(Hebrews 10:37) (Habakkuk 2:2-3) (2 Peter 3:8-9)
(Psalm 86:15) (Isaiah 64:1, 4)

October

Autumn's Abundance

Apple picking and pumpkin pie
Crackling leaves and hayrides
Autumn brings a harvest of blessing.

As the crisp winds of autumn chase away summer's
greenery, take time to notice the fiery display of
new colors. What a creative God he is to make
such a beautiful world for us!

October 1

You will always reap what you sow!

Experience shows that those who plant trouble and cultivate evil will harvest the same. ❧ They have planted the wind and will harvest the whirlwind. ❧ Those who live only to satisfy their own sinful desires will harvest the consequences of decay and death.

The reward of the godly will last. ❧ Those who live to please the Spirit will harvest everlasting life from the Spirit. So don't get tired of doing what is good. Don't get discouraged and give up, for we will reap a harvest of blessing at the appropriate time. Whenever we have the opportunity, we should do good to everyone, especially to our Christian brothers and sisters.

It is possible to give freely and become more wealthy, but those who are stingy will lose everything. The generous prosper and are satisfied; those who refresh others will themselves be refreshed. ❧ Remember this—a farmer who plants only a few seeds will get a small crop. But the one who plants generously will get a generous crop.

It would certainly be a surprise if you planted corn and pumpkins came up. It's a natural law to reap what we sow. If you plant to please your own desires, you'll reap a crop of sorrow and evil. If you plant to please God, you'll reap joy and everlasting life. What kinds of seeds are you sowing? *LAB note for Galatians 6:7-8*

(GALATIANS 6:7) (JOB 4:8) (HOSEA 8:7) (GALATIANS 6:8) (PROVERBS 11:18) (GALATIANS 6:8-10) (PROVERBS 11:24-25) (2 CORINTHIANS 9:6)

October 2

Never be lazy in your work, but serve the Lord enthusiastically.

Whatever you do, do well. For when you go to the grave, there will be no work or planning or knowledge or wisdom. ❧ Work hard and cheerfully at whatever you do, as though you were working for the Lord rather than for people. Remember that the Lord will give you an inheritance as your reward, and the Master you are serving is Christ. ❧ Remember that the Lord will reward each one of us for the good we do.

All of us must quickly carry out the tasks assigned us by the one who sent me, because there is little time left before the night falls and all work comes to an end.

So, dear brothers and sisters, work hard to prove that you really are among those God has called and chosen. Doing this, you will never stumble or fall away. ❧ Our great desire is that you will keep right on loving others as long as life lasts, in order to make certain that what you hope for will come true. Then you will not become spiritually dull and indifferent. Instead, you will follow the example of those who are going to inherit God's promises because of their faith and patience. ❧ Run in such a way that you will win.

Considering the uncertainties of the future and the certainty of death, Solomon recommends enjoying life as God's gift. He may have been criticizing those who put off all present pleasures in order to accumulate wealth, much like those who get caught up in today's rat race. Enjoy God's gifts while you are able! *LAB note for Ecclesiastes 9:7-10*

(ROMANS 12:11) (ECCLESIASTES 9:10) (COLOSSIANS 3:23-24) (EPHESIANS 6:8)
(JOHN 9:4) (2 PETER 1:10) (HEBREWS 6:11-12) (1 CORINTHIANS 9:24)

October 3

It is good to wait quietly for salvation from the LORD.

Has God forgotten to be kind? Has he slammed the door on his compassion? ⚘ In sudden fear I had cried out, "I have been cut off from the LORD!" But you heard my cry for mercy and answered my call for help. Love the LORD, all you faithful ones! For the LORD protects those who are loyal to him, but he harshly punishes all who are arrogant. So be strong and take courage, all you who put your hope in the LORD!

Don't you think God will surely give justice to his chosen people who plead with him day and night? Will he keep putting them off? I tell you, he will grant justice to them quickly! ⚘ Wait for the LORD to handle the matter. ⚘ Be still in the presence of the LORD, and wait patiently for him to act. Don't worry about evil people who prosper.

You will not even need to fight. Take your positions; then stand still and watch the LORD's victory.

Don't get tired of doing what is good. Don't get discouraged and give up, for we will reap a harvest of blessing at the appropriate time. ⚘ Be patient as you wait for the Lord's return. Consider the farmers who eagerly look for the rains in the fall and in the spring. They patiently wait for the precious harvest to ripen.

Asaph cried out to God for courage during a time of deep distress. But as he expressed his requests and doubts to God, his focus changed from thinking of himself to worshiping God. Only after he put aside his doubts about God's holiness and care for him did he eliminate his distress. *LAB note for Psalm 77:1-12*

(LAMENTATIONS 3:26) (PSALM 77:9) (PSALM 31:22-24) (LUKE 18:7-8)
(PROVERBS 20:22) (PSALM 37:7) (2 CHRONICLES 20:17) (GALATIANS 6:9) (JAMES 5:7)

October 4

The LORD's promises are pure, like silver refined in a furnace, purified seven times over.

Your promises have been thoroughly tested; that is why I love them so much. ❧ The law of the LORD is perfect, reviving the soul. The commandments of the LORD are right, bringing joy to the heart. The commands of the LORD are clear, giving insight to life. ❧ Every word of God proves true. He defends all who come to him for protection. Do not add to his words, or he may rebuke you, and you will be found a liar.

I have hidden your word in my heart, that I might not sin against you. I will study your commandments and reflect on your ways. ❧ The laws of the LORD are true; each one is fair. They are more desirable than gold, even the finest gold. They are sweeter than honey, even honey dripping from the comb. ❧ Fix your thoughts on what is true and honorable and right. Think about things that are pure and lovely and admirable. Think about things that are excellent and worthy of praise. ❧ You must crave pure spiritual milk so that you can grow into the fullness of your salvation. Cry out for this nourishment as a baby cries for milk.

As for God, his way is perfect. All the LORD's promises prove true. He is a shield for all who look to him for protection. For who is God except the LORD? Who but our God is a solid rock?

Sincerity and truth are extremely valuable because they are so rare. When we feel as though sincerity and truth have nearly gone out of existence, we have one hope—the word of God. God's words are as flawless as refined silver. So listen carefully when he speaks. *LAB note for Psalm 12:6*

(PSALM 12:6) (PSALM 119:140) (PSALM 19:7-8) (PROVERBS 30:5-6)
(PSALM 119:11, 15) (PSALM 19:9-10) (PHILIPPIANS 4:8) (1 PETER 2:2)
(PSALM 18:30-31)

October 5

You, O God, are my place of safety.

The LORD is my rock, my fortress, and my savior; my God is my rock, in whom I find protection. He is my shield, the strength of my salvation, and my stronghold, my high tower. ▓ The LORD is my strength, my shield from every danger. I trust in him with all my heart. He helps me, and my heart is filled with joy. I burst out in songs of thanksgiving.

They will respect and glorify the name of the LORD throughout the world. For he will come like a flood tide driven by the breath of the LORD. ▓ That is why we can say with confidence, "The Lord is my helper, so I will not be afraid. What can mere mortals do to me?"

The LORD is my light and my salvation—so why should I be afraid? The LORD protects me from danger—so why should I tremble? ▓ Though I sit in darkness, the LORD himself will be my light.

Just as the mountains surround and protect Jerusalem, so the LORD surrounds and protects his people, both now and forever. ▓ I think how much you have helped me; I sing for joy in the shadow of your protecting wings.

For the honor of your name, lead me out of this peril. ▓ Be our strength each day and our salvation in times of trouble.

We become content when we realize God's sufficiency for our needs. Christians who become materialistic are saying by their actions that God can't take care of them—or at least that he won't take care of them the way they want. The only antidote to this insecurity is to trust God to meet all our needs. *LAB note for Hebrews 13:5-6*

(Psalm 59:9) (2 Samuel 22:2-3) (Psalm 28:7) (Isaiah 59:19) (Hebrews 13:6)
(Psalm 27:1) (Micah 7:8) (Psalm 125:2) (Psalm 63:7) (Psalm 31:3) (Isaiah 33:2)

October 6

He leads the humble in what is right, teaching them his way.

God blesses those who are gentle and lowly.

I have observed something else in this world of ours. The fastest runner doesn't always win the race, and the strongest warrior doesn't always win the battle. The wise are often poor, and the skillful are not necessarily wealthy. We can make our plans, but the LORD determines our steps.

I lift my eyes to you, O God, enthroned in heaven. We look to the LORD our God for his mercy, just as servants keep their eyes on their master, as a slave girl watches her mistress for the slightest signal. Show me where to walk, for I have come to you in prayer.

O our God, won't you stop them? We are powerless against this mighty army that is about to attack us. We do not know what to do, but we are looking to you for help.

If you need wisdom—if you want to know what God wants you to do—ask him, and he will gladly tell you. He will not resent your asking.

When the Spirit of truth comes, he will guide you into all truth.

In the Kingdom of Heaven, wealth and power and authority are unimportant. Kingdom people seek different blessings and benefits, and they have different attitudes. Are your attitudes a carbon copy of the world's selfishness, pride, and lust for power, or do they reflect the humility and self-sacrifice of Jesus, your king?   *LAB note for Matthew 5:3-12*

(PSALM 25:9) (MATTHEW 5:5) (ECCLESIASTES 9:11) (PROVERBS 16:9)
(PSALM 123:1-2) (PSALM 143:8) (2 CHRONICLES 20:12) (JAMES 1:5) (JOHN 16:13)

October 7

O LORD, how long will you forget me? Forever? How long will you look the other way? How long must I struggle with anguish in my soul, with sorrow in my heart every day? ※ Do not hide yourself from me. Do not reject your servant in anger. You have always been my helper. Don't leave me now; don't abandon me, O God of my salvation!

When they call on me, I will answer; I will be with them in trouble. I will rescue them and honor them. ※ The LORD is close to all who call on him, yes, to all who call on him sincerely. He fulfills the desires of those who fear him; he hears their cries for help and rescues them.

I will not abandon you as orphans—I will come to you. ※ I am with you always, even to the end of the age.

God is our refuge and strength, always ready to help in times of trouble. ※ I wait quietly before God, for my hope is in him. He alone is my rock and my salvation, my fortress where I will not be shaken.

God's loving concern does not begin on the day we are born and conclude on the day we die. It reaches back to those days before we were born and reaches ahead along the unending path of eternity. Our only sure help comes from a God whose concern for us reaches beyond our earthly existence. *LAB note for Psalm 22:9-11*

(PSALM 22:11) (PSALM 13:1-2) (PSALM 27:9) (PSALM 91:15) (PSALM 145:18-19) (JOHN 14:18) (MATTHEW 28:20) (PSALM 46:1) (PSALM 62:5-6)

October 8

The LORD is king! He is robed in majesty. Indeed, the LORD is robed in majesty and armed with strength. The world is firmly established; it cannot be shaken. Your throne, O LORD, has been established from time immemorial. You yourself are from the everlasting past.

He displays his power. ❧ If God is for us, who can ever be against us? ❧ The God whom we serve is able to save us. He will rescue us from your power. ❧ My Father has given them to me, and he is more powerful than anyone else. So no one can take them from me. ❧ You belong to God, my dear children. You have already won your fight with these false prophets, because the Spirit who lives in you is greater than the spirit who lives in the world.

Not to us, O LORD, but to you goes all the glory. ❧ Yours, O LORD, is the greatness, the power, the glory, the victory, and the majesty. Everything in the heavens and on earth is yours, O LORD, and this is your kingdom. We adore you as the one who is over all things. O, our God, we thank you and praise your glorious name! But who am I, and who are my people, that we could give anything to you? Everything we have has come from you, and we give you only what you have already given us!

Just as a shepherd protects his sheep, Jesus protects his people from eternal harm. While believers can expect to suffer on earth, Satan cannot harm their souls or take away their eternal life with God. If you choose to follow Jesus, he will give you everlasting safety.

LAB note for John 10:28-29

(REVELATION 1:8) (PSALM 93:1-2) (NAHUM 1:3) (ROMANS 8:31) (DANIEL 3:17) (JOHN 10:29) (1 JOHN 4:4) (PSALM 115:1) (1 CHRONICLES 29:11, 13-14)

October 9

The LORD is your security.

Human opposition only enhances your glory, for you use it as a sword of judgment. ❧ The king's heart is like a stream of water directed by the LORD; he turns it wherever he pleases. ❧ When the ways of people please the LORD, he makes even their enemies live at peace with them.

I am counting on the LORD; yes, I am counting on him. I have put my hope in his word. I long for the Lord more than sentries long for the dawn. ❧ I prayed to the LORD, and he answered me, freeing me from all my fears.

The eternal God is your refuge, and his everlasting arms are under you. He thrusts out the enemy before you; it is he who cries, "Destroy them!" ❧ Blessed are those who trust in the LORD and have made the LORD their hope and confidence. They are like trees planted along a riverbank, with roots that reach deep into the water. Such trees are not bothered by the heat or worried by long months of drought. Their leaves stay green, and they go right on producing delicious fruit.

What can we say about such wonderful things as these? If God is for us, who can ever be against us?

How can wrath bring praise to God? Hostility to God and his people gives God the opportunity to do great deeds. God turns the tables of evildoers and brings glory to himself from the foolishness of those who deny him or revolt against him.   *LAB note for Psalm 76:10*

(PROVERBS 3:26) (PSALM 76:10) (PROVERBS 21:1) (PROVERBS 16:7)
(PSALM 130:5–6) (PSALM 34:4) (DEUTERONOMY 33:27) (JEREMIAH 17:7–8)
(ROMANS 8:31)

October 10

A servant is not greater than the master. Nor are messengers more important than the one who sends them. You know these things—now do them! That is the path of blessing.

They began to argue among themselves as to who would be the greatest in the coming Kingdom. Jesus told them, "In this world the kings and great men order their people around, and yet they are called 'friends of the people.' But among you, those who are the greatest should take the lowest rank, and the leader should be a servant. Normally the master sits at the table and is served by his servants. But not here! For I am your servant." ❧ Whoever is the least among you is the greatest. ❧ Whoever wants to be a leader among you must be your servant, and whoever wants to be first must become your slave. For even I, the Son of Man, came here not to be served but to serve others, and to give my life as a ransom for many.

He [Jesus] got up from the table, took off his robe, wrapped a towel around his waist, and poured water into a basin. Then he began to wash the disciples' feet and to wipe them with the towel he had around him.

Lead them by your good example.

Jesus did not wash his disciples' feet just to get them to be nice to each other. His far greater goal was to extend his mission on earth after he was gone. These men were to move into the world serving God, serving each other, and serving all people to whom they took the message of salvation. *LAB note for John 13:12ff.*

(JOHN 13:16-17) (LUKE 22:24-27) (LUKE 9:48) (MATTHEW 20:26-28)
(JOHN 13:4-5) (1 PETER 5:3)

October 11

My heart is confident in you, O God; no wonder I can sing your praises!

The LORD is my light and my salvation—so why should I be afraid?

You will keep in perfect peace all who trust in you, whose thoughts are fixed on you! For those who are righteous, the path is not steep and rough. You are a God of justice, and you smooth out the road ahead of them. ❦ They do not fear bad news; they confidently trust the LORD to care for them. They are confident and fearless and can face their foes triumphantly.

But when I am afraid, I put my trust in you. ❦ He will conceal me there when troubles come; he will hide me in his sanctuary. He will place me out of reach on a high rock. . . . At his Tabernacle I will offer sacrifices with shouts of joy, singing and praising the LORD with music.

After you have suffered a little while, he will restore, support, and strengthen you, and he will place you on a firm foundation. All power is his forever and ever. Amen.

At times the "path" of the righteous doesn't seem smooth, and it isn't easy to do God's will, but we are never alone when we face tough times. God is there to help us, to comfort us, and to lead us. He gives us wisdom to make decisions and faith to trust him.   *LAB note for Isaiah 26:7-8*

(PSALM 108:1) (PSALM 27:1) (ISAIAH 26:3, 7) (PSALM 112:7-8) (PSALM 56:3) (PSALM 27:5-6) (1 PETER 5:10-11)

October 12

Real life is not measured by how much we own.

It is better to be godly and have little than to be evil and possess much. ❧ It is better to have little with fear for the LORD than to have great treasure with turmoil. ❧ True religion with contentment is great wealth. So if we have enough food and clothing, let us be content. ❧ Give me neither poverty nor riches! Give me just enough to satisfy my needs. For if I grow rich, I may deny you and say, "Who is the LORD?" And if I am too poor, I may steal and thus insult God's holy name. ❧ Give us our food for today.

Don't worry about everyday life—whether you have enough food, drink, and clothes. Doesn't life consist of more than food and clothing? ❧ "When I sent you out to preach the Good News and you did not have money, a traveler's bag, or extra clothing, did you lack anything?" "No," they replied. ❧ Stay away from the love of money; be satisfied with what you have. For God has said, "I will never fail you. I will never forsake you."

How do you respond to the constant pressure to buy? Jesus says that the good life has nothing to do with being wealthy, so be on guard against greed. Learn to tune out expensive enticements and concentrate instead on the truly fulfilled life—living in a relationship with God and doing his work. *LAB note for Luke 12:15*

(LUKE 12:15) (PSALM 37:16) (PROVERBS 15:16) (1 TIMOTHY 6:6, 8)
(PROVERBS 30:8-9) (MATTHEW 6:11) (MATTHEW 6:25) (LUKE 22:35)
(HEBREWS 13:5)

October 13

It is the Spirit who gives eternal life.

The Scriptures tell us, "The first man, Adam, became a living person." But the last Adam—that is, Christ—is a life-giving Spirit. Humans can reproduce only human life, but the Holy Spirit gives new life from heaven. He saved us, not because of the good things we did, but because of his mercy. He washed away our sins and gave us a new life through the Holy Spirit.

You are controlled by the Spirit if you have the Spirit of God living in you. . . . Since Christ lives within you, even though your body will die because of sin, your spirit is alive because you have been made right with God. The Spirit of God, who raised Jesus from the dead, lives in you. And just as he raised Christ from the dead, he will give life to your mortal body by this same Spirit living within you.

I have been crucified with Christ. I myself no longer live, but Christ lives in me. So I live my life in this earthly body by trusting in the Son of God, who loved me and gave himself for me. So you should consider yourselves dead to sin and able to live for the glory of God through Christ Jesus.

The Holy Spirit gives spiritual life; without the work of the Holy Spirit, we cannot even see our need for new life. All spiritual renewal begins and ends with God. He reveals truth to us, lives within us, and then enables us to respond to that truth.   *LAB note for John 6:63-65*

(JOHN 6:63) (1 CORINTHIANS 15:45) (JOHN 3:6) (TITUS 3:5) (ROMANS 8:9-11)
(GALATIANS 2:19-20) (ROMANS 6:11)

October 14

The end of the world is coming soon.

I saw a great white throne, and I saw the one who was sitting on it. The earth and sky fled from his presence, but they found no place to hide. ❧ God has commanded that the heavens and the earth will be consumed by fire on the day of judgment, when ungodly people will perish.

God is our refuge and strength, always ready to help in times of trouble. So we will not fear, even if earthquakes come and the mountains crumble into the sea. Let the oceans roar and foam. Let the mountains tremble as the waters surge! ❧ Wars will break out near and far, but don't panic. Yes, these things must come, but the end won't follow immediately.

We will have a home in heaven, an eternal body made for us by God himself and not by human hands. ❧ We are looking forward to the new heavens and new earth he has promised, a world where everyone is right with God. And so, dear friends, while you are waiting for these things to happen, make every effort to live a pure and blameless life. And be at peace with God.

When the disciples asked Jesus when he would come in power and what they could expect then, Jesus pointed out that they should be less concerned with knowing the exact date and more concerned with being prepared. They should live God's way consistently so that no matter when Jesus came, they would be ready. *LAB note for Matthew 24:3ff.*

(1 PETER 4:7) (REVELATION 20:11) (2 PETER 3:7) (PSALM 46:1-3)
(MATTHEW 24:6) (2 CORINTHIANS 5:1) (2 PETER 3:13-14)

October 15

Do you have no respect for me? Why do you not tremble in my presence? I, the LORD, am the one who defines the ocean's sandy shoreline, an everlasting boundary that the waters cannot cross. The waves may toss and roar, but they can never pass the bounds I set. For no one on earth—from east or west, or even from the wilderness —can raise another person up. It is God alone who judges; he decides who will rise and who will fall.

He determines the course of world events; he removes kings and sets others on the throne. He gives wisdom to the wise and knowledge to the scholars. Wars will break out near and far, but don't panic. Yes, these things must come, but the end won't follow immediately.

If God is for us, who can ever be against us? Not even a sparrow, worth only half a penny, can fall to the ground without your Father knowing it. And the very hairs on your head are all numbered. So don't be afraid; you are more valuable to him than a whole flock of sparrows.

When we see evil leaders who live long and good leaders who die young, we may wonder if God is still in control. But God governs the world according to his purposes. You may be dismayed when you see evil people prosper, but God is in control. Let this knowledge give you confidence and peace no matter what happens. *LAB note for Daniel 2:21*

(PSALM 99:1) (JEREMIAH 5:22) (PSALM 75:6-7) (DANIEL 2:21) (MATTHEW 24:6) (ROMANS 8:31) (MATTHEW 10:29-31)

October 16

The enemy.

Be careful! Watch out for attacks from the Devil, your great enemy. He prowls around like a roaring lion, looking for some victim to devour. ▓ Resist the Devil, and he will flee from you.

Put on all of God's armor so that you will be able to stand firm against all strategies and tricks of the Devil. For we are not fighting against people made of flesh and blood, but against the evil rulers and authorities of the unseen world, against those mighty powers of darkness who rule this world, and against wicked spirits in the heavenly realms. Use every piece of God's armor to resist the enemy in the time of evil, so that after the battle you will still be standing firm. Stand your ground, putting on the sturdy belt of truth and the body armor of God's righteousness. For shoes, put on the peace that comes from the Good News, so that you will be fully prepared. In every battle you will need faith as your shield to stop the fiery arrows aimed at you by Satan.

Do not gloat over me, my enemies! For though I fall, I will rise again.

When you feel alone, weak, helpless, and cut off from other believers, you can become so focused on your troubles that you forget to watch for danger. That is when you are especially vulnerable to Satan's attacks. During suffering, seek other Christians for support, keep your eyes on Christ, and resist the Devil—he will flee from you!

LAB note for 1 Peter 5:8–9

(LUKE 10:19) (1 PETER 5:8) (JAMES 4:7) (EPHESIANS 6:11–16) (MICAH 7:8)

October 17

Lord, to whom would we go? You alone have the words that give eternal life. ▓ I know the one in whom I trust, and I am sure that he is able to guard what I have entrusted to him until the day of his return.

In my distress I cried out to the LORD; yes, I prayed to my God for help. He heard me from his sanctuary; my cry reached his ears. They attacked me at a moment when I was weakest, but the LORD upheld me. He led me to a place of safety; he rescued me because he delights in me. He reached down from heaven and rescued me; he drew me out of deep waters. He delivered me from my powerful enemies, from those who hated me and were too strong for me.

I will praise the LORD at all times. I will constantly speak his praises. I will boast only in the LORD; let all who are discouraged take heart. Come, let us tell of the LORD's greatness; let us exalt his name together. I prayed to the LORD, and he answered me, freeing me from all my fears. Taste and see that the LORD is good. Oh, the joys of those who trust in him!

Faced with the tragedy of losing their families, David's soldiers began to turn against him. But David found his strength in God and began looking for a solution instead of a scapegoat. When facing problems, remember that it is useless to look for someone to blame or criticize. Instead, consider how you can help find a solution.   *LAB note for 1 Samuel 30:6*

October 18

All drank from the miraculous rock that traveled with them, and that rock was Christ. ▒ Simon Peter answered, "You are the Messiah, the Son of the living God." Upon this rock I will build my church, and all the powers of hell will not conquer it. ▒ There is salvation in no one else! There is no other name in all of heaven for people to call on to save them.

Fully trusting him . . . without wavering. ▒ A doubtful mind is as unsettled as a wave of the sea that is driven and tossed by the wind.

Can anything ever separate us from Christ's love? Does it mean he no longer loves us if we have trouble or calamity, or are persecuted, or are hungry or cold or in danger or threatened with death? No, despite all these things, overwhelming victory is ours through Christ, who loved us. And I am convinced that nothing can ever separate us from . . . the love of God that is revealed in Christ Jesus our Lord.

Waiting for God to help us is not easy, but David received four benefits from waiting: God (1) lifted him out of his despair, (2) set his feet on solid ground, (3) steadied him as he walked, and (4) put a new song of praise in his mouth. Often blessings cannot be received unless we go through the trial of waiting. *LAB note for Psalm 40:1-3*

(PSALM 40:2) (1 CORINTHIANS 10:4) (MATTHEW 16:16, 18) (ACTS 4:12)
(HEBREWS 10:22-23) (JAMES 1:6) (ROMANS 8:35, 37-39)

October 19

May the words of my mouth and the thoughts of my heart be pleasing to you, O LORD, my rock and my redeemer.

How can I know all the sins lurking in my heart? Cleanse me from these hidden faults. ❧ Look after each other so that none of you will miss out on the special favor of God. Watch out that no bitter root of unbelief rises up among you, for whenever it springs up, many are corrupted by its poison.

I am sure that God, who began the good work within you, will continue his work until it is finally finished on that day when Christ Jesus comes back again. You must live in a manner worthy of the Good News about Christ. ❧ So also, the tongue is a small thing, but what enormous damage it can do. A tiny spark can set a great forest on fire. And the tongue is a flame of fire. It is full of wickedness that can ruin your whole life. It can turn the entire course of your life into a blazing flame of destruction, for it is set on fire by hell itself. No one can tame the tongue. It is an uncontrollable evil, full of deadly poison. ❧ Let your conversation be gracious and effective.

Many Christians are plagued by guilt. Guilt can play an important role in bringing us to Christ and in keeping us behaving properly, but it should not cripple us or make us fearful. God fully and completely forgives us—even for those sins we do unknowingly.

LAB note for Psalm 19:12-13

(PSALM 19:14) (PSALM 19:12) (HEBREWS 12:15) (PHILIPPIANS 1:6, 27)
(JAMES 3:5-6, 8) (COLOSSIANS 4:6)

October 20

Not by force nor by strength, but by my Spirit, says the LORD
Almighty.

Who is able to advise the Spirit of the LORD? Who knows enough
to be his teacher or counselor?

God deliberately chose things the world considers foolish in
order to shame those who think they are wise. And he chose those
who are powerless to shame those who are powerful. God chose
things despised by the world, things counted as nothing at all, and
used them to bring to nothing what the world considers important,
so that no one can ever boast in the presence of God.

Just as you can hear the wind but can't tell where it comes from
or where it is going, so you can't explain how people are born of the
Spirit. ※ Reborn! This is not a physical birth resulting from human
passion or plan—this rebirth comes from God.

My Spirit remains among you, just as I promised. . . . So do not
be afraid. ※ The battle is not yours, but God's.

The LORD does not need weapons to rescue his people. It is his
battle, not ours.

Many people believe that to survive in this world a person must
be tough, strong, unbending, and harsh. But it is only through God's
Spirit that anything of lasting value is accomplished. As you live for God,
determine not to trust in your own strength or abilities. Instead, depend
on God and work in the power of his Spirit!   *LAB note for Zechariah 4:6*

(ZECHARIAH 4:6) (ISAIAH 40:13) (1 CORINTHIANS 1:27-29) (JOHN 3:8)
(JOHN 1:13) (HAGGAI 2:5) (2 CHRONICLES 20:15) (1 SAMUEL 17:47)

October 21

This suffering is all part of what God has called you to. Christ, who suffered for you, is your example. Follow in his steps. He never sinned, and he never deceived anyone. He did not retaliate when he was insulted. When he suffered, he did not threaten to get even. He left his case in the hands of God, who always judges fairly. Think about all he endured when sinful people did such terrible things to him, so that you don't become weary and give up.

Let us strip off every weight that slows us down, especially the sin that so easily hinders our progress. And let us run with endurance the race that God has set before us. We do this by keeping our eyes on Jesus, on whom our faith depends from start to finish. He was willing to die a shameful death on the cross because of the joy he knew would be his afterward. Now he is seated in the place of highest honor beside God's throne in heaven.

Let me say one more thing as I close this letter. Fix your thoughts on what is true and honorable and right. Think about things that are pure and lovely and admirable. Think about things that are excellent and worthy of praise.

Christ never sinned, and yet he suffered so that we could be set free. When we follow Christ's example and live for others, we, too, may suffer. Our goal should be to face suffering as he did—with patience, calmness, and confidence that God is in control of the future.

LAB note for 1 Peter 2:21-22

(1 THESSALONIANS 5:15) (1 PETER 2:21-23) (HEBREWS 12:3)
(HEBREWS 12:1-2) (PHILIPPIANS 4:8)

October 22

The paths of the LORD are true and right, and righteous people
live by walking in them. But sinners stumble and fall along the
way.

He is very precious to you who believe. But for those who reject
him . . . "He is the stone that makes people stumble, the rock that
will make them fall." They stumble because they do not listen to
God's word or obey it, and so they meet the fate that has been
planned for them. ❧ The LORD protects the upright but destroys
the wicked.

Anyone who is willing to hear should listen and understand!
❧ Those who are wise will take all this to heart; they will see in our
history the faithful love of the LORD. ❧ A pure eye lets sunshine
into your soul. ❧ Anyone who wants to do the will of God will know
whether my teaching is from God or is merely my own. ❧ To those
who are open to my teaching, more understanding will be given,
and they will have an abundance of knowledge.

Anyone whose Father is God listens gladly to the words of God.
Since you don't, it proves you aren't God's children. ❧ You refuse
to come to me so that I can give you this eternal life. ❧ My sheep
recognize my voice; I know them, and they follow me.

The book of Hosea closes with an appeal to listen, learn, and
benefit from God's word. All readers have a choice: to listen to the
message and follow God's ways or refuse to walk along the Lord's path. If
you are lost, you can find the way by turning from your sin and following
God. *LAB note for Hosea 14:9*

(HOSEA 14:9) (1 PETER 2:7-8) (PROVERBS 10:29) (MATTHEW 11:15)
(PSALM 107:43) (MATTHEW 6:22) (JOHN 7:17) (MATTHEW 13:12)
(JOHN 8:47) (JOHN 5:40) (JOHN 10:27)

October 23

There is wonderful joy ahead, even though it is necessary for you to endure many trials for a while.

Dear friends, don't be surprised at the fiery trials you are going through, as if something strange were happening to you. Instead, be very glad—because these trials will make you partners with Christ in his suffering, and afterward you will have the wonderful joy of sharing his glory. ✹ Have you entirely forgotten the encouraging words God spoke to you, his children? He said, "My child, don't ignore it when the Lord disciplines you, and don't be discouraged when he corrects you." ✹ No discipline is enjoyable while it is happening—it is painful! But afterward there will be a quiet harvest of right living for those who are trained in this way.

This High Priest of ours understands our weaknesses, for he faced all of the same temptations we do, yet he did not sin. ✹ Since he himself has gone through suffering and temptation, he is able to help us when we are being tempted. ✹ Remember that the temptations that come into your life are no different from what others experience. And God is faithful. He will keep the temptation from becoming so strong that you can't stand up against it. When you are tempted, he will show you a way out so that you will not give in to it.

All believers face trials when they let their light shine into the darkness. We must accept trials as part of the refining process that burns away impurities and prepares us to meet Christ. Trials teach us patience and help us grow to be the kind of people God wants.

LAB note for 1 Peter 1:6–7

(1 Peter 1:6) (1 Peter 4:12-13) (Hebrews 12:5) (Hebrews 12:11)
(Hebrews 4:15) (Hebrews 2:18) (1 Corinthians 10:13)

October 24

Praise the LORD for his great love and for all his wonderful deeds.

Taste and see that the LORD is good. Oh, the joys of those who trust in him! ❧ Your goodness is so great! You have stored up great blessings for those who honor you. You have done so much for those who come to you for protection, blessing them before the watching world.

His unchanging plan has always been to adopt us into his own family by bringing us to himself through Jesus Christ. And this gave him great pleasure. So we praise God for the wonderful kindness he has poured out on us because we belong to his dearly loved Son.

How wonderful and beautiful they will be! The young men and women will thrive on the abundance of grain and new wine. ❧ The LORD is good to everyone. He showers compassion on all his creation. All of your works will thank you, LORD, and your faithful followers will bless you. They will talk together about the glory of your kingdom; they will celebrate examples of your power. They will tell about your mighty deeds and about the majesty and glory of your reign.

God's "unchanging plan" is another way of saying that salvation is God's work and not our own doing. In his infinite love, God has adopted us as his own children. Through Jesus' sacrifice he has brought us into his family and made us heirs along with Jesus. *LAB note for Ephesians 1:5*

(PSALM 107:8) (PSALM 34:8) (PSALM 31:19) (EPHESIANS 1:5-6)
(ZECHARIAH 9:17) (PSALM 145:9-12)

October 25

Lead me by your truth and teach me.

When the Spirit of truth comes, he will guide you into all truth. He will not be presenting his own ideas; he will be telling you what he has heard. ❧ The Holy Spirit has come upon you, and all of you know the truth.

"Check their predictions against my testimony," says the LORD. "If their predictions are different from mine, it is because there is no light or truth in them." ❧ All Scripture is inspired by God and is useful to teach us what is true and to make us realize what is wrong in our lives. It straightens us out and teaches us to do what is right. It is God's way of preparing us in every way, fully equipped for every good thing God wants us to do.

The LORD says, "I will guide you along the best pathway for your life. I will advise you and watch over you." ❧ A pure eye lets sunshine into your soul. ❧ Anyone who wants to do the will of God will know whether my teaching is from God or is merely my own. ❧ It will be only for those who walk in God's ways; fools will never walk there.

Jesus said the Holy Spirit would tell them "about the future"—the nature of their mission, the opposition they would face, and the final outcome of their efforts. They didn't fully understand these promises until the Holy Spirit came after Jesus' death and resurrection.

LAB note for John 16:13

(PSALM 25:5) (JOHN 16:13) (1 JOHN 2:20) (ISAIAH 8:20) (2 TIMOTHY 3:16–17) (PSALM 32:8) (MATTHEW 6:22) (JOHN 7:17) (ISAIAH 35:8)

October 26

We give great honor to those who endure under suffering.

We can rejoice, too, when we run into problems and trials, for we know that they are good for us—they help us learn to endure. And endurance develops strength of character in us, and character strengthens our confident expectation of salvation. And this expectation will not disappoint us. For we know how dearly God loves us, because he has given us the Holy Spirit to fill our hearts with his love.

No discipline is enjoyable while it is happening—it is painful! But afterward there will be a quiet harvest of right living for those who are trained in this way. ▓ Let it grow, for when your endurance is fully developed, you will be strong in character and ready for anything.

I am glad to boast about my weaknesses, so that the power of Christ may work through me. Since I know it is all for Christ's good, I am quite content with my weaknesses and with insults, hardships, persecutions, and calamities. For when I am weak, then I am strong.

We will experience difficulties that help us grow. We can rejoice in suffering, not because we like pain or deny its tragedy, but because we know God is using life's difficulties and Satan's attacks to build our character. Thank God for these opportunities to grow!

LAB note for Romans 5:3-4

(James 5:11) (Romans 5:3-5) (Hebrews 12:11) (James 1:4)
(2 Corinthians 12:9-10)

October 27

The way you live will always honor and please the Lord, and you will continually do good, kind things for others. All the while, you will learn to know God better and better.

Dear brothers and sisters, I plead with you to give your bodies to God. Let them be a living and holy sacrifice—the kind he will accept. When you think of what he has done for you, is this too much to ask? Don't copy the behavior and customs of this world, but let God transform you into a new person by changing the way you think. Then you will know what God wants you to do, and you will know how good and pleasing and perfect his will really is. ✺ Before, you let yourselves be slaves of impurity and lawlessness. Now you must choose to be slaves of righteousness so that you will become holy. ✺ What counts is whether we really have been changed into new and different people. May God's mercy and peace be upon all those who live by this principle. They are the new people of God.

My true disciples produce much fruit. This brings great glory to my Father. ✺ You didn't choose me. I chose you. I appointed you to go and produce fruit that will last, so that the Father will give you whatever you ask for, using my name. I command you to love each other.

Knowledge is not merely to be accumulated; it should give us direction for living. It is not a secret that only a few can discover; it is open to everyone. God wants us to learn more about him and put belief into practice by helping others.   *LAB note for Colossians 1:9–14*

(COLOSSIANS 1:10) (ROMANS 12:1-2) (ROMANS 6:19) (GALATIANS 6:15-16) (JOHN 15:8) (JOHN 15:16)

October 28

I will get up now and roam the city, searching for him.

Return, O Israel, to the LORD your God, for your sins have brought you down. Bring your petitions, and return to the LORD. Say to him, "Forgive all our sins and graciously receive us, so that we may offer you the sacrifice of praise."

Remember, no one who wants to do wrong should ever say, "God is tempting me." God is never tempted to do wrong, and he never tempts anyone else either. Temptation comes from the lure of our own evil desires. These evil desires lead to evil actions, and evil actions lead to death. So don't be misled, my dear brothers and sisters. Whatever is good and perfect comes to us from God above, who created all heaven's lights. Unlike them, he never changes or casts shifting shadows.

Wait patiently for the LORD. Be brave and courageous. Yes, wait patiently for the LORD. ❦ It is good to wait quietly for salvation from the LORD. ❦ Don't you think God will surely give justice to his chosen people who plead with him day and night?

I wait quietly before God, for my salvation comes from him.

When you love someone, you will do all you can to care for his or her needs, even at a cost to your personal comfort. This is demonstrated most often in small actions—getting your spouse a glass of water, leaving work early to attend some function your child is involved in, or sacrificing time to tend to a friend's needs.   *LAB note for Song of Songs 3:1-4*

(SONG OF SONGS 3:2) (HOSEA 14:1-2) (JAMES 1:13-17) (PSALM 27:14)
(LAMENTATIONS 3:26) (LUKE 18:7) (PSALM 62:1)

October 29

God can use sorrow in our lives to help us turn away from sin and seek salvation.

Jesus' words flashed through Peter's mind: "Before the rooster crows, you will deny me three times." And he went away, crying bitterly. ❧ If we confess our sins to him, he is faithful and just to forgive us and to cleanse us from every wrong. ❧ The blood of Jesus, his Son, cleanses us from every sin.

Troubles surround me—too many to count! They pile up so high I can't see my way out. They are more numerous than the hairs on my head. I have lost all my courage. Please, LORD, rescue me! Come quickly, LORD, and help me.

Your sins have brought you down. ❧ Come back to your God! Act on the principles of love and justice, and always live in confident dependence on your God. ❧ Be still in the presence of the LORD, and wait patiently for him to act.

The sacrifice you want is a broken spirit. A broken and repentant heart, O God, you will not despise. ❧ He heals the brokenhearted, binding up their wounds. ❧ The LORD has already told you what is good, and this is what he requires: to do what is right, to love mercy, and to walk humbly with your God.

Sorrow for our sins can result in changed behavior. Many people are sorry only for the effects of their sins or for being caught. Compare Peter's remorse and repentance with Judas's bitterness and suicide. Both denied Christ. One repented and was restored to faith and service; the other took his own life. *LAB note for 2 Corinthians 7:10*

(2 CORINTHIANS 7:10) (MATTHEW 26:75) (1 JOHN 1:9) (1 JOHN 1:7) (PSALM 40:12-13) (HOSEA 14:1) (HOSEA 12:6) (PSALM 37:7) (PSALM 51:17) (PSALM 147:3) (MICAH 6:8)

October 30

These trials are only to test your faith, to show that it is strong and pure.

We are well known, but we are treated as unknown. We live close to death, but here we are, still alive. We have been beaten within an inch of our lives. Our hearts ache, but we always have joy. We are poor, but we give spiritual riches to others. We own nothing, and yet we have everything.

We are pressed on every side by troubles, but we are not crushed and broken. We are perplexed, but we don't give up and quit. We are hunted down, but God never abandons us. We get knocked down, but we get up again and keep going.

Though our bodies are dying, our spirits are being renewed every day. For our present troubles are quite small and won't last very long. Yet they produce for us an immeasurably great glory that will last forever!

So we don't look at the troubles we can see right now; rather, we look forward to what we have not yet seen. For the troubles we see will soon be over, but the joys to come will last forever.

As gold is heated, impurities float to the top and can be skimmed off. Steel is tempered or strengthened by heating it in fire. Likewise, our trials, struggles, and persecutions refine and strengthen our faith, making us useful to God. *LAB note for 1 Peter 1:7*

(1 PETER 1:7) (2 CORINTHIANS 6:9-10) (2 CORINTHIANS 4:8-9)
(2 CORINTHIANS 4:16-17) (2 CORINTHIANS 4:18)

October 31

Love each other in the same way that I love you.

Live a life filled with love for others, following the example of Christ, who loved you and gave himself as a sacrifice to take away your sins. And God was pleased, because that sacrifice was like sweet perfume to him. ❧ This is the message we have heard from the beginning: We should love one another. ❧ Our lives are a fragrance presented by Christ to God.

You have been born again. Your new life did not come from your earthly parents because the life they gave you will end in death. But this new life will last forever because it comes from the eternal, living word of God. ❧ Make them pure and holy by teaching them your words of truth. ❧ No one can enter the Kingdom of God without being born of water and the Spirit. ❧ He saved us, not because of the good things we did, but because of his mercy. He washed away our sins and gave us a new life through the Holy Spirit. ❧ Your promise revives me.

May God, who gives this patience and encouragement, help you live in complete harmony with each other—each with the attitude of Christ Jesus toward the other.

When Christians preach the Good News, it is good news to some and repulsive news to others. Believers recognize the life-giving fragrance of the message. To unbelievers, however, it smells foul, like death—their own. *LAB note for 2 Corinthians 2:14-16*

(JOHN 15:12) (EPHESIANS 5:2) (1 JOHN 3:11) (2 CORINTHIANS 2:15) (1 PETER 1:23) (JOHN 17:17) (JOHN 3:5) (TITUS 3:5) (PSALM 119:50) (ROMANS 15:5)

November

We Give Thanks

Daily necessities and moment-by-moment protection;
Loving guidance and heartwarming friendship;
God's generous character flows into
every area of our lives.

It's the annual season for giving thanks.
As the year nears its end, spend a few moments
appreciating the countless blessings that
are often overlooked in daily life.

November 1

With all my heart I will praise you, O Lord my God.

Giving thanks is a sacrifice that truly honors me. ※ It is good to give thanks to the LORD, to sing praises to the Most High. It is good to proclaim your unfailing love in the morning, your faithfulness in the evening.

Let everything that lives sing praises to the LORD!

Dear brothers and sisters, I plead with you to give your bodies to God. Let them be a living and holy sacrifice—the kind he will accept. When you think of what he has done for you, is this too much to ask? ※ As a sacrifice for sin . . . Jesus suffered and died outside the city gates in order to make his people holy by shedding his own blood. With Jesus' help, let us continually offer our sacrifice of praise to God by proclaiming the glory of his name. ※ Always give thanks for everything to God the Father in the name of our Lord Jesus Christ.

The Lamb is worthy—the Lamb who was killed. He is worthy to receive power and riches and wisdom and strength and honor and glory and blessing.

Thanks should be on our lips every day. When thanksgiving becomes an integral part of your life, you will find that your attitude toward life will change. You will become more positive, gracious, loving, and humble.   *LAB note for Psalm 92:1-2*

(PSALM 86:12) (PSALM 50:23) (PSALM 92:1-2) (PSALM 150:6) (ROMANS 12:1) (HEBREWS 13:11-12, 15) (EPHESIANS 5:20) (REVELATION 5:12)

November 2

If you need wisdom—if you want to know what God wants you to do—ask him, and he will gladly tell you.

Jesus . . . said to her, "Where are your accusers? Didn't even one of them condemn you?" "No, Lord," she said. And Jesus said, "Neither do I. Go and sin no more."

What a difference between our sin and God's generous gift of forgiveness. For this one man, Adam, brought death to many through his sin. But this other man, Jesus Christ, brought forgiveness to many through God's bountiful gift. And the result of God's gracious gift is very different from the result of that one man's sin. For Adam's sin led to condemnation, but we have the free gift of being accepted by God, even though we are guilty of many sins.

God is so rich in mercy, and he loved us so very much, that even while we were dead because of our sins, he gave us life when he raised Christ from the dead. (It is only by God's special favor that you have been saved!) For he raised us from the dead along with Christ, and we are seated with him in the heavenly realms—all because we are one with Christ Jesus. And so God can always point to us as examples of the incredible wealth of his favor and kindness toward us, as shown in all he has done for us through Christ Jesus.

Since God did not spare even his own Son but gave him up for us all, won't God, who gave us Christ, also give us everything else?

Christ offers us the opportunity to be born into his spiritual family—the family line that begins with forgiveness and leads to eternal life. If we do nothing, we receive death through Adam; but if we come to God by faith, we receive life through Christ. To which family line do you now belong?   *LAB note for Romans 5:15-19*

(JAMES 1:5) (JOHN 8:10-11) (ROMANS 5:15-16)
(EPHESIANS 2:4-7) (ROMANS 8:32)

November 3

Make them pure and holy by teaching them your words of truth.

You have already been pruned for greater fruitfulness by the message I have given you. ❧ Let the words of Christ, in all their richness, live in your hearts and make you wise.

How can a young person stay pure? By obeying your word and following its rules. I have tried my best to find you—don't let me wander from your commands.

For wisdom will enter your heart, and knowledge will fill you with joy. Wise planning will watch over you. Understanding will keep you safe.

I have stayed in God's paths; I have followed his ways and not turned aside. I have not departed from his commands but have treasured his word in my heart. ❧ Even perfection has its limits, but your commands have no limit. Oh, how I love your law! I think about it all day long. Your commands make me wiser than my enemies, for your commands are my constant guide. Yes, I have more insight than my teachers, for I am always thinking of your decrees. ❧ You are truly my disciples if you keep obeying my teachings. And you will know the truth, and the truth will set you free.

A follower of Christ becomes pure and holy through believing and obeying the Word of God. He or she has already accepted forgiveness through Christ's sacrificial death. But daily application of God's Word has a purifying effect on our minds and hearts.　　*LAB note for John 17:17*

(JOHN 17:17) (JOHN 15:3) (COLOSSIANS 3:16) (PSALM 119:9-10)
(PROVERBS 2:10-11) (JOB 23:11-12) (PSALM 119:96-99) (JOHN 8:31-32)

November 4

How deep are your thoughts.

We have continued praying for you ever since we first heard about you. We ask God to give you a complete understanding of what he wants to do in your lives, and we ask him to make you wise with spiritual wisdom. ❧ I pray that Christ will be more and more at home in your hearts as you trust in him. May your roots go down deep into the soil of God's marvelous love. And may you have the power to understand, as all God's people should, how wide, how long, how high, and how deep his love really is. May you experience the love of Christ, though it is so great you will never fully understand it. Then you will be filled with the fullness of life and power that comes from God.

Oh, what a wonderful God we have! How great are his riches and wisdom and knowledge! How impossible it is for us to understand his decisions and his methods! ❧ "My thoughts are completely different from yours," says the LORD. "And my ways are far beyond anything you could imagine. For just as the heavens are higher than the earth, so are my ways higher than your ways and my thoughts higher than your thoughts." ❧ O LORD my God, you have done many miracles for us. Your plans for us are too numerous to list. If I tried to recite all your wonderful deeds, I would never come to the end of them.

God is ultimately wise. Although his methods and means are beyond our comprehension, God himself is not arbitrary. He governs the universe and our life in perfect wisdom, justice, and love.

LAB note for Romans 11:33

(PSALM 92:5) (COLOSSIANS 1:9) (EPHESIANS 3:17-19)
(ROMANS 11:33) (ISAIAH 55:8-9) (PSALM 40:5)

November 5

When the Holy Spirit controls our lives, he will produce . . . gentleness.

The humble will be filled with fresh joy from the LORD. Those who are poor will rejoice in the Holy One of Israel.

Unless you turn from your sins and become as little children, you will never get into the Kingdom of Heaven. Therefore, anyone who becomes as humble as this little child is the greatest in the Kingdom of Heaven. ▓ You should be known for the beauty that comes from within, the unfading beauty of a gentle and quiet spirit, which is so precious to God. ▓ Love is patient and kind. Love is not jealous or boastful or proud.

Pursue a godly life, along with faith, love, perseverance, and gentleness. ▓ Take my yoke upon you. Let me teach you, because I am humble and gentle. ▓ He was oppressed and treated harshly, yet he never said a word. He was led as a lamb to the slaughter. And as a sheep is silent before the shearers, he did not open his mouth.

This suffering is all part of what God has called you to. Christ, who suffered for you, is your example. Follow in his steps. He never sinned, and he never deceived anyone. He did not retaliate when he was insulted. When he suffered, he did not threaten to get even. He left his case in the hands of God, who always judges fairly.

Jesus used a child to help his self-centered disciples get the point. We are not to be childish (like the disciples, arguing over petty issues) but childlike, with humble and sincere hearts. Are you being childlike or childish?   *LAB note for Matthew 18:1-4*

(GALATIANS 5:22-23) (ISAIAH 29:19) (MATTHEW 18:3-4) (1 PETER 3:4)
(1 CORINTHIANS 13:4) (1 TIMOTHY 6:11) (MATTHEW 11:29) (ISAIAH 53:7)
(1 PETER 2:21-23)

November 6

He has punished Israel only a little. He has exiled her from her land as though blown away in a storm from the east.

Let us fall into the hands of the LORD, for his mercy is great. Do not let me fall into human hands. ❧ I am with you and will save you, says the LORD. . . . I will not destroy you. But I must discipline you; I cannot let you go unpunished. ❧ He will not constantly accuse us, nor remain angry forever. He has not punished us for all our sins, nor does he deal with us as we deserve. He knows we are only dust. ❧ I will spare them as a father spares an obedient and dutiful child.

Remember that the temptations that come into your life are no different from what others experience. And God is faithful. He will keep the temptation from becoming so strong that you can't stand up against it. When you are tempted, he will show you a way out so that you will not give in to it. ❧ Satan has asked to have all of you, to sift you like wheat. But I have pleaded in prayer for you . . . that your faith should not fail.

To the poor, O LORD, you are a refuge from the storm. To the needy in distress, you are a shelter from the rain and the heat. For the oppressive acts of ruthless people are like a storm beating against a wall.

David wisely chose the form of punishment that came most directly from God. He knew how brutal and harsh men in war could be, and he also knew God's great mercy. When you sin greatly, turn back to God. To be punished by him is far better than to take your chances without him.   *LAB note for 2 Samuel 24:12-14*

(ISAIAH 27:8) (2 SAMUEL 24:14) (JEREMIAH 30:11) (PSALM 103:9-10, 14)
(MALACHI 3:17) (1 CORINTHIANS 10:13) (LUKE 22:31-32) (ISAIAH 25:4)

November 7

Though I sit in darkness, the LORD himself will be my light.

When you go through deep waters and great trouble, I will be with you. When you go through rivers of difficulty, you will not drown! When you walk through the fire of oppression, you will not be burned up; the flames will not consume you. For I am the LORD, your God, the Holy One of Israel, your Savior. ❧ I will lead blind Israel down a new path, guiding them along an unfamiliar way. I will make the darkness bright before them and smooth out the road ahead of them. ❧ Who among you fears the LORD and obeys his servant? If you are walking in darkness, without a ray of light, trust in the LORD and rely on your God.

Even when I walk through the dark valley of death, I will not be afraid, for you are close beside me. Your rod and your staff protect and comfort me. ❧ When I am afraid, I put my trust in you. O God, I praise your word. I trust in God, so why should I be afraid? What can mere mortals do to me? ❧ The LORD is my light and my salvation—so why should I be afraid?

Micah showed great faith in God as he waited on God to bring his people through tough times. We, too, can have a relationship with God that can allow us to have confidence like Micah's. It doesn't take unusual talent; it simply takes faith in God and a willingness to act on that faith.

LAB note for Micah 7:7-10

(MICAH 7:8) (ISAIAH 43:2-3) (ISAIAH 42:16) (ISAIAH 50:10) (PSALM 23:4) (PSALM 56:3-4) (PSALM 27:1)

November 8

Pray as you are directed by the Holy Spirit.

God is Spirit, so those who worship him must worship in spirit and in truth. ❧ All of us, both Jews and Gentiles, may come to the Father through the same Holy Spirit because of what Christ has done for us.

My Father! If it is possible, let this cup of suffering be taken away from me. Yet I want your will, not mine.

The Holy Spirit helps us in our distress. For we don't even know what we should pray for, nor how we should pray. But the Holy Spirit prays for us with groanings that cannot be expressed in words. And the Father who knows all hearts knows what the Spirit is saying, for the Spirit pleads for us believers in harmony with God's own will. ❧ And we can be confident that he will listen to us whenever we ask him for anything in line with his will. ❧ When the Spirit of truth comes, he will guide you into all truth.

Pray at all times and on every occasion in the power of the Holy Spirit. Stay alert and be persistent in your prayers for all Christians everywhere.

To pray as we are "directed by the Holy Spirit" means to pray in the power and strength of the Holy Spirit. He prays for us, opens our mind to Jesus, and teaches us about him. *LAB note for Jude 1:20*

(JUDE 1:20) (JOHN 4:24) (EPHESIANS 2:18) (MATTHEW 26:39) (ROMANS 8:26–27) (1 JOHN 5:14) (JOHN 16:13) (EPHESIANS 6:18)

November 9

If a tree is cut down, there is hope that it will sprout again and grow new branches.

He will not crush those who are weak. ❧ He renews my strength.

God can use sorrow in our lives to help us turn away from sin and seek salvation. We will never regret that kind of sorrow. But sorrow without repentance is the kind that results in death. ❧ No discipline is enjoyable while it is happening—it is painful! But afterward there will be a quiet harvest of right living for those who are trained in this way.

I used to wander off until you disciplined me; but now I closely follow your word.

Do not gloat over me, my enemies! For though I fall, I will rise again. Though I sit in darkness, the LORD himself will be my light. I will be patient as the LORD punishes me, for I have sinned against him. But after that, he will take up my case and punish my enemies for all the evil they have done to me. The LORD will bring me out of my darkness into the light, and I will see his righteousness.

Job's pessimism about death is understandable, since Jesus had not yet conquered death. What is remarkable is his budding hope: If only he could die and live again! When we must endure suffering, we have an advantage over Job. We know that the dead will rise—because Christ rose!

LAB note for Job 14:7-22

(JOB 14:7) (ISAIAH 42:3) (PSALM 23:3) (2 CORINTHIANS 7:10) (HEBREWS 12:11) (PSALM 119:67) (MICAH 7:8-9)

November 10

My Kingdom is not of this world.

Our High Priest offered himself to God as one sacrifice for sins, good for all time. Then he sat down at the place of highest honor at God's right hand. ▧ In the future you will see me, the Son of Man, sitting at God's right hand in the place of power and coming back on the clouds of heaven.

Christ must reign until he humbles all his enemies beneath his feet.

How we thank God, who gives us victory over sin and death through Jesus Christ our Lord! ▧ This is the same mighty power that raised Christ from the dead and seated him in the place of honor at God's right hand in the heavenly realms. Now he is far above any ruler or authority or power or leader or anything else in this world or in the world to come. And God has put all things under the authority of Christ, and he gave him this authority for the benefit of the church. And the church is his body; it is filled by Christ, who fills everything everywhere with his presence. ▧ For at the right time Christ will be revealed from heaven by the blessed and only almighty God, the King of kings and Lord of lords.

Jesus declared his royalty in no uncertain terms. In saying he was the Son of Man, Jesus was claiming to be the Messiah, as his listeners well knew. He knew this declaration would be his undoing, but he did not panic. He was calm, courageous, and determined.   *LAB note for Matthew 26:64*

(JOHN 18:36) (HEBREWS 10:12-13) (MATTHEW 26:64) (1 CORINTHIANS 15:25) (1 CORINTHIANS 15:57) (EPHESIANS 1:19-23) (1 TIMOTHY 6:15)

November 11

What are you doing here, Elijah?

He knows where I am going. O LORD, you have examined my heart and know everything about me. You know when I sit down or stand up. You know my every thought when far away. You chart the path ahead of me and tell me where to stop and rest. I can never escape from your spirit! I can never get away from your presence! If I ride the wings of the morning, if I dwell by the farthest oceans, even there your hand will guide me, and your strength will support me.

Elijah was as human as we are. Fearing people is a dangerous trap, but to trust the LORD means safety. Though they stumble, they will not fall, for the LORD holds them by the hand. They may trip seven times, but each time they will rise again.

Don't get tired of doing what is good. Don't get discouraged and give up, for we will reap a harvest of blessing at the appropriate time. Though the spirit is willing enough, the body is weak! The LORD is like a father to his children, tender and compassionate to those who fear him. For he understands how weak we are; he knows we are only dust.

God is omnipresent—he is present everywhere. Because this is so, you can never escape from his Spirit. This is good news to those who know and love God, because no matter what we do or where we go, we can never be far from God's comforting presence. *LAB note for Psalm 139:7*

(1 KINGS 19:9) (JOB 23:10) (PSALM 139:1-3, 7, 9-10) (JAMES 5:17)
(PROVERBS 29:25) (PSALM 37:24) (PROVERBS 24:16) (GALATIANS 6:9)
(MATTHEW 26:41) (PSALM 103:13-14)

November 12

Now you are free from sin, your old master, and you have become slaves to your new master, righteousness.

No one can serve two masters. . . . You cannot serve both God and money. ⧠ When you were slaves of sin, you weren't concerned with doing what was right. And what was the result? It was not good, since now you are ashamed of the things you used to do, things that end in eternal doom. But now you are free from the power of sin and have become slaves of God. Now you do those things that lead to holiness and result in eternal life.

Christ has accomplished the whole purpose of the law. All who believe in him are made right with God.

All those who want to be my disciples must come and follow me, because my servants must be where I am. And if they follow me, the Father will honor them. ⧠ Take my yoke upon you. Let me teach you, because I am humble and gentle, and you will find rest for your souls. For my yoke fits perfectly, and the burden I give you is light.

O LORD our God, others have ruled us, but we worship you alone. ⧠ If you will help me, I will run to follow your commands.

All people have a master and pattern themselves after him. Without Jesus we would have no choice but to be enslaved to sin. But thanks to him, we can now choose God as our Master. Following him we can enjoy new life and learn how to work for him.

LAB note for Romans 6:16-18

(ROMANS 6:18) (MATTHEW 6:24) (ROMANS 6:20-22) (ROMANS 10:4) (JOHN 12:26) (MATTHEW 11:29-30) (ISAIAH 26:13) (PSALM 119:32)

November 13

Anyone who calls on the name of the Lord will be saved.

Manasseh . . . rebuilt the pagan shrines his father, Hezekiah, had destroyed. He constructed altars for Baal and set up an Asherah pole, just as King Ahab of Israel had done. He even built pagan altars in the Temple of the LORD, the place where the LORD had said his name should be honored. He built these altars for all the forces of heaven in both courtyards of the LORD's Temple. Manasseh even sacrificed his own son in the fire. He practiced sorcery and divination, and he consulted with mediums and psychics. He did much that was evil in the LORD's sight, arousing his anger. While in deep distress, Manasseh sought the LORD his God and cried out humbly to the God of his ancestors. And when he prayed, the LORD listened to him and was moved by his request for help. So the LORD let Manasseh return to Jerusalem and to his kingdom. Manasseh had finally realized that the LORD alone is God!

"Come now, let us argue this out," says the LORD. "No matter how deep the stain of your sins, I can remove it. I can make you as clean as freshly fallen snow. Even if you are stained as red as crimson, I can make you as white as wool." He does not want anyone to perish.

Today, many books, television shows, and games emphasize fortune-telling, séances, and other occult practices. Don't let desire to know the future or the belief that superstition is harmless lead you into condoning occult practices. They are counterfeits of God's power and have as their root a system of beliefs totally opposed to God.

LAB note for 2 Kings 21:6

(ACTS 2:21) (2 KINGS 21:1, 3–6) (2 CHRONICLES 33:12–13)
(ISAIAH 1:18) (2 PETER 3:9)

November 14

When the Holy Spirit controls our lives, he will produce . . . patience, kindness.

I am the LORD, I am the LORD, the merciful and gracious God. I am slow to anger and rich in unfailing love and faithfulness.

Lead a life worthy of your calling, for you have been called by God. Be humble and gentle. Be patient with each other, making allowance for each other's faults because of your love. ❦ Be kind to each other, tenderhearted, forgiving one another, just as God through Christ has forgiven you. ❦ The wisdom that comes from heaven is first of all pure. It is also peace loving, gentle at all times, and willing to yield to others. It is full of mercy and good deeds. It shows no partiality and is always sincere. ❦ Love is patient and kind.

Don't get tired of doing what is good. Don't get discouraged and give up, for we will reap a harvest of blessing at the appropriate time. ❦ Dear brothers and sisters, you must be patient as you wait for the Lord's return. Consider the farmers who eagerly look for the rains in the fall and in the spring. They patiently wait for the precious harvest to ripen. You, too, must be patient. And take courage, for the coming of the Lord is near.

No one is ever going to be perfect here on earth, so we must accept, love, and be patient with other Christians in spite of their faults. Rather than dwelling on a person's weaknesses or looking for faults, pray for him or her. *LAB note for Ephesians 4:2*

(GALATIANS 5:22) (EXODUS 34:6) (EPHESIANS 4:1-2) (EPHESIANS 4:32) (JAMES 3:17) (1 CORINTHIANS 13:4) (GALATIANS 6:9) (JAMES 5:7-8)

November 15

Just as the body is dead without a spirit, so also faith is dead without good deeds.

Not all people who sound religious are really godly. They may refer to me as "Lord," but they still won't enter the Kingdom of Heaven. The decisive issue is whether they obey my Father in heaven.

Seek to live a clean and holy life, for those who are not holy will not see the Lord. ▧ Make every effort to apply the benefits of these promises to your life. Then your faith will produce a life of moral excellence. A life of moral excellence leads to knowing God better. Knowing God leads to self-control. Self-control leads to patient endurance, and patient endurance leads to godliness. Godliness leads to love for other Christians, and finally you will grow to have genuine love for everyone. The more you grow like this, the more you will become productive and useful in your knowledge of our Lord Jesus Christ. But those who fail to develop these virtues are blind or, at least, very shortsighted. They have already forgotten that God has cleansed them from their old life of sin. So, dear brothers and sisters, work hard to prove that you really are among those God has called and chosen. Doing this, you will never stumble or fall away.

Salvation is not a reward for the good things we have done, so none of us can boast about it.

Jesus is more concerned about our walk than our talk. He wants us to do right, not just say the right words. You can only withstand the storms of life if you do what is right instead of just talking about it. What you do cannot be separated from what you believe. *LAB note for Matthew 7:21*

(JAMES 2:26) (MATTHEW 7:21) (HEBREWS 12:14)
(2 PETER 1:5-10) (EPHESIANS 2:9)

November 16

Do you . . . believe?

What's the use of saying you have faith if you don't prove it by your actions? That kind of faith can't save anyone. It isn't enough just to have faith. Faith that doesn't show itself by good deeds is no faith at all—it is dead and useless.

It was by faith that Abraham offered Isaac as a sacrifice when God was testing him. Abraham, who had received God's promises, was ready to sacrifice his only son, Isaac, though God had promised him, "Isaac is the son through whom your descendants will be counted." Abraham assumed that if Isaac died, God was able to bring him back to life again. Don't you remember that our ancestor Abraham was declared right with God because of what he did when he offered his son Isaac on the altar? So you see, we are made right with God by what we do, not by faith alone.

The way to identify a tree or a person is by the kind of fruit that is produced. Not all people who sound religious are really godly. They may refer to me as "Lord," but they still won't enter the Kingdom of Heaven. The decisive issue is whether they obey my Father in heaven. You know these things—now do them! That is the path of blessing.

When someone claims to have faith, what he or she may have is intellectual assent—agreement with a set of Christian teachings—and as such it would be incomplete faith. True faith transforms our conduct as well as our thoughts. If our life remains unchanged, we don't truly believe the truths we claim to hold. *LAB note for James 2:14*

(JOHN 16:31) (JAMES 2:14, 17) (HEBREWS 11:17-19) (JAMES 2:21, 24)
(MATTHEW 7:20-21) (JOHN 13:17)

November 17

May the Lord of peace himself always give you his peace no matter what happens. The Lord be with you all.

Grace and peace from the one who is, who always was, and who is still to come. ❧ You will experience God's peace, which is far more wonderful than the human mind can understand. His peace will guard your hearts and minds as you live in Christ Jesus.

Jesus himself was suddenly standing there among them. He said, "Peace be with you." ❧ I am leaving you with a gift—peace of mind and heart. And the peace I give isn't like the peace the world gives. So don't be troubled or afraid.

The Counselor—the Spirit of truth. ❧ When the Holy Spirit controls our lives, he will produce this kind of fruit in us: love, joy, peace. ❧ His Holy Spirit speaks to us deep in our hearts and tells us that we are God's children.

"I will personally go with you, Moses. I will give you rest—everything will be fine for you." Then Moses said, "If you don't go with us personally, don't let us move a step from this place. If you don't go with us, how will anyone ever know that your people and I have found favor with you?"

God's peace is different from the world's peace. True peace is not found in positive thinking, in absence of conflict, or in good feelings. It comes from knowing that God is in control. Our citizenship in Christ's Kingdom is sure, our destiny is set, and we can have victory over anxiety.

LAB note for Philippians 4:7

(2 Thessalonians 3:16) (Revelation 1:4) (Philippians 4:7) (Luke 24:36) (John 14:27) (John 15:26) (Galatians 5:22) (Romans 8:16) (Exodus 33:14-16)

November 18

We can rejoice, too, when we run into problems and trials, for we know that they are good for us.

If we have hope in Christ only for this life, we are the most miserable people in the world.

Dear friends, don't be surprised at the fiery trials you are going through, as if something strange were happening to you. Instead, be very glad—because these trials will make you partners with Christ in his suffering, and afterward you will have the wonderful joy of sharing his glory when it is displayed to all the world. ※ Our hearts ache, but we always have joy.

Always be full of joy in the Lord. I say it again—rejoice! ※ The apostles left the high council rejoicing that God had counted them worthy to suffer dishonor for the name of Jesus.

I pray that God, who gives you hope, will keep you happy and full of peace as you believe in him.

Even though the fig trees have no blossoms, and there are no grapes on the vine; even though the olive crop fails, and the fields lie empty and barren; even though the flocks die in the fields, and the cattle barns are empty, yet I will rejoice in the LORD! I will be joyful in the God of my salvation.

What a difference it makes to know Jesus! He cares for us in spite of what the world thinks. Don't let circumstances or people's expectations control you. Be firm as you stand true to God, and refuse to compromise his standards for living. *LAB note for 2 Corinthians 6:8-10*

(ROMANS 5:3) (1 CORINTHIANS 15:19) (1 PETER 4:12-13) (2 CORINTHIANS 6:10) (PHILIPPIANS 4:4) (ACTS 5:41) (ROMANS 15:13) (HABAKKUK 3:17-18)

November 19

My eyes are always looking to the LORD for help.

Is anything too hard for the LORD? ✽ Commit everything you do to the LORD. Trust him, and he will help you. ✽ Don't worry about anything; instead, pray about everything. Tell God what you need, and thank him for all he has done. ✽ Give all your worries and cares to God, for he cares about what happens to you. ✽ Take delight in the LORD, and he will give you your heart's desires.

Moses and Aaron were among his priests; Samuel also called on his name. They cried to the LORD for help, and he answered them. He spoke to them from the pillar of cloud, and they followed the decrees and principles he gave them.

I will answer them before they even call to me. While they are still talking to me about their needs, I will go ahead and answer their prayers! ✽ The earnest prayer of a righteous person has great power and wonderful results.

I love the LORD because he hears and answers my prayers. Because he bends down and listens, I will pray as long as I have breath!

"Is anything too hard for the LORD?" The obvious answer is, "Of course not!" Make it a habit to insert your specific needs into the question. "Is the communication problem I'm having too hard for him?" Asking the question this way reminds you that God is personally involved in your life. *LAB note for Genesis 18:14*

(PSALM 25:15) (GENESIS 18:14) (PSALM 37:5) (PHILIPPIANS 4:6) (1 PETER 5:7) (PSALM 37:4) (PSALM 99:6-7) (ISAIAH 65:24) (JAMES 5:16) (PSALM 116:1-2)

November 20

Do people know where to find wisdom?

If you need wisdom—if you want to know what God wants you to do—ask him, and he will gladly tell you. He will not resent your asking. But when you ask him, be sure that you really expect him to answer, for a doubtful mind is as unsettled as a wave of the sea that is driven and tossed by the wind. 🕮 Trust in the LORD with all your heart; do not depend on your own understanding. Seek his will in all you do, and he will direct your paths. 🕮 He is the eternal King, the unseen one who never dies; he alone is God. 🕮 Don't be impressed with your own wisdom.

"O Sovereign LORD," I said, "I can't speak for you! I'm too young!" "Don't say that," the LORD replied, "for you must go wherever I send you and say whatever I tell you. And don't be afraid of the people, for I will be with you and take care of you. I, the LORD, have spoken!"

Go directly to the Father and ask him, and he will grant your request because you use my name. You haven't done this before. Ask, using my name, and you will receive, and you will have abundant joy. 🕮 If you believe, you will receive whatever you ask for in prayer.

Wisdom is not only knowledge, but the ability to make wise decisions in difficult circumstances. Whenever we need wisdom, we can pray to God, and he will generously supply what we need to guide our choices. *LAB note for James 1:5*

(JOB 28:12) (JAMES 1:5-6) (PROVERBS 3:5-6) (1 TIMOTHY 1:17) (PROVERBS 3:7) (JEREMIAH 1:6-8) (JOHN 16:23-24) (MATTHEW 21:22)

November 21

The suffering you sent was good for me, for it taught me to pay attention to your principles.

Even though Jesus was God's Son, he learned obedience from the things he suffered. ❧ If we are to share his glory, we must also share his suffering. Yet what we suffer now is nothing compared to the glory he will give us later. ❧ Whenever trouble comes your way, let it be an opportunity for joy. For when your faith is tested, your endurance has a chance to grow. So let it grow, for when your endurance is fully developed, you will be strong in character and ready for anything.

He knows where I am going. And when he has tested me like gold in a fire, he will pronounce me innocent. For I have stayed in God's paths; I have followed his ways and not turned aside.

Remember how the LORD your God led you through the wilderness for forty years, humbling you and testing you to prove your character, and to find out whether or not you would really obey his commands. So you should realize that just as a parent disciplines a child, the LORD your God disciplines you to help you. So obey the commands of the LORD your God by walking in his ways and fearing him.

Jesus' human life was not a script that he passively followed. It was a life that he chose freely—and a continuous process of making the will of God the Father his own. Because Jesus obeyed perfectly, even under great trial, he can help us obey, no matter how difficult obedience seems to be.

LAB note for Hebrews 5:8

(PSALM 119:71) (HEBREWS 5:8) (ROMANS 8:17-18) (JAMES 1:2-4) (JOB 23:10-11) (DEUTERONOMY 8:2, 5-6)

November 22

No one will succeed by strength alone.

David shouted in reply, "You come to me with sword, spear, and javelin, but I come to you in the name of the LORD Almighty—the God of the armies of Israel, whom you have defied." Reaching into his shepherd's bag and taking out a stone, he hurled it from his sling and hit the Philistine in the forehead. The stone sank in, and Goliath stumbled and fell face downward to the ground. So David triumphed over the Philistine giant with only a stone and sling.

The best-equipped army cannot save a king, nor is great strength enough to save a warrior. But the LORD watches over those who fear him, those who rely on his unfailing love. ❈ Riches and honor come from you alone, for you rule over everything. Power and might are in your hand, and it is at your discretion that people are made great and given strength.

I am glad to boast about my weaknesses, so that the power of Christ may work through me. Since I know it is all for Christ's good, I am quite content with my weaknesses and with insults, hardships, persecutions, and calamities. For when I am weak, then I am strong.

We should be confident of God's ultimate control over the events in our lives, and we should be thankful for the ways God has blessed us. By praising God for all good gifts, we acknowledge his ultimate control over all the affairs of life. *LAB note for 1 Samuel 2:1-10*

(1 SAMUEL 2:9) (1 SAMUEL 17:45, 49-50) (PSALM 33:16, 18)
(1 CHRONICLES 29:12) (2 CORINTHIANS 12:9-10)

November 23

Though the spirit is willing enough, the body is weak!

LORD, we love to obey your laws; our heart's desire is to glorify your name. All night long I search for you; earnestly I seek for God.

I know I am rotten through and through so far as my old sinful nature is concerned. No matter which way I turn, I can't make myself do right. I want to, but I can't. I love God's law with all my heart. But there is another law at work within me that is at war with my mind. This law wins the fight and makes me a slave to the sin that is still within me. ❧ The old sinful nature loves to do evil, which is just opposite from what the Holy Spirit wants. And the Spirit gives us desires that are opposite from what the sinful nature desires. These two forces are constantly fighting each other, and your choices are never free from the conflict.

I can do everything with the help of Christ who gives me the strength I need. ❧ Our only power and success come from God. ❧ My gracious favor is all you need.

We must never use the power of sin or Satan as an excuse, because they are defeated enemies. But without Christ's help, sin is stronger than we are. That is why we should never stand up to it all alone. Jesus Christ, who has conquered sin once and for all, promises to fight by our side.

LAB note for Romans 7:17–20

(MATTHEW 26:41) (ISAIAH 26:8-9) (ROMANS 7:18, 22-23) (GALATIANS 5:17)
(PHILIPPIANS 4:13) (2 CORINTHIANS 3:5) (2 CORINTHIANS 12:9)

November 24

God made Christ, who never sinned, to be the offering for our sin, so that we could be made right with God through Christ.

The LORD laid on him the guilt and sins of us all. ▨ He personally carried away our sins in his own body on the cross so we can be dead to sin and live for what is right. You have been healed by his wounds! ▨ Because one person disobeyed God, many people became sinners. But because one other person obeyed God, many people will be made right in God's sight.

God our Savior showed us his kindness and love. He saved us, not because of the good things we did, but because of his mercy. He washed away our sins and gave us a new life through the Holy Spirit. He generously poured out the Spirit upon us because of what Jesus Christ our Savior did. He declared us not guilty because of his great kindness. And now we know that we will inherit eternal life. ▨ So now there is no condemnation for those who belong to Christ Jesus.

The LORD Is Our Righteousness.

When we trust in Christ, we make an exchange: He takes our sin and makes us right with God. In the world, bartering works only when two people exchange goods of relatively equal value. But God offers to trade his righteousness for our sin—something of immeasurable worth for something completely worthless. *LAB note for 2 Corinthians 5:21*

(2 CORINTHIANS 5:21) (ISAIAH 53:6) (1 PETER 2:24) (ROMANS 5:19)
(TITUS 3:4-7) (ROMANS 8:1) (JEREMIAH 23:6)

November 25

The dust will return to the earth.

Our earthly bodies, which die and decay . . . now disappoint us. . . . They are weak . . . natural human bodies. ❦ Adam, the first man, was made from the dust of the earth.

You were made from dust, and to the dust you will return. ❦ One person dies in prosperity and security, the very picture of good health. Another person dies in bitter poverty, never having tasted the good life. Both alike are buried in the same dust, both eaten by the same worms.

No wonder my heart is filled with joy, and my mouth shouts his praises! My body rests in safety. ❦ After my body has decayed, yet in my body I will see God! ❦ The Lord Jesus Christ . . . will take these weak mortal bodies of ours and change them into glorious bodies like his own, using the same mighty power that he will use to conquer everything, everywhere.

LORD, remind me how brief my time on earth will be. Remind me that my days are numbered, and that my life is fleeing away. ❦ Teach us to make the most of our time, so that we may grow in wisdom.

Stripped of the life-giving spirit breathed into us by God, our bodies return to dust. Stripped of God's purpose, our work is in vain. Stripped of God's love, our service is futile. We must put God first over all we do and in all we do because without him we have nothing.

LAB note for Ecclesiastes 12:7-8

(ECCLESIASTES 12:7) (1 CORINTHIANS 15:42-44) (1 CORINTHIANS 15:47) (GENESIS 3:19) (JOB 21:23-26) (PSALM 16:9) (JOB 19:26) (PHILIPPIANS 3:20-21) (PSALM 39:4) (PSALM 90:12)

November 26

The LORD is more pleased when we do what is just and right than when we give him sacrifices.

The LORD has told you what is good, and this is what he requires: to do what is right, to love mercy, and to walk humbly with your God. ✹ What is more pleasing to the LORD; your burnt offerings and sacrifices or your obedience to his voice? Obedience is far better than sacrifice. Listening to him is much better than offering the fat of rams. ✹ I know it is important to love him with all my heart and all my understanding and all my strength, and to love my neighbor as myself. This is more important than to offer all of the burnt offerings and sacrifices required in the law.

Come back to your God! Act on the principles of love and justice, and always live in confident dependence on your God. ✹ Mary . . . sat at the Lord's feet, listening to what he taught. "There is really only one thing worth being concerned about. Mary has discovered it—and I won't take it away from her."

God is working in you, giving you the desire to obey him and the power to do what pleases him. ✹ May he produce in you, through the power of Jesus Christ, all that is pleasing to him. . . . To him be glory forever and ever. Amen.

Sacrifices are not bribes to make God overlook our character faults. If our personal and business dealings are not characterized by justice, no amount of generosity when the offering plate is passed will make up for it. *LAB note for Proverbs 21:3*

(Proverbs 21:3) (Micah 6:8) (1 Samuel 15:22) (Mark 12:33) (Hosea 12:6)
(Luke 10:39, 42) (Philippians 2:13) (Hebrews 13:21)

November 27

The spirit will return to God who gave it.

The LORD God formed a man's body from the dust of the ground and breathed into it the breath of life. And the man became a living person. ▨ It is God's Spirit within people, the breath of the Almighty within them, that makes them intelligent. But sometimes the elders are not wise. Sometimes the aged do not understand justice.

We are always confident, even though we know that as long as we live in these bodies we are not at home with the Lord. ▨ I long to go and be with Christ. That would be far better for me. ▨ And now, brothers and sisters, I want you to know what will happen to the Christians who have died so you will not be full of sorrow like people who have no hope. For since we believe that Jesus died and was raised to life again, we also believe that when Jesus comes, God will bring back with Jesus all the Christians who have died.

There are many rooms in my Father's home, and I am going to prepare a place for you. If this were not so, I would tell you plainly. When everything is ready, I will come and get you, so that you will always be with me where I am.

It is not enough to recognize a great truth; it must be lived out each day. Elihu [Job's "friend"] recognized the truth that God was the only source of real wisdom, but he did not use God's wisdom to help Job. Becoming wise is an ongoing, lifelong pursuit. Don't be content just to know about wisdom; make it part of your life.   *LAB note for Job 32:7-9*

(ECCLESIASTES 12:7) (GENESIS 2:7) (JOB 32:8-9) (2 CORINTHIANS 5:6)
(PHILIPPIANS 1:23) (1 THESSALONIANS 4:13-14) (JOHN 14:2-3)

November 28

No one can take them from me.

I know the one in whom I trust, and I am sure that he is able to guard what I have entrusted to him until the day of his return. ▓ The Lord will deliver me from every evil attack and will bring me safely to his heavenly Kingdom. ▓ Overwhelming victory is ours through Christ, who loved us. And I am convinced that nothing can ever separate us from his love. Death can't, and life can't. The angels can't, and the demons can't. Our fears for today, our worries about tomorrow, and even the powers of hell can't keep God's love away. Whether we are high above the sky or in the deepest ocean, nothing in all creation will ever be able to separate us from the love of God that is revealed in Christ Jesus our Lord. ▓ Your real life is hidden with Christ in God.

Hasn't God chosen the poor in this world to be rich in faith? Aren't they the ones who will inherit the kingdom God promised to those who love him?

May our Lord Jesus Christ and God our Father, who loved us and in his special favor gave us everlasting comfort and hope, comfort your hearts and give you strength in every good thing you do and say.

Paul was in prison, but that did not stop his ministry. He trusted God to use him regardless of his circumstances. If your situation looks bleak, give your concerns to Christ. He will guard your faith and safely keep all you have entrusted to him until the day of his return.

LAB note for 2 Timothy 1:12

(JOHN 10:29) (2 TIMOTHY 1:12) (2 TIMOTHY 4:18) (ROMANS 8:37-39)
(COLOSSIANS 3:3) (JAMES 2:5) (2 THESSALONIANS 2:16-17)

November 29

You will not be condemned for doing something you know is all right.

Keep away from every kind of evil. ▨ We are careful to be honorable before the Lord, but we also want everyone else to know we are honorable. ▨ It is God's will that your good lives should silence those who make foolish accusations against you.

If you suffer, however, it must not be for murder, stealing, making trouble, or prying into other people's affairs. But it is no shame to suffer for being a Christian. Praise God for the privilege of being called by his wonderful name!

For you have been called to live in freedom—not freedom to satisfy your sinful nature, but freedom to serve one another in love. ▨ The Kingdom of God is not a matter of what we eat or drink, but of living a life of goodness and peace and joy in the Holy Spirit. ▨ You must be careful with this freedom of yours. Do not cause a brother or sister with a weaker conscience to stumble. ▨ If anyone causes one of these little ones who trusts in me to lose faith, it would be better for that person to be thrown into the sea with a large millstone tied around the neck. ▨ When you refused to help the least of these my brothers and sisters, you were refusing to help me.

As Christians, we cannot avoid every kind of evil because we live in a sinful world. We can, however, make sure that we don't give evil a foothold by avoiding tempting situations and concentrating on obeying God.   *LAB note for 1 Thessalonians 5:22-24*

(ROMANS 14:16) (1 THESSALONIANS 5:22) (2 CORINTHIANS 8:21) (1 PETER 2:15) (1 PETER 4:15-16) (GALATIANS 5:13) (ROMANS 14:17) (1 CORINTHIANS 8:9) (MATTHEW 18:6) (MATTHEW 25:45)

November 30

Awake, O sleeper, rise up from the dead, and Christ will give you light.

Wake up, for the coming of our salvation is nearer now than when we first believed. ▨ So be on your guard, not asleep like the others. Stay alert and be sober. Night is the time for sleep and the time when people get drunk. But let us who live in the light think clearly, protected by the body armor of faith and love, and wearing as our helmet the confidence of our salvation.

Let your light shine for all the nations to see! For the glory of the LORD is shining upon you. Darkness as black as night will cover all the nations of the earth, but the glory of the LORD will shine over you.

Think clearly and exercise self-control. Look forward to the special blessings that will come to you at the return of Jesus Christ. ▨ Be dressed for service and well prepared, as though you were waiting for your master to return from the wedding feast. Then you will be ready to open the door and let him in the moment he arrives and knocks. ▨ If you do these things, your salvation will come like the dawn. Yes, your healing will come quickly. Your godliness will lead you forward, and the glory of the LORD will protect you from behind.

The imminent return of Christ should motivate us to live for him. This means being mentally alert ("think clearly"), disciplined ("exercise self-control"), and focused ("look forward"). Are you ready to meet Christ? *LAB note for 1 Peter 1:13*

(EPHESIANS 5:14) (ROMANS 13:11) (1 THESSALONIANS 5:6-8) (ISAIAH 60:1-2) (1 PETER 1:13) (LUKE 12:35-36) (ISAIAH 58:8)

December

The Giver of Life

Creator and Provider

Comforter and Friend

Eternal, infinite, awesome God

In this special season of giving, take a minute to

reflect on God's generosity to you. He truly is the

giver of all good things. How is your life changed

by God's greatest gift on that first Christmas?

December 1

The Word became human and lived here on earth among us. He was full of unfailing love and faithfulness. And we have seen his glory, the glory of the only Son of the Father. ※ Your promises are backed by all the honor of your name.

He will be called Immanuel (meaning, God is with us). ※ Jesus, for he will save his people from their sins.

Everyone will honor the Son, just as they honor the Father. ※ God raised him up to the heights of heaven and gave him a name that is above every other name. ※ He is far above any ruler or authority or power or leader or anything else in this world or in the world to come. And God has put all things under the authority of Christ. ※ A name was written on him, and only he knew what it meant . . . King of kings and Lord of lords.

We cannot imagine the power of the Almighty. ※ What is his name—and his son's name? Tell me if you know!

In a time of great darkness, God promised to send a light who would shine on everyone living in the shadow of death. He is both "Wonderful Counselor" and "Mighty God." This message of hope was fulfilled in the birth of Christ and the establishment of his eternal Kingdom. *LAB note for Isaiah 9:2-6*

(ISAIAH 9:6) (JOHN 1:14) (PSALM 138:2) (MATTHEW 1:23) (MATTHEW 1:21) (JOHN 5:23) (PHILIPPIANS 2:9) (EPHESIANS 1:21-22) (REVELATION 19:12, 16) (JOB 37:23) (PROVERBS 30:4)

December 2

You judge all people according to what they have done.

No one can lay any other foundation than the one we already have—Jesus Christ. If the work survives the fire, that builder will receive a reward. But if the work is burned up, the builder will suffer great loss. The builders themselves will be saved, but like someone escaping through a wall of flames. ❧ For we must all stand before Christ to be judged. We will each receive whatever we deserve for the good or evil we have done in our bodies.

When you give to someone, don't tell your left hand what your right hand is doing. Give your gifts in secret, and your Father, who knows all secrets, will reward you. ❧ There will be glory and honor and peace from God for all who do good.

It is not that we think we can do anything of lasting value by ourselves. Our only power and success come from God. ❧ LORD, you will grant us peace, for all we have accomplished is really from you.

It is tempting to use honor, power, wealth, or prestige to measure people. We may even think that such people are really getting ahead in life. But God weighs us by different scales. Only the faithful work we do for him has eternal value. *LAB note for Psalm 62:9-12*

(PSALM 62:12) (1 CORINTHIANS 3:11, 14-15) (2 CORINTHIANS 5:10)
(MATTHEW 6:3-4) (ROMANS 2:10) (2 CORINTHIANS 3:5) (ISAIAH 26:12)

December 3

Make every effort to live a pure and blameless life. And be at peace with God.

Now you are no longer a slave but God's own child. And since you are his child, everything he has belongs to you.

You should consider yourselves dead to sin and able to live for the glory of God through Christ Jesus. Do not let sin control the way you live; do not give in to its lustful desires. Do not let any part of your body become a tool of wickedness, to be used for sinning. Instead, give yourselves completely to God since you have been given new life. And use your whole body as a tool to do what is right for the glory of God. ▨ Obey God because you are his children. Don't slip back into your old ways of doing evil; you didn't know any better then. But now you must be holy in everything you do, just as God—who chose you to be his children—is holy. ▨ If you keep yourself pure, you will be a utensil God can use for his purpose. Your life will be clean, and you will be ready for the Master to use you for every good work.

So, my dear brothers and sisters, be strong and steady, always enthusiastic about the Lord's work, for you know that nothing you do for the Lord is ever useless.

We should not become lazy and complacent because Christ has not yet returned. Instead, we should live in eager expectation of his coming. What would you like to be doing when Christ returns? That is how you should be living each day. *LAB note for 2 Peter 3:14*

(2 PETER 3:14) (GALATIANS 4:7) (ROMANS 6:11–13) (1 PETER 1:14–15)
(2 TIMOTHY 2:21) (1 CORINTHIANS 15:58)

December 4

I no longer call you servants, because a master doesn't confide in his servants. Now you are my friends, since I have told you everything the Father told me.

And God has actually given us his Spirit (not the world's spirit) so we can know the wonderful things God has freely given us.

When I think of the wisdom and scope of God's plan, I fall to my knees and pray to the Father, the Creator of everything in heaven and on earth. I pray that from his glorious, unlimited resources he will give you mighty inner strength through his Holy Spirit. And I pray that Christ will be more and more at home in your hearts as you trust in him. May your roots go down deep into the soil of God's marvelous love. And may you have the power to understand, as all God's people should, how wide, how long, how high, and how deep his love really is. May you experience the love of Christ, though it is so great you will never fully understand it. Then you will be filled with the fullness of life and power that comes from God.

"God's deep secrets" refers to God's unfathomable nature and his wonderful plan—Jesus' death and resurrection—and to the promise of salvation, revealed only to those who believe that what God says is true. Those who believe in Christ's death and resurrection and put their faith in him will know all they need to know to be saved. *LAB note for 1 Corinthians 2:10*

(1 CORINTHIANS 2:10) (JOHN 15:15) (1 CORINTHIANS 2:12) (EPHESIANS 3:14-19)

December 5

Revive us so we can call on your name once more.

It is the Spirit who gives eternal life. ❦ And the Holy Spirit helps us in our distress. For we don't even know what we should pray for, nor how we should pray. But the Holy Spirit prays for us with groanings that cannot be expressed in words. And the Father who knows all hearts knows what the Spirit is saying, for the Spirit pleads for us believers in harmony with God's own will. ❦ Pray at all times and on every occasion in the power of the Holy Spirit. Stay alert and be persistent in your prayers for all Christians everywhere.

I will never forget your commandments, for you have used them to restore my joy and health. ❦ The old way ends in death; in the new way, the Holy Spirit gives life. ❦ If you stay joined to me and my words remain in you, you may ask any request you like, and it will be granted! ❦ We can be confident that he will listen to us whenever we ask him for anything in line with his will.

How can anyone pray at all times? One way is to make quick, brief prayers your habitual response to every situation you meet throughout the day. Another way is to order your life around God's desires and teachings so that your very life becomes a prayer. *LAB note for Ephesians 6:18*

(PSALM 80:18) (JOHN 6:63) (ROMANS 8:26-27) (EPHESIANS 6:18)
(PSALM 119:93) (2 CORINTHIANS 3:6) (JOHN 15:7) (1 JOHN 5:14)

December 6

Let us come boldly to the throne of our gracious God. There we will receive his mercy, and we will find grace to help us when we need it.

Don't worry about anything; instead, pray about everything. Tell God what you need, and thank him for all he has done. If you do this, you will experience God's peace, which is far more wonderful than the human mind can understand. His peace will guard your hearts and minds as you live in Christ Jesus. So you should not be like cowering, fearful slaves. You should behave instead like God's very own children, adopted into his family—calling him "Father, dear Father."

Yes, ask anything in my name, and I will do it! So, dear brothers and sisters, we can boldly enter heaven's Most Holy Place because of the blood of Jesus. Let us go right into the presence of God, with true hearts fully trusting him. For our evil consciences have been sprinkled with Christ's blood to make us clean, and our bodies have been washed with pure water. "The Lord is my helper, so I will not be afraid. What can mere mortals do to me?"

Prayer is our approach to God, and we are to come "boldly." Some Christians approach God meekly with heads hung low, afraid to ask him to meet their needs. Others pray flippantly, giving little thought to what they say. Come with reverence because he is your King. But also come with bold assurance because he is your Friend and Counselor.

LAB note for Hebrews 4:16

(HEBREWS 4:16) (PHILIPPIANS 4:6-7) (ROMANS 8:15) (JOHN 14:14)
(HEBREWS 10:19, 22) (HEBREWS 13:6)

December 7

When darkness overtakes the godly, light will come bursting in.

Who among you fears the LORD and obeys his servant? If you are walking in darkness, without a ray of light, trust in the LORD and rely on your God. ※ Though they stumble, they will not fall, for the LORD holds them by the hand. ※ These commands and this teaching are a lamp to light the way ahead of you. The correction of discipline is the way to life.

Do not gloat over me, my enemies! For though I fall, I will rise again. Though I sit in darkness, the LORD himself will be my light. I will be patient as the LORD punishes me, for I have sinned against him. But after that, he will take up my case and punish my enemies for all the evil they have done to me. The LORD will bring me out of my darkness into the light, and I will see his righteousness.

A pure eye lets sunshine into your soul. But an evil eye shuts out the light and plunges you into darkness. If the light you think you have is really darkness, how deep that darkness will be!

If we walk by our own light and reject God's, we become self-sufficient, and the result of self-sufficiency is torment. When we place confidence in our own intelligence, appearance, or accomplishments instead of in God, we risk torment later when these strengths fade.

LAB note for Isaiah 50:10-11

(PSALM 112:4) (ISAIAH 50:10) (PSALM 37:24) (PROVERBS 6:23)
(MICAH 7:8-9) (MATTHEW 6:22-23)

December 8

That couldn't happen even if the LORD opened the windows of heaven!

Have faith in God. ❧ It is impossible to please God without faith. ❧ With God everything is possible.

Was I too weak to save you? Is that why the house is silent and empty when I come home? Is it because I have no power to rescue?

"My thoughts are completely different from yours," says the LORD. "And my ways are far beyond anything you could imagine. For just as the heavens are higher than the earth, so are my ways higher than your ways and my thoughts higher than your thoughts." ❧ I will open the windows of heaven for you. I will pour out a blessing so great you won't have enough room to take it in!

The LORD is not too weak to save you, and he is not becoming deaf. He can hear you when you call. ❧ O LORD, no one but you can help the powerless against the mighty! Help us, O LORD our God, for we trust in you alone. It is in your name that we have come against this vast horde. O LORD, you are our God; do not let mere men prevail against you.

We expected to die. But as a result, we learned not to rely on ourselves, but on God who can raise the dead.

Sometimes we become preoccupied with problems when we should be looking for opportunities. Instead of focusing on the negatives, develop an attitude of expectancy. To say that God cannot rescue someone or that a situation is impossible demonstrates a lack of faith.

LAB note for 2 Kings 7:2

(2 KINGS 7:2) (MARK 11:22) (HEBREWS 11:6) (MATTHEW 19:26) (ISAIAH 50:2) (ISAIAH 55:8-9) (MALACHI 3:10) (ISAIAH 59:1) (2 CHRONICLES 14:11) (2 CORINTHIANS 1:9)

December 9

Here on earth you will have many trials and sorrows. ❧ For we know that all creation has been groaning as in the pains of childbirth right up to the present time. And even we Christians, although we have the Holy Spirit within us as a foretaste of future glory, also groan to be released from pain and suffering. We, too, wait anxiously for that day when God will give us our full rights as his children, including the new bodies he has promised us. ❧ Our dying bodies make us groan and sigh.

These are the ones coming out of the great tribulation. They washed their robes in the blood of the Lamb and made them white. That is why they are standing in front of the throne of God, serving him day and night in his Temple. And he who sits on the throne will live among them and shelter them. They will never again be hungry or thirsty, and they will be fully protected from the scorching noontime heat. For the Lamb who stands in front of the throne will be their Shepherd. He will lead them to the springs of life-giving water. And God will wipe away all their tears.

As Christians we should expect continuing tension with an unbelieving world that is "out of sync" with Christ, his Good News, and his people. At the same time we can expect our relationship with Christ to produce peace and comfort because we are "in sync" with him.

LAB note for John 16:31-33

(Isaiah 60:20) (John 16:33) (Romans 8:22-23) (2 Corinthians 5:4)
(Revelation 7:14-17)

December 10

The LORD is good to everyone. He showers compassion on all his creation.

All the wild animals, large and small, and all the birds and fish will be afraid of you. I have placed them in your power. I have given them to you for food, just as I have given you grain and vegetables. ▨ As long as the earth remains, there will be springtime and harvest, cold and heat, winter and summer, day and night.

The LORD is good. When trouble comes, he is a strong refuge. And he knows everyone who trusts in him. ▨ Then God heard the boy's cries, and the angel of God called to Hagar from the sky, "Hagar, what's wrong? Do not be afraid! God has heard the boy's cries from the place where you laid him." Then God opened Hagar's eyes, and she saw a well. She immediately filled her water container and gave the boy a drink.

Don't worry about having enough food or drink or clothing. Why be like the pagans who are so deeply concerned about these things? Your heavenly Father already knows all your needs. ▨ Trust . . . in the living God, who richly gives us all we need for our enjoyment.

Think about the storms in your life—the situations that cause you great anxiety. Whatever your difficulty, you have two options: You can worry and assume that Jesus no longer cares, or you can resist fear, putting your trust in him. When you feel like panicking, confess your need for God and then trust him to care for you. *LAB note for Mark 4:38-40*

(MARK 4:38) (PSALM 145:9) (GENESIS 9:2-3) (GENESIS 8:22) (NAHUM 1:7) (GENESIS 21:17, 19) (MATTHEW 6:31-32) (1 TIMOTHY 6:17)

December 11

Your faithful work.

This is what God wants you to do: Believe in the one he has sent.

Faith that doesn't show itself by good deeds is no faith at all—it is dead and useless. What is important is faith expressing itself in love. Those who live only to satisfy their own sinful desires will harvest the consequences of decay and death. But those who live to please the Spirit will harvest everlasting life from the Spirit. We are God's masterpiece. He has created us anew in Christ Jesus, so that we can do the good things he planned for us long ago. He gave his life to free us from every kind of sin, to cleanse us, and to make us his very own people, totally committed to doing what is right.

We keep on praying for you, that our God will make you worthy of the life to which he called you. And we pray that God, by his power, will fulfill all your good intentions and faithful deeds. God is working in you, giving you the desire to obey him and the power to do what pleases him.

The Thessalonians had stood firm when they were persecuted. Paul commended these young Christians for their faithful work, loving deeds, and anticipation of the Lord's return. These characteristics are the marks of effective Christians in any age. *LAB note for 1 Thessalonians 1:3*

(1 THESSALONIANS 1:3) (JOHN 6:29) (JAMES 2:17) (GALATIANS 5:6)
(GALATIANS 6:8) (EPHESIANS 2:10) (TITUS 2:14)
(2 THESSALONIANS 1:11) (PHILIPPIANS 2:13)

December 12

This is what God has testified: He has given us eternal life, and
this life is in his Son.

The Father has life in himself, and he has granted his Son to
have life in himself. He will even raise from the dead anyone he
wants to, just as the Father does.

I am the resurrection and the life. Those who believe in me, even
though they die like everyone else, will live again. They are given
eternal life for believing in me and will never perish. ▨ I am the
good shepherd. The good shepherd lays down his life for the sheep.
The Father loves me because I lay down my life that I may have it
back again. No one can take my life from me. I lay down my life
voluntarily. For I have the right to lay it down when I want to and
also the power to take it again. For the Father has given me this
command. ▨ I am the way, the truth, and the life. No one can come
to the Father except through me. ▨ So whoever has God's Son has
life; whoever does not have his Son does not have life. ▨ For you
died when Christ died, and your real life is hidden with Christ in
God. And when Christ, who is your real life, is revealed to the
whole world, you will share in all his glory

Jesus has power over life and death as well as power to forgive
sins. This is because he is the Creator of life. He who is life can surely
restore life. When we realize his power and how wonderful his offer to us
really is, how can we not commit our lives to him? *LAB note for John 11:25-26*

(1 JOHN 5:11) (JOHN 5:26, 21) (JOHN 11:25-26) (JOHN 10:11, 17-18) (JOHN 14:6)
(1 JOHN 5:12) (COLOSSIANS 3:3-4)

December 13

Then the LORD did exactly what he had promised. Sarah became pregnant, and she gave a son to Abraham in his old age.

Trust in him at all times. Pour out your heart to him, for God is our refuge. ❧ David found strength in the LORD his God. ❧ God will surely come for you, to lead you out of this land of Egypt. He will bring you back to the land he vowed to give to the descendants of Abraham, Isaac, and Jacob. ❧ I have seen the misery of my people in Egypt. I have heard their cries. So I have come to rescue them. Now go, for I will send you to Egypt. And by means of many miraculous signs and wonders, he led them out of Egypt, through the Red Sea, and back and forth through the wilderness for forty years. ❧ All of the good promises that the LORD had given Israel came true.

God can be trusted to keep his promise. ❧ God is not a man, that he should lie. He is not a human, that he should change his mind. Has he ever spoken and failed to act? Has he ever promised and not carried it through? ❧ God also bound himself with an oath, so that those who received the promise could be perfectly sure that he would never change his mind. ❧ Heaven and earth will disappear, but my words will remain forever. ❧ The grass withers, and the flowers fade, but the word of our God stands forever.

Who could believe that Abraham would have a son at one hundred years of age—and live to raise him to adulthood? But doing the impossible is everyday business for God. Our big problems won't seem so impossible if we let God handle them.   *LAB note for Genesis 21:1-7*

(GENESIS 21:1-2) (PSALM 62:8) (1 SAMUEL 30:6) (GENESIS 50:24) (ACTS 7:34, 36)
(JOSHUA 21:45) (HEBREWS 10:23) (NUMBERS 23:19) (HEBREWS 6:17)
(MATTHEW 24:35) (ISAIAH 40:8)

December 14

He will save his people from their sins.

You know that Jesus came to take away our sins, for there is no sin in him. ▦ He personally carried away our sins in his own body on the cross so we can be dead to sin and live for what is right. ▦ He is able, once and forever, to save everyone who comes to God through him.

He was wounded and crushed for our sins. He was beaten that we might have peace. He was whipped, and we were healed! All of us have strayed away like sheep. We have left God's paths to follow our own. Yet the LORD laid on him the guilt and sins of us all. He was oppressed and treated harshly, yet he never said a word. He was led as a lamb to the slaughter. And as a sheep is silent before the shearers, he did not open his mouth. From prison and trial they led him away to his death. ▦ It was written long ago that the Messiah must suffer and die and rise again from the dead on the third day. . . . Take this message of repentance to all the nations, beginning in Jerusalem: "There is forgiveness of sins for all who turn to me." ▦ He came . . . to remove the power of sin forever by his sacrificial death for us.

Then God put him in the place of honor at his right hand as Prince and Savior. ▦ In this man Jesus there is forgiveness of your sins. Everyone who believes in him is freed from all guilt and declared right with God—something the Jewish law could never do. ▦ Your sins have been forgiven because of Jesus.

Jesus came to earth to save us because we can't save ourselves from sin and its consequences. No matter how good we are, we can't eliminate the sinful nature present in all of us. Only Jesus can do that. Thank Christ for his death on the cross for your sin, and then ask him to take control of your life. *LAB note for Matthew 1:21*

(MATTHEW 1:21) (1 JOHN 3:5) (1 PETER 2:24) (HEBREWS 7:25) (ISAIAH 53:5-8) (LUKE 24:46-47) (HEBREWS 9:26) (ACTS 5:31) (ACTS 13:38-39) (1 JOHN 2:12)

December 15

The Philistine commanders demanded, "What are these Hebrews doing here?"

Be happy if you are insulted for being a Christian, for then the glorious Spirit of God will come upon you.

You will not be condemned for doing something you know is all right. ▧ Be careful how you live among your unbelieving neighbors. Even if they accuse you of doing wrong, they will see your honorable behavior, and they will believe and give honor to God when he comes to judge the world.

Don't team up with those who are unbelievers. How can goodness be a partner with wickedness? How can light live with darkness? And what union can there be between God's temple and idols? For we are the temple of the living God. As God said: "I will live in them and walk among them. I will be their God, and they will be my people."

You are a chosen people . . . so you can show others the goodness of God, for he called you out of the darkness into his wonderful light.

Christ will send his Spirit to strengthen those who are persecuted for their faith, but not all suffering is the result of good Christian conduct. It may take careful thought or wise counsel to determine the real cause of our suffering. We can be assured, however, that whenever we suffer because of our loyalty to Christ, he will be with us all the way.

LAB note for 1 Peter 4:16

(1 Samuel 29:3) (1 Peter 4:14) (Romans 14:16) (1 Peter 2:12)
(2 Corinthians 6:14, 16) (1 Peter 2:9)

December 16

He calls his own sheep by name and leads them out.

God's truth stands firm like a foundation stone with this inscription: "The Lord knows those who are his." ❧ On judgment day many will tell me, "Lord, Lord, we prophesied in your name and cast out demons in your name and performed many miracles in your name." But I will reply, "I never knew you. Go away; the things you did were unauthorized." ❧ For the LORD watches over the path of the godly, but the path of the wicked leads to destruction.

I have written your name on my hand. ❧ Place me like a seal over your heart, or like a seal on your arm. For love is as strong as death, and its jealousy is as enduring as the grave. ❧ The LORD is good. When trouble comes, he is a strong refuge. And he knows everyone who trusts in him.

There are many rooms in my Father's home, and I am going to prepare a place for you. If this were not so, I would tell you plainly. When everything is ready, I will come and get you, so that you will always be with me where I am.

Jesus exposed those who sounded religious but had no personal relationship with him. Many people think that if they are "good" people and say religious things they will be rewarded with eternal life. In reality, faith in Christ is what will count at the judgment.

LAB note for Matthew 7:21-23

(JOHN 10:3) (2 TIMOTHY 2:19) (MATTHEW 7:22-23) (PSALM 1:6) (ISAIAH 49:16)
(SONG OF SONGS 8:6) (NAHUM 1:7) (JOHN 14:2-3)

December 17

He will keep you free from all blame on the great day when our Lord Jesus Christ returns.

You who were once so far away from God . . . were his enemies, separated from him by your evil thoughts and actions, yet now he has brought you back as his friends. He has done this through his death on the cross in his own human body. As a result, he has brought you into the very presence of God, and you are holy and blameless as you stand in it firmly. Don't drift away from the assurance you received when you heard the Good News. ※ Live clean, innocent lives as children of God in a dark world full of crooked and perverse people. Let your lives shine brightly before them.

And now, all glory to God, who is able to keep you from stumbling, and who will bring you into his glorious presence innocent of sin and with great joy. All glory to him, who alone is God our Savior, through Jesus Christ our Lord. Yes, glory, majesty, power, and authority belong to him, in the beginning, now, and forevermore. Amen.

The guarantee to be "free from all blame" is not because of our great gifts or our shining performance but because of what Jesus Christ accomplished for us through his death and resurrection. All who have received the Lord Jesus as their Savior will be considered blameless when he returns. *LAB note for 1 Corinthians 1:7-9*

(1 CORINTHIANS 1:8) (COLOSSIANS 1:21-23) (PHILIPPIANS 2:15) (JUDE 1:24-25)

December 18

We are lying if we say we have fellowship with God but go on living in spiritual darkness. We are not living in the truth. But if we are living in the light of God's presence, just as Christ is, then we have fellowship with each other, and the blood of Jesus, his Son, cleanses us from every sin. ▨ Let us strip off every weight that slows us down, especially the sin that so easily hinders our progress.

I will teach you wisdom's ways and lead you in straight paths. If you live a life guided by wisdom, you won't limp or stumble as you run. Do not do as the wicked do, or follow the path of evildoers. Avoid their haunts. Turn away and go somewhere else. Look straight ahead, and fix your eyes on what lies before you. Mark out a straight path for your feet; then stick to the path and stay safe. Don't get sidetracked; keep your feet from following evil.

The Lord will deliver me from every evil attack and will bring me safely to his heavenly Kingdom. To God be the glory forever and ever. Amen.

How does Jesus' blood cleanse us from every sin? Jesus died for the sins of the world. When we commit our life to Christ and thus identify ourselves with him, his death becomes ours. He has paid the penalty for our sins, and his blood has purified us. *LAB note for 1 John 1:7*

(1 SAMUEL 2:9) (1 JOHN 1:6-7) (HEBREWS 12:1)
(PROVERBS 4:11-12, 14-15, 25-27) (2 TIMOTHY 4:18)

December 19

Try to understand what the Lord wants you to do.

God wants you to be holy. ❧ Stop quarreling with God! If you agree with him, you will have peace at last, and things will go well with you. ❧ This is the way to have eternal life—to know you, the only true God, and Jesus Christ, the one you sent to earth. ❧ We know that the Son of God has come, and he has given us understanding so that we can know the true God. And now we are in God because we are in his Son, Jesus Christ. He is the only true God, and he is eternal life.

We have continued praying for you ever since we first heard about you. We ask God to give you a complete understanding of what he wants to do in your lives, and we ask him to make you wise with spiritual wisdom. ❧ God, the glorious Father of our Lord Jesus Christ, . . . give you spiritual wisdom and understanding, so that you might grow in your knowledge of God. I pray that your hearts will be flooded with light so that you can understand the wonderful future he has promised to those he called. I want you to realize what a rich and glorious inheritance he has given to his people. I pray that you will begin to understand the incredible greatness of his power for us who believe him.

Being made holy is the process of living the Christian life. The Holy Spirit works in us, conforming us to the image of Christ. Do you seek for holiness in your daily life, with the Holy Spirit's help?

LAB note for 1 Thessalonians 4:3

(EPHESIANS 5:17) (1 THESSALONIANS 4:3) (JOB 22:21) (JOHN 17:3) (1 JOHN 5:20) (COLOSSIANS 1:9) (EPHESIANS 1:17-19)

December 20

Be strong with the special favor God gives you in Christ Jesus.

You will be strengthened by his glorious power so that you will have all the patience and endurance you need. May you be filled with joy. ❦ Just as you accepted Christ as your Lord, you must continue to live in obedience to him. Let your roots grow down into him and draw up nourishment from him, so you will grow in faith, strong and vigorous in the truth you were taught. Let your lives overflow with thanksgiving for all he has done. ❦ The LORD has planted them like strong and graceful oaks for his own glory. ❦ We are his house, built on the foundation of the apostles and the prophets. And the cornerstone is Christ Jesus himself.

And now I entrust you to God and the word of his grace—his message that is able to build you up and give you an inheritance with all those he has set apart for himself. ❦ May you always be filled with the fruit of your salvation—those good things that are produced in your life by Jesus Christ—for this will bring much glory and praise to God.

Fight the good fight for what we believe. ❦ Don't be intimidated by your enemies.

Just as we are saved by God's special, undeserved favor, we should live by it. This means trusting completely in Christ and his power and not trying to live for Christ in our strength alone. Receive and utilize Christ's power. He will give you the strength to do his work. *LAB note for 2 Timothy 2:1*

(2 TIMOTHY 2:1) (COLOSSIANS 1:11) (COLOSSIANS 2:6–7) (ISAIAH 61:3) (EPHESIANS 2:20) (ACTS 20:32) (PHILIPPIANS 1:11) (1 TIMOTHY 6:12) (PHILIPPIANS 1:28)

December 21

And the Spirit of the LORD will rest on him—the Spirit of wisdom and understanding, the Spirit of counsel and might, the Spirit of knowledge and the fear of the LORD. He will delight in obeying the LORD.

Listen as wisdom calls out! Hear as understanding raises her voice! She stands on the hilltop and at the crossroads. At the entrance to the city, at the city gates, she cries aloud, "I call to you, to all of you! I am raising my voice to all people. How naive you are! Let me give you common sense. O foolish ones, let me give you understanding. Listen to me! For I have excellent things to tell you. Everything I say is right, for I speak the truth and hate every kind of deception. Good advice and success belong to me. Insight and strength are mine."

The LORD Almighty is a wonderful teacher, and he gives the farmer great wisdom. ▓ If you need wisdom—if you want to know what God wants you to do—ask him, and he will gladly tell you. He will not resent your asking. ▓ Trust in the LORD with all your heart; do not depend on your own understanding. Seek his will in all you do, and he will direct your paths.

God takes all our individual circumstances and weaknesses into account, much as the farmer uses special tools to plant and harvest the fragile plants. God deals with each of us sensitively. We should follow his example when we deal with others. Different people require different treatment.   *LAB note for Isaiah 28:23-29*

(ISAIAH 9:6) (ISAIAH 11:2-3) (PROVERBS 8:1-7, 14) (ISAIAH 28:29) (JAMES 1:5) (PROVERBS 3:5-6)

December 22

Mighty God.

You are the most handsome of all. Gracious words stream from
your lips. God himself has blessed you forever. Put on your sword, O
mighty warrior! You are so glorious, so majestic! In your majesty,
ride out to victory, defending truth, humility, and justice. Go forth
to perform awe-inspiring deeds! Your throne, O God, endures
forever and ever. Your royal power is expressed in justice. ※ Who is
this . . . with his clothing stained red? Who is this in royal robes,
marching in the greatness of his strength? "It is I, the LORD,
announcing your salvation! It is I, the LORD, who is mighty to save!"

See, God has come to save me. I will trust in him and not be
afraid. The LORD God is my strength and my song; he has become
my salvation. ※ But thanks be to God, who made us his captives and
leads us along in Christ's triumphal procession.

The Son reflects God's own glory, and everything about him
represents God exactly. He sustains the universe by the mighty
power of his command. After he died to cleanse us from the stain of
sin, he sat down in the place of honor at the right hand of the
majestic God of heaven. ※ Glory to God, who is able to keep you
from stumbling, and who will bring you into his glorious presence
innocent of sin and with great joy. . . . Amen.

What a glorious day it will be when Jesus Christ comes to reign
over the earth! Even now we need to express our gratitude to God,
thanking him, praising him, and telling others about him. From the
depths of our gratitude, we must praise him. And we should share the
Good News with others. *LAb note for Isaiah 12:1ff.*

(ISAIAH 9:6) (PSALM 45:2-4, 6) (ISAIAH 63:1) (ISAIAH 12:2)
(2 CORINTHIANS 2:14) (HEBREWS 1:3) (JUDE 1:24-25)

December 23

Everlasting Father.

Hear, O Israel! The LORD is our God, the LORD alone.

The Father and I are one. The Father is in me, and I am in the Father. 🦋 Since you don't know who I am, you don't know who my Father is. If you knew me, then you would know my Father, too. 🦋 Philip said, "Lord, show us the Father and we will be satisfied." Jesus replied, "Philip, don't you even yet know who I am, even after all the time I have been with you? Anyone who has seen me has seen the Father! So why are you asking to see him?" 🦋 Here I am— together with the children God has given me. 🦋 When he sees all that is accomplished by his anguish, he will be satisfied. 🦋 "I am the Alpha and the Omega—the beginning and the end," says the Lord God. "I am the one who is, who always was, and who is still to come, the Almighty One." 🦋 I existed before Abraham was ever born! 🦋 I AM THE ONE WHO ALWAYS IS. . . . I AM has sent me.

To his Son he says, "Your throne, O God, endures forever and ever." 🦋 He existed before everything else began, and he holds all creation together. 🦋 In Christ the fullness of God lives in a human body.

Monotheism—belief in only one God—was a distinctive feature of Hebrew religion. Many ancient religions believed in many gods. Then and today there are people who prefer to place their trust in many different "gods." But the day is coming when God will be recognized as the only one. He will be the king over the whole earth.   *LAB note for Deuteronomy 6:4*

(ISAIAH 9:6) (DEUTERONOMY 6:4) (JOHN 10:30, 38) (JOHN 8:19) (JOHN 14:8-9)
(HEBREWS 2:13) (ISAIAH 53:11) (REVELATION 1:8) (JOHN 8:58) (EXODUS 3:14)
(HEBREWS 1:8) (COLOSSIANS 1:17) (COLOSSIANS 2:9)

December 24

Prince of Peace.

Help him judge your people in the right way; let the poor always be treated fairly. May the mountains yield prosperity for all, and may the hills be fruitful, because the king does what is right. Help him to defend the poor, to rescue the children of the needy, and to crush their oppressors. May he live as long as the sun shines, as long as the moon continues in the skies. Yes, forever! ❧ Glory to God . . . and peace on earth to all whom God favors.

Because of God's tender mercy, the light from heaven is about to break upon us, to give light to those who sit in darkness and in the shadow of death, and to guide us to the path of peace. ❧ There is peace with God through Jesus Christ, who is Lord of all.

I have told you all this so that you may have peace in me. Here on earth you will have many trials and sorrows. But take heart, because I have overcome the world. ❧ I am leaving you with a gift—peace of mind and heart. And the peace I give isn't like the peace the world gives. So don't be troubled or afraid. ❧ God's peace . . . is far more wonderful than the human mind can understand. His peace will guard your hearts and minds as you live in Christ Jesus.

What qualities do we want most in our leaders? God desires all who rule under him to be just and righteous. Think how the world would change if world leaders would commit themselves to these two qualities. Let us pray that they will! *LAB note for Psalm 72:1-2*

(ISAIAH 9:6) (PSALM 72:2-5) (LUKE 2:14) (LUKE 1:78-79) (ACTS 10:36) (JOHN 16:33) (JOHN 14:27) (PHILIPPIANS 4:7)

December 25

Thank God for his Son—a gift too wonderful for words!

Shout with joy to the LORD, O earth! Worship the LORD with gladness. Come before him, singing with joy. Enter his gates with thanksgiving; go into his courts with praise. Give thanks to him and bless his name. ❧ For a child is born to us, a son is given to us. And the government will rest on his shoulders. These will be his royal titles: Wonderful Counselor, Mighty God, Everlasting Father, Prince of Peace.

For God so loved the world that he gave his only Son. ❧ Since God did not spare even his own Son but gave him up for us all, won't God, who gave us Christ, also give us everything else? ❧ There was only one left—his son whom he loved dearly. The owner finally sent him. ❧ Everyone who believes in him will not perish but have eternal life. ❧ The whole world and life and death; the present and the future. Everything belongs to you, and you belong to Christ, and Christ belongs to God.

Let them praise the LORD for his great love and for all his wonderful deeds to them. ❧ Praise the LORD, I tell myself; with my whole heart, I will praise his holy name.

Oh, how I praise the Lord. How I rejoice in God my Savior!

God's love is not static or self-centered; it reaches out and draws others in. Here God sets the pattern of true love, the basis for all love relationships—when you love someone dearly, you are willing to give freely to the point of self-sacrifice.   *LAB note for John 3:16*

(2 CORINTHIANS 9:15) (PSALM 100:1-2, 4) (ISAIAH 9:6) (JOHN 3:16) (ROMANS 8:32) (MARK 12:6) (JOHN 3:16) (1 CORINTHIANS 3:22-23) (PSALM 107:21) (PSALM 103:1) (LUKE 1:46-47)

December 26

Be strong and steady, always enthusiastic about the Lord's work.

You know that nothing you do for the Lord is ever useless. ▧ Just as you accepted Christ Jesus as your Lord, you must continue to live in obedience to him. Let your roots grow down into him and draw up nourishment from him, so you will grow in faith, strong and vigorous in the truth you were taught. Let your lives overflow with thanksgiving for all he has done. ▧ Those who endure to the end will be saved.

Stand firm in your faith.

All of us must quickly carry out the tasks assigned us by the one who sent me, because there is little time left before the night falls and all work comes to an end.

Those who live only to satisfy their own sinful desires will harvest the consequences of decay and death. But those who live to please the Spirit will harvest everlasting life from the Spirit. So don't get tired of doing what is good. Don't get discouraged and give up, for we will reap a harvest of blessing at the appropriate time.

Because of the Resurrection, nothing we do is useless. Knowing that Christ has won the ultimate victory should affect the way we live right now. Don't let discouragement over an apparent lack of results keep you from doing the work of the Lord enthusiastically as you have opportunity.

LAB note for 1 Corinthians 15:58

(1 CORINTHIANS 15:58) (1 CORINTHIANS 15:58) (COLOSSIANS 2:6-7)
(MATTHEW 24:13) (2 CORINTHIANS 1:24) (JOHN 9:4) (GALATIANS 6:8-9)

December 27

He is able, once and forever, to save everyone who comes to God through him.

I am the way, the truth, and the life. No one can come to the Father except through me. ❧ There is salvation in no one else! There is no other name in all of heaven for people to call on to save them.

My sheep recognize my voice; I know them, and they follow me. I give them eternal life, and they will never perish. No one will snatch them away from me ❧ God, who began the good work within you, will continue his work until it is finally finished on that day when Christ Jesus comes back again. ❧ Is anything too hard for the LORD?

And now—all glory to God, who is able to keep you from stumbling, and who will bring you into his glorious presence innocent of sin and with great joy. All glory to him, who alone is God our Savior, through Jesus Christ our Lord. Yes, glory, majesty, power, and authority belong to him, in the beginning, now, and forevermore. Amen.

No one can add to what Jesus did to save us; our past, present, and future sins are all forgiven, and Jesus is with the Father as a sign that our sins are forgiven. If you are a Christian, remember that Christ has paid the price for your sins once and for all.   *LAB note for Hebrews 7:25*

(HEBREWS 7:25) (JOHN 14:6) (ACTS 4:12) (JOHN 10:27-28) (PHILIPPIANS 1:6) (GENESIS 18:14) (JUDE 1:24-25)

December 28

For Christ himself has made peace between us.

For God was in Christ, reconciling the world to himself, no longer counting people's sins against them. This is the wonderful message he has given us to tell others. For God made Christ, who never sinned, to be the offering for our sin, so that we could be made right with God through Christ. ❧ By him God reconciled everything to himself. He made peace with everything in heaven and on earth by means of his blood on the cross. As a result, he has brought you into the very presence of God, and you are holy and blameless as you stand before him without a single fault. ❧ He forgave all our sins. He canceled the record that contained the charges against us. He took it and destroyed it by nailing it to Christ's cross.

I am leaving you with a gift—peace of mind and heart. And the peace I give isn't like the peace the world gives. So don't be troubled or afraid.

There are many barriers that can divide us from other Christians: age, appearance, intelligence, political persuasion, economic status, race, theological perspective. Fortunately, Christ has knocked down the barriers and unified all believers into one family. His cross should be the focus of our unity. *LAB note for Ephesians 2:14-22*

(EPHESIANS 2:14) (2 CORINTHIANS 5:19, 21) (COLOSSIANS 1:20, 22)
(COLOSSIANS 2:13-14) (JOHN 14:27)

December 29

Your sins are forgiven.

I will forgive their wickedness and will never again remember their sins. ▨ Who but God can forgive sins!

I—yes, I alone—am the one who blots out your sins for my own sake and will never think of them again. ▨ Oh, what joy for those whose rebellion is forgiven, whose sin is put out of sight! Yes, what joy for those whose record the LORD has cleared of sin, whose lives are lived in complete honesty! ▨ Where is another God like you, who pardons the sins of the survivors among his people?

God through Christ has forgiven you. ▨ The blood of Jesus, his Son, cleanses us from every sin. If we say we have no sin, we are only fooling ourselves and refusing to accept the truth. But if we confess our sins to him, he is faithful and just to forgive us and to cleanse us from every wrong.

He has removed our rebellious acts as far away from us as the east is from the west. ▨ Sin is no longer your master, for you are no longer subject to the law, which enslaves you to sin. Instead, you are free by God's grace.

God wants to forgive sinners. Forgiveness has always been part of his loving nature. He announced it to Moses; he revealed it to David; and he dramatically showed it to the world through Jesus Christ. He forgives rebellion, puts sin out of sight, and clears our record of sin.

LAB note for Psalm 32:1-2

(MARK 2:5) (JEREMIAH 31:34) (MARK 2:7) (ISAIAH 43:25) (PSALM 32:1-2)
(MICAH 7:18) (EPHESIANS 4:32) (1 JOHN 1:7-9) (PSALM 103:12) (ROMANS 6:14)

December 30

You saw how the LORD your God cared for you again and again here in the wilderness, just as a father cares for his child.

I brought you to myself and carried you on eagle's wings. ❦ In his love and mercy he redeemed them. He lifted them up and carried them through all the years. ❦ Like an eagle that rouses her chicks and hovers over her young, so he spread his wings to take them in and carried them aloft on his pinions. The LORD alone guided them.

I will be your God throughout your lifetime—until your hair is white with age. I made you, and I will care for you. I will carry you along and save you. ❦ For that is what God is like. He is our God forever and ever, and he will be our guide until we die. ❦ The steps of the godly are directed by the LORD. He delights in every detail of their lives. Though they stumble, they will not fall, for the LORD holds them by the hand.

Give your burdens to the LORD, and he will take care of you. He will not permit the godly to slip and fall. ❦ Don't worry about everyday life—whether you have enough food, drink, and clothes. Your heavenly Father already knows all your needs.

God wants us to give our burdens to him, but often we continue to bear them ourselves even when we say we are trusting in him. Trust the same strength that sustains you to carry your cares also.

LAB note for Psalm 55:22

(DEUTERONOMY 1:31) (EXODUS 19:4) (ISAIAH 63:9) (DEUTERONOMY 32:11-12) (ISAIAH 46:4) (PSALM 48:14) (PSALM 37:23-24) (PSALM 55:22) (MATTHEW 6:25, 32)

December 31

Much land remains to be conquered.

I don't mean to say that I have already achieved these things or that I have already reached perfection! But I keep working toward that day when I will finally be all that Christ Jesus saved me for and wants me to be.

You are to be perfect, even as your Father in heaven is perfect. Make every effort to apply the benefits of these promises to your life. Then your faith will produce a life of moral excellence. A life of moral excellence leads to knowing God better. Knowing God leads to self-control. Self-control leads to patient endurance, and patient endurance leads to godliness. Godliness leads to love for other Christians and finally you will grow to have genuine love for everyone.

I pray that your love for each other will overflow more and more, and that you will keep on growing in your knowledge and understanding.

No eye has seen, no ear has heard, and no mind has imagined what God has prepared for those who love him.

There is a special rest still waiting for the people of God. Your eyes will see the king in all his splendor, and you will see a land that stretches into the distance.

Our culture often glorifies the young and strong and sets aside those who are older. Yet older people are filled with the wisdom that comes from experience. They are very capable of serving if given the chance and should be encouraged to do so. Believers are never allowed to retire from God's service. *LAB note for Joshua 13:1*

(JOSHUA 13:1) (PHILIPPIANS 3:12) (MATTHEW 5:48) (2 PETER 1:5-7)
(PHILIPPIANS 1:9) (1 CORINTHIANS 2:9) (HEBREWS 4:9) (ISAIAH 33:17)